TAXES, TARIFFS, AND SUBSIDIES

Volume 2

AF721955

J. HARVEY PERRY

TAXES, TARIFFS, & SUBSIDIES

A history of Canadian fiscal development

Volume 2

Sponsored by the Canadian Tax Foundation

UNIVERSITY OF TORONTO PRESS

Copyright, Canada, 1955
University of Toronto Press
Printed in Canada
Reprinted in 2018
ISBN 978-1-4875-8189-3 (paper)
London: Geoffrey Cumberlege
Oxford University Press

Contents

VOLUME 2

PART VII: FINANCING WORLD WAR II, 1940–46

Tables

TEXT, VOLUME 2

APPENDIX C

Part VII

FINANCING WORLD WAR II
1940-46

21 WORLD WAR II, 1940–46

Revised Philosophy of War Finance

DESPITE THE FACT that it prevented the immediate implementation of the Rowell-Sirois Commission's main tax proposals, World War II affected few aspects of our national life more profoundly than the tax system. The harsh reality of the emergency forced the immediate adoption of measures designed to make it an effective and efficient instrument of national policy. At one stroke the Wartime Tax Agreements resolved almost all the internal conflicts of jurisdiction in the area of direct taxation. These structural changes were paralleled by an equally remarkable revolution in the attitude towards the role of taxation in a modern economy. Pre-war thought, as we have seen, had hardly accepted taxation as a dynamic instrument of economic policy; but in the urgency of the war years the role came to be recognized without question. In few countries was taxation employed on as broad a front to facilitate the job of converting an economy from peacetime to wartime operation, and in few countries was the job done with better public co-operation and understanding.

The developments leading to the Wartime Tax Agreements are fully discussed in chapter 25 in the context of intergovernmental fiscal arrangements, and will not be dealt with here. In the present chapter it is intended to review some of the basic principles governing the role of taxation in wartime, and to consider its limitations in giving effect to these principles. This subject was examined in a general way in the chapter dealing with World War I, and of course has been discussed by many other Canadian writers. The next two chapters will present a case study of some of the specific measures of taxation adopted in World War II.

Basic Objectives of Wartime Finance

The immediate and specific objective of any tax programme is, of course, the provision of revenues adequate for the support of the services of government. Governments, like individuals, must meet their liabilities if they are to retain the services of employees and the goodwill of suppliers and contractors. This is true alike in peace and war. Funds must be available for meeting bills as they come due, and a chronic inability to make full payment would, even under wartime conditions, soon lose a government its credit standing in the community. It is not exclusively the job of taxation to provide such funds, since a government can borrow or issue new money. On the other hand it is generally accepted that no government can retain its credit if it borrows or debases its money indefinitely and indiscriminately, and that the maximum possible share of its expenditures should be financed from tax revenues *in the long run.*

This is a simple, urgent, immediate, and understandable objective, and if it were not that the demands of governments were so immensely enlarged in war as compared with peace, the subject of wartime finance would require no special attention. However, the very size of a wartime tax programme makes it not just a larger programme but a programme of a different kind.

The nature and consequences of this difference will be discussed in a moment. First, however, the record of wartime taxation in Canada should be measured simply on the test of its effectiveness in meeting the cost of government—in this case of the federal government. Table XXVII gives the record for the seven fiscal years of the war and post-war period. In that period revenues (mainly from taxation) covered 56.6 per cent of expenditures (mainly for war), although in individual years the ratio was considerably higher. As a long-run basis of opera-

TABLE XXVII

DOMINION EXPENDITURE AND REVENUE IN WORLD WAR II, SEPTEMBER 1, 1939, TO MARCH 31, 1946
(in millions of dollars)

Fiscal year	Total expenditure	Total[a] revenue	Ratio of revenue to expenditure
1939–40[b]	464.2	328.3	70.7
1940–41	1,249.6	872.2	69.8
1941–42	1,885.1	1,488.5	79.0
1942–43	4,387.1	2,249.5	51.3
1943–44	5,322.3	2,765.0	52.0
1944–45	5,245.6	2,687.3	51.2
1945–46	5,136.2	3,013.2	58.7
	23,690.1	13,404.1	56.6

[a] Excludes refundable taxes.
[b] September 1, 1939, to March 31, 1940.

tion, it would not be regarded as sound policy to borrow nearly one-half of the funds necessary to carry on a government. For a wartime period, however, to cover by taxation more than one-half of expenditures represents almost the maximum of accomplishment, and is more than most countries achieved. As the table shows, it meant increasing federal revenues ninefold in the short period of five years, an accomplishment that would not have been deemed possible in 1939.

The expenditure figures in the table will also serve to illustrate the vastly enlarged scale of operation of the federal government in wartime. In several years its annual budgetary outlays were at least ten times those of pre-war years, and there were additional cash outlays, not reflected in the budget, which had the same general economic effect. The economic consequences of expenditures on this astronomic scale were extremely significant. At the peak of the war effort the federal government was taking almost half of the total output of the country and commandeering the services of a large fraction of the adult working population. No economy can support an additional levy of this magnitude without a curtailment in the purchases of private individuals, a curtailment offset only to the extent that production in total can be increased.

The essential issues in an operation of this scale cease to be financial and become economic. Furthermore, the economic problem is of a complexity and urgency unparalleled in peacetime experience. The insatiable appetite of war for materials and men must be met without stint or pause. But more industrial countries are normally geared to production for civilian needs. The rapid conversion to wartime requirements therefore represents a major upheaval—a head-on collision between the economy of war and the economy of peace. To assure that the conversion is made, a war government must do much more than simply place orders, enlist men, and stand prepared to pay the bills. These are essential steps, and a nation advances not a whit closer to preparedness until they are taken. But it would be extremely rare and improbable circumstances in which these were the only steps that were required.

The necessity for these other steps may not be immediately apparent at the outset. The impact of war orders and service enlistments on the civilian economy may be eased temporarily by the existence of slack in the form of unused plant and unemployed workers. Such was the case in 1939. As the economy becomes taut, however, it will soon be apparent that governments and individuals are both bidding for increasingly scarcer supplies of materials and labour. In this contest there can be no doubt of the outcome, since on it may depend the very survival of the nation. The demands of the civilian economy *must* be overridden and the civilian purchases that would otherwise be made *must* be curtailed. There is no way of postponing the real cost of war—the men and materials devoted to its needs are lost to other purposes. Every national emergency, of course, presents a challenge for increased output in all quarters, and an entirely negative approach that stressed only sacrifice and curtailment would lose the real psychological values of a positive emphasis on greater effort. A general concentration on serious effort during work hours may make enough difference in output to carry a substantial defence programme without serious disturbance to the civilian economy. However, in a major war, when every possible ounce of material and manpower must be unstintingly devoted to the one cause, it would be out of the question to maintain all output at peak levels. Civil demands must suffer.

A government has one method of enforcing its demands in wartime which is the crudest of all—simply to outbid the civilian population by the use of unlimited quantities of newly created money. Most national governments have this power, exercisable either through the printing of new paper money or the creation of new government drawing accounts through the banking system. Armed with this unlimited source of supply, the government can outbid all contenders, and force the price of materials and labour to prohibitive heights. This is monetary inflation. To a large extent the financing of World War I was of this character, and no conflict has been entirely without it. Its unfairness as a means of exacting a sacrifice from the civilian population is self-evident. Those in a position to increase their incomes, and possibly even to make enormous gains by speculative dealings in scarce supplies, bear the least of the burden, while those on small and fixed incomes bear the most.

At the other extreme one might visualize a nation of super-intelligent individuals who without any prompting or instruction from their government immediately on the outbreak of war reduced their level of personal consumption and increased their own efforts as producers to the point where a wide and ample leeway was provided for the war programme. Each such individual would automatically gauge his own sacrifice so that it was equal to that of his neighbour, and all would make the exact sacrifice required by the war effort. The financial aspect of the government's programme would then be reduced to a simple choice of the most convenient means for effecting payment. Financing the war would have no other implications than simply to assure that persons and suppliers who dealt with the government were compensated for their efforts.

Such a state of affairs, of course, has never existed at any time. Perhaps it was most closely approached in the primitive society where the individual literally beat his ploughshare into a sword—and his ploughshare was one of his most valued possessions. In a modern society the closest counterpart would be those individuals (and there are many in wartime) who voluntarily contribute a part of their wealth and income to the government as a gift.

Like most extremes, the above positions serve mainly to mark the boundaries of possibility. The normal case lies between. No government would willingly pursue the inflationary process to its ultimate, if for no other reason than that, once started, a rapid price rise is almost impossible to stem. On the other hand, in a modern complex society individuals are not sufficiently aware of the problems of manpower and materials voluntarily to reduce their consumption by just the right amount. Furthermore the very psychology of a war period combined with the inflationary character of spending for war production (an increase in purchasing power is created without any compensating increase in the production of consumable goods) militate against the achievement of this state of intelligent self-interest.

Between the undesirable extreme of monetary inflation and the improbable extreme of completely intelligent self-interest, taxation stands as a reasonable compromise. Within its limitations it achieves the purpose of forcing a reduction of civilian consumption with the maximum of fairness and equality. It compels the sacrifice of civilian expenditure by taxing away income that might otherwise have been spent, or by making goods more expensive that might otherwise have been purchased. Within its limitations it assures the equitable achievement of this result by the conscious direction of specific taxes towards incomes having the greatest surplus over basic requirements and towards goods the purchase of which can be postponed with least permanent sacrifice. Taxation furthermore recaptures the abnormal incomes that sometimes emerge during wartime because of spectacular increases in the value of scarce commodities or of wages paid for rare skills and because of the generally increased tempo of economic activity directly attributable to the war effort. Re-negotiation has removed much of the possibility of "profiteering" on government contracts, but high taxes retrieve whatever abnormal profits may be made here as well.

Taxation is, of course, a normal device of government financing, but the major difference between its use in peace and war is crucial. Under peacetime conditions it is employed primarily to fill the public purse, while in wartime its primary use is to empty the private purse. It is less important in wartime to obtain income for the government by taxation (it could be provided in other ways) than it is to take income away from the people. The real struggle is not for money, but for the men and materials that money left in private hands can divert from the war effort. Governments must ensure that they obtain adequate production and service enlistments by reducing private competition for materials and labour to the minimum; in facilitating this process taxation becomes a major weapon in the arsenal of economic controls which, within its limitations, achieves the desired end with the greatest possibilities of equity.

What are the limitations on the use of taxation in wartime? Why is it not made to carry the whole burden of financing a war? There are several reasons. If the final hope for victory in a war rested on increased effort and output one could in fact make an excellent case on psychological grounds that taxes should be reduced, rather than increased. Ordinarily to rob a business firm or an individual of all incentive for increased profits or higher earnings by taxing away a large part of both would not be regarded as a step likely to result in higher production. High taxes undeniably stultify the normal instincts of progress and improvement, and only cease to have this effect to the extent that other and stronger urges—the urge of self-preservation in war—command the individual to action. The dampening effect of high taxation has positive advantages for restricting unnecessary investment and consumer expenditure, but the removal of the normal forces of economic motivation can be pressed too far. The problem is further complicated by the fact that high business taxes designed to discourage expansion and expenditure may have the diametrically opposite result by putting a premium on any outlay that can be deducted from taxable income. Thus waste may be encouraged rather than forestalled. There are major psychological problems, therefore, that a minister of finance must take into account which need not concern an economist intent on gauging only the mathematical implications of withdrawing a given number of dollars from private hands.

Further, to deprive a whole generation of all the surplus income it might ordinarily expect to retain for use in later years would have consequences which no government would be prepared to face. Taxation at, say, twice the level of that of World War II would bankrupt all private provision for savings and retirement, for the purchase of homes, and so on. Insurance would lapse, mortgages would be defaulted, and all other payments dependent on the retention of some surplus over immediate living requirements would have to be dropped. For large sections of the population the result would be disastrous.

Taxation is also much less precise an instrument than is commonly supposed. It cuts deep, but with the violence of the butcher's knife rather than the finesse of the surgeon's scalpel. Its flexibility has definite limitations. The administrative mechanism can support only a minimum deviation from standard rules. Beyond a certain point, red tape and confusion take over. The simplest law makes for the easiest administration, but simple law and fair law are often not compatible. The more account that is taken of individual variations the greater the resulting complications. Furthermore, even if it were possible to administer them, it is not at all clear what provisions can or should be made in law to cover many common differences between individuals and firms. Perhaps the ultimate development in "total" taxation for "total" war would be to have the government receive *all* income and profits in the first instance and then to pay over to the individual or firm only whatever amount they could prove was necessary for their continued existence.

There are other objections to "total" taxation, but the discouragement to incentive, the disruption of private arrangements, and the inevitable greater hardship for some individuals than for others establish the main limitations. In effect, therefore, taxation is a fair and efficient fiscal aid to conversion from peace to war only up to a point. Beyond that point (the determination of which represents one of the most delicate of judgments) it must be supplemented by measures which leave the ultimate decision to the individual, such as mass appeals for savings through the sale of victory bonds, and by more precise and rigorous measures of general control, intended usually to forestall further expansion rather than to secure an absolute reduction, such as ceilings on prices, wages, and profits and the rationing of scarce goods.

One general reservation should be made respecting all these devices, including taxation: their ultimate success depends in large measure on the extent to which they are understood and accepted by the whole people. If powerful individuals or groups in the community attempt to pass on to weaker individuals or groups, by higher prices or by demands for higher wages, the burden of taxation they were intended to bear, then the principle of equal sacrifice is lost. If wartime borrowing represents merely the conversion of one form of existing saving into another form without any net curtailment of consumption then its purpose is to a large extent defeated. If masses of the consuming public conspire to evade the price ceiling and rationing restrictions then they may as well not have been imposed. In the final analysis, therefore, a major war can be successfully conducted only if most of the members of the community are dedicated to its prosecution and are ready to support all measures directed to this end.

One of the notable features of the Canadian financial programme in World War II was the insistence with which the tax system was pressed forward towards its maximum practicable bounds and the frankness with which the limitations governing these bounds were recognized. No opportunity for an exposition of the basic problem of wartime finance was overlooked, and the constant repetition of the theme in the annual budget speech and elsewhere undoubtedly gave the general public a grasp of the essentials that in large measure was responsible for the success achieved. At the same time there was also a ready willingness to make a breach in the formidable tax wall, or even to dismantle a part of it, when it appeared to be impeding progress.

Nowhere is this perception of the basic problem of war finance revealed more clearly than in the budget speeches of the years 1939 to 1945, a record which has been allowed to speak for itself on every possible occasion in this volume. The main theme of the wartime finance policy was stated in the special war budget of September, 1939. The following excerpts will serve to demonstrate the comprehensive character of this statement:

> First of all let me emphasize that however we finance the cost of the war, whether by taxation or by borrowing or by inflation, we cannot escape its real costs. By the real costs I mean the goods and services which have to be sacrificed out of our current production to meet the needs of war. . . .
>
> We can, however, lighten the burden imposed by this real sacrifice if we expand our total employment and production. To the extent that we can put our unemployed men and equipment to work producing what we need for war, we will have to divert less resources away from normal uses. . . .
>
> Whatever such offsets may be, it is important to emphasize that, as I have already said, the real costs of war must come out of current production, out of the goods and services produced during the war. . . . Taking it by and large the fact is that the shells that are fired and the other goods and services that are used up in the course of a war must be produced during the period of the war. This being the case, it follows that, and I repeat it again, in real terms, namely, in terms of the loss to the nation of this production, a war is paid for substantially during its duration. Obviously this simple fact has very important implications for any program of war finance. There may be some who feel that borrowing at home may enable us to shift part of the

burden to the next generation. . . . Borrowing at home is merely one means of diverting our production into war requirements, a means which is less painful at the time but which ultimately requires a somewhat greater resort to taxation. When we borrow a hundred dollars from one of our citizens and spend it on war supplies, he is thereby prevented from spending that hundred dollars on his own consumption or investing it to enable someone else to spend it on some kind of capital production. In future years we will have to pay him not only the principal but interest as well. Obviously we could accomplish the same diversion by taxing the hundred dollars away from him. Diversion by this method alone, that is to say, by a 100 per cent taxation or pay-as-you-go policy would seem at first sight to represent the ideal policy of war finance; in principle it would appear to be the most logical, the most equitable, the least likely to create disturbances and dislocations. But, in the first place, this takes no account of the desire, indeed the necessity, of individuals making some savings to provide for a rainy day, and an effort to take so much in taxation that individual savings would be practically wiped out, would become so disruptive in character as inevitably to produce disorganization and public discontent. In the second place, realism compels us to admit that a pay-as-you-go policy has to take account of the psychological reactions to taxation. In other words, we must recognize that when diversion by means of taxation rather than borrowing is carried too far the average citizen begins to feel that there is no use in his working for any additional income and therefore he does not put his best effort into his work with the result that efficiency and production fall off. If we cannot maintain our production at maximum efficiency we may lose the war, and at least the real costs of the war will increase. It is by a reasonable balancing of these various considerations that we have to decide how much to tax and how much to borrow.

We can also divert our resources to war purposes by inflation. We can create additional supplies of money and use them to purchase what we need. In this case, just as in the others, what we take for war purposes someone else must do without. Instead of taking money from the individual citizen in the form of taxes or loans, we put our new money into competition with his old money and take the goods and services away from him by forcing prices up against him. . . . It must be realized that this inflationary method of financing a war is easily the most unfair and inequitable of all the methods of diverting labour and materials to war-time purposes. It represents merely a thinly disguised scheme of taxation of a most unjust type. It throws a grossly unfair proportion of the burden upon the person of small or medium income, the wage earner, the salaried man and those who have savings deposits, insurance policies or securities of any kind whose value is fixed in money. It represents a complete violation of the principle of taxation in accordance with ability to pay.

It is with these fundamental considerations in mind that we have decided upon our policy of war finance. Because we believe it is the part of wisdom, we shall follow as far as may be practicable a pay-as-you-go policy. In imposing the new tax burdens which this policy will require we shall be guided by the belief that all our citizens will be ready to bear some share of the cost of the war, but we shall insist on the principle of equality of sacrifice on the basis of ability to pay. We shall not of course be able to meet all war costs by taxation, because, as already indicated, there is a limit to the taxes that can be imposed without producing inefficiency, a lack of enterprise, and serious discontent. As the first necessity is to win the war as quickly as possible and without undue cost, we cannot carry taxes beyond the point where they seriously interfere with production. But we are not prepared to be timid or lighthearted in judging where this point lies, if need arises. What we cannot meet by taxation we shall finance by means of borrowing from the Canadian public at rates as low as possible.

The Minister of Finance drove home the point again in the following passage of his budget speech of June, 1940:

If an appropriate financial policy is not followed the ultimate result will inevitably be that the government will be frustrated in its attempt to procure goods for war purposes by the competition of consumers who seek to spend their increased buying power to satisfy civilian wants. In that event, also, the familiar spiral of rising prices, then rising wages and costs, and then prices rising still further would begin to work. Prices would rise more rapidly than wages and salaries, and, by this indirect, hidden and most inequitable process, the civilian population and particularly the wage and salary earners and the receivers of fixed incomes, would be forced to curtail their consumption not only of luxuries but of comforts and necessaries as well. Eventually in such a process our entire economic life would be disorganized; a hectic period characterized by feverish speculation, waste and extravagance would develop; and a collapse of the inflationary structure would be as inevitable as it was at the close of the last war.

The government's financial and economic policies have been so designed as to try to safeguard against that type of situation. They have been evolved with the aim to avoid unjustified price increases or speculative excesses, to keep our economy functioning as effectually as possible and to secure the necessary diversions of man-power, equipment and materials to war purposes in a way which would be the least dangerous to the economy and the most equitable as between different individuals and groups.

And again in the budget speech of April, 1941:

. . . the budgetary task of these years of war is that of devising financial policies which will assist in attaining the single object of both the government and parliament, the mobilizing of the maximum war strength of this country. In planning these policies, the government set for itself two objectives:

First, to bring the country as rapidly as possible to the full use of its resources and man-power. For this, financial policy could not be the sole nor even the chief instrument, but it was necessary that it should help and not hinder, that it should keep step with the work of industrial and military organization.

The government's second objective was to follow "as far as may be practicable a pay-as-you-go policy." This it derived not from any dogma of financial orthodoxy, whatever that may be, but from the known and proved inequities and the disorganizing and shattering effects of inflationary rises in prices and incomes.

By 1942 a full complement of direct controls in the form of price ceilings, rationing of goods, and controls over manpower had been installed, and the Minister was able to review his financial policy as part of a broader scheme. He nevertheless urged the necessity of further tax increases, and supported them with the following argument:

> These fiscal measures are necessary also to success in our four-front battle against inflation. The price ceiling, control and rationing of supplies, the direction of man-power, and fiscal policy are complementary, not alternative measures. The offensive must be maintained on all four fronts. No one front can be held unless the others are held. The price ceiling, a sound policy which is being administered with great courage and imagination, cannot itself defeat inflation. If I may venture another military metaphor, it can prevent the enemy from winning by infiltration.

As the long struggle dragged on, and no one saw the end, the role of the financial programme—for many people the most oppressive aspect of the war—was justified and explained again and again. In March, 1943, the budget speech carried the following message:

> As I have said frequently, financial measures are but one of the means through which we link the whole war programme together. They are instruments and not ends in themselves. They are instruments which must be used wisely lest we frustrate our efforts now and sow the seeds of intolerable conditions later. Financial measures are one of the means through which each person has his share in this war. Taxes and loans are not exactions from the people by a government. They are weapons which the people through their elected representatives and the free methods of democracy have fashioned for their own use and their common purpose. We cannot all man guns and planes and ships; we cannot all build guns and planes and ships, but the Canadian people have shown by the reception which has been given to each succeeding wartime budget that they are ready to wield these weapons, each according to his strength and all against the people's enemies. They are ready to accept their share in each increase in the effective organization for war of which the budget is but the financial counterpart.

By June, 1944, however, the end appeared to be in sight, and the Minister of Finance began to turn to the consideration of post-war tax problems. In introducing some minor alleviations he stated:

> It is no more than prudent to give sober consideration to some of the problems which will arise when we are able to release some portion of our

productive capacity for the purposes of peace. Let no one misunderstand me. This is no time to begin the execution, as distinguished from the making, of post-war plans. There is other work for every pair of hands at the moment. I am concerned only with clearing away some of the uncertainties of fiscal policy—opening the way for business firms, both large and small, to proceed on as definite as possible a basis with the drawing up of plans for the post-war conversion and expansion of industry and trade on which employment after the war will depend. If the planning and designing can be done, the execution of the plans will come in good time.

Finally, in October, 1945, in the flush of victory, the same Minister who had presented the first wartime budget of September, 1939, Hon. J. L. Ilsley, had the satisfying privilege of reviewing the wartime programme in retrospect. His words provide not only an epilogue to this chapter, but a compact summary of the major wartime developments in all aspects of the financial programme:

Mr. Speaker, in presenting to the house tonight the government's proposals for meeting the financial requirements of the present fiscal year in a budget, which is the first to follow the cessation of hostilities both in Europe and in the Pacific, I am reminded that six years and one month ago, on September 12, 1939, I presented at the special session of parliament, on behalf of the then Minister of Finance, the first budget following the outbreak of war.

I was impelled to warn at that time against expecting the war "to be a short and only moderately expensive one" and said further, "We must make our plans now with the full realization that we may be in for years of strenuous national effort". Though we foresaw the kind of problems we would have to meet and something of the magnitude of the effort, none of us realized how strenuous or how long those years would be.

It is a matter for great thankfulness that we have accomplished the task and that we can now confront, in good order and in good heart, a future which is filled with problems and difficulties but also with promise.

It was helpful to me in preparing this budget, and I think it will be helpful to the house, to take a glance back over the rugged path which we have travelled before turning our attention to the road ahead.

In the budget speech of September 1939, certain broad principles of war finance were laid down. The first one was that we should "follow as far as may be practicable a pay-as-you-go policy". It was explained that in the view of the government this meant a rapid increase in the level of taxation as our war effort and national income expanded, having due regard to the needs of war, the necessity of preserving incentive, and the need for allowing individual savings to be made. In the course of the war, the government was seldom criticized for not pressing forward rapidly enough on this policy.

The income tax was increased by 20 per cent in 1939 and moved in three more swift steps to the full war level established in the budget of 1942. The increase to this level of income taxation with the provision for refundable taxes was made possible by the withdrawal of the provincial governments from the income tax fields under the agreements of 1941. In 1943, without increasing the general level of the personal income tax, the pay-as-you-earn system was adopted and collections put on a current basis. In the course of these changes, by advancing the dates of payment we were able to augment the revenue of the war years substantially. With the exception of the cancellation of the refundable feature of the personal income tax in 1944 and of minor amendments, the taxation of personal incomes remains at the level established in 1942.

The Excess Profits Tax Act, provisionally enacted in the fall of 1939, was given its present form in 1940, and in 1942 the rate of the "excess profits" was increased to 100 per cent of which 20 per cent is to be refunded.

Succession duties were first imposed in 1941 and have not been changed since except in minor degree.

In 1940 and 1941 new and increased commodity taxes were imposed for exchange reasons, to encourage transfer to war production and for revenue. Since 1942 the main increases in taxation have been in indirect taxes applying to commodities and services which were not necessaries of life and of which frequent purchase gave some evidence of ability to pay.

By about the middle of the war we had thus reached nearly the full wartime level of taxation. By previous Canadian standards, the level of taxes was enormously high. It was, however, by no means the highest tax level among comparable countries and, generally speaking, the taxation of the lower incomes was less severe than in other countries.

The result of the balance we endeavoured to keep between taxation and borrowing has been that up to March 31, 1945, after meeting all other expenditures, we covered about 45 per cent of our war expenditures out of current revenues.

The second principle enunciated in September 1939 was that, after an initial credit expansion, designed to facilitate a rapid increase in production, we should endeavour to limit our borrowings as closely as possible to the genuine savings of the country. In pursuit of this principle, our initial borrowing was from the chartered banks, followed by a war loan offered to the public but not distributed among individuals by the intensive effort which has characterized the victory loans. In May 1940, war savings certificates were instituted and the campaign to increase savings which is still being carried on was begun. With the first victory loan of May 1941, full emphasis was given to borrowing the savings of individuals, and the organization which later became the national war finance committee began the notable and patriotic work which they are still carrying on with such great initiative and thoroughness. In the first victory loan the number of individual cash subscriptions was 946,549. In the eighth victory loan of last May, the number of individual subscriptions was 3,178,275. I trust that in the ninth victory loan which is being offered to the public this month this great number will be maintained or exceeded. It is difficult to estimate the importance for the future of the very large savings now held by individuals in this country. It is possible to make a rough estimate only of the savings held by Canadian individuals in certain liquid forms. Such an estimate, which cannot be too wide of the mark, indicates that as of May 31, 1945, in currency, bank deposits, refundable taxes and Dominion government securities, Canadian individuals held savings of more than nine and a half billion dollars and that these savings had increased by more than six and a half billions since the end of 1938. The major item in these savings is dominion government securities estimated at five and a quarter billion dollars. These figures do not, of course, include all the savings of individuals but only savings held in the liquid forms specified. They do not include savings in the form of insurance, pensions, homes, or corporate securities.

The third principle which we set out at the beginning of the war was that in our borrowings we would endeavour to set the rates of interest as low as possible. We began our public borrowings in January 1940 with the issue of a 3¼ per cent bond having an average maturity of ten years. The long-term issue which is being offered in the ninth victory loan has a term of twenty years and ten months and carries a rate of 3 per cent. At the rates now obtaining, a ten-year bond such as was issued at 3¼ per cent in January 1940 could now be issued at 2.59 per cent. As of March 31, 1939, the average rate of interest paid on the funded debt was 3.52 per cent. On March 31, 1945, the average rate had fallen to 2.51 per cent.

The fourth principle laid down for wartime financial policy was part and parcel of the other principles. It was a definite rejection of the methods of inflationary finance. That principle has affected all our operations in the fields of taxation and borrowing but its pursuit has also led us to many major decisions in other fields. It emerged in its most comprehensive form in the historic decision of October 1941, to consolidate our wage controls, institute salary control and impose a comprehensive price ceiling as of that period. The progressive development of many additional controls over the supply and distribution of goods lent support to this structure.

These simple principles have led us a long way. They have permeated war-time financial and economic policies and have given them solidity and coherence. The carrying out of these policies throughout the fields of finance and economic stabilization has been recognized, I think, as one of the most substantial of our war-time achievements and one most appreciated by the people of this country.

22 WORLD WAR II, 1940–46

Excess Profits Tax: A Case Study

THE PREVIOUS CHAPTER has reviewed the principles of war taxation in World War II. It is proposed in the present and the following chapter to consider some actual measures by which these principles were carried into effect. To do full justice to all the details of this extremely significant epoch in Canadian tax history would require far more space than can be allotted here, and it has been found necessary, therefore, to resort to some short cuts. For example, as many as possible of the details have been reduced to tabular form and are given in various tables in the Appendix. These tables, the relevant statutes, and the budget speeches of the period, accessible to most readers, provide the basic material for anyone wishing to delve more deeply. The main purpose here is rather to consider the larger aspects of each form of tax for whatever lessons may be derived for future reference. One is above all conscious of the fact that in these troubled times this is far from being an academic exercise.

The excess profits tax will be dealt with separately in this chapter, and the following chapter will be devoted to the personal income tax, the commodity taxes, and miscellaneous other taxes.

Excess Profits Tax

There is abundant evidence that the excess profits tax would be regarded by many as the most spectacular aspect of taxation in World War II. Indeed, no other single tax gave rise to more than a fraction of the literature in the legal, accounting, and economic journals. While its detailed operations have already been fairly extensively documented elsewhere there will be some advantage in attempting to sort out in perspective some of the main strands in the development of corporate taxation in the war period.

First, a word on the general purpose and nature of an excess profits tax. One of the principal justifications for a charge in the form of a levy on "excess" profits during wartime is generally accepted to be the recapture for the use of the state of all or substantially all of the profits derived by business from a level of activity regarded as directly attributable to the war. "Taking the profit out of war" is a worthy and desirable objective with which few would disagree. Modern methods of contracting for defence supplies, with protracted re-negotiations following completion of the contract, remove much of the possibility of direct "profiteering" on such contracts, but this device does not touch the industries which are indirectly stimulated by defence buying. An excess profits tax in some sense serves the same purpose in regard to these. Also, it is popularly regarded as fair that when ceilings have been imposed on salaries and wages, a "ceiling" should also be imposed on corporation profits. As a deterrent to capital investment during wartime the tax is probably effective in the case of certain long-term assets having a low rate of tax write-off. For short-term outlays the possibility of recapturing a large part of the initial cost through write-offs under a high rate of tax may, of course, have a stimulating rather than a depressing influence. This last danger has led to some disagreement regarding the anti-inflationary effects claimed for the tax. On the one hand it is argued that by removing the possibility of making extra profit the incentive for raising prices is also withdrawn; on the other, that by imposing a tax of such weight all the normal barriers against waste are removed and the forces of business that normally hold down costs and prices are frustrated. The net effect, therefore, may well be to increase prices. Strong arguments can be marshalled on both sides of this question.

The *nature* of the tax is clearly implied by its name. It is a tax on profits which, measured against some "normal" standard of profits for a business, are determined to be *excess profits*. Two main types of standard are generally used. One is a measurement based on a comparison of the profits earned in wartime with profits earned in peacetime. This form of tax may most properly be called a wartime *excess* profits tax, since it simply attempts to tax profits of the individual company that are higher in wartime than in peacetime. The other standard is a return on the capital employed in the business. Normally a flat rate of return is established as proper for all industries, although, as in the business profits war tax of World War I and in all the United States excess profits taxes, the rate may be graduated with the amount of capital employed. Since the capital employed is not that of some previous peacetime period but that of the actual year being taxed, this method suggests that it is *excessive* profits—beyond some rate of return presumably regarded as fair—rather than *excess* profits, that are sought to be taxed.

When introduced in the Special War Budget of September, 1939, to be effective for 1940, the first excess profits tax of World War II embodied both these forms of standard as alternatives. It was explained that this solution had been adopted to provide for industries where capital employed was not significant. The taxpayer was given the option of paying a tax based on a graduated scale of rates of return on capital employed, or a tax based on the excess of his earnings over average profits of the years 1936 to 1939. Under the latter method the rate of tax was to be 50 per cent of the excess, after deducting the normal corporation profits tax. Under the capital employed method the rates of tax were as follows:

On profits not in excess of 5 per cent of the amount of capital employed by the taxpayer in the business	nil
On profits in excess of 5 per cent but not exceeding 10 per cent of the capital employed	10 per cent
On profits exceeding 10 per cent but not exceeding 15 per cent of the capital employed	20 per cent
On profits exceeding 15 per cent but not exceeding 20 per cent of the capital employed	30 per cent
On profits exceeding 20 per cent but not exceeding 25 per cent of the capital employed	40 per cent
On profits exceeding 25 per cent	60 per cent

No taxes were paid under this Act, since it was entirely repealed in 1940 when a new and revised law was enacted. Under it the optional tax based on capital employed was abandoned. The Canadian excess profits tax of World War II therefore employed a standard based only on pre-war earnings as measured by 1936 to 1939 experience. There were many important exceptions to this general rule for special circumstances which will be discussed later. Before delving into these intricate aspects, however, it would be advisable to broach the more elementary matter of the tax rates in connection with which the standard period was employed.

The normal peacetime corporation tax rate remained unchanged during the war, with one exception. In 1939, applicable to corporation fiscal year ending after March 31, 1940, the rate was increased from 15 per cent to 18 per cent. Minimum taxes imposed under the excess profits tax, however, had the same effect as an increase in the normal rate. Under the revised Act, applicable to income earned after January 1, 1940, the tax was the greater of 12 per cent of total profits or 75 per cent of excess profits. There was thus a minimum total tax rate of 30 per cent, i.e., 18 per cent normal plus 12 per cent "excess." For 1941 the minimum rate was increased to 22 per cent under the excess profits tax, giving a minimum total tax of 40 per cent, i.e., 18 per cent normal plus 22 per cent "excess." The alternative rate on actual excess profits was left at 75 per cent. This schedule was applied also to the first six months of 1942, but for the balance of the war years a more complicated scheme was adopted. The minimum rate under the excess profits tax was reduced to 12 per cent, and in addition the greater of a tax of 10 per cent on total profits or 100 per cent on excess profits was made payable. Where the 100 per cent rate applied a portion of the tax equal to 20 per cent of profits in excess of 116⅔ per cent of standard profits was to be refundable after the war. Thus, if current profits were less than 116⅔ per cent of standard profits the tax rate was 40 per cent on *total* profits (including the normal 18 per cent); if current profits were greater than 116⅔ per cent of standard profits, the tax was 30 per cent of standard profits and 100 per cent of excess profits (116⅔ per cent of standard profits was the point at which the 100 per cent rate on excess profits became greater than the 10 per cent rate on total profits). One effect of this plan was that *all* profits over 116⅔ per cent of standard profits went to the government, subject to the 20 per cent post-war refund; another was that no company could retain during the period of the war following mid-1942 more than 60 per cent of its standard profits.

The *effective* or *average* rate of tax applicable to corporations under the 1940, 1941, and 1942 rate schedules was as shown in Table XXVIII. It will be apparent that the principal result of the adjustments in 1941 and 1942 was to increase the taxes payable by corporations whose profits had increased least over standard profits. For those companies having substantially increased profits a very high rate was adopted from the outset, and, excluding the refundable tax, the 1941 and 1942 adjustments made little change. For companies earning profits only moderately above their standard profits the 1940 rate was comparatively lenient, and it was in these ranges that the 1941 and 1942 increases made the deepest impression.

The above description of rates is applicable only to corporations. Sole proprietors and partners operating a business were also taxable. For 1940 the tax was the greater of 12 per cent on total profits or 75 per cent on excess profits. In 1941 the 12 per cent rate was raised to 15 per cent, and following mid-1942 the 75 per cent rate was raised to 100 per cent. Where the 100 per cent rate applied 20 per cent of profits over 117.64 per cent of standard profits were refundable after the war.

TABLE XXVIII

MARGINAL AND EFFECTIVE RATES ON CORPORATION PROFITS (COMBINED NORMAL AND EXCESS PROFITS TAXES) FOR 1940, 1941, AND 1942–5

Current year profits (standard profits taken as 100)	Marginal rates[a]				Effective rates[b]			
	1940	1941	1942–5 (inc. refund)	1942–5 (exc. refund)	1940	1941	1942–5 (inc. refund)	1942–5 (exc. refund)
$	%	%	%	%	%	%	%	%
100.00 (or less)	30.00	40.00	40.00	40.00	30.00	40.00	40.00	40.00
116.67	30.00	40.00	100.00	80.00	30.00	40.00	40.00	40.00
120.00	30.00	40.00	100.00	80.00	30.00	40.00	41.67	41.11
124.25	75.00	40.00	100.00	80.00	30.01	40.00	43.67	42.44
150.00	75.00	40.00	100.00	80.00	38.50	40.00	53.33	48.89
155.69	75.00	75.00	100.00	80.00	40.00	40.01	55.04	50.02
200.00	75.00	75.00	100.00	80.00	48.75	48.75	65.00	56.66
250.00	75.00	75.00	100.00	80.00	54.90	54.90	72.00	61.33
300.00	75.00	75.00	100.00	80.00	59.00	59.00	76.67	64.44
500.00	75.00	75.00	100.00	80.00	67.20	67.20	86.00	70.66

[a]Rate applicable to the next dollar of profits over amount shown in left-hand column.
[b]Total tax as per cent of total income.

The dramatic feature of the 1942 schedule, of course, was the 100 per cent rate on excess profits. There would be a better basis for judging its significance if exact information as to the number of companies and the aggregate amount of profits to which it applied were available. Unfortunately only an analysis of experience for the taxation year 1944 has been published by the Department of National Revenue, and to some extent the value of this compilation has been marred by subsequent substantial adjustments arising out of re-negotiation of war contracts. It is now apparent, however, that the total amount of refundable tax paid by taxpayers subject to the 100 per cent rate was about $220 million, attributable to profits earned between July 1, 1942, and December 31, 1946.

A great deal of space could be devoted to further analysis of these admittedly very complicated rate schedules, but enough has been said to indicate their general character. Of more permanent significance are the complex situations that must be dealt with when profits are subjected to extremely high rates of tax, whatever may be the particular form of the rates employed. Among the most varied and intransigent of all the problems in taxation, these will be discussed very briefly in the following pages.

The Scope of the Tax

Perhaps the issue of first importance is, to whom the tax shall apply. In principle it might be argued that it would be equitable to apply a tax of the character of an excess profits tax to all income—salary, wages, professional earnings, and so on. In actuality, however, the administrative problems of establishing a base or standard for every wage earner in the country, quite apart from other considerations, makes such an approach impracticable. Excess profits taxes have traditionally been limited, therefore, to profits of a business or trade.

Corporations in general clearly fall within the scope of the tax, although as a matter of policy certain kinds of organizations were not subjected to it in World War II. These included life insurance companies (except on the amount credited to shareholders' account), personal corporations, non-resident-owned investment corporations, Canadian investment corporations, co-operatives and credit unions, foreign business corporations, and such organizations as mutuals, charitable institutions, labour and farm associations, clubs and municipal undertakings, which are generally also exempted from income tax. The "business" status of individuals and partnerships, however, becomes a matter almost of sorting out the sheep from the goats. One starts with the presumption that employed persons and persons in a profession where personal qualifications are the governing factors (doctors, lawyers, dentists, accountants, etc.) are not carrying on a business in the usual sense. But this is only the initial hurdle. As an example of the problems encountered, consider two common classes of case that created serious difficulties—travelling salesmen and insurance agents. After consideration it was ruled that travelling salesmen who were employees of a firm were *not* taxable, while those carrying several lines on a commission basis *were* taxable, and that life insurance salesmen (who are virtually employees of one life insurance company) were *not* taxable, while agents selling fire, casualty and other insurance (who generally act for several companies) *were* taxable. Needless to say decisions of this degree of fineness are difficult to make and even more difficult to sustain.

The following is a partial list issued by the Department of National Revenue drawing a line between professional and non-professional (i.e. business) activities:

Individuals within the exemption i.e., non-taxable	*Individuals outside the exemption* i.e., taxable
1. Clergy	
lawyers, notaries	
doctors, dentists	druggists and drug companies
accountants, auditors, actuaries	business consultants, (i.e., taxpayers engaged in the business of business consultants)
teachers (e.g., private schools or business schools unless owned by a company)	
2. Engineers	
e.g., architects	builders
civil engineers	
mining engineers	metallurgists and gold refiners, assayers and analysts
chemical engineers	
3. Artists	
e.g., musicians	musical and dramatic agents and entrepreneurs
actors, radio entertainers	
writers, artists	printers, advertising agencies, photographers, publishers
4. Professional athletes	
e.g., golf pros (except profits from shops)	promoters, proprietors of arena, etc.
hockey players	
5. Personal services	
life insurance agents (who are virtually employees of one life company)	insurance agents (other than life)
	brokers
	commission agents
barbers, hairdressers	tailors
masseurs	real estate agents
chiropractors	insurance adjusters

The inclusion of sole proprietorships and partnerships also gave rise to some complications in the definition of income. The proceeds of businesses operated under these forms of ownership are normally taxed as personal income of the partners or proprietors. But for the excess profits tax it was necessary to create an artificial entity separate from the individuals concerned. One result was that certain deductions allowed for personal income tax were disallowed or allowed on a different basis for excess profits tax. On the other hand a deduction was allowed, for excess profits tax calculations, of salary not exceeding $5,000 paid to a working proprietor, which would not be allowed for establishing personal income tax liability.

Another problem in connection with the coverage of the tax was the large number of small businesses, whether incorporated or run by individuals or partners, where the difficulty and expense of establishing a standard profit would almost outweight the revenue that could be derived from the tax. A great mass of these were exempted entirely from the 100 per cent rate by a provision that in no case would the standard profit be less than $5,000, with the result that the 100 per cent rate was not payable until profits exceeded $5,833. Partnerships and sole proprietorships were not required to pay even the minimum flat rate when their earnings, before drawings, were $5,000 or less, and corporations having profits of $5,000 or less were favoured with an exemption from the 10 per cent rate. They thus paid a rate of 30 per cent (18 per cent plus 12 per cent) where the larger corporations in comparable circumstances paid a 40 per cent rate. They were also protected by a proviso that where the 10 per cent rate was applicable it should not operate to reduce current profits, after deducting the 30 per cent tax, below $3,500. These concessions not only assisted the small business but also relieved many thousands of them from the necessity of determining a standard profit.

The Measurement of the Excess

The two general forms of "standard" profit—a return on capital employed and average pre-war earnings for a period—have been discussed above. As was stated, the general standard under the excess profits tax of World War II was the average of earnings of the four calendar years 1936 to 1939 inclusive. Before calculating the average, the actual profits of the years 1936, 1937, and 1938 were increased or reduced by 7½ per cent of the change in capital employed between the beginning of these years and the commencement of the 1939 year, in order to obtain as nearly as possible uniform treatment of each year in the base period. Where a company had a fiscal year different from the calendar year it was also required to determine its standard by apportioning its earnings of the base years to the above calendar years. Where a taxpayer had not been in business for the whole of the standard period he could take as his standard the average of his earnings during the period in which he actually had been in business. If the period were only one year he could, if he wished, take the earnings of that year as his standard (although under certain conditions he could apply to the Board of Referees to have a standard determined for his business; see below). In general, losses in the standard period were not required to be deducted from income of the other years in the standard period, but the loss years had to be counted in determining the average; in short, loss years were counted as zero in working out the average.

These were adjustments of general application to all taxpayers. In addition, however, many situations appeared in which adjustments of a more fundamental character were necessary to establish a reasonable and equitable basis for measuring the excess. These arose from two main causes: first, deficiencies and abnormalities in the base period experience which made it unrepresentative for the business; and second, changes in the character of the corporation or the nature of its business during the years of taxation which outmoded the experience of 1936–9 as a reasonable standard. The principal adjustments for abnormal or deficient experience in the base period years were as follows:

(i) *Where profits of a year in the base period were abnormally low.* An alleviation was provided under which, if the profits of any one year in the base period was less than 50 per cent of the average of the other years, that year could be dropped from the base period and the standard profit be calculated as the average of the profits of the other years.

(ii) *Where a business was depressed during the standard period.* Where the business was depressed in the standard period, because of conditions peculiar either to itself or to the industry, provision was made for a special determination of standard profit. The taxpayer was permitted to calculate a standard profit on such basis as he thought just, but not in an amount in excess of 10 per cent of capital employed at the commencement of the last year of his standard period. The Minister of National Revenue was authorized to accept the taxpayer's determination or to refer the case to a Board of Referees, established for this purpose in November, 1940. The Board was given authority to determine the standard profit in an amount "equal to the average yearly profits of the taxpayer during the standard period or to interest at the rate of not less than five nor more than ten per cent per annum on the amount of capital employed at the commencement of the last year or fiscal period of the taxpayer in the standard period." However, a wide latitude was granted the Board where it was satisfied that a standard based on capital employed "would result in the imposition of excessive taxation amounting to extreme hardship or extreme discrimination or would jeopardize the continuation of the business," because capital was not an important factor in the business, because it had become abnormally impaired, or because it was abnormally low owing to other extraordinary circumstances. In these conditions the Board was allowed to determine the standard profit "on such basis as it thinks just having regard to the standard profits of taxpayers in similar circumstances engaged in the same or an analogous class of business."

(iii) *Where the firm was not in business throughout the standard period.* Although, as stated above, a taxpayer who had been in business for only a part of the standard period could base his standard profits on the experience of that period, he had the alternative, if he commenced business on or after January 1, 1938, and before January 1, 1939, of applying to the Board of Referees for a standard profit. Where a business was commenced after January 1, 1939 (i.e., where there was not a complete year of experience in the standard period) it was mandatory that the standard profit be set by the Board of Referees. In either of these cases the Board was authorized to allow the same rate of return on capital employed in the business as was earned during the standard period by taxpayers in similar circumstances and engaged in the same or a similar line of business. For a new business, therefore, the Board was not limited to establishing a standard within the range from 5 to 10 per cent on capital employed. Furthermore, it could grant a standard "on such basis as it thinks just having regard to the standard profits of taxpayers in similar circumstances" if it was satisfied that a return on capital employed would not be a fair basis for establishing the standard. Apparently this last power was quite frequently employed to grant such a standard as the Board felt to be fair and reasonable.

Thus the principal classes of abnormality in the base period for which special relief was provided were years of loss, depressed conditions, and incomplete earnings experience. Reliefs were also given for changes in the character of the corporation or the nature of its business in the following circumstances:

(i) *Where capital employed in the business increased or decreased from capital employed in the standard period.* For all businesses, whether the standard profit was determined on the basis of 1936 to 1939 earnings or by the Board of Referees on the basis of capital employed, an adjustment was made in the standard profit where the capital employed in the taxation year was greater or less than at the commencement of the 1939 taxation year. The adjustment was made by deducting from or adding to the standard profit an amount equal to 7½ per cent of the increase or decrease in capital, an adjustment designed presumably to compensate for a change in the earning power of the corporation due solely to an alteration in the invested capital. In general the adjustment was made only if the change in capital employed was accompanied by an alteration in the outstanding capital stock. A reduction in the standard was provided where capital employed had been decreased without any change in capital stock, but this reduction was limited to the amount of the aggregate net increase made in the standard by the adjustments for changes in capital employed during the base period.

(ii) *Where capital employed in the business increased by one-third or more over the standard period.* In general, where capital employed in the business had increased by one-third or more over the capital employed in the standard period (again, in the case of a corporation, only if accompanied by an equivalent increase in capital stock) the taxpayer could apply to the Board of Referees to have his standard profit ascertained as though he were carrying on a new business.

(iii) *Where the capital employed in 1944 had increased, without changes in capital stock, over capital employed in 1939.* As a special recognition of increases in capital during the war period which had not been accompanied by an increase in capital stock, taxpayers were permitted to increase their standard profit by an amount of 5 per cent of the change in capital employed between 1939 and 1944 which had not been accompanied by an increase in capital stock.

(iv) *Where the capital employed was less in 1945 and later years than in 1944.* The relieving adjustment just described was accompanied by a penalty adjustment for reductions in capital employed following 1944 even though not accompanied by a reduction in capital stock. The standard profit was reduced by 5 per cent of the reduction in capital employed in 1945 and later years as compared with 1944, irrespective of whether capital stock was reduced.

(v) *Where the business carried on in the taxation year was substantially different from the business carried on in the standard period.* A measure was introduced in 1944, applicable to that year and the following years of the excess profits tax, which permitted the Minister to have the Board of Referees determine the standard profit where he was satisfied that the business carried on by the taxpayer had become substantially different from the business carried on during the standard period. Many businesses underwent a complete metamorphosis during the war, and experience of a four-year period which commenced eight years before often did not provide a fair comparison of like with like. A committee of officials in the Taxation Division known as the Business Classification Committee was set up to determine the cases that should be referred to the Board for establishment of a standard as a new business.

The application of this measure was considerably broadened under order in council in August, 1945, when its scope was extended to require the determination of a standard profit by the Board of Referees where a different business than that of the standard period was carried on in any year after 1939. This extension was later confirmed by an amendment to the law.

Since the concept of "capital employed" was significant in many of the adjustments just described, its definition merits comment. In general it meant equity capital employed in the business, and was determined from the assets, valued at cost, less certain deductions. On the one side the total value of all tangible and intangible assets used in the business was established, including both assets acquired by cash purchase and assets acquired for considerations other than cash. The valuation of assets was made as of the date of their acquisition, in many instances a figure considerably different from the current value. Accounts receivable and money or bank deposits actually used in the business were also included. Against the aggregate of these amounts there were offset subsidies received from a government to assist in the acquisition of any asset, total depreciation taken since 1917 on fixed assets, and such deductions for depletion write-offs as the Board of Referees deemed "fair and reasonable." Deductions were also made for borrowed money and debts (except income bonds or debenture where the interest payment had not been allowed as a deductible expense and such non-interest-bearing inter-company loans as the Minister determined to be "in the nature of permanently invested capital"), investments yielding tax-free income and investments that were neither acquired nor required for the purpose of the business. The whole calculation was made as at the beginning of the year, for the adjustment of the base period profits described earlier, but for determining capital employed as at the beginning of the taxation years further adjustments were made for changes during the year. These included increases or decreases in capital stock made during the year and between 1940 and 1943 the deduction of 50 per cent of cash dividends declared during the year was required. In 1944 and following years the amount of cash dividends declared during the year was to be deducted only to the extent that they reduced capital employed at the beginning of the year, and never was more than 50 per cent of the dividend to be deducted. Contrary to the calculation made for the base period years, however, dividends declared and unpaid at the beginning of the year were not treated as a liability in determining capital employed at the commencement of the 1940 and later taxation years. This was compensated for by the fact that cash dividends actually paid during 1940 and later years were required to be deducted in whole or in part from the capital employed as determined at the beginning of the year.

On the theoretical side this definition differed from both the American and British by excluding any recognition of borrowed capital (except the limited recognition of inter-company loans), a feature having both its exponents and its critics. Undoubtedly any future use of the concept will again bring forth similar divergences of opinion. Of the main practical difficulties encountered one would include the problem of valuation of assets for which no cash had been paid, and for many of which the original consideration would be less than their existing balance sheet amount (mining properties, power rights, land, patents, copyrights, goodwill, etc.). The determination of whether cash on hand was actually employed in the business was troublesome, as was the determination of whether inter-company loans were "permanently invested" in the subsidiary. Adjustments for changes in capital during the course of the year also provoked arguments. Indeed, several aspects of the matter were fraught with extreme complexity. One business man, in an address before the Canadian Economic and Political Science Association, in 1941, probably expressed the general sentiment of the business community when he said:

> I do not think that it is an exaggeration to say that the utmost confusion has surrounded the question of the ascertainment of capital employed and its application to a specific case. . . . Many companies have been through various sorts of mergers, capital reorganizations, and so on, which makes historical cost very difficult to determine and which raises the most unbelievable complications and doubts, to such an extent that I am strongly inclined to the belief that the theory of a return on capital, while sound in principle, is unworkable in practice.[1]

[1]C. W. Leach, "Excess Profits Taxation in Canada—A Business Man's View," *Canadian Journal of Economics and Political Science*, vol. VII (1941), pp. 368–9.

So much for the rather involved history of the adjustments in the rules for determining excess profits. Technical as this description may appear, the significance of any one of the possible relieving adjustments cannot be over-estimated when considered in the light of a 100 per cent rate of tax. A most realistic appraisal of this fact was given by a Montreal chartered accountant during the war, in the following words: "With rates of taxes at 75 per cent and now 100 per cent of the amount in excess of the average or standard profits in the period from 1936 to 1939 having to be paid to the government, the successful application for, and the receiving of, an adequate standard profit from the Board of Referees, is possibly the most important and profitable work which can be undertaken by the executives of any company."[2]

Some Correctives for High Taxation

So far only the more technical aspects of the excess profits tax have been dealt with. Of more general concern are the effects on economic incentives and business practices of taxation as burdensome as that described above, effects which are by no means uniform. Pressures are created which work in almost opposite directions. Where long-term capital expenditures are in question the negligible profit after tax is usually insufficient to encourage corporations to undertake the risk involved in very heavy outlays. Particularly is this true of heavy capital expenditures incurred primarily for defence production. By the same token, where the life of a company is entirely dependent on a limited natural resource, and the only hope of obtaining a return of the original investment is through the exploitation of that resource (e.g., a mine or an oil well) the owners of that company will feel an understandable reluctance to push forward such exploitation during a period when most of the fruits will go to the government. By contrast with this depressing effect, there are certain types of business expenditure for which high tax rates provide a positive stimulus. Where, for example, the whole amount of an expenditure may be written off in the year the saving under very high tax rates provides an almost irresistible attraction.

Both these classes of problem were encountered in World War II. One class had to be dealt with to ensure that essential investment was forthcoming and the other to ensure that the revenue was not undermined. Measures adopted under the first heading are discussed below.

[2]E. C. Leetham, "The Preparation and Presentation of a Brief before the Board of Referees, *Canadian Chartered Accountant*, vol. XLIV (Feb. 1944), pp. 73–4.

(i) *War Contracts Depreciation Board.* Expansion of wartime facilities, most of which were expected to be of little post-war value, was encouraged by the granting of accelerated depreciation—the privilege of writing off a capital asset over a period shorter than that normally adopted. Such accelerated depreciation was awarded on capital outlays for the production of war materials which seemed likely to "have no reasonable post-war value" and for "capital expenditures incurred under a war contract." Awards were granted by the War Contracts Depreciation Board, established in August, 1940. No fixed formula was laid down for the Board, but it is understood that accelerated depreciation was normally granted over a three- to five-year period. To the end of 1944, when the Board had almost completed its work, such depreciation had been granted on expenditures exceeding $275 million.

(ii) *War Exchange Conservation Act.* A serious problem of the wartime period was the acute shortage of U.S. funds prior to the Hyde Park agreement. During the first three years of the war serious efforts were made by the Canadian government to encourage imports from the sterling area, to discourage imports from the United States, and, in addition, to stimulate exports to the United States. Accelerated depreciation was the main device used to achieve this last purpose. Under part III of the War Exchange Conservation Act, 1940, the Minister of Finance was authorized to enter into agreements with companies to allow them a rapid write-off of expenditures on assets that would increase our exports to the United States and which would not otherwise have been undertaken. These expenditures amounted in total to about $59 million, and the industries affected were mainly mining, lumbering, oil, and power. In some cases the concession took the form of a special depletion allowance or a tax credit, depending on the requirements of the individual circumstance. These agreements, all of which tabled in Parliament, were negotiated directly between the companies concerned and the Minister of Finance, without the intervention of a special board or other agency. After mid-1943, when the currency problem became less acute, no further agreements were written under this authority.

(iii) *Special agreements for depreciation.* Accelerated depreciation was given under separate agreements for substantial investments, amounting to about $180 million, incurred by the Aluminum Company of Canada for expansion of power and production facilities.

(iv) *Special depreciation instituted in 1944.* The three forms of wartime accelerated depreciation indicated above were succeeded by the broader system inaugurated late in 1944. This plan, providing for the rapid write-off of capital expenditures, was intended primarily as a post-war measure, and will be discussed fully later. It is mentioned here only because in actual fact it came into operation prior to the end of hostilities and before there had been any substantial tax reductions. Certain projects not primarily of a defence character were encouraged to go ahead in the last days of the war as a result of this step. A companion measure was the rate concession given for the first year of new businesses started after June 26, 1944. They were taxed at the minimum rates only, i.e. 40 per cent.

(v) *Encouragement given the extractive industries.* Measures of an order different from the above were adopted to encourage primary industries to speed up the exploitation of depletable resources such as minerals, petroleum, timber, and so on. These took several forms. For gold mines and oil wells the standard profit was recalculated each year by adjusting the actual average profit of the standard period upward by the increase in physical production in the taxation year over average annual physical production in the standard period. Thus no excess profits could arise from an increase in production alone; they would come about only if there had been an increase in the unit profit. It will be noted that this provision was limited to gold and petroleum. Following the income tax precedent established in 1936 a three-year exemption from excess profits tax was granted for new base metal and strategic mineral mines coming into production between January 1, 1943, and December 31, 1945, and this was extended to any metalliferous mine that came into production after January 1, 1946. The mining and oil industries were also both assisted by a broadening of the write-off of exploration expenses to include off-property exploration and by other concessions.

The timber industry was assisted by means of a special rate of depletion. Where timber companies were taxable at the highest rate (75 per cent or 100 per cent) they were allowed to deduct an additional amount of depletion, equal to one-third of their normal depletion, on the increase in the timber cut in the taxation year over the average cut in the base period. Pulp and paper companies were also given an additional depletion deduction of 15 cents per cord on pulpwood cut. These allowances were both in effect from 1941 onward until repealed after the war.

(vi) *Deferred maintenance and repairs.* A problem of a similar order to those just mentioned arose in connection with the maintenance and repair of plant and equipment. Much of the normal expenditure of this kind could not be undertaken during the war because of material and labour shortages, and the suggestion was commonly advanced that businesses should be allowed to establish a reserve to meet such expenditures later on when it became possible to make them. Otherwise, it was argued, the government was permanently depriving industry of funds which had been demonstrated by experience to be necessary for proper maintenance. The government showed itself sympathetic with this argument, but not to the extent of allowing a reserve. Instead it was indicated that after the war a period would be selected in respect of which one-half the expenditures on maintenance and repairs could be carried back to the accounts of a wartime year in which the company paid the 100 per cent rate of excess profits tax. Apparently post-war economic activity was so buoyant, however, that the government did not feel justified in adding the inflationary pressure of the incentive offered by this formula, and it never became effective.

(vii) *Reserve against inventory losses.* Only one reserve of any consequence was allowed; this was an inventory reserve. Its allowance was within the discretion of the Minister, and only a company taxed at the highest rate was eligible. Its purpose was to make a "reasonable provision as a reserve against future depreciation in inventory values . . . having regard to a normal quantity of stock in trade necessary for the business as indicated by the quantities on hand during the standard period." On such "normal" quantities the taxpayer was to be protected against depreciation below either the prices governing inventory at the end of his 1939 taxation year or during the month of August, 1939. The allowance was by no means automatically granted, and each taxpayer seeking it had to prove that he was entitled to it. Provision was made for adding back the reserves in the post-war period in the event that prices did not depreciate, and one would judge that many of them were found to be unnecessary, although no statistics on the matter have ever been made public.

(viii) *General relieving measures.* Finally, in addition to the several specific measures of relief outlined above, some general measures were adopted during the war which helped to overcome the inevitable inequities and unavoidable discouragement of punishing taxation. Probably the most important of these was the introduction of the loss carry-over, of great assistance to the feast and famine industries which otherwise would have been bankrupted by an excess profits tax levied at a 100 per cent rate. The first step was taken in the 1942 budget, and provided for a one-year carry-forward, effective for losses incurred in

1942 and thereafter. In the 1943 budget the allowance was extended to a two-year carry-forward for farmers, the general rule remaining at one year. A much broader general measure was provided in the 1944 budget, however. Losses sustained in 1944 and any year thereafter could be carried back one year and forward three years.

So much for the relieving aspects of this Spartan tax measure. The specific suppressive measures need only be briefly mentioned. They included limitations on advertising expenditures and charitable donations. One might also include here the measures adopted to prevent businesses from increasing their total standard profits by creating new corporations. Advertising outlays allowable as a deductible expense were restricted by an administrative memorandum issued in 1942 to an amount comparable to expenditures in the base period, making allowance for changes in the character of the business. This restriction was in effect until January 1, 1946. The limitation on charitable donations was introduced in 1944, after it had become apparent that extremely heavy emphasis was being given in certain campaigns to the tax savings possibilities of deducting a charitable donation from income taxed at a 100 per cent rate. The maximum tax saving on charitable donations made by companies in excess of a previous average level of donations was limited to 40 per cent. In the case of individuals carrying on a business subject to excess profits tax, the maximum tax saving allowed on the increased donations was 15 per cent. The level by which the increase was measured was the average amount of donations in the last two fiscal periods ended before July 1, 1942. This restriction came into operation with respect to fiscal years ending in 1944 and was terminated with respect to fiscal years ending after June 30, 1947.

A limitation aimed specifically against the possibility of obtaining a higher aggregate standard profit by splitting one business operation into several corporations was also introduced. It was fairly drastic. Where new companies were organized as the controlled subsidiaries of an existing corporation in 1940 or subsequently, the total standard profit of all such subsidiaries was limited to an aggregate of $5,000. Exceptions were made only for new corporations established to carry out a defence contract and to the cases where the Minister could be satisfied that there had been an actual increase in the capital employed by reason of the split-up.

As a final comment, it should be said that it is doubtful whether any excess profits tax could long withstand the pressure to increase wages and salaries without some independent control over these forms of business expense. The general powers of the administration to disallow unreasonable outlays are totally inadequate to cope with this problem. The salary and wages ceiling of the last war were therefore an almost inevitable complement to an excess profits tax.

23 WORLD WAR II, 1940–46

Personal Income and Other Taxes

THE PERSONAL INCOME TAX undoubtedly ranks with the excess profits tax as an unforgettable feature of taxation in World War II. This revenue source was exploited with an energy that surpassed all previous expectations. Rates were raised to levels which seem almost as unbelievable in retrospect as they would have seemed in anticipation. Through this medium direct taxation of individuals was given a greater prominence in the federal budget than ever before or since.

An essential preliminary to the intensive development of this field by the Dominion was the withdrawal of the multitude of provincial and municipal income taxes, a purpose which was achieved through the Wartime Tax Agreements. These arrangements unquestionably contributed in large measure to the success of the federal programme of direct taxation during the war (see chap. 32). Once having obtained a free hand the Dominion rapidly increased rates and broadened the coverage of its tax by lowering exemptions. Prior to the war the personal income tax applied only to some 200,000 to 250,000 persons, or perhaps 5 per cent of the working population. Less than one-fifth of the total revenue came from incomes below $5,000. Within five years the combined effect of reduced exemptions and higher incomes had increased its scope tenfold, until every second person in the working force was paying income tax, and over half the total revenue was coming from incomes of $5,000 or less.

This upheaval came about in four main stages. The first was a flat 20 per cent increase in existing rates for 1939. The second was effected in 1940 by further rate changes and by the introduction of the national defence tax, patterned after the Manitoba wages tax. The distinctive feature of the national defence tax was that it applied to the total income at a flat rate (3 per cent for single persons, 2 per cent for married) in addition to the graduated tax, and was deductible at the source from most income payments. Another new feature introduced with this form of levy was the tax credit for dependents. The basic exemptions were fixed by law at $600 for single status and $1,200 for married (for 1940) but for each dependent (e.g., a child) the taxpayer was allowed to deduct an amount of $8 per annum (for 1940) from his tax. It will be recalled that the *Report* of the Rowell-Sirois Commission had proposed the adoption of such tax credits. In form the national defence tax was retained throughout the wartime period, although after the revision of 1942 it was embodied into the rate structure as a "normal" tax. The final rates were 7 per cent for single persons with incomes up to $1,800, 8 per cent for single persons with incomes over $3,000. The tax credit principle was retained and indeed extended in 1942 to the main graduated tax.

The third step in 1941 followed the pattern of reduced exemptions and increased rates, but in 1942, the last phase, the whole system was revised. The national defence tax became the normal tax, a refundable tax portion (to be discussed in a moment) was introduced, and except for a basic deduction of $660 granted all taxpayers under the graduated tax all exemptions were converted into either tax credits or "starting" incomes. (A "starting" income is a point below which the income is totally exempt but above which it is totally taxable.) A married taxpayer did not start to pay the 7 per cent normal tax until his income exceeded $1,200, and he was allowed $28 tax credit for each dependent other than the one for whom he claimed married status. Under the graduated tax he was allowed a tax credit of $150 for his wife (or dependent of the same class) and $80 apiece for other dependents, but in no case was to pay tax if his income were below $1,200.

One disturbing consequence followed from the "starting" point principle. It initially introduced a marginal rate of 100 per cent on additional income in a narrow range above the starting point. To illustrate: the 7 per cent normal tax applied to the total income of a single person once that income exceeded $660, and as a result the tax absorbed all the additional income over $660 until the total income exceeded $733. The area was even broader for married persons, without dependents, earning over $1,200, where it extended to $1,362. The inequity of this result was recognized in the budget of 1943 by a provision that in no case would the tax payable exceed two-thirds of the additional income immediately over $660 and $1,200. Since one-half the tax was refundable, this change gave an effective marginal pure tax rate of 33⅓ per cent. Thus the worst "notch" (in the language of the trade) was considerably ameliorated by this change. The "notches" at $1,800 and $3,000 in the normal tax on single persons, where theoretically one cent of extra income could increase the tax as much as $30, remained however, until the normal tax was abandoned in 1947.[1]

The theoretical arguments regarding the tax credit for dependents have never been resolved to everyone's satisfaction. The Rowell-Sirois *Report* (and the official budget speeches) supported the method on the ground that the relief for dependents should be uniform for all taxpayers and that the wealthy person should not receive the greater tax saving (because of his higher marginal rate) that followed from an income deduction. On the other hand it has been argued that the greater value of the income deduction for the wealthy person is only in proportion to the greater penalty he suffers under graduated rates of tax; in short, it is illogical to regard it as the bestowal of a favour if a deduction from income taxed at a marginal rate of 95 per cent is of more value than a deduction from income taxed at a marginal rate of 25 per cent.

A structural change in the rate not yet mentioned was the abandonment in 1941 of the graduated tax on investment income and the substitution of a flat rate of 4 per cent, still in effect.

The refundable tax feature, introduced in the revision of 1942, was an experiment launched under the highest auspices. The late Lord Keynes had argued for the adoption of a system of compulsory savings as a means of achieving the ends of wartime finance and at the same time building up a fund of consumer purchasing power for the post-war period. The plan was accepted in England and Canada, and for a brief period in the United States. In Canada it was announced in the budget of 1942 as part of the substantial tax increase of that year. Here it took the form of a measure designed to enforce saving only on those taxpayers who were not saving through certain other mediums. These other forms were selected not on the basis of their desirability as methods of saving, however, but rather on the basis of the penalty that would fall on the taxpayer if he were forced to abandon them. This proved to be a difficult line to hold, and in one or two instances compromises had to be effected.

The savings portion of the tax was determined by a rather complicated formula. In general it was one-half the tax, but there were

[1]For a more detailed description of the personal income tax structure of the early war period see the bulletins on *National Defence Tax* (1940 and 1941) and the bulletin *Your 1942 Income Tax* issued by the Taxation Division, Department of National Revenue. An analysis of the effect of structural changes in rates has also been made by Wm. C. Hood in a note in the *Canadian Journal of Economics and Political Science* for May, 1949: "Structural Changes in the Dominion Personal Income Tax, 1932–49."

upper limits. For a single person it could not exceed 8 per cent of taxable income with a maximum of $800; for a person having married or equivalent status it could not exceed 10 per cent of the taxable income, with a maximum of $1,000; and for dependents the percentage was increased by 1 per cent but not to exceed $100 for each dependent. Against this portion of the tax could be offset certain forms of voluntary savings. These were of four main types: (1) contributions to superannuation, retirement, or pension funds; (2) premiums on life insurance policies; (3) payment on annuities and certain forms of savings contracts, and (4) principal payments on a mortgage or agreement of sale. At first, payments on a Dominion government annuity were disallowed on the ground that their postponement would not result in substantial loss to the taxpayer, but this position had to be abandoned in 1943.

Few aspects of the wartime tax programme aroused more contention than the refundable tax. Among the smaller problems were the extremely difficult distinctions that had to be made between alternative forms of savings. In general the deductions were restricted to liabilities of the taxpayer outstanding before June 23, 1942, but a limited concession was made for life insurance of narrowly specified types purchased on or after that date. At first the line was held at mortgages registered on that date in the name of the taxpayer, but so many taxpayers had, for business or other reasons, placed their residence in their wife's name that the limit had to be extended to cover such situations when *bona fide*. The general rule that the alternative savings were to be of such a form that their postponement would result in *substantial* loss to the taxpayer was also probably difficult to convey to the public at large, and undoubtedly the Minister of Finance received constant requests for the deduction of savings that in the eyes of the taxpayer were equally desirable.

The greatest objection, however, appears to have come from those taxpayers who were forced to pay the refundable portion. Because it represented such a large part—one-half—of the tax in the lower incomes its deduction at the source took a substantial bite out of take-home pay. This might not have had such ill effects had it not been for a widespread doubt that the savings would be repaid as promised. Despite continued efforts of the Minister of Finance and certain of the larger employers to enhance the prestige of this forced saving it appears not to have been accepted with any confidence by the majority of workers. Had it been administratively feasible to inform the wage earner of the portion of his tax deduction that was for savings and to inform him at short intervals of the accumulated total standing to his account, some of the dissatisfaction might have been overcome. These and other difficulties with the tax were frankly recognized by the Minister of Finance in 1944 when he announced its abandonment as from July 1 of that year. It had been in effect for half of 1942, all of 1943, and half of 1944. A total of some $296 million was collected, and paid back with interest at 2 per cent per annum in the amount of $59 million in March, 1948, and $237 million in March, 1949. The 1948 payment related to the year 1942, and the 1949 payment to the other two years. Thus the fears of taxpayers were proved to be groundless, but whether a system of compulsory savings through tax deductions could be made palatable in another war remains an open question.

Another aspect of the personal income tax fraught with problems was the taxation of the armed services and related groups. In general this experience illustrated the enormous difficulties encountered in confining within proper limits an outright exemption from tax. Prior to the war, service income was fully taxable. Early in the war, before any appreciable numbers of servicemen had been sent overseas, an exemption was granted for the ranks in Canada while officers in Canada remained fully taxable. The result of this arrangement was that certain of the men in the ranks holding the position of staff sergeant or warrant officer and receiving trades pay were netting two or three hundred dollars more in tax-free pay than the lowest grade of commissioned officer could retain after paying income tax. The effects on morale may be imagined. The problem was overcome by switching to an exemption in terms of earnings, regardless of rank. An unusual device was adopted to achieve this result. Since it was not felt necessary to give the exemption in a form that would benefit any but the lower paid groups, it was given as a tax credit which, for a single man, completely offset the tax payable on $1,600 of pay. This tax credit, however, was reduced in the ratio that the pay exceeded $1,600, so that when the pay reached $3,200 (an excess of 100 per cent over $1,600) the credit had vanished entirely. Thus a single member of the armed forces in Canada receiving more than $3,200 annual pay was taxable in the same way as a civilian; if he received less than $1,600 he was fully exempt, and between $1,600 and $3,200 he was partially exempt. A higher tax credit was given for married personnel (to offset the fact that dependents allowances were taxable to him as service pay) but the same principle of diminution was applied. With the important exceptions noted below this was the wartime tax system for service personnel in Canada.

The more acute problems arose, however, from the treatment of service personnel stationed overseas. These were completely exempt from tax on all their pay and dependents' allowances. This outright exemption led to several complications. For example, in recognition of the risk involved in their duties it was necessary to follow this precedent and exempt completely certain service personnel in Canada whose duties were normally performed in aircraft or afloat. A special category also had to be established for armed forces in the Western hemisphere but outside Canada (Newfoundland, Alaska, Kiska, etc.) who were taxed at only half the rates applicable to personnel in Canada. Service personnel returning to Canada from overseas were granted exemption from tax for six months after their return home if they remained in the service.

The continual movement of men of all ranks from one taxable status to another (they could be in two or three different categories in a year) created a great deal of confusion. It is understandable, too, that the discrimination in favour of personnel overseas as opposed to those stationed in Canada, especially where the overseas post entailed no particular risk, might be a cause of some dissatisfaction. The greatest complaint, however, came from groups closely related to the armed forces, often undergoing comparable risks, who received less favourable treatment than the service personnel. Overseas these groups included the auxiliary service supervisors (Y.M.C.A., Canadian Legion, etc.), the members of Fire-Fighters Corps, war correspondents, radio commentators, etc. On and over the seas the merchant marine and the Ferry Command laid claim for recognition, and at home civilian flying instructors teaching service personnel, test pilots, employees of shell-filling plants, and others at various times argued for special recognition of the dangers of their occupation. Partial concessions were made for some of the groups overseas and for the Ferry Command and merchant marine, but complete exemption was never given.

It is apparent that this is a very unhappy phase of wartime taxation, in which reasonable solutions are unlikely to emerge. The emotional reaction to the great sacrifices made by fighting men prevents a detached consideration of the endless complexities and discriminations involved in attempting to compensate for that sacrifice through a privilege as jealously guarded and as zealously sought after as income tax exemption. In 1947 the peacetime position of full taxability was restored, but in 1951 new arrangements were introduced for troops engaged in the Korean war.

Another thorny problem for which there seems to be no permanently satisfactory answer is the tax treatment of the working wives of taxable husbands. In wartime concessions are made to encourage wives and mothers who can do so to take a job in a war industry. Commendable as this may be for the production programme, its effects cut across a basic principle of income tax. As nearly as possible the rule is followed that the allowance for a dependent is granted in recognition of the support of that dependent by the taxpayer. Normally the amount of income of the dependent is used as the test of dependency. The pre-war rule was that as soon as a wife earned enough to be taxable herself her husband was regarded as not wholly supporting her, and he was therefore deprived of the married allowance and taxed as a single person. The effect of this rule, it was alleged by employers, was that many wives worked only until they had earned an amount just less than that which would deprive their husbands of the married exemption, and then quit for the year. Such were the entreaties addressed to the Minister of Finance that the rule was suspended, and a wife was allowed to earn any amount of income from an employment without affecting her husband's position. This apparently had the desired result of keeping the wives at work. On the other hand it had the inequitable result of allowing an exemption (at wartime levels) of only $1,200 where the husband was the sole provider, and of $1,860 where there were two earners in the family. This concession was removed shortly after the end of the war, to the general disgruntlement of working wives. This problem, of course, is only a segment of the broader question of the taxation of family income.

These were some of the more transient wartime problems, for which temporary provision was made. Several other changes were adopted of a more permanent character, designed mainly to increase either the equity or the efficiency of the tax. Among these are the extension of the allowances for dependents to include in-laws and illegitimate children, the introduction in 1942 of an allowance for unusual medical expenses, and the gradual adoption of a pay-as-you-go system of tax collection, culminating in the 1943 cancellation of one-half the outstanding tax and the concurrent inception of a system of deduction at the source designed to collect by pre-payment most of the tax on salaries and wages. On the pre-war basis of payment once a year, the wartime tax rates would have been an unmanageable burden, and the pay-as-you-go system has so many advantages for both the treasury and the taxpayer that it has become in peacetime a permanent feature of the personal income tax.

While deduction at the source was an administrative change of tremendous significance, it had other consequences that were equally important. Undoubtedly the one that gave most concern during the war was the effect of wage deductions on incentive. Absenteeism was perhaps often blamed unfairly on the income tax, but the feeling was commonly expressed that the government took so much of the ordinary wage in income tax that the net loss from staying away from work was negligible. In the case of overtime work it was constantly alleged that such a large part of the extra rate of pay went to income tax that the additional effort was not worth while. Indeed one of the suggestions most frequently heard during the war was that overtime pay be completely exempted from tax.

A secondary result of the deduction of the tax on wages at the source was the feeling that wage and salary income was caught in the maw of a device that allowed no escape or evasion, while popular sentiment, to some extent with justification, was inclined to regard with suspicion the possibilities for tax evasion left open to those taxpayers who did their own accounting and paid their tax directly. The tax prosecutions of the post-war years have demonstrated that in many instances the law has had the last say, but when tax rates are as high as those of World War II the resentment may be acute.

The irritation with the flaws in a tax system increases in proportion to the burden of tax rates. Inequities and discouragements that are easily tolerated at low rates become major issues of tax policy when rates are drastically increased. This leads to the final and crucial question regarding the personal income tax of World War II: were the rates too high?

Of course there is no definitive answer to this question and the reader's judgment, based on the recollection of his own experience, is probably as valid as that of any tax expert. Most assuredly the rates were *very* high. In fact, in terms of pre-war and post-war standards the very significant *marginal* rates of tax were astonishingly high. Table XXIX gives a dramatic demonstration of the comparison. It shows the peak wartime rate of tax that applied to the income in excess of specific amounts of "taxable" income, compared with a pre-war and post-war year. Taxable income is the amount of income in excess of the exemptions, which were $1,000 for a single person and $2,000 for a married person in 1939 and 1949, and $660 and $1,200 respectively in 1942–3. Thus for a single person the rate applying to the first dollar of "taxable" income would be the rate on the first dollar over a gross income of $1,000 in 1939 and 1949, and over a gross income of $660 in 1942–3. Other brackets may be read accordingly.

TABLE XXIX

MARGINAL RATES OF PERSONAL INCOME TAX

Taxable income[a] exceeding	Pre-war marginal rate on additional dollar	1942–43[b] marginal rate on additional dollar		1949 marginal rate on additional dollar
		Inc. savings	Exc. savings	
$	%	%	%	%
0	3.0	37.0	19.0	15.0
1,000	4.0	44.0	36.0	17.0
2,000	5.0	49.0	41.0	19.0
3,000	6.0	50.0	42.0	19.0
5,000	8.4	59.0	51.0	22.0
10,000	13.7	64.0	56.0	35.0
15,000	22.1	69.0	63.7	45.0
20,000	28.4	74.0	70.0	45.0
30,000[c]	31.5	83.0	80.3	54.0
50,000	36.8	88.0	86.0	59.0
100,000	49.4	98.0	97.2	69.0
200,000	58.8	98.0	97.6	74.0
500,000	69.3	98.0	97.8	84.0

[a]Income in excess of the statutory exemptions.
[b]Where different rates of tax applied to single and married persons (e.g., national defence tax and normal tax), the rate for single persons was used.
[c]In calculating the above rates it has been assumed that all incomes up to $30,000 are entirely earned incomes and that incomes of more than $30,000 include earned income of that amount and additional investment income to make up the total, except in the pre-war year, where under the tax then in effect all income in excess of $14,000 was taxed as "investment" income.

One instance alone will serve to illustrate the severity of the peak wartime rates. A single person earning about $50 a week and liable to pay the full compulsory savings tax would find that 49 per cent, or about one-half, of any additional earnings would go to the government. Small wonder that in a public discussion of the personal income tax during the war A. K. Eaton, chief of the Taxation Division of the federal Department of Finance, made the following statement:

> Canadian experience reveals another important limiting factor in the vigorous use of taxing power to curb inflation. I refer to the effect of high marginal tax rates on the incentive to work. It is said that high taxes are an important factor contributing to absenteeism and reluctance to work overtime. The advantage of moving from, say, low paid unnecessary work to higher paid important work may be very considerably reduced if taxes absorb too large a portion of the higher wages. These are very serious charges in wartime when maximum production, particularly in certain directions, is so vitally important. It is extremely difficult to know how much

weight to attach to these charges. They have given us some concern in Canada.[2]

Commodity Taxes

Although the direct tax increases attracted most attention, some very substantial upward adjustments were made in existing commodity taxes and many new taxes were introduced. In some respects familiar patterns were followed. Sharp increases were made, for example, in the traditional taxes on spirits and tobacco, and the combined revenue from these sources increased over seven times, from a pre-war level of about $50 million to nearly $370 million at the wartime peak. The one conspicuous example of a major tax source that remained unchanged in the face of heavy revenue needs was the general sales tax. It was apparently not felt necessary to change the 8 per cent rate in the early stages of the war and by the time revenue requirements were more acute a general price ceiling had been imposed. The task of policing throughout the whole of the economy the infinite number of price adjustments resulting from an increase in the sales tax would probably have shattered the mechanism of price control. The wartime Minister of Finance gave this reason, along with the government's desire to stress direct taxation in the over-all financial programme, for not making an increase. Sales tax changes therefore were limited to removing from the exempt list prepared meats and fish, domestic electricity and gas, and building materials.

While the need for revenue is a self-evident reason for tax increases, two other purposes were also served through these commodity tax measures. The first was the diversion of materials and labour to war purposes by reducing the consumption of certain goods. The second—essentially an international aspect of the first—was the relief of the drain on resources of U.S. dollars by the imposition of taxes on goods of a type that had a high content of imported American parts or materials.

The whole programme of wartime commodity taxation is given in summarized form in Table XXX. Some of the conspicuously successful revenue producers were the war exchange tax, which gave a peak revenue of $118 million in 1943–4, the gasoline tax, which yielded $36 million in 1946–7, the tax on transportation and communications (transportation tickets, parlour car seats, berths, long distance calls, etc.), producing $27 million in 1946–7, and amusements, which annually brought in $13 to $14 million. By contrast the taxes on semi-

[2]A. K. Eaton, "Canadian Experience in Curbing Inflation through Fiscal Devices" *Curbing Inflation through Taxation* (New York Tax Institute, 1944), p. 196.

TABLE XXX

CHANGES IN INDIRECT LEVIES IN WORLD WAR II
(combined excise taxes and excise duties)

	Pre-war tax	Highest wartime tax
Amusements		
Admissions	none	20%
Night clubs	none	25%
Pari-mutuel bets	none	5%
Playing cards	10c pack	20c pack
Phonographs	none	25%
Radios	none	25%
Slot machines	none	25%
Beverages		
Beer (on malt)	6c per lb.	16c per lb.
Other beer	22c per gal.	45c per gal.
Canadian brandy	$3 per gal.	$9 per gal.
Carbonic acid gas	none	50c per lb.
Soft drinks	no tax	25% plus 1c per bot.
Spirits	$4 per gal.	$11 per gal.
Wines		
non-sparkling	7½c per gal.	50c per gal.
sparkling	75c per gal.	$2.50 per gal.
Clothing		
Furs	none	25%
Food and confectionery		
Candy	none	30%
Chewing gum	none	30%
Glucose	½c per lb.	1c per lb.
Sugar	1c per lb.	2c per lb.
Household goods		
Electrical and gas appliances	none	25%
Ornaments, silverware, etc.	none	25% (retail)
Importations		
War exchange tax	none	10%

TABLE XXX—*Continued*

	Pre-war tax	Highest wartime tax
Personal accessories		
Cameras and supplies	none	25%
Fountain pens and pencils	none	35%
Jewellery, watches, etc.	none	25% (retail)
Lighters	20%	25%
Smoking accessories (pipes, etc.)	none	35%
Trunks, purses, luggage	none	35%
Services		
Domestic phone extensions	none	25c per month
Long distance telephone calls	6% (max. 25c)	15% (max. 75c)
Letters and post cards	1c each	2c each
Parlour car chairs	10%	15%
Sleeping berths	10%	15%
Telegrams and cables	5c each	7c each
Transportation tickets	none	15%
Tobacco and related products		
Cigarettes (per 1000)	$4.00	$10.00
Cigars (graduated with value per 1000 cigars)	$3.50 on $40 or less to $19 on $200 or more	25% plus $1 per 1000
Cigarette papers (per 100)	2c	8c
Cigarette tubes (per 100)	2c	14c
Manufactured tobacco (per lb.)	20c	67c
Canadian raw leaf tobacco (per lb.)	no tax	28c
Matches (per 100)	¾c	1c
Toilet soap and toilet articles		
Toilet articles	10%	25%
Toilet soap	5%	5%
Vehicles		
Automobiles	valued to $650—no tax valued over $650—5% on excess over $650	less than $900—25% $900 to $1,200—40% over $1,200—80%
Buses	same as autos	5%
Tires	2c per lb.	5c per lb.
Tubes	3c per lb.	5c per lb.
Gasoline	none	3c per gal.

durable goods which, particularly in the case of automobiles, were at an unprecedented level, produced almost no revenue because of the almost complete cessation of production of such goods for civilian consumption.

Total revenue from indirect taxes increased from about $300 million in pre-war years to over $800 million by the end of the war. Despite this increase their importance declined from about two-thirds of tax revenues before the war to little more than one-third at the end of the war.

Of the taxes imposed to reduce the consumption of specific articles using scarce materials, those on automobiles and electrical appliances were leading examples. Steel is chronically in short supply during wartime, and heavy levies on these steel-using articles acted as an advance guard for the direct controls of the later period. Skilled labour normally occupied in producing these goods was also released for employment in the war programme.

Less obviously but in large measure for the same purpose were such new taxes as the heavy charge imposed on railway and other travel during the war. The extreme pressure on every travel facility and the priority that had to be given troop and other essential movements might have warranted a general system of travel rationing, but for various reasons this was not considered feasible. A heavy tax—in reality fiscal rationing—was imposed to exert a deterrent effect which still left the choice to the individual and did not require the creation of a new and elaborate control system.

The several taxes imposed to assist the exchange conservation programme represented probably the most direct use of commodity taxes as measures of economic control. The detailed reasons for the shortage of United States dollars need not concern us here; but basically it arose from the breakdown of the triangular arrangement which enabled Canada to use its surplus of sterling to meet its deficit in dollars, the problem thus created being accentuated by a simultaneous and sharp increase in Canada's imports from the United States which magnified the normally heavy current account deficit with that country. Within a week of the declaration of war in September, 1939, exchange control had been instituted, but attention was first directed mainly towards preventing a flight of capital, and no restrictions were placed on trade, on tourist movements, or on the payment of interest or dividends.

This form of control, while saving the exchange position from the disruptive movement of large-scale capital withdrawals, failed to cope with the growing deficit of United States dollars on current account. As in many other emergencies, the first measure adopted to this end was the imposition of taxes. In the budget of June, 1940, the Minister of Finance took the fairly drastic step of introducing a tax of 10 per cent—the war exchange tax—on all imports from non-sterling countries, and at the same time announced a sharp increase in the tax on automobiles, aimed at their high American content (as well, of course, at their Canadian content of steel). These taxes undoubtedly helped to slow the growth of the dollar deficit by discouraging civilian importations, but were inadequate to stem it. During the summer of 1940 restrictions on tourist travel were introduced, and efforts were made to find markets for Canadian exports in the United States and to stimulate the production of gold for export.

Despite these steps, so serious had the situation become by December, 1940, that the Minister of Finance found it necessary to embark on a further series of measures. These relied heavily on quotas, tariffs, and taxation. Under the War Exchange Conservation Act lists of goods were established the importation of which from hard currency countries was either completely prohibited or allowed only under permit. The same Act provided for the removal of the tariff on certain imports from the United Kingdom, including textiles, bituminous coal, jellies, jams and marmalade, and furniture, to encourage the substitution of sterling for hard-currency imports. The measures to provide accelerated depreciation on assets acquired for production for export to hard-currency countries have already been mentioned.

Concurrently with these steps, aimed specifically against imported goods, a series of taxes of domestic application were imposed to prevent any indirect stimulus to the import of raw materials and to discourage the development of new Canadian production facilities to replace the goods prohibited under the Act. Again automobiles were prominent in this list, and a graduated schedule was introduced which taxed at 80 per cent the value of any private passenger vehicle in excess of $1,200. At the same time several existing taxes—on radios, phonographs, cameras, etc.—were increased from 10 per cent to 25 per cent and new taxes at 25 per cent were levied on a long list of electrical and gas appliances.

Of other tax measures adopted to assist in the exchange problem before the Hyde Park agreement finally brought relief in 1942, undoubtedly the most important was the gasoline tax of 3 cents per gallon. This preceded the institution of direct rationing and was designed to slow up the flow of petroleum from the United States for civilian consumption.

The wartime use of commodity taxes in an attempt to influence the foreign trade balance was not only significant in itself but has interest as well for the precedent it set for a similar experiment under peacetime conditions—the "radio speech" tax programme of 1947.

In the case of the tariff almost all the wartime changes were of a short-term character related to the state of emergency. Its traditional role as an instrument of industrial and commercial policy, as traced in earlier pages, was almost entirely suspended during the war. The only important change of a permanent character was the final granting of complete exemption from duty for agricultural implements in 1944. This completed a cycle that had been in course for decades, the last substantial reduction having been effected under the Canada–U.S. trade agreements of the 1930's which brought the general level down to 7½ per cent. Some other changes of a permanent character were also made, but were relatively minor in effect.

Far more significant were the wartime changes effected by the War Exchange Conservation Act, already discussed, and the temporary reductions and revisions introduced without fanfare under the authority of orders in council. The latter were intended for the most part to relieve the pressure of foreign prices on the Canadian price ceiling. Three general orders in council were passed, and a variety of individual orders. P.C. 9888, December 19, 1941, suspended all special or dumping duties except in respect of fruits and vegetables. P.C. 9889, of the same date, authorized the use of the export selling price of a good as the valuation for duty, and under this authority special valuations were established for passenger automobiles, raw cotton, dried fruits, essential oils, canned orange juice, parts for electric stoves, rice, vegetable oils, and miscellaneous other items. Another general order —P.C. 62/450, January 20, 1942—provided that duties and taxes imposed in the country of origin were to be disregarded in making valuations for Canadian duty.

Of even greater consequence were a great variety of individual orders in council under which customs duty, war exchange tax, and, in some instances, even an internal excise tax, were removed or reduced to relieve pressure on a price ceiling. The goods so affected covered a wide range. They included coal, both anthracite and bituminous, crude rubber, tea and coffee (the additional duties imposed in September 1939, were removed by order in council in 1942), sugar (the excise tax was reduced by ½ per cent per lb. in 1943 by order in council), bananas, peanuts, potatoes and other fruits and vegetables (for various periods), crude petroleum imported into British Columbia ports, various fabrics for clothing, and so on. Some duties were lifted for comparatively short periods of a few months; others for periods extending over several years.[3]

A final word on a practical aspect of commodity tax administration in wartime. As production became increasingly devoted to defence orders, paid for directly by the Canadian government or in many instances by foreign governments, the collection of tax on this large segment of economic activity created special problems. It is a general rule of the Dominion government to pay its own taxes on its own purchases, largely as a matter of administrative convenience. It is also a rule of Canadian federal tax laws that goods exported to foreign purchasers leave Canada free of Canadian taxes as far as it is possible to achieve this end. In the context of war production, therefore, the implications of this system were that production for Canadian account was taxable but production for foreign account was tax-free. The first approach to the problem thus posed was to allow Canadian manufacturers to import and purchase materials and parts for production for foreign governments free of duty and tax, but at the same time to require them to pay tax on materials and parts for Canadian production. Since many manufacturers were turning out identical products for both foreign and Canadian governments, and in frequent instances the ultimate consignee of the goods was subject to last minute change, the task of maintaining a separation between taxed and tax-free inventory became extremely involved for the producer. Indeed, the accounting problems became so snarled that on April 1, 1943, this system was abandoned. It was replaced by a plan under which manufacturers purchased all materials and parts subject to tax, and the federal government itself undertook to refund the tax to the foreign purchaser. This system in the end worked out fairly well, but because it took some time to inaugurate the rebate procedure (it was necessary, for example, to carry out elaborate studies to determine the "tax content" of an aircraft or automotive vehicle being sent abroad) the initial effect was to swell the revenues, particularly from the tariff and the sales tax, while in later years, when refunds were catching up, the revenues were artificially reduced. The artificial inflation may be seen in the increase in customs revenue in the first year of the new plan to

[3]For complete details of these changes see *Report*, Wartime Prices and Trade Board, January 1, 1946, to December 31, 1946, Appendix J.

$168 million from $119 million in the previous year, while sales tax at the same time rose to $339 million from $250 million. The offsetting factor of heavy refunds occurred later on. From a normal level of $10 to $20 million a year, refunds on sales tax jumped to $195 million in 1944–5. A distortion of some considerable proportions was introduced, therefore, in the annual revenue figures for indirect tax during the war on this account. In this connection it might have been mentioned earlier too that because in many instances corporations did not distinguish between their tax payments for the normal tax and those for the excess profits tax, and also because of the difficulty of estimating the appropriate annual reserve for the refundable portion of the excess profits tax, revenue figures as reported for these years in the published accounts are to be used with caution. A more accurate statistical distribution has since been made and has been published in the Taxation Statistics of the Department of National Revenue.

Other Federal Development of the War Period

In the Dominion field the principal other main development was the introduction of a national death duty in 1941. Based on the same principles as the existing provincial duties—a combination of estate and inheritance tax—this new levy was apparently intended, from its inception, to become a permanent part of the national tax structure. It has remained in effect ever since, and under the tax agreement arrangements entered into in 1947 and 1952 it has supplanted the provincial levy in eight of the ten provinces.

Provincial Wartime Developments

The Wartime Taxation Agreements, deàlt with in later chapters, suspended further activity for the period of the war in the major provincial areas that had been so thoroughly ploughed and harrowed during the depression. At the same time the disappearance of heavy outlays on relief and the necessity of postponing many capital and other expenditures because of material and labour shortages brought budgets into balance. Most provinces and many municipalities reduced debt during the war, and emerged in a sounder financial position than they had experienced in decades. Of the tax changes that helped to contribute to this position undoubtedly the most significant was the introduction of a 2 per cent provincial retail sales tax in Quebec in 1940. It will be recalled that Saskatchewan was the only other province in the field at the time, although Montreal had already tapped this source. A 10 per cent retail tax on tobacco was also adopted in Quebec in 1940, and in the same year New Brunswick adopted a similar tax. In the following year Prince Edward Island levied a 10 per cent tax on both liquor and tobacco. In 1943, on an appeal from the New Brunswick tobacco tax, the Judicial Committee of the Privy Council gave what is generally considered as the final blessing for direct retail sales taxes in the *Atlantic Smokes Shops* case. Retail sales taxes thus appeared on the Canadian scene as a new and apparently permanent feature of provincial taxation.

Other wartime developments in provincial taxation were unimportant, and may be found in the chronological survey in the Appendix.

Epilogue

One of the first acts of the federal government at the onslaught of the emergency was to impose taxes—and one of its first at the cessation of hostilities in Europe was to remove taxes. Hardly had a week passed after the capitulation of Germany when, by order in council under the War Measures Act, most of the taxes on semi-durable goods, including automobiles, were reduced to 10 per cent, the sales tax was removed from building materials, and the war exchange tax was taken off imported machinery and apparatus and building materials. Lest it be assumed, however, that this step was taken by way of light-hearted celebration, the preamble to the order in council should be noted. Consistent to the last, the government gave as its reason that the taxes enumerated were imposed "by reason of the war to discourage production and purchases" and their removal was contemplated because "their continuation would delay and complicate transition to essential civilian production."

Part VIII

THE POST-WAR EXPERIMENT
1946-54

24 THE DOMINION, 1946–54

New Philosophy for Peacetime

DURING THE WAR, as preceding chapters have shown, there was a rapid, vigorous, and sustained application of a new fiscal policy. Taxation measures designed for a variety of purposes besides the raising of revenue became commonplace. This experience fairly conclusively demonstrated that fiscal devices, despite definite limitations, could be used as a potent influence on economic activity when supported by the unanimity of purpose found in wartime. But a vastly different set of circumstances—economic, social, and psychological—quickly reappeared on the cessation of hostilities. Objectives again became diffused and fragmented, the natural human preoccupation with personal welfare reasserted itself, and encroachments on individual freedom by the state were more grudgingly accepted than when catastrophe threatened. Several questions demanded an immediate answer in this change of climate. Had any principles of permanent value been proved by the wartime experience with the new fiscal policy? If so, was there reason to believe that these principles could be applied in peacetime, when one of the essential elements of success, public acceptance, might be less readily forthcoming? If there were such reason, what form of tax system would best carry out the purpose of retarding too rapid expansion or of stimulating too timid activity? On the answer to these questions rested the whole basis of post-war fiscal policy. As will be seen in a moment, the Dominion Government accepted the challenge, announced its conviction that important lessons for peacetime had been derived from the wartime experience, and in practice based a large part of its post-war financing on this belief.

Almost equally as far-reaching as the adoption of a new theoretical approach to taxation has been the change in the form and content of the tax system in post-war years. The war left an array of federal taxes that bore unmistakable signs of hurried conception, since the atmosphere of emergency seldom allowed time for mature development. The taxing statutes had also become deeply overlaid with patches and stitches. In particular the administrative machinery of the direct taxes had almost bogged down under the enormous load thrust upon it. As in many other spheres reform was in the air, and editorial discussions of "a long-overdue overhauling" to remove "anomalies and inequities" were frequent in the post-war press.

The Liberal Government, which was in power throughout the post-war period, espoused the general revision of federal tax measures as a major part of its programme, and the Opposition has steadily reminded the Government of its promises. To a remarkable extent the goal of an over-all revision has been achieved. In gradual stages significant changes have been made in all the major tax measures, and the federal structure today probably shows a greater degree of effectiveness, efficiency, and simplicity than ever before. Even in the face of sharply increased rates necessitated by the outbreak of the Korean war and the launching of the defence programme it has been possible to hold the progress that had been previously made, and in some cases to adopt further improvements.

In the federal sphere these two major themes—the developing philosophy and the improving practice—dominate the years since World War II ended. The first provides the subject of the current chapter, and the latter, along with the closely allied subject of the general trend of tax rates, of the next chapter.

Post-war Fiscal Policy of the Dominion Government

It may be stated at the outset that the Dominion Government, in a series of significant public declarations, adopted as its basic fiscal policy a programme involving the conscious use of the tax structure to influence economic behaviour. In language now common place, it announced its adherence to the concept of "contra-cyclical budgeting." The influence of the war in bringing about this decision is amply clear. It should also be recalled, however, that the Rowell-Sirois Commission had formally proposed the adoption of this basic approach to public financing, and the Government in a sense was morally and politically bound to revive consideration of the recommendations that had been shelved in 1941. While by many the *Report* had been all but forgotten by 1945, in retrospect it would appear that the wartime experience had added weight and authority to some of its major recommendations, rather than the reverse. If some of the specific proposals had been out-distanced by the rapidly moving events of the five years following its submission the *Report* remained, none the less, as a concrete proposal for specific action. It stood, therefore, as the inescapable starting point for any new plan.

For convenience all aspects of post-war fiscal policy relating to Dominion-provincial relations are dealt with in a later part of this book. This should be kept in mind in reading the present chapter, since federal-provincial relations have been almost as significant an influence on post-war fiscal policy as have general economic conditions. In the meantime, however, it is the latter aspect that will be considered.

On this aspect the Dominion Government very early made its position known. In April, 1945, before the European war had ended, it outlined its policy in a White Paper on *Employment and Income*,[1] presented to Parliament by the Minister of Reconstruction, Mr. Howe. This White Paper set forth objectives of post-war policy in every important segment of the economy. The general target was "to accomplish a smooth, orderly transition from the economic conditions of war to those of peace and to maintain a high and stable level of employment and income." "The Government," it said, "adopts this as a primary object of policy." In special fields specific proposals for action were outlined. Under the heading of "Government Finance," the traditional peacetime approach to the budget was abandoned in three sentences and a new concept installed in its place:

> The Government will be prepared, in periods when unemployment threatens, to incur the deficits and increases in the national debt resulting from its employment and income policy, whether that policy in the circumstances is best applied through increased expenditures or reduced taxation. In periods of buoyant employment and income, budget plans will call for surpluses. The Government's policy will be to keep the national debt within manageable proportions, and maintain a proper balance in its budget over a period longer than a single year.

It is significant that full credit was given in the adoption of this policy to the influence of the wartime experience. The acknowledgment was in the following words: "Fiscal policy during the war has necessarily been based on economic as much as purely financial considerations. It is proposed to extend that practice into the post-war years and apply war experience to the problems of peace."

In the crucial area of capital investment the Paper particularly stressed the importance of taxation as an influence on economic behaviour. It oriented certain measures already adopted in 1944 as the beginning of a post-war programme designed to encourage reconversion and research expenditures, and outlined a general policy for after the war:

> The Government recognizes that wartime taxation, both in its form and rates, is discouraging to new investment. It was deliberately designed to

[1]Department of Reconstruction, *Employment and Income, with Special Reference to the Initial Period of Reconstruction.*

be discouraging in order that more resources could be used for the purposes of war. Because war expenditures are so inflationary in effect, wartime taxation must be restrictive and deflationary. After the war, a quite different taxation policy will become an appropriate part of policies directed to the maintenance of employment and income. The Government proposes not only to reduce taxation as rapidly as possible but to develop its fiscal policy so as to encourage the increase of private investment to a high and stable level. It is proposed particularly to eliminate or minimize taxation which contributes to a higher level of production costs.

Four months later in the presentation of the Dominion's proposals to the provinces at the Conference on Reconstruction (August, 1945) the new policy of contra-cyclical budgeting was made the central theme. The Dominion based its proposal for renewal of agreements granting it exclusive rights in the major direct tax fields on the necessity for removing any impediment to the fullest possible implementation of this policy, the nature of which it represented to the provinces as follows:

In periods of declining business activity, arising perhaps from depressions abroad, it is proposed that these expenditures will be boldly expanded. Tax rates might be reduced at the same time, but whether this is done or not revenues will obviously fall off sharply and large deficits will result. The Government is not only prepared to accept these but will deliberately plan for them in periods of threatened depression in order to give the economy a stimulus and relieve unemployment. As a corollary the Government will also plan for substantial budgets and debt retirement in periods of high business activity. This is simply saying that the Government will budget for a cycle rather than for any one fiscal year, and that the Government will design both its spending policies and its tax policies throughout the cycle to levelling out the deflationary valleys and inflationary peaks. The great growth in government revenues and expenditures made necessary by the war makes a responsible policy of this sort an obligation, and at the same time, with our increased knowledge of fiscal techniques, makes it a practical policy in the sense that it can have a really significant effect on the business cycle. The modern governmental budget must be the balance wheel of the economy; its very size to-day is such that if it were allowed to fluctuate up and down *with* the rest of the economy instead of deliberately *counter* to the business swings it would so exaggerate booms and depressions as to be disastrous.[2]

And again the close relationship between capital investment and taxation was stressed:

The creation of conditions under which the initiative and skill of private enterprise will result in new investment on a scale far exceeding pre-war

[2]Dominion-Provincial Conference on Reconstruction, August, 1945, *Proposals of the Government of Canada*. See also Speech of Minister of Finance, Proceedings, Plenary Session, August 7, 1945.

levels is one of the principal problems of reconstruction policy. The tax policies of all governments can be a fundamental factor in the removal of undesirable and unnecessary obstacles. The elimination or reduction of taxes on costs, the removal of tax penalties upon enterprise, and the effect of taxes upon the taking of risks are basic considerations in determining a satisfactory system of Dominion-provincial financial relations.[8]

In his fall budget of October, 1945, the Minister of Finance returned to this theme. In justifying tax reductions in that budget, despite an anticipated deficit for the fiscal year, he stressed "economic" considerations and added: "The government has adopted, as a major aim of government policy, the maintenance of a high and stable level of income and employment. Accordingly it becomes a major consideration in budget policy."

At the sterile conclusion of the protracted Reconstruction Conference in May, 1946, the Minister of Finance, in making a final appeal for the Dominion's tax proposals, again stressed the desirability of single control and uniform administration of the major direct tax fields to assist in carrying out the new fiscal policy. An appeal couched in the same terms accompanied his modified offer of tax agreements in the budget speech of June, 1946. "Of particular importance," he said, "was the belief that the right tax policies, varying with the needs of the times, would lead to a broadening and expansion of the tax base, that is to say, the size of personal and national incomes, and consequently reduce the real burden of taxation."

Numerous further statements might be cited to demonstrate that in the months following the end of the war the federal Government adopted and attempted to popularize a concept of contra-cyclical budgeting in the fullest meaning of the expression. The presentation of this policy in the White Paper of April, 1945, and in the *Proposals* to the Reconstruction Conference in August, 1945, constitute probably the most unreserved declaration of acceptance of the Keynesian approach by any national government. However, following the failure to attain universal agreements with the provinces, and with the emergence of specific problems requiring specific remedies, in later references to the policy there was a perceptible modification of the theoretical approach. Attention was centred on the advantages of reducing the debt during good times, and on the anti-inflationary aspects of high taxation. For example, the Minister of Finance in his 1947 budget speech (the Hon. D. C. Abbott had just succeeded the Rt. Hon. J. L. Ilsley) said:

[8]*Proposals*, p. 7.

It is a sensible and far-sighted policy to reduce the national debt in good times and permit it to increase in times of economic adversity. We must expect, I believe, that at times when our employment, production and incomes are below satisfactory levels, our revenues will fall short of our expenditures. Indeed, at such times it will probably be necessary to incur expenditures of various kinds to assist in restoring better levels of employment and income. It is a necessary corollary of this that we should aim at a surplus in times of prosperity and very high levels of income and employment, such as we have at the present time. Only by efforts to maintain our revenues under such conditions can we hope to avoid indefinite and undesirable accumulation of debt over the long run.

Despite this justification for a continuing high tax policy sizable reductions were announced in the same speech. But in the bleak and barren budget of May, 1948, when, having just announced a surplus for the previous year of $670 million, the Minister of Finance asked the public to be content with trifling reductions in minor taxes, the Minister evidently felt obliged to give a lengthy defence of his position. By this time the change in economic climate was apparent in the emphasis on anti-inflationary devices. The theoretical outlines of 1945 had taken concrete shape in actual measures for a specific problem. Mr. Abbott's statement was as follows:

I believe that all parties in this parliament and most Canadians share the view that the national budget is no longer merely a matter of the government accounts that should be balanced every twelve months on some financial rule of the thumb. We view the national budget now as an integral part of the nation's business, influenced by and having an influence upon the state of employment, income and prices. I think we would all agree that in times of widespread unemployment and insufficient demand for goods and services our expenditures should be increased in order to support employment and incomes, and that they could and should exceed our revenues under such conditions. Now we are at the opposite extreme and we should follow the opposite course. We should deliberately budget, as a matter of policy, for substantial surpluses in times like these. Only that way can we hold inflationary forces in check. Only that way, over the course of many years, can we make up at least in part for the deficits we shall have in less favourable years, and prevent an indefinite spiralling up of our national debt already at a very high level as the sequel to two wars. Now is the time to lay the foundation for employment budgets in future, while fighting inflation at present.

The following budget of 1949 gave substantial tax reductions, and press-writers regarded it as a rejection by the Government of its anti-inflationary policy in preparation for an election in that year. There was no evidence that the policy had been abandoned in principle, however, and some relaxation of taxes in the light of softening business conditions might have been justified on economic grounds. In the light of subsequent events the point is, at any rate, academic. The Korean episode and the accompanying expansion of the defence programme required the reimposition of much of the tax load that had been lifted in post-war years. It also required serious consideration of the alternative means for combating the inevitable stimulus to the post-war inflation that would result from heavy defence expenditures. Up to the time of writing the Dominion Government has affirmed its faith in fiscal devices by relying on them almost entirely, along with credit restrictions, in support of the defence programme. This is in sharp contrast to the situation in United States, where a price ceiling and other direct controls were instituted early in the revival of defence spending.

So much for the declared principles on which federal post-war tax policy has based. It is pertinent then to enquire to what extent this policy has been carried into practice.

Judged solely on the basis of surpluses in the government's accounts it has been followed with considerable consistency. There has been a surplus in every post-war year. In 1946–7, the first complete year following the cessation of hostilities, the surplus was $374 million. In 1947–8 it was $676 million, in 1948–9 $596 million, in 1949–50 $131 million, in 1950–1 $211 million, in 1951–2 $248 million, in 1952–3 $24 million, and in 1953–4 $46 million. As a result since the end of the war net debt has been reduced by over $2¼ billion.

The bare presentation of such figures, of course, gives no more than an indication that the first step in a contra-cyclical policy was taken. It is recognized that the amount and character of government expenditures and their relationship to other expenditures in the economy are in themselves of considerable significance irrespective of the over-all budgetary position. Heavy outlays on public works, for example, are likely to be more inflationary in their effect than most other forms of expenditure. It is also recognized that without the support of a complementary policy of debt management and monetary control the attainment of a surplus is not necessarily of final significance in itself. To illustrate—if money is taken through taxes from one group of citizens and given back to the same or another group of citizens through the redemption of war bonds, the net deflationary effect may be negligible. The nature of the debt redemption, therefore, plays as significant a role as the attainment of the initial surplus, and similarly the regulation of the supply of money in circulation and the level of the interest rate may be equally significant. It is not incumbent on us here, however, to examine these aspects of the post-war Canadian economy. For the present purpose it is sufficient that an attempt appears to have been made to meet the first requirement of a well-rounded fiscal programme in the post-war period by the attainment of governmental surpluses.

This broad standard gives no indication of the extent to which individual tax sources were used to affect economic behaviour. Attention centred on capital expenditure, the most significant tax stimulus undoubtedly being the plan of "double depreciation." In announcing this plan in the June, 1944, budget the Minister of Finance gave the following explanation of its purpose:

> First, it will allow the taxpayer to recover a part of his capital whenever earnings are good but will still leave all the income or profit actually realized from the venture over its whole life subject to taxation; second, it will allow him, in respect of such new investment carried out at a time when the Government has declared the conversion and expansion of industry to be desirable, to transfer some of his income from a period when wartime tax rates may still be in effect to a later period when he may expect normal taxation to be lower. To this extent, it will relieve such investment for post-war purposes from such wartime taxation of business profits as may still be in effect at the time the work of conversion or expansion is carried out.

The scheme was brought into actual operation by order in council on November 10, 1944, and by subsequent extensions applied to all expenditures on approved projects made between this date and March 31, 1949. Newly acquired plant, buildings, and equipment for use in *industry* only were eligible, while assets acquired by service enterprises—transportation, communication, light, heat, power, laundering, garages, warehousing, and financial and commercial establishments—were excluded. Projects were required to be approved by the Department of Reconstruction, and a certificate of eligibility was issued to the income tax administration. No applications were accepted after March 31, 1947. The taxpayer had the option of taking depreciation at any rate varying from one-half to double the normal rates, up to 80 per cent of the cost of the asset, in respect of expenditures on the project made before March 31, 1949.

A detailed study of the effects—economic and industrial—of this measure was published by the Department of Reconstruction and Supply. The experience under it is summarized in the following extract from this report:

> Special depreciation has been approved for investment expenditures of \$1.4 billion which reporting companies expect to spend between November

10, 1944, and March 31, 1949. This outlay involves 8,054 different projects planned by 4,212 companies. It entails the conversion, modernization and expansion of 3,668 existing plants and the establishment of 1,174 new plants. Broadly, about two-fifths of all business investment and some four-fifths of total manufacturing investment undertaken in the transition period has been or is making use of special depreciation provisions.[4]

It should be stressed, as the report emphasized, that "special depreciation provisions were not by themselves responsible for this large volume of investment." To measure the effects of the plan would necessitate having knowledge of the amount of expenditure that would have gone forward without depreciation assistance—an impossible requirement. It can probably be assumed that many less certain projects went ahead because of the assurance of a write-off, but how large a proportion of the total these represented no one can say.

Two other forms of special depreciation, of less significance than the above, were also provided in the post-war era. Rental housing was the subject of one, and ships of the other. Under Order in Council P.C. 1095 of March 25, 1947, depreciation at not less than half nor more than double the normal rates was extended for rental housing erected between March 31, 1947, and December 31, 1949, and under Order in Council P.C. 2487 the same privilege was extended in respect of ships acquired from War Assets Corporation or built for the taxpayer in a Canadian shipyard in the period from April 1, 1947, to December 31, 1949.

In this context the general revision in 1949 of the system of depreciation allowances, the increase in the general rates concurrently with the adoption of the diminishing balance principle, and the introduction of an obsolescence allowance are also significant. These steps, while not intended primarily for this purpose, have undoubtedly given some stimulus to capital investment by assuring that costs may be recovered under any circumstances. The reintroduction of special depreciation allowances for defence investments, and the reversal of the post-war approach through the adoption in 1951 of a plan of *deferred* depreciation to discourage certain capital expenditures are also in this category. They are discussed more fully in later pages.

The above measures were of particular significance in relation to capital investment, but several other changes of greater or less importance were also adopted. The extension of the losses carry-over provision to allow a one-year carry-back and a five year carry-forward

[4]*Encouragement to Industrial Expansion in Canada: Operation of Special Depreciation Provisions November 10, 1944–March 31, 1949*, p. 9.

was presented by the Minister of Finance as a significant step in creating a climate in which enterprise would take risks because the government would in effect be a partner in these risks. The step taken to remove in part the double taxation of corporate earnings through the 10 per cent tax credit for dividends, introduced in 1949, was intended among other purposes to attract investment capital to business financing. The introduction of a graduated tax rate for corporations, with a reduced rate on income of $10,000 or less, was also designed to encourage the launching of new small businesses. In the extractive industries the increase in the depletion allowance for gold mines from 33⅓ per cent to 40 per cent and the perpetuation in the post-war period of most of the wartime concessions granted the mining and petroleum industries for exploratory expenses are also income tax measures of "economic" significance. Other instances could be cited, but enough have been given to demonstrate that Dominion government fiscal policy of recent years has shown an acute consciousness of the economic consequences of the income tax. Perhaps the most conclusive evidence of this awareness was the fact that the income tax was the first and most frequent tax to be reduced in the post-war period. Only the renewal of large-scale defence expenditures decreed the reversal of a decisive downward trend in rates.

Under the heading of commodity taxes the case of the removal or reduction of excise taxes on electrical appliances and automobiles in May, 1945, cited at the conclusion of the previous chapter, was a typical example of the new policy. Its avowed purpose was to assist the manufacturers of these articles to get into peacetime production as rapidly as possible. The concurrent removal of the sales tax from building materials was designed to stimulate housing and other construction. Closely related with the income tax measures designed to stimulate capital investment was the removal, in the October, 1945, budget, of the sales tax from machinery and apparatus used directly in the manufacture or production of goods. This change lifted from Canadian industry a very substantial burden in the form of an 8 per cent charge on the cost of its new purchases of machinery and apparatus. These two major sales tax changes—the exemption of building materials and of machinery and apparatus for use in production—represented a substantial loss of sales tax revenue.

Of equal significance in economic influence was the adoption of an emergency programme of commodity taxes in November, 1947, as part of a general attack on the growing trade deficit with United States. Following the pattern of 1940 and 1941, excise taxes were levied on a wide range of goods having a high American content. The taxes on electrical appliances, removed in 1945, were replaced, the automobile tax was increased, and wholly new taxes were levied at the outset at a 25 per cent rate on firearms, motorcycles, outboard motors, musical instruments, pipe organs, pleasure boats, sporting goods, and miscellaneous other products. These taxes, it should be made clear, applied to all goods, whether manufactured in Canada or imported. They were designed solely to discourage the purchase of goods for which it was apparent from the import statistics that large quantities of raw materials or semi-finished parts were imported or else of which there was a large direct importation of finished products. These taxes were gradually removed as the exchange position improved, and in July, 1948, the last of the increases were repealed. As an indication of the fact that this programme had not been designed to provide increased revenue it might be pointed out that as part of it the sugar tax was eliminated, the tariff on tea and coffee was repealed, and electricity and gas used in domestic dwellings were exempted from the sales tax.

Other instances of the use of commodity taxes for non-revenue purposes in the post-war period could be cited. However, details of all recent changes are set out in tables in the Appendix, and there is no point in duplicating the information here. The main purpose in giving these instances has been to illustrate that in a variety of ways effect was given to the announced policy of using the tax mechanism as a device for influencing business decisions and economic behaviour in general.

It is unlikely that anyone, and certainly not the present writer, could yet say to what extent the fiscal policy of the post-war era has been a "success." The experience is still too recent and the context still too inflammable politically for final judgment. In some individual areas it is possible to isolate and examine results. It is freely acknowledged that in the petroleum industry, for example, the tax incentives given for widespread exploration for new fields has been a major factor in the discovery of extensive new petroleum resources in recent years. Undoubtedly also the measures designed to stimulate capital investment played some part in setting the stage for the investment boom of the post-war period, and tax measures also contributed when efforts were made to slacken the pace of the boom. But a final assessment of the general shape of the whole policy—fiscal, monetary, and debt management—will have to await maturer reflection and a longer perspective. In the meantime, however, one authoritative expression of opinion has been given, in mid-stream as it were, by the Royal Commission on Prices. The second volume of the Commission's *Report* provides an excellent review of war and post-war economic conditions and is recommended to the general reader as a source of background information. The Commission also reviewed and commented on the fiscal and monetary policies of the federal Government. Of post-war tax policy (it will be left to the reader to examine, if he has not already done so, the comments on other aspects of policy) the Commission said:

> Looking at the matter only in the light of what was economically desirable, and leaving out of account the question of acceptability, we are inclined to think that taxes might have been maintained at a somewhat higher rate. No doubt prices would still have risen, but the rate of increase would probably have been smaller, and the resulting pressure on those with relatively fixed incomes, less severe.
>
> When account is taken of over-all government spending and investment, rather than merely those particular forms of expenditure that happen to be included in the budget, the surplus of government intake over government outgo in the past few years has not been large.[5]

The Commissioners, however, realistically modified this statement with the observation that "In assessing post-war tax policy it is necessary to take account of public acceptability as well as economic desirability." They conceded that public acceptability of high taxation during periods of high incomes and inflationary price movements was conditioned by all the theoretical and practical difficulties encountered when taxation is pushed beyond its "optimum" level, most of which have been examined in earlier chapters. This "optimum" level, of course, is almost entirely a relative thing. It is undoubtedly much lower in peacetime than in the midst of active hostilities, and it is certainly higher under conditions of buoyant prosperity than in a depression. At the same time, under conditions of full employment and rising prices such as the years following World War II have witnessed, there are encountered some particularly acute problems in the public acceptance of high taxation. It is indeed one of the ironies of the situation that whereas the contra-cyclical budgeting principle had its birth in and to a large extent was influenced by the depression of the thirties it has been given its first serious trial during the most buoyant and inflationary period in our history.

By and large this has meant that its peacetime inauguration has been not only in different circumstances but also in many respects in more difficult circumstances than those for which it was originally

[5]Royal Commission on Prices, *Report*, vol. II, pp. 169–70.

conceived. It is self-evident that to increase taxes in times of prosperity merely to produce a budget surplus will commend itself much less readily to the public than to reduce taxes in a depression. Tax reductions are always popular, but in the midst of hard times they would be particularly so. Common sense would suggest such a course to most people as reasonable and sensible, provided deficits did not reach such a size that confidence in the financial stability of the government was undermined. The effect of such a step would be immediate, visible, and beneficial. On the other hand the economic reasoning by which high taxes and large government surpluses are justified under buoyant and inflationary conditions is infinitely more subtle. Such action will inevitably appear to many citizens as being diametrically opposed to their personal interests. This can give rise to a feeling of resentment, expressed sometimes in the statement that the government appears to feel that it knows better how to spend the citizen's money than he does himself. To many people also the logic of imposing commodity taxes, which themselves *increase* prices, as a means of combating inflation is not self-evident. Furthermore such ultimate anti-inflationary effect as may result from any programme of high taxation is obscured usually by many other factors. The one convincing result is that prices stop rising or even begin to fall. But this may not happen. If inflationary pressures are particularly strong the result may be that prices rise less than they would have otherwise. This objective is equally worthy, but the extent to which it is achieved is almost impossible of proof.

To overcome completely these and related problems of public acceptance would in peacetime call for a degree of economic sophistication unusual, and perhaps unattainable, in the average citizen. Nevertheless some degree of understanding and acceptance is essential to success. While this was not recognized initially by all economists, it has been obtaining broader acceptance in recent years. The following quotation from a recent article by an economist with wide experience both inside and outside the federal government of the United States is indicative of this realistic approach. The statement was made in discussing American anti-inflationary taxation for the defence programme:

> If taxation is to perform successfully its anti-inflationary function, tax increases must not give rise to compensatory increases in the incomes of those on whom the tax is intended to rest. The purpose of a tax program is to distribute the burden of taxes among the various taxpayers in a fair and economically sound manner. If any major economic group is able to escape the burden of the tax by securing a larger income, the intended burden

distribution will be frustrated, and the tax will not achieve its anti-inflationary goal, since it will not reduce spending. It will then be necessary to increase the burdens and reduce the spending of other economic groups. This is unfair and necessitates an unnecessarily large total volume of taxation, intensifying all the problems which high taxes produce.

The principle that tax increases must be absorbed by the persons who are intended to carry them has a direct bearing in applying wage contracts where wage increases are based on increases in the cost of living. . . .

This principle that tax increases should not result in compensatory income increases also has a bearing on agriculture. . . .

Under this principle also, prices would not be raised by either private or public action because of increases in corporate income or profits taxes. . . .

The government by the people will not work unless we have a responsible public which puts the national interest ahead of private interest. If important segments of the American public assume that they must be protected against sacrifice, if groups with large economic power insist that their incomes after taxes must be kept sufficiently high to maintain their accustomed habits of expenditure, then there is no remedy except to impose compulsory direct controls. Only as farmers, workers, businessmen, and other major groups in the American economy see the dangers of selfishness and understand the nature of the economic problems of the defense economy [or any inflationary economy], will these problems prove to be reasonably solvable.[6]

[6]Roy Blough, "Fiscal Policy in a Defense Economy," *National Tax Journal*, vol. III, no. 4 (Dec., 1950), pp. 279–82.

25 THE DOMINION, 1946–54

Personal Income Tax Reform

SIGNIFICANT AS WAS the ideological background of the post-war period it can hardly overshadow several measures of concrete tax reform that were justifiable simply on the grounds of sound public policy and efficient tax administration. These reforms were concentrated largely in the income tax, although the indirect taxes did not escape the broom.

One of the marked features of the immediate post-war period was the ground swell of discontent with the income tax. People had accepted a Spartan regime during wartime in fairly good heart; but with peace the income tax seemed to become the popular whipping boy. Everything was wrong with it. The rates were too high; the exemptions were too low; the calculations were too complicated; the law was uncertain; the statute was cumbersome; the administration was arbitrary; appeals were costly; there was "double taxation" of company earnings; some forms of income–life annuities and undistributed profits–paid too much tax while others–income of mutuals and co-operatives–paid too little. And so it went on. The income tax and its alleged deficiencies became front-page copy for newspapers, the Senate had an investigation, and an Income Taxpayers Association was formed, aimed primarily against co-operatives but carrying the crusade as well into other fields. Undoubtedly the formation of the Canadian Tax Foundation also was an echo of this general public agitation, although the organization was in fact destined for longer-term purposes. Even the federal Minister of Finance, with unusual candour, admitted that all was not well. In 1946 he stated that "Our income tax is now unnecessarily cumbersome . . . not only is the tax structure itself complex but as the house well knows its drafting leaves much to be desired."

The outcome of this agitation and of the receptive attitude of post-war federal ministers of finance has been a remarkable series of revisions in both the personal and corporate income tax, including a complete redrafting of the statute law.

Structure and Rates of the Personal Income Tax

One of the major jobs—and in point of public appeal one of the more significant—was the simplification of the personal income tax. It will be recalled that the wartime version had two separate taxes—a normal tax (with three rates) and a graduated tax—each with its own set of exemptions and allowances, which were a combination of tax credits and income deductions. Into this complex system in 1942 there had been introduced a refundable portion, with fairly involved calculations. In mid-1944 the refundable portion had been withdrawn, in 1945 a 4 per cent reduction in tax was enacted, and in 1946 a 16 per cent reduction. As if this were not sufficient complexity, in mid-1945, with the inauguration of family allowance payments, supplementary taxes were introduced on taxpayers with dependent children in order to remove as completely as possible the duplication of benefit between the cash payment and the deduction allowed for the same child under the income tax, as directed in the Family Allowances Act.

The experts of the tax administration achieved miracles in 1945 and 1946 in reducing this hodge-podge to short-cut formulae and by the use of simplified forms reduced to a minimum the number of taxpayers who were exposed to the full rigour of these calculations. But for a large segment of the taxpayers who were not eligible to use these simplified methods the calculation of the tax was complicated and tedious.

In a general clean-up in 1947 all these complexities were swept away. For the normal tax, the graduated tax, the "notch" provisions, the non-payable refundable tax, and the family allowance recovery tax there was substituted a single graduated schedule of rates. The composite of income deductions and tax credits through which recognition was granted for single or marital status and for dependents was replaced by a simple plan of deductions from income. In the process the basic exemptions were raised from $660 to $750 for single status and from $1,200 to $1,500 for married status, a change which at the time eliminated about 600,000 taxpayers, or approximately one-quarter of the existing tax roll. At the same time a revised method for making the family allowance adjustment was introduced. The fact that the parents of a child under 16 were eligible to receive a cash payment was compensated for under the income tax through the granting of a smaller deduction for that child. A taxpayer claiming support of a child under 16 was allowed a deduction of $100 for that child in 1947, whereas a dependent over the age of 16 or otherwise ineligible for family allowance payments the deduction was set at $300.

Another problem dealt with was the relationship for tax purposes between a husband and wife who both have incomes. The anomalous situation that was deliberately created during the war to encourage wives to take employment has already been explained. This was removed in 1947. Henceforth where husband and wife each had taxable incomes in excess of the minimum exemption ($750 for 1947) each would be taxable as a single person. This in effect meant reverting to the pre-war status. In addition, however, the Government took the further logical step of providing that where a wife had any income at all (other than a nominal $250) the husband's allowance granted for her support would be correspondingly reduced. This return to normality met with some outcry from married women, but appears not to have had the dire consequences then predicted.

The 1947 revision set the general pattern for the post-war personal income tax. It has remained basically a simple combination of a single graduated rate structure with allowances in the form of deductions from income, a pattern departed from only for the temporary defence surtax enacted for 1951 and the new 2 per cent old age security tax which became effective in July, 1952.

Very substantial reductions in the actual burden of personal income tax were effected before it became necessary to reverse the trend for defence purposes in 1950. It has already been mentioned that in 1945 there was a 4 per cent reduction and in 1946 a 16 per cent. The 1947 revision just discussed effected as well a reduction in tax which amounted to 10 to 15 per cent for most taxpayers. This reduction had been provided in the 1946 budget, but in the 1947 budget, for extremely interesting reasons, the Minister of Finance recommended and Parliament enacted a further reduction that aggregated about 29 per cent. This second reduction had two main purposes—to restore incentive for work and to reduce the attractiveness of emigration to United States, a trend then causing concern, by making the Canadian tax more comparable to the American. The Minister of Finance frankly admitted these motives:

> . . . people are still smarting so much from their wartime experience that even after the substantial reductions made in the last two budgets the present levels of personal income taxes are regarded as excessive by a large proportion of the public. Therefore, whatever may be argued from the point of view of immediate economic effects or long-term debt policy, one must reach the conclusion that those who must bear them are not ready to support income taxes on the present scale. In fact, I am sure that were our present levels of personal income tax to be continued, they would constitute a serious impediment to a full working effort and a brake upon the drive and initiative of men and women in all groups and classes.
>
> There is another important point. We in Canada must always remember

the effect upon us and our policies of our proximity to the United States. . . . It would appear that if Canadians are asked to carry tax burdens which, after making due allowance for lower cost of living or lower cost of doing business or other offsetting factors, are significantly heavier than those imposed by the United States, there is a risk of serious drain of Canadian personnel to the south by this reason alone.

Taking account of the further 29 per cent reduction in 1947 (which came into effect from the middle of the year)it was estimated that the rates on average were then down to about one-half the wartime peak, *excluding* the refundable tax. No further reductions were made in 1948 although a popular concession was made for older taxpayers by the granting of an additional deduction of $500 for persons 65 years of age or over. But in the spring of 1949 the most substantial post-war reduction was made. Effective from the beginning of the year the exemptions were increased from $750 to $1,000 for single status and from $1,500 to $2,000 for married. The deductions for dependents were also raised from $100 to $150 and from $300 to $400. It was estimated that these higher exemptions would remove about 750,000 taxpayers from the scope of the personal income tax. At the same time very substantial reductions in rates were also made. Following this reduction the rates of personal income tax were down, on the average, to about one-third of the wartime peak. No further general changes were made until the defence surtax of 10 per cent was introduced for 1951.

The effect of these changes on the tax of individual persons is shown in Tables XXXI and XXXII. Table XXXI gives a comparison of the peak wartime rates and those of 1949 for a married taxpayer without dependents. The percentage of income paid in tax (the effective rate) is given for a range of income. It will be seen that up to $5,000 the reduction was two-thirds and more, while at both $10,000 and $15,000 it was 50 per cent.

Another comparison, perhaps even more significant, is between the rates that applied to each additional dollar of income—the "marginal" rate. This is shown for the same years in Table XXXII. In many instances there was a reduction of more than half from the wartime peak.

While these figures indicate clearly that substantial tax reductions were made (estimated, as previously stated, to be about two-thirds on the average), employment and incomes of the post-war period have been so buoyant that in 1951, even omitting the defence surtax, revenue from the personal income tax was almost as high and taxpayers almost as numerous as in 1946. When the revenue loss estimated

TABLE XXXI

EFFECTIVE RATES OF INCOME TAX, WARTIME PEAK AND 1949
MARRIED TAXPAYER—NO DEPENDENTS

Gross income $	Wartime peak[a] %	1949 %
1,500	6.7	0.0
2,000	11.6	0.0
3,000	19.5	5.0
5,000	27.6	10.2
10,000	37.6	16.6
15,000	46.2	22.4
20,000	51.4	27.6
30,000[b]	58.1	33.9
50,000	67.1	42.5
75,000	73.6	48.9
100,000	78.0	53.1
200,000	87.0	62.9
500,000	92.4	71.8
1,000,000	94.2	75.4

[a]Excludes refundable tax.
[b]All incomes over $30,000 are assumed to include $30,000 of earned income, the balance being investment income.

TABLE XXXII

MARGINAL RATES OF INCOME TAX, WARTIME PEAK AND 1949

Taxable income[a] exceeding $	Wartime peak[b] %	1949 %
1	19.0	15
1,000	36.0	17
2,000	41.0	19
3,000	42.0	19
5,000	51.0	22
10,000	56.0	35
15,000	63.7	45
20,000	70.0	45
30,000[c]	80.3	54
50,000	86.4	59
100,000	97.2	69
200,000	97.6	74
500,000	97.8	84

[a]Income in excess of the statutory exemptions.
[b]Excludes refundable tax.
[c]All incomes over $30,000 are assumed to include $30,000 of earned income, the balance being investment income.

for each individual step in the reduction is taken into account this becomes all the more astonishing. The original 16 per cent reduction was estimated to mean an annual loss of $115 million a year; the reduction of June, 1946, a loss of $155 million a year; the reduction of April, 1947, a loss of $175 million, and that of March, 1949, a loss of $270 million. All these total $715 million. In the fiscal year 1945–6, a year barely affected by the rate reductions, total revenue had been $691 million. One would assume therefore that the personal income tax would have vanished as a revenue item in the federal budget. In fact, in the fiscal year 1950–1, a year which should have reflected the accumulated result of all these reductions, including that of 1949, the revenue from the personal income tax was $652 million, or less than 6 per cent lower than that of 1945–6. Similarly, despite the fact that two increases in exemption levels were estimated to have together dropped some 1¼ million taxpayers out of a total in 1945 of 2¼ million, by 1951 it was estimated that there were again over 2½ million persons subject to income tax.

The explanation of this apparent enigma lies, of course, in the "leverage" of progressive tax rates on rapidly rising incomes. It is estimated that in general the relationship of change, under recent federal tax rates, between personal incomes and personal income tax revenues is of the order of one to two. This means that when personal incomes rise by 1 per cent there will be in general a 2 per cent rise in income tax revenues. Between 1945 and 1950 total personal incomes increased by about 50 per cent. While it would be mistaken to draw an exact mathematical conclusion from these two facts, the combined effect of the "leverage" and the general upward trend of incomes appears to have approximately offset the revenue losses resulting from the tax reductions outlined above.

In order to round out this description, several other adjustments in the rates and allowances may conveniently be mentioned here. For example, during the war the age limit for eligible dependents was reduced from twenty-one to eighteen. This restriction was relaxed first by excluding from it students and nurses in training between the ages of 18 and 21, and was finally abandoned in the 1949 revision of the Act by increasing the general age limit to the pre-war level of 21 years. The medical expenses allowance has also been extended in some manner almost annually. The period in respect of which expenses could be claimed was changed from the taxation year to any twelve months ending in the taxation year; the maximum amounts of allowable deductions were increased from $600 to $750 for a single person, from $900 to $1,000 for a married person, and from $150 to $250 for each dependent, the maximum for dependents being also increased from $600 to $1,000. Deductible expenses were extended in 1949 to include the cost of wheel chairs, and a deduction of $500 was granted to taxpayers confined throughout the year to a bed or wheel chair. In 1951 a significant step was taken in extending the allowance for the first time to a specific list of drugs, i.e., insulin, cortisone, ACTH, liver extract and vitamin B12 for pernicious anaemia, and in 1952 the maximum limits were doubled.

Extremely significant changes affecting the taxation of pensions and annuities arose out of the *Report* of the Royal Commission on the Taxation of Annuities and Family Corporations. In Canada for some years the practice had been followed of taxing the *whole* of the proceeds of a contractual annuity (including an endowment policy), no account being taken of the portion of the payments that represented the return of the cost of the annuity. This was and still is the English system, and is well supported by a long list of cases in the English courts. It was hardly surprising that the legal subtleties were not convincing to most taxpayers, but it was rather astonishing that a matter affecting a relatively small segment of the total taxpaying public could generate as much heat. There were frequent editorial references to the "iniquitous" practice (despite its British origin!) and the mail of the Minister of Finance was jammed with letters of protest. Some complicated problems had also arisen regarding the taxation of periodic payments under wills and trusts.

The peak of this agitation coincided with the recognition of serious anomalies under the existing treatment of pensions. Briefly, under one alternative, which any pension plan was free to adopt, the pension was tax free, but no deduction was allowed for the individual contribution to the fund, and the income of the fund was taxable. The effect of this arrangement was that the individual contributor sacrificed only the tax on his contribution, and received back his own money, his employer's contribution, and the interest on both these elements free of any further tax. Under the other alternative a deduction was allowed for the contribution to the fund, but the resulting pension was fully taxable. The disparate advantages under these alternatives and the question also of the appropriate maximum amount of deduction to be allowed for contributions to a pension fund were of considerably more practical importance under high wartime rates than they had been in pre-war days. In the case of the latter there was in general a limit of $300 per employee, restricted until 1944 to contributions in respect of the year of current service. In 1944 an equal allowance had been provided for contributions in respect of past services.

To advise the Government on a fitting solution to these problems (and an unrelated problem involving undistributed surpluses of closely held corporations, discussed in later pages) a Royal Commission was appointed in November, 1944, which, after its chairman, became known as the Ives Commission. The *Report* of the Commission, filed in March, 1945, was accepted by the Minister of Finance almost *in toto*, and made the basis of several amendments to the income tax law in 1946. The existing system of annuity taxation was abandoned, and replaced by one which in effect exempted from tax the capital portion of a contractual annuity. The method for accomplishing this end was to exclude from tax the present value of the annuity or series of payments at the time of commencement, taking into account the life expectancy of the annuitant and employing a rate of interest approved by the Minister of National Revenue. The amount so calculated is divided by the life expectancy of the annuitant, and only the part of each payment in excess of the figure so obtained is taxable. In effect only interest accruing *after* the annuity period commences is taxable. This elaborate system was not extended to annuities paid under wills and trusts, but such payments were exempt to the extent that they were paid out of the capital of the trust or estate.

The pension revisions were equally drastic. The double system was abandoned, and all pension plans were put on a basis under which deductions are allowed for the contributions of both employer and employee, the income of the fund is tax exempt, and the pension is fully taxable. The accrued rights of pensioners under the old optional treatment were perpetuated by a system under which their pensions are pro-rated into taxable and non-taxable parts. The maximum deduction for pension contributions was also increased from $300 to $900 in the case of the contributions both for current services and for past services.

No changes of consequence have since been made in the treatment of pensions and annuities established in 1946, although some revisions in the tax treatment of lump-sum receipts from pension plans and a statutory basis governing the taxation of profit-sharing plans have been enacted.

A great many other significant changes in the personal income tax have been made in the post-war period without the attention of a Royal Commission. To discuss these fully would require many more pages than can be spared here. The following list, however, indicates the wide variety of aspects of the tax that were involved: the exemption for the 4 per cent investment income surtax was increased from $1,500 to $1,800 in 1947 and to the greater of $2,400 or the personal exemptions deductible for the graduated tax in 1949; the deduction for dependents was extended to include dependents living outside of Canada; a system of averaging was introduced for farmers and fishermen, first on a three-year averaging period, later revised to a five-year period, and a system for taxing the disposal of cattle from a basic herd was inaugurated; authors, composers, and similar persons were allowed to spread their payments for the sale of a work over a two- or three-year period, depending on the time spent in producing it; members of provincial legislatures were allowed to receive a tax-free expense allowance not exceeding one-half the normal sessional indemnity; measures were introduced to alleviate the impact of progressive rates on certain forms of accumulated income, such as a death benefit and other accrued amounts received after the death of a taxpayer; the payment of tax on income accumulating in a blocked currency was allowed to be postponed; finally, a significant departure from past policy was made in recent years by the gradual introduction into the statute of provisions allowing the deduction of certain expenses incurred in earning salaries and wages. Some of these, such as salesmen's travelling expenses and away-from-home costs incurred by railwaymen, bus, truck, and transport drivers, had been allowed previously by administrative ruling. A significant extension into new fields was made in 1951, however, with the granting of deductions for union dues, fees paid to associations to which the employee was required to belong, and travelling expenses incurred in carrying on any employment.

Finally, some extremely significant changes in the personal income tax affecting the relations between corporations and their shareholders have been made in recent years. These may best be reviewed under the general headings of "double taxation" and "undistributed surpluses."

Double Taxation

The historic background of "double taxation" will be recalled from earlier chapters. The last official champion to sponsor its abolition had been Mr. Bennett, who made his ill-fated attempt in 1931. Some public interest was evidenced during the depression, but no further attention was given to the subject even semi-officially until the Rowell-Sirois *Report* urged that remedial steps be taken. During the war years there were renewed signs of restiveness from the business community, press editorials alleged generally that the situation was outrageous, and the Dominion Association of Chartered Accountants published specific proposals for action. The subject again attracted official attention in 1946 when the Dominion offered the assurance, as an inducement to the provinces to enter into a new deal, that universal agreements would enable it to proceed to remove "double" taxation. As will be seen in the next chapter, the Senate Special Committee of 1945–6 heard several influential witnesses criticize the existing position, and in its report urged that "double" taxation be avoided, and the Royal Commission on Co-operatives shared the same experience. "Double" taxation therefore was a particular bogey of the post-war period.

The first actual remedial step in over twenty years of agitation was taken by the federal Minister of Finance, Hon. D. C. Abbott, in his budget proposals of 1949. Conditions had been sufficiently prosperous in the post-war period to enable some progress to be made even without universal taxation agreements with the provinces. The measure he offered was typically Canadian, being very similar to that proposed by the Rowell-Sirois Commission. Particularly did it differ from the British system, generally regarded as the model. The Canadian venture—admitted to be but a first step—took the form of a deduction from personal income tax of 10 per cent of the amount of dividends received by Canadians from Canadian taxpaying companies. This system was described as administratively simple, but its overriding advantage was that it limited the area of the tax concession to Canadian taxpayers. If the concession had taken the form of a reduction in the corporation income tax, its benefit would have extended, owing to the large foreign ownership of Canadian businesses, beyond the limits the Government felt obliged to cover. This change was accompanied by a reduction to 10 per cent in the rate of corporation tax on the first $10,000 of income, so that at the time of introduction the two changes together almost removed double taxation of the income of small companies. This symmetry was disturbed during the defence financing period when the lower rate went to 20 per cent, but was restored in 1953 when the dividend tax credit was increased to 20 per cent.

Undistributed Surpluses

Equally radical, but of more restricted public interest, have been the changes in the tax treatment of undistributed profits. In chapter 14 the various measures adopted to the beginning of the depression to prevent the tax-free withdrawal of such surpluses through redemptions, capitalizations, etc., were described. It was also mentioned that in

1930 a concession was introduced under which corporations were permitted to distribute, free of tax, on a winding up, discontinuance, or reorganization, surpluses accumulated prior to 1930. This was the law until July 3, 1934, when the previous position was restored, so that all such distributions again became taxable to the extent of undistributed income on hand.

The position remained unchanged during the depression and throughout World War II. However, one of the unfortunate results of wartime tax rates that appears to have been increasingly impressed on the Minister of Finance was the confiscatory effect of combined income tax and succession duties when there was a large forced distribution from a closely held company on the death of a principal shareholder. The penalty was most severe when the only estate of a deceased person was represented by his share of the accumulated earnings of a corporation whose stock was so closely held that the other shareholders often did not have sufficient capital to buy up a large block of stock of a deceased shareholder. In order to obtain funds for the payment of succession duties under these circumstances it was necessary to declare a large dividend to all shareholders for the benefit of the estate of the deceased. But this large dividend was subject to personal income tax at steeply progressive rates, with the result that in some instances it was almost impossible to declare a dividend sufficiently large to leave, after paying the appropriate income tax, a balance for the payment of succession duty—the original purpose of the whole transaction.

The unmitigated operation of this process of attrition, or the fear of its potential operation among the living shareholders who were its intended victims, had created an extremely unwholesome atmosphere. If it did operate, the result was the draining of the business of its liquid assets, perhaps requiring its termination. Much more frequently, however, it meant that shareholders shed themselves of this liability by selling the whole business, sometimes at bargain prices, or perhaps as often resorted to other practices, legal enough but not entirely consistent with the "spirit" of the law, which enabled them to withdraw the earned surplus as a capital sum, and therefore non-taxable. This whole situation reached such a state towards the end of the war that the Ives Commission was asked to study it and recommend a solution.

The temporary plan proposed by the Commission was adopted intact by the Government. A private company (defined initially as one having not more than 50 shareholders, later extended to 75) was to be permitted to pay a tax on the amount of its undistributed surplus accumulated up to 1939 and thereafter pay out such surplus as a tax-free dividend. The tax was calculated on a graduated schedule of rates proposed by the Commission which applied to the individual segment of the surplus allocable to each shareholder. The aggregate of the taxes on each segment was the tax payable by the corporation.

This measure was greeted with acclaim. There appears to have been an intensive cultivation of the benefits it offered, since in all the federal government received some $59 million under it. Quite obviously, however, it did not offer a permanent solution. In the war and post-war years extensive capital expansion has required the ploughing back of a substantial portion of profits, and within a decade of the cut-off date for the Ives formula there was ample evidence that the shareholders of many firms were again facing a serious problem—and that some of the earlier practices and some new ones were being adopted to avoid these problems.

In addition to the temporary solution accepted by the Government, the Ives Commission had also suggested a formula for permanent adoption. The Minister of Finance had not found this formula acceptable, but in rejecting it he had virtually promised that after full consideration the Government would put forward a solution of its own. This step was taken in 1950. Its basic principle was the granting of a right to capitalize undistributed income on hand, and thus create "tax-paid" undistributed income, on the payment of a 15 per cent tax. The plan covered two phases. First, undistributed surpluses up to the end of the 1949 taxation year could be cleared by paying a tax of 15 per cent thereon. This could be done at any time, but it could only be done in a single operation and had to be done before the second phase could be entered on. Secondly, a corporation, having cleared its pre-1949 surplus, could at any time thereafter pay a 15 per cent tax on an amount of its later accumulations of surplus equal to the amount of its dividends declared in the later period. In short, a corporation could earn the right to pay the 15 per cent tax on a dollar of undistributed surplus by declaring a dollar of dividends. It should be noted that payment of the 15 per cent tax does not permit, as did the Ives formula, the declaration of a tax-free dividend. It allows companies to perform the act of capitalizing undistributed surplus on hand without such capitalization being deemed to have put taxable income in the hands of the shareholders. However, there is no further tax payable by the shareholder when, for example, there is a redemption of a redeemable preferred share issued in capitalization of undistributed surplus on which the 15 per cent tax has been paid.

This treatment was first extended to companies having 75 shareholders or less, but in 1951 was made available to all companies. It is not apparently anticipated that any large company with a wide share-distribution would be interested in taking advantage of the measure. That many closely held companies have taken advantage of the plan is indicated by the receipts from the tax. To March 31, 1954, some $120 million had been received.

While they are too detailed to discuss further here, several important changes were made in related provisions of the law as a result of the introduction of the 15 per cent tax formula. In general these were designed to tighten up existing protective provisions so as to discourage practices for which the 15 per cent tax payment provided a substitute, and also in some instances to discard protective provisions which appeared to be unnecessary with the new regimen in operation. An adaptation of the 15 per cent "company" tax was made in 1953 when companies were given the right to redeem preferred shares at a premium on payment of a tax, in this case at a 20 per cent rate. In 1954 the Government, apparently having concluded that this privilege was being abused, raised the rate to 30 per cent.

26 THE DOMINION, 1946–54

Corporate Income Tax Reform

The Excess Profits Tax

IT MAY BE AS WELL, at the outset of a consideration of post-war business taxation, to dispose first of the last days of the excess profits tax. We left this fearsome weapon in chapter 22, spiked with a 100 per cent rate, of which 20 per cent was refundable, and barbed, for greater security, with a minimum rate of 40 per cent (including the 18 per cent normal rate).

The first relaxation in the excess profits tax was made for fiscal years ending after December 31, 1945. Standard profits of less than $25,000 were increased by the addition of one-half the difference between the actual standard and $25,000. This measure had the effect of raising the minimum standard, formerly $5,000, to $15,000, and it also raised in some degree all standards of less than $25,000. At the same time the rate structure was simplified, the effective rate was reduced, and the refundable portion withdrawn. The simplification as such merely codified what had previously been the net effect of the complicated rate structure. The rates became 22 per cent on total profits (a minimum of 40 per cent including the 18 per cent normal rate) and, in addition, 20 per cent of profits in excess of 116⅔ per cent of standard profits. Under this arrangement, therefore, the rate was 40 per cent up to 116⅔ per cent of standard profits and 60 per cent on profits over that mark, no part of the tax being refundable.

For 1947 a revision was made which involved the first increase since 1939 in the normal rate—from 18 per cent to 30 per cent. Concurrently the excess profits tax was limited in its application to profits in excess of 116⅔ per cent of standard and reduced in rate to 15 per cent. The effect of the new arrangement, therefore, was that profits up to 116⅔ per cent of standard bore 30 per cent; profits over that mark bore 45 per cent. This arrangement was in effect to the end of 1947, when the excess profits tax was finally repealed, two years after it had disappeared in the United States, and one year after it had been repealed in the United Kingdom. The Minister of Finance acknowledged on several occasions that as a tax measure it had outlived its prime and that its continuation into the peace, with each year making more remote and less realistic the standard period based on a decade before, had possibilities of serious hardship. He justified its retention in 1946, however, on the grounds that "we are still living in highly abnormal times, the shadow of war is still upon us and . . . the financial burdens on the Dominion budget arising out of the war are still of huge proportions," and in 1947 as follows: "If business conditions had now returned to normal and we could rely upon the forces of competition and bargaining to keep profits at normal levels, we would be justified in repealing this tax. . . . If business needed larger profits to encourage and enable it to provide additional employment by greater expenditures, we should repeal the tax forthwith. Neither of these conditions exists at present." In the same budget, however, he announced the repeal of the tax at the end of 1947.

Even its final repeal did not immediately remove the tax from the centre of interest it had occupied during the war. The greater discretion given for the adjustment of standard profits for cases of hardship and for new businesses had produced such a spate of applications to the Board of Referees that a deadline of 1947 was set to bring a conclusion to this form of activity. Although the Board underwent a change of personnel it was not finally disbanded until 1949, having disposed of some eight thousand appeals on standard profits.

Work of Board of Referees

No official study has been published in Canada on the over-all results of the Board's activities, but a certain amount of information regarding its work is available.

Most of the hearings were held in Ottawa, but the Board often held hearings in other cities. This assisted taxpayers who could not travel to Ottawa, and also enabled the Board to get first-hand knowledge of business conditions in other parts of the country. In 1945, the Board adopted the practice of making written offers to claimants, with the understanding that if the offers were unacceptable, hearings would be given. Out of 1,480 such offers, 68 per cent were accepted without hearings. Not all first hearings were held by the Board, those of taxpayers with standard profits of less than $50,000 being held in the district offices by special committees of technical personnel. Some 2,572 agreements between taxpayers and the committees were made in this way, and 2,034 of them were later confirmed by the Board.

There was no appeal from, and no reasons given for, the Board's decisions; the taxpayer was merely told the amount of standard profit awarded. But as there were few public complaints by industries, professional groups, or newspapers, it may be concluded that there was general satisfaction with the decisions. Nor were there many disagreements between the Board and the Minister—a dozen or so out of over 8,000 total claims, of which only one went to the Treasury Board.

No hard and fast rule was applied by the Board in determining standard profits, each case being given special study. Information was taken from public records or from evidence supplied by the Department of National Revenue. Statistical data compiled early in the war period in Canada and the United States tended to show that in "non-depressed" industries profits during the base period averaged around 60 to 70 per cent of the profits made in the period 1927–30; and this was sometimes used as a guide. Firms applying for relief were given all the possible concessions available under the statute. The Act limited standard profits, under the "depressed business" provision, to between 5 and 10 per cent of invested capital; but if the Board felt that a claimant was entitled to more than the 10 per cent, it often advised him to file a new claim under other relief provisions, such as the "new business" or the "capital impairment" clause. Only a small proportion of businesses, however, applied for relief under the "depressed business" clause, as about 85 per cent of hardship claims were adjusted without regard to invested capital in the base period.

The Board was not concerned with the actual tax consequences of its decisions, which were solely on the matter of awarding standard profits. It did not therefore keep any record of tax savings resulting from the awards; and since there is no record of actual standard profits earned, it is not possible to compute the amount of refunded taxes. The only statistics available, which are for the period ending December 31, 1949, concern the number of cases dealt with and the dollar amounts of the awards. These show that in all 8,125 awards were made, 6,895 to corporations and 1,230 to individuals; while the dollar total of the awards amounted to $515 million, out of total claims of $729 million.

Two main criticisms of the Board's work were made. One was that it was too slow, largely because the processing of claims through the Department of National Revenue took too long. The other was that as the Board became more accustomed, during the war years, to higher levels of profits, their awards became more lenient, so that the later claims were made, the more generously were they treated. It was felt that this fact, well known in the business world, might prove a source of trouble if ever the tax were reimposed.

Corporation Income Tax—Rate Revisions

The first post-war change in the rate of corporation income tax has already been mentioned. In 1947 the rate was increased from 18 per cent to 30 per cent. Taken in conjunction with the elimination of the minimum rate of excess profits tax in the same year, this had the effect of a reduction from 40 per cent to 30 per cent in the aggregate minimum rate applicable to corporations. While other circumstances may also have played a part, the undertaking given by the Dominion under the Wartime Tax Agreements to reduce its corporate rate by 10 points in the year following the expiration of the agreements was the immediate reason given by the Minister of Finance for the change.

The most significant rate alteration in the whole history of the tax was introduced in 1949 with the adoption of a two-step graduation. The flat 30 per cent rate was abandoned for an initial rate of 10 per cent on profits not in excess of $10,000 combined with a 33 per cent rate on profits over that amount. The explanation for this change was that the Government felt it desirable to foster the establishment and growth of small businesses. The "small business" movement in Canada has never reached the intensity of the American agitation, but the innovation was nevertheless well received. Taken in conjunction with the tax credit of 10 per cent against individual income tax in respect of dividend income, previously explained, the reduced rate had the effect of almost eliminating "double" taxation of the income of small corporations.

This rate graduation has been retained in later increases. In September, 1950, as part of the defence programme, the 10 per cent rate was raised to 15 per cent and the 33 per cent rate to 38 per cent. From January 1, 1951, a 20 per cent surtax was imposed on the higher rate, giving a combination of 15 per cent and 45.6 per cent. By the same budget (April 10, 1951) the long-standing right to file consolidated returns on payment of a rate usually 1 per cent or 2 per cent higher than the standard rate was withdrawn in respect of fiscal years ending after December 31, 1951. Both rates were increased by a further 2 per cent, effective from January 1, 1952, for financing of old age pensions, under the provisions of the Old Age Security Act. (A later chapter reviews most recent developments.)

This completes the description of the course of the rates to 1951 except in one particular. It should be mentioned that the reduced rate has been hedged with restrictions to prevent companies from watering down their total taxation by splitting up into numerous small companies. In general only one company of a group of "related" companies has been allowed the reduced rate. The concept of "relationship" has undergone some changes since it was first introduced. Originally a company was considered to be related if controlled by another company or subject to joint control. Later this was relaxed to the extent that ownership of less than 70 per cent of the shares of a company did not constitute control for this purpose. The most common cause of complaint after this relaxation was against the rule of law which deemed all companies to be related if controlled by or subject to the joint control of persons not dealing "at arms length." Since persons not dealing "at arms length" were deemed to include relatives, situations arose in which brothers, for example, living at opposite ends of the country, in different lines of business and having no financial ties, were forced to elect which of them would claim the lower rate. This situation was relieved by an amendment in 1951, retroactive to 1949, allowing all companies controlled by persons not dealing "at arms length" to take the reduced rate if there were no common ownership of shares between such persons, and by a narrower definition of relationship enacted in 1952.

Structural Changes

Several alterations and innovations in the scope and form of the corporation income tax command even more attention than the rate revisions just described. Some of these fundamental changes have already been indicated in preceding chapters and require only elaboration here. Others represented new departures not hitherto mentioned.

An aspect of the corporation tax that has always attracted attention in all countries is the position of co-operatives, mutuals, and similar organizations. Canada has been no exception. During the war, the advantage such organizations enjoyed under the laws enabled them to accumulate substantial reserves and to expand their activities at a time when businesses not so organized were being drained of their profits by extremely heavy taxation. (In Canada the co-operative movement is almost entirely confined to agriculture and fishing, and has reached its most advanced development in wheat marketing in the western provinces.) Starting from an initial impetus given by the private grain trade in the West, of which the formation of the Income Taxpayers Association was the most marked evidence, a fairly strong feeling developed in the business community throughout Canada, as the war progressed, against the apparently privileged position of co-operatives, mutuals, and similar organizations. There were indications, too, that the leaders of the co-operative movement in Canada, following a conference in Winnipeg in 1944, were anxious to have their status under the tax laws clarified, in view of the obscure terms of the provisions under which they claimed exemption.

Taking heed of both these developments, the federal Government in November, 1944, appointed a Royal Commission[1] (the second devoted to taxation in the post-war era) to recommend a solution. The Commission submitted its *Report* in September, 1945, and its general recommendations were adopted by the Government and became law in 1946.

The Commission held public hearings throughout Canada, in the course of which a considerable amount of heat was both generated and dissipated in the friction caused by contact between standard and co-operative principles of business. The point at issue was extremely elusive. In theory it is possible for a group of people to organize a business operation in such a way that no annual profit emerges from it. Consumers, for example, can organize an agency to purchase goods for resale to themselves at cost, plus a fee to cover the agency expenses, or producers can set up an agency to sell their produce and return the full proceeds to themselves less an amount to cover the necessary costs of the agency. If each year's transaction were to be completed before the close of the year the receipts and disbursements of the agency would result in a zero profit for the agency. This is the essence of a true mutual or co-operative, and in fact many small business operations are carried on in this manner.

More commonly, however, the agency—usually a corporation and therefore a separate legal person—ends the year with a surplus, which the members agree to leave with the agency to be returned to them in a future repayment or in a future reduction of costs and prices. But the income tax is an annual affair, and looking at the year's operations it is reasonable to ask what real distinction there is between this surplus and the profit that emerges as a result of the year's operations of any private company. In general if the surplus is retained by the co-operative as a reserve not allocated to specific members who may draw it out if they wish, then there is little to distinguish it from undistributed profit. However, if the surplus that emerges at the end of the year is distributed to customers or made available to them in accordance with an announced plan, then there is ground for argument

[1] Royal Commission on Co-operatives, *Report* (1945).

that the surplus is not income of the co-operative—that it does not "belong" to the co-operative.

Every aspect of this beguiling phase of tax theory was canvassed, pro and con, before the Commission. It is interesting that many witnesses directed their main offensive not against the mutual principle but against the existence of double taxation. The problem of taxing co-operatives arose, it was maintained, only because there was a *corporation* income tax. It was the advantages co-operatives had in being able to minimize or escape the corporation tax, not the individual income tax applicable to its members, that was the real rub. Ergo—remove the advantages by removing the corporation income tax.

The Commission recommended in its *Report* that the tax exemption granted under the law be repealed and that co-operatives be subject to tax. But it also recommended that patronage dividends paid or made available to members be deductible in calculating the income to which tax would apply. In order not to create or perpetuate discriminations it also recommended that *all* businesses be allowed to pay patronage dividends and deduct them from taxable income, provided that certain conditions were met. It recommended the same general treatment for mutual, fire, casualty, and automobile insurance companies, i.e., dividends and rebate of premiums were to be deductible. For organizations deriving all their income from the insurance of churches and schools and for credit unions it recommended continuation of the existing exemption. It also recommended that *bona fide* new co-operatives be given an exemption from tax for their first three years.

The one minor change adopted by the Government in implementing the *Report* was the introduction of a requirement that a co-operative could not reduce its taxable income below an amount equal to a return of 3 per cent on its capital employed by the payment of patronage dividends. Against this part, however, it could offset any amount paid in interest on its capital, and tax would be payable only on the balance, if any. In introducing this modification the Minister of Finance gave the following explanation: "The principle underlying this rule is that amounts set aside out of taxable income to be distributed in proportion to patronage by a cooperative or company which does not pay at least three per cent on the capital employed in its business contain earnings which arise from the employment of capital and ought not to escape tax entirely."

With minor revisions which have not altered the basic pattern the system adopted in 1946 has been retained unchanged.

Undoubtedly the most far-reaching revisions affecting the calculation of income have been those made in the allowance for the write-off of fixed assets. Under the old methods the cost of fixed assets was allowed to be written off in equal annual amounts while the asset was in use. The rates were applied on a straight-line basis, and there were a variety of them for different kinds of assets. Certain allowances, such as that permitting the amortization of pre-production expenses of mines, were granted which did not appear to have much basis in law. No allowance was made for obsolescence, and the only provision for the recapture of depreciation on assets sold at a price in excess of their written-down value was restricted to immovable assets (excluding machinery and equipment) that had been subject to "special" depreciation (for the most part accelerated write-offs allowed during the war) and to plant and equipment for which post-war accelerated depreciation had been taken.

In place of these arrangements a system having several new features was enacted in 1948, to take effect in 1949. A relatively few rates, each applicable to a class of assets of roughly similar nature, were substituted for the existing schedules. It was provided that an annual write-off could be taken for all assets in each class at the appropriate rate, on the "diminishing balance basis," i.e., the rate is applied each year to the original cost less the aggregate of the write-offs previously taken for these assets. Under the new system an addition is made to the balance remaining in each class each year for new assets purchased and a subtraction for old assets sold. As long as there is any balance left in the class an annual write-off may be taken, regardless of whether the assets are still in use or even still in the ownership of the taxpayer.

It is obvious, of course, that, under this system, sales from a class of assets will reduce the balance to be written off. Where a sale is large enough to more than extinguish the balance remaining (indicating liquidation at a price in excess of the written-down value of the class of assets) the amount of the sale will be taken into income, but only to the extent of any depreciation previously taken in respect of the asset or assets sold. No attempt is made under the new system to recapture a capital gain represented by any excess of the sale price over original cost. In order to bring the scheme into operation with respect to existing assets, the original cost less depreciation taken to the commencement of the 1949 taxation year was established as the unamortized cost for the new plan.

A feature of considerable significance in the new plan was the approximate doubling of depreciation rates concurrently with the switch to the diminishing balance method of calculation. Its essential merit, however, was that it granted in effect a write-off for obsolescence, coupled with a recapture as income of previous write-offs when an asset is sold at a price in excess of the written-down value. Several other forms of write-off, too detailed to discuss here, were given a statutory basis in the revision.

A host of other important and interesting organic alterations in the corporation income tax must be dismissed with scant notice. The extension from three years to five years in the period over which losses might be carried forward has been mentioned. Comment was also made on the perpetuation of the wartime allowances for exploration expenses in the mining and petroleum industries. The three-year exemption for new mines has also been carried forward, a larger depletion allowance has been granted to gold mines, and the shareholders' depletion allowance on dividends has been graduated in accordance with the proportion of the dividend attributable to mineral or petroleum production. In unrelated fields which have attracted wide attention in United States solutions have also been found. To obviate potential abuses of "charitable foundations" their exemption has been made contingent on the distribution of nearly all their income each year for charitable purposes. Any tax advantages in the "sale and lease-back" type of transaction have been nullified by the denial of a deduction for depreciation or other expenses to the seller-lessee, in respect of the property involved, in excess of what he could claim were he the owner of the property.

Overhauling the Statute

Finally, one of the distinctive features of the post-war period, particularly in regard to business taxation, has been the marked progress achieved in the complete reconstruction of the statute law, a process in which the Income War Tax Act was scrapped and replaced by a new measure, the Income Tax Act.

A useful role in this development was served by a Special Committee of the Senate, appointed by that body in October, 1945, "to examine into the provisions and workings of the Income War Tax Act and the Excess Profits Tax Act, 1940, and to formulate recommendations for the improvement, clarification and simplification of the methods of assessment and collection of taxes thereunder and to report thereon." This Committee held public hearings in the fall of 1945 and the spring of 1946, and received representations from the Canadian Manufacturers' Association, the Canadian Bar Association, the Dominion Association of Chartered Accountants, the Canadian Chamber of Commerce, and about twenty other influential persons and organizations. One of its principal witnesses was Mr. C. F. Elliott, the Commissioner of Income Tax. While many of the briefs it received covered ground well outside the Committee's terms of reference it was able nevertheless to glean from them a sufficient cross-section of opinion to support certain recommendations which did fall within the ambit of its purview. These were set forth in the Committee's reports of May 28, 1946, and July 31, 1946.

Its principal findings were summed up in the following paragraphs:

> 1. There is dissatisfaction with the appeal procedure as now found in the Income War Tax Act and with the lack of facilities afforded taxpayers to have cases decided rapidly and objectively. Co-existing with this feeling is the more technical and less widely held objection to the use of ministerial or administrative discretion and to the absolute authority of the administration in many matters of substantive importance.
>
> 2. Secondly, a portion of the criticism which has been received deals with the phraseology of the statute itself. There appears to be a growing feeling among economists, lawyers and accountants throughout Canada that the language of the present Dominion Income War Tax Act is no longer capable of permitting the legislation to fill its proper place in the vastly changed economic structure of the country in the face of concepts of profit and necessary expenditures which now exist when compared with those whose presence helped to shape the original statute in 1917. . . . Almost without exception the witnesses who appeared before your Committee urgently advocated a complete revision of the taxing statute to the end that not only may clarity and coherence be achieved but that its provisions be brought into conformity with modern business practice. With this suggestion your committee is in complete accord.
>
> 3. The third head under which criticism falls is that pertaining to the administrative framework of the Taxation Division itself. Most of those objections are directed to the low salaries paid, delays within the Department in assessing and the disposition of individual cases, and to the inability of the public to obtain the various inter-office administrative directives that are issued to the District Offices by the Deputy Minister at frequent intervals.[2]

To facilitate appeal procedure and reduce the use of discretionary powers, which were not subject to review by the courts, the Committee suggested that a Tax Appeal Board be established. The fee for an appeal to this Board should not exceed $25, and it should have full power to amend any assessment issued by the Minister of National Revenue and to confirm or vary any exercise of his discretionary powers. Of these powers the Committee listed approximately ninety

[2]Special Committee, *Proceedings* (Session 1946), p. 378.

individual instances in the Income War Tax Act, many of no great importance. With regard to the drafting of the Act it recommended: that section 6(1)(a), the general definition of income, be amended "to conform with modern accounting practice," possibly along the lines suggested by the English Income Tax Codification Committee of 1926; that specific statutory provision be made for the accrual basis of accounting; that the tax liability of shareholders arising out of changes in the capital structure of a company having undistributed surplus on hand be made less ambiguous; that section 32A (a protective measure giving very broad powers to the Treasury Board) and the provision which segregated primary from secondary sources of income be eliminated; that depreciation be allowed as a matter of right rather than of ministerial discretion; that no interest accrue after two years of the filing of a tax return if no assessment notice has been issued, and that interest only recommence to accrue after an assessment has been sent; that the deduction of tax at the source be retained; that the provisions relating to expenses not laid out to earn income and to reserves, contingent accounts, and sinking funds be reviewed in the light of modern business practices, and that the sections covering the withholding tax on non-residents and deductions from the gift tax be clarified. The Committee did not issue the part of its report that was intended to carry its recommendations on the operation of the Department, but did observe that "current salaries appear in the main to be inadequate in view of the national importance and the high degree of responsibility inherent in the nature of the functions performed. . . ."

As mentioned above, the Committee carried on its hearings in the fall of 1945 and the spring of 1946, submitting partial reports on its conclusions in May and July, 1946. Its apparent intention of renewing its proceedings at the following session and of issuing further reports did not materialize. This suspension of activity was undoubtedly a direct consequence of the announcement made by the Minister of Finance in his budget speech of June, 1946, that an interdepartmental committee had been established to redraft the entire income tax law with explicit instructions to explore the possibility of reducing to the minimum the number of discretionary powers. The Government thus demonstrated clearly that it was fully aware of the deficiencies of the existing legislation and was as anxious as anyone else to see it revised.

The results of this spate of interest were not long in coming. The first appeared in 1946, with the amendment of the law to authorize the establishment of an Income Tax Appeal Board. It also provided for an

Advisory Board, independent of the Appeal Board, to which a taxpayer could require the Minister of National Revenue to refer, for hearing, consideration, and advice, decisions made by the Minister in the exercise of specific discretionary powers. The Appeal Board was authorized to hear appeals, on payment of a $15 fee, from departmental assessments for income of 1946 and later years, and was given authority to confirm the assessment or direct that the department amend it as the Board thought fit. The Advisory Board on discretions was never established (the later repeal of most of the discretions made it unnecessary), but the Appeal Board came into active operation early in 1949, and by the end of 1954 had heard nearly a thousand cases. Throughout most of its existence it has been constituted as a three-man board, although in 1954 a fourth member was appointed. Appeals from the Board's decisions may be taken to the Exchequer Court.

By far the most significant event of the "reform" period was the adoption by Parliament in 1948 of a completely revised income tax statute, to come into effect on January 1, 1949. This action was the culmination of over two years of intensive work by the interdepartmental committee, composed of officials of the Departments of Justice, Finance, and National Revenue. The general instructions given this committee were to simplify, clarify, revise, and rearrange the existing statute law, to eliminate as many as possible of the discretionary powers, to embody as statute law all existing practices of the department or to provide for their codification in regulations, and to recommend such improvements in practices as might be made without altering the underlying principles of the law.

The committee, working within this directive, produced a bill which, after extensive consideration by the Minister of Finance, was presented to Parliament late in the 1947 session. A unique procedure was followed in order to assure the fullest examination of its provisions by members of Parliament, lawyers, accountants, and the public at large. The redrafted measure, known as Bill 454, was allowed to stand over between the 1947 and 1948 sessions. During this period it was studied intensively by the Canadian Tax Foundation, the Canadian Bar Association, the Dominion Association of Chartered Accountants, and scores of other organizations and individuals, many of whom presented oral or written submissions to the Minister of Finance on its provisions. In the 1948 session, the bill was again presented to Parliament, many of its sections having been altered in some respect as a result of the intensive study it had received. This measure, Bill 338, was referred to the Standing Committee on Banking and Commerce, again an unprecedented step in the case of a taxing law. This Committee heard the Minister of Finance, Hon. D. C. Abbott, and members of the interdepartmental drafting committee explain the general character of the revision. (The published minutes of these hearings provide an excellent review of the new law.[3]) On passage by the House and Senate, Bill 338 became known as The Income Tax Act, to succeed on January 1, 1949, to the Income War Tax Act.

Unfortunately it would be a major undertaking to review in detail all the changes effected in the revision. Many have already been mentioned. Several very important changes of form and procedure were also made. Of the departmental (ministerial) discretions that had been so castigated by every witness before the Senate Special Committee, all but one or two of slight importance were deleted. Undoubtedly the most significant alteration in this regard was the transformation of the depreciation provision from the form of a negation of any deduction except in the discretion of the Minister (a form adopted in 1940 after the first *Pioneer Laundry* case[4]) to a positive allowance for a deduction for capital cost at rates required by statute to be established by regulation of the Governor in Council. The import of the "capital cost" concept has been explained previously. It was almost as great a revolution in the administration of the Act, however, that henceforth depreciation rates were to be made known to the taxpaying public at large, on the authority of the Governor in Council, and that the old system under which taxpayers learned only through experimentation what rates would be accepted by the department was to be abolished.

The revolutionary character of the removal of the discretionary powers and the codification in legal rules of many existing departmental "practices" is most clearly seen when considered in juxtaposition with the establishment of the Tax Appeal Board. Whereas the administration of income tax in Canada for thirty years had been markedly barren of adjudication by the courts, at one stroke the discretionary powers which were not subject to review by the courts were replaced by statutory rules, and at the same time a new and easy access to a court of law for appealing the application of these rules was provided. Thus simply was the whole concept of income tax administration converted from one basis to another, each with its own relative merits.

[3]*Minutes of Proceedings and Evidence* (Session 1947–8, House of Commons), pp. 547–728.

[4][1940] A.C. 127.

Other changes affecting business taxation may be only briefly mentioned. The concept of residence was clearly established as the basis of liability for full tax, with the concept of "carrying on business" as the basis of liability for non-residents, thus introducing clarity where the basis was neither clear nor uniform before; income from a business was to be the "profit" for the year, a concept well defined by English and Canadian courts; a new method of dealing with bad debts and reserves for doubtful debts was introduced; the conditions under which interest on borrowings could be deducted were restricted slightly; the general rules governing the deductibility of expenses were brought into closer conformity with actual administrative practice; the lesser of cost or market was established as the statutory basis for the valuation of inventories, with power given to provide for other bases by regulation; several new measures to protect the revenue were introduced and several old ones refurbished. Section 32A was not repealed.

It is with regret that we pass over here other changes made by the new law along with the extremely successful job of streamlining forms and procedures undertaken by the Taxation Division in the years following the war. These details may be obtained elsewhere, and sufficient has been said in the present and preceding chapter to demonstrate that in many respects the post-war period has represented an epoch of progress unparalleled in the history of the tax.

Dominion Succession Duties

Before we leave the direct taxes it should be mentioned that only one or two changes of significance have been made in the succession duty law in the post-war period. Undoubtedly the change of widest interest was the increase in the general exemption from $5,000 to $50,000 in 1948. This was estimated by the Minister of Finance to have eliminated from duty about 90 per cent of the estates, at a revenue loss of only $5 million. Another amendment was made as a result of the failure to obtain a general suspension of the provincial succession duties under the tax rental agreements. The Dominion doubled its rates to apply in the provinces where the local levy had been dropped, and to preserve approximately the previous position for residents of Ontario and Quebec it allowed a deduction from its duty, up to one-half, for duty paid to a province in respect of the same estate. This new system came into effect in 1947. Some further changes, discussed later, were made in the 1952 budget.

27 THE DOMINION, 1946–54

Commodity Taxes and Tariffs

IN ORDER TO CARRY the narrative forward to present events, two more or less related aspects of federal developments in recent years remain to be dealt with. These are (*a*) the post-war revision of the commodity taxes; (*b*) the post-war tariff changes under the General Agreement on Tariffs and Trade. A brief chapter will follow later on the unwelcome return of high taxes to finance the large-scale defence expenditures set in motion by the Korean war.

Commodity Taxes

As the description of wartime developments in chapter 23 has shown, commodity taxes were exploited on a very broad front by the Dominion. Few old taxes remained unchanged, and few new sources remained unchallenged. The relative importance of revenue from indirect taxes declined, but this was owing to the considerably greater leeway for increases in the income and other direct taxes rather than to any shortfalls in the effort on the indirect side. As in most other fields, the wartime experience with indirect taxes was without precedent in our history.

Some of the steps in the descent from this pinnacle have already been noted. The reductions in May, 1945, on the crest of the victory over Germany, were particularly marked on automobiles and electrical appliances. For automobiles a flat 10 per cent rate replaced a schedule that carried an 80 per cent charge on the value in excess of $1,200. On a wide range of electrical appliances a wartime tax of 25 per cent was dropped entirely. The exemption of building materials from sales tax in this same operation was also notable, marking an early return to a position that had existed for a short time prior to the war.

The only other decreases of any moment in the immediate aftermath of the war were the repeal of the 10 per cent war exchange tax and the exemption of machinery and apparatus for manufacturing industries in October, 1945, and the repeal of the 3 cents per gallon gasoline tax in April, 1947. This last was a friendly gesture in the direction of the provincial premiers, some of whom had protested against the Dominion's retention in peacetime of this traditional provincial source of revenue. Withdrawal of the Dominion tax was the signal for a general rise in provincial rates although not in every province to the full extent of the three cents suspended by the Dominion.

1947 Exchange Conservation Programme

The momentous radio speech of the Hon. Douglas C. Abbott, Minister of Finance, in November, 1947, inaugurated a period of feverish activity in the commodity tax field. As part of a temporary programme to save dollars by cutting down on imports of goods from the United States, a long list of new and increased taxes was introduced on November 18. The fact that these taxes were first announced in a radio speech and had no statutory basis for several months had interesting parliamentary repercussions that must be neglected here. Suffice it to say that the Minister of Finance was apparently convinced that the crisis was sufficiently grave to warrant taking such drastic action, relying on a subsequent session of Parliament to support him with retroactive legislation. More important is the fact that the federal Government appeared to be confident that a formula that had produced good results in a specific limited field under the stimulus of wartime emergency conditions would work equally as well in the less demanding and more relaxed atmosphere of peacetime.

The range of new taxes announced at the outset of this programme surpassed in some respects all previous efforts. A long list of new excises were imposed—generally at a 25 per cent rate—to apply on both imported and internally manufactured goods for the duration of the exchange emergency. These included almost every form of electrical appliance (washing machines being an exception), electric and gas refrigerators, stoves and water heaters, oil burning equipment, sporting goods for golf, tennis, badminton, squash, polo, billiards, pool, bowling, and curling, fishing rods and reels, firearms, pleasure boats, outboard motors, motor cycles, musical instruments, film projectors, and toilet articles not previously taxed. The automobile tax went up once more from a flat 10 per cent to a graduated schedule having a top rate of 75 per cent, and taxes on radios and cameras were increased from 10 per cent to 25 per cent. A notable exception to the upward trend, undoubtedly intended to underline the fact that the tax increases were for exchange conservation purposes and not for revenue, appeared in the form of several tax reductions. The exemption from sales tax of gas and electricity used in homes was restored, the sugar tax (of chequered history) was repealed, and substantial reductions were made in the tariff on tea and coffee.

The history of the long and impressive list of new taxes in the months following the original announcement would seem to carry some sort of lesson for future reference. The purpose of the original announcement was undoubtedly to enunciate in the clearest and sharpest terms the crucial character of the exchange crisis. All the principal articles selected for taxation were either imported directly from the United States in quantity or else had a substantial element of imported components. Some of the less significant articles had to be included in order to maintain balance and equity within competitive ranges. Like many another tax programme, however, this one suffered considerable erosion when exposed to the acid of public trial. The Minister of Finance was in the unusual position that, having introduced these taxes without parliamentary action, he could just as easily withdraw them before Parliament enacted them as law. Petitions for such withdrawal were not long in coming from almost everyone affected. Within a month the tax on stoves (both gas and electric), church organs, and tooth brushes had been withdrawn, the tax on pleasure boats restricted to apply only to the engines in the boats, and the tax on refrigeration and oil burning equipment restricted to apply only to models for household use and to installations in places of entertainment, amusement, or recreation. These changes were effective from December 8. By the end of the following January the tax on oil burning equipment had been completely withdrawn, the tax on sporting goods had been first amended to exclude golf shoes and then withdrawn *in toto*; pianos and electric organs had been excluded from the tax on musical instruments, combs, brushes, and mirrors costing 25¢ or less had been dropped from the tax on toilet articles, and the tax on several electrical appliances had been limited to apply to household models. During February the tax on engines for pleasure boats was dropped (but outboard motors were left taxable) and tax on the remaining musical instruments was abandoned, along with the tax on electric grills and hot-plates. After all these deletions and amendments the taxes finally enacted at the spring session of Parliament applied to automobiles, motor cycles, certain electrical appliances, firearms, outboard motors, cameras, radios, and film projectors. An unprecedented provision in the law that enacted these remaining taxes gave the Governor in Council power to remove them by proclamation "where he deems it advisable either in order to avoid restricting production of goods for export from Canada or otherwise." Under this authority all the new taxes were repealed and all the old ones returned to their pre-November 18 rates by proclamation on July 31, 1948. The explanation for the final repeal was given in an official statement by the Minister of Finance:

> These taxes, like other parts of the exchange conservation program, were an emergency measure and I have made it clear on a number of occasions that the Government intended to remove them as soon as possible. They were imposed originally, not for revenue purposes, but as part of the program to curtail the use of United States dollars. The continuing improvement in our exchange position, the increasing effectiveness of direct measures of control over imports and the positive efforts to increase exports, seem sufficiently encouraging to justify the removal of these taxes now.

One would judge from the evidence that this whole experience had been rather a novel one for both the tax authorities and the public. The primary purpose of the general programme was to cut down certain lines of consumer expenditure and capital investment that were burning up U.S. dollars at an excessive rate. Heavy excise taxes played an integral part in achieving this result by discouraging the consumption of goods having a high American content. At the same time they tended to forestall an investment boom in Canadian industries sheltered by the direct import restrictions that formed the major part of the programme. To have taken no steps to counteract the very real protection afforded by these quota restrictions might have defeated the whole purpose of the programme by stimulating the importation from the United States of primary steel and other materials difficult to ration. But it was this very aspect of the tax measures that was most difficult to "sell" to the business community. On the contrary, when any particular tax appeared to be having a dampening effect the Government was roundly criticized by all concerned. It was evident that few business men were ready to accept the philosophy that the state should deliberately use its taxing powers to curtail their volume of business, or even slacken their rate of growth, under peacetime conditions. Particularly was it difficult to justify this result in small industries which were specialized (organ building) or localized (boat building) and which had been swept into the programme to maintain fair treatment between competitors. The whole experience threw up some extremely provocative problems of economics, equity, and tax administration which deserve further exploration by students in this field. Not the least of the problems worth considering are the effects on tax administration and taxpayer compliance of such swiftly changing conditions as those experienced between November, 1947, and July, 1948, an aspect of contra-cyclical budgeting practices seldom considered by academic writers.

Changes in commodity taxation apart from those affected by the exchange conservation programme were not of much consequence during this period. Some further friendly motions towards the provincial governments were evidenced in the repeal of the Dominion's taxes on amusements, pari mutuel bets, and night clubs in May, 1948, and minor concessions were made to the consuming public in the same budget by the exemption of substantially all remaining food items not previously exempted under the sales tax (mainly canned and packaged foods) and the exclusion from the retail purchase tax of alarm clocks selling for $10 or less and plated knives, forks, and spoons. A tax on spirits used in vinegar was also repealed in this budget.

The 1949 Overhaul

The budget of March, 1949, brought a major shake-up of the whole commodity tax structure—the most sweeping in its history. The general purpose of this overhauling was to throw out most of the wartime "nuisance" taxes and to eliminate many taxes which fell mainly on business. The form of those taxes that were left was also simplified. Of the taxes that were entirely repealed the more important were the taxes on soft drinks, candy, chewing gum, long distance telephone calls, telegrams and cables, domestic telephone extensions, transportation tickets, and sleeping-car berths and parlour-car chairs. The 25 per cent retail tax, an orphan in the Dominion's tax family, was repealed and replaced by a 10 per cent tax at the manufacturer's level (this tax applies mainly on watches, jewellery, ornaments, etc.). Most of the remaining taxes were also brought to a common 10 per cent rate. Fountain pens and pencils, luggage, leather goods, and smokers' accessories, previously 35 per cent; toilet articles, cigarette lighters, and slot machines, previously 25 per cent; matches, previously taxed at a rate per 100, and tires and tubes, previously taxed on a poundage basis, were all converted to the *ad valorem* 10 per cent rate. Following this revision the only excise taxes not levied at the 10 per cent rate were the taxes on tobacco products and cigarette papers and tubes, playing-cards, cheques, and wines. The order of magnitude of the tax reductions granted in this revision is indicated by the fact that revenue from these sources before the changes was expected to be $260 million and after the changes, taking account of the effect of the reductions in a full year, was expected to be about $160 million, a reduction of 40 per cent.

Some further reductions were made in October, 1949, and in March, 1950, on the eve of the sharp increases necessitated by the defence programme. The major change in the fall of 1949 was the exemption of fuel oils under the sales tax. In the spring of 1950 the only changes were the repeal of the 5 per cent tax on toilet soap, and the removal of the sales tax from ice cream and from purchases by public institutions providing shelter for children or for the aged.

By the spring of 1950 the low point of commodity taxation in the post-war period had been reached, although it is to be noted that no reductions had been made in the two major revenue sources—liquor and tobacco. Tables in the Appendices give in concise form a summary of all the various changes described above.

The Sales Tax Today

Despite the fairly drastic rate revisions in the post-war period, the internal workings of the commodity taxes had been spared anything comparable to the intensive inspection and introspection to which the income tax had been subjected. The absence of any change in the rate over a long period had reduced public and parliamentary curiosity about the sales tax to a minimum. For two decades there had been nothing comparable to the serious discussions of the twenties. However, at the time of writing there are signs of a renewed interest. Mr. Abbott, the federal Minister of Finance, not only attracted attention to the tax by increasing its rate from 8 per cent to 10 per cent in 1951, but provoked further interest by taking the offensive against a long-standing allegation that the tax was regressive, and therefore "iniquitous," etc. In the 1951 budget debate he presented calculations, based on family expenditure surveys made by the Dominion Bureau of Statistics, to illustrate that for the great mass of the public the tax was not regressive at all but on the contrary was reasonably proportional. This result was of course attributed mainly to the exemption granted foods.

In the challenge of this new and authoritative claim for respectability, the sales tax has undergone closer public scrutiny than in many years past. On the whole it appears to have survived the ordeal without serious damage. The most penetrating and objective of these examinations was made under the auspices of the Canadian Tax Foundation by John F. Due, Professor of Economics, University of Illinois. In a book published by the Foundation under the title *The*

General Manufacturers Sales Tax in Canada this American observer presented the most thorough analysis of all aspects of the tax yet to appear. His independent study of the incidence of the tax bore out the claims of the Minister of Finance regarding its proportional character. He expressed a personal preference for a retail tax to avoid the pyramiding effect he found under the manufacturer's form of levy, but conceded that long strides had been taken under the Canadian law to remove its other defects. Among several recommendations for further improvement he included the exemption as far as possible of business expenditures still taxable (e.g., railway equipment, trucks, consumable materials, and certain industrial machinery and equipment), the exemption of certain foods and building materials still taxable, the payment of compensation to local governments for continued application of the tax to their purchases, and simplification of the rules governing the taxability of materials and containers. On the administrative side he urged that wider publicity be given to departmental rulings, that information in easily understood form be published on certain features of the tax (e.g., the unlicensed wholesale branch provisions), and that audits be improved and made more frequently. These recommendations were discussed at both the 1951 and 1952 Conferences of the Tax Foundation and attracted some attention. At later conferences the Foundation has urged the desirability of simplifying the exemption structure and of introducing a statutory definition which would more clearly reflect the bases on which the tax is applied in practice.

Tariff Developments—the Latest Phase

Canadian trade and tariff history, as traced in the previous pages, has presented a many-sided pattern. In the beginning there was almost complete dependence on the French and later on the British markets, a trade that was sheltered by mercantilist restrictions and fostered by preferential tariffs. The final repeal of the Trade Laws and the abandonment of the preferential rates on colonial produce by Great Britain during the 1840's marked the conclusion of this phase. In the succeeding period the Reciprocity Treaty with United States was the predominant factor, and Canadian natural produce flowed freely into the American market under its terms. Some protectionist sentiment was apparent before Confederation in embryonic Canadian manufacturing circles, as reflected in the Galt and Cayley Tariffs of the late 1850's. This trend appeared to be on the wane in the 1860's, and the Confederation tariff of 1867 was a distinct compromise with earlier levels. But protectionist sentiment was revived in the 1870's by hard times and disappointment over the American refusal to continue the reciprocal arrangements. Espousal of a high tariff programme by the Conservatives culminated in their return to office in 1878 and inauguration of the National Policy in 1879. This protective policy was modified in 1897 by the restoration, this time on Canadian initiative, of preferential duties on imports from Great Britain and other Empire countries, a development which, however, had no noticeable effect on the direction of trade for some time. Revenue needs of World War I brought generally higher tariff rates, but these were abandoned after 1918. During the twenties politically organized agricultural sentiment was influential in forcing a moderate downward revision. This trend was reversed abruptly in the early thirties, when the highest tariffs in Canadian history were adopted partly to shield the Canadian economy from invasion by foreign products and partly in reprisal for sharply increased American tariffs. In the wake of this development two extremely important events ensued. First, the Imperial Economic Conference of 1932 at Ottawa established—for the first time in the history of the Empire—a system of tariff preferences on a contractual basis, a result for which Canada had laid the groundwork in 1897. Secondly, from 1935 onward, trade agreements were entered into with United States which granted substantial concessions on both sides. Temporary tariff changes of major consequence were made during World War II for exchange and price ceiling purposes, but most of these had been terminated by the end of 1947.

The framework within which post-war trade and tariff negotiations have been conducted is characteristic of many aspects of post-war international relations. Here, as in other spheres, under the general aegis of the United Nations an attempt has been made through broad participation in international conferences, and by negotiation of agreements that adhered to some accepted general principles, to create conditions in which international trade might revive and flourish. The original impetus behind this movement was provided largely by the Americans, and was stimulated undoubtedly by recollection of the thirties when international trade channels had been choked by every form of restriction, including quotas, discriminatory tariffs, and blocked currencies. Plans for a concerted attack on these restrictions were forming long before the end of the war. Countries entering into Lend-Lease Agreements with the United States pledged themselves to the elimination of "all forms of discriminatory treatment in international commerce, and to the reduction of tariffs and other trade barriers . . ." (Article 7). Canada, although not a signatory of a Lend-Lease Agreement, gave the same undertaking in an exchange of notes with the United States in 1942. London was the scene in 1943 of a meeting of Commonwealth trade experts gathered to explore the possibilities of post-war revisions, and Canadian representatives also attended meetings in Washington in 1944. As the end of the war approached concrete plans began to take shape, and of these the most significant was undoubtedly that contained in a document forwarded in 1945 by the United States government to the other governments of the world setting forth, in the words of its title, *Proposals for Expansion of World Trade and Employment*. The principal theme advanced in these *Proposals* was that there should be formed under the auspices of the United Nations an international trade organization. The member nations of this organization would agree to adhere to certain principles established in its charter. In general these principles would govern such matters as trade barriers, restrictive business practices, intergovernmental commodity arrangements (state trading), and the international aspects of domestic employment policies. A specific plan for the structure of the organization was outlined in the *Proposals*.

The *Proposals* were issued in December, 1945. In February, 1946, the first meeting of the Economic and Social Council of the United Nations passed a resolution that a conference be called to consider the establishment of an international trade organization. A "preparatory committee" of 19 countries was set up to prepare a draft charter for the organization. For this purpose it held a meeting in the fall of 1946. A second document issued by the United States, *Suggested Charter for an International Trade Organization*, which was essentially an elaboration of the *Proposals*, was used as a basis for discussion at this meeting, and after revision was adopted as a charter to be submitted to a conference of all the important trading nations of the world. This larger conference was held at Geneva in 1947 and resulted in the General Agreement on Tariffs and Trade, a document of extreme importance in relation to post-war international trade.

As one of the leading trading nations of the world Canada had followed closely the events leading up to the Geneva Conference, and Canadian representatives had taken part in all the conferences preceding it. In the June, 1946, budget, after referring to the impending general negotiations, the Minister of Finance set aside all but a few trivial tariff changes on the ground that it would be inadvisable "to introduce at this time anything in the nature of comprehensive or important tariff changes or changes of a type that may soon be the subject of tariff negotiations with other countries from which we may desire and reasonably expect tariff concessions." In the April, 1947, budget speech, delivered after the Conference at Geneva had commenced, the Minister gave a more general expression of the Canadian attitude towards the objectives of the negotiations. He said: "The ultimate objective of these negotiations is to make possible the restoration of multilateral trade on a large scale, which is the best possible basis for Canadian prosperity and stability." Of the position that Canada would take in attaining these objectives he gave the following indication:

> I have already referred to the tariff negotiations now taking place in Geneva. These are of the greatest importance to Canada. We hope and expect that out of them will come sufficient reduction in tariffs to make it practicable to establish an international trade organization and to agree upon a code of international behaviour in regard to import restrictions, export subsidies and other commercial policies. Canada is, of course, prepared to make tariff reductions in preferences in exchange for tariff reductions by the United States and by other countries. We do not expect one-sided bargains. We are ready to do our full share.

While thus pledging close co-operation in the work of the Conference he nevertheless stressed two conditions which he considered essential to its successful outcome: first, the United States must be prepared to reduce its tariffs—"Unless large scale American imports provide the world with an adequate supply of United States dollars, the rest of the world cannot hope to follow the liberal, multilateral and non-discriminatory trade policy which the United States has been urging upon it with our support and that of others. A positive lead in real tariff reductions by the United States is, therefore, needed if success is to be achieved at Geneva"; second, if too many qualifications and escape clauses (particularly in relation to quantitative restrictions on trade) were included in the proposed agreement the benefit that countries expected to receive would be seriously undermined. The Canadian frame of mind therefore appears to have been compounded of willingness and prudence in about equal portions.

The Geneva Conference in 1947 accomplished two main purposes. First, using the draft prepared at the earlier conferences it formulated a charter for an International Trade Organization. Second, it succeeded in effecting very important tariff reductions among the leading trading nations of the world.

The Charter for the International Trade Organization was unique among international documents in that it set forth rules for the conduct of trade between nations and provided for the establishment of an organization to police these rules. The Geneva Conference was attended by some 23 nations, and this broad and representative group of countries devoted several months to discussion and refinement of the provisions of the Charter. As a result of this discussion the Conference drafted a final proposal which it urged be considered by a broader group of countries at the earliest possible time.

While not adopted at Geneva, the Charter nevertheless exerted a pervasive influence on the tariff negotiations carried on there, since these were conducted in the light of the major principles set forth in the Charter. In fact these major principles were embodied in the final document that gave effect to the tariff changes, and the signatory countries pledged themselves to abide by them until they were superseded by the adoption of the Charter. As events have turned out, the Charter has not yet been adopted by any important trading country, despite the consideration it was given by a conference of over 50 countries in Havana, Cuba, in the fall of 1947, and in 1952 there did not seem much hope that it ever would be adopted. The principles set forth in the Geneva Agreement are therefore of interest, since they represent the rules of conduct which in general were followed in drawing up the tariff revisions and which have since governed, in a general way, the trade and tariff policy of the signatory countries.

In the negotiation of the tariff reductions probably the most important principle followed was that a concession granted to any individual country would be extended also to all other signatory countries. This is the basic characteristic of a "multilateral" as contrasted with a "bilateral" agreement. Further (and this rule was of particular interest to the British preferential group) it was accepted that no existing preferences would be enlarged and such preferences as remained after the agreement had been signed would be subject to further negotiation between countries with a view to their reduction. Of the rules governing general trade and tariff policy, many were in the more or less standard form found in bilateral trade agreements, and gave undertakings affecting the application of internal taxation to imported articles, freedom of transit, anti-dumping and countervailing duties, valuations for customs purposes, formalities connected with the importation and exportation of goods, marks of origin, publication and administration of trade regulations, and so on. In addition, however, the provisions of the draft Charter prohibiting quantitative trade restrictions (quotas) were also embodied in the agreement. This was an important step, although the exceptions under which such restrictions might be invoked have allowed several countries, including Canada, to use this device in recent years. The broadest general exception was that made for countries encountering foreign exchange difficulties. Further rules governed the manner in which quota restrictions were to be applied should they become necessary. In general they were to be administered without discrimination between foreign countries, although again exceptions to this rule were allowed. Further refinement of these rules, and the examination of alleged infractions of them, have occupied a good part of the time of delegates at subsequent trade and tariff conferences.

The tariff revisions negotiated at Geneva within the framework of these general rules were both broad and deep. The official Canadian government press release described the final document in which they were embodied as "the most far-reaching and comprehensive agreement of its kind in Canadian history. The Canadian portion of the multilateral instrument is a vital part of what is probably the most comprehensive multilateral trade agreement ever attempted." Negotiations extended over months, and culminated with the signature of the General Agreement by 23 countries on October 30, 1947. The effective work of the Conference was the conclusion of over 100 sets of bilateral tariff negotiations between individual nations. In final presentation these treaties were consolidated in schedules to the General Agreement, so that under Schedule v, the Canadian schedule, all tariff concessions granted by Canada to any one country were granted equally to all other countries signing the agreement, unless any individual country was entitled to a lower or special preferential rate. In the latter class in particular fell the other countries of the British Empire, which under the British Preferential system in effect before the Conference were entitled to rates lower than those granted other countries. The system of British Preferences was therefore retained, although these rates in themselves were subject to negotiation between Empire countries. No new preferences were created, however, nor was any existing margin of preference made more favourable. Where a preferential rate was lowered the rate granted to any most-favoured-nation country was also lowered to preserve the same margin of preference. At the same time Canada joined other Empire countries in opposing any narrowing of existing preferential margins by the device of raising the preferential rate, and in general succeeded in upholding this point of view.

Under the Canadian schedule of the Agreement there are some 1,050 items or sub-items, of which 590 represented reductions in most-favoured-nation rates and 460 the binding or consolidation of most-favoured-nation rates then in effect. On some 100 items or sub-items the British preferential rate was reduced directly, and in respect of some 50 more items or sub-items a reduction was made indirectly. On the other hand substantial concessions were secured by Canada from other countries, and in particular from the United States. These included the reduction or binding of rates on wheat, wheat flour, coarse grains, cattle, seed potatoes, turnips, apples, berries, dairy products, eggs, cheese, butter, liquor, cod fillets and other fishing products, lumber, base metals, non-metallic minerals, and many manufactured and miscellaneous goods. In relation to United States it is said that Canada retained practically all the advantages granted in former trade agreements and obtained some new and important further concessions.

The countries with which Canada completed negotiations, in addition to the United Kingdom and the United States, included Belgium, Luxembourg, and the Netherlands (the Benelux union), Brazil, Chile, China, Cuba, Czechoslovakia, France, Lebanon-Syria, Norway, the Union of South Africa, Ceylon, India, and Pakistan. In most of these countries the terms of the Agreement came into effect on January 1, 1948, and were to be in effect for a three-year period—i.e., to January 1, 1951.

Since the Geneva Conference there have been several other international trade parleys and consultations, but none of comparable importance. As indicated earlier, the Charter for an International Trade Organization was further developed and expanded at a conference of over 50 countries in Havana in November, 1947. This conference adopted a draft, since known as the Havana Charter, and recommended it for adoption by all governments concerned. No government had adopted it formally at the time of writing, and indications were that it had become an unimportant issue. The guiding spirit of the move for implementation had been the American administration, and on several occasions it requested the Congress to enact necessary legislation, without success. Eventually the charter was dropped as a lost cause. For Canada this outcome has been of little significance, since the provisions of the Charter most closely affecting Canadian commercial interests were in any event embodied in the Geneva Agreement on Tariffs and Trade.

In 1949 negotiations were carried on at Annecy, France, with several countries which had not entered the original agreement. As a result of these discussions eight additional countries became "members of the club," and tariff changes were adopted which came into effect for the most part on January 1, 1950. These were of considerably less interest to Canada, however, than those covered in the original agreement. Of greater significance was the conference at Torquay, England, which extended over the fall and winter of 1950–1. The occasion of this conference was the approaching lapse of the General Agreement, by its own terms fixed to expire on January 1, 1951. The pattern of this conference was similar to that of the Geneva and Annecy negotiations. In general the previous arrangements, with some modifications, were extended for a further period of three years, i.e., to January 1, 1954. Six new members became signatories—Austria, the German Federal Republic, Korea, Peru, the Phillipines, and Turkey. The admission of Western Germany as a "member of the club" was indicative of the new attitude being adopted towards that country by the major powers. As a result of this development important reductions were made in the American tariff on several items of trade important to Germany, which, under the multilateral principle adopted at Geneva, were available also to all other countries. The treaty concluded at Torquay between Canada and the United States represented the fourth important agreement on trade since 1935.

The most recent meetings of the Contracting Parties have been held in Geneva. The principal accomplishment of a conference in the fall of 1953 was the extension of the main terms of the General Agreement for another eighteen months, i.e., until July 1, 1955. The admission of Japan as a Contracting Party was discussed, but action was deferred. (Canada has since entered into a trade treaty with Japan directly.) It was also at this conference that it was agreed to hold a series of meetings in the fall of 1954 to review the whole Agreement, and meetings for this purpose commenced in Geneva late in October. Since some countries have given signs of restiveness with its existing terms the prospect of substantial revision of the whole scheme is not remote.

Canada–United States Trade Relations

Against the previous background of almost three-quarters of a century when no trade negotiations were carried on between Canada and the United States, the historic significance of the period since 1935, and particularly of the several substantial revisions effected since 1947 through the General Agreement, is strikingly apparent.

The touchstone of this development, as previously mentioned, was the act first passed in 1934 by the United States Congress, the United

States Reciprocal Trade Agreements Act. It gave the President authority over a ten-year period to enter into agreements to reduce American tariff rates by 50 per cent from the level established in the Tariff Act of 1930, and thus opened the way for the Canada-United States trade agreements of 1935 and 1938. When most of the area for reduction under the 1934 Act had been exhausted, the administration requested and received from Congress authority to enter into agreements for further reductions. Under this Act reductions up to 50 per cent from the 1945 rates could be made. This authority was used in negotiating the General Agreement, and as a result some rates under the American tariff have been reduced by 75 per cent from the level of 1930.

The President's powers under the Reciprocal Trade Agreements legislation have recently been renewed only for one year at a time, and since reductions are still based on rates in effect in January, 1945, little room is left for further cuts.

In 1953 an enquiry was instituted to advise President Eisenhower on the course that should be followed in trade negotiations in the future. This was the Commission on Foreign Economic Policy, more generally known as the Randall Commission, after its chairman, Clarence B. Randall, Chairman of the Board of Inland Steel. Public enquiries were held in the latter part of 1953, and in January, 1954, a report was submitted to the President and Congress. Regarding the Reciprocal Trade Agreements Act the Commission proposed a three-year extension, during which period the President would be authorized to negotiate, by treaty, reductions not exceeding 5 per cent of 1954 rates in each of the three years. He would also be authorized to reduce by not more than 50 per cent the 1945 rates on goods of negligible import volume, and to reduce to 50 per cent rates which exceeded an ad valorem duty of 50 per cent.

In a message to Congress on March 30 the President asked that these and other proposals be implemented, but the most that Congress was willing to do was to extend for another year the Reciprocal Trade Agreements Act, which is now almost ineffectual, since practically all duties that could be lowered have already been reduced. One of the imponderables of the next year will be what action the American Congress will take when the Agreements legislation comes up for further discussion prior to its expiry on June 30, 1955.

Specific points of interest in trade relations between Canada and the United States in recent years have involved American quota restrictions on the import of cheese and dairy products (in contravention of the General Agreement) and more recently hearings of the Tariff Commission on fish fillets, oats, and lead and zinc. An infant but fast-growing Canadian industry has recently been given a set-back by higher tariffs on pre-cooked and breaded "fish sticks," although the President in July rejected a recommendation of the Tariff Commission that import restrictions be raised against Canadian fish fillets. The threat of high tariffs against Canadian oats was overcome by the voluntary imposition of export quotas by the Canadian government, and during 1954 President Eisenhower rejected increases in tariffs on lead and zinc which had been recommended by the Tariff Commission.

The Sterling Area

Quota restrictions imposed in some of Canada's markets in the sterling area, as permitted under the General Agreement when emergency conditions threaten, have limited the benefit originally derived from tariff concessions granted by those countries. This was particularly true of South Africa and Australia. However, these quota limitations are gradually being eased. It is an interesting commentary that the other major country to violate the General Agreement (along with the United States) was the United Kingdom. Discriminatory treatment against foreign products under the purchase tax was contrary to one of the main terms of the Agreement, and under protests from the other Contracting Parties the discrimination was eventually removed.

The Course of Canadian Trade

As is clearly revealed by Table XXXIII, whereas until 1944 the United Kingdom and the United States were about equally important as customers of Canada, since that year American purchases have been more than twice the level of the British.

The increasing flow of goods from Canada to the United States has been in sharp contrast to the diminution, both relative and absolute, in the flow to the United Kingdom and the rest of the sterling area. This trend has reflected the harsh realities of the post-war exchange position of the sterling area, which has required the rationing of scarce dollar reserves by means of quantitative restrictions and such other methods as are available under the Geneva Agreement. In the perspective of the last one hundred years this development is of great historical interest. Almost exactly a century has passed since England, for quite different reasons, took steps which resulted in a sharp decline in Canada's exports to the British market and a counter-balancing increase in our trade with the United States.

TABLE XXXIII

CANADIAN EXPORTS TO UNITED STATES AND UNITED KINGDOM (excluding gold)

Calendar year	Exports to			Percentage of total exports to	
	U.S.A.	U.K.	All countries	U.S.A.	U.K.
		($ million)		%	%
1936	345	396	951	36	42
1937	372	403	1,012	36	40
1938	279	341	849	32	41
1939	390	329	936	41	35
1940	452	512	1,193	38	43
1941	610	661	1,640	37	41
1942	897	748	2,385	38	31
1943	1,167	1,037	3,001	39	35
1944	1,335	1,238	3,483	38	36
1945	1,227	971	3,267	37	30
1946	909	599	2,339	38	26
1947	1,057	754	2,812	37	27
1948	1,522	689	3,110	49	22
1949	1,524	709	3,022	50	24
1950	2,050	473	3,157	65	15
1951	2,334	636	3,963	59	16
1952	2,349	751	4,356	54	17
1953	2,463	669	4,173	59	16
1954	2,363	662	3,946	60	17

SOURCE: D.B.S., Annual Reports on Trade of Canada.

28 THE DOMINION, 1946–54

Taxes for Security—National and Social

HAD IT NOT BEEN for two major developments which came after 1949 the record of post-war federal taxation would have closed with the preceding chapter. By the end of the fourth year following the war there were good reasons for believing that a period of relative calm lay ahead. The important job of reforming the income tax legislation had been all but completed, and major improvements had been made as well in other parts of the federal tax system. A series of tax reductions had eased the general burden to its lowest post-war level. The Minister of Finance, in his budget speech of the spring of 1950, expressed his own view that a budget of about $2.4 billion could be counted on as a permanent level, and the likelihood of further substantial tax reductions therefore seemed remote. At the same time there was little cause for expecting that taxes would rise.

By contrast with this promise of relative stability the ensuing five years—1950 to 1954—instead brought major upheavals. These were due to two causes: first, the return of large-scale defence spending following the outbreak of war in Korea in 1950; second, the introduction of a major new social security measure, the contributory old age pension. Together these developments in national security and social security resulted in the temporary restoration of tax rates at levels as high as those of World War II, and the stabilizing of federal expenditures at a new plateau of $4½ to $5 billion annually, or about twice the level predicted by the Minister of Finance in 1950.

DEFENCE PROGRAMME

The Over-all Objective

It was recognized from the outset that in the absence of general hostilities the over-all objective would be considerably different from that of 1939. Then there was no alternative but an all-out effort, to which every resource of the nation must be dedicated. The goal was defeat of a known enemy, and all other ends were subordinated to that goal. By contrast in 1950 the objective was to achieve a reasonable state of military preparedness against a potential, rather than an actual enemy, and to reach this state within a reasonable period of time without drastic disruption of the normal tenor of the economy. The Minister of Finance summed up the three prongs of this policy in the following words: "First, we must achieve a high degree of military security without which all else may fail. Second, we desire the highest quality of political freedom and individual liberty. Third, we want to promote economic stability and progress, both on a national scale and in terms of sustained and improved individual standards of living."[1]

The general objective then was to be peace with security; defence with economic growth; or, as some have put it, guns *and* butter.

The Military Objective

At the wartime peak the strength of the active forces had been in excess of 780,000, but by 1948, following a period of rapid demobilization, it had declined to about 35,000. Furthermore training camps had been closed, except for the older permanent stations, and equipment had not been kept up to date. In broadest terms, therefore, the military objective was to build up our defence forces again to a level that would enable Canada to meet its immediate commitments for the security of the free world, and to bring our defence industries to a point of preparedness where they could rapidly meet any larger commitments. More specifically, there have been three main divisions within the general programme: first, NATO—the North Atlantic Treaty Organization; second, the war in Korea; and third, the protection of Canada proper.

NATO had come into being in April, 1949, and some steps had been taken to implement Canada's undertakings. At a special fall session in 1950 further emergency measures were approved. However, it was not until the session of 1951 that the Government outlined its main defence programme. Since these general objectives, as announced by the Minister of National Defence on February 5, 1951, have been altered only in detail, it is worth presenting them here in summary form.

Manpower. The strength of our active armed forces was to be increased by 80 per cent from 64,000 to about 115,000 and civilian defence employees were to be increased by about 30 per cent to about 33,000. In total, this meant an increase from slightly less than 90,000 full-time employees to 148,000, an increase of about two-thirds.

[1]*House of Commons Debates*, Sept. 7, 1950, p. 419.

These forces were eventually to comprise the following military units: Army, 50,000 men, including commitments of forces to be stationed in Europe and Korea; Navy, 100 ships and many small craft, of which 52 ships are to be seconded to NATO; Air Force, 41 squadrons (originally 40) with more than 3,000 aircraft of which 12 squadrons (originally 11) were to be stationed in Europe for NATO.

Equipment. World War II equipment of the United Kingdom design was to be replaced by equipment of the latest available American design and the Navy was to modernize or replace all its ships.

Facilities. Barracks, camps, stations, depots, warehouses, airfields, and so on were to be reconstructed. In the past the final large-scale battle training of our army had to be done outside the country. Fighting grounds for this final training on a scale up to divisional strength were also to be provided in Canada.

This programme was presented as one on which about $5 billion would be spent over a three-year period, i.e. in the fiscal years 1951–2 to 1953–4 inclusive. The fact that it was so described unfortunately gave the public the impression that a total outlay of $5 billion over a period of three years would be the sum total of the defence effort. In fact the general "stretch-out" of the build-up in all the western powers has meant that even the immediate objectives have not been attained in the three years, while the processes of inflation and the increasing cost of equipment has meant that the $5 billion price-tag had by 1954 become almost a nominal one. Much of the original plan had been completed by then to be sure, but much also remained to be done. Furthermore, the maintenance of personnel and facilities and the replacement of equipment made it quite evident that military spending would be maintained at a high level for years to come. But this is a problem of the future, rather than of the build-up period.[2]

The Economic Problem

For several reasons the defence build-up offered a challenging economic problem for the Government. The most acute danger was the threat of a price inflation. Whereas in 1939 there was a great deal of slack in the economy, with both materials and labour in abundant supply, in 1950 the situation was the reverse. There had been several years of almost continual price rise, of almost full employment, of heavy consumer expenditure, and of private capital expenditures at

[2]Discussion of the military programme has been necessarily limited. For further details see the annual white paper issued by the Department of National Defence, *Canada's Defence Programme*, and *The National Finances*, issued annually by the Canadian Tax Foundation.

unprecedented levels. Some goods and materials had not returned to adequate supply, and the public retained a lively memory of war-time shortages, so that the dangers of panic buying were real. The forty-hour week had become fairly general in industry, and the general attitude towards hard work had become complacent, to say the least. Government expenditures at all levels were high by any previous standards, and gave little promise of contraction. In short Canada was in the midst of a boom that with only one or two signs of hesitation had been gathering momentum since the end of the war. Into this busy drama, where all the available actors already appeared to be fully engaged and little interested in changing parts, there had to be crowded a new act—an act that would change the whole meaning of the performance.

That the play would suffer considerably by this intrusion was pointed out early and often by the financial authorities. The Minister of Finance in his budget speech of September 7, 1950 (Special Session), and on many subsequent occasions, warned that there would have to be an adjustment to the new situation. Some restriction of consumer goods—in particular of the type that required metals—would have to be suffered, but more especially there would have to be an easing up in the capital investment programme, which was the strongest competitor for scarce materials and labour and also represented the most dangerous inflationary threat. The Government would play its part by following a pay-as-you-go fiscal policy and would minimize waste expenditures, and the public was urged to do the same. And over and over the public was asked to increase output. This was the positive side of the programme; the emphasis on more production as the alternative to less consumption was frequently driven home.

This warning and prodding was by now more or less familiar to a war-conditioned public, and was readily accepted for the most part. However the Government, no doubt wisely, felt compelled to take several positive steps to support this reluctant acquiescence. Consumer credit restrictions were introduced in November, 1950, and remained in effect, with some alterations, until May, 1952. Funds available for mortgage lending under government housing programmes were temporarily curtailed. The Bank of Canada raised its rediscount rate and in an almost unprecedented move "advised" the chartered banks not to increase their aggregate volume of loans over a ceiling figure. Direct controls on several materials were also introduced. For the strategic metals these were essential. Steel particularly was in short supply, and the control over this product was among the first to be introduced.

Fiscal policy along pay-as-you-go lines was pursued with such vigour that the federal budget continued to show surpluses, although smaller than those of previous years. Tax policy followed lines which the war and earlier post-war years had made familiar, but there was one wholly new device—deferred depreciation. This is described along with other aspects of the defence fiscal programme, in the following pages.

Undoubtedly the most contentious aspects of the general anti-inflationary programme was the Government's refusal to impose a price ceiling. Both in and out of Parliament it was roundly criticized for not adopting what to many seemed the obvious method for controlling inflation. But on this point it was adamant. Despite the fact that in the United Kingdom rationing and price ceilings were still in effect from World War II and that price ceilings had been reimposed in the United States, the Canadian Government throughout adhered to its position that devices of this sort were not suited for a short-period emergency and would do more harm than good. Its arguments were stated on many occasions, and could be quoted at length. In general they may be summed up as follows: first, price ceilings do not cure inflation, they merely hide it; second, they are tolerable only when used as a last resort after fiscal and monetary policies have been pressed to the maximum limits; third, even under these circumstances they will work only if supported by unanimous public understanding and sympathy; fourth, only an emergency far more drastic than that faced would bring forth the necessary degree of public co-operation; fifth, much of the Canadian rise in price was being imported from abroad, particularly in high American prices, and a Canadian price ceiling would not change this fact; finally, to impose a price ceiling in the knowledge that none of the conditions essential for its successful operation were present would seriously disrupt the economy and with it the defence effort. Much the same sort of argument was used, as will be seen in a moment, for not imposing an excess profits tax.

In short, the Government followed the course of attempting to guide the economy in the desired directions by means of indirect hedges and restraints rather than to steer it there by direct control. To assess the wisdom of its decision is beyond our purpose here, and indeed at this proximity to events it would be an effrontery to try. It would appear on the one hand that events may have justified the gamble. A burst of inflation did take place in 1951 and 1952, but by 1953 prices had levelled off and it was apparent that by then the economy had fully adjusted itself to the defence programme. By 1954, in fact, it was becoming painfully obvious that the economy was showing slack, and that defence spending was by then only a sustaining influence, and certainly not an inflationary one. Objective economic analysis in general supported the Government's policy, although there had been only a dribble of academic writing in the whole field of post-war economic policy to 1954. Certainly also if business sentiment, international esteem, and election results are any guide the Canadian Government's policy for defence has been a resounding success.

On the other side of the picture was the undoubted fact that, while the price rise had stopped by 1953, in the previous two years it had been steeply upward. Indeed in the one year 1951 wholesale prices rose by nearly 14 per cent over 1950, equal to about half the previous rise in the whole post-war period. The consumer price index also rose, but in a less spectacular way. The effect of course was to turn the screws even tighter on all those people in the community whose fixed incomes had already suffered a sharp fall in real value from the previous round of price increases. (The introduction of a universal old age pension plan in 1952, the subject of a later part of this chapter, was almost an admission that the community owed a debt to at least the older people in this unfortunate segment of the population.) Further, the credit restrictions and in some respects the tax changes fell with undue penalty on certain groups or individuals. The restrictions on instalment buying were very hard on the automobile and home furnishing businesses, simply because in those lines credit has become essential. The ceiling on bank credit, even though informal, placed individual banks and their branch managers in a position where an aggressively negative attitude was the role of least resistance, often with cruel results for clients who were temporarily over-extended. There was always room for "doubting Thomases" to believe that the Government was forcing others to assume responsibility for carrying out tough jobs that it would not tackle directly itself.

So run some of the arguments that might be advanced on either side. Time and mature reflection will alone sort them out, and they are put down here only superficially. More will be said in a moment on the subject of fiscal policy; perhaps the most that can be said now of the general economic policy for defence is that in the short run it appears to have succeeded, and in public affairs there are few other tests but success or failure.

Financial Developments: Fiscal Policy

While the economic policy has already been discussed in its general outline the largest single element in the over-all picture was fiscal policy, which has only been touched on. Previous chapters dealing with the experience of World War II and the years immediately following have stressed the predominant role of fiscal policy throughout, and it is therefore not surprising that with the emergence of a new challenge it should again play a leading part.

In the main two trends are discernible—and there are few other trends to be discernible in any fiscal policy—in the years 1950 to 1954. On the one side there was the implementation of the pay-as-you-go policy, which meant imposing sufficiently heavy taxes to keep the budget in balance, or better than in balance, if possible. On the other side was the deployment of the individual tax sources in the best order for serving the main strategy of curtailing capital investment and of reducing consumer expenditure on semi-durable goods. It will be recognized that these two objectives are scarcely separable, and that the second is in some respects only a refinement of the first.

Pay-As-You-Go Taxation

The essential facts of the financial picture on the eve of the defence period in 1950 were that taxes had been reduced to the lowest point of the post-war era and that defence expenditure, from a peak of nearly $4,500 million in 1943–4, when it represented over 85 per cent of total expenditure, had declined to the almost nominal amount of $385 million in the fiscal year 1949–50, when it represented only 15.7 per cent of total expenditure. By steps which for two successive years meant an approximate doubling of the expenditures of the previous year, followed by an increase of about half again, defence expenditures were raised to a level of approximately $2 billion within three years. Despite this relatively sharp climb, in no year have expenditures approached, much less exceeded, the target set in the programme for that year.

As a proportion of total federal expenditures defence now occupies roughly three times as prominent a position as it did prior to Korea; in short it now accounts for about 45 per cent of total expenditures. Table XXXIV gives both defence and total expenditures for the six fiscal years ended March 31, 1950 to 1955 inclusive.

Despite this rapid rise in defence and total expenditure the overall budget balance has been on the favourable side in every year of the build-up period. In two years the surpluses exceeded $200 million, and for the five-year period, 1951–2 to 1954–5 inclusive, totalled approximately $500 million. In Table XXXV will be found figures of revenue, expenditure, surplus, and net debt outstanding for these five

TABLE XXXIV

DEFENCE AND TOTAL EXPENDITURES FOR FISCAL YEARS ENDED (OR ENDING) MARCH 31, 1950 TO 1955

Year	Defence expenditures ($ million)	Total budgetary expenditures ($ million)	Defence as a % of total
1950	384.9	2,448.6	15.72
1951	782.5	2,901.2	26.97
1952	1,447.4	3,732.9	38.77
1953	1,972.9	4,337.3	45.49
1954	1,857.8	4,350.5	42.68
1955	1,954.8[a]	4,513.8[a]	43.31

[a]Main and supplementary estimates.

years and the immediately preceding year. (These figures exclude both revenues and expenditures of the Old Age Security Fund.)

It will be noted from this table that on the revenue side there has been an increase of roughly $2 billion during the defence build-up period. In the Appendices there will be found detailed tabulations and notations of the tax changes which brought about this result. The following summary will serve to highlight the major changes and also to indicate the extent to which the inflationary process was a complementary factor in raising the tax base.

1950–1951. In the budget speech of September 7, 1950, tax changes were introduced intended to yield about an extra $59 million in the

TABLE XXXV

REVENUE, EXPENDITURE, SURPLUS, AND NET DEBT OUTSTANDING FOR FISCAL YEARS ENDED (OR ENDING) MARCH 31, 1950 TO 1955
($ million)

Year	Revenue	Expenditure	Surplus[a]	Net debt outstanding at end of fiscal year
1950	2,580.1	2,448.6	131.5	11,644.6
1951	3,112.5	2,901.2	211.3	11,433.3
1952	3,980.9	3,732.9	248.0	11,185.3
1953	4,360.8	4,337.3	23.5	11,161.7
1954	4,396.3	4,350.5	45.8	11,115.9
1955	4,464.0[b]	4,460.0[b]	4.0[b]	11,111.9[b]

SOURCES: Public Accounts of Canada; Budget Speech and Budget Papers.

[a]Equivalent to reduction in net debt.
[b]Forecast.

balance of fiscal year 1950–1 and about $190 million in a full fiscal year. Of these the principal were increases in corporation income tax, new taxes on soft drinks, candy, and chewing gum, higher taxes on alcoholic beverages (on which there had been no reduction from the wartime peak), an increase from 10 per cent to 15 per cent in the broad range of excise taxes (automobiles, radios, etc.), and several new commodities brought in at 15 per cent, mainly of the postponable consumer goods class (electrical appliances, firearms, motorcycles, golf and fishing equipment).

As revised for these tax increases the revenue estimate for the fiscal year March 31, 1951, was $2,669 million. In fact revenue for that year came to $3,112 million, or $443 million over the estimate. Of this excess almost 40 per cent arose under the corporation income tax, and most of the balance from personal income tax, sales tax, and import duties. A large part of the excess was undoubtedly accounted for by price inflation.

1951–1952. The budget speech of April 10, 1951, brought the heaviest tax changes of the build-up period. A range of increases, touching almost every important source, was made to produce an estimated $405 million in the fiscal year 1951–2 and $578 million in a whole fiscal year. These included 20 per cent defence surtaxes on both personal and corporate income taxes, an increase from 8 per cent to 10 per cent in the sales tax (the first increase since 1936), an increase in the general excise tax rate from 15 per cent to 25 per cent, new taxes at 15 per cent on stoves, refrigerators, and washing machines, and an increase in the cigarette tax (in which there had been no peacetime reduction from the wartime peak rate).

As revised for these increases the revenue for 1951–2 was expected to be $3,730 million. Again, actual revenues of $3,981 exceeded this forecast, in this case by a margin of $281 million. The major factor was an excess of corporation income tax revenues, but of the balance personal income tax accounted for a considerably larger portion than in the previous year. Undoubtedly much of this unexpected margin was also due to the inflation of prices, profits and incomes.

1952–1953. The budget speech of April 8, 1952, was delivered in an atmosphere considerably more relaxed than the previous two. The defence programme was beginning to hit its stride, the worst pressure of the inflation was over, and the tax increases of previous years had provided funds in embarrassing abundance. There was therefore room for some minor adjustment of tax rates. Furthermore some of the increases had proven troublesome. The high tax on cigarettes had induced a wave of smuggling across the American border. Housewives who found that washing machines, stoves, and refrigerators continued to remain plentiful in the stores failed to understand what connection there could be between the tax of 15 per cent and the defence effort once the Government had allowed such items to be produced. The tax on soft drinks appeared to have fallen heavily on an industry pinched between rising costs and a fixed price, and, finally, the Minister of Finance by his own word had accepted only as a temporary measure peacetime corporation taxes in excess of 50 per cent and the high marginal rates of personal income tax produced by the 20 per cent defence surtax.

This was a buget, therefore, of adjustments and reductions, which were to cost about $116 million in the balance of the fiscal year 1952–3 and about $146 million in a whole year. The personal and corporate income tax changes were largely of a technical character, but involved some relief. The principal revenue changes were the reduction to 15 per cent in the general excises and the tax on soft drinks, the repeal of the previous taxes of 15 per cent on stoves, washing machines, and refrigerators, and the abandonment of the increase in the cigarette tax.

Even the tax reductions, however, turned out to cost less than had been anticipated, just as the tax increases had produced more. The budget forecast, revised for the reductions, had been $4,279 million. The actual revenue for the year was $4,361 million, or $82 million over the forecast. Therefore the cost of the tax reduction was offset, except for $34 million, by unanticipated revenue.

1953–1954. The budget speech of February 19, 1953 is one that taxpayers recall with pleasure. Certainly the economic climate fully justified some easing of anti-inflationary measures, and indeed by that time almost all the other measures (e.g. credit restrictions, material controls) had been abandoned. The fiscal restrictions could well be relaxed with little danger. What made the occasion an even happier one for the Government, however, was that this state of affairs by chance coincided with an election year. All the signs were therefore favourable.

The reductions affected every important source and represented a revenue sacrifice of $361 million for a full year and $237 million in the fiscal year 1953–4. The effect of the personal income tax reduction was that rates were put back at the level of 1950, the post-war low. Other significant changes under the personal income tax were an increase in the dividend tax credit from 10 per cent to 20 per cent and a reduction in the ineligible amount of deductible medical expenses from 4 per cent of income to 3 per cent. The Minister of Finance was also able under the corporation income tax to achieve his oft-postponed objective of reducing the rate below 50 per cent, the effect of the change being to establish a rate of 18 per cent on the first $20,000 of income and 47 per cent on the excess (excluding old age security taxes of 2 per cent, as explained later). Some less significant reductions were also made in the indirect taxes. A further cut was made in cigarette taxes, the stamp tax and security transfer tax were repealed entirely, and sales tax exemptions were extended. (This was also the budget in which the radio licence was abandoned and revenue from radio and TV taxation earmarked for the Canadian Broadcasting Corporation.)

For this year the forecast came closer to the actual. Indeed for the first time in many years the actual did not reach the forecast. The revised revenue figure, taking account of the tax reductions, had been $4,473 million. The actual final revenue figure was about $4,400 million, a shortfall of about $73 million.

1954–1955. By the spring of 1954 the piper had called to be paid. The inflation had come to a halt, there were no more surpluses running into the hundreds of millions, and the tax reductions of the previous year had foreclosed any possibility of further major reliefs. Nevertheless in the budget of April 6, 1954, it was still possible to make a gesture. With an estimated margin of only $40 million in hand the Minister of Finance made dramatic use of the occasion by entirely exempting several large classes of items from the special excise tax and reducing the rate on many others from 15 per cent to 10 per cent. However, on automobiles and other big revenue producers, such as radios and television sets, no reductions were made.

Summary. The level of taxes in effect in mid-1954 compared roughly as follows with that of the immediate pre-Korea era: personal income tax—the same (except for old age security tax, explained later); corporation income tax—18 per cent on the first $20,000 of income and 47 per cent on the excess (excluding 12 per cent old age security tax) as compared with 10 per cent on the first $10,000 and 33 per cent on the excess, to which, for comparability, there should be added the 5 per cent provincial tax imposed by the agreeing provinces, which was part of the federal rate in 1954, giving earlier rates of 15 per cent and 38 per cent; the general sales tax—raised from 8 per cent to 10 per cent, although by 1954 revenue from only 8 per cent was going into the general budget; liquor tax—increased to $12.00 per proof gallon as compared with $11.00, but on the other hand cigarette taxes reduced from $10.00 per thousand to $8.00 per thousand; the main special excise taxes—a 15 per cent rate as compared with 10 per cent pre-Korea. This in broad outline was the position of the defence tax programme after four years. The conspicuous survival was the fairly drastic increase in the corporation tax rate, which for many companies represented a burden as heavy as they had suffered during World War II.

Another way of measuring the development of the period is to relate the federal tax "take" to the gross national product. The ratio, expressed as a percentage, was as follows: 1950–14.6; 1951–17.3; 1952–17.7; 1953–17.2. This series indicates that a fairly sharp rise took place between 1950 and 1951. There was only a modest rise in 1952, and 1953 actually showed a decline. Tax revenues increased in all these years, but gross national product was increasing more rapidly.

Perhaps the most illuminating observation is simply that by 1954 the federal government was deriving almost twice the revenue from a tax system which, with the conspicuous exception of the corporation income tax, was not remarkably higher than that of 1950. This had come about as the result of a considerable expansion in the tax base, the composite result of a growing population, higher productivity, and some very substantial degree of inflation.

Taxation for Economic Control

At least four aspects of the defence tax programme deserve specific mention. These are (1) the absence of an excess profits tax; (2) the novel experiment with deferment of depreciation; (3) the more orthodox use of accelerated depreciation for assets for defence production, and (4), the renewed use of high excise taxes on semi-durable consumers' goods.

Absence of an excess profits tax. In the face of the prompt resort to this levy (the most fearsome device in the tax chamber of horrors) by both the British and American governments, the decision of the Canadian authorities to avoid it at all costs indicated an originality of approach and no little political courage. The parliamentary Opposition brought constant pressure, and appeared to have won considerable public support. The Canadian Government could hardly be accused of being unwilling to impose this form of levy, however, since it had acted quickly at the outbreak of World War II and had retained its war tax longer in peacetime than either the United Kingdom or the United States. Perhaps indeed it was the extent of its previous experience that made it reluctant to engage in the venture again. At any rate it refused, and again, as in the case of a price ceiling, its gamble appeared to have paid off.

The Government's position, which was adhered to throughout the defence period, was stated by the Minister of Finance in his budget speech of September 7, 1950, in the following words:

> We have, of course, given thought to suggestions that we should reintroduce an excess profits tax, but I think members in all parts of the house who had experience with our wartime excess profits tax will agree that such a tax is not desirable under present circumstances. To be efficient and fair an excess profits tax needs a recent base period representing normal operating conditions for various classes of business, and a tax related to the average profits of the last three years would not be likely to yield much revenue during the next year or two. But the more important objection at this stage is that an excess profits tax, particularly one at a high rate, becomes an invitation to extravagance and waste in corporate management, whereas, as I have already said, what we need most urgently now is maximum efficiency and production. I have no doubt that all honorable members know or will have heard of cases of such waste and extravagance. Furthermore, in spite of our best efforts to make an excess profits tax as fair as possible there are bound to be severe inequities under this kind of legislation. Under conditions of total war, many businesses would be compelled to accept these inequities and hardships. I am reluctant, however, to impose this severe type of regulation under present circumstances.[3]

The alternative—high standard corporation tax rates for all companies—was applied, as earlier pages here indicated, with considerable vigour. The sole exception to the general pattern is therefore all the more conspicuous, and its conception and development represented in itself an incident in the defence tax programme. Here it may be touched on only briefly. The incident opened with the following statement by the Minister of Finance in his 1951 budget speech, when the 20 per cent defence surtax was introduced:

> I am conscious of the fact, however, that this 20 per cent surcharge will weigh very heavily on those kinds of companies which for a variety of reasons, public control of rates or otherwise, are never able to earn more than a very modest rate on their capital. To such companies the next few years can offer little expectation of increased profits, yet many of them are engaged in activities which will require them to raise very large sums of additional capital for essential expansion. If we are not to cripple their borrowing capacity we must not cripple their capacity to earn their normal profits after tax. For these reasons I propose that the 20 per cent defence

[3]*House of Commons Debates*, Sept. 7, 1950, pp. 422–3.

surcharge shall not operate so as to reduce the net income after federal tax, but before any provincial income taxes, of any company to a point below a five per cent return on capital employed.[4]

To implement this proposal the resolution introducing the defence surtax carried the proviso that the increase was subject to "a right of refund of such tax to the extent that it would reduce the corporation's taxable income after payment of the ordinary income tax to an amount less than 5 per cent of its capital employed".[5]

The next episode came at first as a surprise. The whole provision was withdrawn during the budget debate. When the Minister explained that he had been beaten by that ancient horror—"capital employed"—there were many who sympathized with his dilemma. In all the years of excess profits tax there had never ceased to be confusion and complaint regarding this concept, and no satisfactory definition had ever been found. And apparently the problems were still there. The Minister gave as another reason that the majority of the companies he was attempting to help had been found to be earning better than 5 per cent in any event. However he was pressed to give further consideration, and promised to do so before the next budget.

At the next session a change was introduced which was narrower in scope and therefore more capable of precise definition. The substance of the provision was that a company which derived more than half of its gross revenues from the generation or distribution of gas, electricity, or steam would be limited to a tax rate of 43 per cent on its net profit from these activities, the general tax rate at this time being 50 per cent. Compared to the proposal of the year before, which, even if it was intended to help only companies operating under "rate-regulated" conditions, would have embraced banks, railways, bus and other taxable transit companies, telephone and other communication companies, and perhaps even milk and bread companies, this was indeed a narrowly drawn circle. In effect it was the same group of companies whose tax was being shared to the extent of one-half with the provinces (chap. 33). This classification provided a definition, but hardly a rationale.

The reduced rate came into effect from January 1, 1952, and was still in the law at the time of writing.

Deferred depreciation. The experiment with the compulsory deferment of the depreciation deduction on certain forms of assets was an attempt to strike directly through the tax structure at the capital construction boom that was thought to be one of the main causes underly-

[4]Budget speech, 1951, p. 14. [5]*Ibid.*, p. 19.

ing the inflation. It was introduced by the Minister of Finance in his budget speech of April 10, 1951, as a measure to provide "a stiff financial deterrent that will affect particularly the businessman who is considering the kind of investment which is attractive, not because of its long-term soundness, but because it can be written off out of the unexpected high profits of the next few years at a time when he expects the rate of corporate income tax to be abnormally high." In particular the measure was aimed at "projects of uncertain long-run value" and also at "capital expenditures on frills, gadgets and generally 'dressing-up' offices, stores and buildings."[6]

The plan which was introduced pursuant to this announcement established three main classes of assets (based on the income tax categories), each with its own treatment. For one class the restrictions were not to apply at all; for a second they could be lifted by obtaining a departmental permit, and for the residual group they would not be lifted under any circumstances. The general character of the scheme was that for assets of the second class for which a permit could not be obtained and for all assets of the third class, if acquired after April 10, 1951, no depreciation could be written off for a period of four years.

In general, assets in the unrestricted class were those used by public utilities and by individuals in farming, fishing, and professional services, and included also patents and franchises and residential property. In the class for which permits could be applied were assets acquired to fulfil a defence contract or sub-contract or for purposes contributing to the defence of Canada, for the production and distribution of primary products in the farming, fishing, mining, petroleum, lumber, and pulp and paper industries, for direct use in transportation and communication, and for assets used in commercially operated hospitals. The third, or residual group, was comprised mainly of property constructed or acquired for retail or whosesale trade, for an office or hotel, or for commercial or financial service or for renting for other than human habitation.

The two immediate objections raised against the plan were that it applied to construction already in process or machinery already contracted for in good faith before April 10, when acquired by a new owner after that date. It was urged that if the purpose of the measure was only to affect business intentions it should not apply to the result of decisions already taken which could not be altered, or to assets already in existence the acquisition of which put no strain on current material supplies. Since the impact of the plan depended to a large

[6]Budget speech, 1951, pp. 12–13.

measure on a fairly rigid administration no cognizance was taken immediately of these appeals, but in time, after the main psychological shock had been achieved, some relaxations were introduced. In June, 1951, the restrictions were lifted for inherited properties, and properties transferred between associated taxpayers, and properties acquired by purchase of a whole business in an arm's-length deal after April 10 were made eligible for certification by permit. In November, 1951, the other main point of complaint was met. Properties in existence, under construction, or under contract, which the taxpayer was under a genuine obligation to purchase on April 10, were made eligible for lifting of the restrictions by permit.

As indicated earlier in this chapter, for several reasons the period of acute emergency following the inauguration of the new defence programme was of much shorter duration than had been expected. By the end of 1952 almost all other restrictions but the direct controls on strategic materials had been withdrawn. While the period of deferment had originally been announced as four years, apparently by the end of 1952, some 21 months after first introduced, it was felt possible to withdraw the restrictions entirely. The removal took the following form: (1) no restrictions whatever would apply to assets acquired on and after January 1, 1953; and (2) for assets acquired between April 10, 1952, and December 31, 1953, depreciation could be taken for the first time in the fiscal years of the taxpayer that commenced on or after January 1, 1953.

While no official appraisal of experience with this device has been published, an article in the *Canadian Tax Journal* by the Associate Deputy Minister of Trade and Commerce (whose department administered the permit regulations) may be accepted as an authoritative appraisal.[7] Figures given in this article revealed that permits were issued for assets in the amount of about $912 million during the period April 10, 1951, to December 31, 1952, and permits were denied on a total of $228 million of assets in the same period. The test of the effectiveness of the measure in the final analysis was the amount of investment that was postponed by reason of the restrictions, and of course this is an indeterminable quantity. No doubt the original threat of a four-year deferment did have a deterrent effect, but it is certainly open to doubt that a second use of the measure would now be effective, in view of the fact that on the first application the actuality fell so far short of the threat.

[7]M. W. Sharp, "Deferred Depreciation," *Canadian Tax Journal*, vol. I, no. 3 (May-June 1953).

Accelerated depreciation. In February, 1951, early in the defence build-up period, accelerated depreciation was announced for assets used in defence production. Such assets would be eligible only on certification by the Department of Defence Production.

Two classes of assets were established, based on the income tax categories. The first class included most assets that would be acquired for defence production, with the conspicuous exception of machinery. For this first broad group the taxpayer was permitted to take a write-off of 30 per cent per annum, in addition to the rate ordinarily applicable, provided that the aggregate of the deduction so taken did not exceed 70 per cent of the certified cost. For machinery the accelerated rate of write-off was 20 per cent per annum, with the similar proviso that the total write-off so taken might not exceed 50 per cent of the certified cost. Certified cost was as determined by the Department of Defence Production and was understood to take into account any residual value the asset might have after termination of the defence contract.

These provisions for accelerated depreciation were still in effect at the time of writing in mid-1954.

Commodity taxes. Of all the aspects of defence taxation the one which commanded least public support was the high taxation laid on household electrical appliances, automobiles, and other purchases now regarded as essential to our way of life. Partly this resulted from a misjudgment of the material supply, since shortages of almost every strategic commodity were overcome much more rapidly than had been expected, and the direct controls were therefore able to cope with the emergency period. Primarily, however, these taxes were designed to "mop up excess purchasing power." This of course is an expression which all economists can understand, but the unfortunate truth is that economists represent a tiny segment of the buying public. Not one housewife in a thousand would admit to having "excess purchasing power." And not one in ten thousand could be persuaded that there is the remotest connection between the defence effort and her purchase of a needed washing machine or stove which the Government has permitted to be manufactured and put on sale. Least of all can she understand why a government running a very substantial surplus feels it necessary to levy a stiff tax that puts some essential article beyond her reach.

Perhaps the economic objective—making the very charitable assumption that the economist has promulgated the right one—can be served without general public understanding. One has the feeling, however, judging from all experiences with "psychological taxation" in Canada to date, that there are many rules of the art yet to be mastered. So far are we from the point of mastery as yet that even the suggested title for a study—"Taxes and the Housewife" or something of the sort—seems incongruous.

Social Security

The second big issue of the period 1950 to 1954, the financing of a universal old age pension, was of minor importance compared to defence. Still, it added a permanent annual burden of $250 million at the minimum to the federal budget and is therefore not to be overlooked.

As a prelude to a description of the tax changes enacted for this purpose the reader must be given some background information on Canadian experience with old age pensions. This will be brief, since the subject is dealt with again in another context in later chapters.

Old age pensions for persons 70 and over were introduced first in Canada in 1927 on the basis of a 50-50 sharing of the cost between the Dominion and provincial governments. The provinces only slowly entered into the arrangement, but after the Dominion's share was increased to 75 per cent in 1931 they were less reluctant. By 1936 pensions were being paid in all provinces. The amount of the pension was gradually increased from $20 monthly at the outset to $25 in 1943, $30 in 1947, and $40 in 1949. Some provinces paid an additional amount of $5 or $10 but the federal government did not contribute to the cost of this supplement.

The distinctive feature ot this plan was that to become eligible a person was required to pass a "means test." In practice this meant that the income from the pension plus other income could not exceed a specified amount, and a considerable apparatus for investigating claims was in operation. As prices rose the allowable income was also raised, and this, combined with the increase in the amount of the pension and the fact that relatively more people were reaching the age of 70 and surviving for some years, meant that the total cost of the plan was rising rapidly in the post-war period. The federal share had increased from about $40 million in 1946 to an estimated $110 million had the scheme been in effect for the full fiscal year 1951–2. The total cost of the scheme in its last year, including the provincial share, would have been $136 million. By that time almost one-half the persons over 70 in Canada were in receipt of the old age pension.

The more immediate context of the change under discussion was the offer made by the federal government at the Conference on Reconstruction in 1945 and 1946 to assume the full cost of a universal pension at age 70 (i.e. without means test). This was intended to relieve the provinces of all further cost and to recognize a growing public discomfort with the means test. With the collapse of that Conference no further action was taken, but the proposal continued to be pressed by provincial authorities and by members of Parliament. The outcome of this agitation was the appointment in March, 1950, of a Joint Committee of the Senate and House of Commons on Old Age Security, which in addition to its representations from both House and Senate reflected as well the views of all parties. In the public hearings held by the Committee there appeared before it representatives of practically all the leading labour, business, and welfare organizations, as well as various prominent individuals. Information and expressions of opinion were also called for from provincial governments. While there were considerable divergencies in the actual details of proposals, and one or two conspicuous departures from the general view, the notable feature of this evidence was the strong condemnation of the means test and the general support for a universal pension financed by earmarked taxes.

The Committee, in its report dated June 28, 1950, reviewed the available alternatives, and reduced these to three in number.[8] First, there was old age assistance, i.e. the system of providing additional income to the needy aged, which was the plan in effect. The Committee pointed out correctly that the means test was the feature of this scheme that had been most roundly condemned. Second, there was old age insurance, i.e. insurance in the usual sense, in which the regular premiums were paid and the amount of the benefit was related to the size and duration of the premiums. Of this approach the Committee conceded that the great virtue was its actuarial soundness and the direct sense of responsibility on the part of the individual, but pointed out that it had the disadvantages that those entering the plan late in life would have only a small pension and that experience had proven in other countries that it was impossible to obtain universal coverage through an insurance scheme. The problem of need in old age would therefore remain. Third, there was a scheme the Committee termed as the "universal pay-as-you-go system," i.e. one under which pensions were paid to all in the eligible age group and the current cost was met by special taxes. The scheme avoided the

[8]Joint Committee of the Senate and House of Commons on Old Age Security, *Report*, pp. 104 ff.

problem encountered under the insurance approach that coverage would not be universal, and at the same time the use of earmarked taxes, which all would pay, created a sense of direct contribution towards the cost of the pensions without the complications involved in collecting and recording payments by millions of wage-earners and others.

In view of the importance that attached to this particular scheme it would be advisable to reproduce the precise wording the *Report* used in describing it. The relevant passages follow:

> The universal pay-as-you-go system of old age security is designed to avoid the chief weaknesses of the insurance approach by assuring benefits to the entire population in the eligible age group. It does not attempt to relate the benefit which an individual receives or the amount of that benefit to the individual record of contributions. Under a universal pay-as-you-go system it is still necessary to face up to the total costs involved and to collect from those who will ultimately benefit a portion of their earnings in order to meet the cost of paying pensions to those who are now eligible. By this device of pay-as-you-go, the necessity for the accumulation of a reserve fund can be avoided, and it becomes unnecessary to keep records of the amount or number of individual contributions.
>
> There is, the Committee recognizes, in the universal pay-as-you-go system, some loss of the psychological values inherent in the insurance approach, arising out of the fact that no direct relationship exists between the record of prior contributions and the right to benefit. For this reason it is important that any universal pay-as-you-go system should be solidly based on a revenue system that involves direct contributions for old age security purposes from the largest possible number of citizens.[9]

The Committee also considered the responsibility of government towards those aged 65 to 69, and came to the view that for this group old age assistance, i.e. a scheme employing a means test, would be sufficient.

Its recommendations therefore were: (1) that a universal pay-as-you-go pension of $40 a month for all persons 70 and over be instituted by the federal government, to be paid for by earmarked taxes; and (2) that a means-test pension of $40 a month be instituted for persons aged 65 to 69, the cost to be shared equally by the federal and provincial governments.

The Committee estimated that the total cost of the new programme for the federal government would be about $350 million in the first year. However, since about $100 million was already being spent on the existing pensions the net additional cost would be $250 million. It made no concrete recommendations as to how this amount might

[9]*Report*, p. 106.

be raised, on the grounds that "The raising of revenues is a technical problem which bears a close relation to fiscal policy in general, and the Committee did not feel that it should suggest more than the main outlines and principles to be followed."[10] However, it did put forward, as one of many schemes worthy of consideration, a three-way division of cost between individuals (by way of a direct tax on earnings), employers (by way of a direct payment on the analogy of the unemployment insurance scheme), and the general revenues of the federal treasury. But the *Report* contained estimates of revenues from alternative sources, and the Committee appeared to be content to leave this disagreeable aspect of the matter to the Government.

Finally, on the basis of an opinion given by the Deputy Minister of Justice, the Committee suggested that an amendment to the B.N.A. Act be obtained to give Parliament the necessary authority to levy "earmarked" taxes for social security.

Thus recommended the Parliamentary Committee, by unanimous vote, late in June, 1950. Within a week following the appearance of its *Report* the North Koreans had crossed the boundary into South Korea, and overnight the world had changed. A whole new set of conditions appeared, all unfavourable to the introduction of a major new social security measure. It was obvious that taxes would have to be raised sharply for defence, and there would be little room for additional levies for old age pensions. Furthermore a period in which every effort would have to be made to resist inflationary pressures hardly seemed appropriate for the introduction of a measure that would give a considerable stimulus to consumer buying.

Yet from all sides the pressure mounted for implementation of the proposals, no matter what the consequence. Most powerful was the argument that it was the aged who had become the victims of the post-war inflation and that the rest of the community, which by and large was prospering under boom conditions, owed them at least this much in compensation. Furthermore the Government was in the position that the change in circumstances after Korea would force it to disappoint almost every expectation that had been raised by the calling of a Dominion-Provincial Conference for December, 1950. Of all these the least easily forgiven would be a default on the old age pension plan, particularly since it had been the Dominion's own proposal in 1945 and the unanimous support of the Parliamentary Committee was fresh and undeniable evidence that the elected representatives of the people were strongly in favour of it.

[10] *Report*, p. 111.

In the light of these circumstances the Dominion apparently concluded that it had no alternative, and at the conference with the provinces in December, 1950, announced, in solemn words, because the Korean war had by then taken on sombre implications, that it was prepared to go on with both the universal pensions for those aged 70 and over and the shared-cost "means-test" pensions for persons aged 65 to 69 if the provinces so wished. The provincial representatives accepted the offer, and the die was cast. At the spring session in 1951, legislation for the means-test pensions was enacted under the Old Age Assistance Act (and incidentally for continuation of pensions for the blind under the Blind Persons Act), and in May the Imperial Parliament made the necessary amendment to the B.N.A. Act for the introduction of earmarked taxes for the universal old age pensions at seventy. This came too late for the introduction of enabling legislation at the spring session of 1951, but at a fall session the measure was passed as the Old Age Security Act. It provided for the introduction of pensions of $40 a month from January 1, 1952, and also for earmarked taxes for financing these pensions.

The so-called "2–2–2" formula of taxes that was adopted is by now well known, and will be mentioned further in a moment. The discussion, both official and private, which preceded this decision in retrospect has some interesting facets. The Committee itself invited conceptual confusion by using the term "contributory" to describe its final proposal, and the federal Government, no doubt deeply anxious to impress the public that it could not have free pensions, compounded the confusion by couching its own undertakings in terms of a "contributory" scheme. In discussions this led to a certain amount of tilting at windmills for a period, designed to demonstrate the impracticability of the "insurance" principle.

This semantic problem would not have arisen if discussion had been carried on in the more accurate terms of a "pay-as-you-go" programme, but it at least served to clear the air of lingering illusions that payment of pensions for all at 70 could be made compatible with any sort of test of eligibility, the insurance principle simply involving the substitution of the payment of premiums test for the old means test. It also served to demonstrate that once it had abandoned the means-test principle, the Parliamentary Committee had been right in its conclusion that no other test could be reintroduced in its place. The earmarking of *general* taxes was the only appropriate device for a *general* pension plan, and there would be real value, both in the cause of prudent finance and public acceptability, in having higher taxes plainly marked. Parliamentary Committees are seldom so clearly vindicated.

Less can be said, however, of the Committee's tentatively advanced specific scheme for earmarking. It became amply apparent on examination that it had failed to mention the only tax of mass application in the federal structure, the sales tax. If it had been seeking a source through which all would contribute in a roughly proportionate way, it would not have passed up this tax. The unpopularity of the tax in Parliament no doubt accounted for this reserve, but its very unpopularity would be its greatest strength in reducing the pressure from Parliament for perpetually higher pensions. The administrative impracticability of collecting small individual amounts directly from millions of new taxpayers through reducing the income tax exemptions also pointed to the sales tax as an acceptable means of accomplishing the same result indirectly. On the strength of these and other arguments one expert advanced the view that the whole cost of the new plan be paid for by way of the sales tax.[11]

The actual plan of financing, announced by the Minister of Finance in the fall of 1951 as described by him, was the "2-2-2 formula." The individual elements represented by this formula were: (1) 2 per cent of the sales tax, the increase of 2 per cent (from 8 to 10 per cent) enacted in the spring budget being withdrawn from the general revenue; (2) 2 per cent additional rate of corporation income tax, on both brackets; and (3) 2 per cent additional rate on taxable personal income, but not to exceed $60 annually. In explaining his choice the Minister said at the outset that "it seemed most sensible to utilize the main taxes which at present support our revenue systems,"[12] and took some pains to justify his selection of the sales tax and his substitution of an addition to the corporation income tax for a payroll tax on employers. The sales tax was in his view almost ideal for financing social security, on the grounds that, "Where under social security provisions the benefits are to be universal, it is only right that contributions to the fund should likewise be universal."[13] Further: "Taxation for social security finds justification in the benefit principle of taxation. All pensioners, rich and poor, receive equal benefits. From this it could quite reasonably be argued that all should make equal contribution towards the fund, but such a system might be regarded as harsh and impracticable. Under the sales tax method of financing, the burden

[11]Monteath Douglas, *Financing Old Age Pensions: A Personal View* (1951). For the most exhaustive discussion of the alternatives see D. C. MacGregor, *The Proposed Old Age Pension* (Oct., 1951).

[12]*House of Commons Debates*, Oct. 25, 1951, p. 388.

[13]*Ibid.*

through a wide income range will be roughly proportional. . . . In the light of these facts, I suggest that any argument about unfairness of using sales tax for financing old age pensions is not impressive."[14] He rejected the payroll tax on the grounds that it would be a most difficult one to collect from all the small employers in the country; that certain employers—hospitals, school boards, universities, churches, charitable organizations and provincial and municipal governments—would strongly resist such a tax and would in some cases suffer hardship; that it would increase the production costs of our exporters, and would require new government machinery to administer a tax of this sort.[15]

These separate taxes were enacted as part of the Old Age Security Act, their proceeds are earmarked for the Old Age Security Fund, and they are now known as Old Age Security taxes. This has caused a certain amount of confusion both in the tax statutes and in public accounts. For example, although the sales tax for all business purposes is charged at a 10 per cent rate the Excise Tax Act discloses only an 8 per cent rate, the other 2 per cent appearing in the Old Age Security Act. The same of course is true for the personal and corporate income taxes. Similarly in using either revenue or expenditure figures for the federal government it must now be explicitly stated whether these include or exclude the operations of the Old Age Security Fund. The separate fund is justified as a device for keeping before the public the fact that the pensions must be paid for from taxes, and that if disbursements from the fund increase its tax revenues must be increased correspondingly. At the same time the novelty of a fund supported from tax revenues in the federal budget has required some adjustment in public thinking.

To round out this episode requires only brief mention now of subsequent events. The sales tax transfer and the corporation income tax increase came into effect on January 1, 1952, concurrently with the introduction of a federal scheme of universal pensions of $40 per month for those aged 70 and over. The personal income tax change was postponed to July 1, 1952, to coincide with a revision of the personal income tax schedule, which somewhat eased the introduction of the additional levy. For 1952, therefore, the maximum tax was $30, but since, with the tax in effect for full taxation years, it has been $60. There has been some pressure from the C.C.F. party to remove this maximum, but consistent with the originally announced principle that the charge would be on the benefit basis the Government has resisted this proposal. Since the pension is of nominal value to the

[14] *Ibid.*

[15] *Ibid.*, p. 387.

upper income groups in any event, being subject to income tax, the removal of the limit on the old age security charge would only add a substantial additional rate to the already high graduated rates of personal income tax.

As predicted by the Minister of Finance the fund was substantially in deficit for the first year, but, as was probably not anticipated, it has been very slow in emerging from a deficit position in later years. The annual operations of the fund for its first three years were as follows: 1951–2, revenue $26.4 million, expenditure $76.1 million, deficit, $49.7 million; 1952–3, revenue $223.6 million, expenditure $323.1 million, deficit, $99.5 million; 1953–4, revenue $294.0 million, expenditure $338.8 million, deficit $44.8 million. In view of the fact that a deficit of $144.3 million had been accumulated and not written off by March 31, 1954, it was expected by many that some adjustment might be made in the 1954 spring budget to increase the tax revenues of the fund. However, in place of such a step the deficit of about $100 million accumulated to March 31, 1953, was written off against a reserve account, and no change was made in taxes. Apparently the federal treasury was willing to take the chance that in time the present sources would meet the needs of the fund as had been originally expected, although the problem may remain chronic, since the annual payments, about $350 million in 1954–5, were expected to reach $500 million by 1971.

29 THE PROVINCES AND MUNICIPALITIES, 1946–54

Latent Problems Become Pressing

CHANGES AT THE PROVINCIAL and municipal level in the post-war years, while less volcanic than the upheavals that have taken place in the federal sphere of taxation, have also been important.

The provinces and municipalities entered the post-war era in fairly good financial condition. Early in the war the upsurge of economic activity rapidly dissipated the burden of relief, still a serious problem in 1939. For six years the competing demands of war production for labour and materials forced the postponement of much of the normal expenditure on roads, schools, and other public works. At the same time, with the support of the payments from the Dominion under the Wartime Tax Agreements, revenues were more stable than they had been for decades, despite the fact that gasoline and liquor rationing prevented receipts from these sources from keeping pace with the increase in economic tempo. The municipalities benefited particularly from the war-inspired prosperity. Tax arrears, accumulated during the depression, became liquid assets as property-owners paid their debts, and properties seized for tax sale found a ready market. At the same time current tax levies were being paid up in full.

As a result of this combination of reduced expenditures and increased revenues there were budget surpluses at both provincial and municipal levels of government. Treasuries that had been on the verge of bankruptcy were restored to fiscal health, and all provinces and many municipalities were enabled to reduce their debts, in some cases substantially. In a financial sense, therefore, the wartime prosperity repaired a good part of the damage that had been wrought by the depression.

By contrast with this state of comparative calm, a convulsive change has occurred in the post-war period. A few general facts will best illustrate the course of events. Between 1946 and 1954 provincial expenditures on current and capital account increased from about \$480 million to over \$1,350 million (the latter figure an estimate), an increase of more than 180 per cent. Revenues increased from $495 million to an estimated $1,310 million, an increase of nearly 165 per cent. Further, the increase in provincial direct and guaranteed debt in the same period has more than wiped out the reductions made during the war. Total provincial direct and guaranteed borrowings stand today at the highest levels in history. Almost similar changes have occurred as well at the municipal level. The figures, given in Table XXXVI, for current tax levies and net debenture debt in the larger cities illustrate this marked trend.

Two main causes lie behind this revolution. First, provincial and municipal governments, either directly or through their agencies, in a short span of years have been attempting to provide the new highways, roads, water services, sewers, schools, transportation services, power developments, and other capital facilities necessitated by the tremendous economic growth of the post-war period, and to make up for the neglect of the war and to some extent of the depression as well. An indication of the magnitude of this effort is given in the official survey *Private and Public Investment in Canada 1926–1951* and subsequent annual reports issued by the federal Department of Trade and Commerce. These reports show that in the eight post-war years 1946 to 1953 new investments in durable physical assets by provincial and municipal governments and their agencies amounted to $5,435 million. This was almost 200 per cent more than the total of $1,825 million spent in the previous *fifteen* years.[1] In the provincial budgets the financial reflection of this change is most apparent in highway expenditures. These have recently been running at about $370 million a year, as compared with about $137 million in 1946 and $89 million in 1939. The increase in educational expenditures and in part the increase in expenditures on conservation of natural resources also reflect this heavy capital investment programme.

The second major cause has been the increase in provincial and municipal expenditures on activities usually grouped together as "public welfare." Between 1946 and 1954 provincial expenditures on this account increased from $100 million to an estimated total of almost $325 million. More generous scales of assistance for indigents, higher allowances for widows and others, increased hospital and other grants, and the introduction of state-sponsored compulsory hospitalization plans in two provinces, British Columbia and Saskatchewan, accounted for a large part of this increase. The inauguration in Janu-

[1]Derived from a table on page 146, *Private and Public Investment in Canada 1926–1951.*

TABLE XXXVI

Current Tax Levy and Net Debenture Debt of Leading Canadian Cities For Fiscal Years Ended Nearest December 31

(millions of dollars)

(1) Current tax levy
(2) Net debenture debt

Fiscal year	Halifax		Saint John		Montreal		Quebec		Toronto		Ottawa	
	(1)	(2)	(1)	(2)	(1)[a]	(2)	(1)[a]	(2)	(1)	(2)	(1)	(2)
1941	2.3	9.7	2.1	4.6	27.1	217.0	4.3	27.9	32.4	97.8	6.2	12.5
1945	2.8	8.1	2.5	3.6	27.2	214.5	4.3	25.2	28.8	64.9	5.6	7.8
1946	3.0	8.9	2.5	3.8	27.4	207.9	4.4	26.1	31.4	56.2	5.9	7.2
1947	3.6	10.9	2.6	4.3	29.2	201.7	4.5	24.2	35.7	56.3	7.2	7.1
1948	3.7	12.8	2.9	3.5	32.2	192.1	4.9	23.2	36.6	62.2	7.9	6.7
1949	4.0	12.4	3.2	5.4	34.0	184.6	4.9	25.4	41.5	64.2	8.8	13.6
1950	4.1	13.8	3.3	6.6	36.0	175.0	5.1	24.6	45.1	80.5	10.5	21.4
1951	5.1	17.9	3.4	7.9	43.5	171.6	5.2	28.0	54.6	98.5	12.7	27.9
1952	6.3	18.1[c]	3.7	7.5	46.5	182.1	6.6	32.8	59.3	102.1	13.7	29.2

Fiscal year	Hamilton		Winnipeg		Regina		Edmonton		Calgary		Vancouver		Victoria	
	(1)	(2)	(1)	(2)	(1)	(2)	(1)	(2)	(1)[b]	(2)	(1)[b]	(2)	(1)	(2)
1941	6.3	19.0	8.3	23.9	2.2	5.7	3.7	21.3	2.8	11.5	10.8	32.7	1.4	12.3
1945	6.0	11.7	8.5	15.5	2.1	3.3	4.4	16.9	3.0	10.2	11.7	33.5	1.7	11.7
1946	6.4	10.5	9.4	16.8	2.2	3.9	4.7	16.5	3.3	9.5	12.6	35.8	1.7	11.7
1947	7.2	10.0	10.0	17.5	2.3	3.5	5.0	17.2	3.8	8.9	13.5	36.2	1.9	11.8
1948	8.7	10.8	11.6	20.7	2.6	5.1	5.4	18.9	4.4	8.5	14.5	45.4	2.0	12.3
1949	9.3	11.3	13.5	23.2	2.8	6.4	6.0	21.7	5.1	14.6	15.4	54.7	2.4	12.9
1950	10.4	19.6	14.5	25.7	2.9	6.4	7.4	29.5	5.4	16.0	15.8	60.6	2.5	13.2
1951	13.0	26.4	15.9	30.8	3.3	7.3	9.3	40.6	6.2	17.7	17.3	67.4	2.8	12.8
1952	16.4	27.4	17.1	32.6	3.5	10.5	11.6	45.6	7.6	20.8	20.3	79.2	2.9	13.0

Sources: Current tax levy—municipal officials and Dominion Bureau of Statistics; net debenture debt—Dominion Bureau of Statistics.
[a]Real property taxes.
[b]Excludes business taxes.
[c]Includes $3,400,000 serial debentures issued by Public Service Commission.

ary, 1952, of universal pensions, financed by the Dominion, for all persons 70 or over relieved the provincial governments of a formidable outlay. However, the cost of sharing with the Dominion one-half the expense of paying old age pensions on a means-test basis to persons between 65 and 70 from the same date will partially offset this saving.

These two costly phases of post-war provincial-municipal finances have been combined with a general increase in the standard of normal current services and a consequent rise in their cost. Salary and wage expenses have, of course, increased with the higher cost of living.

The financing of this post-war transition has been a relatively easy matter for some provinces, and a most difficult one for others. The fundamental disparities in their relative position remain today much as they were described in the Rowell-Sirois *Report.* If the war had the effect of restoring the *financial* position of all provincial governments it did so with varying degrees of permanency, and did little to rectify the underlying maladjustments of the Canadian economy. Indeed it has been argued on behalf of the eastern provinces that it aggravated these maladjustments by further intensifying the concentration of industry in central Canada. Happily recent developments in some regions are helping to right the balance. The discovery of large oil deposits in Alberta and the rapid post-war industrialization of British Columbia have probably assured both these provinces of a bright future. The generally high levels of income in the post-war era have also given some stimulus to all parts of the economy, and made more tolerable the basic disparities. Nevertheless they remain, and their effect is fully apparent in certain provinces. Throughout the post-war period the budgets of the Maritime Provinces, for example, have almost continuously shown deficits on combined current and capital account.

The burst of economic growth in post-war Canada also aggravated the financial problems of the municipalities. The war gave them a breathing space, as it did the provinces, in which they were able largely to mend the ravages of the depression, but post-war developments have caught them up in a spending spree that in the nature of their functions is almost impossible to resist. New housing developments have required new roads, sewers, water mains, schools, and transportation facilities, and new factories have had to be similarly serviced. So closely enmeshed with the whole economic machinery are such municipal activities that they can be delayed only to a limited extent. Along with this capital expansion there has been a marked increase in the cost of providing normal municipal functions.

Police and fire protection require increasingly elaborate and expensive equipment, health and sanitation measures are ever broadening in their scope, the provision of cultural and recreational facilities is increasingly expensive, demands of motorists for snow removal and road maintenance become more exacting each year. Most important of all, the many social and public welfare functions, including education, which in the past have devolved on the municipalities, represent a responsibility that grows continually more burdensome.

There have also been severe growing pains of an institutional character in recent years. The mushroom development of suburban areas on the fringes of every large Canadian city has created new and unprecedented problems. Small suburban areas there have been in the past, and these have been rapidly and easily absorbed into the parent city by a slight extension of municipal boundaries and services. The marked change that has taken place in recent years, however, is that the *major* urban developments are now taking place in these fringe areas, while the population of the cities is remaining static or growing only slowly. The general character of this trend, and some of the problems it creates, are graphically summarized in the following paragraphs from a recent report on municipal problems in Nova Scotia:

> This phenomenon of large cities spilling over their legal boundaries into the surrounding area is by no means peculiar to Halifax. With increasing industrial expansion, the development of rapid means of transportation and especially the rapid rise in urban population during the war, it has become almost universal. The result has been the Metropolitan Area: an urban social and economic unit, which has many problems of area-wide concern but no corresponding unit of local government to solve them.
>
> The pattern of growth in a Metropolitan Area is always the same. People from the city move to nearby rural areas to build their homes, hoping to gain the advantages of low-cost land, lower taxes and rural living, and at the same time to retain the urban advantages of industrial or commercial employment and urban amusements and recreation. For a period these advantages are enjoyed, but eventually services which at first were merely a convenience to be foregone for the sake of economy become a necessity. Larger schools are required; sewage and garbage disposal facilities and a central sanitary water supply become necessary to health; fire protection and increased public health and welfare services become imperative; and the lack of community planning becomes impressively apparent. In short, a rural community becomes suburban. Those who have fled the high costs of urban living find themselves trapped into providing most of the services responsible for those high costs and, at the same time, paying perpetually the psychic costs of living in a community that grew without proper planning and control.
>
> At the same time, the parent city must continue to supply services for

these people who continue to live their economic and cultural lives within its borders. Usually, too, the parent city is left with large areas of vacant, and hence unproductive, land. This is true only to a slight degree in Halifax, for the city has comparatively little vacant land suitable for building. On the other hand, this shortage of land has been one of the main factors responsible for the movement of population from the city into the fringe.[2]

While this development is creating new problems for some of the larger Canadian centres, it does not appear as yet to have reached the acute stage now apparent in the United States. There many of the larger cities have suffered an actual decline in population in the last two decades and the phenomenon has become so intensive as to become known as "the disintegration of the cities." The serious concern of tax authorities in the United States over the problems posed by this development is illustrated by the following typical statement:

> Urban decentralization is rapidly changing the pattern of local government finance in America. The outward push of population and industry continually gather momentum. The cities are losing population in the upper and middle income groups. Replenishments—to the extent to which they are arriving—are more likely to be in the low-income or relief category. The incoming groups not only have less capacity to help shoulder the city's fiscal burdens, but also add more to the city's relief and welfare expenditures.
>
> Concurrently, the outgoing population likewise increases the city's fiscal problems by settling in the outlying regions and maintaining commuter or frequent visitor contact with the central city, thereby greatly enhancing its traffic difficulties.
>
> Thus the current decentralization development is spearing the city on several sharp fiscal prongs. The situation is serious and will probably become more so.[3]

Experience in Canada and elsewhere suggests that the traditional solution of absorption into the parent city is workable today only in limited circumstances. Where the area of dispersion of population is not too wide, and where local pride and local services are not too far developed, it may still provide an answer. The principal obstacle under such circumstances appears to be the reluctance of the residents of the fringe areas to share the usually higher taxes of the parent city. Where, as is commonly the case, the fringe areas are in themselves moderate sized cities with deeply rooted community pride and adequate equipment to provide their own fire, police, and other services, complete absorption presents almost insurmountable political, administrative, and physical problems. Unfortunately the same is true

[2] *The Reorganization of Provincial Municipal Relations in Nova Scotia* (1949), pp. 73–4.

[3] Tax Institute Inc., *Tax Policy: The State and Local Revenue Outlook* (Sept., 1951), pp. 6–7.

where an extensive population is widely dispersed over areas at distances of fifteen, twenty, or twenty-five miles from the parent city. Where fringe areas are found in both these stages of development the complexities are multiplied.

While complete amalgamation may still be feasible in some areas, provincial and municipal authorities are turning their attention increasingly to the possibilities of joint action over a wide range of activities through a metropolitan form of government, or of co-operation in selective fields of activity through special metropolitan boards. The expense, inconvenience, and inefficiency of unco-ordinated effort in fire protection and policing, in the provision of health and hospital services and the control of communicable diseases, in the provision of water, the location of garbage dumps, and the disposal of sewage, in the placing of secondary schools, libraries, and other cultural facilities, and in a myriad other aspects of municipal "housekeeping," have compelled joint action in many of these spheres. This trend toward large and specialized administrative units that cut across the lines of existing political entities is not limited to urban municipalities. Drainage and local improvement districts in rural areas have been common in the past, and today the trend is towards larger local areas of administration for education, health, welfare, and other services. In the rural areas the broadening scope of the educational unit in particular has been a universal phenomenon, the causes of which are summarized by Horace L. Brittain:

> The small school district led everywhere to unequal opportunities for the schooling of children who have equal rights to a sound education. Many small units were quite unable to provide modern school buildings, adequate equipment or even passable sanitary services. They were greatly handicapped in obtaining, and even more in retaining, properly qualified teachers and many had to close their schools or accept teachers without professional training. The large number of local authorities increased the difficulty of maintaining adequate provincial inspection and supervision. As a result there has been for some years a strong movement toward increasing the size and decreasing the number of local school authorities particularly in rural areas.[4]

The same authority made the further comment:

> The most spectacular development during the last decade has been the increase in area and reduction in number of local school administrative units. In 1938 it was estimated by the Citizens Research Institute of Canada that there were about 23,000 local school authorities in Canada. By 1948 the number of autonomous authorities responsible for the financial administration of the schools within their jurisdiction has possibly been reduced to 10,000 or 11,000 or even less.[5]

[4]Horrace L. Brittain, *Local Government in Canada* (1951), p. 30.

All these developments in local government have posed in new and urgent form a whole catalogue of questions always latent in the Canadian federation. Are the existing municipal units, both urban and rural, the ideal size and constitution for efficient distribution of workload between the provinces and the municipal units? Given an efficient distribution, to what extent should the municipal units be required to finance the functions allocated to them? Assuming continuation of the property tax as the mainstay of municipal revenues, is there evidence that it is now too burdensome? What steps should be taken to remove some of the obvious defects of the property tax? Are there other tax sources which might be used to supplement the property tax? Assuming that as much as possible has been done to improve municipal arrangements and increase municipal revenues, to what extent should the province then give aid by grants? If grants are paid, by what standard should they be allocated among the municipalities? Should the grants be general or for specific purposes? If for specific purposes, how much control should the province exercise to be assured the purposes are carried out?

Fundamental to all these issues is the ancient riddle of how to combine efficiency with responsibility in public administration. Faith in government at close contact with the citizens and taxpayers is fortunately still vigorous in Canada. One finds often that even when it is amply apparent that a function might be performed more efficiently by a senior government it is left at the municipal level because of the advantages of intimate relations with the taxpaying public. At the same time strong forces have been working in the opposite direction. The mounting cost of services which by tradition have devolved on the local governments (social welfare, education, roads, etc.) and the increasingly apparent anomalies of tax administration in a multitude of small self-contained areas are pressures forcing the gravitation of financial responsibility to senior levels of government. This trend is no doubt stimulated by chronic but heartfelt complaints from property-owners that the burden of the property tax is becoming intolerable, that assessment methods are antiquated and their application unfair, and so on. Municipal councils, always sensitive to this cry, have pleaded for a larger share of the tax pie in the post-war period rather than for an authorization of new tax sources.

In most provinces this plea has been met (but not silenced) by more and more provincial grants. The most marked changes have occurred in the financing of education. Provincial governments gener-

[5] *Ibid.*, p. 43.

ally are now assuming a share of educational costs by grants to school boards far in excess of their pre-war participation. The basis on which these grants are made varies from province to province, but the over-all magnitude of the increase may be judged from the fact that provincial government expenditures on education have soared from about $38 million in 1939 to an estimated $240 million in 1954. Municipal authorities have argued that because of the sharp increase in total educational expenditures these grants have not given the relief that would be assumed, since their own expenditures on education have risen despite the grants. Nevertheless it is obvious that had the provincial grants not been given municipal educational costs would today be much higher than they are.

The increased participation of the province in other local expenditures is reflected in part also in the rise in provincial public welfare expenditures from $98 million in 1939 to an estimated $320 million in 1954, and in the increase in general municipal subsidies from $5 million to an estimated $42 million between the same years. Provincial participation in the cost of building and maintaining local roads has also risen. These developments have awakened the traditional cry that all governments should be financially independent, a principle extremely difficult to adopt in practice. No less serious are the practical issues involved in the search for a satisfactory formula of allocation for the grants. One inevitable result has been to expose the inadequacies of existing local assessments, which have been traditionally used in such formulas as a measure of local tax potential.

To assist in finding solutions to all the wide ramifications of this post-war municipal development there has been one or more royal commissions or similar inquiries in almost every province, and increasingly the dispassionate advice of the expert is being sought and accepted. The reports of these enquiries represent in the aggregate an unprecedented attempt to discover objective criteria in this most complex of fields, and represent a most encouraging aspect of the post-war period. They are touched on very briefly in the following chapter.

Influence of Other Factors

In addition to the very broad underlying influences outlined above certain factors of a more concrete character have affected post-war provincial and municipal taxation.

(*a*) *The Tax Rental Agreements.* The influence of the agreements between certain provincial governments and the Dominion under which provincial and municipal taxes were suspended in return for compensation is self-evident. Had these agreements not existed the course of post-war tax events would have been radically different. In a later chapter they are dealt with in the light of the historic subsidy mechanism, but their terms relating specifically to taxation may appropriately be mentioned here. Two sets of agreements are involved: the so-called 1947 Agreements, entered into for a five-year period by all provinces but Ontario and Quebec, and the 1952 Agreements, entered into for a further five years by all provinces but Quebec.

Taking the periods of the two agreements together they have had the following effect:

1. For the calendar years 1947 to 1956, inclusive, the agreeing provinces and their municipalities have undertaken not to impose personal income taxes, corporation income taxes or corporation taxes (taxes on paid-up capital, places of business, etc.).

2. In respect of deaths occurring between April 1, 1947, and March 31, 1957, the provinces and their municipalities, except for Ontario, have undertaken not to impose succession duties. (Ontario opted to retain its succession duties.) It will be noted that in this respect the post-war agreements are broader than the Wartime Agreements, which did not affect succession duties.

3. During the period 1947 to 1951 the provinces were permitted to levy a tax of 5 per cent on corporation profits allocated to their jurisdiction according to rules set out in the agreement. This tax was administered by the Dominion government, and by virtue of an offset made against its payment, which operated whether or not the province imposed the tax, there was a financial compulsion on the province. All imposed this tax as a result. It was in effect for the full term of the agreement, 1947 to 1951 inclusive, its purpose being to enable any province not wishing to enter into an agreement with the Dominion to impose a tax of at least 5 per cent without discriminating against its corporations. This tax was withdrawn under the 1952 agreement, and in its place, to achieve the same effect, the federal government offered a tax credit against its corporation profits tax for a similar tax paid to a non-agreeing province.

4. Precise definitions were formulated in the new agreement to give clarity to certain concepts, such as "royalty" and "rental," which had been passed over in the Wartime Agreement. At the same time a formula was established by which an agreeing province could impose a tax on income from mining operations without conflicting with the spirit of the agreement. A similar tax might also be imposed on income

from logging operations. The Dominion undertook to allow a deduction from income subject to its own profits tax for both such taxes. Following the establishment of these definitions the royalties and rentals imposed in the agreeing provinces were brought into conformity where necessary and several provinces imposed mining profits taxes in the specified form.

5. The municipal tax provisions were also made more exact. In particular specific exceptions were made for gross receipts taxes not in excess of a 3 per cent rate on public utilities in lieu of property taxes on poles, lines, wires, tracks, etc. A municipal business tax on gross receipts was also allowed if imposed under legislation enacted prior to June 27, 1946, and at a rate not in excess of the general municipal property rate.

(*b*) *Repeal of certain federal taxes.* Another factor which exerted an influence was the repeal by the Dominion of its gasoline tax of 3 cents per gallon an April 1, 1947, and of its amusement taxes in May, 1948. The first of these was particularly significant, since it allowed all provinces to increase their own taxes concurrently with the repeal of the federal levy.

(*c*) *Offer of indirect retail sales tax amendment.* The Dominion offered, at a conference in December, 1950, to request an amendment to the B.N.A. Act to allow the provinces to levy an indirect retail sales tax, if they could agree among themselves on the character of the amendment desired. This offer was accepted and a draft circulated for approval. Quebec finally withheld its support of the amendment, and in 1954 the issue appeared to be dead. At least one province, Nova Scotia, temporarily abandoned its announced intention of imposing a retail sales tax because of the failure of the proposed amendment.

(*d*) *Payment of taxes on federal properties.* A federal development of less general importance, but nevertheless of significance for other reasons, was the announcement of a policy to govern the making of payments in lieu of property taxes to municipalities.[6] The new policy, announced by the Minister of Finance on November 14, 1949, was based on the principle that the Dominion should sustain its tax exempt status under the B.N.A. Act, but that it should make a payment to compensate a municipality where there was an "abnormal concentration" of federal property. The test for "abnormal concentration" was established from the actual average proportion of federal property to total municipal assessments throughout Canada, which, as

[6]For discussion of this measure see *House of Commons Debates*, 1951 Session, pp. 4216–27, 4355–83.

the result of a survey, was found to be 4 per cent. Where the ratio of federal property exceeded 4 per cent, therefore, a condition of "abnormal concentration" was recognized.

The specific proposal made by the Minister was that in a municipality where the 4 per cent ratio was exceeded the federal government would pay a grant equal to 75 per cent of a proportion of the tax levy for municipal and school purposes, the proportion to be the same as the percentage by which the ratio of federal property to the total taxable assessment exceeded 4 per cent. In short, if the ratio was 8 per cent, the grant would be 75 per cent of 4 per cent of the total municipal and school levy, excluding business taxes. The net effect is that the federal government pays a grant of three-quarters of the tax otherwise payable on any amount of excess of its property over 4 per cent of the total taxable property in the municipality.

Ancillary to the main proposal it was announced that when the federal government acquired any property formerly taxable in a municipality receiving a grant, it would pay full taxes for the year of acquisition and half the annual taxes in the second year. Where no grant was being paid, it would meet full taxes in the year of acquisition, full taxes in the following year and in the succeeding three years pay 75 per cent, 50 per cent, and 25 per cent of full taxes.

The municipalities, who were no doubt hoping for a general federal bonus to relieve their hard-pressed finances, have expressed disappointment with the plan, and demands for more generous treatment continue to be made. Some extension of the measure was to have been made at the 1953–4 session, according to government announcements, but legislation was held over finally until 1955.

30 THE PROVINCES AND MUNICIPALITIES, 1946–54

Tax and Other Changes in Summary

As a sequel to the review of general issues in the preceding chapter the following pages present in brief outline some of the actual changes in provincial and municipal taxation in the post-war period.

Newfoundland

Provincial

One of the notable events of the post-war period was the advent of Newfoundland as the tenth Canadian province. The circumstances under which the Island, after a postponement of over eighty years, came into the Confederation on April 1, 1949, have been recounted many times, and the tax implications of this move have been described by the present author in *Taxation in Canada.*[1] It will be sufficient to state here, therefore, that with Confederation the new province gave up its main previous source of revenue, its tariff, and henceforth, of course, is to be restricted to direct taxation. In return it has received subsidies along the traditional lines from the Dominion, supplemented by a liberal "transitional grant." The new province also entered into a Tax Rental Agreement with the Dominion, and under it, in return for compensation, suspended its pre-Confederation income and corporation taxes for the period January 1, 1949, to December 31, 1951, and its death duties for the period April 1, 1949 to March 31, 1952. As in other "agreeing" provinces a 5 per cent tax on corporation profits was levied for 1949, 1950, and 1951. In 1952 the province renewed its agreement with the Dominion for a further five years.

The principal taxation developments following Confederation were the imposition of a gasoline tax of 14 cents per gallon (increased to 15 cents per gallon in 1954) and the levying of a retail sales tax at a rate of 3 per cent, which came into effect on November 15, 1950. The province has also imposed some minor taxes on persons paying insurance premiums and on the use of telephones, and royalties on

[1] Chap. 14, 2nd ed., pp. 255 ff.

mining operations in the province have been revised to accord with the terms of the tax agreement with the Dominion.

Municipal

One of the distinguishing features of Newfoundland is the virtual absence of a local level of government. Only in the last decade has any progress been made in the establishment of organized municipalities. Of these St. John's, the largest centre of population, most closely approaches the concept of an urban municipality throughout the rest of Canada, although even here fire and police protection are still financed largely by the province. More than thirty other municipalities had been formed by 1953, and the efforts of the provincial government to have further units organized under provisions of the Local Government Act passed in 1949 are slowly bearing fruit. An encouraging sign of growing interest in the movement was the formation of the Newfoundland Federation of Municipalities, which held its first convention in 1951.

The tax system of the Newfoundland municipalities is described in some detail in the chapter of *Taxation in Canada* previously referred to and will not be elaborated on here. Suffice it to say that except in St. John's the traditional source of local revenue, the real property tax, is either entirely lacking or is elementary in form. In St. John's a tax is levied on the rental value of real property, and since union the former business tax (stock tax), which applied on the inventory of merchants, has been converted to a tax on the rental value of business premises in the more familiar Canadian pattern. It would thus seem that the transition from a business tax based largely on the personal property of merchants to one based on some more general measurement, which took place in the Canadian provinces for the most part early in the twentieth century, has been long delayed in Newfoundland. Other St. John's revenues include an amusement tax and taxes on users of phones and persons paying fire and casualty insurance premiums, and in 1954 a water tax was introduced to pay for water and sewage extensions. In the newer municipalities the principal tax is a poll tax ($3 to $10), supplemented by a stock tax on inventories, a processing tax, an entertainment tax, and business licences and fees. In 1952 the first Assessment Act governing the imposition of property taxes was passed, and this almost universal form of municipal levy is gradually being adopted.

St. John's suffered a considerable loss of revenue as a result of the disappearance of certain tax sources at Confederation (for example, a share of the former tariff on coal imported into the city) and of the suspension of others (mainly taxes on corporations) under the tax agreement entered into in 1949. Apparently in compensation for these losses the province introduced an annual grant of $100,000 for the city in 1950, which, however, was discontinued in 1952. Grants are also paid to encourage the organization of municipalities throughout the province.

Several interesting proposals, some of which have been implemented, were made by H. Carl Goldenberg in a report on the Greater Corner Brook Area, a region dependent almost entirely on the Bowater's paper mill.[2]

Prince Edward Island

Provincial

The major development of the post-war period in the smallest province was the repeal in 1948 of the provincial tax on property. This had been one of the oldest taxes in Canada, having been in effect almost continuously since 1877. In the same year another set of charges that were at least half a century old—the poll and horse taxes under the Road Act—were also repealed.

The province assumed the full amount of the repealed Dominion gasoline tax in 1947, thus raising its rate from 10 cents to 13 cents per gallon. There have been no other significant changes.

Municipal

The only significant municipal tax development took place in Charlottetown, where in 1954 a business tax on the Ontario model was introduced as an alternative to the personal property tax. In general personal property continues to be taxed on a broader basis than in any other province, apparently with little concern to the citizens, judging at least by the absence of comment in the press or elsewhere. Outside the few organized areas the school districts assess and collect their own property taxes. Most have found it necessary to absorb all or the greater part of the levy formerly imposed by the province.

Until recently there have been few financial contacts between the province and the municipalities. Under the Wartime Tax Agreement the province paid $18,000 to Charlottetown in lieu of corporation taxes suspended under its provisions, and this amount was continued under the 1947 agreement. In 1949, however, the province inaugurated

[2]*Report on Municipal Administration and Services in the Greater Corner Brook Area of Newfoundland* (1950).

grants of $1 per capita to Charlottetown and the towns. In 1951 it increased this grant to $1.50 per capita, and if experience in other provinces is any guide future years will bring further increases. Grants were also introduced in 1951, at 50 cents per capita, to encourage the organization of villages under the Village Act, a statute of long standing. Two or three villages had been formed by 1954.

The province assumes a considerable share of school district expenses, however, through direct payments on teachers' salaries. On average these amount to more than two-thirds of the salary paid. The need for consolidation of school districts is evident in the fact that there are over 450 schools for a population of less than 100,000.

Small grants have also been made to organized municipalities for assistance with "market" roads.

Nova Scotia

Provincial

The province has made two increases in its gasoline tax, one of 3 cents per gallon in 1947, and another of 2 cents per gallon in 1951. The latter change brought the rate to 15 cents per gallon, the highest in Canada. It was part of a round of increases, enacted at a three-day special session in June, 1951, in place of a retail sales tax in indirect form forecast earlier for which expected authority had not been obtained. Other changes in June, 1951, included raising the pari-mutuel bets tax from 5 to 10 per cent, increasing a charge on long distance calls from a straight 5 cents per call to 5 cents per each 50 cents of the charge, increasing the amusement tax applicable to theatres and sporting events and charges levied on film servicing businesses. In December, 1951, the amusement tax was extended to apply to charges made for admissions to skating rinks, provision for which is made in the statute.

In 1952 the province brought in a levy designed to obtain revenue from one of the few mineral resources it possesses—gypsum. Since most of the deposits are privately owned there has always been considerable doubt regarding the province's right to impose a tax or royalty that would come within its constitutional powers. The first tax imposed, in 1952, took the form of a charge of 6 cents per ton on all gypsum extracted where more than 20,000 tons a year was mined. So levied the charge probably applied only to two or three large corporations, and undoubtedly was challenged by the federal authorities as being a corporation tax, which infringed on the tax rental agreements, and probably as being also an indirect tax, and therefore beyond the constitutional powers of the province. In any event the tax was revised in 1953 to convert it to a levy on the profits from mining gypsum at a rate of 33⅓ per cent, with a minimum of 6 cents per ton mined in the year. In this form it comes within the terms of the tax rental agreement.

In 1947 the poll and property taxes levied under the Public Highways Act, which local units had collected for some four decades and turned over to the province, were repealed with the exception of the property tax in rural areas. In discussing possible means of obtaining new revenues the provincial Premier in his budget speech of April 17, 1950, pointed out that the rate of this latter tax had been unchanged at 6 mills for 30 years and might have to be increased. However, no increase had been made up to mid-1954.

There have been no official enquiries into provincial finances in Nova Scotia since the Royal Commission on Provincial Development and Rehabilitation in 1944. This Commission, of which R. M. Dawson was chairman, stressed the disadvantageous position of Nova Scotia in the Canadian economy and expressed the view that "there is every reason to believe that Nova Scotia's general position in the federation has been worsened rather than bettered by events since 1939."[3] It foresaw that in the post-war period the province would be compelled to increase its income by the imposition of more or higher taxes, and recommended consideration of a provincial income tax, a retail sales tax, a small tax on electric power, and heavier charges on buses and trucks operating on the public highways. But the possibilities in this direction had definite limitations. The *Report* said: "Heavier taxes in any form, however, must be levied in Nova Scotia with great circumspection, for it must never be forgotten that the economy is not operating at such a level that it can absorb very much in the way of additional burdens."[4] The only hope for real improvement in Nova Scotia's position lay in an intelligent and constructive national policy of resources development to help the fishing, mining, steel producing, and other industries, and a judicious use of grants from the Dominion to bolster provincial finances. The Commission argued in general for adoption of the recommendations of the Rowell-Sirois Commission.

Municipal

There have been few notable developments in municipal taxation in Nova Scotia in recent years. Perhaps the most unusual situation is that of Halifax, where the rate of tax on residential property was fixed at

[3]Nova Scotia, Royal Commission on Provincial Development and Rehabilitation, *Report* (1944), p. 46.
[4]*Ibid.*, p. 53.

35 mills in 1942. Increased revenues have had to be found by raising the business rate, which was 101.7 mills in 1953. Personal property continues in form to be taxed in most other municipalities, although there appears to be a trend towards a household tax, as yet unauthorized by statute, in lieu of the personal property tax on residents.

A wealth of material on recent provincial-municipal developments in Nova Scotia, and in other provinces as well, is contained in the excellent report prepared in 1949 for the Government of Nova Scotia by D. C. Rowat, Director of Research of the Nova Scotia Municipal Bureau.[5] This survey grew out of a provincial-municipal conference held at Halifax in 1947. Pending its completion the province in 1947 relieved the municipalities of any contribution towards road maintenance by repealing the highway poll and property taxes, except the property tax in rural municipalities. It also relieved the local governments of all costs for the special treatment of tuberculosis patients and the mentally ill. In 1948 existing payments to municipalities were increased from $150,000 to $410,000 through a per capita grant of 150 per cent of the highest amount of revenue raised by any city, town, or rural municipality under the taxes suspended by the Dominion-provincial tax agreement, and in 1949 this annual grant was further increased to $600,000. In the same year a 50 per cent increase in hospital grants was made.

No action had been taken up to mid-1954 to implement the major recommendations of the Municipal Bureau report. Press reports indicated that a provincial-municipal conference was held at Halifax early in 1952, the first since 1947. The Union of Nova Scotia Municipalities pressed strongly for direct provincial grants towards a substantial increase in teachers' salaries. At the conference, however, the provincial Premier, Hon. A. L. MacDonald, left this issue entirely with the municipalities, but promised a percentage increase in the per capita payments to local governments equal to the anticipated increase in the guaranteed minimum payment under the new tax agreement with the Dominion. A more liberal scheme of tax payments to municipalities by the Maritime Telegraph and Telephone Company was also promised. Both these promises were subsequently implemented.

As in other provinces educational finance is an ever pressing issue. The appointment of a Commission to enquire into educational matters in March, 1953, reflects the growing concern of provincial authorities, and may result in significant changes. The Commission began public hearings in March, 1954, and its report appeared late in the same year.

[5]*The Reorganization of Provincial-Municipal Relations in Nova Scotia.*

New Brunswick

Provincial

The important development in New Brunswick in the post-war period was the introduction of a retail sales tax in 1950 under the Social Services and Education Tax Act. As in other provinces employing this tax it quickly became a major source of revenue, although a reduction in rate from 4 per cent to 3 per cent in 1954 will lessen its importance in the future. The gasoline tax was increased in 1947 by 3 cents, bringing the rate up to 13 cents per gallon, and in 1954, concurrently with the reduction in sales tax, was raised to 15 cents per gallon. The province abandoned its levies for road construction in rural areas under the Highways Act in 1945.

The substantial increase in tax burden imposed by the retail sales tax was contrary to the advice of an officially appointed Committee on Reconstruction, of which N. A. M. MacKenzie was chairman. Its *Report*, issued in 1944, was devoted mainly to the economy of the province, but also contained some observations on the future prospects for provincial taxation. On the whole it took an even gloomier view than the Nova Scotia commission: "On the revenue side," it stated, "it is submitted that the upper limits of taxable capacity in New Brunswick, as far as the provincial administration is concerned, have been reached. While it is difficult, if not impossible, to measure the incidence of the tax burden, and to place any accurate limits on taxable capacity, there are good grounds for positive statements regarding limits within the framework of provincial jurisdiction and administration."[6] Of taxes on surpluses, such as profits taxes, it said: "Taxes on surpluses cannot be made to yield much revenue, simply because the federal government is already exploiting this field heavily." Nor was there much hope from other taxes: "Taxes on consumption and costs are already very high, and it is doubtful if the economy could tolerate further increases in the long run."[7]

It appeared, therefore, that finances for the major post-war reconstruction programme would have to come from the Dominion. The *Report* urged that the Dominion should assume fiscal and administrative responsibility for all social services, that financial assistance should be given by the Dominion for highway construction and the raising of educational standards, and that in return for the transfer of the major direct tax fields to it the Dominion should pay in addition the National Adjustment Grants recommended by the Rowell-Sirois Commission.

[6]*Report* (1944), pp. 230–1. [7]*Ibid.*, p. 233.

Municipal

In the New Brunswick municipalities the long-term trend away from personal property taxes on business is still working itself out. In Saint John and Fredericton such taxes were replaced by other levies in 1936 and 1944. In 1942 Moncton adopted a rental value tax on both residential and business properties. In 1947 Saint John introduced for retailers and wholesalers a business tax based on a percentage of turnover of the previous year. Poll taxes continue to be a widely used source of revenue, one-sixth of the municipal taxes commonly being raised in this manner. In 1952 Saint John was authorized to charge a "city services tax" not exceeding $20 in lieu of the prevailing $12 poll tax.

In 1948 Fredericton repealed its personal property levy and substituted specific taxes on motor vehicles only, following recommendations of a special Commission, of which J. R. Petrie was chairman.[8] The motor vehicle tax was $3 on motorcycles, $10 on passenger automobiles, and $100 on buses. Other recommendations of the Commission have also been implemented. Under the City of Fredericton Assessment Act, 1948, the poll tax was increased to $15 for every male over 21 not paying the occupancy tax and left at $6 on every other resident. Housewives whose husbands pay the poll tax and old age pensioners are exempt. The occupancy tax applicable to tenants was revised to apply to the actual rent paid if greater than 10 per cent of the assessed value, and the business tax was increased through upward revision in the percentage of assessed value to which it applied. The classification of rates was also broadened.

With the advanced development of income and corporation taxes in New Brunswick municipalities their suspension under the tax rental agreement between the province and the Dominion has meant a substantial revenue loss. The province has compensated for this by general grants. Under the Wartime Agreements these were fixed at $1,384,410 a year, but in 1947 the total was increased to $2,056,000. When the sales tax was imposed in 1950 it was indicated in the budget speech that the revenue might be shared with the municipalities and school boards, but no evidence has been found that this was done. The province has been increasing its share of educational costs, both for construction and maintenance, in the post-war period. Of ten million dollars spent on education in 1950 in the province approximately one-third came from the provincial government—twice the share of two decades ago. The Country School Finance Act (under which a county

[8]Commission to Investigate Taxation in the City of Fredericton, *Report* (1947).

levy is made to provide a minimum educational programme, expenditures in excess of that minimum being paid for out of local taxation) and the Rural School Assistance Act have brought rapid improvements in rural education. With an increase in grants in 1951 designed to bring the provincial share of operating costs up to 40 per cent for towns and cities and 50 per cent for counties the total provincial share of current educational costs will no doubt have exceeded 40 per cent. Counting in capital grants it would probably be as much as one-half.

In 1945 the provincial government took over the full expenses of hospitalizing tuberculosis patients in the province and reduced the municipal payments towards the support of mental patients. Grants are made to towns and cities for winter road ploughing and in rural areas the total cost is carried by the province.

As in the other provinces the lack of uniform standards in property assessment has marred the use of this index of local "tax potential" as a basis for grants. The provincial and municipal authorities have therefore been devoting increasing attention to the introduction of uniform methods. An Association of Assessing Officers was organized in 1944, and the municipal division of the Department of Education and Municipal Affairs has set up an annual assessors' school and in other ways has improved methods of assessment. The principal impetus behind this movement has been the consolidation of schools into the "county unit," with school taxes imposed over the county area. Equalization of parish assessments for this purpose has been done hitherto through the county chief assessor and through the county board of valuators. Where a town within a county made its own assessments, however, its values and procedures were more often than not different from the rest of the county.

Recommendations on many of these matters were made in 1951 by the Royal Commission on Rates and Taxes, of which R. T. Love was chairman.[9] Most of these still remained to be implemented three years later. In the realm of municipal taxation probably the most significant proposal was that the personal property tax on stock-in-trade finally be abandoned in all municipalities and replaced by a business tax. Like Nova Scotia the province was also in 1954 seeking new light on the cost of education through a Royal Commission on School Financing.

Quebec

Provincial

Quebec, like Ontario, in the absence of a new agreement with the

[9]Royal Commission [on the] Rates and Taxes Act, *Report* (1951).

Dominion, was free in 1947 to reintroduce taxes on personal income and on corporations. The post-war tax structure is therefore very similar to that suspended by the Wartime Tax Agreements in 1940. A corporation profits tax was reinstated at a 7 per cent rate, as compared with the pre-war 5 per cent. Place of business taxes were renewed at the pre-war rates, and the tax on paid-up capital was reinstated at 1/5 of 1 per cent, or double the pre-war rate of 1/10 of 1 per cent. Taxes on insurance companies were also renewed, at the pre-war rates. The provincial personal income tax levy, which had been in effect only in 1939 and 1940, was not immediately revived. However, in the spring of 1954 the provincial legislature enacted a new measure, modelled on the federal act, to tax personal income in the province for the years 1954, 1955, and 1956. The rate of tax was higher under the measure than the credit of 5 per cent allowable under the federal law—on average the rates were about 15 per cent of the federal—although the announcement by the federal government early in 1955 that it would replace the 5 per cent credit with a reduction of 10 per cent gave promise that most of the overlapping would be removed. Revenue from this new tax, estimated at $22 to $25 million a year, was to be used to support education and for other purposes.

Apart from its significance as marking a sharp change in recent fiscal development in Canada the new Quebec income tax was notable in that its imposition preceded the report of a Royal Commission that had been established to advise the provincial authorities on matters of this kind. Known from its president, Mr. Justice Thomas Tremblay, as the Tremblay Commission,[10] this enquiry was still in the midst of its public hearings in the spring of 1954, when the new tax was enacted.

Another feature of Quebec taxation has been the sharp increase in gasoline taxes. In 1947 the 8 cent rate was increased to 11 cents per gallon, and in 1950 a second increase of 2 cents brought the rate to 13 cents per gallon.

A measure of relief under the provincial succession duty for beneficiaries in the direct line was introduced in December, 1951, at a fall-winter session of the legislature. The law before this amendment exempted bequests to such beneficiaries only if the total estate was $10,000 or less. If it exceeded that amount the estate was dutiable in full. Under the amendment the $10,000 was altered to become a deduction from the amount of the estate passing, the effect being that only the excess over $10,000 is taxable, although an upper limit restricts this concession to estates under $50,000. At the same time the ad-

[10]Royal Commission of Inquiry on Constitutional Problems (1953).

ditional exemption allowed to a preferred beneficiary of $1,000 for each child under 21 years of age was increased to $1,500 for each child under 25 years of age.

Since 1946 provincial taxing powers have been put to interesting use under the Progress of Education Act. This legislation imposed taxes of 15 cents per cord of wood cut for the manufacture of pulp or paper by every holder of timber limits or owner of wooded territories and 15 cents per 1,000 kilowatt hours of electricity generated by any owner or lessee of a power site in the province. In 1947 there were added taxes of ⅓ of 1 per cent on the paid-up capital of petroleum refining and telephone companies in the province, telephone companies having a capital of less than $1 million being exempt. The proceeds of these taxes—about $3 million—along with an annual contribution of $2.8 million from the Hydro-Electric Commission and one-half the revenues from the provincial retail sales tax, are set aside in an Education Fund created by the Act. This Fund is used to meet payments of interest and principal on debts of school commissions assumed by the province under a general reform of school financing. Under this plan the province offered to assume the debts of school commissions incurred on or before April 17, 1946, in accordance with conditions set out in the Progress of Education Act. By the end of 1950 almost all of the 1,051 school commissions eligible for this offer had accepted it, and more than 95 per cent of the 1946 school debt, in an amount exceeding $100 million, had been assumed by the province. Out of the revenues of the Education Fund a substantial amount of the debt issued by the Quebec Municipal Commission to refinance the assumed school debts has been paid off. Increased grants to school commissions have also been paid in recent years from the fund. In 1948, for example, school grants, mainly for construction and teachers' salaries, were increased about 20 per cent. In 1951 the financing problem of school boards was alleviated by a provision that the payment of the grant for teachers' salaries would in future be made as an advance rather than as a refund.

Municipal

The distinctive feature of the Quebec municipal tax system today is the extensive use of retail sales taxes, revenues from which account for from 15 to 25 per cent of total tax receipts. The Quebec municipalities stand alone in this respect, and it will be recalled that Montreal was the first jurisdiction of any sort to levy a retail sales tax in Canada (in 1935). Administered by the province, these taxes apply over broad areas of urbanized population rather than simply within municipal boundaries. Collections are made over the whole area and receipts are allocated to the municipalities on the basis of collection, or, where that is not feasible, on the basis of population. By 1954 a tax at a 2 per cent rate was being charged in all important urban areas in Quebec, the notable exception being Hull, where the proximity to Ottawa in Ontario probably rules out the use of such a tax.

The sales tax has also been used, along with increased educational grants from the province, as a means of bolstering the revenues of several municipal school commissions. The Montreal School Commission was first given permission in 1949 to receive the proceeds of a 1 per cent rate levied in addition to the total of 4 per cent imposed by the province and municipality, and in 1950 this right was extended to the Catholic School Commission in Quebec City. School commissions in other municipalities have since been granted similar permission, so that in total a 5 per cent retail tax is payable in many urban centres in Quebec.

Despite the prominence of the retail sales tax the real property tax is still the largest single source of tax revenue for local governments. In the smaller municipal units—villages and towns where no sales tax is levied—it provides the bulk of the revenue. The same is true of the smaller school boards, which total almost 1,800. Such school boards may levy and collect their own tax directly from property owners or may require the local municipal corporation to collect it on their behalf. In practice many boards collect their own taxes, although the municipal assessment is used for this purpose. In Quebec (as in Ontario) the counties, having responsibility mainly for certain courthouses and registration buildings and county roads, bridges, and streams, obtain their revenues through a levy on the municipal corporations within their boundaries, both urban and rural, in proportion to their assessment of taxable real estate.

A distinctive feature of municipal government in Quebec is the religious parish. Under the Parish and Vestry Act authority is granted for the appointment of trustees in a parish through commissioners who have jurisdiction over a diocese. Such trustees are appointed to carry out, under supervision, the construction and maintenance of a church, sacristy, or presbytery, and are given authority to make a levy on the real property of Catholic owners in the parish in the amount necessary to carry out such work. In effect, therefore, a real property tax is used as the means of providing a formal and systematic contribution to the construction and maintenance of religious buildings.

As in other provinces the provincial authorities have paid increasing attention in recent years to the improvement of assessing methods. Representatives of the Department of Municipal Affairs have visited most of the 60 or 70 larger centres and are attempting with some success to impress councils, officials and taxpayers. A re-assessment in Montreal, which was to have come into effect in 1954, encountered such strong opposition that the city fathers postponed its introduction for at least a year. Early in 1955 the Paquette Commission proposed an equalization for Metropolitan Montreal, but the fate of this proposal will depend on the reception of its larger plans for a metropolitan government.

Other taxes that may be imposed in the villages and rural municipalities include a poll tax of $1 on males over 21, a tax of 5 per cent on rents paid by tenants and a tax not exceeding 1/10 of 1 per cent on inventories of merchants. In practice few village or rural municipalities use these sources, but some revenue is derived from specific business taxes and licences, which may not exceed $100, and from amusement taxes, which may be imposed at a 12½ per cent rate, being a 10 per cent basic rate plus a surtax of 25 per cent. The municipality is entitled to keep half the 10 per cent rate and 2 per cent of the surtax, the balance going to the province.

It is in the larger towns and cities that supplementary tax sources are used most extensively. Business taxes, levied either as a fixed charge or on the rental value of the premises, are general, and several cities levy occupancy taxes on tenants. In Montreal the business tax rate was increased from 10 per cent to 11 per cent in 1951, and there is a monthly tax of 25 cents on each telephone line and 10 cents for each extension, both of which have been in effect since 1940. The attempts of Quebec City to bolster its tax sources in 1951 with a bevy of new charges attracted dramatic attention because of "strikes" on the part of the business community, and in general failed to achieve necessary provincial support. However, revenue from an increase from 15 per cent to 20 per cent in the business tax rate and a grant of $250,000 in lieu of taxes on its property from the provincial government no doubt eased the city finances somewhat.

Ontario

Provincial

The immediate post-war provincial tax pattern in Ontario was very similar to that of Quebec. Having abstained, like Quebec, from renewing its tax agreement with the Dominion in 1947, it was free to reimpose any of its pre-war taxes. These were all revived with the exception of the personal income tax. A corporation profits tax was levied for the years 1947 to 1951 at a rate of 7 per cent as compared with the pre-war rate of 5 per cent, and the insurance premium taxes were reduced slightly; other changes were insignificant.

The province made a gesture towards a personal income tax in 1950 when it enacted statutes authorizing both a tax levy (equal to 5 per cent of the federal tax) and a collection agreement with the federal government. The federal government was unreceptive to suggestions that it collect the tax on behalf of the province and the levy was not proclaimed. The province appeared to have set its face against the new federal tax agreement offer made in 1950, but in August, 1952, Premier Frost announced that he had decided to sign. (See chapter 33.) A special session of the legislature in the fall passed the enabling legislation, and the agreement was signed on October 29. Its main effect was to withdraw, for the years 1952 to 1956 inclusive, the 7 per cent profits tax and the corporation taxes on places of business and paid-up capital. The province elected to retain its succession duties, suffering a deduction from its compensation under the agreement as an offset.

Ontario followed the general trend in 1947 and assumed the full amount of the former Dominion gasoline tax. Beyond this 3 cent increase, which brought the tax to 11 cents per gallon, there had been no further change to mid-1954. Ontario was one of the provinces, however, which took advantage of the repeal of the federal amusement tax in 1948. No amusement tax had been collected by the province since 1937 and the repeal of the Dominion levy provided an opportunity of returning to this field. The new tax was at a 20 per cent rate, applied to admissions in general and to cabaret and night club charges, and the proceeds were set aside (as provided in the Hospital Tax Act under which it was levied) for grants to Ontario hospitals. The rate was reduced to 15 per cent in 1950 and to 12½ per cent in 1951, and receipts now go into the general funds of the province, the original earmarking plan having been abandoned in 1950. The provincial take from race-track betting has also been revised periodically in recent years. In 1950 the pari-mutuel bets tax was increased from 10 per cent to 12½ per cent; in 1951 graduated rates were substituted which had the effect of reducing the total charge; in 1953 a flat rate tax of 8 per cent was restored, and in 1954 the flat rate was reduced to 7 per cent.

A significant step was taken by the province in 1949 under its succession duty legislation. The exemption granted for estates passing to beneficiaries in the direct line was increased from $25,000 to $50,000. The effect was to relieve many moderate sized estates entirely from tax and to bring the Ontario exemption for this class of estate up to the federal level. The "notch" created by estates just over the $50,000 was relieved by a further amendment in 1953.

A sizable increase was made in the provincial tax on mining in 1947. The graduated rates under the mining profits tax, which applies to mining profits in lieu of the general profits tax, were raised respectively from 3, 5, and 6 per cent to 6, 8, and 9 per cent. In 1950 the province broke new ground in forestry taxation by introducing a tax on logging profits, calculated in accordance with an elaborate formula. The tax applies to all companies cutting logs, including pulp and paper companies, and is levied at a rate of 9 per cent.

Two recent royal commissions, devoted respectively to the problems of mining and forestry, are indicative of the key position of natural resources in the wealthiest of the Canadian provinces. The first, of which N. C. Urquhart was chairman, was on mining, and made its report in 1944.[11] Among its observations on many problems affecting the industry the Commission had some to make on taxation. For the most part these were hardly relevant to provincial taxation, however, since the Commission appeared to regard the Dominion as the principal offender, and addressed most of its recommendations to the federal income tax. It urged that the federal depletion allowance of 33⅓ per cent for the company and 25 per cent for the shareholder should be raised to 50 per cent for both. The tax paid by mines under the Ontario Mining Tax Act should be allowed as an expense under the Dominion income tax, on the grounds that it is a royalty. (Since 1947 it has been so allowed.) The incentive allowance granted by the Dominion during the war for "off-property" exploration expense should be made a permanent part of the tax law. (It is not yet permanent, but in fact was still being allowed in 1954.) Finally, the discouraging effect of high tax rates on risk-taking in the exploration for and exploitation of natural resources was emphasized, and a plea made for a "sound" post-war federal tax policy for mining.

Regarding provincial taxation the Commission proposed that the tax on mineral lands be increased from 5 cents to 10 cents per acre, that authority be given the provincial government to suspend the tax on gas production in designated areas by order in council, that the deduction of the federal income tax as an expense in calculating the

[11]Royal Ontario Mining Commission, *Report* (1944).

Ontario mining tax be discontinued, that certain other steps be taken to increase municipal revenues from mining, and that the province consider to what extent investment in mining might be suffering discouragement from the imposition of succession duties.

The forestry commission (Howard Kennedy, Commissioner) issued its report in 1947.[12] It dealt mainly with means of improving the efficient use of forestry resources, and had less to say about the complex problems of forestry taxation. It made significant proposals, however, for simplification of the system of stumpage and other charges made for the use of provincial forest resources. These were contained in the following paragraphs:

> In the case of other industries such as iron-ore mining, the producer does not quote different selling prices depending upon the ultimate destination of the product, whether it be used for making ploughshares or rails, pen nibs or battleships, but treats all users alike. I consider the Government should similarly standardize its stumpage rates per cubic unit of any given species, regardless of the final disposal of the timber. Natural economic forces would then come into play and the logs or bolts would automatically find their best market.
>
> I am certain that the method of levying government charges on forest operations could be simplified and improved. I recommend that, instead of several different assessments, only two be applied.
>
> One of these, which might be termed "forest rental", would cover all items of expense which continue regardless of the size of the annual cut. It would include the revenues necessary for the maintenance of staffs at Headquarters and in the field, together with the cost of their various activities such as research, forest protection (including fire fighting), air service, etc. Needs could be estimated with accuracy and rentals set for a period of five or more years. I suggest that any portions of the estimated fire fighting costs remaining unexpended in a particular year should be carried forward to succeeding years within the period, as a cushion against disaster. At the end of the period a rebate should be made or, if a deficit exists, the assessment for the ensuing period should be raised to reimburse the Treasury.
>
> The other charge might be called "stumpage" and would include government revenue for timber cut and all items dependent upon the quantity of wood cut. Zones of special stumpage rates could, if necessary, be established to take care of wide differences in operating conditions or for other reasons such as Government tolls on roads or for other improvements constructed for limit holders at public expense. Variations of this kind should only be permitted on the broadest possible basis, such as differentiating between timber on watersheds draining into the Great Lakes and timber on watersheds draining into James Bay or Hudson Bay, with no effort made to adjust differences between individual stands or operators. Endless argument and inconsistencies would result if the basis were to be narrowed.

[12]Ontario, Royal Commission on Forestry, *Report* (1947).

> Stumpage rates could properly be raised or lowered in conformity with the economic cycle applying to forest industries. I see no reason why industries, which in past times of stress have applied for and received rate-reductions from the Department, should not, within reason, share periods of prosperity with the same Department. There are sound arguments for raising provincial charges on timber in times of high federal taxation on industrial profits. While there is no quarrel with the idea that the Federal Government should derive such benefits in wartime, I point out that low provincial stumpage rates are reflected in enhanced federal revenues from taxes on profits and excess profits.[13]

At the beginning of 1955 no significant change had yet been made in the general scheme of forestry charges, although signs of continuing provincial study and concern were evident in the issuance of a white paper on forestry in February, 1954.

Municipal

There has hardly been a single significant change in municipal taxation in Ontario in the post-war years. Municipal tax revenues are drawn almost exclusively from the real property tax, levied on 100 per cent of the assessed value of both land and improvements, and a business tax, levied on varying percentages of the same assessment. School boards derive their tax revenues from property taxes on the municipal assessment which are collected for them by the municipal corporation or township.

In Ontario each city, town, or village is a school section and taxes are levied for both school and local purposes within the boundaries of the corporation. In rural areas school sections depend on the township for their tax revenues. In each township the yield of a uniform levy is allotted to teachers' salaries, and in addition a section rate is levied in each school section within the township to meet the individual requirements of the section board. In recent years the trend has been towards township school areas, with unified control over elementary education throughout the whole township. In this way over half the former school sections have been absorbed into the larger units. The same broadening out of jurisdiction and taxation is taking place in the case of high school districts, which normally contain several townships.

The county, an intermediate level very similar to that of Quebec, controls certain court-houses, jails, registration buildings, roads, bridges, homes, etc. It derives its revenues from a levy on the municipal corporations within its boundaries in proportion to their assess-

[13] *Ibid.*, pp. 180–1.

ments. For many of these expenditures the county (or township) also receives substantial grants from the province.

The municipal income taxes have remained in limbo. The personal income tax was repealed in 1936, and the tax on corporations last applied in 1943, having been repealed under the Wartime Tax Agreement and not reinstated. Furthermore the Tax Rental Agreement signed by the province in 1952 effectively ends any chance of revival of such taxes before 1957. Poll taxes are rare, and there is no personal property tax. Since 1935 a moderate revenue has been received from the province from the sharing with the municipality of 20 per cent of the revenue from the gallonage tax and from the licensing of beverage rooms within the municipality. A minor change which affected only two or three municipalities that were employing the levy was the repeal of the mortgage tax in 1953.

As in every other province the problems of municipal and educational finance were receiving increasing attention in Ontario. At the time of writing the whole area of provincial-municipal relations was still being studied by a provincial committee, of which H. J. Chater was chairman.[14] The launching of this study was the culmination of many developments, including a Provincial-Municipal Conference in 1948, various apparently unsuccessful attempts of the provincial authorities to arrive at an acceptable basis of grants for municipal and educational purposes, the contentious report of the Royal Commission on Education[15] (the Hope Commission), and the emergence of metropolitan problems in their most acute form in the Toronto region. The inauguration of a federal form of metropolitan regional government in 1954 in the Toronto area represented an interesting attempt to cope with the most urgent of these problems, and preliminary reports of the Committee[16] proposing a schedule of per capita grants have been immediately implemented as a device for providing provincial assistance to the new entity. However, general relations between levels of government in the rapidly changing Ontario economy are in a state of flux, and it is doubtful if the Committee's report can provide more than a general scheme of approach. But even this will be a help to the provincial government, since its post-war relations with the municipalities have been lacking in any guiding principle. The abandonment of the former general one mill subsidy was dictated by the growing inequality of assessments among the municipalities, but the conditional

[14]Ontario Provincial-Municipal Relations Committee.

[15]Royal Commission on Education in Ontario, *Report* (1950).

[16]*First Report*, December 19, 1952; *Second Report*, February 4, 1953.

grants for police, fire, and other services which were introduced as a replacement encountered almost universal hostility from municipal councils. As a result the most recent trend has been towards per capita grants graded with the population of the municipality, the larger the population the larger the per capita grant. Educational grants have been based on more complicated formulae, too detailed to discuss here.

In 1954 there was evidence from the interim reports of the Provincial-Municipal Committee and from partial measures actually implemented that the province might finally attempt to evolve a grants system in which per capita payments and a provincial uniform assessment are both factors. A system of per capita payments had already been introduced at the time of writing, but what role would be finally taken by uniform assessments, if any, remained obscure.[17]

Several municipalities have undergone complete reassessment in recent years. The most ambitious undertaking of this sort was the assessment by the Greater Toronto Assessment Board on a uniform basis of the property in thirteen municipalities in metropolitan Toronto, preparatory to the establishment of the metropolitan government. The provincial authorities in Ontario have also been working in various ways towards improving and equalizing assessments. The Department of Municipal Affairs now has a staff of assessment experts who train local assessors in their own municipality without charge.

The problem of equalization for the county assessment is a chronic one. As mentioned earlier, provision for such equalization was made in the Assessment Act of 1850. In 1866 county councils were authorized to appoint valuators to carry out an equalization of local assessments. In 1904 these valuators were given power to inspect and value from 5 to 8 per cent of the lands in a municipality to establish a basis for adjusting the local assessment. This system apparently never worked satisfactorily, and in 1940 provision was made for a county assessor, with authority to make uniform the preparation of assessment rolls by the municipalities in the county, to supervise the local assessment, and to provide advice to local assessors, rather than simply to make an adjustment of existing local assessments to obtain rough uniformity. In 1944 the county valuators were abolished and the report of the county assessor made the basis of the equalization of assessment.

[17]For further discussion of problems facing Ontario municipalities see *Submission to the Committee on Provincial-Municipal Relations*, by the Citizens Research Institute, Toronto, and also *Municipal Finance* (1950).

A significant step was taken in 1947 with the establishment of an Assessment Branch in the Department of Municipal Affairs to assist municipal assessors with local problems. This new branch has been active in furthering efforts to produce uniform assessment procedures and in improving equalization for county levy purposes. The County Assessor is a key figure in this development.

Another factor leading towards a degree of uniformity is the scheme introduced in 1952 for payments of amounts in lieu of taxes on certain provincial administrative properties. These properties are to be assessed by the Department of Municipal Affairs on the basis prevailing in the individual municipality. Indirectly the Department may thus be enabled to influence the adoption of greater uniformity than now prevails.

MANITOBA

Provincial

Comparative stability has been the key-note to post-war provincial taxation in Manitoba. The gasoline tax was increased 2 cents per gallon (to 9 cents) in 1947, and in 1948 the amusement tax was increased from 10 per cent to 25 per cent, following suspension of the federal levy, but in 1953 was reduced to 17½ per cent. The province has been striving for a more rational system of charges for its natural resources, the trend being towards the replacement of volumetric royalties with taxes based on profits. In 1954 a producing areas tax was enacted, oil fields of some promise having been discovered in the province the previous year.

Municipal

Mention was made earlier of special taxes imposed in Winnipeg in 1932 on automobiles, liquor purchases, and gas and electricity bills. The automobile and liquor levies were dropped in 1942, but the charges on gas and electricity are still in effect at rates of 2½ per cent on domestic consumption and 5 per cent on commercial. Apart from these special taxes the revenues of Manitoba municipalities are derived primarily from taxes on land and improvements, the latter assessed at two-thirds of value, except in rural municipalities, where farm buildings are exempt. Business taxes are on the rental value basis, and a permissible alternative tax on personal property of businesses is sometimes used. Poll taxes are allowed only in urban centres, and even there are rare.

The provincial government has provided various forms of increased assistance to local units since the end of the war to relieve pressure on municipal budgets. In 1947, following a Provincial-Municipal Conference the province announced that it would pay annually to the municipalities one-half the increase it obtained in the guaranteed minimum payments under its tax agreement with the Dominion. The increase was \$5½ million, and the amount payable to the municipalities was therefore \$2¾ million. This annual amount of \$2¾ million is paid out through various grants towards specific services. The province also paid over to the municipalities one-half of a rebate it received in 1947 from the Dominion on relief debt, an amount of \$2.7 million, which it shared in proportion to municipal relief expenditures. In 1949 a levy on municipalities towards payment of old age pensions was repealed, provision was made for the payment of municipal business taxes by various government enterprises, and annual grants were instituted for assistance with medical and child welfare and relief. The province also assists the municipalities with grants towards local highways, and grants to hospitals.

The latest phase in the Manitoba developments arose out of the establishment of a Provincial-Municipal Committee under the chairmanship of Hon. Douglas Campbell, Premier of the province. The Committee was established following the submission by Winnipeg in 1948 of a brief prepared by Carl Goldenberg[18] and general expressions of dissatisfaction from other municipalities. In February, 1953, the report of the Committee was tabled,[19] and in view of its official sponsorship was immediately implemented. It touched on twelve main areas of provincial-municipal relations, in which the province either assumed responsibility or greatly increased its grants-in-aid. The main increases were in the grants for education, but increases were also made for welfare, market roads, and major bridges, and in grants in lieu of taxes on non-commercial provincial lands.

Manitoba, like the other western provinces, has progressed farther towards uniform and equalized assessments than the central and eastern provinces. Such equalization, it will be recalled, was necessary for the provincial property taxes, and, though the last of these taxes has recently been repealed, the mechanism for equalization has survived. In Manitoba the Assessment Commission, established in 1921, was replaced in 1948 by the Manitoba Equalization and Appeal Board. The functions of the Board are to establish equalized assessments

[18]*Brief on Provincial-Municipal Relations Submitted to the Government of the Province of Manitoba.*

[19]Provincial-Municipal Committee, *Report* (1953).

every two years for purposes of the municipal commissioner's levy and to hear assessment appeals. At the same time by an amendment to the Municipal Act there was created a Provincial-Municipal Assessment Branch of the Department of Municipal Commissioner to make or direct assessments in all municipal corporations or local government districts except cities and suburban areas.

Consolidation of school districts had not, by 1954, taken place to any extent in Manitoba.

Saskatchewan

Provincial

Saskatchewan assumed 2 cents of the repealed Dominion gasoline tax in 1947 (bringing its rate to 10 cents per gallon). A further increase of 1 cent per gallon was made in 1953. The most significant post-war change was the increase in the retail sales tax in 1950 from 2 per cent to 3 per cent. At the same time it was renamed the education and hospitalization tax. Revenues from the previous educational tax had been devoted exclusively to the support of education. The addition of the reference to "hospitalization" is a reflection of the inauguration in the post-war period of a plan of hospital insurance for residents of the province. Costs are financed partly from general provincial revenues and partly from a specific charge which until 1954 was $10 per person, with a maximum of $30 per family, but was increased in that year to $15 per person with a maximum of $40 per family.

Saskatchewan until 1953 had the distinction of imposing the only province-wide tax on property in Canada today, the public revenue tax. By legislation enacted at the 1952 session the tax was repealed from January 1, 1953.

In the area of natural resources the province completely revised its Mineral Taxation Act in 1948 by providing a new profits tax as an alternative to volumetric royalties. The recent discoveries of petroleum and uranium will undoubtedly attract further attention to the basis of taxation of resources.

Municipal

Saskatchewan municipalities conform with the general pattern in relying almost completely on property taxes. Vestiges of the single tax movement still remain, however, in the assessment of improvements at 60 per cent of value or less in villages, towns, and most cities and their complete exemption in rural areas. One source of revenue that has been left to the municipalities entirely is the amusement tax. It is usually imposed by the provincial governments elsewhere.

Recommendations on provincial-municipal relations and municipal taxation were made in 1951 in the *Report* of a provincial-municipal committee, of which G. E. Britnell was chairman.[20] Of these the principal so far implemented are the establishment of a permanent Municipal Advisory Commission and the repeal of the provincial property tax. The 1 cent per gallon increase in the gasoline tax in 1953 was also in partial fulfilment of one of the Committee's proposals. (The Committee proposed a 2 cent increase, and also that a 1 cent tax be levied on farm fuels.) Increased grants to tuberculosis sanatoria and higher grants to rural municipalities for bridge building also follow the *Report*'s recommendations.

To ensure uniformity throughout the province for the provincial property tax, all assessment, except in the larger cities, was done after 1943 by provincial assessors. Originally under the jurisdiction of the Assessment Commission, this work was transferred in 1948 to the Assessment Branch of the Department of Municipal Affairs. A province-wide reassessment has recently been completed, and it is the responsibility of a valuator, of which there is one in each of 13 assessment districts into which the province is divided, to keep the assessment for municipal purposes up to date. Undoubtedly this system will be continued even though the provincial tax has been repealed. Although the provincial assessors are directly responsible only for centres having less than 15,000 population, the 1949 provincial budget speech mentioned that Moose Jaw had requested that they revise its assessment roll.

ALBERTA

Provincial

The beneficent influence of that modern miracle worker, oil, loomed large in post-war Alberta. By 1954 the new resources discovered in 1948 had brought enough revenue to the province that on balance it was out of debt. This happy position gave partial confirmation of the earlier prediction of Premier Manning that the prospect of a tax-free debt-free province was not "too visionary."

Despite this bright outlook not all tax changes had been downward in Alberta in the post-war period. One significant reduction was made in 1947 with the abandonment of the social service tax (provincial property tax) which had been levied since World War I. In 1949 the

[20]Committee on Provincial-Municipal Relations, *Report* (1951).

wild lands tax was also repealed. During the same period, however, the gasoline tax was raised from 7 cents to 9 cents per gallon in 1947 and in 1951 from 9 cents to 10 cents per gallon, although in the latter year motor vehicles licences were reduced, and the 1 cent per gallon charge on farm fuels removed. The amusement tax was also increased in 1948.

In 1949 a new Mines and Minerals Act was introduced which revised the existing charges for mineral exploitation, and in 1951 a substantial increase in oil royalties was introduced.

A recent Privy Council decision regarding mineral rights in lands granted by the Dominion in certain periods prior to the assumption of provincial control in 1930 was of particular moment for Alberta. The effect of this decision is to remove any doubt as to the right of the three western provinces to levy royalties on petroleum or minerals discovered on such lands.[21]

In general, with the exception of the repeal of the provincial property tax, there had been no significant downward trend in provincial taxation to mid-1954.

Municipal

Municipal taxation in Alberta is distinguished by a greater reliance on assessment of personal property than anywhere outside the Maritimes. This tendency appears to be growing. Few marked changes occurred in the post-war period in the general outlines of the local tax system. An episode of the period was the revision of the Assessment Act in 1950 requiring that all lands, buildings, improvements, and personal property be fully assessed in all municipalities (except cities) for purposes of the school requisition, and giving the Director of Assessments authority to revise such assessment if necessary in the interests of equity. Reassessment of property values has been common in Alberta, and in 1951 seven cities were undergoing complete revision, in the case of Edmonton the first since 1933. The Provincial Director of Assessments was given authority in 1949 to carry out the assessing in any town, village, or municipal district, at the request of the local council.

Most of the problems of financial readjustment being encountered in other rapidly developing Canadian municipalities were to be found in post-war Alberta, some of them alleviated but others aggravated by the prosperity that has come with oil. In particular Edmonton has

[21]*Attorney-General for Alberta and another* v. *Huggard Assets Ltd. and Attorney-General for Canada and others*, [1950] A.C. 420.

suffered serious growing pains due to the combined influence of its proximity to the new oil fields and its strategic location as a point of departure to the developing north.

In dealing with these problems the provincial authorities, as elsewhere, sought the advice of a Royal Commission, which reported in 1948.[22] In this province the enquiry was conducted by the Deputy Minister of Municipal Affairs, J. W. Judge, after whom the report is known as the *Judge Report.* The authorities have gone far beyond the proposals in this report for grants and assistance, and today Alberta has a broad scheme of assistance involving outright grants and low interest rate loans for municipal and educational purposes.[23] Undoubtedly some further changes in provincial policies will result from the recommendations of the Royal Commission on Metropolitan Development of Calgary and Edmonton which was holding public hearings late in 1954.

One feature of the administrative structure in Alberta is worthy of mention. During the last decade the consolidation of school districts and municipal districts (rural areas) has gone ahead rapidly. Some 143 municipal districts have been consolidated into less than sixty units, and 3,720 school districts have also been reduced to less than sixty divisions. The Division Boards in charge of these large units administer the schools in place of the former school district boards, and charge the municipalities within their boundaries for the expenses.

Even more radical is the form of organization now being established under the Alberta County Act 1950. In this form of "county" government all the usual local functions in a rural area—municipal, school, hospital, etc.—are placed under one elected body, by contrast with the usual practice of establishing separate boards or councils. The new Alberta "county" has control over its own budget and levies its own taxes, again in distinction from the eastern type of county, which is dependent on a requisition on other bodies for its funds. Reports of the experience so far are generally favourable.

British Columbia

Provincial

British Columbia, like the other provinces, increased its gasoline tax in 1947, in this case by 3 cents per gallon. In 1948, after long and

[22]Royal Commission on Taxation, *Report* (1948).

[23]For a detailed description of post-war developments see E. J. Hanson, "Provincial Grants in Alberta," *Canadian Tax Journal* (Sept.-Oct., 1953).

careful study, the province took the step of imposing a retail sales tax, at a 3 per cent rate. In the same year the amusement tax was increased from 5 per cent to 25 per cent, the pari-mutuel bets tax was increased to 12 per cent, the coal and coke taxes, of long standing, were repealed, and a new Mining Tax Act, to replace the levy previously imposed in the Taxation Act, was enacted. No significant general changes were made in 1949, but in 1950 the amusement tax was reduced to 17½ per cent and the remains of the provincial poll tax, in recent years levied only where a municipal poll tax was not charged, was finally abandoned. No important changes in general tax sources were enacted in 1951 or 1952, but the new Social Credit Government put through several revisions in 1953 and 1954. The spring budget of 1953 (except for a reduction in motor vehicle licences) was held over for an election during the summer, in which the Social Credit party won a more secure majority, and was implemented at a fall session. The important changes included introduction of a logging profits tax (on the Ontario model) at a 10 per cent rate; a new tax of 1 per cent on timberland held under certain types of leases and licences; an increase from 4 per cent to 10 per cent in the mining profits tax; a tax of 10 per cent on liquor purchased in licensed premises and to all purchases in cabarets and night clubs and an increase to $1.00 (from 50¢) in the exemption for meals under the sales tax, which incidentally was renamed the social services tax. At the spring session of 1953 a reduction of 10 per cent in motor vehicle licences had been enacted; other changes were adopted also at the fall session affecting municipal taxes.

Like Saskatchewan, British Columbia in the post-war period inaugurated a province-wide plan of hospital insurance. This service has been financed from the proceeds of part of the sales tax revenue, from grants out of general revenues, and from premiums paid by residents of the province. At the outset of the plan in 1948 these premiums were $33 for the head of a family and $21 for a single person. In 1951 after the hospital insurance fund had shown substantial deficits on its operations, these rates were increased to $42 and $30 respectively, and the cost of the first ten days of hospitalization was to be paid by the patient to the extent of from $2.00 to $3.50 per day. In mid-1952, however, easier conditions permitted a reduction in rates. The $42 family charge was reduced to $39 and the $30 charge to $27. The daily charge for the hospitalization was maintained, but was converted to a flat $1 per day for every day spent in hospital in place of the former charge of $3.50 for the first ten days. The most drastic change was made in 1954, however, when the premiums were entirely abandoned and to provide revenue in their place the provincial sales tax was increased from 3 per cent to 5 per cent, where it stood at the time of writing.

Other changes at the 1954 session included the repeal of the 10 per cent cocktail lounge tax introduced at the previous session, the reduction of the amusement tax from 17½ per cent to 15 per cent, and the exemption of children's shoes and clothing from sales tax.

New trends in forestry taxation are gradually appearing as part of a forest management policy adopted following the 1945 *Report* on forest resources, (G. McG. Sloan, Commissioner).[24] The general tenor of this *Report* was that efficient utilization and sustained operation of the province's forest resources would succeed only if the operator, hitherto regarded as a transient reaper, were given a permanent interest in a timber area and encouraged by every means, including taxation, to maintain that area. The future objective should be "a regulated policy of forest management, leading eventually to a programme ensuring a sustained yield from all our productive land area,"[25] but to achieve this objective "new systems of tenure and taxation need to be formulated to encourage private forestry and to remove causes compelling liquidation."[26] The recommendations regarding provincial taxation were summed up in the following words: "It seems to me therefore, if private forestry is to be encouraged . . . then owners of revertible tenures should be permitted to retain these lands, when classified as best suited for the purpose of tree-farming, at a nominal annual license fee of 1 cent per acre, plus the fire-protection tax, and subject to a yield tax at 12½ per cent of prevailing stumpage values payable when the final crop, or any interim cutting thereof, is harvested."[27] The necessity for increased fire protection was stressed throughout the *Report*, but the Commissioner was of the view that the limit had been reached for obtaining the required finances through the fire-protection tax, then 6 cents per acre. He recommended that there should be a greater allocation of general forestry revenues for this purpose, and that "because of the benefits accruing to the people of Canada from the forests of this Province that the Dominion Government should shoulder some of the financial responsibility for the protection and conservation of this national asset."[28] The Dominion could also help the general cause of forest management in another way. "The practice of private forestry is an

[24]Royal Commission on the Forest Resources of British Columbia, *Report* (1945).

[25]*Ibid.*, p. 127. [26]*Ibid.*, p. 128. [27]*Ibid.*, p. 145. [28]*Ibid.*, p. 134.

important step toward the perpetuation of our forests. In my view therefore the Dominion Government should be prepared to facilitate this development by allowing the operator to charge annually current operations with all reasonable costs incurred during that year in the reforestation of logged-off lands under his control or management."[29]

Finally, the Commissioner pointed out a source of revenue which he thought the province should consider. A large tract of forests on Vancouver Island had been granted by the Dominion government to the Esquimalt and Nanaimo Railway Co., from lands originally conveyed to it by the province. Sections of this land had been sold by the railway company in the past without any return to the province. The Commissioner proposed that on future alienations by the company the province should charge a tax that would provide it with approximately the same return as would a royalty at the current rate.[30]

Important taxation changes pursuant to the *Report* were made in 1947 and 1951. The 1947 changes affected operations on Crown-owned forest land, which constitute about 90 per cent of the total. Under amendments to the Forest Act a new tenure called a "management licence" was introduced. Contracts were to be entered into to give effect to this form of tenure, and to provide as well for taxation concessions designed to encourage forest conservation.

The 1951 changes affected privately owned lands. The land tax charged under the Taxation Act on forest land was reduced from 3 per cent to 1 per cent for any area qualifying as "tree-farm land." This was defined as land which would find its best economic use under forest crop and on which there was (*a*) a stock of young growth not less than the standard set by the Forest Service or (*b*) an approved reforestation plan or (*c*) mature timber which would, according to an approved plan, be harvested on a sustained yield basis. Just as important as the reduction in rate was the new basis of valuation adopted for tree-farms. Hitherto the value of timberland had included the value of the timber stand on the land at the time of assessment. This practice, it was alleged, had tended to discourage conservation, because standing timbers represented a tax liability. The new basis, although in form a property tax, is in some respects a yield tax. The value of tree-farm land in the future is to be determined by capitalizing the annual net income from growing trees where there is an annual cut. Where there is a periodic cut the assessment will be determined as the present value of the future prospective net income. This basis of valuation, while presenting complex administrative

[29] *Ibid.*, p. 146.

[30] *Ibid.*, pp. 173–84.

problems, is thought to be more scientific and equitable than that previously used.

The provincial government also adopted the suggestion in the Sloan *Report* for a tax on future alienations of timber lands in the Esquimalt and Nanaimo Railway belt. The manner in which this was done was unusual. In February, 1946, it announced a tax of 25 per cent, payable only once, on the assessed value of land disposed of by the railway company on or after February 20, 1946. The assessed value for purposes of the tax was to be its actual value at the date of alienation, and was to include the value of the timber on the land. Issue was taken with this tax on various grounds by both the company and the Dominion government, and its validity was challenged in the courts. The province's action was sustained, however, in a judgment given by the Privy Council in 1950.[31]

The 1953 changes have been previously mentioned. These appear to stem mainly from a desire to obtain more revenue from the logging and lumber industries and to counteract allegedly favourable arrangements granted in years gone by for holding timber land under certain forms of lease.

A recent study has presented an informative analysis of the total burden of various forms of tax on timber lands in British Columbia.[32] The general conclusions of this study were that forest lands were paying taxes second only to improved lands, and several times the tax payable on coal lands, farm lands, and wild lands; that the level of timberland taxation has increased sharply in recent years, and that, as the Sloan *Report* had stated, existing methods of taxation were detrimental to the best use of the forest resources.

In submitting his first *Report* Commissioner Sloan had recommended that the whole matter of forest management be reviewed again after ten years. Late in 1954 the government announced that Mr. Justice Sloan himself had agreed to act as a Royal Commission to undertake this review.

Municipal

In the municipal realm undoubtedly a milestone in the post-war period was the introduction of a general business tax for the first time in Vancouver in 1948. British Columbia municipalities have been exceptional until recent years in not imposing such a tax, although

[31]*Attorney-General for British Columbia* v. *Esquimalt and Nanaimo Railway Co.*, [1950] A.C. 87.

[32]Lowell Besley, *Taxation of Crown-Granted Timberlands in British Columbia* (1951).

their business licences have been considerably higher than elsewhere in partial compensation for this fact. After serious consideration of the forms now in use in other Canadian cities and having regard to restrictions imposed on income and similar taxes by the tax agreement with the Dominion, the city selected rental value as the basis.[33] This tax has also been adopted by New Westminster, and probably would have been adopted generally had it not been for the generous assistance received by municipalities in the post-war period. This assistance undoubtedly has also enabled Vancouver and New Westminster to reduce their rates of tax from the 1948 levels of 8 per cent and 11 per cent to 6 per cent and 9 per cent respectively in 1951.

In recent years Vancouver has also adopted a revised approach to an old municipal tax problem—the taxing of the property of public utilities. Land and buildings owned by public utilities are assessed and taxed on the usual basis. But special "statutory assessments" have been provided in the governing legislation of most provinces for the pole-lines, cables, wires, and similar property of telephone, telegraph, electric light, and power companies, the mains and conduits of gas companies, and the tracks and wires of street railways. The common practice is to establish arbitrary "statutory" valuations on such property at a fixed amount per mile of lines, track, etc. Vancouver had followed this basis, but in 1947 the charter was amended to substitute a tax on gross revenues of public utilities—i.e., rental from subscribers within the city in the case of a telephone company, the revenues received from customers in the city in the case of a gas, electric light, or power company, and the fares received by a street railway within the city. The initial rate of tax was 1½ per cent. Undoubtedly the precedent for this change was found in Ontario, where telephone companies have been taxed on this basis for some years. It was adopted first in British Columbia under the Electric Power Act, 1945, which required the new government-owned Power Commission to pay to municipalities a tax of 3 per cent of its gross revenues from a municipality in lieu of the special assessments.

The poll tax has been attracting increasingly unfavourable comment from residents of British Columbia municipalities. Vancouver repealed its tax in 1951, and other cities have been following suit. It will be recalled that the provincial tax was abandoned in 1950.

[33]See R. M. Clark, *A Brief on the Proposed Business Tax By-law for Vancouver* (1948), and the same author on "The Municipal Business Tax in Canada," *Canadian Journal of Economics and Political Science*, (Nov., 1948), pp. 491–501, and the Royal Commission on Provincial-Municipal Relations (British Columbia), *Report*, chap. 6.

By far the most fundamental developments in municipal and school district revenues in the post-war period have followed from the *Report* by M. A. Cameron in 1945 on school financing[34] and the *Report* by H. Carl Goldenberg in 1947 on provincial-municipal affairs.[35] Because they preceded the enquiries in other provinces both these reports have exerted an important influence on all developments elsewhere. Regretfully a full discussion of their contents must be passed up here.

The Cameron *Report* was reflected in several amendments passed at the 1946 session of the legislature. Under amendments to the Public Schools Act in 1946, 77 large school districts were created where there had previously been about 650. A new system of school grants was also instituted; in general the grant was to be the difference between the yield of a 5 mill tax on the full value of land and on 75 per cent of the value of improvements, and a minimum cost of school operation. The extension of the school districts brought almost all rural land into a district and therefore subject to the district school tax, but in areas still remaining outside a 5 mill tax is collected by the province. With this change a 2 mill special land tax collected by the province on lands outside school districts since 1932 under the Taxation Act was removed.

In 1947 a significant move in the direction of personal property taxation was made by the inclusion, in the school assessment of rural areas and villages, of industrial and commercial machinery and fixtures. This beginning culminated with the extension in 1953 of the same basis of taxation to all areas for school tax purposes.

Amendments to the Public School Act have also provided for the appointment of a Commission to enquire into the whole problem of equalization of assessment. In 1948 the province set up an Assessment Equalization Board to investigate and recommend adjustment of assessment for purposes of school grants where an appeal was made to it by a certain number of ratepayers in a school district. This development culminated later in the passage of the Assessment Equalization Act, 1953, under the provisions of which an equalization was made in 1954 which is to be used for purposes of school taxes and grants in 1955.

There have been almost annual changes in the school grants. In 1948 general educational grants were raised and special aid exceed-

[34]Commission of Enquiry into Educational Finance, *Report* (1945).

[35]Royal Commission on Provincial-Municipal Relations (British Columbia), *Report* (1947).

ing $1 million was provided to rural school districts. Further special aid was given rural school districts in 1950, and the province borrowed $10 million to be used for school construction grants. *Ad hoc* grants were being increasingly used, and the rejection of the so-called "Rolston" formula in 1953 had left the future nature of the educational grants system in considerable obscurity for some time. However the 1955 budget speech established a new and more generous formula to take effect immediately.

Several important changes in provincial-municipal finances have taken place since the Goldenberg *Report* was submitted. The limit was removed from the motor vehicle grant and an increased share of certain social welfare expenses was assumed. The most important development, however, was of a different character. In 1948, as previously mentioned, the government took the step of imposing a 3 per cent retail sales tax, and of the proceeds of the tax the yield of 1 per cent was to be paid unconditionally to the municipalities. The municipal share of the tax is distributed on a per capita basis which takes account of school population as well as general population. The tax first came into effect in July, 1948, and it was expected that in a full year it would yield $12 million and that the municipalities would therefore receive $4 million. In fact, in the first full year in which it was in effect, the fiscal year ending March 31, 1950, receipts, after deduction of collection expenses, were nearly $25 million, and the municipalities therefore received over $8 million as their share. Undoubtedly at current levels of business activity the regular annual return to the municipalities will exceed $10 million. The municipalities were also to have received half the proceeds from the new tax of 10 per cent on liquor and night club purchases, but this prospect appears to have been removed by the subsequent repeal of the tax at the 1954 session. They were to continue to receive the yield of 1 per cent of the sales tax on its increase to 5 per cent at the same session, but in the drastic revision of school grants made in the 1955 budget both this grant and the grant from motor vehicle licences were abolished.

Of more permanent significance were the substantial increases in municipal licence charges enacted in 1953 (in many cases the new rates were double or more than double the old) and the amendment to the Municipal Act which permits any council to assess industrial and commercial machinery and fixtures for general municipal purposes as is being done under the Public Schools Act for educational purposes.

Part IX

SUBSIDIES AND FISCAL ARRANGEMENTS
1867-1954

31 SUBSIDIES

The First Seventy Years, 1867-1940

THE COURSE OF DEVELOPMENT of one aspect of Canadian fiscal arrangements, the taxing power, has been traced to its latest phase in the previous chapters. There remains but to examine the other main aspect—the intergovernmental subsidy payments. This will be done in considerably less detail, since the subsidy mechanism, while throughout Canadian history an ever present alternative to taxation, is nevertheless secondary to the main subject of this volume.

The review in the following pages will commence with 1868, the Confederation financial arrangements of the previous year having been described in an early part of this volume. The present chapter will trace developments from 1868 to the outbreak of World War II.

This period of some seventy years falls naturally into two subdivisions. The first sub-division covers the forty years to 1907, and the second the following thirty-odd years to World War II.

The year 1907 marked the climax of a continuous struggle to meet every problem that arose by fitting it as nearly as possible into the Confederation mould of grants, which came to be known in time as the "statutory subsidies." The general revision of that year fixed the basic pattern of statutory subsidies so firmly that there has been no important change in it since. Such minor changes as were made have been restricted to the one variable element in the pattern, the special grant. The second period brought experiments with payments outside the scope of statutory subsidies, including grants-in-aid of specific functions of government and heavy grants of assistance during the depression to the provinces and municipalities for relief and related purposes. Special grants to compensate for regional disabilities (some of which became statutory) were also more readily given than in the earlier period.

STATUTORY SUBSIDIES, 1868 TO 1907

Despite the declaration that the financial terms of the British North America Act were to be in full and final settlement, the ink had scarcely dried on the document before some of the provinces were clamouring for a new deal. The initial discontent was most acute in Nova Scotia, but anomalies created by the adaptation of the original terms to new provinces, the increase in provincial responsibilities beyond those contemplated by the Fathers of Confederation, and the slack budgets of the years of the Great Depression commencing in 1873 brought increasing pressure for a general revision, finally effected in 1907.

It will be recalled that immediately following Confederation the Dominion was faced with heavy financial outlays for railways—the Intercolonial in the east and the Canadian Pacific in the west—and that the financial problem thus presented was aggravated by the depression following 1873. As a result it reacted to provincial agitation for better terms with a series of compromises and stratagems reflecting the conflict between the political necessity for preserving the union and the financial stringency that dictated a cautious approach. On the whole a reasonably successful attempt was made to maintain in outward form the original financial terms, although increasing reliance on "special grants" represented a departure from the per capita equality for which the Fathers had striven. This departure was perhaps the price of preserving the union. It could have been badly shaken by an unyielding adherence to the original and exact terms of the financial arrangements. It was also in part the price for avoiding the imposition of provincial direct taxes, shunned in those provinces where they had not been in effect at Confederation. Of course this purpose was achieved only temporarily, since by 1907, when a major subsidy revision was made, most of the provinces had already been forced to tax successions and corporations. Subsidy revisions were inadequate to forestall this event permanently.

That the new union survived the period (not an easy one) is a credit to the statesmanship of the day as much as to the soundness of the terms of union. Thirty years later it emerged as a rounded-out Dominion of nine provinces, and it was under these conditions that, as the result of buoyant national development with the opening of the West and the emergence of the wheat trade, the Dominion was able to effect a general readjustment of the financial terms.

In the following pages a brief chronological survey is made of events leading up to this revision. (The general reader not wishing to follow developments in detail may skip these paragraphs and pick up the thread with the 1907 revision at page 517.)

1868: Early discontent centred in Nova Scotia, where a trade depression following abrogation of the Reciprocity Treaty with the

United States (1854–66), and a slump in business conditions after the Civil War, were laid at the door of Confederation. Substantial budget deficits prevailed. Urgent representations were made to the Dominion by A. W. McLenan outlining these and other grievances and specifically requesting an increase in debt allowance from $8,000,000 to $10,000,000. Joseph Howe's campaign for "Better Terms" was also stirring Nova Scotia to unrest.

1869: To meet the serious provincial financial position the Dominion increased the Nova Scotia debt allowance to the same per capita amount as that of New Brunswick ($27.77) giving a total of $9,186,756. At the same time an additional grant of $83,000 was given to Nova Scotia for ten years from July 1, 1867. (A similar special grant of $63,000 for ten years had been given to New Brunswick in 1867.) The effect of these two adjustments was to increase the annual payments from $325,000 to $465,000. This temporarily appeased Nova Scotia but brought protests from Ontario and Quebec against tinkering with the final terms of union in favour of the smaller provinces.

1870: The Dominion Government purchased the Northwest Territories, Rupert's Land, and Ungava from the Hudson's Bay Company for £300,000 and the Province of Manitoba was created and admitted to Confederation in the same year. Though there had been no previous provincial government an attempt was made to apply the same financial provisions as had been worked out for the older provinces. The province was given a debt allowance grant of $23,600 per annum (5 per cent on $472,000, being the Nova Scotia–New Brunswick rate of $27.77 on an estimated population of 17,000); a grant of $30,000 per annum in support of government, and $13,600 as a general grant (80 cents per capita), the latter to be increased with population until a population of 400,000 was reached, as in the final arrangement with Nova Scotia and New Brunswick. In total these grants amounted to $67,200, and were in full and final settlement. Crown lands in the new province were retained by the Dominion, for national purposes of settlement and transportation, contrary to the previous policy of leaving them with the provinces. This was the origin of the "natural resources" question that was to disturb relations between the Dominion government and the Prairie Provinces in later years.

1871: British Columbia entered the union. A debt allowance was given at a rate of $27.77, along with an annual grant of $35,000 for support of government and a general grant of 80 cents per capita on an assumed population of 60,000, the actual population probably being in the neighbourhood of 34,000. A condition of union was the construction of a transcontinental railway, and, in consideration of the transfer of lands twenty miles on either side of the railway right of way to the Dominion, the province was given an additional grant of $100,000 a year. This additional grant was also needed to bring the total to the amount of $216,000, approximately that estimated by the provincial authorities as being necessary for their purposes. The older provinces protested against the promise to construct the railway because of the higher taxes that would be required to meet its cost.

1873: Prince Edward Island was admitted to union; although represented at the early negotiations, the Island had turned strongly against union and had kept out until financial difficulties growing out of heavy railway financing forced a reconsideration in 1873. Because of the enormous increase in debt (from $3 per capita in 1864 to $41 per capita in 1873) the debt allowance was set at $50 per capita, as compared with $27.77 in the other Maritime Provinces. A grant of $30,000 per annum was given for support of government, and a grant of 80 cents per capita amounting to $75,000. Finally, an additional annual grant of $45,000 was allowed in compensation for the fact that about two-fifths of the former Crown lands had been alienated from the province and were owned by absentee landlords. These grants amounted in total to $193,000 a year. Provision was also made for a loan not exceeding $800,000 to enable the Island government to repurchase alienated Crown lands.

In the same year, New Brunswick protested that it could not meet its expenditures, that it was contributing disproportionately to Dominion customs revenue, that its people would not accept the imposition of direct taxes, and, finally that it had had to give up its right to collect timber export dues as a result of the negotiation with United States of the Treaty of Washington. The Dominion thereupon agreed to pay the province an additional annual grant of $150,000 per annum.

Also, in 1873, because of the difficulty of allocating the payment of 5 per cent interest on the excess of debt over the "debt allowance" granted Ontario and Quebec, the Dominion assumed the excess and revised the debt allowance of the other provinces (except P.E.I.) upward in the same proportion. This adjustment increased the payments to the other provinces under the "debt allowance" by $150,000 a year. (In 1884 this revision was made retroactive to 1867, and the resulting interest credits were added to the capital amount of the debt allowances.)

1874: The Dominion government under an enactment of Parliament was authorized to advance to any province funds for local improvements to the amount of the excess of the province's debt allowance over the actual debt assumed by the Dominion. Manitoba in particular made heavy drawings under this authority. (After 1885 passage of an act by the provincial parliament was necessary before the Dominion would make an advance.)

These first six years were significant. They brought subsidies into an even more prominent place in most provinces than they held at Confederation. By 1874 the following proportions of total revenue were derived from subsidies: New Brunswick, 92 per cent; Nova Scotia, 81 per cent; Prince Edward Island, 75 per cent; British Columbia, 62 per cent; Ontario and Quebec, 40 to 50 per cent. The adjustments following 1867 had increased the total annual Dominion payment by about $1 million.

For the next twenty years only minor upward adjustments were made. The heavy commitments assumed by the federal government for railways and the depression that commenced in 1873 and persisted for almost twenty years stiffened its resistance to provincial demands. Nevertheless some concessions were made.

1876: Manitoba protested that it was not receiving "equal" treatment with the other provinces because it received no special grant; under pressure the Dominion increased the population grant to the province by $26,700 in anticipation that the 1881 census would show an increased population.

1877: The special grants of $63,000 and $83,000 to New Brunswick and Nova Scotia respectively expired. They were not renewed.

1878–83: Prince Edward Island, Nova Scotia, and Manitoba continued to press for further aid, and in 1883 for the first time Quebec also entered a claim for an increased subsidy.

During this period the Maritime Provinces put forward a claim to a share of the $4,500,000 received by the Dominion from the United States for fishing privileges in Canadian waters under the Halifax Award. This claim the Dominion refused to recognize. Nova Scotia continued to argue the inadequacy of her basic subsidies during this period.

Manitoba argued needs based mainly on the rapid growth of the province and the resulting increase in government expenditures. Her claims were met by an addition of $15,900 to the grant of $26,500 given in 1876, and by a general revision in 1882 which increased the basic population grant to 80 cents on 150,000 of population instead of 17,000, raised the grant for government from $30,000 to $50,000, and also gave the province a new grant of $45,000 a year in lieu of lands alienated by the Dominion. These adjustments, to be effective for ten years, brought the total Manitoba subsidy to $230,000. (It had been $67,000 at Confederation.)

1884: As mentioned previously, the increased debt allowances of all provinces resulting from the adjustment of 1873 was extended back to 1867. Interest at 5 per cent per annum that the Dominion would have paid on the difference between the new debt allowances and the previous amounts, and interest on that interest, were added to the capital amount of the debt allowances themselves. These adjustments in total brought the per capita debt allowances to $32.43 and increased the annual grants by $360,000 (through increasing the amount on which the Dominion was paying interest at 5 per cent to the provinces).

1885: Manitoba subsidies were again increased; the annual payment under the debt allowance was increased by $148,000, and the lands grant from $45,000 to $100,000. These adjustments almost doubled the total grants to an amount of $443,000 in 1885–6. Provision was made for adjustment of the population subsidy on the basis of a quinquennial census and on estimates of the years between. Along with the increased grant for lands, all swamp land in the province and 150,000 acres of fair land for the support of a university were given to the provincial government.

1886: The Fielding Government was elected in Nova Scotia on a secession platform, and in May the legislature adopted a repeal resolution. When the Government failed to take any further steps the agitation declined.

1887: A conference at Quebec, attended by all provincial premiers except the premiers of Prince Edward Island and British Columbia, drew up a programme for a revised system of subsidies and presented it to the Dominion Government. The plan was not accepted.

1897: Requests from Prince Edward Island for increased aid in compensation for lack of Dominion government capital expenditures, for further communication facilities with the mainland, and for part of the Halifax Award, were met by a Dominion government appropriation of $180,000 for a further steamship, but by no other action.

1898: The Manitoba debt allowance was adjusted by restoration of $267,000 representing the cost of erecting Parliament Buildings, previously deducted under 1874 authority.

1901: An additional annual grant of $30,000 was paid to Prince Edward Island in recognition of insularity, lack of mineral wealth, etc.

1902: A second interprovincial conference, again called by the Premier of Quebec, urged adoption of revisions similar to those proposed by the 1887 conference. Arguments for increased payments were based on grounds of increase in Dominion revenues and rapid growth in provincial population. Ontario and Quebec particularly argued for revision of their population grants, which had not been increased since Confederation, being based on their 1861 population as agreed at the time of union.

1905: Alberta and Saskatchewan entered the union as provinces. They each received in total approximately $1,125,000, as follows:

(*a*) Debt allowances at $32.43 per capita (the rate to which all provinces had been raised by the 1884 adjustment) on populations of 250,000 apiece; annual payments were $405,375.

(*b*) An annual grant for government of $50,000 apiece.

(*c*) Population grants of 80 cents per capita on population as indicated by decennial and quinquennial census and estimates for years between increasing to a maximum of 800,000 population; initial annual payment was $200,000.

(*d*) Crown lands were retained by the Dominion, but compensation was paid on the basis of provincial population. Each province was to receive $375,000 per annum.

(*e*) An additional annual grant of $93,750 was given each province for five years for the construction of public buildings.

1906: Sir Wilfrid Laurier called a conference of provincial premiers to discuss statutory subsidies and other matters. All provinces joined in requesting better terms. The Dominion Government was particularly anxious to satisfy all provinces so that an arrangement could be made that would be final and unalterable. By this time the country had emerged from the twenty years' depression and the federal Government could well adopt a more generous attitude than in the earlier period when deficits were chronic.

1907: A revised scale of subsidies was enacted by an amendment to the British North America Act as a result of the conference of the previous year. Every effort was made by Laurier, the Prime Minister of the day, to have it understood that this was a "final" settlement; the resort to an amendment to the B.N.A. Act (all previous adjustments having been made by enactment of the Dominion legislature) and a strongly worded "finality" clause were directed to this end. The principal feature of the new arrangements was the removal of the limit of 400,000 of population which previously restricted the amount payable under the 80 cents per capita grant. This step was greatly to the initial advantage of Ontario and Quebec where population had far exceeded the old limit. The grant in support of government and legislature was increased about three times. A special payment was made to British Columbia for ten years. In detail the new arrangements were as follows:

(*a*) Grants in support of government and legislature: population under 150,000–$100,000; 150,000 to 200,000–$150,000; 200,000 to 400,000–$180,000; 400,000 to 800,000–$190,000; 800,000 to 1,500,000–$220,000; over 1,500,000–$240,000.

(*b*) Per capita grants–80 cents per capita up to 2,500,000 of population; 60 cents per capita for excess (population to be determined by last decennial census, except in the Prairie Provinces where quinquennial censuses and estimates for mid-years were to be made).

(*c*) No change in debt allowances.

(*d*) British Columbia given a special grant of $100,000 for ten years in token of its mountainous terrain and sparse settlement; no other changes in special grants.

(*e*) No change in Dominion's policy on western natural resources.

In Table XXXVII a comparison is made of the amount payable under each type of grant to the individual provinces following the 1907 adjustment and the amount payable at the time of entrance of each individual province into Confederation.

Taking into account the 1907 revisions, statutory grants increased in total from a net payment of $2.2 million in 1867–8 to about $9.3 million in 1907–8. Despite this absolute increase, attributable in part to the entrance of new provinces, their aggregate importance in provincial finances declined markedly, particularly following the 1890's when direct taxes and other revenue sources began to take a more prominent place. From a ratio of more than half of provincial revenues in 1868, by the end of the period they had declined in relative importance to about a quarter. They rose temporarily to about 30 per cent following the 1907 revision, but, with an increase of provincial revenue from other sources, had within five years fallen back to less than 25 per cent. These aggregates, of course, conceal wide differences in the relative position of individual provinces. In the Maritime Provinces and the new western provinces the proportion was considerably higher than the average; in Ontario and Quebec it was lower.

A similar change had taken place in the position of subsidies in the Dominion budget. Accounting for about one-fifth at Confederation,

TABLE XXXVII

Comparison of Subsidies at Union and after 1907 Revision

	Aid to government		Population grants		Special grants		Interest on debt allowance		Total	
	At union	1907	At union	1907	At union	1907	At union	1907	At union	1907
	($000)	($000)	($000)	($000)	($000)	($000)	($000)	($000)	($000)	($000)
P.E.I.	30	100	75	87	—	95	131	39	236	321
N.S.	60	190	265	368	83	—	48	53	456	611
N.B.	50	180	202	265	63	150	—	26	315	621
Que.	70	240	889	1,319	—	—	[a]	127	959	1,686
Ont.	80	240	1,117	1,746	—	—	[a]	142	1,197	2,128
Man.	30	190	14	293	—	100	71	179	115	762
Sask.	50	220	200	206	469	469	405	405	1,124	1,300
Alta.	50	190	200	200	469	469	405	405	1,124	1,264
B.C.	35	190	48	143	100	200	64	29	247	562
Total	455	1,740	3,010	4,627	1,184	1,483	1,124	1,405	5,873	9,255

SOURCE: *Summary of Legislation Relating to Subsidies to Provinces*, Dept. of Finance.

[a]Due to excess of Ontario and Quebec debt over allowance an actual deficit resulted at union. For the period 1867 to 1884 the deficits amounted to $1,593,755 and $602,669 respectively. By the 1884 adjustment the deficits were made up to the provinces.

they fell to 10 per cent within a few years, with other outlays expanding, and remained below that level until 1907–8. The 1907 adjustment raised them briefly over the 10 per cent mark but they diminished rapidly in succeeding years and by 1920 accounted for less than 2 per cent of Dominion expenditures.

SPECIAL SUBSIDIES AND GRANTS-IN-AID, 1907 to 1940

It can hardly be said that events realized Sir Wilfrid Laurier's hopes that the 1907 terms would be final, but it is apparent in retrospect that a gradual change began to occur in the nature of Dominion-provincial financial relationships. While statutory subsidies continued to form the backbone of financial relationships, they were supplemented by further special grants to provinces and by grants in aid of particular provincial functions (including agricultural instruction, technical education, highway construction, employment offices, and old age pensions). The extension of special grants to individual provinces heralded the abandonment of the test, as the ultimate yardstick, of equal per capita payments. With the end of the formative period of Confederation, when demands had to be appeased by one stratagem or another, it became possible to adopt a more selective and discriminating policy towards the provinces.

Two minor adjustments in the unconditional subsidies were made on the heels of the 1907 revision. Of these one was for Manitoba and represented a further modification of the second "final" settlement of 1907. Manitoba argued that her position was inferior to that of the other western provinces with regard to her debt allowance and grant in lieu of land and boundaries, and also represented that population and the demand for services were outstripping the province's financial resources. In 1912 the Dominion acted on this petition. The debt allowance was recalculated at a per capita rate of $32.43 (the same as that previously applied to Alberta and Saskatchewan) on an assumed population of 250,000. After this amount had been reduced by certain previous payments to the province that were to be taken into account, there resulted an increase of $308,000 in the debt allowance payment. At the same time substantial additional grants were given in compensation for the lack of public lands, on a basis similar to those previously allowed to Alberta and Saskatchewan, increasing the grant from $100,000 to $409,000. Both these adjustments were made retroactive to 1908, and the resulting arrears of over $2 million were paid to the province in a lump sum. Concurrently the Manitoba boundaries were extended northward to the 60th parallel.

The other adjustment was also made in 1912, for Prince Edward Island. This province advanced a claim based on alleged disadvantages arising out of Confederation, and was granted a further annual payment of $100,000.

Since these 1912 adjustments no further changes have been made in the terms of the unconditional statutory subsidies, with the sole exception of the Maritime Subsidies Act of 1942, discussed later. In fact from 1912 to 1927, when the Duncan Commission grants for the Maritime Provinces were instituted, no further unconditional grants in any form were instituted. It would be most misleading to suggest that this lack of change reflected a final accord on Dominion-provincial financial matters, however. On the contrary, in 1913 the provinces urged another subsidy revision, the surpluses of the easy period since 1904 having come to an end. The proposal then favoured was that the provinces be paid, in addition to their existing subsidies, one-tenth of the Dominion's annual revenue from customs and excise duties. In the following year the western provinces pressed for the return of the natural resources but refused to accept the offer of Sir Robert L. Borden, then Prime Minister, to return them the lands on condition that the compensatory payments in lieu of lands be suspended. The western demands were not pressed during the period of World War I, but were revived immediately on the return of peace. The Dominion renewed its former offer, and the provinces again refused to accept. They argued that the existing payments were in compensation for lands already permanently alienated and that they should be continued in perpetuity.

Maritime Claims

During the early twenties the Maritime Provinces pressed with growing insistence long-standing claims for compensation for the alleged disabilities suffered as a result of Confederation and of national government policies. Chronic economic problems of the region were aggravated by the persistence of post-war depression conditions, from which the rest of the country had made a buoyant recovery, and by declining or static populations. The agitation for remedial action was fostered by a "Maritime Rights" movement, and meetings in Charlottetown and Moncton in 1925 to study economic problems of the area attracted wide attention. Public feeling ran high and the familiar talk of secession again was heard.

This agitation culminated in the appointment by the Dominion of a Royal Commission, known after its chairman as the Duncan Commission, to investigate the claims and propose a solution.[1] In September, 1926, after hearing the submissions of the provincial governments, the Commissioners reported their conclusions that "the Maritime Provinces have not prospered and developed, either in population, or in commercial, industrial or rural enterprise, as fully as other portions of Canada." While they were "unable to take the view that Confederation is, of itself, responsible for this fact," certain features of the financial developments since Confederation, particularly the more favourable arrangements with the western provinces regarding debt allowances and payments in lieu of lands, were thought to have been less than fair to the Maritime Provinces.

While not accepting all the financial and other proposals, the Dominion agreed to make additional annual grants of $875,000 to Nova Scotia, $600,000 to New Brunswick, and $125,000 to Prince Edward Island, as recommended by the Commission, until such time as the whole question could be reconsidered. At the same time the Maritime Freight Rates Act was passed, providing for a reduction of 20 per cent on freight rates on eastern lines, the railways to be reimbursed by the Dominion.

Western Natural Resources

In the meantime, another old fire was smouldering. A general Dominion-Provincial Conference in 1927 brought forth a round of claims for adjustment from practically all the provinces, but the issue that persistently came to the fore was the growing demand in the Prairie Provinces for a settlement of the natural resources question. The western governments wanted not only the remaining lands returned but also compensation for the losses they had suffered because of the alienation that occurred while the lands were under the stewardship of the Dominion. It will be recalled that these lands had been withheld originally from Manitoba in 1870 and from Alberta and Saskatchewan in 1905 when these provinces entered union. Their control by the Dominion had contributed immeasurably to settlement and railway development but had given the western governments the opportunity to argue that they had suffered a loss of revenue in comparison with the older provinces, even though they were being compensated for this loss by the Dominion.

The upshot of the continued agitation was that in August, 1928, the Dominion Government appointed the Turgeon Commission[2] to

[1]Royal Commission on Maritime Claims, *Report* (1927).

[2]Royal Commission on the Transfer of the Natural Resources of Manitoba, *Report* (1929).

investigate the Manitoba claims, and in 1933 and 1934 the Dysart Commissions[3] to consider respectively the position of Alberta and Saskatchewan. In 1930 the Dominion took a long step towards a solution of the problem by turning over to the provinces the remaining unalienated areas. In addition, however, all Commissions recommended the payment of compensation for past alienations. Manitoba accepted a settlement of $4,584,000 as proposed by the Turgeon Commission, but Saskatchewan refused, and Alberta delayed acceptance of, awards of $5,000,000 apiece proposed by the Dysart Commissions. A final settlement in the case of these latter provinces was postponed until 1947 when both accepted payment of $8,031,000, being $5,000,000 at 5 per cent interest from the date of the original offer. In 1930 the Dominion returned to British Columbia land which it had held in the railway belt and the Peace River Block (the latter being 3,500,000 acres assigned to the Dominion in 1884 to make up the deficiencies in the railway belt land).[4] In every case the previous annual grant to the province in lieu of land was continued after the return of the remaining lands.

British Columbia: Further Maritime Claims

Other changes in a familiar pattern also took place during this period. In 1935 a special interim subsidy of $750,000 was granted to British Columbia (the culmination of an agitation extending over a quarter-century). It was paid annually until 1941. This increase had in turn been precipitated by the award of larger grants to the Maritime Provinces as recommended by the White Commission[5] appointed in 1934 to conduct the further study proposed by the Duncan Commission. As a result of a re-examination the annual awards were increased from $125,000 to $275,000 for Prince Edward Island, from $875,000 to $1,300,000 for Nova Scotia, and from $600,000 to $900,000 for New Brunswick, as a "final equitable settlement." These payments were made until 1941, although they were suspended during the period of the Wartime Tax Agreements. However, in 1947 they were renewed and are now paid as part of the ordinary statutory subsidies to these provinces under the terms of the Maritime Subsidies Act, 1942.

The White Commission enquiry deserves further discussion in one respect. The evidence submitted by the provinces, particularly Nova

[3]Royal Commission on the Natural Resources of Alberta, *Report* and Royal Commission on Natural Resources of Saskatchewan, *Report* (1935).

[4]Royal Commission on Reconveyance of Land to British Columbia, *Report* (1928).

[5]Royal Commission on Financial Arrangements between the Dominion and the Maritime Provinces, *Report* (1935).

Scotia, and the contents of the *Report* itself, disclose for the first time in the history of subsidy negotiations a discussion of the concept of "fiscal need."

The provinces argued that there were impelling grounds for a grant from the national government when it could be shown as a result of an objective study that taxation in a province equal to the average burden in other provinces would not support services of the general average provincial level. The basis for grants, it was urged, should be "fiscal need" as measured by the deficiency so shown. The majority of the Commissioners did not accept this argument. While admitting that "financial necessity has lain at the basis of most, if not all, of the revisions and special grants of subsidies to Provinces since Confederation" (*Report*, p. 5), the Commissioners (one member dissenting) after considering the theoretical, practical, and political aspects of the "fiscal need" principle, stated: ". . . we feel obliged to reject this proposal of 'fiscal need' and proceed to consider on other grounds the claims of the Maritime Provinces for increased subsidies" (*Report*, p. 7). However, this was not the last to be heard of the question. Within five years "fiscal need" was given the blessing of the Rowell-Sirois Commission as a basis for provincial subsidies.

Special Grants during the Depression

While the depression wrought general havoc with provincial finances, its ravages were deepened and prolonged in the West by crop failures which recurred after improved conditions had appeared in the rest of Canada. The financial resources of the Prairie Provinces, sapped by the exhausting years of depression, were reaching the breaking point by 1936, as, particularly in Saskatchewan, each year brought worse drought. Following an urgent request for emergency assistance the Dominion Government, acting jointly with the premiers of Manitoba and Saskatchewan, asked the Bank of Canada, then newly organized, to make a special examination of the financial position of those provinces and to recommend what might best be done. The Bank's proposal that special payments be made to Manitoba and Saskatchewan in the amount of $750,000 and $1,500,000 was accepted by the Dominion, and the payment to Saskatchewan was supplemented by an extra $2,000,000 for 1938 and 1939, following the most disastrous crop failures in the history of the province. A similar examination of Alberta's finances at the request of the provincial Premier led the Bank to recommend a payment of $600,000 on condition of full payment of interest on the province's debt. Since the province had, in fact, defaulted on its bonds and was paying only one-half of its interest liability the Dominion made no payments at the time but in 1945, after the province had settled its defaulted liabilities, the Dominion made a retrospective payment of $600,000 a year for the four fiscal years from 1938 to 1941.

These grants were in addition to substantial payments from the Dominion for relief, which are discussed on a later page.

Grants-in-Aid

Concurrently with the developments described in the previous pages an experiment had been going on with a form of payment designed to assist the provinces in financing specific projects. These were known as conditional subsidies, or grants-in-aid, as they are more often called.

Agricultural instruction. Grants-in-aid had their genesis in Canada in the Agricultural Instruction Act of 1913, a measure the purpose of which was rather loosely conceived to be the encouragement of an interest in agricultural education. Its adoption reflected the concern of all governments with the growing drift of the farm population to the cities, and also their interest in fostering the adoption of scientific agricultural methods. Ten million dollars were provided to be spent in co-operation with the provinces over a period of ten years. Payments were to commence with an initial annual outlay of $700,000 and rise by $100,000 to a maximum of $1.1 million a year. A further grant of $900,000 was made in the eleventh year. The problem of allocating the funds between individual provinces was met on the traditional per capita basis, with a slight variation. A flat grant of $20,000 per annum was first given to each province and the same amount to each veterinary college. The balance was then distributed among the provinces on the basis of population. In all, about $11 million were paid out in the period between 1912 and 1924.

The results of this experiment were somewhat mixed, according to authorities. Apparently no fixed standards of performance were established, supervision over projects after initial approval by the Dominion was not sufficiently strict, and the fact that the provinces were under no obligation to share in the costs left little incentive for care or economy. The programme thus lacked most of the basic requisites of a successful grant-in-aid plan, and the results achieved depended largely on the enterprise of the individual provinces. In some provinces permanent buildings were erected with the Dominion funds, while in others it was less evident that any permanent advantage had been gained.

Technical Education. Closely related to the agricultural instruction measure was a similar co-operative venture in technical education. Interest in this phase of education antedated World War I when the growing needs of industrialism for special technical training had resulted in the appointment of a Royal Commission[6] in 1910 to inquire into the subject. The Commission recommended that the Dominion give subsidies to assist the provinces in providing this form of training. World War I postponed action, but in 1919 the Technical Education Act was passed.

Like the Agricultural Instruction Act, the measure provided for the distribution of $10 million over a ten-year period on the same ascending scale. Each province was to receive a flat annual grant of $10,000 and the balance of the annual amount was to be allocated in proportion to population. The measure differed from its predecessor, however, in the important respect that the provincial government was required to match the federal grant dollar for dollar.

When part of the original allotment remained unspent at the end of ten years, the offer was renewed for additional periods of five years at a time, to allow the provinces that were less able financially, and less interested in technical education, to take up their share. The requirement that the provinces share in the expenditure undoubtedly had the desirable effect of curbing extravagance, but it had the disadvantage of barring the less wealthy provinces from participation or else it forced them to strain their resources in order to participate. This is a criticism made in general against grants-in-aid, and undoubtedly the conflict between considerations of administrative efficiency and political and social desirability is inherent in the plan.

In 1931, some years after the first legislation had expired, a measure to provide renewed assistance for vocational education was passed by the Dominion Parliament. It contemplated an annual expenditure of $750,000 for fifteen years through grants to the provinces, but the financial crisis of the depression prevented its implementation. No further measures were taken until World War II and the post-war period.

Highway construction. Another 1919 measure, equally indicative of the changing times, was the Highway Construction Act. It provided $20 million to be distributed among the provinces over a five-year period to assist in construction of main highways. An annual grant of $80,000 was given each province and the balance distributed on the basis of population. In place of the equal sharing of cost under the

[6]Royal Commission on Industrial Training and Technical Education, *Report* (1913).

technical education plan the province had to meet 60 per cent of the cost and was also required to submit a plan for a five-year development programme. No funds were paid by the Dominion until the project had been completed and approved by a federal inspector. The depression of the early twenties prevented some provinces from using their full allotment, and two extensions of two years each were required before the full $20 million was taken up.

On the whole, experience with this measure was fairly satisfactory, according to one student of these grants, Professor J. A. Maxwell. "It is very probable that the federal Act not only encouraged a greater provincial expenditure on highways, but also that the expenditure got better results than would have been achieved without federal advice and supervision."[7] It is interesting to note that in 1949 the shared cost plan for highway construction was revived with the passage of the Trans-Canada Highway Act.

Employment offices. The years 1918 and 1919 also saw the introduction of two other conditional subsidy measures: the Employment Offices Co-ordination Act, and the project for assistance in combating venereal diseases.

The former was intended to encourage provinces which had no employment offices to set them up and also to facilitate the exchange between provinces of information on employment opportunities. In 1922 the grant was fixed at $150,000 a year and although expenditures ran in excess of this amount in the early years, owing to the extra cost of placing the demobilized troops, it remained the same until the Dominion took over the employment offices with the establishment of national unemployment insurance in 1941. The grant was allocated to each province in the ratio that its individual expenditures bore to the total provincial expenditure on such offices.

At the time the Act was passed Quebec, Ontario, and Saskatchewan already had offices, and within a year or two most of the other provinces established them. A fairly successful attempt was made by the Dominion to maintain uniformity of procedure, and the provincial governments were required to maintain a provincial and interprovincial clearance system as a condition of obtaining the grant. For the expenditure of only $150,000 per annum comparatively good results were achieved.

Venereal diseases. Another fairly satisfactory programme was the attack, in co-operation with the provinces, on venereal disease, a serious

[7]J. A. Maxwell, *Federal Subsidies to the Provincial Governments in Canada* (1937), pp. 219–20.

civilian problem following World War I. Originally $200,000 a year was provided to assist in furnishing treatment in clinics and hospitals, in providing hospital beds, and for related purposes. This amount was gradually reduced to $150,000 in 1924, and to $100,000 in 1927, and was eliminated altogether in 1932. In all, over $1,700,000 was distributed, which, although there are inherent difficulties in measuring the results of this form of outlay, appeared to have been well spent.

Old age pensions. The most important of the co-operative ventures was inaugurated in 1926 with the introduction of old age pensions on a shared-cost plan. Agitation for public pensions for the aged had appeared in Parliament before World War I, but nothing had been done. Interest in the plan revived during the election of 1921, when the Liberals promised the introduction of a plan in their campaign. Because the Department of Justice had ruled that jurisdiction lay with the provinces, the Dominion was forced to restrict its role to offering assistance to any province that would undertake to introduce a pension plan of its own. A committee of Parliament set up to investigate various proposals in 1924[8] recommended a scheme involving an equal contribution from Dominion and provincial governments.

A bill authorizing a fifty-fifty sharing of the cost of pensions of $20 a month for persons over seventy years of age, with certain qualifications, was adopted by Parliament late in 1926. The applicant had to be a British subject who had resided in Canada for twenty years, with an annual income not in excess of $365. British Columbia came in under these conditions almost immediately, Manitoba and Saskatchewan followed in 1928, and Alberta and Ontario in 1929. As a result of an increase in the Dominion contribution in 1931 to 75 per cent, the Maritime Provinces came in—Prince Edward Island in 1933, Nova Scotia in 1934, and New Brunswick in 1936. Quebec was the last of the original provinces to act, holding off until 1936, and Newfoundland came under the plan on its entry into union in 1949. Pensions for blind persons aged forty or over were introduced in 1937 on the same shared-cost basis, and were immediately adopted in all provinces.

The Dominion's annual expenditures for old age and blind pensions increased from a mere $131,000 in 1927–8, when British Columbia was the only participating province, to an annual outlay of about $30 million by 1940. Subsequent changes in the war and post-war period brought this grant to the fore, before it was superseded in 1952 by the universal federal old age pension plan, as the largest of all conditional payments. In 1950–1 the total grant under it exceeded $100 million.

Relief grants-in-aid. In dismal pre-eminence over all other subsidies

[8]*Journal of the House of Commons*, 1924, App. 4.

of the period prior to 1940 were the grants to the provincial and municipal governments for relief. Unemployment in the early thirties on a national scale thrust forth an emergency financial problem which, under existing constitutional arrangements, was the responsibility of provincial and local governments. Provincial governments quickly discovered that revenue resources which had yielded handsomely in the prosperous twenties dwindled rapidly with falling prices and incomes. Despite efforts to bolster finances with new and increased taxes most provinces were quickly engulfed in difficulties and the stronger financial resources of the Dominion had to be employed to prevent a general financial *débâcle*. While refusing to recognize any alteration in the constitutional position as a result of its participation, the Dominion made extensive contributions through outright grants. From 1930 to 1934 it shared one-third of the cost of direct relief, with the province and municipality sharing the balance in approximately equal proportions. Following August, 1934, however, the Dominion adopted the practice of making a monthly grant-in-aid, which varied in amount with seasonal and other requirements. The Dominion also shared in the cost of approved employment-creating construction projects and carried on its own programme of works designed to relieve unemployment. The Dominion's own expenditures under the annual relief acts from 1930 to 1940 inclusive totalled $394 million, of which about $317 million, or over three-quarters, was paid to the provinces. Table XXXVIII gives the provincial breakdown of this

TABLE XXXVIII

DOMINION DISBURSEMENTS TO PROVINCES UNDER RELIEF LEGISLATION
(under 1930 to 1940 Relief Acts, as at March 31, 1941)
(thousands of dollars)

	Grants-in-aid	Material aid	Public works	Other	Total
Prince Edward Island	151	118	1,021	49	1,339
Nova Scotia	2,040	1,646	4,137	258	8,081
New Brunswick	988	636	4,174	297	6,095
Quebec	29,686	23,209	12,235	1,557	66,687
Ontario	35,317	35,953	31,223	375	102,868
Manitoba	9,088	8,350	7,621	2,412	27,471
Saskatchewan	13,092	26,074	5,028	13,430	57,624
Alberta	6,743	5,488	4,514	1,828	18,573
British Columbia	8,807	10,252	5,869	3,685	28,613
Total	105,912	111,726	75,822	23,891	317,351

SOURCE: Department of Labour, Ottawa (fiscal year ending March 31, 1941), *Report of the Dominion Commissioner of Unemployment Relief*, p. 40.

amount of $317 million under the various headings of expenditure.

In addition to these grants, the Dominion advanced to the four western provinces funds required to meet their own share of relief expenses, for meeting maturing bond issues, and, to some extent, for ordinary government expenditures. In the aggregate these advances amounted to over $175 million, of which a substantial part was subsequently written off.

Summary of Payments in Period 1907–40

Following the 1912 adjustments for Manitoba and Prince Edward Island, no further changes were made during the period in the basic components of the statutory subsidies—per capita grant, debt allowance, and grant for government and legislature. The payments under these headings increased in absolute amount with increasing population as provided under the 1907 settlement. The annual payment increased gradually from about $9 million in 1908 to $13.7 million by 1939.

During the period further "special grants" were paid, of which only those awarded to the Maritime Provinces as a result of the Duncan and White Commissions have become a permanent part of the statutory subsidies. Other special grants of a less permanent nature were also paid to British Columbia, Manitoba, and Saskatchewan. In 1940 these interim payments, including the White awards to the Maritime Provinces, were as follows:

Prince Edward Island	$ 275,000
Nova Scotia	1,300,000
New Brunswick	900,000
Manitoba	750,000
Saskatchewan	1,500,000
British Columbia	750,000
	$5,475,000

During the period grants-in-aid for agricultural instruction, technical education, highways, employment offices, old age pensions, and other projects introduced a new factor into intergovernmental financial relations. In total the outlay on these conditional subsidies amounted to about $230 million, of which the lion's share of $172 million was for old age pensions. Of these measures only the old age pensions plan became permanent, although in recent years conditional grants for health services and for the Trans-Canada Highway have revived this trend.

Finally, the enormous drain of relief on provincial and municipal finances during the depression necessitated Dominion support for local budgets on a scale unprecedented except in the early period of Confederation.

In the years between 1907 and 1940 total intergovernmental payments increased about tenfold. They rose from an annual figure of about $9 million at the outset to a level of $90–$100 million by 1940. While the importance of payments from the Dominion gradually declined from about a quarter of provincial revenues in 1908 to less than a tenth in 1929, during the depression they rapidly mounted to over a third in the aggregate, and in some provinces to 60–70 per cent. Outlays of this magnitude also placed a greater strain on Dominion finances than any since the subsidies of the early years of Confederation. Total payments to the provinces represented less than 4 per cent of Dominion expenditures in 1929, having declined from a level of 8–10 per cent in the previous twenty years. During the depression, however, they absorbed over 15 per cent of total outlays in most years, and in 1938 accounted for almost 20 per cent.

The period closed with general concern over the maladjustments in the financial structure of Canadian government, a concern expressed as we have seen in the appointment of the Royal Commission on Dominion-Provincial Relations in 1937. The taxation aspects of the Commission's *Report,* filed in 1940, have been discussed in earlier chapters. Its recommendations in the field of intergovernmental payments, and the alternative plan adopted during World War II, are discussed in the following chapter.

32 SUBSIDIES

Major Revisions for Wartime, 1940-46

IN THE HISTORY of intergovernmental financial relations in Canada the developments of World War II are of immense significance. The *Report* of the Rowell-Sirois Commission in 1940 marked the opening of the period and the Reconstruction Conference of 1945–6 marked its close. Both were events of historic importance, and were intended to result in the reshaping of the federal financial structure. On neither occasion was the anticipated result achieved, however. As has happened often enough in Canadian affairs, both attempts produced a compromise that was short of the original objective. The Wartime Tax Agreements were the compromise that grew out of the Rowell-Sirois *Report*; and the Tax Rental Agreements of 1947, discussed in the next chapter, took the place of the larger plans submitted by the Dominion to the Reconstruction Conference in 1945. Both these compromise measures were in themselves of extreme importance, but each again demonstrated the apparently inescapable influence of political considerations on financial arrangements within the Canadian confederation.

ROWELL-SIROIS COMMISSION RECOMMENDATIONS

While the precise recommendations of the Commission in the area of intergovernmental payments were not adopted, its analysis of past developments and the conclusions drawn from that analysis have certainly influenced subsequent events.

In general the attitude of the Commissioners towards the financial arrangements that had developed between levels of government in Canada was highly critical. They examined the solutions adopted in the past to cope with the underlying financial maladjustments and expressed the view that these had only temporized with fundamental dislocations. They urged a broad approach to intergovernmental finance. They insisted on the necessity of a franker recognition of regional differences of wealth and income and a more vigorous effort on the part of the Dominion to reduce these disparities.

Much of the existing financial structure was to be discarded in the process of re-confederation they visualized. The existing subsidy system was found to be "chaotic and illogical"[1] and should be replaced. The conditional grant was found to be "under Canadian conditions, an inherently unsatisfactory device. It may be used in some special cases and for some limited purposes. . . ."[2] The Commission regarded the early experiments with conditional grants, including the old age pensions arrangement, as reasonably satisfactory, but it rejected such grants as a "method of financing major functions of government and of providing for necessary intergovernmental transfers in a federal state. . . ." The product of the historical development described in the previous chapter was to be completely recast to fit modern requirements, although the Commissioners felt that this could be done without any fundamental breach with the basic pattern and principles of Confederation. They explained that except in one respect their financial proposals were of the same general character as the arrangements adopted then. "The principle is basically the same as that underlying the Confederation settlement, but the major changes which have occurred since Confederation in the relative taxable capacity and governmental responsibilities of the different provinces make it necessary to discard the assumption that equal per capita payments would provide for real equality of fiscal position. This assumption has, in fact, long been discarded. . . ."[3]

Specific Financial Proposals

The Commission's specific financial recommendations were presented in two alternative plans. As a counterpart to its tax transfer proposals the Commission recommended the assumption by the Dominion of provincial debts and of responsibility for relief for employable unemployed, and the payment also of grants to the provinces. This was Plan I, which, as summarized in the *Report*,[4] is given below. Plan II, offered as a second best, contemplated only the transfer of relief for employable unemployed to the Dominion, the rest of the existing financial structure to remain unchanged.

Plan I (excluding tax recommendations)

Relief to the provinces

Relieve the provinces (and the municipalities) of the whole burden of relief for the employable unemployed and their dependents.

[1]Royal Commission on Dominion-Provincial Relations, *Report*, Book II, p. 83.
[2]*Ibid.*, Book I, p. 259. [3]*Ibid.*, Book II, p. 127. [4]*Ibid.*, p. 86.

The Dominion would assume the whole of the provincial (but not the municipal) debts, and would, in effect, bear the dead-weight cost of this debt, as it would collect from the provinces no more than the return which they receive today from their revenue producing assets. The provinces would thus have no further provisions to make for sinking funds.

In the case of Quebec, where the provincial debt is an unusually low proportion of combined provincial and municipal debt, the Dominion would assume 40 per cent of the net, or dead-weight, cost of combined provincial and municipal debt service.

Surrender of subsidies

The provinces would surrender all existing subsidies.

New Dominion provincial revenue sources

The Dominion would pay annually a National Adjustment Grant to certain provinces. The amount of the Grant would be such as to enable each province (including its municipalities) without resort to heavier taxation than the Canadian average, to provide adequate social, educational and developmental services. The weight of taxation is estimated by comparing the provincial and municipal taxation with the total income of the province. The test of adequacy of social and educational services is found in the Canadian average for these services. The adequacy of developmental services is tested by what the province itself has done in years which may be considered normal.

The original adjustment grants would be irreducible. Increases would be granted (on the advice of the proposed Finance Commission) at appropriate intervals if they were needed, in order to enable a province to perform its functions adequately without exceptionally heavy taxation.

In addition to the National Adjustment Grants payable to some provinces, the Dominion would pay an Emergency Grant to a province in which abnormally bad conditions prevailed. Such a Grant would be made for a year at a time, reduced as soon as possible, and eliminated as soon as possible.

Future borrowing

Future provincial and municipal borrowing would have to be in lawful money of Canada.

Future provincial borrowing might be either (*a*) as today on the sole credit of the province, in which case the debt charges could not be counted as part of the financial need of the province if it applied for a National Adjustment Grant (if it were not receiving one) or for an increase in its grants; or (*b*) on the credit of Canada if the proposed Finance Commission is asked to approve it, and after reviewing all the circumstances does so.

Freedom of provinces

No control of provincial expenditures is contemplated. Every province would be quite free to improve its services by specially heavy taxation, or to have specially light taxation by reducing its services, or to develop some services in excess of the Canadian average at the expense of others which would remain below it.

Fiscal Need Grants

Of main interest to our present purposes is the specific recommendation that the statutory subsidies be withdrawn for all provinces and replaced by permanent National Adjustment Grants payable to all provinces except British Columbia, Alberta, and Ontario. These were to be supplemented by temporary Emergency Grants which would be payable only during periods of stress.

The National Adjustment Grants were to assist individual provinces to provide educational and welfare services equivalent in quality to the national average, and to maintain development expenditures at their individual 1928–31 averages, without resort to heavier taxation than the average. The payments were, therefore, to be "fiscal need" subsidies in the accepted sense of that expression. They were to be fixed at an irreducible minimum for all time, but every five years a Federal Finance Commission would review the amounts and increase them on proof by any province that it would suffer a budget deficit by providing social services and education equivalent to the national average without increasing the burden of its taxation above the Canadian average. This taxation burden was to be estimated by comparing the total provincial and municipal taxation with the total income of the province. The national statistical average for welfare and education expenditures was to be the arithmetic average of the dollar expenditures per capita for these purposes in the nine provinces, although in some instances—the Maritime Provinces and British Columbia—the Commission professed to use a different concept—"the real national per capita average"—in calculating the size of the initial grant.

Thus for a given province a grant would in general be forthcoming to offset its budget deficit after making certain adjustments in its accounts. The actual deficit would be adjusted in accordance with deviations of tax burden and levels of services from the national average. Its actual revenues would be reduced to the extent that its tax burden was above average, or *vice versa,* while its actual expenditures would be reduced to the extent that its level of services was above average, or *vice versa.* The final grant based on this "adjusted" deficit would in no circumstance be less than the irreducible minimum based on 1937 conditions.

The additional Emergency Grants would be payable for a year at a time during a period of emergency, and would expire with the end of the emergency. It would also be the responsibility of the Finance Commission to recommend the amount of such grants to the Dominion government.

Financial Effect of Proposals

In view of the heavy financial burdens for relief and for provincial debt to be assumed by the Dominion under Plan I, it is perhaps misleading to consider the National Adjustment Grants proposed by the Commission except in the context of the over-all settlement. However, for the sole purpose of indicating the magnitude of the intergovernmental payments under the new plan in relation to existing arrangements, those suggested by the Commission for 1938 are shown in Table XXXIX and compared with the aggregate of the statutory subsidies and special grants actually paid to each province in the same year.

TABLE XXXIX

GRANTS PROPOSED BY COMMISSION COMPARED WITH EXISTING GRANTS

	Total of existing subsidies	Proposed National Adjustment Grants
	($ 000)	($ 000)
Prince Edward Island	657	750
Nova Scotia	1,953	800
New Brunswick	1,567	1,500
Quebec	2,592	8,000
Ontario	2,941	—
Manitoba	2,453	2,100
Saskatchewan	5,620	1,750[a]
Alberta	1,776	—
British Columbia	1,625	—
	21,184	14,900

[a]Plus an Emergency Grant for 1938 of $4,000,000.

It is apparent from this comparison that unconditional subsidies would have been reduced by only about one-third under the proposal. Of much greater financial significance, therefore, was the proposed assumption by the Dominion of the outstanding provincial and municipal debt and the cost of relief for employable unemployed. At the time of the *Report* the annual interest charges on this debt were approaching $65 million, and relief expenditures were running at an annual level of $50 to $60 million, making a gross current outlay, including the grants, in the neighbourhood of $135 million. Against this outlay would have been offset a saving of about $21 million in the discontinued subsidies, and an increase in revenue of $65 to $75 million from assumption of all the taxes suspended by the provinces.

On balance, under immediate pre-war conditions, the Dominion's net position resulting from the implementation of the financial aspects of Plan I would have been an increase in annual outlay of $40 to $50 million, or about 10 per cent. Ultimately there would also be the problem of repaying the provincial debt.

The immediate fate of the Commission's proposals may be briefly stated. A recommendation that the British North America Act be amended to allow the Dominion to set up employment offices and an unemployment insurance plan was implemented in 1940 and given practical effect by 1941, but the main proposals did not fare as well. Their flat rejection by certain provinces at a two-day Dominion-Provincial Conference in January, 1941, left the whole issue of fiscal relations within the federation in a state of uncertainty and confusion.

The Wartime Tax Agreements

At the conclusion of this abortive Conference, J. L. Ilsley, then Dominion Minister of Finance, had felt it necessary to warn the provincial premiers in the strongest terms that the overriding financial needs of the war would compel increases in Dominion taxes to a level hitherto never contemplated. He predicted that as a result of the failure of the Conference, provincial finances would suffer severe dislocation from the measures the Dominion would be forced to take and that the residents of provinces where taxes were heaviest would bear a harsh and inequitable burden in such an event. The first foretaste of the truth of his prediction was not long in coming. Three months later he announced drastic increases in personal and corporation income taxes that were overshadowed only by even more drastic measures in the following year.

Offer of Temporary Tax Agreements

Mr. Ilsley made it clear in announcing these increases in his budget speech of April, 1941,[5] that, while he could not help but be concerned by the serious problem of the unequal burden that would fall on residents of the various provinces as a result of existing provincial taxes, he had been forced to the conclusion, "after the most careful consideration of all the questions involved . . . that the rates of personal and corporation income taxes should be raised by the Dominion to the maximum levels which would be reasonable at this time, *if the provinces were not in those fields.* Our plans are drawn, therefore, on that basis. . . ." The Dominion Government thereby declared that

[5]*House of Commons Debates*, April 29, 1941.

it was preparing to go ahead, agreement or no agreement. But having made this declaration, the Minister went on to say that he was ready to make one more try at some kind of an agreement. He said: "... but these increases if taken together with the existing provincial rates would result in too heavy a burden and it is proposed, therefore, as a temporary expedient for the duration of the war only, to ask the provinces to vacate these two tax fields." He then announced that he was writing that day to the provincial premiers, proposing to them an agreement covering income and corporation taxes only. The broader plan envisaged by the Rowell-Sirois Commission would be held over until after the war, but the war itself had created an imperative need for a temporary redistribution of taxing powers.

Nature of the Offer

Specifically he proposed that, in return for an undertaking from a province that it would not impose personal income taxes or corporation taxes for the period of the war and one year thereafter, the Dominion would pay, for each year in which the undertaking was in effect, an amount calculated on whichever of the two following bases a province might select, at its own option: (*a*) the revenues which the province and its municipalities actually obtained from these tax sources during the fiscal year ending nearest to December 31, 1940, or (*b*) the cost of the net debt service actually paid by the province in the fiscal year ending nearest to December 31, 1940 (not including contributions to sinking funds), less the revenue obtained from succession duties during that period.

In addition these payments would be supplemented by fiscal need subsidies to any province where the necessity for additional revenue could be shown. The existing statutory subsidies would remain unchanged, but in recognition of the proposal to pay fiscal need subsidies the existing special grants, amounting in all to $5,475,000, would be suspended. As a complementary measure the Minister also offered a guarantee of provincial gasoline tax revenues, which he foresaw might suffer from rationing measures and from a new Dominion tax of 3 cents a gallon which was announced in the same budget. Revenues from this source would be underwritten at their level for the fiscal year ended nearest to December 31, 1940.

The offer, made in April, was accepted within a few months with varying degrees of alacrity by all the provinces. Four of them—the three Maritime Provinces and Saskatchewan—found that the debt option was to their best advantage, and the rest elected the tax revenue base. Extreme care was taken to determine accurately which base would be in the province's best interest and detailed calculations of the payments resulting under each option was incorporated in the text of the individual agreements.

Financial Effect of Agreements

The tax reimbursement grants and the other subsidies under the taxation agreement are set out in Table XL. The main grants for the

TABLE XL

ANNUAL PAYMENTS UNDER WARTIME TAX AGREEMENTS

	Statutory Subsidies	Tax reimbursement grants	Fiscal need subsidies	Loss of revenue subsidies	Total annual payments under agreement
	$ 000	$ 000	$ 000	$ 000	$ 000
P.E.I.	382	265	175	262	1,084
N.S.	705	2,585	—	326	3,616
N.B.	732	3,279	300	71	4,382
Que.	2,808	20,586	—	—	23,394
Ont.	3,155	28,964	—	—	32,119
Man.	1,718	5,055	600	—	7,373
Sask.	2,092	4,330	1,500	—	7,922
Alta.	1,795	5,828[a]	—	—	7,623
B.C.	1,003	12,048	—	—	13,051
	14,390	82,940	2,575	659	100,564

[a]Increased from $4,080,000 in 1945 on completion of bond refunding; Dominion allowed Alberta to change to debt option.

tax sources amounted in all to about $83 million but statutory, fiscal need, and loss of revenue subsidies brought the total to over $100 million. In return the Dominion received full and unrestricted tenure of the personal income tax, corporation income tax, and corporation tax fields for the crucial war and immediate post-war period.

The payments were made annually for six years beginning with the fiscal year ended nearest to December 31, 1941, and terminating with the fiscal year ended nearest to December 31, 1946. A feature of the payment plan was the so-called "hold-back" under which the Dominion withheld from each province an amount which was not to exceed one year's payment as an offset for revenues the province continued to collect for tax liabilities incurred prior to the repeal of the taxes in question. These "hold-backs" were paid over to each province within thirty days of the termination of its agreement, and amounted in total to about $64 million.

The provinces also received substantial reimbursements under the guarantee of their gasoline tax revenues. For the total period these amounted to $34.1 million. When the Dominion brought in liquor rationing in 1943 it also guaranteed provincial liquor revenues at their level of that year; but no payments were required to be made under this guarantee because of the sustained high level of provincial liquor profits.

Comparison with Rowell-Sirois Financial Proposals

While the Wartime Tax Agreements were undoubtedly the offspring of the Rowell-Sirois recommendations and achieved, in the field of taxation, the purpose sought by the Commission, the payments made under them were considerably different in character from the National Adjustment Grants proposed by the Commission. The Commission's purpose was to relieve the social and economic disparities between regions of Canada, and it was inherent in its plan that proportionately the largest payments would go to the least wealthy provinces. By contrast the tax agreement payments were essentially the price that had to be paid to rent from the provinces their rights to impose certain direct taxes for the period of the war, and it was inevitable, therefore, that the largest payments would be received by the provinces where the tax fields had most value.

It is not inconsistent with the traditions of intergovernmental subsidies in Canada that the tax agreement payments were something more than simply a dollar for dollar reimbursement for the value of the tax fields given up. The rigid application of such an approach in all provinces would have produced an amount unacceptable to at least four of them, and therefore a second option had to be provided, based on revenue needs rather than on the value of revenue resources. The option so designed embodied one of the most burdensome of the provincial expenditures—debt interest—and took into account revenue from the remaining important direct tax source not being given up, i.e., succession duties. Even this degree of compromise was apparently not sufficient, and the historic reliance on special grants reappeared in the form of the so-called "fiscal need" subsidies and "loss of revenue" subsidies, both required simply to enable certain provinces to meet their financial obligations. Neither of these appear to have been based on any such precise calculations as those suggested by the Rowell-Sirois

Commission. They were simply conceded by the Dominion as additional compensation.

In annual amount the tax agreements payments were the largest transfers between the Dominion and provincial governments up to that time. The total fixed annual payment of about $100 million (including statutory subsidies but taking no account of the gasoline tax guarantee payments) considerably exceeded the relief transfers of any single year during the depression. Along with the payments for old age pensions and other transfers they boosted the share of provincial revenues derived from the Dominion to about one-third during the war years, as compared with about one-fifth immediately before the war.

Reconstruction Conference, 1945–6

The Wartime Tax Agreements just discussed were due to expire shortly after the conclusion of hostilities. With this contingency in mind the Dominion Government called representatives of the provinces to a Reconstruction Conference in Ottawa in August, 1945. The purpose was to consider measures for the continuation of co-operation in the tax field and for a co-operative venture in a broad programme of social security, public investment, and employment-sustaining measures.

Specific Proposals

For the consideration of the Conference the Dominion made proposals which differed in many important respects from the recommendations of the Rowell-Sirois Commission. They are outlined briefly below under their various headings.[6]

1. *Natural resources and public investment proposals*

The Dominion proposed to give grants to assist in raising provincial standards of protection and development of natural resources, in providing new roads into undeveloped mining and forest resources, in constructing transportation facilities of national importance ordinarily within the provincial field (e.g., Trans-Canada Highway), and in the promotion of particular construction programmes, such as hospitals and schools for technical education. Emphasis was placed on the *timing* of public investment, to achieve the maximum beneficial effect

[6]The proposals were presented in summary form in the "Green Book," *Proposals of the Government of Canada*, with supporting details in special studies.

of the expenditures. The Dominion proposed to make its assistance contingent on and varying with the timing of provincial expenditures, and offered a grant to enable a province to carry out the necessary research for a planned investment programme.

2. *Social security proposals*

The social security proposals fell under three subheadings—health, old age pension, and unemployment assistance.

(i) *Health.* The Dominion proposed to pay grants for planning and organization of provincial health insurance programmes; to share the expense of health insurance programmes by a basic grant of one-fifth of the initial *estimated* cost of a service and a further payment of one-half of the additional *actual* cost, up to a maximum contribution of $12.86 per capita under a complete programme. The total health insurance programme, to be adopted piecemeal at the option of each province, was estimated to cost $250 million—$150 million for the Dominion and $100 million for the provinces.

In addition a variety of conditional grants exceeding $13 million a year were proposed to assist the provinces in improving existing health services or in introducing new services. These included a general public health grant and specific grants for tuberculosis, mental illness, and venereal disease control, crippled children, professional training, research, and civilian blind. The Dominion also proposed to assist in the construction of hospitals by granting loans at very low rates of interest.

(ii) *Old age pensions.* The Dominion proposed to assume the full expense of a pension of $30 a month to all men and women over 70, without means test, at an estimated annual cost of $200 million, and to share to the extent of 50 per cent of the cost of paying pensions between the ages of 65 and 69 with a means test. The cost of the shared pension over 65 would be $17 million for each level of government, so that the cost of the total programme was estimated at about $235 million.

(iii) *Unemployment assistance.* The Dominion's proposal in regard to unemployment assistance was to extend the coverage of unemployment insurance on as broad a scale as possible. It offered to pay assistance at 85 per cent of the normal insurance benefits to able-bodied unemployed who were either not covered by insurance or whose insurance coverage had been exhausted. In effect this meant the assumption by the Dominion of the cost of relief to employable unemployed. No attempt was made to estimate the potential cost.

3. *Financial arrangements*

Like the other proposals, those in the taxation and financial fields had the objective of achieving the most favourable circumstances for the maintenance of a buoyant national income, high employment, and a uniform national level of governmental services and taxation.

(i) *Tax proposals.* It was proposed that the wartime suspension of provincial personal income tax and corporation taxes be continued for a further three years, and, in addition, that succession duties also be suspended for the three years.

(ii) *Payment proposals.* The Rowell-Sirois proposal that the existing statutory subsidies be eliminated was revived. In their place the Dominion proposed to pay each province a guaranteed minimum payment calculated at $12 per capita on the 1941 population of the province. This amount would be only a guaranteed minimum. The actual payment in any year would be an adjusted amount calculated by increasing the minimum payment in the same ratio as the increase in the provincial population and in the gross national product per capita between 1941 and the year preceding the payment year.

The total guaranteed minimum payment to all provinces under this offer was $138 million, which may be compared with provincial receipts of about $125 million under the Wartime Tax Agreement, made up of $100 million of payments from the Dominion (including statutory subsidies) and $25 million in succession duty revenue that would be surrendered under the new proposal. However, this minimum payment of $138 million would have exceeded $200 million in 1947 after adjustment for increased population and per capita gross national product.

This financial offer again differed from the recommendations of the Rowell-Sirois Commission in the omission of any direct proposal for fiscal need payments. The single uniform per capita amount was to be substituted for the National Adjustment Grants and the Emergency Grants proposed by the Commission.

Failure of the 1945–6 Conference

These proposals were presented by the Dominion at the opening conference in August, 1945, and were finally abandoned in May, 1946.[7] In the interim they were considered in Ottawa by a Coordinating Committee, composed of representatives of all govern-

[7]For a full report of proceedings of the Conference over the nine-month period see Dominion-Provincial Conference, 1945, *Dominion and Provincial Submissions and Plenary Conference Discussions* (1946).

ments, whose deliberations were supplemented by a fact-finding "Economic Committee" composed of governmental technical experts. Certain of the provinces, particularly Ontario, submitted alternative recommendations and these too were studied by the Co-ordinating Committee.

It was revealed subsequently that in these meetings (held *in camera*) the Dominion granted further concessions to the provinces and in particular increased the amount of the grants it proposed to pay. At a meeting of the Co-ordinating Committee in January, 1946, the Dominion agreed to increase the minimum payments from $138 million to $180.4 million. The methods used to bring about this result were an increase from $12 to $15 in the basic per capita amount, a switch to 1942 as the base year, and the introduction of an undertaking that no province's payment would fall below 150 per cent of its Wartime Tax Agreement payments (applicable to British Columbia) or would be less than $2 million (applicable to Prince Edward Island). The calculations for the adjusted payment were to be based on the ratios of the adjustment factors in the three years prior to the year of payment, rather than on just one year, and the adjustment factors would be calculated on 1942 as the base year, rather than on 1941. So calculated over the three years the payment would be more stable and would be sustained for a longer period if the national income were to fall off. It was proposed, however, in view of the increased payments offered to British Columbia and Prince Edward Island, that the compensation to these provinces would not be subject to the adjustment.

The Dominion at this time also undertook not to increase certain of its taxes, and promised to seek again an amendment to the British North America Act to allow the provinces to impose an indirect retail sales tax in the event of general agreement being reached. Important modifications were also introduced in January in the public investment and social security measures, mainly designed to increase the Dominion's share of the expenditure.

Despite these modifications no decision was reached in January, and it was agreed that the committee should meet again at the end of April. In a two-day closed session late in April the Dominion offered some further concessions. One of these would have allowed any province to remain in the field of succession duties at its own option. Another would have allowed a province to base its minimum payment on the greater of its 1941 or 1942 population. Under a third the Dominion offered to withdraw its gasoline tax of 3 cents per gallon in return for appropriate compensation from the provinces and to share with all provinces one-half of its income tax receipts from companies engaged in the generation or distribution of electrical energy, gas, or steam. Other minor adjustments were also proposed but the Dominion would not accept proposals advanced by several provinces, particularly Ontario and Nova Scotia, that it should withdraw unconditionally from certain tax fields traditionally left to the provinces in pre-war years—succession duties, gasoline, amusements, pari-mutuel bets, etc.

Apparently matters reached a stalemate at this final closed meeting and on the motion of the Premier of Ontario the conference moved into open session. There followed a week of public discussions, notable principally for the introduction of an alternative compensation proposal by the Premier of Ontario, George Drew, on the basis of which he stated that his province was willing to enter into an agreement. The proposal called for compensation on a formula somewhat different from that advanced by the Dominion. The guaranteed minimum was to be $12 for every person in the population in the year preceding the year of payment or in the year 1941, whichever was the greater. The adjusted payment was to be determined by adjusting the amount of $12 by the increase between 1941 and the year preceding the year of payment in the per capita gross national product, and the resulting figure was to be multiplied by the actual population of the province in the year preceding the year of payment. The existing statutory subsidies were to be retained and paid in addition to these amounts. Other parts of the proposal called for the repeal of certain Dominion taxes, including its succession duties, and required the Dominion to undertake not to enter any fields of direct taxation, other than income tax, for the life of the agreement. The Dominion was also to assume the full cost of relief for unemployed employables, old age pensions, and pensions for the blind.

The Ontario payment proposal had been introduced in the form of an algebraic formula in which the basic factor, the per capita payment, had originally only been identified as "X" and had remained in this state of obscurity until Thursday afternoon of the week. When "X" was finally given a value of $12 by the Ontario Premier, the Dominion Minister of Finance, Mr. Ilsley, replied after consideration that the Dominion could not accept the proposals on the ground that they would involve an additional cost to it of at least $134 million per annum, and it was not prepared to accept this extra burden.

The Premier of Quebec, Mr. Duplessis, had not outlined the terms on which his province would have entered an agreement. Some of the seven remaining premiers had serious reservations on certain aspects of the Dominion proposals, but, in general, appeared to be willing to accept them as the basis for an agreement. However, events were to take another shape. Having exhausted every possibility of attaining a general arrangement satisfactory to all parties the conferees ended their deliberations on a motion of the Dominion Minister of Finance to adjourn *sine die*. This general Conference was never recalled.

33 SUBSIDIES

The Tax Rental Period, 1946-54

WITH THE COLLAPSE of the Conference that lasted for nine months and ended in failure the Dominion Minister of Finance was faced, as in 1941, with the task of preparing the general framework of the future federal tax structure—now one that must be adapted to peacetime conditions—without any assurance that his policies would not clash head-on with those of the provinces. Similarly the provincial treasurers laboured in the dark so far as their future relations with the Dominion were concerned.

A Compromise Proposal

Apparently under the conviction that a return to pre-war competitive taxation at post-war rates would be undesirable the Dominion Government again sought a compromise solution, despite the dismal failure of its earlier efforts. In the budget speech of June, 1946, the Minister of Finance brought forth new proposals in the form of an offer which could be accepted or rejected by individual provinces and which, like the 1941 offer, was limited to taxation alone.

In introducing this proposal he gave the following explanation:

> If no new agreements are made, the provinces will again become dependent on what they can collect from income and corporation taxes. Unfortunately, the income and corporation tax base is very unevenly divided as between provinces. Even before the war those provinces which were less fortunately placed in this respect were driven to uneconomic methods of taxation in attempting to meet their budget requirements. Apart from duplication and overlapping of taxes, provinces were forced to adopt arbitrary and make-shift devices which bore heavily on costs and hampered production. In spite of this, some provinces could not meet their minimum requirements without loans and temporary subsidies from the Dominion. Their autonomy and ability to discharge their constitutional responsibilities were seriously threatened.
>
> If the prewar situation was unsatisfactory, the post-war position will, in the absence of new agreements, become intolerable. Provincial expenditures have expanded greatly. Overall provincial budgets, brought down for the

current year, call for expenditures higher by about $200,000,000 than in 1940. This is an increase of roughly two-thirds. If the provinces again become dependent on income and corporation taxes, some will be forced to adopt taxation expedients far more drastic than those employed before the war. Financial pressure on the less favoured provinces will give rise to increasingly arbitrary and discriminatory taxation, will lead to interference with interprovincial trade and to the extension of government ownership and operation of business merely in order to obtain additional provincial revenues which of course would mean loss of revenues to the Dominion. Even with all this, it is difficult to see how some provinces could retain their solvency and any degree of financial autonomy. Moreover, the arbitrary and discriminatory provincial taxes would come on top of Dominion taxes which, while substantially less than at present, would still be considerably higher than before the war. The Dominion cannot stand aside and allow such a situation to develop. It would seriously impair the capacity of private enterprise to provide high and expanding employment. It would weaken and perhaps destroy our federal system.

The government has reached the conclusion that it would be irresponsible in the extreme if it allowed such a situation to develop without a further attempt to prevent it. It has been convinced that it would be shirking its responsibility to the people of Canada if it did not seek to devise some modified proposal which could be accepted by those provinces which wished to accept it and be left aside by those which did not desire it or felt they had no need for it. Such a modified proposal we have devised.[1]

Actual Terms

The terms of the new offer were: (*a*) an agreeing province would undertake for a period of five years (the rejected proposals had been for three years) not to levy personal income taxes, corporation income taxes, corporation taxes, or succession duties, but any province was to have the option of retaining succession duties if it wished, and this would be facilitated by the allowance of a credit against the Dominion duty; (*b*) in the expectation that the non-agreeing provinces would impose new taxes on corporation profits the agreeing provinces would be asked to impose a profits tax of 5 per cent to remove at least to this extent any discrimination against corporations in the non-agreeing provinces (this tax was to be administered by the Dominion, and the revenue from it would be turned over to the province, but the payment under the agreement would be reduced accordingly); (*c*) an agreeing province would be allowed to impose in addition a special tax on the income of corporations engaged in mining or logging operations.

In compensation for the taxes repealed the Dominion offered to make payments on the basis of the last formula submitted to the Conference. At the same time it renewed its offer to share with every

[1] *House of Commons Debates*, June 27, 1946.

province, whether agreeing or not, one-half of its own income tax from companies whose main business was generating or distributing electrical energy, gas, or steam to the public.

Negotiations with Individual Provinces

Immediately following the Minister's announcement the provinces were almost equally divided between those that expressed willingness to enter into an agreement and those that indicated varying degrees of reluctance. Negotiations were commenced in Ottawa in the fall of 1946 in closed sessions with representations of those provinces wishing to participate. During the course of these proceedings it became apparent that, extracted from the other proposals in the field of social security and public investment, the agreement payments by themselves would in some instances not be adequate for provincial purposes. Further consideration was also given to the fact that it had not been contemplated that the payments to Prince Edward Island and British Columbia would be subject to upward adjustment by the acceleration formula as in the case of the other provinces. Under the original proposals payments to these two provinces were to be fixed for the period of the agreement, but in view of the rising trend of costs and prices this rigidity was felt to hold some risk for the future, even though by most measurements the basic amounts were defensible.

This last situation was first corrected by the Dominion's concession that the payments to both provinces would be subject to the same adjustment for increase in population and per capita gross national product as the payments to the other provinces. But having thus departed from the terms of its initial general offer in favour of two provinces the Dominion was faced with a demand from the others for reconsideration of the whole basis of compensation. To this it acceded, and in January, 1947, proposed an entirely new scheme of payments.

Final Offer

The new compensation proposals provided for two general formulae, either of which a province might select as the basis for determination of its guaranteed minimum payment. A third option—a flat sum of $2,100,000—applied only to Prince Edward Island. The two general options were as follows:

First option—an amount made up of three components: (i) $12.75 per capita on the 1942 population of the province; (ii) 50 per cent of the revenue of the province from income and corporation taxes for the year ending nearest to December 31, 1940, as agreed for purposes of the Wartime Tax Agreements; (iii) the amount of the statutory subsidies payable to the province in 1947. This option would provide the greatest amount in the case of New Brunswick, Quebec, Ontario, Manitoba, Alberta, and British Columbia.

Second option—an amount made up of two components: (i) $15 per capita on the 1942 population of the province; and (ii) the amount of the statutory subsidies payable to the province in 1947. This second option would provide the greatest amount to the provinces of Nova Scotia and Saskatchewan.

In discussing these options in Parliament D. C. Abbott, who succeeded J. L. Ilsley as Minister of Finance late in 1946, described what he believed to be their respective merits. Of the first option he said:

> It will be noted that it has the great merit of including in the guaranteed minimum payments the amounts of the statutory subsidies payable to the various provinces, which have been the product of eighty years of historical development and negotiation. For the rest this particular option is based on a reasonable compromise between the principle of basing the annual grants on equal per capita payments and the principle of adjusting the grants to the varying capacity of the provinces to raise revenues from the tax sources which they are renting to the Dominion. The greatest weight is placed on the principle of equality but at the same time reasonable weight is given to the principle of tax ability or tax potential, which is of advantage to the more favoured provinces, and reasonable weight also to the principle of need, which is reflected in the statutory subsidies and which is, of course, of greatest advantage to the less favoured provinces.

Of the second:

> This is the option which proves most favourable to the provinces of Nova Scotia and Saskatchewan. In the case of Nova Scotia the province had not been cultivating the fields of income and corporation taxes as intensively as other provinces in the base year of the Wartime Tax Agreement and in the case of Saskatchewan prevailing economic conditions in that province had led to a relatively low yield from these tax fields in 1940. It could have been contended, therefore, that the first option would not be fair to either of these two provinces, and consequently the second option was worked out to meet their special situations.[2]

Agreements with Eight Provinces

On the basis of these options and the other terms outlined above agreements were signed between the Dominion and seven provinces in 1947 and early 1948. The same basic agreements were adopted in 1948 in revising the financial arrangements between the Dominion and the Yukon Territories, and after Newfoundland entered Confederation in

[2] *House of Commons Debates*, July 9, 1947.

1949 a similar agreement was worked out for it. Throughout the period 1947 to 1951 neither Ontario nor Quebec entered into an agreement, although Mr. Drew, the Premier of Ontario, suggested on several occasions that the adjourned conference be reconvened.

Financial Implications

An indication of the financial implications of the basis of compensation finally agreed upon may best be given by a comparison of the guaranteed amounts with the payments under the Wartime Tax Agreement and the offers that had been made during the course of the negotiations. This comparison is made in Table XLI, which includes as well the payments that would have been made to Quebec and Ontario had they entered into agreements. The last column in this table also shows the *adjusted* payment for 1951 (the final year of the agreement) the computation of which is explained below.

In comparison with the Wartime Tax Agreement payments of $124.5 million the aggregate guaranteed payments to all provinces under the three proposals would have been $138 million, $181.4 million, and $206.5 million, with an adjusted payment for 1951 of $332.6 million.

TABLE XLI

COMPARISON OF PAYMENTS UNDER WARTIME TAX AGREEMENTS AND VARIOUS PROPOSALS, AUGUST, 1945, TO JANUARY, 1947
($ million)

	Wartime Tax Agreement[a]	Guaranteed minimum payment[b]			1951 Adjusted payment[b]
		Aug. 1945 offer	April 1946 offer	Jan. 1947 offer[c]	Jan. 1947 offer
P.E.I.	1.2	1.14	2.0	2.1	3.1
N.S.	4.2	6.9	8.9	10.9	16.1
N.B.	4.8	5.5	7.0	8.8	13.3
Que.	31.3	40.0	50.9	56.4	90.4
Ont.	44.3	45.5	58.3	67.2	106.7
Man.	8.0	8.8	10.9	13.5	19.5
Sask.	8.2	10.8	13.4	15.3	20.0
Alta.	8.2	9.6	11.9	14.2	22.0
B.C.	14.3	9.8	18.1	18.1	32.0
Total	124.5	138.0	181.4	206.5	332.6

[a]Includes statutory, loss of revenue, and fiscal need subsidies and succession duty revenue.
[b]Includes statutory subsidies.
[c]The basis on which agreements were actually entered into with all provinces but Ontario and Quebec; for comparative purposes excludes Newfoundland.

For the seven provinces which entered into the agreements in 1947 (i.e., excluding Quebec, Ontario, and Newfoundland) the comparable amounts were $48.9 million for the Wartime Agreements and $52.5 million, $72.2 million, $82.9 million respectively for the three post-war offers. The 1951 adjusted payment to these provinces was $135.5 million.

It must be emphasized that the *guaranteed minimum payments* under these agreements were only the amounts below which the payments could not fall in any year. The actual payments made were considerably higher in each of the five years than these minima, due to the operation of the adjustment formula. In fact the last column in the table indicates that the payment made in the fifth year of the agreement to each province in most cases was 50 per cent or more above the minimum for that province.

Nature of the Adjustment Formula

The constituent elements in the adjustment formula were ratios of change in per capita gross national product and in provincial population, in the three years preceding the year of payment, in relation to 1942. The application of these factors was somewhat complicated, but may be described briefly as follows: in each of the three years prior to the year of payment a composite ratio of the ratios of change in per capita gross national product and provincial population over the same factors for 1942 was calculated; this composite ratio was applied to the guaranteed minimum annual payment, thus giving three amounts, each being an adjustment of the minimum; these three amounts were totalled and averaged, and the resulting figure was the actual payment for the year.

The amount for each year, calculated on the basis of information provided for this purpose by the Dominion Statistician, was paid in four equal quarterly instalments beginning on September 30. There was then recalculation of these payments in the following year on the basis of revised information, and there was also a final adjustment following the termination of the agreement for the whole period of five years on the basis of finally revised statistics of gross national product per capita and provincial population for the whole period.

In each year the payments so calculated were subject to a deduction for the statutory subsidies payable in that year and also for the collections under the 5 per cent provincial corporation income tax mentioned above. For the agreeing provinces these amounts were approximately $12½ million and $20 to 25 million a year respectively. As events transpired the process of collection and assessment of the provincial tax fell behind the agreement payments, so that the agreement period closed with a substantial balance of taxes yet to be collected and offset against the agreement payments. Since this amount was in fact owed to the Dominion by the provinces a bulk settlement was made under which it was agreed that the Dominion would simply retain for itself the outstanding liabilities under the provincial 5 per cent tax as they were collected.

In addition to the principal payments under the agreement the Dominion also paid to all provinces (including Ontario and Quebec) one-half of its revenue from the corporation income tax on power, gas, and steam producing companies. This amount varied from year to year, but on average was about $3½ million annually.

The Agreements in the Federal Budget

The complexity of the various adjustments and offsetting payments in this five-year period makes almost impossible a simple presentation of the actual transactions under the 1947 agreement. In Table XLII the payments and reimbursements of the federal government are given for the relevant fiscal years (1948 to 1952). This presentation indicates as nearly as is possible under these conditions the aggregate financial impact of the agreements on the federal budget.

Because of the involved character of the annual accounting these

TABLE XLII

DOMINION PAYMENTS TO PROVINCES UNDER 1947 AGREEMENTS
FISCAL YEARS 1948 TO 1952
($ million)

Fiscal year	Statutory subsidies[a]	Tax agreement	5% Corp. inc. tax collections	½ Dom. tax on utilities[a]	Total
1948	17.3	59.5	—	—	76.8
1949	17.1	84.4	—	—	101.5
1950	19.2	76.9	20.2	1.4	117.7
1951	18.7	94.1	17.4	4.6	134.8
1952	20.1	96.9	25.1	3.7	145.9
					576.7

[a]Includes payments to Quebec and Ontario; in the case of the sharing of the tax on utilities payments relating to the five-year period were also made in 1953 and 1954 in the amount of $4.4 million and $4.0 million respectively

payments bore no constant relationship to the rest of the federal budget. For the whole period they represented about 3.8 per cent of federal revenues and 4.3 per cent of expenditures.

The Agreements in the Provincial Budgets

The relative weight of the payments in provincial budgets varied markedly. In Prince Edward Island, for example, in all years they accounted for more than half of total provincial revenues. The proportion in the other provinces was lower than half in every case, being just under half in Manitoba, 35 to 40 per cent in Nova Scotia and New Brunswick, around 30 per cent in Saskatchewan, and in the neighbourhood of one-quarter in Alberta and British Columbia. These proportions were considerably less, it will be noted, than the share of revenues derived from the Dominion at the time of union, when some provinces received 80 to 90 per cent of their revenues from the Dominion and few received less than 50 per cent.

The abstention of Quebec and Ontario meant that in their case only the traditional statutory subsidies were paid. These amounted respectively to $2.9 million and $3.2 million annually.

As a result of the 1951 census the statutory subsidies of all provinces were revised in 1952, the aggregate effect being to increase the total annual amount payable from $18.7 million to $20.1 million. It is self-evident that these subsidies are now much less important in the complex of federal-provincial payments than ever before.

Terms for Newfoundland

Before passing on to the latest phase of recent developments—the 1952 agreements—the financial terms on which Newfoundland entered union in 1949 should be explained. The essential condition of course was to avoid any radical departure from the traditional pattern of Canadian federal finance. After protracted negotiations a plan of subsidies was evolved which conformed reasonably well with that objective. The annual "statutory" subsidy was set at $1,540,000, being the total of (*a*) $260,000 (80 cents per capita on a population of 325,000); (*b*) $180,000, and (*c*) $1,100,000. The second two amounts were calculated to be comparable to the subsidies for support of government and the various special grants paid to the existing Maritime Provinces, the latter being justified in the case of Newfoundland by the nature of its terrain and the sparse and scattered nature of its population.

More significant for the immediate future were the so-called "transitional" grants, totalling $42,750,000. These grants were to be at the amount of $6.5 million for the first three years, declining thereafter by $850,000 a year until $1.4 million is reached in the ninth year, and thereafter the decline will be $350,000 a year until at the end of the twelfth year the transitional grants will cease.

Other terms of union provided for assumption of most of the provincial debt by the Dominion, and for the retention by the province of a surplus of $40 million accumulated during the war. The province was to spend this money on development projects. Finally, after union the province accepted the federal offer of a tax rental agreement on terms comparable to those of the other agreeing provinces. In this case the period was for the three years 1949 to 1951 inclusive, and the province was given a guaranteed minimum payment of $6,208,765, calculated under the option applicable also to Nova Scotia and Saskatchewan.

Federal-Provincial Conference, December, 1950

In fulfilment of an undertaking that it would call a conference at least one year before the expiry of the 1947 tax agreements to consider new arrangements, the Dominion summoned all ten provinces to a meeting at Ottawa in December, 1950. Many subjects in the field of federal-provincial relations were suggested for discussion, but in view of the serious international situation that had developed with the war in Korea the agenda was held down to two issues: (1) the basis for new tax agreements, and (2) the introduction of contributory old age pensions without a means test (see p. 561). The Dominion submitted concrete terms for a new tax agreement that would run from April 1, 1952, to March 31, 1957, and cover the same taxes as the 1947 agreement. The new basis of compensation would be the guaranteed minimum payments under the 1947 agreements (which it will be recalled was based on factors relating mainly to 1942) increased by the ratio of gross national product per capita and provincial population between 1942 and 1948. The existing guaranteed payments would in effect be permanently raised to the level of these indices of economic activity as they stood in 1948.

One new alternative was offered, however. Any province could elect a guaranteed minimum payment equal to the total of the following amounts:

1. The yield of a personal income tax at 5 per cent of 1948 federal rates applied to 1948 incomes in the province.

2. The yield of a tax of 8½ per cent on corporation profits earned in

the province in 1948. (The rate of 8½ per cent, it was explained, was taken to represent in terms of a single rate of corporation profits tax the combined effect of the separate or specific taxes traditionally levied by provinces and a tax of 7 per cent on corporate profits.)

3. The average revenue received by the province from succession duties. (The figure taken for the agreeing provinces was the average of the revenues received during the last two years before their succession duties were suspended, and for Ontario and Quebec, the average of the three fiscal years 1946–7, 1947–8 and 1948–9.)

4. Statutory subsidies payable to the province for 1948.

On the basis of calculations made by the Dominion, this option, intended to represent a fair revised appraisal of the value of the tax sources being rented, would be more favourable only to the province of Ontario.

The Dominion also proposed that under the new agreement the adjusted payments be calculated on the basis of the two years prior to the year of payment rather than on three years, and that the concept "gross national product at factor cost" be substituted for "gross national product at market prices" as an adjustment factor, the purpose being to eliminate the effect of changes in indirect taxes on the adjustment factor.

The guaranteed minimum payments under the new proposal are compared in Table XLIII with the guaranteed minimum payments under the 1947 agreement.

These proposals were discussed at a three-day conference, which

TABLE XLIII

GUARANTEED PAYMENTS—1947 AGREEMENT AND 1950 OFFER
($ thousand)

	1947 agreement	1950 offer
Newfoundland	6,209	9,151
Prince Edward Island	2,100	2,911
Nova Scotia	10,870	15,666
New Brunswick	8,773	12,758
Quebec	56,382	84,598
Ontario	67,158	101,801
Manitoba	13,540	18,855
Saskatchewan	15,291	19,831
Alberta	14,228	20,243
British Columbia	18,120	30,229
Total	212,671	316,043

adjourned to give the provincial representatives a further opportunity to consider them. (As previously indicated, at this same Conference the Dominion, at the request of several provinces, undertook to sponsor an amendment to the British North America Act that would allow the provinces to impose an indirect retail sales tax.)

Post-Conference Developments

Only scant information has been made public on the nature of the negotiations which followed the Conference. The indications are that requests were received from all or most of the provinces for a higher level of guaranteed payments and perhaps for other concessions as well. The details of these representations were not revealed, but their existence was acknowledged in a letter addressed by Mr. Abbott to all provinces in January, 1952. In this letter Mr. Abbott explained that the federal government thought it unwise to accede to provincial requests for higher payments because of "the continuing heavy burden on the federal treasury for defence and other outlays" and in view of "the extreme uncertainty of the years immediately ahead." However, he offered a compromise. He agreed that there was validity in the argument advanced by some provinces that even with the reduction of the adjustment period from a three-year to a two-year average the payments might still not be buoyant enough to meet the pressure of a period of rapid development. He therefore offered, on behalf of the federal government, to allow any province the option of having its actual payment calculated on the basis of the adjustment factors relating to the *single* year immediately preceding the year of payment.

Apparently the provincial authorities were content to proceed without a further public conference. On the basis of the original offer, as modified by the alternative just mentioned, which all provinces elected to take, the original eight provinces renewed without more ado. The new contract, while covering essentially the same subject matter as the previous one, was redrafted throughout for greater clarity and simplicity. The payment schedule was retained on a quarterly basis but the time of the first payment was advanced to June 30 in place of September 30. The provisions for arbitration in the event of a dispute were drastically altered, and some modifications were made in less significant terms.

The most marked departure from the 1947 agreement was in the commitments given by the Dominion for the period following expiry. The previous agreement had carried a guarantee that for *one* year after its expiry the Dominion would allow tax credits for personal and corporate income taxes and succession duties imposed by a province. Under the new agreement this guarantee is for a *five*-year period, and the credit to be allowed for a corporation profits tax is raised to 7 per cent in place of 5 per cent under the former agreement. The other undertakings—for a credit up to 50 per cent of the federal death duty and up to 5 per cent of the federal personal income tax—remain unchanged.

The extension to five years of the guarantee of tax credits appears to have been made as a result of pressure from British Columbia, and was undoubtedly influential in the decision of this province and probably one or two others to renew.

By 1951 relations between Ontario and the federal government were marked by a greater degree of cordiality than had prevailed for some time. But Premier Frost had said nothing, following the 1950 conference, that indicated he would accept the federal offer. On the contrary, according to the press he was reported to have said, at the time of the revisions made in January, 1952: "I don't think this offer means a great deal to Ontario. We don't want to accept something which is artificial and far removed from the realities of Ontario's tremendous growth in recent years." Further evidence of indifference appeared in the spring session of the Ontario legislature. The Frost Government then argued that the Dominion was obliged to pay to Ontario the amount of revenue the province could obtain by levying a personal income tax equal to the 5 per cent allowable credit, and requested that it do so. This request received some editorial support in the province but the federal government turned it down promptly.

This was the position reached by late spring, 1952. As a result, the announcement by the Ontario Premier in late August that his Government had concluded an agreement on substantially the basis offered at the 1950 Conference came as some surprise. On the whole, however, the move appeared to have been well received by the public. At a special session held in the fall to adopt the necessary legislation there was little criticism. On the other hand casual remarks by federal officials indicated that the heavy payments to Ontario had been a less than welcome addition to the national budget.

The position of Premier Duplessis, Quebec, as viewed from the perspective of late 1954, has developed from an attitude of enigmatic amiability at the 1950 Conference to one of firm rejection of the tax agreement approach and belligerent assertion of provincial financial autonomy. Many of his own public utterances could be quoted to this effect, but most convincing evidence is the establishment of the so-called Tremblay Commission and the adoption of a provincial personal income tax. Both have been mentioned previously (chap. 29). While there were signs towards the end of 1954 that a *rapprochement* between Quebec and the federal authorities might be in the offing, there was no suggestion that this would be on the basis of acceptance of a tax rental agreement by Quebec. Indeed Premier Duplessis' reaction to the Dominion's announcement early in 1955 that it would give a 10 per cent reduction in a province taxing personal incomes in place of the 5 per cent credit confirmed this view. He applauded, but said the Dominion should go higher still.

Financial Summary

Table XLIII demonstrated the effect of the upward adjustment in the guaranteed minimum payment as offered at the 1950 Conference. The change in the adjustment period to a one-year basis has of course exerted a most important influence on the payments actually received. In Table XLIV the 1954 adjusted amounts are given for all provinces, including and excluding Quebec for comparative purposes. As a standard for comparison the amounts of the 1947 and 1952 guaranteed

TABLE XLIV

COMPARATIVE PAYMENTS RELATING TO 1952 AGREEMENT[a]
($ million)

	Estimated adjusted payment 1954	Estimated adjusted payment for 1952		Guaranteed minima	
		One-year adjustment	Three-year adjustment	1952 agreement	1947 agreement
Nfld.	13.9	12.2	10.7	9.2	6.2
P.E.I.	4.5	3.9	3.4	3.0	2.1
N.S.	22.2	20.1	17.7	15.3	10.9
N.B.	18.4	16.6	14.6	12.6	8.8
Que.	129.3	114.4	99.9	85.1	56.4
Ont.	156.0	137.4	118.3	101.8	67.2
Man.	27.5	24.6	21.6	18.6	13.5
Sask.	28.2	24.6	21.9	20.0	15.3
Alta.	33.4	28.7	24.8	21.0	14.2
B.C.	46.6	41.2	35.6	29.6	18.1
Total	479.9	423.8	368.5	316.2	212.7
Total ex. Quebec	350.6	309.4	268.6	231.1	156.3

[a]Subject to deduction of statutory subsidies in all cases and of federal succession duty credits in the case of Ontario and Quebec.

minima are again given, and figures for 1952 are also given to demonstrate the effect in that year of the change from the three-year to the one-year adjustment basis.

The Agreements in the Federal Budget

In the federal budget of approximately $4.5 billion, statutory and tax agreement subsidies of $340 million in 1953 (tax agreement, statutory subsidies, share of income tax on utilities, and transitional grant to Newfoundland) accounted for 9 per cent.

The Agreements in the Provincial Budgets

In the aggregate, payments related to the tax agreements represented about 35 per cent of the revenue of the agreeing provinces in 1953. But as in the past the relative importance of the payments in individual provincial budgets varies markedly. In that year as a percentage of total revenues they ranged from a high of 59.8 in Prince Edward Island to a low of 24.0 in Alberta (based on preliminary figures). The specific percentage in each province, in order of magnitude, was as follows: Prince Edward Island, 59.8; Manitoba, 49.9; Nova Scotia, 44.2; Newfoundland, 42.4; Ontario, 40.6; New Brunswick, 38.7; Saskatchewan, 30.6; British Columbia, 24.4, and Alberta, 24.0. In Quebec the statutory subsidy payments account for only slightly more than one per cent of provincial revenues.

So much for the status of federal-provincial payments relating to tax transfers in 1954. In view of rumours current in late 1954 of an imminent provincial conference at which new proposals would be offered by the federal government, it was not certain at the time of writing that the agreements would run their course to maturity in 1956. Whatever alternative, if any, is adopted, it is safe to assume on the basis of the historical development traced in these pages that it will continue to involve very substantial payments from the Dominion to several of the provinces.

Other Federal-Provincial Subsidies

In addition to the tax agreement payments substantial amounts are still being paid by the federal governments as grants-in-aid of specific provincial services and projects. At least three new programmes—health grants, Trans-Canada highway grants, and university grants—have been instituted in the post-war period. The assumption by the Dominion of the full responsibility for pensions of $40 a month to all persons 70 and over in 1952 brought to an end the oldest and largest of the joint schemes, but federal-provincial co-operation has been continued in this field with the inauguration of pensions for persons in the 65-to-69 age group, subject to a means test.

Old age pensions. It will be appropriate, before going on to new matters, to put on the record some of the data relating to the joint scheme for old age pensions which terminated on January 1, 1952. Under this arrangement, it will be recalled, the federal government paid three-quarters of the cost of pensions to persons over seventy who could qualify under a means test. It also shared in the cost of pensions to blind persons. Actual administration was in provincial hands, the federal government simply sharing in the expense, subject to audit control.

In 1950–1, the last full fiscal year in which pensions were paid, the federal share of the cost was about $103 million, and in future years would have remained in excess of $100 million. This compared with a pre-war outlay of $30 million. This increase of more than threefold was due to two factors: (1) successive raises in the amount of the pension, and (2) relaxation of the means test.

Prior to World War II the rate of pension had been $20 a month. In 1943 it was increased to $25 a month, in 1947 to $30 a month, and in 1949 to $40 a month, in recognition of the decreased value of money in the war and post-war period. Due to this factor alone the federal contribution doubled in less than ten years.

The relaxation of the means test was of considerable significance as well. Prior to the war a single person was allowed only a total income (including the old age pension itself) of $365 a year. This was increased to $425 in 1944 and to $600 in 1947. For a married couple the original allowance was $730, but was subsequently raised to $1,080. The granting of pensions to persons other than British subjects, the reduction of the age of eligibility for blind pensions from 40 to 21, and the increasing proportion of persons over 70 in the population also contributed to raise the cost. At the time this scheme was ended about 45 per cent of the 650,000 persons in Canada then over 70 were in receipt of an old age pension.[3]

The introduction of pensions for persons 65 to 69 in 1952 followed from the proposal made by the Dominion at the 1950 Conference to meet one-half the cost of a pension of $40 a month to persons eligible under a means test. Authority was granted for agreements with the

[3]For a full description of the pre-1952 old age pensions plan see Joint Committee of the Senate and House of Commons on Old Age Security, April and May, 1950, *Minutes of Proceedings and Evidence.*

provinces in the Old Age Assistance Act, 1951, and subsequently these were entered into with nine provinces at the full monthly rate. Newfoundland, the tenth, has an agreement for payment of $30 a month. The maximum allowable annual income, including the amount of the pension, was increased under the new plan to $720 (formerly $600) for single persons and to $1,200 for married couples (formerly $1,080). Where one spouse is blind the allowable income is $1,320 a year. In general applicants must have resided in Canada for the previous 20 years to be eligible.

The federal contribution for the fiscal year 1953–4 was over $20 million, and would rise with an aging population.

For most of the provinces the outlay for one-half the cost of pensions under the new plan was as large as that made for one-quarter of the cost of the former pensions. Although relieved of the major responsibility for persons seventy and over with the introduction of the federally financed scheme in 1952, their net financial position has been left relatively unchanged.

Pensions for the blind have been continued under new legislation passed in 1951—The Blind Persons Act. The federal government provides three-quarters of the cost of pensions of $40 a month for blind persons 21 years of age or over. The means test limit is higher than for old age assistance, being $840 a year for a single person or $1,320 a year for a married couple. Persons receiving other federal assistance are not eligible. Federal payments in 1953–4 amounted to about $3 million.

Health grants. Of the post-war innovations undoubtedly the health grants plan is the most important. When the very comprehensive health proposals advanced at the Reconstruction Conference in 1945 failed to elicit provincial support the whole scheme was temporarily dropped. However, in 1948 the Prime Minister announced that the federal government was prepared to implement that part of the proposals which called for grants in support of specific health services. He announced a five-year programme, under which $30 million or more would be made available annually.

The grants take several forms, of which those for hospital construction, for improving general public health services, for tuberculosis and cancer control and for mental health bulk largest. Others include assistance for completion of surveys of health service requirements, venereal disease control, aid to crippled children, professional training, and public health research. In some cases the province must make a matching grant, in others not. Hospital construction grants, which accounted for about 40 per cent of the total over the initial five-year period, are distributed on the basis of $1,000 per bed for active treatment beds and $1,500 per bed for chronic or convalescent beds, on condition that the province match or exceed the Dominion contribution and also that in no case will the Dominion grant exceed one-third of the total cost of the hospital. Most of the other grants give a flat minimum to each province, with the balance being distributed on a per capita basis, and without any requirement of provincial matching.

In all during the first five-year period about $167 million was made available to the provinces by annual appropriation, which rose gradually from about $30 million in 1948–9 to $36½ million in 1952–3. Of this amount, however, only about $94 million was taken up in total, actual expenditures rising from about $7½ million in 1948–9 to about $27 million in 1952–3. The growing importance of these grants to the provinces is indicated by the fact that in 1948–9 they accounted for 9 per cent of their health expenditures and in 1952–3 for over 12 per cent.

Annual federal expenditures in the five fiscal years 1948–9 to 1952–3 under the various grants are set out in Table XLV.

In 1953 it was announced that the grants would be carried on for another five years on an expanded basis. It was estimated that some $219 million (including a revote of $21 million for hospital construction) would be available in the new period. Along with the services pre-

TABLE XLV

FEDERAL HEALTH GRANTS
($ thousand)

	1948–9	1949–50	1950–1	1951–2	1952–3	Total
Health surveys	60	161	198	74	27	521
Hospitals	2,223	6,804	6,897	9,166	10,544	35,635
Public health	782	2,081	2,908	3,605	3,893	13,268
T.B. control	2,586	2,427	3,166	4,046	4,299	16,523
Mental health	439	1,928	2,645	3,724	4,546	13,282
V.D. control	325	493	484	480	463	2,246
Crippled children	104	187	244	350	399	1,285
Prof. training	232	381	453	521	605	2,192
Public health research	43	149	231	314	444	1,181
Cancer control	867	1,135	1,693	2,042	2,127	7,864
	7,661	15,746	18,919	24,322	27,349	93,997

viously supported new grants were announced for (*a*) laboratory and radiological services; (*b*) rehabilitation of disabled persons, and (*c*) medical services for mothers and children. The first two of these new grants are to be distributed on a per capita basis and the third in accordance with the rate of births and infant deaths. For most projects the provinces will be required to make a matching grant.[4]

Trans-Canada Highway. Another major programme was introduced in 1949 with the passage of the Trans-Canada Highways Act. It provides for a federal contribution of up to 50 per cent of the cost of completing a highway across Canada, a project that was started in the depression to create employment. Much of the road in outlying areas is completed with gravelled surface, and by paving these sections, joining up existing paved highways, and filling in the many remaining gaps it is hoped to achieve the goal of a coast-to-coast highway by the end of 1956. Federal participation is limited under the Act to a total of $150 million. It is interesting that it proposes to share in the cost of expenditures on the route made since April, 1928, when the Canada Highways Act, 1919, expired.

Agreements have been negotiated between the Dominion and nine provinces (all but Quebec) covering a projected route.

Annual federal grants in the first four years were as follows:

1950–1	$ 7,205,000
1951–2	12,791,000
1952–3	13,953,000
1953–4	14,200,000

University grants. The third significant post-war innovation was the introduction of federal grants in aid of university education. The Dominion had previously given aid to provincial technical and other specialized schools, but had fairly scrupulously refrained from entering the area of general education, which is fraught with constitutional, religious, racial, and other hazards in Canada. It was induced to inaugurate the scheme of university grants in 1951 on the recommendation of the Royal Commission on Canadian Arts and Culture, of which the Rt. Hon. Vincent Massey (now Governor General of Canada) was chairman. The Commission proposed that a grant should be paid to educational institutions of university standing. The basis proposed was 50¢ per capita of the population in each province, the allocation among the individual universities in the province to be in the proportion that the number of enrolments in courses leading to a university degree in

[4]For further details see Dept. of National Health and Welfare, *Five Year Report, National Health Programme* (Ottawa, 1954).

each university bore to the total of such enrolments in all universities in the province.

An amount of $7 million was first appropriated in the fiscal year 1951–2, and slightly larger amounts have been set aside in later years. Except for Quebec the provincial governments have raised no serious objections to this "invasion" of one of their traditional fields; on the contrary several have openly welcomed it. In Quebec, however, the scheme met firm resistance from the beginning. At first the provincial authorities agreed to allow the universities to accept the grants on condition that the provincial Minister of Finance join with the federal Minister of Finance in making the awards. But even this concession finally did not satisfy Quebec sensibilities, and the universities were ordered to refuse the 1952–3 and 1953–4 grants. The province itself now gives its own grants to universities from the proceeds of the personal income tax introduced in 1954.

With the exclusion of Quebec the actual payments under the measure are just in excess of $5 million.

Miscellaneous Other Grants and Programmes

In addition to the major programmes just outlined there are many arrangements of lesser importance which involve either joint Dominion-provincial action or Dominion assistance with a function traditionally provincial. These include grants for various forms of vocational, apprenticeship, and youth training; grants for land protection, reclamation, and development, such as those made under the Eastern Rocky Mountain Forest Conservation Act and the Maritime Marshland Rehabilitation Act, and special appropriations for major irrigation, storage, and flood control measures, such as the Fraser Valley Dyking Scheme and the Red River and Upper Thames flood control projects; grants for the improvement and protection of forests under the Canada Forest Act of 1949, which authorizes a sharing of one-half the cost of making provincial forest inventories and one-quarter of the cost of programmes of reforesting provincial Crown lands. These and other instances represent direct co-operative measures. While it goes somewhat outside the area of this survey, it might also be mentioned that several direct federal measures in which the provincial governments do not participate in some degree relieve them of financial responsibilities. Among these would be included the national scheme for unemployment insurance inaugurated in 1941; the family allowance scheme introduced in 1945; the universal old age pensions scheme introduced in 1952, and various forms of agricultural assistance and development, principally under the Prairie Farms Assistance Act and the Prairie Farms Rehabilitation Act.

Summary

Tables 21 and 22 in Appendix C give a statistical tabulation of all the major payments made by the Dominion to the provinces from 1868 to 1954. The interesting conclusion to be drawn from this tabulation is that in the eight and one-half decades or so since Confederation nearly three billion dollars has been paid in one form or other by the Dominion to the provincial governments. By contrast, had the original and "final" terms of settlement been carried through unchanged this amount would have been in the neighbourhood of $200 million.

Epilogue

THE DROPPING of our curtain on the Canadian scene in the early spring of 1955 is a purely arbitrary event dictated only by the iron rules of time. It is as indefensible "theatre" as dousing the lights just when the lead players are returning to the stage for yet another episode in the drama. None of the conflicts have been resolved, and the performance is as crowded and confusing as it has ever been. But here is the end of the script; whatever is to come now can only be revealed by the passage of time.

However, if the exact shape of events is obscure, it should at least be possible to give some general idea of the setting in which they will work themselves out.

THE GENERAL LEVEL OF TAXATION

It would appear from the vantage point of early 1955 that expenditures at all levels of government in Canada will remain in the neighbourhood of $6½ to $7 billion for the foreseeable future. The aggregate at this time is made up of $4½ to $5 billion of federal expenditure and $2 billion of combined provincial and municipal expenditure. The distribution may change but it hardly seems likely that the total will decline. A defence programme requiring a peacetime outlay of $1½ to $2 billion a year for many years will be the largest single element in the federal budget. Defence expenditures and outlays for welfare programmes, interest on the public debt, and payments to provinces (if the present scale continues) will make up about three-quarters of the total. The balance will go for the many ordinary functions of government, the cost of which it may be possible to contain but which with a growing population and an expanding economy will be difficult to reduce.

Provincial and municipal expenditures will be heavily committed to highways, education, and welfare programmes, which will easily account for two-thirds of their budgets. The traffic problem on the highways and city streets will become more pressing with an increasing population and more cars, and its solution will involve outlays of a magnitude unparalleled in previous experience. The education of children already born will require a substantial increase in school facilities, and there is no indication of slackening in the growth in school population. For the immediate future the financing of these budgets will necessitate maintaining rates of tax heavier than in previous peacetime experience. For a time this might mean rates on corporation profits of 45 to 50 per cent; rates on personal incomes at more than double prewar levels; provincial gasoline taxes at new highs; possible additions to the ranks of the five provinces now levying retail sales taxes; and continuing pressure on the real property tax.

This prospect quite naturally causes some concern to government and business leaders, economists, and others in early 1955. How long can an economy go forward under tax conditions which give so little incentive for enterprise and investment? How can Canadian exporting industries successfully meet tough competition for foreign markets while carrying this heavy tax burden at home? What effect is the massive machinery of government finance having on the regional distribution of industry and on the saving and spending habits of the people? Will the cessation of the postwar upward movement of prices and incomes reveal that the bad effects of high taxes have previously been glossed over by inflation, and that only more inflation or lower rates will provide a remedy? Has the time arrived for a deliberate programme of tax reductions and deficit financing to stimulate lagging business conditions? What are the prospects for some new welfare programme, such as a health insurance scheme for the country, which would add several hundred millions to the federal budget?

The outlook is serious enough, but perhaps not quite as black as these questions, so baldly posed, would suggest. Resting on a gross national product of about $24 billion this tax load is much more of a burden than it would be if the gross national product were, say, $30 billion. There is a fair prospect that this figure might be reached over a decade, so that the load will gradually lighten over the long run, assuming that no large-scale warfare intervened. Furthermore there is still evidence of economic growth on every hand at the beginning of 1955, despite gloomy prognostications, and a younger generation of businessmen who have known nothing but the present level of taxation seem as eager to go ahead as their forefathers ever were. Much sorrow is also being salved by the beneficent influences of tax-free capital gains for the upper classes and family allowances and old age pensions for the masses. What is most important of all is that the role Canada has adopted in the cold war defence programme is unquestioned by the taxpayers, who are meeting the heavy burden it imposes in reasonably good spirit. Certainly there is no cause for complacency, but there seem grounds for reasonable hope that the country will survive its ordeal.

Intergovernmental Relations

In this phase of Canadian federal finance, whose turbulent career has been traced in earlier chapters, all is in flux and confusion at the beginning of 1955. The tax rental agreement device, which in federal-provincial relations bridged the gap for the war and postwar years, is being challenged on all sides. New men, both in Ottawa and in many provincial capitals, who had no active part in the negotiation of the present arrangements, are questioning their value. There is much talk of more autonomy for provincial governments in the levying of taxes, but at the same time there is talk of more money for the provinces too, and there is only one place the money can come from—the federal government. For its part the federal government seems to have become restive under the yoke of the agreements, which saddle it with both heavy expenditures for general grants and heavy responsibilities for over-all tax policy, despite which the provinces continually press for other assistance with specific functions—roads, education, health, welfare, and so on. Some part of this restiveness grew out of an understandable desire to let the provinces stand on their own feet to test their manliness, and about as much again out of a lessening of enthusiasm for the role of "great centralizer" voluntarily assumed after World War II. In this atmosphere the meetings which Mr. St. Laurent has invited provincial premiers to attend in 1955 might well mean the end of the tax agreements. The Province of Quebec of course will in any event be guided by its own view of its own destiny, so that any solution that is adopted will have to take into account at least one province that is unwilling to enter into any form of agreement with the national government, and there will probably be more. As always the solution will have to contain as one of its ingredients some form of payments to the less prosperous provinces, the historical imperative of federal financial relations in Canada. In short it begins to look as though the wheel is spinning once again, undoubtedly to stop at some position of compromise which will please no one but which the majority will accept in order to get on in relative peace with the important matter of governing the country. In the process of bargaining a great many extravagant statements may be made and a certain amount of heat generated but none of this will be novel in Canadian experience. Indeed it is clear that much of what has transpired since union was shrewdly foreseen by one of its most bitter critics. His words were the sharp words of a parliamentarian in opposition, and therefore barbed and scathing. And yet he spoke true in many ways. Here are the cynical and brilliant words of Mr. Christopher Dunkin, member for the constituency of Brome, spoken in the Legislative Assembly of the Province of United Canada in 1865 in the debates on Confederation:

> . . . engineers say that the measure of strength of a fortified place is the strength of its weakest part. And this principle is here applied to our provinces in a financial point of view. The need of the neediest is made the measure of the aid given to all. The most embarrassed is to have enough for its purposes, and the rest are to receive, if not exactly in the same ratio, at least so nearly up to the mark as that they shall all be satisfied.
> . . . And before I go further, there occurs to me this consideration, arising out of this state of things . . . one consideration, I say, connected with this, which should not be lost sight of when we are talking about the application of anything in the least like responsible government to our provinces. I never yet heard of an elected legislative body that had much control over a government, unless it had hold of the strings of a purse from which the government wanted to get something.
> . . . the provincial governments will, in a quiet way, want money, and the provincial legislators and people will want it yet more; grants for roads and bridges, for schools, for charities, for salaries, for contingencies of the legislative body—for all manner of ends they will be wanting money, and where is it to come from? . . . the easiest way for it to get money will be from the General Government. I am not sure, either, but that most members of the provincial legislatures will like it that way the best. (Hear, hear.) It will not be at all unpopular, the getting of money so. Quite the contrary.
> . . . when the time comes for making that sort of demand, depend upon it that it will sound singularly reasonable in the ears of the provinces whose representatives shall make it; and if two or three provinces shall join in the demand, my word for it, the thing will soon be done.
> . . . for everything so given, much or little, to whatever province, you will have to do the like for all the rest, and the figure will be alarming before you get to the end. And even this is not all.
> . . . For any local work in which it can be at all pretended that it is of general interest, pressure may be brought to bear upon the General Government and Legislature, and whenever one province succeeds in getting any such grant, every other province must be dealt with in the same way. (Extracts taken from pp. 517–20.)

In the area of provincial-municipal relations major changes will undoubtedly continue to take place. It is becoming increasingly evident that the property tax (even if greatly improved) will not in the future be adequate to finance the demands on municipalities for education, streets, and a multitude of other services. Already large grants are being made by provincial governments for these purposes. Undoubtedly the amounts of these grants will continue to grow, and there may also be some transfer of functions from municipality to province. But the way to the best solution is by no means clear. There is much to be done yet in reorganizing municipalities and school districts into their most efficient operational areas, and this is a slow process, largely because for sentimental and other reasons the citizen himself resists it. The sort of function that may safely be transferred to provincial hands is by no means self-evident, and there is still a strong faith in the salutary effect of administration in close contact with the people. Particularly is this true of education, where tax-paying parents have no substitute as a lively watch-guard over the schools. By the same token it would be essential that provinces avoid giving grants so large that local governments become subservient to their control. And yet almost unanimously the tax-paying public is opposed to more municipal taxation of any sort, so that the dilemma is a real one. Fortunately there are signs that this dilemma has been recognized, and much serious thought has been devoted to it in all provinces in recent years. The progress towards its solution will be one of the major developments of 1955 and the years ahead, although here again the problem alters with changing times, and each period requires its own compromise.

The Tariff

Finally, there is one of the oldest members of the cast—the tariff. Today more than ever before almost exclusively regarded as an arm of commercial policy rather than as a source of revenue, its role in the piece is as lively as at any time. At the outset of 1955 long months of studied horse-trading at Geneva resulted in an undertaking among the GATT countries to extend the treaty arrangements substantially unchanged for two and one-half years following June 30, 1955, and for three-year periods thereafter. The treaty has yet to be submitted to the various legislatures for ratification, and undoubtedly in Canada its parliamentary reception will be marked by some friction. Lagging business and serious unemployment in the electrical manufacturing and textile industries are being blamed on imports from abroad, and requests for increased tariff protection are being voiced. The suggestion of a revived "National Policy" can be faintly discerned in public discussion for the first time in years. With the current government holding staunchly to its low tariff policies—apparently with the support of the majority of the business community—the treaty seems sure to become law. Nevertheless it is clear enough that if heavy unemployment continues in industries that are suffering from foreign competition the government will be under increasing pressure for some form of protection.

To give a clear statement of the philosophical basis of the present Canadian tariff is a challenge the present writer will happily pass on to persons better qualified than himself. However it is probably safe to venture that its basic role is still its traditional one—to help in creating a Canadian nation in defiance of the bonds which hold us to Great Britain and the forces which attract us toward the United States. This role was more apparent when our struggle upwards from the status of a colony to a strong and autonomous nation was in its earlier stages. Today we take much of this for granted, but our tariff is still in a sense the price we pay for being Canadians. This price of course can be too high if our tariffs invite retaliatory action by other countries to keep out of their market the products we must export to survive. This is the price that every Minister of Finance has been forced to estimate since Confederation, and the calculations are becoming increasingly fine as we engage ever more closely in the United States economy without becoming a part of it.

Apology

The above is most of what the author wanted to say in this rather rambling tailpiece. There might have been more, however, had he not realized that he was engaged in a futile attempt to have the last word, whereas events may have belied every thought expressed in this Epilogue before it appears in print. Chastened with this realization the author is content to lay down pen and join the reader as a spectator of the passing parade in one of the most eventful periods of civilization.

APPENDIXES

Appendix A—Main Events in Taxation, 1650-1954

circa
1650 *New France*—first known tax in Canada levied in form of export duty on beaver and moose pelts at 50% and 10% respectively, payable in kind
1653 *N.F.*—export duty on beaver pelts reduced to 25%
1662 *N.F.*—10% tax on all imports introduced for six years to pay colonial debt
1664 *N.F.*—dry goods exempt from 10% duty
1665 *N.F.*—dry goods taxable under 10% duty
1670 *N.F.*—10% duty removed; specific duties roughly equivalent imposed on imported tobacco, wine, and brandy
1703 *N.F.*—duties on wine, brandy, and tobacco increased one-third
1707 *N.F.*—export duty of 25% on beaver pelts abolished
1716 *N.F.*—property tax imposed in Montreal to pay for cost of stone wall built around city
1743 *N.F.*—duties on wines and liquor increased
1747 *N.F.*—further substantial increases on wines and liquor
1748 *N.F.*—general 3% tariff introduced; food and certain other essentials exempted; general 3% export duty also provided—moose pelts retained at 10%, but beaver pelts subject to 3%; neither tariff nor export duties brought into effect immediately, but operative at time of conquest
1750 *N.F.*—annual levy based on property introduced in Quebec City for support of garrison
1751 *N.S.*—first tax, duty of 6¢ per gallon on spirits sold in province
1758 *N.S.*—first revenue legislation levied tariff and excises on spirits only
1759 fall of Quebec
1760 *N.S.*—charge based on tonnage of ships leaving Halifax
1763 British régime formally instituted in Canada by Treaty of Paris; French revenue system of tariffs and fur royalties continued substantially unchanged; Navigation Laws applicable to new colony
1764 *N.S.*—import duties on sugar, bricks, lumber, and billiard tables levied
1765 *N.S.*—excises on tea, coffee, and playing-cards imposed; new taxes also levied on "persons" for support of counties
1769 P.E.I. became separate province, formerly being part of Nova Scotia
1772 *N.S.*—first land tax levied for temporary period
1774 Quebec Revenue Act established permanent revenue system for colony
1775 *N.S.*—capitation tax, "varying with circumstances and abilities to bear and pay such rate," imposed on every male over 21; lapsed after a year
1778 by Declaratory Act (18 Geo. III, c. 12) Imperial government undertook to levy colonial tariffs for purposes of trade regulation only and to leave revenue in colonies to be used for local purposes
1779 *N.S.*—real property tax levied for one year

1782 *N.S.*–2½% general tariff on imports by non-residents
1784 New Brunswick, formerly part of Nova Scotia, became separate colony
1785 *N.B.*–Saint John (oldest incorporated municipality in Canada) given charter
N.S.–tobacco and chocolate added to tariff
1786 *N.B.*–specific duties enacted on rum and other liquors and 5% tariff on all imports, except necessities from foreign countries
1787–8 restricted trade with United States via Lake Champlain given legal sanction
1789 *N.S.*–10% tariff on American imports; lumber, grain, and cattle exempt
1791 Constitutional Act divided Quebec into provinces of Upper and Lower Canada; Imperial government retained regulation of trade and tariffs, but new provincial governments were also allowed henceforth to levy their own customs duties in addition to Imperial duties
N.S.–elementary form of income tax (capitation tax) levied, moderate rate graduation
1792 *N.S.*–2½% general *ad valorem* tariff introduced; 10% American tariff continued
1793 *Upper Canada*–first municipal Assessment Act (33 Geo. III, c. 3) adopted; imposed a moderately graduated tax on total property, real and personal
1795 *N.S.*–1791 capitation tax repealed
1796 Jay's Treaty allowed trade with United States in non-prohibited items without imposition of discriminatory rates of duty
Lower Canada–first municipal Assessment Act adopted
1807 *Upper Canada*–provincial licences on pedlars introduced
1810 *Upper Canada*–provincial licences for billiard tables introduced
1811 *N.S.*–10% tariff on American imports expired
1813 *Upper and Lower Canada*–general *ad valorem* tariff rate of 2½% introduced
N.S.–10% tariff on American imports re-enacted
1813–21 Imperial tariff granted substantial preferences in British market on wheat (Corn Laws) and lumber from British North America which persisted in some form for three decades
1817 Bank of Montreal opened
1819 *Upper Canada*–first effective local assessment Act (59 Geo. III, c. 7), taxing land, houses, mills, factories, and certain forms of personal property
1820 *Upper Canada*–first effective provincial tax on land introduced, rate extremely low, many exemptions; revenue turned over to local magistrates for local purposes
1822 *Canada Trade Act* formalized terms of trade of the Canadas with United States following disruption of War of 1812–15; in general, natural products of United States were admitted but manufactured and processed products were prohibited
N.B.–Municipalities required to levy poll and property taxes
1825 prohibited items from United States reduced
1826 *N.S.*–general upward revision of tariff rates
–7 *Upper Canada*–residents allowed for first time to cut timber for commercial sale; stumpage dues introduced for this privilege
1825–35 periodic amendments in Imperial colonial tariff increased intercolonial preferences
1830 *N.S.*–obtained complete control over tariff
1831 *N.B.*–municipalities required to levy poll, property, and income taxes (first municipal income tax), ⅛ of revenue to be raised by poll tax, balance by other taxes

1832 *Lower Canada*—Montreal and Quebec given charters (suspended in 1836)
1834 *Upper Canada*—Toronto incorporated (previously Town of York)
1835 *N.B.*—granted complete control over tariff
N.S.—income included in municipal tax base
1837 *Upper and Lower Canada*—uprisings; Toronto adopts annual value basis of assessment
1838 *Upper Canada*—personal property given clear definition in revised municipal assessment act which also provided that real property be assessed at 20% of its value and income at full value
1839 Lord Durham's *Report* proposed union of Upper and Lower Canada, responsible government, and strengthened municipal system
1840 Act of Union joined Upper and Lower Canada in province of United Canada; Imperial government retained right to regulate colonial trade by tariffs; Montreal and Quebec given permanent charters with power to levy real and personal property tax; first general municipal legislation passed in Lower Canada but not effective
1841 *United Canada*—colonial tariff revised and consolidated, with increase in general rate from 2½% to 5%; tax on bank note circulation imposed
N.S.—Halifax given charter, with right to impose general property tax
1842 British Possessions Act repealed all Imperial colonial duties on empire products and left only duties on foreign imports; Corn Law amended to increase preference on Canadian wheat in British market, but reduction of duty on Baltic timber threatened Canadian preference in timber
1843 *United Canada*—substantial element of agricultural protection introduced into tariff
N.S.—Halifax levied taxes on real estate and "profits" of banks and fire and marine insurance companies
1845 *Lower Canada*—municipal law adopted with elective principle for councils; revenue from tavern licences given to local authorities, as well as power to impose real property taxes
1846 British Corn Laws repealed; Canada's preferred position in wheat to be entirely removed within 3 years; in same year all Imperial intercolonial preferences abolished
Upper Canada—Kingston and Hamilton incorporated
1847 *United Canada*—tariff rates increased on luxury and manufactured products, and general rate increased from 5% to 7½%
Lower Canada—new municipal law passed
1848 *N.S.*—Halifax imposed clearly defined tax on income in excess of £150
N.B.—Fredericton incorporated
1849 *United Canada*—general rate under tariff increased to 12½% and many specific duties increased; Baldwin Municipal Act provided first general municipal legislation; Select Committee of the Legislature of United Canada on Forests and Timber Operations and enactment of Act for "The Sale and Better Management of Timber and Public Lands"
N.S.—Halifax exempted salary and wages but continued taxes on business profits
1850 colonies in British North America extend reciprocal tariff concessions on foodstuffs and raw materials.
Lower Canada—revised Municipal Act passed
Upper Canada—new Assessment Act (13 & 14 Vict., c. 67) continued annual value of real and personal property basis of assessment in cities, towns, and villages; capital value in counties and townships; income over £50 taxed as personalty unless exceeded by amount of other personal property.

N.B.—Fredericton (inc. 1848) given statutory right to levy poll and income taxes; consolidation of Rates and Taxes Act carried on valuation of property at 20%, provided that ⅛ of revenue be raised by poll tax and balance by taxes on property and income

1851 preference in Canadian timber in British market further reduced

Upper Canada—annual ground rent for timber lands introduced; farmers exempted from income tax by municipalities in Upper Canada

Lower Canada—Montreal given power to levy duty on all businesses and occupations

N.B.—"An Act Relating to Municipalities" passed

1853 *Upper Canada*—Consolidated Assessment Act (16 Vict., cc. 163 and 181) revised full general property tax in municipalities; income tax exemptions extended and corporate personal property exempted from tax with shares to be taxed as personal property of shareholders; this legislation formed basis of municipal taxation for some decades in Ontario, with revisions

1854 Reciprocity Treaty (Elgin-Marcy) with United States negotiated, bringing free trade on substantially all native products of both countries

United Canada—increases in tariff rates on manufactured products, with general rate increased from 12½% to 15%; further hearings on forest resources by a Select Committee

1855 *Lower Canada*—Municipal Roads Act provided first effective general municipal legislation; municipalities incorporated under it authorized to tax real property and also income and profits of business and professions. Quebec City given power to levy duties on all businesses and occupations

Upper Canada—Ottawa incorporated

P.E.I.—Charlottetown incorporated as town with right to impose real and personal property tax

1856 Grand Trunk Railway between Toronto and Montreal opened

1857 *N.S.*—Halifax restored tax on earned income

1858 *United Canada*—Cayley Tariff further increased rates on manufactured and processed goods and established broad classifications dutiable at *ad valorem* rates; Decimal system introduced

N.B.—Saint John charter amended to remove "double tax" on corporate income

1859 *United Canada*—Galt's first tariff elaborated classifications under *ad valorem* rates of 10%, 25%, and 30%, with general N.O.P. rate of 20%; duties on liquor and tobacco imports 100% and 40% respectively; internal excise duty on spirits increased from 2*d.* to 6¢ per wine gal.

Lower Canada—Municipal code adopted in substantially present form

1860 *B.C.*—New Westminster incorporated

Vancouver Island—land tax and gross revenue tax on businesses and occupations levied

1862 *United Canada*—excise duty on spirits increased from 6¢ to 9¢ per wine gal.

B.C.—Victoria incorporated

1864 Charlottetown and Quebec Conferences on Confederation

United Canada—excise duty on spirits increased from 9¢ to 30¢ per wine gal.

1865 Reciprocity Treaty abrogated by United States effective following year

Vancouver Island—1% tax enacted on salaries over £150

1866 *United Canada*—rates of tariff reduced to conform more closely to Maritime Provinces' rates: general rate reduced from 20% to 15%

Upper Canada—Consolidation Act (29–30 Vict., c. 53) abandoned annual value basis of property assessment in municipalities and specifically included income as personal property subject to municipal tax; $300 income exemption replaced £50 exemption; new regulations issued revising system of auctioning and establishing minimum "upset" price on sales of timber

1867 British North America Act brought about confederation of Ontario, Quebec, Nova Scotia, and New Brunswick effective July 1; United Canada tariff of 1866 continued without much basic change in new national tariff; excise duties on spirits increased from 30¢ to 60¢ per wine gal.; other excise duties were 1¢ per lb. on malt (beer); 3¼¢ per gal. on beverages fermented from substances other than malt (called malt liquor); 10¢ per lb. on manufactured imported tobacco; 5¢ per lb. on Canada Twist (domestic unmanufactured); graduated tax on cigars; cigarettes at same rate as manufactured imported tobacco; snuff at 10¢ per lb.

1868 *Dom.*–tariff changes enacted on a range of imports, particularly flour, meal, grain, and breadstuffs (to be free, removing 10% duty imposed previous year) and molasses (duty to be reduced); sugar duties revised, and other changes affected animals, books, wine, beer, porter, and iron products; export duty introduced on pine logs and shingle bolts; excise duty on spirits increased to 63¢ per gal. and new duty of 5¢ per gal. imposed on refined petroleum (mostly kerosene)

Ont.–provincial duty on tavern keepers ($12, $10 & $5); royalty of 2% to 10% on gold and silver mines.

1869 *Dom.*–no tariff changes; western territory purchased from Hudson's Bay Co. for £300,000 and 1/20 of land in territory

N.S.–consolidated Mines and Minerals Act included 3% royalty on gold

Ont.–provincial tavern and liquor shops licences increased; Assessment Act revised and consolidated; under General Mining Act 1869 royalties on gold and silver abandoned

1870 *Dom.*–upward trend in tariff rates forerunner of National Policy; general increase of 5% of existing charges along with specific duties of 50¢ per ton on coal and coke, 4¢ per bush. on wheat, 3¢ on coarse grains, 25¢ bbl. on wheat and rye flour, 3¢ on other flour, and 5¢ bush. on salt; customs duty on cigars changed from *ad valorem* to poundage (45¢ lb.) basis; customs also increased on wines and other tobacco and alcoholic products; machinery (free) put under 15% rate; excise duties increased on spirits from molasses to 65¢ per gal., on manufactured foreign tobacco, snuff, and cigarettes from 10¢ to 15¢ per lb., on Canada Twist from 5¢ to 7¢ per lb. and also on cigars; new excise duties imposed on vinegar (3¢ per prf. gal.) and methylated spirits (12¢ per prf. gal.)

P.E.I.–legislation for towns and villages passed

Que.–Municipal Code revision removed right of towns, villages, and counties to levy income taxes and authorized real estate, stock-in-trade, poll, and business taxes

Manitoba enters Confederation

B.C.–3% probate duty introduced

1871 *Dom.*–all tariff increases of 1870 repealed; authority given to put raw materials and machinery on free list by o/c

British Columbia entered Confederation

1872 *Dom.*–tariff on tea and coffee removed

N.S.–gold royalty reduced to 2%

1873 *Dom.*–no changes

Prince Edward Island entered Confederation

N.S.–Consolidated Mines and Minerals Act royalty of 2% on gold, 9⁷⁄₁₀¢ per ton on coal, 3¢ per ton on iron ore, and 5% on other minerals; local taxation for support of schools made compulsory

Ont.–Municipal Institutions Act revised and consolidated

Man.–Winnipeg given charter

B.C.–Wild Lands Tax introduced to tax all unimproved land in province at 1% of assessed value; Road Ordinance, 1869, amended ($2 poll tax and land tax for roads)

1874 *Dom.*–major changes for revenue; under tariff 15% general rate on unenumerated articles increased to 17½%; tea and coffee tariff reimposed, increases in tariff on wines, spirits, luxury goods, sugar, cigars, iron goods, machinery, and others; excise duties increased on spirits from 63¢ to 75¢ per wine gal., on tobacco, cigarettes, and snuff from 15¢ to 20¢ per lb., on Canada Twist from 7¢ to 10¢ per lb., and on cigars from 30¢ to 40¢ per lb.

B.C.–city of Nanaimo incorporated; charter exempted improvements 100%

1875 *Dom.*–no significant tariff changes; excise duty on spirits altered from 75¢ per wine gallon (prf.) to 90¢ per imperial gallon (prf.); export duty removed from stave-bolts and oak logs

N.B.–General Assessment Act, 1875, abandoned 20% valuation of property (henceforth 100%); proportion of revenue in cities, towns, and parishes from poll tax raised from ⅛ to ⅙; Moncton re-incorporated with same tax powers as in General Act

Que.–provincial government imposed a tax in form of a licence on all new and renewal premiums received within the province at a rate of 3% in case of fire insurance and 1% for life insurance (c. 7)

1876 *Dom.*–no changes

Que.–Montreal introduced rental value business tax

B.C.–income tax (½ of 1% if over $1500), land tax (⅓ of 1%), personal property tax (⅙ of 1%), and wild land tax (5¢ per acre) imposed under Assessment Act; School Tax Act ($3 poll tax) passed; road tax repealed

1877 *Dom.*–tariff on crude petroleum reduced from 15¢ to 6¢ per gal; excise duty of 5¢ per gal. on petroleum removed at same time; substantial revenue loss recouped by additional tariff of 2¢ per lb. on tea and an increase in excise duties on malt from 1¢ to 2¢ per lb. and on malt liquor from 3¼¢ to 8¢ per gal; other minor tariff adjustments

P.E.I.–introduced provincial land tax under Assessment Act, 1877, which also imposed $1 poll tax on males over 21 (balance not raised by poll tax to be raised by land tax); Summerside incorporated with right to levy poll, property, and income tax

N.B.–Rates and Taxes Act consolidated with minor changes; Municipalities Act provided law for county municipalities

Ont.–Public Lands Act in R.S.O. continued authority for Lieut.-Governor to set timber dues

1878 *Dom.*–no changes

N.S.–royalty levied on copper at 10¢ per ton

Que.–Privy Council decision in *Queen* v. *Queen Insurance Company*, (1878) 3 App. Cas. 1090, declared 1876 charges on insurance premiums *ultra vires* of province in existing form

Ont.–Select Committee on Taxation and Exemptions

B.C.–all Chinese over 12 required to take out quarterly licence ($10) in lieu of all other taxes

1879 National Policy instituted by newly elected Conservative Government; protective tariff introduced with substantial increases in rates, particularly on manufactured and processed goods to yield $2,200,000 in increased revenue; specific duties replaced many *ad valorem* rates; general rate reduced in scope, increased from 17½% to 20%; at same time however tariff on tea, sugar and molasses reduced; in revenue terms significant tariff increases were: 2½% increase in general rate, $750,000; breadstuffs, $250,000; anthracite coal, $175,000; bituminous coal, $100,000; iron bars, $200,000; woollen goods, $180,000; silk goods, $150,000; cotton goods, $100,000; spirits and wines, $110,000; excise duty on spirits increased from 90¢ per imp. gal. prf. to $1.00; duty on Canada Twist reduced to 4¢ per lb. and on malt from 2¢ to 1¢ per lb.

P.E.I.—poll tax limited to residents of Charlottetown and Summerside

N.S.—21 year tax exemption provided for any new cotton mill or sugar refinery

1880 *Dom.*—tariff on coal further increased from 50¢ to 60¢ a ton; other changes not significant; excise duty on spirits amended to impose duty of $1.02 and $1.03 per gal. on spirits made of malted barley and molasses respectively; 14¢ per lb. on tobacco and 30¢ per lb. on cigars manufactured from domestic leaf; vinegar duty increased from 3¢ to 4¢ per prf. gal. and duty on methylated spirits increased from 12¢ to 15¢ per prf. gal.

P.E.I.—Summerside right to levy income tax withdrawn but Charlottetown granted right in same year

Que.—Mining Act amended to introduce royalty of 2½% on value of gold and silver produced and 50¢ per ton on phosphate of lime

B.C.—income tax increased to ¾ of 1%, land tax to ½ of 1%, and personal property tax to ¼ of 1%

1881 *Dom.*—numerous but minor tariff adjustments

N.S.—2% royalty on silver

B.C.—provincial school tax repealed and replaced by provincial revenue tax ($3 poll tax on males over 18)

1882 *Dom.*—tariff changes include removal of duty on tea, coffee, and tin, and several other changes, mainly reductions; total revenue loss estimated at $1 m. reducing total customs revenue to $19.5 m.; excise duty on tobacco and cigars manufactured from Canadian leaf reduced from 14¢ to 8¢ per lb.; and from 30¢ to 20¢ per lb. respectively; stamp tax on notes and bills of exchange repealed

P.E.I.—land tax and poll tax under Assessment Act, 1877, repealed

N.B.—Saint John Assessment Act consolidated, dropping 20% valuation of property; poll tax to be $1

Que.—introduced new provincial taxes on insurance companies, banks, loan, navigation, telegraph, telephone, and railway companies and incorporated companies generally (latter tax on capital and places of business); (45 Vict., c. 22)

1883 *Dom.*—reductions in tariff by placing on free list many raw materials used by Canadian manufacturers; duty on newspapers removed; general effect to reduce revenue by $1 to $1¼ m.; increases were effected on cotton textiles and numerous other articles, including farm equipment and steel ingots; bounty of $1.50 per ton on pig iron produced in Canada introduced; excise duty on tobacco reduced from 8¢ to 2¢ per lb. on manufactured domestic leaf, from 20¢ to 12¢ on manufactured foreign leaf, from 4¢ to 2¢ per lb. on Canada Twist, and from 20¢ to 8¢ on snuff, dry, or 12¢ on snuff, moist; tax on cigars converted to $1.50 per thousand if manufactured from Canadian leaf and $3.00 per thousand if foreign leaf used (these rate changes were prompted largely by reductions in

American rates); excise duty on malt liquor reduced from 8¢ to 4¢ per gal.; bill stamps abolished

N.S.—copper royalty revised; Halifax abandoned income tax

Ont.—Liquor Licence Act 1883 passed

N.W.T.—"Ordinance Respecting Municipalities" passed authorizing property taxes, including taxes on income

1884 *Dom.*—tariff changes unimportant, but designed mainly to give manufacturers lower duty or free importation of materials; no excise duty changes

Ont.—liquor and tavern licences drastically increased under Licence Duties Act

N.W.T.—School Ordinance provided taxes up to 5 mills on real and personal property and incomes

B.C.—Chinese Regulation Act imposed $10 annual tax on all Chinese over 14; Timber Act provided licences for cutting timber on ungranted Crown land, with royalty charge

1885 *Dom.*—further numerous but unimportant additions of manufacturer's materials to free list or to lower rate schedule in tariff; excise duties on cigars doubled (foreign leaf $6 per thousand; Can. leaf, $3 per thousand), tobacco (including cigarettes) manufactured from foreign leaf increased from 2¢ to 5¢ per lb. and foreign leaf from 12¢ to 20¢ per lb. (35¢ if in package of 1/20 lb. or more); Canada Twist increased to 5¢ per lb.; excise duty on spirits increased from $1.00 to $1.30 per prf. gal. (other rates $1.32 and $1.33 respectively); Chinese Immigration Act passed—$50 head tax, 25% of revenue to be turned over to provinces

Que.—Montreal extended business tax on rental value of premises occupied and special taxes on breweries and distillers, banks, insurance companies, brokers, and agents

N.W.T.—towns authorized to levy $2 poll tax

B.C.—Chinese Regulation Act, 1884, declared *ultra vires* of province by Supreme Court of British Columbia in *Regina* v. *Wing Chong* (B.C. Rpt., vol. I, Pt. 2, p. 150); under new Act, Chinese immigrants barred from province and required to pay $50 to enter

1886 *Dom.*—duties on tea and coffee imported direct from country of origin removed; other tariff changes limited largely to substitution of specific duties for *ad valorem* duties on a range of importations to sustain revenues then declining with falling world prices; excise duty on snuff increased and new excise duty of 8¢ per lb. on oleomargarine manufactured in Canada introduced (an import duty of 10¢ per lb. had been imposed in same budget)

Que.—city of Sherbrooke levied income tax under authority given in 1879

Ont.—liquor licences revised

N.W.T.—school districts allowed to tax land only

B.C.—Vancouver incorporated; authorized to tax real and personal property

1887 *Dom.*—tariff removed from anthracite coal and increased on pig iron from $2 to $4 per ton; substantial increases also on blooms and billets, bars and rails of iron; bounty of $1.50 per ton on domestic pig iron extended to June 30, 1889; other minor changes, including requirement that spirits be stored for two years prior to sale

Que.—Provincial corporation tax of 1882 declared constitutional by Privy Council in *The Bank of Toronto* v. *Lambe* (1887) 12 App. Cas. 575; Quebec City introduced business tax of 12.5% on rental value of premises occupied

Ont.—Assessment Act amended (R.S.O. 1887, c. 193); personal property exempt under $100; income exempt under $700; other exemptions included public property, churches, cemeteries, schools, farm income, government bonds, etc.; basis of assessment established generally as actual value

B.C.—tax on real estate increased to ⅔ of 1%, on personal property to ½ of 1%, on wild lands to 8½¢ per acre (Assess. Act)

1888 *Dom.*—no tariff changes; excise duty on cigarettes established as separate duty at 60¢ per M. to 3 lbs.; $1.00 per M. over 3 lbs.

P.E.I.—Charlottetown income tax withdrawn

N.S.—Towns Incorporation Act passed; Assessment Act revised

Ont.—First Report of Commission on Municipal Institutions condemned municipal personal property tax

B.C.—Assessment Act consolidated; New Westminster chartered and authorized to tax land and personal property

1889 *Dom.*—no tariff changes; reduced excise duty of 15¢ per gal. given for spirits used in chemical composition; duty on cigarettes increased to $1.50 per M. and $6.00 per M. respectively; bounty on domestic pig iron reduced to $1.00 per ton

N.B.—Saint John poll tax raised to $2.00

Que.—Sorel authorized to levy income tax

Ont.—Second Report of Commission on Municipal Institutions

1890 *Dom.*—trend back to *ad valorem* rates in tariff amendments of this year; increase in duty on woollens, flour, and meats, latter strengthening agricultural protection considerably; tariff on window glass and molasses reduced; export duty on lumber and logs removed by o/c Oct. 15, 1890

N.B.—Moncton incorporated

Que.—Mining Act amended to empower collection of royalty of 3% on value of production of a broad list of minerals; gold and silver royalty retained at 2½%

Ont.—Assessment Act amended to permit substitution of 7½% tax on premises of merchants in lieu of personal property tax

1891 *Dom.*—major tariff change with removal of duty on raw sugar ($3.5 m. reduction); to compensate, tariff on tobacco and spirits increased and excise duty on spirits increased from $1.30 to $1.50 per gal., on malt from 1¢ to 2¢ per lb. and on malt liquor from 4¢ to 10¢ per gal., and on tobacco from 20¢ to 25¢ per lb.; special rate of $7 per M. imposed on cigars in pckgs. of less than 10; duty on snuff increased; export duty on logs repealed

Ont.—General Mining Act restored royalties of 3% on silver, nickel, or copper, and not over 3% on other minerals

B.C.—municipalities authorized to take over $3 poll tax within their boundaries and tax renamed revenue tax; wild land tax increased from 8½¢ per acre to 2½% of value; Municipalities Act authorized municipalities to exempt improvements at their option

1892 *Dom.*—no tariff changes; bounty on pig iron increased from $1.00 to $3.00 per ton

N.S.—succession duties introduced (very similar to Ontario); Consolidated Mines & Minerals Act shows 2% royalty on gold and silver, 10¢ per ton on coal, 4¢ per unit on copper, 2¢ per unit on lead, 5¢ per ton on iron, and 5% on all other minerals

N.B.—corporation taxes introduced (55 Vict., c. 22) and also succession duties

Que.—succession duty and tax on transfers of real estate introduced; "An Act respecting direct taxes on certain persons" levied provincial taxes on members of certain professions and on civil servants; Sherbrooke adopted rental value buisness tax

Ont.–Succession Duty Act (c. 6) introduced for support of provincial asylums and hospitals; Ontario was first province to levy succession duties; Assessment Act revised and consolidated; Mines Act, 1892, abandons all existing royalties but levies new ones on new nickel, silver, or copper mines at 3%, iron at 2%

B.C.–Consolidated Municipal Act provided improvements be not assessed for more than 50% of value

1893 *Dom.*–no significant tariff changes

Que.–Hull authorized to levy income tax

Ont.–Report of Commission on Municipal Taxation

Man.–"The Succession Duties Act" introduced; personal property tax in Winnipeg abandoned and business tax based on floor space substituted

N.W.T.–graduated rates for municipal income taxes; business taxes on gross receipts; but by vote municipalities could tax land only

B.C.–25¢ per acre levied on mineral lands held under Crown grant

1894 *Dom.*–first major revision and rearrangement of tariff since 1878; reductions on iron and steel products (principally agricultural implements), cotton and woollen goods, and long list of other articles; increases on scrap iron and rice and miscellaneous other goods; net revenue loss $1.5 m. bounty on pig iron limited to iron from domestic ores and extended at $2 per ton for 5 years; puddled iron also to receive bounty; excise duty on malt reduced from 2¢ to 1½¢ per lb; vinegar duty increased from 4¢ to 6¢ per gal.

P.E.I.–income tax (1%, farmers not taxed, exemption for residents $350), corporation taxes (insurance, trust, telegraph, banks), and succession duties introduced; land tax (repealed 1882) reinstated applicable to all land outside Charlottetown and Summerside but improvements erected after 1894 exempted (Assessment Act, 1894)

N.B.–Municipal Tax Commission Report proposed several reforms but none adopted

Ont.–mining royalty reduced to 2% and expenses of mining allowed

Man.–"Manitoba Insurance Act," fees and taxes on fire and life insurance companies

N.W.T.–Calgary given city charter; land, improvements, income, and personal property to be taxed

B.C.–succession duties introduced; Railway Assessment Act to tax property for province

1895 *Dom.*–tariff on raw sugar imposed at ½¢ per lb. (⅓ of pre-1891 rate) to provide $1.2 m. revenue; excise duty on spirits increased from $1.50 to $1.70 per gal. (tariff also increased)

N.B.–income tax exemption in towns raised to $600

N.W.T.–Village Ordinance authorized taxes on real and personal property

B.C.–Vancouver exempted 50% of value of improvements; exemption granted mines from provincial taxes withdrawn; new municipalities not to tax railways

1896 *Dom.*–no changes

N.B.–general legislation for incorporation of towns adopted

Que.–provincial taxes of 1892 on persons repealed

Ont.–succession duty rates amended

B.C.–1% tax on value of mineral output levied under Assessment Act; timber royalty made 50¢ per 1000 B.F. on some timber; 25¢ on all other; Vancouver exempted 50% of assessment of improvements

1897 *Dom.*—first Liberal Government since 1879 introduced preferential feature in tariff; minor reductions on agricultural products, crude oil and coal oil, pig iron, cottons and woollens, binder twine (free), and sugar; increases on spirits and tobacco products, preferential feature offered rate reduction to any country reciprocally favouring Canada, reduction to be ⅛ of ordinary rates from April 23, 1897, to June 30, 1898, and ¼ after July 1, 1898, except for large revenue items such as spirits, sugar, and tobacco products, excise duty on spirits increased from $1.70 to 1.90 per gal. and new duty of 4¢ per gal. imposed on acetic acid; duty on vinegar reduced from 6¢ to 4¢ per gal; new duty of 10¢ on imported raw leaf tobacco and higher duties on cigarettes; bounty on iron production increased to $3.00 per ton and extended to steel

P.E.I.—land tax rate set at ⅙ of 1% with all improvements taxable

N.B.—Moncton Assessment Act passed

Que.—real estate transfer tax repealed

Ont.—Privy Council broadened interpretation of provincial rights to collect licences; *Brewers and Maltsters* v. *Ontario*, [1897] A.C. 231.

N.W.T.—General Municipal Ordinance gave towns option of exempting personal property and improvements; village poll tax increased from $1 to $1.25

B.C.—under Assessment Act income tax revised to reduce exemption from $1,500 to $1,000 and make true exemptions; rates ranging from 1¼% to 1¾% introduced minor degree of progression; rates on real estate increased to ⅘%, on personal property to ¾%, and on wild lands to 3%; new tax of 1% on output replaces tax on real and personal property of mine

1898 *Dom.*—tariff revised by introduction of exclusively British Preferential Tariff schedule in place of general reciprocal reductions (12½ and 25%) of previous year; preferential rates extended to West Indies, New South Wales, and British India (had been extended to Great Britain following 1897 budget); polariscopic system of sugar duties reintroduced to encourage lower grade West Indies sugars

Ont.—all logs cut on crown land must henceforth be manufactured in province

N.W.T.—village poll tax set at $2

1899 *Dom.*—no changes; iron and steel bounties extended on descending scale to 1907

Ont.—Supplementary Revenue Act introduced corporation taxes

B.C.—succession duty rates revised

1900 *Dom.*—British Preferential Tariff schedule, formerly 25% lower than general schedule, to be 33⅓% lower

P.E.I.—corporation taxes raised and extended to breweries

Ont.—Special Commission appointed to investigate operation of municipal assessment laws; under Mines Act tonnage charges replaced *ad valorem* royalties

Man.—Corporation Tax Act imposing taxes on certain companies introduced; also Railway Taxation Act, imposing 2% on gross income; city of Brandon authorized to impose business tax based on rental value at 12½%

B.C.—tax of 5¢ per ton on coal and 9¢ per ton on coke levied under Coal Tax Act in lieu of land tax on coal mines; mining output tax raised from 1% to 2%; income tax rates graduated from 1½% to 4% (sharp rise from 1897 rates)

1901 *Dom.*—Chinese immigration tax increased from $50 to $100

P.E.I.—road tax (75¢ poll tax & 25¢ horse tax) levied under Public Roads Act, 1901

Ont.—Succession Duty Act amended

N.W.T.—Ordinance gave villages option of exempting personal property, improvements, and income.

B.C.—under Assessment Act taxes imposed on income of corporations carrying on business in the province by bringing them under general tax on net income, payable if greater than personal property tax; mines and railways exempt; timber royalty extended to railway lands

1902 *Dom.*—no changes

P.E.I.—income tax raised to 1½% and tax on banks increased

Ont.—Report of Special Commission on Assessment Act condemned municipal personal property tax as a failure

1903 *Dom.*—no significant tax changes; bounty on steel rods to be made into wire and on lead introduced

N.S.—corporation taxes introduced on minor scale, full scale of customary levies not imposed, however, until 1912; Sydney incorporated

Ont.—motor vehicle licence fee introduced, $2 per vehicle

N.W.T.—Succession Duties Ordinance passed; Regina incorporated; school districts allowed $2 poll tax; exemption under income tax raised from $600 to $1,000

B.C.—Assessment Act revised and consolidated; real estate rate increased to 1% personal property to 1% and wild lands to 5%; income tax rates slightly lower; net income of banks subject to special rate and 1% rate levied on gross revenue of certain other corporations in lieu of taxes on net income and personal property; 25¢ per acre tax on unworked Crown-granted mineral claims retained

1904 *Dom.*—moderate tariff increases in British Preferential rate on woollens, twine, and cordage, and reductions on china and window glass; tariff on coal oil reduced from 5¢ to 2½¢ per gal. and bounty of 1½¢ per gal. on domestic crude oil production instituted; crude oil put on free list; dumping duty introduced for first time to be in amount the difference between value of commodity in market of origin and import price into Canada; Chinese immigration tax increased to $500; 50% of revenue to go to provinces

Ont.—provincial tax on railway companies sharply increased; Assessment Act amended to abolish municipal personal property tax and to substitute a business tax based on value of real estate occupied, with variation in portion of value taxed depending on class of business; at same time the basis of municipal income tax (1866) was revised to broaden application and improve collections

Alta.—Edmonton receives charter, improvements to be entirely exempt from tax, business tax based on rate per square foot of floor space occupied, the rate varying with nature of business; poll and income taxes also authorized, but not personal property tax; system of government in local improvement districts revised

1905 *Dom.*—Tariff Commission (of Government Ministers) established to prepare over-all revision of tariff; minor adjustments only in 1905 budget

Ont.—succession duty rates and exemptions increased

provinces of Alberta and Saskatchewan created

B.C.—coal tax made additional to royalties and in place of tax on mine improvements; special rates under Assessment Act for coal lands and timber lands in lieu of wild land and real estate tax; rates were 1% on Class A coal lands and 2% on Class B; timber land 2%; real estate tax reduced to 3/5% on property under $2,000, personal property rate reduced to 2/3%, wild lands to 4%, and income tax rates revised; net income of banks taxed at ordinary rates applied to individuals; Special Assessment Commission submits its reports, recommended repeal of personal property tax; instead province increased personal income tax rates and made greater of personal property or income tax rate payable; in effect personal property tax became a minimum tax; exemption remained $1,000

1906 *Dom.*—no significant tariff changes at first session; general revision postponed to second session in fall; this revision completely overhauled tariff schedules by classifying articles under eleven general classes, with free items included with appropriate group rather than in one list at end of tariff; at same time rates were classified for each item under three general tariff schedules—general, intermediate, and British Preferential; the former perpetuated largely the former general tariff, the latter the former British Preferential, although with a general overhauling of the flat 33⅓% reduced rate to provide a rate appropriate to each article of trade; rate structure also simplified by avoiding odd fractions; intermediate tariff to be extended to countries outside Empire giving Canada favourable tariff concessions; duty-free importations for government abolished; maximum dumping duty fixed at 15%, iron and steel bounty moderately increased; tariff on citrus fruits and rice reduced; on raw sugar increased; export tax on Yukon placer gold introduced (c. 39, ss. 85–87)

P.E.I.—companies taxes increased and extended to utilities, brewers, distillers, etc.

N.B.—Report of Assessment Law Commissioners of Saint John issued

Que.—succession duty revised to increase rates and graduation based on relationship of beneficiary; motor vehicle fees and stock transfer tax introduced

Ont.—tax on railways doubled; new Mines Act passed, all previous royalties abandoned

Man.—Assessment Act of 1906 provided for abolition of personal property tax in towns and villages on proclamation and substitution of a tax on rental value of premises, not to exceed 12½% rate

Sask.—Regina and Saskatoon personal property tax abolished and taxes on lands, businesses, income and franchises adopted

Alta.—Railway Taxation Act passed

B.C.—Timber Manufacture Act prohibited export in unmanufactured state of timber from Crown-granted lands; Vancouver increased exemption of improvements from 50% to 75%

1907 *Dom.*—no tax changes

N.B.—Fredericton Assessment Act consolidated to close 20% valuation of property and fixed poll tax at $5; certain companies to pay flat tax in lieu of personal property tax

Ont.—provincial mining profits tax introduced under Supplementary Revenue Act; rate 3% on profits over $10,000, credit against tax to be allowed for municipal income tax; taxes on acreage (2¢) and natural gas output (2¢ per 1,000 ft.)

Man.—Winnipeg business tax converted to uniform rate of 8⅓% of rental value of premises occupied (floor space factor dropped)

Sask.—supplementary revenue tax on land in local improvement districts imposed for support of education; Corporations Taxation Act introduced, imposing first corporation taxes on banks, insurance, loan, trust, telegraph, railway express co's., etc.

Alta.—Corporations Taxation Act and Educational Tax Act (on land outside organized school districts at 1¼¢ per acre) introduced; Villages Act continued right of villages to exempt personal property and improvements

B.C.—probate duty changed to 1% on near relatives and 5% on others; wife and children exempt; personal property rate ⅗%; salmon canneries special tax of 2¢ per case and 1% on sales of other salmon (in lieu of personal property tax); Railway Assessment Act revised, rural district school taxes first levied locally

1908 *Dom.*—general revision of excise duties on tobacco products to simplify without increasing burden; general purpose to adopt uniform stamps and to place more emphasis on taxation of raw leaf than of manufactured product; no tariff changes; lead bounty extended 5 years

P.E.I.—"Act to Prohibit use of Motor Vehicles on the Public Highways of this Province" passed

N.S.—provincial poll tax and property tax imposed under Highway Act on municipalities

N.B.—provincial poll tax and tax on real and personal property and income imposed as road tax under the Highway Act, 1908, on municipalities.

Ont.—Supplementary Revenue Act (corp. taxes) revised and consolidated

Man.—"The Towns and Villages Business Tax Act" passed, allowing at local option repeal of personal tax and substitution of business tax on rental value in villages and towns; also first provincial tax on motor vehicles of $5 per annum under Motor Vehicle Act; Winnipeg reverted for one year to floor space business tax

Sask.—Railway Taxation Act levied taxes on railways at rate not to exceed 3% of gross revenue; Cities and Towns Acts amended to abolish personal property tax and install taxes on land, businesses, income and franchises as principal sources (Edmonton system); in towns and villages buildings and improvements to be assessed at 60% of value

B.C.—coal tax increased from 5¢ to 10¢ and coke tax from 9¢ to 15¢ per ton

1909 *Dom.*—moderate changes in sugar tariff only

N.B.—Saint John Act raised poll tax to $5 and revised income tax exemptions

Que.—Quebec Companies Tax Act passed to revise previous corporation taxes

Man.—Winnipeg charter amended, following report of Phippen Commission, to reduce assessment of improvements to 66⅔% of value and to again adopt rental value as basis of business tax (6⅔%)

Sask.—Railway Taxation Act rates amended; Rural Municipality Act passed authorizing land taxes; grazing leases brought under Supplementary Revenue Tax

B.C.—minor amendments to Succession Duty Act

1910 *Dom.*—no changes; bounty on pig iron and steel billets terminated

P.E.I.—Land Assessment Act consolidated (rate ⅙ of 1% on assessed value)

N.S.—2% royalty on gold, silver, and tungsten under Mines Act

Man.—minor amendments in succession duties and railway taxation

Alta.—Edmonton repealed poll tax and income tax

B.C.—under Assessment Act real estate and personal property tax reduced from ⅗% to ½%; income tax rates also reduced; net income tax on banks converted to specific tax on branches in province; Vancouver gave complete exemption for improvements

1911 *Dom.*—no changes

P.E.I.—Income Tax Act consolidated c. 4 (rate unchanged at 1½% but exemption increased from $350 to $500)

N.S.—Consolidated Mines Act indicated existing royalties imposed on gold, silver, tungsten, copper, lead, iron, tin, precious, and other reserved metals

N.B.—motor vehicle fees revised; taxes on insurance co's., and banks amended and new tax levied on fire insurance agents

Que.—10¢ per acre tax under Mining Act

Ont.—stock transfer tax introduced, tax of $200 per day on race track meets and increased taxes on railways and express co's. under Supplementary Revenue Act

Man.—succession duty rates revised; Moving Pictures Act imposed fees; motor vehicle tax increased from $5 to $6 per annum; municipal assessment act amended and consolidated

Sask.—cities and towns authorized to reduce assessment of improvements (then fixed at 60%) by an additional 15% a year until fully exempt; assessment of improvements optional with local councils in villages

Alta.—Edmonton repealed business taxes; Calgary reduced assessment of improvements from 100% to 50% of value and repealed income tax

B.C.—Taxation Act introduced to replace Assessment Act and consolidate all previous provincial statutes imposing taxes on income, persons (poll), real property, personal property, wild lands, coal and timber land, corporations, mineral output, canneries, coal and coke, railways, etc. (c. 222); Victoria and New Westminster extended 100% exemption for improvements; Royal Commission on Taxation submitted report

1912 *Dom.*—no changes

P.E.I.—Road Act consolidated, raising poll tax to $1.50 and horse tax to 40¢; dog tax introduced; Land Assessment Act also revised

N.S.—Domestic, Dominion, and Foreign Corporations Act passed, revising rates of annual fees on corporations carrying on business in Nova Scotia and Supplementary Revenue Act introduced first effective specific corporation taxes in Nova Scotia; motor vehicle taxes extended; Succession Duty Act revised and consolidated

N.B.—licence fees on theatres introduced; motor fees increased

Que.—succession duties amended; paid-up capital tax and place of business taxes reduced; Sherbrooke income tax dropped

Ont.—no changes

Man.—Corporations Taxation Act amended imposing new taxes on loan, land, trust, and insurance co's.

Sask.—fire prevention tax levied on fire insurance co's.

Alta.—provincial fees under Motor Vehicle Act first levied; Calgary reduced assessment of improvements to 25% of value; complete exemption of improvements made compulsory in towns, villages, and rural municipalities

B.C.—forest protection tax introduced

1913 *Dom.*—minor adjustments of tariff to give effect to trade treaty with West Indies; reductions in tariff on cement, typesetting machines, and other minor changes; lead bounty extended for 5 years

P.E.I.—Fox Tax Act passed imposing 1% on value of the annual offspring; legislation prohibiting motor vehicles repealed

N.S.—succession duties amended; municipal income tax exemption raised to $800

N.B.—first taxes imposed on railways; road tax (poll) reduced; Rates and Taxes Act revision replaced 1874 Assessment Act

Que.—succession duty rates revised and duty imposed on transmissions of moveable property situated outside province

Ont.—minor revision in succession duty exemptions; city of Toronto electors favour single tax in plebiscite, but provincial government refused to authorize change; income tax exemptions under Assessment Act increased from $1,200 to $1,500 in cities and from $900 to $1,200 in towns and villages; investment income exemption from $300 to $400

Man.—Corporations Taxation Act revised and consolidated; rates increased; Towns' and Villages' Business Tax Act confirms rental value business tax

Sask.—rates on banks and telegraph co's. raised and new tax levied on timber lands under Corporations Taxation Act; Rural Municipality Act amended to impose surtax of 6¼¢ per acre for municipal purposes; provincial licences levied on pool rooms, bowling alleys, restaurants, travelling shows, and circuses; valuation of land exclusive of improvements in rural municipalities made compulsory 1914 onward; at 2nd session Corporations Act consolidated and rates increased; timber areas tax under separate act at 1½¢ per acre; theatre licences introduced and circus fees raised; export tax on silver and red foxes under Game Act

Alta.—unearned increment tax (5%) passed; general increases in corporation taxes; Towns Act amended to permit imposition of business taxes and poll tax to replace tax on improvements; Villages Act amended to permit poll tax and restore personal property tax under certain conditions; first oil discovered in Alberta

B.C.—provincial poll tax ($3) abolished, coke tax reduced to 10c per ton; tax of 4¢ per case and additional taxes on cured fish substituted for personal property and income tax on canneries; forest royalties raised; tax on banks increased 50%; Moving Pictures Act passed

1914 *Dom.*—pre-war budget increased tariff on heavy steel, wire rods, building stone, and caustic soda; tariff on binders, reapers and mowers reduced; minor other changes. August, war budget: tariff increases: coffee ($0.5 m.); sugar ($5.0 m.); spirits ($2.5 m.); cigars, cigarettes and tobacco ($0.2 m.); excise duty increases: spirits, from $1.90 to $2.40 per gal.; malt liquor, from 10¢ to 15¢ per gal.; malt, from 1½¢ to 3¢ lb.; cigars, from $2 to $3 per 1,000; cigarettes, from $2.40 to $3 per 1,000; tobacco, from 5¢ to 10¢ per lb.: total revenue from excise duty increases $6.6 m.

N.S.—minor revisions in corporation taxes on banks, life insurance, loan, and trust co's. under Supplementary Revenue Act

N.B.—Moncton Assessment Act consolidated; income tax exemption raised to $600 and poll tax fixed at $5; certain companies subject to special taxes in lieu of personal property tax

Que.—motor vehicle fees increased; succession duties legislation revised to overcome *Cotton* case; Privy Council in *Cotton* v. *The King*, [1914] A.C. held Succession Duties Act *ultra vires*

Ont.—Supplementary Revenue Act replaced by Corporation Tax Act and rates sharply increased on banks, railways, loan, insurance, trust, telephone, gas, electric, express, and street railway co's.; revenue increased over 50%; race track tax increased to $500 per day; Separate Mining Tax Act passed; succession duties raised and amended to bring in all gifts made since 1892; Theatres and Cinematographs Act in R.S.O.

Man.—minor amendments in corporation taxes and succession duties

Sask.—no changes

Alta.—wild lands tax (1% on all uncultivated land outside municipalities), travelling shows fees, and timber areas tax (2½¢ per acre) introduced;

Succession Duties Act enacted to replace 1903 ordinance; educational tax extended and patriotic fund levy (5 to 10% of salary) imposed on provincial civil servants; liquor licence and motor fees raised

B.C.—Timber Royalty Act passed revising royalties formerly levied under Forest Act

1915 *Dom.*—tariff increases enacted under Customs Tariff War Revenue Act in form of special *ad valorem* duty on all goods, whether dutiable or free, of 5% on imports under Br. Pref. Tariff and 7½% under general and intermediate tariffs; important exceptions included wheat, flour, coffee, tea, anthracite coal, sugar and tobacco; new indirect taxes were imposed under Special War Revenue Act on bank note circulation (¼ of 1% on average for quarter), trust and loan co. gross income (1%), insurance premiums other than life (1%), telegrams and cables over 15¢ (1¢), domestic railway and steamship tickets (over $1 to $5, 5¢; over $5, 5¢ for each additional $5), and on foreign steamship tickets at other rates, berths (10¢) and parlour car seats (5¢); stamp taxes on cheques, bank receipts, bills of exchange, express and post office money orders (2¢); postal notes, letters, and post cards (1¢); bill of lading (2¢); patent medicines and perfumes (1¢ for each 25¢ of retail price); wine, non-sparkling (5¢ per quart); champagne and sparkling wines (25¢ per pint)

P.E.I.—Companies Tax Act revised all previous Acts imposing corporation taxes; extra-provincial co's. $100 each

N.S.—imposed special provincial war tax of 1 mill on property in cities and towns for gift to England and put 1% on gross income of public utilities

N.B.—provincial taxes on insurance, express, telephone, telegraph, street railway, trust, and loans co's. and banks revised and increased; Succession Duties Act amended and consolidated; motor vehicle fees revised; Saint John City Council appointed Commission to revise Assessment Law (reported 1917)

Que.—minor amendments to Succession Duty Law and License Act

Ont.—Provincial War Tax Act of 1 mill on real property passed to be collected by municipalities; gross premium tax on insurance companies replaced by flat levy of $30,000 apiece, minor changes in taxes on banks, electric, gas, and telephone co's.

Man.—corporation taxes on insurance companies amended; motor fees raised to $10 per annum, and Theatre and Automatic Vending Machine Tax Act passed

Sask.—minor changes

Alta.—Calgary repealed personal property tax and substituted a business tax based on rental value (effective 1916)

B.C.—no changes

1916 *Dom.*—tariff increases limited to minor changes in duty on apples and petroleum; major feature of budget was introduction of business profits war tax of 25% on profits in excess of 7% of capital employed in an incorporated business and in excess of 10% employed in an unincorporated business, if capital over $50,000; applicable to 1915 and later years, to expire Dec. 31, 1917

P.E.I.—War and Health Tax Act, 1916, provided for levy for 1916 of one-third increase in all existing taxes except road tax

N.S.—no provincial tax changes; City of Halifax Assessment Act amended to abolish personal property tax and substitute business tax (on assessed value) and household tax (ditto)

N.B.—railway taxation increased from $50 to $100 per mile operated; liquor prohibition enacted; patriotic tax imposed on towns, cities, and municipalities to be collected in addition to usual property tax with alternative of imposing poll tax (effective 1917); theatre licences increased; Report of Civic Assessment Commission, Saint John

Que.—under Licence Law adopted provincial amusement tax (including racetrack fees); increased motor vehicle fees, mining royalties, and taxes on banks and telephone co's.; liquor controls tightened; succession duty rates revised

Ont.—Amusement Tax Act (1¢ per ticket) passed; race tracks tax increased from $500 to $1,250 per day; tax on loan company deposits imposed; liquor prohibition enacted

Man.—Public Amusement Act replaced 1915 legislation; taxes and fees imposed on all public entertainments; taxes increased on street railways and express co's.; patriotic levy of 1½ mills on total assessment of municipalities introduced; municipal commissioner's levy for mother's allowance introduced; Temperance Law enacted

Sask.—patriotic revenues tax passed (1 mill on property in municipalities; 1¢ per acre elsewhere)

Alta.—theatre goers tax introduced (general admissions to amusements); tax on express and gas co's. revised and tax imposed on authorized capital of all corporations not otherwise taxed; timber areas tax reduced to 1¢ per acre; towns and villages restored right to tax improvements up to 60% of value and given authority for business tax on rental value

B.C.—minor tax changes; liquor prohibition enacted

1917 *Dom.*—business profit war tax amended by increasing rates to 50% on profits exceeding 15% but not exceeding 20% of capital and 75% where they exceeded 20% on capital; 25% rate retained for lower amounts; no other changes announced in budget speech but during 1917 session first national income tax (Income War Tax Act) on individuals and corporations was enacted, the latter at a 4% rate, to be paid if greater than business profits tax; personal income tax exemptions, single, $2,000 and married, $3,000; normal tax was 4% and a graduated supertax ran from 2% to 25%; 50% depletion rate for gold mines and 25% for base metal mines and oil wells (for both operators and shareholders)

P.E.I.—war and health tax extended for a year: fox tax converted to tax of 1½% on income from fox sales; stricter liquor control measures enacted

N.S.—land tax on occupants of 500 acres or more and theatres tax introduced; provincial property and poll taxes under Highway Act revised; new Succession Duties Act adopted; tax on telephones, long distance calls, electric meters, and public utility profits imposed under Supplementary Revenue Act; motor licences increased

N.B.—wild lands tax introduced, applicable where more than 500 acres held; tax on telephone companies (25¢ per instrument); motor licences increased

Que.—royalties under Mining Act enforced for first time commencing in 1917; first mineral subject to duty was asbestos at rate of 5% on gross return less certain deductions, amended after May 1, 1917 to 2% on gross return

Ont.—rates on nickel and nickel-copper mines increased from flat 3% to 5% on first $5 m., 6% on next $5 m., 7% on next $5 m., etc. under Mining Profits Tax Act; mining acreage tax increased from 2¢ to 5¢ per acre; higher profits tax also applied to profits of other mines if in excess of $1 m., fire protection tax on holdings under Crown Timber Act levied

Man.—patriotic fund levy increased from 1½ to 2 mills; railway brought under Corporations Tax Act and rates increased

Sask.—patriotic revenue tax increased from 1 to 1½ mills and poll tax of $2 levied on male non-taxpayers over 21; 2nd session. Supplementary Licence Act consolidated; surtax under Rural Municipalities Act (s. 295, c. 14, 1917) repealed effective Jan. 1, 1918, and replaced by Wild Lands Tax at 1% of assessed value for provincial purposes; liquor control tightened; timber areas tax revised; Succession Duty Act consolidated

Alta.—under Patriotic Tax Act municipalities authorized to impose additional rate on property to make contribution to Alberta Patriotic Fund; minor succession duty changes

B.C.—Amusement tax passed, poll tax ($5) re-introduced under Poll Tax Act, rates on successions increased and under Taxation Act income tax exemption increased from $1,000 to $1,500; real and personal property rate increased to 1%, wild land to 5%, income tax rates raised; liquor prohibition in force Oct. 1; corporations formerly subject to specific tax only made subject to income tax; gross revenue tax raised from 1% to 2%; in addition to these increases under Surtax Act 1917 further surtaxes were levied for one year of ½% on real and personal property, 1% on wild land and timber lands, 2% on coal lands; graduated surtax on income and further taxes on corporations

1918 *Dom.*—corporation income tax rate raised from 4% to 6% and minimum capital exemption reduced from $50,000 to $25,000 under business profits war tax; personal income tax exemptions reduced to $1,000 and $2,000, supertax rates increased, and surtax levied; $200 exemption for children introduced; excise duties on tobacco products were about doubled, additional customs duties levied on tobacco, tea and coffee, existing excise taxes on railway berths and seats raised to 10¢ or 10%, and new taxes levied on matches, (1¢ per 100), playing cards (8¢ per pack), and at 10% on automobiles, phonographs, records, mechanical pianos and rolls, and jewellery; also on moving picture films at 15¢ per day

P.E.I.—Fox Tax Act revised but rate unchanged; war and health tax extended for a year

N.S.—tax on life insurance premiums increased; exemptions under municipal income tax increased to $1,000 and $1,500 for single and married

N.B.—Wild Lands Tax Act re-enacted; admissions tax introduced, road tax increased, patriotic fund tax renewed to end of war; forest protection tax of ½¢ per acre enacted

Que.—increased amusement tax; asbestos royalty increased to 3½% and royalty imposed on pyrites; bachelor tax levied in Montreal

Ont.—minor revision in succession duty rates; municipalities authorized to impose dog tax and tax of 1/10 of 1% on mortgages (mortgage tax)

Man.—Supplementary Revenue Act (1 mill on equalized assessment in organized areas and school districts), Amusements Taxation Act, and Unoccupied Land Tax Act (½% on value) passed; patriotic levy reduced from 2 mills to 1½ mills and extended to 1923 (but actually expired after 1919)

Sask.—patriotic revenue tax renamed public revenue tax and increased to 2 mills (1917 laws)

Alta.—provincial supplementary revenue tax on land in urban units (1 mill)

and in rural units (4¢ per acre) levied on municipalities; Mine Owner's Tax of 5¢ per ton levied; new rates of succession duties enacted; amusements tax replaced theatre goers' tax; Edmonton reimposed business tax on rental value and tax on improvements at 60% of value and introduced income tax; Calgary given authority to levy income tax and to increase assessment of improvements up to 50%

B.C.—Vancouver abandoned complete exemption of improvements; assessment at 25% instituted

1919 *Dom.*—corporation income tax increased from 6% to 10%; personal income tax rates again increased; business profits war tax extended at existing rates to end of 1919; tariff reductions included removal of 5% special war tariff on Br. Pref. goods and exemption of some goods from 7½% special war rate under intermediate and general tariff, reductions in rates on tea, coffee, and cement, reciprocal free importation for wheat, flour, and potatoes, and substantial reductions on agricultural implements

P.E.I.—Education Tax Act imposing poll tax and tax on real property outside municipalities enacted; War and Health Tax extended for another year

N.S.—new provincial tax of 1/20 of 1% of capital of all companies imposed under Supplementary Revenue Act and Domestic, Dominion and Foreign Corp. Act amended, increasing existing corporation taxes; Income Tax Act passed imposing graduated rates on individuals and 1½% on corporations, but not proclaimed; motor vehicle fees increased

N.B.—City of Saint John Assessment Act revised to exempt 50% of tangible personal property and 100% of intangible personal property

Que.—Prohibition Law enacted, prohibiting all but sale of light beer and wines for which heavy licences were imposed

Ont.—provincial war tax on property repealed; personal exemptions for municipal income tax raised (Assessment Act) and municipalities given authority to exempt part of value of improvements where assessment under $4,000

Man.—tax on banks, insurance, and trust co's. increased patriotic levy reduced to ½ mill; supplementary levy increased to 1½ mills; assessment of improvements in cities, towns, villages, and rural municipalities reduced from 100% to 66⅔%; Report of Assessment and Taxation Commission issued

Sask.—Corporations Taxation Act revised, with general increase in rates; tax imposed on all companies not otherwise taxed under Act (form of tax not specified)

Alta.—educational tax amended to apply at uniform rate of 1 mill; provincial licences for bowling alleys and pool rooms enacted; Calgary increased rate of assessment for improvements from 25% to 50%

B.C.—greater of coal tax or income tax made payable by mines; same for coke tax; other minor amendments; Vancouver increased rate of assessment for improvements from 25% to 50%

1920 *Dom.*—business profits tax rates revised to 20% on profits exceeding 10% but not over 14% on capital employed; over 15% to 20%, 30% tax; over 20% to 30%, 50% tax; over 30%, 60% tax; rate 20% on excess over 10% of capital where capital between $25,000 and $50,000; tax to expire Dec. 31, 1920; income tax amended to introduce 5% surtax and to tax stock dividends and income from a trust or estate; general sales tax introduced; stamp tax on cheques, etc. increased; stock transfer tax introduced and special taxes imposed at rates from 3% to 50% on a long list of luxury and semi-luxury goods including clothing, house furnishings, sporting goods, smoking accessories, candy, musical instruments, patent medicines, playing-cards, liquors, automobiles, etc. (c. 71, 1920); these came into force on May 19, and most were repealed on Dec. 12 of same year

P.E.I.—Taxation Act passed revising income tax and imposing a provincial personal property tax, tax on lobster canneries, higher corporation taxes, and poll tax; land tax and succession duties increased and amusement tax passed; new Road Act increased poll tax and horse and dog tax

N.S.—amusement tax broadened and tax on loan and trust co's. raised

N.B.—succession duties increased; Corporation Tax Act, 1920, introduced to revise and increase rates; wild lands tax increased (to 2¢ per acre)

Que.—asbestos royalty increased to 5%

Ont.—flat tax on insurance co's. converted to tax on gross premiums and tax on banks and race tracks increased; amusement tax extended to cabarets; licences on passenger and freight carriers introduced; income tax returns made mandatory and exemption of dividend income previously granted under municipal business tax abolished by amendment to Ontario Assessment Act and exemptions for householder increased to $2,000 and non-householder to $1,000; Ontario Municipal Tax Exemption Act, 1920, gave authority to municipalities to exempt improvements at their option—apparently no advantage was taken of it

Man.—new tax on pool and billiard rooms and bowling alleys under Amusement Tax Act (latter 1¢ per string); supplementary revenue tax increased to 2 mills; succession duty rates revised; permanent Tax Commission appointed

Sask.—1st session: succession duty rates increased; theatre licences raised; 2nd session: supplementary revenue tax (1907) repealed; fees on travelling shows increased; new Timber Taxation Act passed; Corporations Taxation Act again consolidated with increased rates; Towns Act amended to allow towns to tax incomes, with exemptions of $1,000 for single and $1,500 for married persons; City Act amended to allow cities to impose amusement taxes and increase income tax exemption for married persons from $1,500 to $2,000

Alta.—supplementary revenue tax rate raised to 2 mills effective 1921, and Assessment Equalization Board appointed to equalize assessment throughout province; fur tax levied under Game Act; Medicine Hat allowed to impose business tax on rental value and $10 poll tax; Calgary authorized to impose motor vehicle tax

B.C.—personal income tax exemptions revised to provide separate exemptions for single ($1,200) and married ($1,500) and $200 for dependents; provincial poll tax allowed to be adopted by municipalities at their option; amusement tax increased and ½ revenue to be returned to municipalities; Privy Council in *Canadian Pacific Rlwy.* v. *Workmen's Compensation Board of British Columbia*, [1920] A.C. 184, upheld levy by board

1921 *Dom.*—Excise duty on spirits increased from $2.40 per gal. (plus $2.00 luxury tax) to $9.00 except for medical and other licensed purposes; sales tax increased from 1% to 1½% on manufacturer's sales to wholesalers and jobbers and from 2% to 3% on sales to retailers; sales tax on imports also increased; elaborate system of luxury taxes imposed in 1920 repealed except taxes on playing-cards, non-sparkling and sparkling wines

P.E.I.—no tax changes

N.S.—The Provincial Revenue (Corporations) Act revised and increased corporation tax rates formerly imposed under Supplementary Revenue Act, 1919, and under An Act Respecting the Taxation of Certain Companies, 1919 (general capital tax); rates under Domestic, Dominion and Foreign Corp. Act also increased; poll and property taxes under Highways Act revised and renamed "municipalities highway tax"

N.B.—tax on telegraph and extra-provincial companies amended and special licences for commercial vehicles introduced under the Motor Vehicle Act; assessment on municipalities under School Act increased

Que.—new and increased licences on hotels, restaurants, circuses, amusements, race tracks (including admission tax and bets tax), auctioneers, peddlars, billiard tables, bowling alleys, brokers, etc.; Montreal Metropolitan Commission established

Ont.—several major tax changes including new tax on real estate transfers and bank reserves; increases in succession duties, railway and mining taxes, daily race track tax, and amusement tax; investment income exempt to $800 under municipal income tax if total income not over $1,500

Man.—2% tax on corporation profits not otherwise taxed levied for 1921 only; motor vehicle fees and unoccupied land tax increased to 2%

Sask.—no changes

Alta.—educational tax (on land) increased to 3 mills; rates on amusements and travelling shows raised; Edmonton income tax withdrawn; service tax instituted in Edmonton, Calgary, and Lethbridge

B.C.—depletion allowance granted mines; amusement tax extended at 10% to race track admissions, taxes on personal property and income overhauled and enacted under separate Income and Personal Property Taxation Act, the greater tax only being payable; first fully graduated rate schedule introduced; in place of net income and personal property tax new 2% tax on gross revenue of certain corporations (insurance, loan, trust, telegraph, telephone, express, gas, electric, etc.); banks to pay place of business tax in lieu of income tax; province agreed to pay municipalities ⅓ of motor vehicle revenues, all amusement tax from race tracks, and 50% of liquor control profits

1922 *Dom.*—normal tax revised and children's exemption increased from $200 to $300 under income tax; sales tax increased from 4% to 6%; under Special War Revenue Act tax on insurance premiums increased to 5% on policies with British and foreign companies not registered in Canada; excise taxes were also increased on cables and telegrams, cheques and money orders, matches, stock transfers, and new taxes were levied on automobiles, candy, soft drinks, ale, beer, porter, stout, and cigars; excise duties on cigars reduced and raised on cigarettes and a new duty levied on sugar produced from sugar beets; tariff reduced on sugar, agricultural implements, textiles, boots, and shoes

P.E.I.—Motor Vehicles Act imposed new taxes on motor vehicles; poll tax under Road Act reduced

N.S.—Provincial Tax Commission Bill defeated in legislature; minor adjustment in succession duty rates

N.S.—property assessment on municipalities under Highway Act and School Act increased from 25 mills to 40 mills

Que.—succession duty rates and motor vehicle licences increased; minor amendments to corporation taxes; City and Town Act revised; asbestos royalty reduced to 2½%; Montreal bachelor's tax repealed; Privy Council in *Alleyn Sharple* v. *Barthe,* [1922] 1 A.C. 215 upheld Succession Duties Act

Ont.—5% tax on race track bets imposed under Corporation Tax Act; exemption for elderly persons and children under municipal income tax increased

Man.—government proposals to introduce gasoline and income taxes rejected by electorate; 50% of liquor profits in future to go to municipalities

Sask.—Assessment Commission established

Alta.—first provincial gasoline tax introduced at 2¢ per gal.; coal tax increased to 10¢ per ton; new taxes levied on grain companies, general capital stock tax increased and broadened, and special taxes on insurance premiums and express offices increased; succession duty rates amended and wild lands tax increased

B.C.—Taxation Act revised and consolidated and Income and Personal Property Taxation Act, 1922, repealed, these subjects again being taxed under Taxation Act; apparently no change in rates, which were as follows: improved land, 1%; wild land, 5%; coal land, class A, 1%, class B, 4%; income at rates graduated from 1% on $2,500 to 15% on $25,000; coal and coke, 10¢ per ton; mineral output, 2%; personal property, 1%; gross income of certain corporations, 2%; banks on property and branches; railways on track; canneries on output

1923 *Dom.*—technical amendments to income tax, including introduction of "chief occupation" rule and allowance of interest on borrowed capital; 10% reduction in Br. Pref. rates exceeding 15% except on spirits, tobacco, and sugar; tariff negotiations with U.S. authorized but no agreement entered into; excise duties on cigarettes reduced and beet sugar duty repealed; Chinese Immigration tax repealed; excise tax on wines reduced and soft drinks tax changed to tax on carbonic acid gas; maximum cheque tax $1 instead of $2, sales tax made uniform rate at 6%, and further items added to exempt list

P.E.I.—no tax changes

N.S.—Motor Carriers Act introduced special taxes on carriers; exemption for married increased to $2,000 under municipal income tax

N.B.—new tax imposed on travelling shows and circuses

Que.—no changes

Ont.—no changes

Man.—gasoline tax (1¢ per gal.), personal income tax, and grain futures tax introduced (on 1,000 bushels—flaxseed 12¢, wheat 6¢, oats, barley, or rye 3¢); pari-mutuel bets tax of 3% also introduced in Revised Amusement Tax Act; succession duty rates revised

Sask.—succession duties increased under revised Act; Report of Saskatchewan Assessment Commission on Municipal Income Tax issued

Alta.—tax on coal operators converted from 10¢ per ton to 2% of gross revenue; tax introduced at 3¢ per acre on mining lands under Mineral Taxation Act; timber area tax increased from 1¢ to 3¢ per acre and education tax increased; new tax imposed on beverages (including soft drinks) at 3% on gross sales, and on slot machines; succession duties increased

B.C.—tax on personal property and farm lands reduced by 50%; amusement tax on certain entertainment reduced from 10% to 7%; tax of ½¢ per gal. on fuel oil and 3¢ per gal. on gasoline introduced; auto licences reduced 25%

1924 *Dom.*—administration of Income War Tax Act transferred from Department of Finance to Department of Customs and Excise; income tax exemption for dependents increased from $300 to $500 and various technical amendments made affecting inter-company sales, non-residents carrying on business in Canada, incomes of partners, and liens for tax; tariff revised to reduce rates on instruments of production in primary industries and materials for same, tea duty revised; sales tax reduced from

6% to 5%, instruments of production for primary industries were made totally exempt, and half rate (2½%) granted for boots and shoes, canned vegetables and fruits, jams and preserves, biscuits, creosoted railway ties, and other articles

P.E.I.—Taxation Act, 1920, repealed and two acts, Land Assessment Act, 1924, and Income and Personal Property Taxation Act substituted, the former carrying forward the provincial land tax and latter the main taxes on income, personal property, and corporations; gasoline tax of 2¢ per gal. introduced.

N.S.—taxes on fire insurance co's., banks, and succession duties amended

N.B.—no changes

Que.—gasoline tax of 2¢ per gal. introduced; Motor Vehicle Act revised and consolidated

Ont.—Provincial Land Tax Act (unorganized territories) enacted; 1917 Mining Profits Tax rates on nickel and nickel-copper extended to all mines; Municipal Tax Exemption Act, 1920, repealed

Man.—substantial increase in succession duty rates; unoccupied land tax levy reduced to ½%

Sask.—Vehicles Act revised; Report of Assessment Commission issued

Alta.—motor licences revised under consolidated Vehicles and Highway Traffic Act

B.C.—minor technical changes

1925 *Dom.*—lien for income taxes enacted in previous year repealed; tariff on slack coal increased from 14¢ to 50¢ per ton; grapefruit put on free list and duty on well-drilling equipment reduced; sales tax removed from minor items; excise tax on cheques, etc., under $5 removed; tax on playing-cards reduced to 10¢ per pack and on carbonic acid gas removed; tax on export of electricity brought into effect for first time under The Electricity and Exportation Act, 1907

P.E.I.—taxation of insurance companies revised; Succession Duties Act amended

N.S.—gasoline tax of 3¢ per gal. enacted (effective Jan. 15, 1926)

N.B.—no changes

Que.—Mining Act royalties replaced by profits tax similar to Ontario mining tax; rates graduated 3% to 7%; gasoline tax increased from 2¢ to 3¢ per gal.; consolidated statutes contain new Corporation Tax Act, Amusement Tax Act, and legislation to tax land transfers

Ont.—Gasoline Tax Act introduced tax of 3¢ per gal.; race tracks subject to daily tax of $7,500, subject to rebate of $2,500 a day; luxury tax imposed on soft drinks, wines, and light beer; railway fire charge (fire protection tax on railway lands) and minor amendments to succession duties enacted.

Man.—gasoline tax increased from 1¢ to 3¢ per gal.; Income Tax Act amended to allow deduction for Dominion income tax and dependent children; Privy Council in *Attorney General for Manitoba* v. *Attorney General for Canada*, [1925] A.C. 561, held grain futures tax *ultra vires*

Sask.—minor technical amendments; Moose Jaw increased rate of assessment of improvements from 45% to 50% and Saskatoon from 25% to 45%

Alta.—minor technical changes

B.C.—personal income tax rate reduced and further 10% rebate given on personal property tax; tax on timber land reduced from 3% to 1½%

1926 *Dom.*—income tax exemptions increased from $1,000 to $1,500 for single and from $2,000 to $3,000 for married; personal income tax rates revised and reduced and corporation tax rate dropped from 10% to 9%; dividends, previously exempt from normal tax, made fully taxable; substantial tariff reductions on coffee, spices, pineapples, raw sugar, automobiles, and tin plate; excise tax on receipts and 1¢ postage removed

P.E.I.—gasoline tax increased from 2¢ to 3¢ per gal.

N.S.—motor carrier taxes increased

N.B.—gasoline tax of 3¢ per gal. introduced; corporation taxes and amusement taxes increased; under An Act to Aid in the Raising of Revenue provision made for assessment on the municipalities of additional taxes to be levied on real and personal property and income; power was given provincial authorities to equalize and if necessary increase assessment for this purpose

Que.—liquor licences and duties increased; Educational Fund Act authorized duties on natural resources (not proclaimed); 5% tax on meals in hotels and restaurants in cities and towns imposed under Quebec Public Charities Act

Ont.—minor technical changes

Man.—pari-mutuel bets tax increased to 5%; income tax deductions revised

Sask.—City Act revised

Alta.—timbers areas tax reduced from 3¢ to 2¢ per acre; minor reductions in tax on grazing leases under educational tax and supplementary revenue tax; Oil and Gas Wells Act (regulatory) passed

B.C.—no changes

1927 *Dom.*—general 10% reduction in income tax and children eligible to age 21 (formerly 18); sales tax reduced from 5% to 4%; graduated cheque tax reduced to flat 2¢ on cheques over $10; tax on matches reduced from 1¢ per 100 to ¾¢ per 100; 1927 consolidation of Special War Revenue Act showed taxes on bank note circulation, gross income of trust and loan co's., insurance premiums, cables and telegraphs, railway and steamship tickets, seats and berths, cheques and bills of exchange, etc., stock transfers, matches, automobiles, beverages, cigars, playing-cards, and wines

P.E.I.—land tax reduced 20%; income tax exemptions increased from flat $500 to $750 for single and $1,000 for married persons, and motor fee reduced from $5 to $2.50

N.S.—gasoline tax increased from 3¢ to 5¢ per gal. (effective March 7, 1928); land tax made applicable to occupant of over 1,000 acres (formerly 500)

N.B.—Revenue Act of previous year repealed; capital tax on extra-provincial companies increased

Que.—minor amendments to stock transfer and amusement taxes; municipalities over 5,000 population prohibited from levying taxes on non-residents employed therein

Ont.—tickets under 25¢ exempt from amusement tax; race track tax reduced from $7,500 per day to $5,000 per day; 10¢ per gal. luxury tax repealed on beer; motor vehicle operators' licence fee of $1 introduced; Mining Tax Act revised and consolidated; Assessment Act exemptions for income tax increased from $2,000 to $3,000 for householders and from $1,000 to $1,500 for non-householders; Mortgage Tax Act in consolidated statutes; Assessment Act revision introduced to be considered for adoption at 1928 session; the revision provided for exemption of dividends of Canadian manufacturing companies from municipal personal income tax but increased tax on businesses was to offset revenue loss; businesses to be assessed for income tax in municipality where chief place of business (rather than head office) is situated (see 1928)

Man.—supplementary levy reduced from 2 mills to 1¼ mills; income tax reduced 20%; tickets 25¢ or less exempt from amusement tax

Sask.—public revenue tax reduced from 2 to 1½ mills; slight revision in corporation taxes; revised Towns Act passed

Alta.—5% tax on pari-mutuel bets introduced; gasoline tax increased from 2¢ to 3¢ per gal; Public Vehicles Act passed

B.C.—historic provincial personal property tax abolished; gross revenue levy enacted for all businesses, payable if greater than net income tax; two classes of taxpayers set up under gross income levy: Class A (professions, brokers etc.) paid rate of ½ of 1%, Class B paid rate of 1/10 of 1%; tax on bond income of banks substituted for repealed personal property tax; income tax exemptions increased from $1,500 to $1,800 for married persons and from $200 to $300 for dependents; ½ of the amount of an annuity was exempted from income tax, and life insurance premiums up to $500 allowed as deduction from income; succession duty rates reduced; Privy Council in *Attorney General for British Columbia* v. *Canadian Pacific Railway*, [1927] A.C. 934, held fuel oil tax *ultra vires*

1928 *Dom.*—Income tax rates reduced by a further 10% (to 80% of the tax otherwise payable) and children over 21 dependent by reason of mental and physical infirmity made eligible; corporation income tax reduced from 9% to 8%; general sales tax reduced from 4% to 3%; tariff reductions on machinery and articles used in mining and fishing, textiles and yarns and textile machinery; excise tax on gross revenue of trust and loan co's. repealed

P.E.I.—gasoline tax increased from 3¢ per gal. to 5¢ per gal.; horse tax reduced

N.S.—no tax changes; Privy Council in *City of Halifax* v. *Fairbanks Estate et al.*, [1928] A.C. 117, upheld Halifax business tax

N.B.—fire prevention tax on fire insurance premiums increased; gasoline tax increased from 3¢ to 5¢ per gal.; tax on life insurance agents increased

Que.—gasoline tax increased from 3¢ to 5¢ per gal.; minor amendments to succession duties

Ont.—2nd session—minor technical amendments in succession duties and land tax; major Assessment Act changes not adopted

Man.—supplementary revenue tax reduced to 1 mill; 50% liquor profits rebate to municipalities (1922) cancelled

Sask.—gasoline tax of 3¢ per gal. introduced; Wild Lands Tax Act revised; Public Vehicles Act passed to tax public carriers; revised Villages Act passed

Alta.—no tax changes; Advisory Committee on Taxation issued report; Privy Council in *The King* v. *Caledonian Collieries, Ltd.*, [1928] A.C. 358, held Mine Owners' Tax Act *ultra vires*; Calgary business tax set at flat rate of 8%

B.C.—further tax reductions: 10% income tax cut for 1927 and thereafter; pension contributions deductible from income; Class B coal lands tax reduced from 4% to 2%; depletion allowance adjusted to actual cost basis in case of mines; rate of gross income levy on Class A reduced to ¼ of 1% on first $2,000; poll tax age raised from 18 to 21

1929 *Dom.*—sales tax reduced from 3% to 2%; excise taxes repealed on insurance premiums, cables and telegrams, railway and steamship tickets, and berths and seats; stock transfer tax revised to graduated *ad valorem* schedule; depletion rate on base metal mines (25% since 1917) increased to 33⅓% (golds 50% from 1917 to 1935); minor tariff changes

P.E.I.—no changes

N.S.—minor amendment to insurance taxes and succession duties; Mines Act amended to introduce tax on profits as option to royalties

N.B.—insurance company taxes increased

Que.—tavern duties in Montreal and Quebec revised

Ont.—gasoline tax increased from 3¢ to 5¢ per gal.

Man.—no changes

Sask.—minor amendments to Corporations Taxation Act and Travelling Shows Act; revised Rural Municipalities Act passed

Alta.—gasoline tax increased from 3¢ to 5¢ per gal.; Electric Power Taxation Act authorized province to impose 5 mill tax on property of electric companies outside a city, town, or village; Assessment Commission replaced Assessment Equalization Board

B.C.—output tax on fishing industry abolished and replaced by personal property tax at rate of 1½% of property used in canning or curing fish, tax payable as alternative to income tax, whichever greater; succession duty exemption increased and life insurance proceeds exempt for calculation of duties; collection of rural school district taxes taken over by provincial Surveyor of Taxes

1930 *Dom.*—sales tax reduced from 2% to 1%; income tax amended to allow $500 deduction for dependent parents and for charitable donations up to 10% of income; government and like annuities to $5,000 and co-operatives exempt; distribution of surpluses to shareholders on winding-up made non-taxable; stock transfer tax rates increased; tariff on iron and steel products completely revised, seasonal tariffs for fruits and vegetables introduced, duties were reduced on tea, porcelain, chinaware, and meats and increased on beans and butter; at 2nd session rates were increased on agricultural products, printed matter, paper manufactures, iron and steel items, textiles and boots and shoes, and other goods; fur export tax brought into effect (Dec. 31, 1929) by Ordinance under s. 10, Northwest Territories Act

P.E.I.—no tax changes

N.S.—Municipalities Highway Tax revised

N.B.—no changes

Que.—succession duty rates increased and minor amendments to corporation taxes

Ont.—mining tax schedule amended by eliminating 7% bracket; municipal income tax exemptions of $3,000 for married and $1,500 for single to apply to all income, including investment income

Man.—Income Tax Act amended to introduce 2% tax on corporation profits, effective 1931; gasoline tax increased from 3¢ to 5¢ per gal.; supplementary revenue levy abolished; succession duties reduced; new Highway Traffic Act enacted

Sask.—gasoline tax increased from 3¢ to 5¢ per gal.; Succession Duty Act revised; other minor amendments

Alta.—no changes

B.C.—gasoline tax increased from 3¢ to 5¢ per gal.; wild lands tax reduced from 5% to 3%; Privy Council in *Macdonald Murphy Lumber Co.* v. *Attorney-General for British Columbia*, [1930] A.C. 357, held provincial tax on timber exported from province *ultra vires*

1931 *Dom.*—sales tax increased from 1% to 4%; special excise tax of 1% levied on imports; exemption from stamp tax reduced from $10 to $5 and postage stamps permitted to be used; excise taxes on insurance premiums, postal notes, and letters restored; tariff increases on long list of items including tea, steel plate, motor vehicles, various textiles, coal and coke, leather and leather products; importation of second-hand motor vehicles prohibited

P.E.I.—Domiciled Companies Act passed; succession duty rates increased

N.S.—no changes

N.B.—no changes

Que.—succession duties increased; gasoline tax raised from 5¢ to 6¢ per gal.; meals tax extended to eating places outside cities and towns; various licences on hotels, restaurants, etc. increased

Ont.—Corporations Tax Act amended by introducing new general tax of 1/10 of 1% on paid up capital of corporations not already subject to special corporation taxes

Man.—unoccupied land tax turned over to rural municipalities

Sask.—no changes

Alta.—Corporation Taxation Act amended to provide 2% tax on gross life insurance premiums; municipal assessment of electricity companies limited to 5 mills on property

B.C.—increase in banks taxes; telegraph and express co. taxes revised; The Special Revenue Act of 1931 levied a tax of 1% on all wages over $25 a week (married), $15 a week (single), and other income in excess of $1,300 (married) or $780 (single) a year and additional 1/4% surtax imposed on gross revenue companies

1932 *Dom.*—corporation income tax raised from 10% to 11%, 20% rate reduction under personal income tax removed and 5% surtax on incomes over $5,000, all effective for 1931; exemptions reduced from $1,500 to $1,200 and from $3,000 to $2,400; sales tax increased from 4% to 6%; special import tax increased to 3%; excise taxes reimposed on cables and telegrams, seats (10¢), and berths (10%); new tax on long distance calls; stamp tax increased to 3¢ up to $100 and 6¢ over $100; at fall session major tariff changes following the Imperial Economic Conference were enacted; excise duty on spirits reduced from $9 to $7 per prf. gal.

P.E.I.—gasoline tax increased from 5¢ to 6¢ per gal.

N.S.—gasoline tax increased from 5¢ to 6¢ per gal.; general increase in taxes on banks, insurance, chain stores, and other corporations; general capital stock tax also increased; succession duty rates raised

N.B.—gasoline tax increased from 5¢ to 7¢ per gal.; succession duties increased and special taxes on banks, insurance co's., and agents levied

Que.—general corporation profits tax (1½%) introduced in addition to existing corporation taxes; security transfer and amusement tax increased; unemployment tax (on liquor) enacted and meals tax extended and re-enacted as hospital duty

Ont.—gasoline tax increased from 5¢ to 6¢ per gal.; Corporations Tax Act amended to impose new 1% profits tax and $50 for each place of business in province; capital stock tax retained at 1/10 of 1%; amusement tax increased and extended; luxury tax replaced by tax of 10¢ per gal. on wine under Supplementary Revenue Act, 1932; tax of ½¢ per gal. enacted under Fuel Oil Tax Act (not proclaimed)

Man.—Special Revenue Tax Act imposed 15% surtax on succession duties, increased amusement tax and corporation taxes, raised profits tax from 2% to 5% and gasoline tax from 5¢ to 7¢ per gal.; personal income tax exemptions reduced and rates increased for 1931; special taxes on automobiles and gas and electricity levied in Winnipeg

Sask.—gasoline tax increased from 5¢ to 6¢ per gal.; public revenue tax increased from 1½ mills to 2 mills; provincial personal income tax and profits tax (4%) introduced under Income Tax Act and power of municipalities to tax income withdrawn; taxes on banks, insurance, finance, and oil co's. increased; succession duty exemptions reduced and surtax imposed where estate over $20,000; 10% tax on mortgage interest levied; Public Service Vehicles Act replaced Public Vehicles Act

Alta.—general corporation profits tax (4%) and provincial personal income tax introduced under Income Tax Act; general 10% increase in corporation taxes provided; rates of automobile fees, amusement taxes, and succession duties raised; Fuel Oil Tax Act passed

B.C.—Gasoline tax increased from 5¢ to 7¢ per gal.; amusement tax broadened; separate Income Tax Act passed, reducing exemptions to $500 for married person and $200 for each dependent, and increasing rates (1% on 1st $1,000 to 19% on amount between $18,000 and $19,000 and 10% on total if over $19,000) applicable to 1931; tax paid under Special Revenue Act for 1931 allowed as credit against new tax; gross revenue tax on special corporations fixed at 2¼%; Special Revenue Tax Act repealed; special 5 mill tax on land outside school districts levied under Taxation Act

1933 *Dom.*—corporation income tax raised from 11% to 12½% for 1932 and $2,000 exemption removed (consolidated rate 13½%); personal income tax exemptions reduced from $1,200 to $1,000 and from $2,400 to $2,000, children from $500 to $400; rates increased; 5% withholding tax on interest and dividends going abroad instituted; new excise taxes imposed on sugar (2¢ lb.), cigarette papers (2¢ per 100), tubes (5¢ per 100), malt syrup (50¢ lb.), tires and tubes, toilet articles (10%), toilet soaps (5%); increases in tax on matches, cheques, postal notes, and stock transfers; excise duties on spirits used for certain licensed manufacturers set at $2.50 per gal. and $1.00 for spirits used in fortifying mines; validation fee of 20¢ per gal. on exported spirits imposed by order-in-council of Dec. 2, 1933

P.E.I.—amusement, corporation, and succession duties increased; gasoline tax increased from 6¢ to 8¢ per gal.

N.S.—no tax changes

N.B.—no changes

Que.—minor changes only

Ont.—succession duty rates increased and 10% surtax imposed

Man.—Special Income Tax Act of 2% on income where total income in excess of $960 for married person and $480 for single person; deducted at source from wages and salary but applicable also to other income; provincial tax of 2% imposed on land and improvements in unorganized territories; Winnipeg gas and electricity taxes expired after one year

Sask.—5% tax levied on pari-mutuel bets under Horse Racing Regulation Act; personal income tax exemptions reduced

Alta.—gasoline tax increase from 5¢ to 6¢ per gal.; 10% increase in corporation taxes continued; Pipe Line Taxation Act (5 mill property tax on pipe lines) introduced; Privy Council in *Provincial Treasurer of Alberta* v. *Kerr*, [1933] A.C. 710, declared Succession Duties Act *ultra vires*

B.C.—succession duties increased; surtax levied on individual incomes over $5,000 at graduated rates from 1% on $5,000–$7,500 to 18% over $47,500 effective after Sept. 29, 1932; for purposes of surtax, income included dividends and interest (exempt from standard income tax); school tax reduced from ½% to ⅙%; amusement tax made general at 5% rate; meals tax (5% if over 50¢) passed under Hospitals Aid Act; rate of special school tax reduced to 2 mills

1934 *Dom.*—excise taxes reduced on sugar (to 1¢ per lb.), cigarette tubes, and wines; taxes increased on postal notes; excise duty of 3¢ per lb. on malt used in beer and 12½¢ gallonage excise tax consolidated into one poundage duty on malt of 7½¢ per lb.; Bullion Tax Act enacted to impose tax of 25% on difference in value of gold between former price of $20.67 per ounce and new price of $35; Dominion Income Tax offset against bullion tax; major reductions in Br. Pref. Tariff on jute yarns, steel plates, salt cake, and artificial silk yarns; special excise tax reduced from 3% to 1½% on Br. Pref. imports

P.E.I.—succession duties amended to exempt life insurance left for payment of duty

N.S.—gasoline tax increased from 6¢ to 8¢ per gal.; Fuel Oil Tax Act passed (not proclaimed); sharp increase in all corporation taxes Provincial Revenues (Corporations) Act; Report of the Royal Commission of Economic Inquiry

N.B.—gasoline tax increased from 7¢ to 8¢ per gal.; special taxes on banks and insurance co's. extended

Que.—minor technical changes

Ont.—Succession Duties Act revised and consolidated

Man.—Succession Duty Act consolidated

Alta.—10% surtax on corporation taxes extended for 1934 and 1935; new Succession Duties Act to meet *Kerr* decision; amendment to Income Tax Act, including revised schedule and repeal of surtax

Sask.—succession duties amended; insurance taxes increased 50%

B.C.—Probate Duty and Succession Duty Acts consolidated; income tax exemptions increased to $600 (single), $1,000 (married); meals tax repealed; Privy Council in *Attorney-General for British Columbia* v. *Kingcome Navigation Co. Ltd.*, [1934] A.C. 45, held fuel oil tax *intra vires;* Report of Municipal Taxation Commission

1935 *Dom.*—corporation income tax rate raised from 12½% to 13½% for 1934; surtax on investment income over $5,000 (all income over $14,000) at graduated rates (also for 1934) and gift tax introduced effective 1934; depletion allowance for precious metal mines reduced from 50% to 33⅓% for company and from 50% to 20% for shareholders, on base metals from 33⅓% to 20% for shareholders and on oils from 25% to 20% for shareholders; excise duty on spirits reduced from $7 to $4 per gal. and new tax levied on cigarette lighters of 20% (10% on combination with pencils, etc.); several items exempt from sales tax and further reductions in Br. Pref. rates; bullion tax expired

P.E.I.—no tax changes

N.S.—rates of general capital stock tax increased and succession duties revised; amusement tax broadened

N.B.—no tax changes

Que.—profits tax increased from 1½% to 2½%; capital tax broadened; mining profits tax and succession duties raised; 45% surtax levied on bank taxes; Montreal introduced retail sales tax (2%), personal income tax at 10, 15, or 20% of the Dominion tax, depending on the amount of latter, and special business taxes

Ont.—10% surtax on succession duties increased to 15% and Corporations Tax Act consolidated

Man.—unorganized land tax amended; Winnipeg adopted graduated rates (from 5% to 15%) under "rental value" business tax in place of flat 6⅔%

Sask.—gasoline tax increased from 6¢ to 7¢ per gal.; profits tax raised from 4% to 5% and personal income tax rates increased (both for 1934) and Timber Taxation Act repealed

Alta.—corporations to pay greater of corporation taxes or profits tax; gasoline tax increased from 6¢ to 7¢ per gal.; Report of Alberta Taxation Inquiry Board on Provincial and Municipal Taxation issued; full-time Director of Assessments replaced Assessment Commission

B.C.—no changes

1936 *Dom.*—corporate income tax increased from 13½% to 15% for 1935; 3-year exemption for new mines and half rate for non-resident-owned investment companies begun; $300 limit on employee pension contributions introduced; sales tax increased from 6% to 8% and crushed stone for roads, paper for periodicals, and other items exempt; automobile tax revised to apply at 5% on value over $650; excise duty on Canadian brandy and medicinal spirits reduced; major tariff revisions affected automobiles, cotton yarns, fabrics and clothes, and other items, mainly by reductions in British Pref. rate; Canada–United States Trade Agreement implemented

P.E.I.—taxes on chain stores and succession duties increased

N.S.—succession duties revised

N.B.—Corporation Tax Act amended and broadened; Saint John adopted business tax on assessed value of property occupied

Ont.—provincial personal income tax introduced (effective 1935) and right of municipalities to impose withdrawn

Man.—married exemption under special income tax increased from $960 to $1200; Winnipeg automobile taxes reduced

Sask.—Report of Commission of Enquiry into Provincial and Municipal Taxation (Jacoby Commission) recommended 2% retail sales tax; wild lands tax (1917) repealed

Alta.—Retail Sales Tax Act (Ultimate Purchasers Tax) imposed tax at 2%; profits tax increased from 4% to 5% for 1935; supplementary revenue tax (land tax) replaced by social services tax and increased from 2 to 3 mills; wild lands tax repealed and automobile licences reduced; corporation tax surtax extended for 1937

B.C.—amusement tax increased to 10%; minor amendments to Succession Duty Act

1937 *Dom.*—Royal Commission on Dominion-Provincial Relations appointed; second Canada–United States Trade Agreement came into effect; First Can.–U.S. Income Tax Convention became effective for taxable years beginning on and after Jan. 1, 1936; other minor changes

P.E.I.—gasoline tax increased from 8¢ to 10¢ per gal.; minor changes in income and corporation taxes

N.S.—chain store taxes increased

N.B.—alternative tax based on places of business or retail sales provided for extra-provincial companies; municipalities authorized to exempt improvements for two years; new Motor Carrier Act passed

Que.—no changes

Ont.—Succession Duty Act revised and rates increased; amusement tax repealed

Man.—Income Taxation Act passed to consolidate previous ordinary income tax and special income tax; tax on land in unorganized territories repealed; Privy Council in *Attorney-General for Manitoba* v. *Forbes*, [1937] A.C. 260, held tax on wages *intra vires*

Sask.—education tax (2% retail sales tax) introduced and corporation taxes increased

Alta.—Grazing Lease Taxation Act passed imposing tax equal to rent paid under lease; 10% surtax on corporation taxes extended for 1938 and taxes on insurance premiums, authorized capital, loan, railway, and other co's. sharply increased; ultimate purchasers tax suspended; Bank Taxation Act passed

B.C.—forest protection tax extended to Crown-granted timberland whether or not logged

1938 *Dom.*—gift tax rates increased; under income tax provision made for lump sum payments by employees into pension funds, s. 32A and exemption for companies with 75% of capital outside Canada introduced; building materials, gopher poison, harness, fur-bearing animal food, etc. exempt from sales tax.

P.E.I.—Income and Personal Property Tax Act (1924) replaced by two new acts, Income Tax Act and Personal Property and Special Companies Taxation Act, the former modelled after Income War Tax Act imposing graduated tax on individuals and corporations at rates unchanged since 1920; $200 allowance granted for children

N.S.—gasoline tax increased from 8¢ to 10¢ per gal.

N.B.—general corporation profits tax (1%) introduced under revised Corporations Tax Act; general capital tax of ⅛ of 1% imposed and other taxes revised; gasoline tax increased from 8¢ to 10¢ per gal.

Que.—additional 1932 corporation taxes extended for further period; minor amendments to succession duties and to Montreal and Quebec taxes

Ont.—minor tax changes

Man.—5% profits tax replaced by graduated schedule rising from 1% on first $1,000 to 10% on total income if over $19,000; alternative schedule adopted for profits of mining co's. rising from 5% on $100,000 to 10% over $1,300,000. Winnipeg adopted taxes on gas and electricity and liquor purchases

Sask.—Provincial Tax Commission established to administer tax laws; Succession Duties Act consolidated and Fuel Petroleum Products Act, 1938, passed

Alta.—Mineral Taxation Act, 1938, levied ⅓¢ per acre tax on mineral lands; under Agricultural Land Relief Act tax of 7/100 of all agricultural produce authorized; 1938 Securities Tax Act authorized tax of 2% on principal sums owing on interest in land; 50% surtax levied on banks; pipe lines and electric power taxes increased to 10 mills; wild lands tax raised to 2¢ per acre; loan and trust co. taxes increased; 10% surtax on corporations extended to 1939 and 20% surcharge levied for succession duties; 5% profits tax replaced by graduated schedule from 3% on first $2,000 to 7% of all net income if over $10,000; unearned increment tax increased from 5% to 10%

B.C.—life insurance premiums taxed at 2¾%

1939 *Dom.*—1st session: credit against income tax for 10% of capital expenditures made in year following May 1, 1939; 3% special excise on imports repealed except for general tariff; 3-year exemption for new mines renewed; duty on spirits used in vinegar increased from 27¢ to 60¢ per gal. 2nd session: first war budget introduced excess profits tax on fiscal periods ending after March 31, 1940, with alternative standard profits of percentage of capital employed or profits of previous four years; corporation income tax increased from 15% to 18%; surtax of 20% on personal income tax; excise duties and tariff on spirits, beer, and tobacco increased and tariff on tea and coffee sharply raised; 8% sales tax applied to domestic electricity and gas, salted, smoked, and canned meats and fish; moderate tax on carbonic acid gas

P.E.I.—no tax changes

N.S.—general corporation profits tax (1%) introduced under Corporation Tax Act, 1939 and other corporation taxes revised and increased

N.B.—no tax changes

Que.—new Corporation Tax Act passed making numerous changes, including increased taxes on capital and places of business and revision of other specific taxes; profits tax rate maintained at 2½%; gasoline tax increased from 6¢ to 8¢ per gal.; Quebec City authorized to levy personal income tax not exceeding 20% of Dominion tax

Ont.—new Corporation Tax Act passed, increasing profits tax from 1% to 2% and reducing capital stock tax from 1/10 of 1% to 1/20 of 1%; gas, electric, and loan and trust companies taxed on profits instead of under specific taxes; Race Tracks Tax Act and Stock Transfers Tax Act re-enacted separately, the latter with rates same as Dominion; gasoline tax increased from 6¢ to 8¢ per gal.; succession duty surtax, formerly 15% on all rates, increased to 20% on class 2 and 25% on class 3; Assessment Act amended to increase from 1% to 2½% allowable municipal tax on mining profits over $2⅓ m. (under $2⅓ m. rate of 1½% retained); Mining Tax Act amended to allow Assessment Act tax credit in full

Man.—The Amusements Act revised and consolidated; other changes minor; Report of Royal Commission on the Municipal Finance and Administration of the City of Winnipeg.

Sask.—Corporations Taxation Act amended

Alta.—10% corporation tax surtax and 50% surtax on banks extended to 1940; amusements tax broadened; Privy Council in *Attorney-General for Alberta* v. *Attorney-General for Canada* and others, [1939] A.C. 117, declared Bank Taxation Act, 1937, *ultra vires*

B.C.—no changes

1940 *Dom.*—June, 1940: personal income tax exemptions reduced to $1,500 (married) $750 (single) and rates increased; national defence tax at 2% and 3% with exemptions of $1,200 (married) and $600 (single) introduced from July 1 deductible at source; corporation income tax rate fixed at 18% for 1940 and Excess Profits Tax Act, 1940, passed replacing 1939 Act, providing for one standard base (1936–9 profits) and 75% rate on excess over this base but not less than 12% of total profits; 10% war exchange conservation tax on all imports introduced and drastic increases in automobile taxes; excise taxes increased on matches, cigarette papers and tubes, furs, cigars, tires and tubes, and carbonic acid gas; new taxes imposed on cameras; excise duties and tariff on tobacco products increased; tea tariff increased. Aug., 1940: War Contract Depreciation Board set up. Nov., 1940: Board of Referees for Excess Profits Tax set up. Dec., 1940: War Exchange Conservation Act introduced; drastic increase in tax on cars and new excise taxes on electric fixtures and electrical home appliances and apparatus, such as stoves, refrigerators, washing machines, vacuum cleaners, etc.; same Act (part III) granted authority for special depreciation on assets that would increase foreign exchange

P.E.I.—amusement tax and succession duties revised

N.S.—profits tax increased from 1% to 2½%

N.B.—profits tax increased from 1% to 2½%; other corporation taxes revised and increased; Tobacco Tax Act (10% tax) enacted; succession duty rates increased

Que.—Retail Sales Tax Act and Tobacco Tax Act enacted imposing a 2% provincial retail sales tax and a 10% tobacco tax respectively; corporation profits tax increased from 2½% to 5%; provincial personal income tax introduced for 1939 income equal to 15% of Dominion income tax; Quebec City authorized to levy 2% retail sales tax; Montreal authorized to impose annual licences or taxes on radios, telephones, and motor vehicles

Ont.—corporation profits tax for 1939 and 1940 increased retroactively from 2% to 5%, and 25% surtax levied on specific taxes payable by banks and insurance, railway, telegraph, telephone, express, and car co's.; numerous minor amendments to personal income tax and succession duties

Man.—Income Taxation Act, Corporations Taxation Act, Succession Duty Act, and others revised and consolidated; Winnipeg tax on gas and electricity reduced

Sask.—minor amendments to Corporation Taxation Act and Income Tax Act

Alta.—surtax on banks and other corporations extended for 1941; personal income tax increased

B.C.—no changes

1941 *Dom.*—personal income tax rates increased, 4% tax on investment income introduced, payment by instalments made optional, and national defence tax rates raised to 5% and 7%; minimum excess profits tax increased to 22% of total profits; one year additional depletion allowance of 33⅓% allowed for timber; under excess profits tax oil well operators west of Ontario given 33⅓% depletion rate (was 25%); 5% withholding tax on non-residents increased to 15% and rates of gift tax raised; limit of 5% of payroll (max. $300) put on employer pension contributions; first Dominion succession duty introduced; existing taxes increased on insurance premiums, long distance calls, cigarette papers and tubes, wines, playing-cards, automobiles, lighters, cameras, radios, sugar, soft drinks, carbonic acid gas, and toilet articles, and duties on beer and malt raised; new taxes imposed on travel tickets, gasoline, admissions, pari-mutuel bets; buildings materials made subject to sales tax; offer made to provinces to vacate fields of direct taxation for period of war; Can.–U.S. Income Tax Convention abrogated by U.S.

P.E.I.—10% health tax on retail tobacco and liquor sales introduced; minor amendments to income tax and succession duties

N.S.—no tax changes

N.B.—no changes

Que.—rates of personal income tax reduced by repeal of former tax equal to 15% of Dominion tax and substitution of new separate rate schedule; exemptions of $1,000 and $2,000 for single and married persons provided; Montreal and Quebec retail sales taxes broadened in scope and Montreal authorized for one year to impose personal income tax

Ont.—corporation tax on telephone co's. revised and 1940 increases in profits tax and corporation taxes extended for another year; other minor amendments in corporation taxes, personal income tax and succession duties

Man.—minor amendment to personal income tax

Sask.—technical amendments only

Alta.—Amusement Act and Vehicles and Highway Traffic Act consolidated;

banks and corporation surtaxes extended for 1942; succession duty amended re gifts; new Mineral Taxation Act passed

B.C.–minor changes

1942 *Dom.*–personal income tax exemptions lowered, rates increased and revised; national defence tax absorbed as *normal* tax at rates of 7, 8, and 9% and part of new tax to be refunded after war; deduction at source for individual incomes and instalment payment for corporations made compulsory; ministerial approval of pension plans introduced; medical expenses allowance introduced; gift tax rates again increased; excess profits tax rate increased to 100%, part to be refundable after war; 1 year carry-forward of business losses instituted, effective for 1943; pulpwood producers allowed extra 15¢ per cord deduction (until 1946); minor amendments to succession duties; existing taxes on almost all commodities further increased and new levies imposed on candy, chewing gum, films, cabarets, luggage, jewellery, etc.; second Can.-U.S. Income Tax Convention signed to be effective from abrogation of first Convention

P.E.I.–an Act to Suspend Temporarily the Imposition of Income Taxes, Corporation Taxes and Taxes on Securities passed (c. 2)

N.S.–an Act to Authorize an Agreement between the Government of the Dominion and the Government of the Province (c. 2); Halifax residential property rate fixed at 35 mills

N.B.–an Act to Suspend the Imposition of Income Taxes, Corporation Taxes and Taxes on Securities (c. 6) passed; succession duties raised; road tax reduced; Moncton adopted rental value tax on both residential and business properties

Que.–an Act Respecting an Agreement between the Dominion and the Province for the Suspension of Certain Taxes in Wartime passed (c. 27); other minor changes

Ont.–The Corporations and Income Tax Suspension Act passed to implement tax agreement with Dom.; charitable bequests allowance under succession duties extended from 50% to 100% of estate

Man.–Taxation Suspension Act (c. 1) passed; Gasoline Tax Act consolidated; Winnipeg taxes on automobiles and liquor purchases repealed

Sask.–Taxation Agreements Act, 1942 (c. 2); Travelling Shows Act revised

Alta.–The Tax Collection Temporary Suspension Act (c. 9) passed

B.C.–Dominion-Provincial Agreement Act (c. 7) passed

1943 *Dom.*–personal income tax put on pay-as-you-go basis by cancellation of 50% of liability for 1942; taxation system for armed forces overhauled; new deductions allowed for oil and mineral exploration expenses and oil depletion rate increased from 20% to 33⅓%; west coast loggers allowed $1 per m.b.m. extra write-off; $300 for pension arrears; rates on liquor and tobacco increased and additional 1¢ tax levied on postage

P.E.I.–no changes

N.S.–succession duty rates increased

N.B.–no changes; in *Atlantic Smokes Shops* v. *Conlon*, [1943] A.C. 550, Privy Council upheld tobacco tax

Que.–new Succession Duties Act passed without major changes

Ont.–minor changes only; municipal corporation income tax applied for last time

Man.–aviation gas exempt from gasoline tax; Highway Traffic Act revised

Sask.–Report of Urban Assessment Committee

Alta.–no changes

B.C.—no changes

1944 *Dom.*—refundable portion of personal income tax abolished from July 1; other minor alleviations introduced; carry-over of losses extended to 3 years forward and 1 year back for all taxpayers in business; deduction for oil and mineral exploration expenses renewed and deduction allowed for scientific research expenditures; authority given for double depreciation in post-war period; minor amendments in commodity taxes and excess profits tax; agricultural implements made exempt under tariff; Schedule I of War Exchange Conservation Act (prohibited entry list) repealed

P.E.I.—no changes

N.S.—highways tax on property in towns and cities increased; Report of the Royal Commission on Provincial Development and Rehabilitation

N.B.—Fredericton adopted business tax on assessed value of premises; Report of New Brunswick Committee on Reconstruction

Que.—minor revision in rates of stock transfer tax; minimum price of meal for meals tax increased from 35¢ to 60¢; further goods exempt from retail sales tax

Ont.—Municipal Health Services Act to permit municipal property or poll tax for health plans; Report of Royal Ontario Mining Commission

Man.—no changes

Sask.—1st session, no changes; 2nd session, Provincial Tax Commission disbanded; Mineral Taxation Act passed

Alta.—minor changes in succession duties

B.C.—Taxation Act amended to exempt entirely farm improvements under property tax

1945 *Dom.*—by P. C. 3408 (May) excise taxes removed from electrical and gas appliances, reduced to 10% on automobiles, cameras, radios, phonographs; building materials exempted from sales tax and war exchange tax; Dominion-Provincial Conference on Reconstruction (August); fall budget made 4% reduction in personal income tax for 1945 and 16% for 1946 and changes adopted implementing Report of Royal Commission on Annuities and Family Corporations, including exemption of capital element of annuities and payment of special tax on undistributed surpluses of private companies; 5(1)(h) pension plans repealed; increase in employee pension contribution from $300 to $900 for both past and current service; 5% limit for employers removed and $900 per employee substituted; other income tax changes affected armed forces, Alberta debt adjustment, petroleum and mineral exploration expenses, etc; under excess profits tax, individuals and partners exempt from 15% rate, 20% refundable portion repealed, minimum standard profit raised from $5,000 to $15,000, and rate on excess profits reduced to 60%; provision made for relief of quick successions; War Exchange Tax abolished; sales tax removed from apparatus and machinery used in manufacturing and production; fur tax revised; minor tariff revisions

P.E.I.—5% tax on pari-mutuel bets enacted

N.S.—Succession Duties Act revised and consolidated

N.B.—road tax (poll and property taxes) under Highways Act abolished

Que.—no tax change

Ont.—minor changes

Man.—pari-mutuel bets tax increased from 5% to 10%; Motive Fuel Users Tax Act passed (7¢ tax)

Sask.—gasoline tax increased from 7¢ to 8¢ per gal.; succession duty surtax increased from 10% to 20%

Alta.—Mineral Taxation Act revised and tax fixed at 5¢ per acre
B.C.—no changes; Report of the Commissioner relating to Forest Resources of British Columbia; Report of the Commission of Inquiry into Educational Finance

1946 *Dom.*—budget made new offer to provinces for agreements; also major tax changes for 1947, including revision of personal income tax structure and increase in exemption from $600 to $750 and from $1,200 to $1,500, corporation tax rate increased from 18% to 30%, and excess profits tax reduced from 20% to 15%; individuals and partners exempted and minimum rate repealed; Report of Royal Commission an Co-operatives implemented; other income tax measures included 3-year averaging for farmers and fishermen, Income Tax Appeal Board, expense allowances for elected members, special treatment for authors and artists, revision of armed forces taxation, ½ rate of tax for new mines after Jan. 1, 1947, oil and mineral exploration allowances extended, etc.; succession duty rates doubled with credit for provincial duties, minor revisions of taxes on security transfers, cigars, insurance premiums; minor tariff changes
P.E.I.—no tax changes
N.S.—suspended corporation profits tax increased from 2½% to 5%—not proclaimed
N.B.—no changes
Que.—Progress of Education Act passed imposing tax of 15¢ on 1,000 K.W.H. of electricity generated and 15¢ per cord of wood cut
Ont.—mining acreage tax increased from 5¢ to 10¢; extensive revisions to Assessment Act (municipal property tax); minor succession duty changes
Man.—no changes
Sask.—retail sales tax removed from foodstuffs, meals, and lunches
Alta.—succession duties amended for "quick" successions
B.C.—gasoline tax increased from 7¢ to 10¢ per gal. (effective April 1, 1947); special school tax repealed; tax under Public Schools Act revised and increased; forest protection tax extended to wild lands

1947 *Dom.*—budget: further reduction in personal income tax effective July 1, 1947; mineral exploration allowances extended another year; 5% tax levied on dividends going to parent company abroad; excess profits tax repealed from Dec. 31, 1947; gasoline tax repealed; other minor changes; additional $500 exemption allowed persons over 65 under income tax; Bill 454 (Revised Income Tax Act) introduced for public consideration; Tax Agreements entered into with seven provinces

Nov., 1947: taxes on sugar and household gas and electricity removed and tariff on tea and coffee reduced at same time as new temporary taxes imposed or increased on many semi-durable goods as part of dollar exchange conservation proposal; these included automobiles, cameras, electrical and gas appliances, firearms, bicycles and motorcycles, outboard motors, toilet articles, musical instruments, etc.; depletion allowances set by regulation as follows: producers, base metals, 33⅓%; golds, 40% or $4 per oz.; asbestos, 33⅓%; oil wells, 33⅓%; gas wells, 25%; coal mines, 10¢ per ton
P.E.I.—gasoline tax increased from 10¢ to 13¢ per gal.; taxes suspended under new agreement with Dominion
N.S.—gasoline tax increased from 10¢ to 13¢ per gal.; taxes suspended under new agreement with Dominion; highway poll and property taxes repealed except for property tax in rural municipalities
N.B.—gasoline tax increased from 10¢ to 13¢ per gal.; taxes suspended under new agreement with Dominion; Report of the Commission to

Investigate Taxation in the City of Fredericton; Saint John adopts special business tax for retailers and wholesalers based on fraction of sales of previous year

Que.—new Corporation Tax Act reimposed suspended profits tax at 7% and other specific taxes on paid-up capital and places of business; gasoline tax increased from 8¢ to 11¢ per gal.; new taxes on petroleum and telephone co's. under amendments to an Act to Insure the Progress of Education; personal income tax suspended for 1947

Ont.—gasoline tax increased from 8¢ to 11¢ per gal.; corporation profits tax reimposed at 7%; mining tax rates increased from 3, 5, and 6% to 6, 8, and 9% respectively; personal income tax suspended for 1947; corporation taxes on paid-up capital, places of business, etc., and other special taxes re-enacted; Report of Ontario Royal Commission on Forestry; Fire Department Act, Police Act, and Highway Improvements Amendment Act passed

Man.—gasoline tax increased from 7¢ to 9¢ per gal.; taxes suspended under new agreement with Dominion

Sask.—gasoline tax increased from 8¢ to 10¢ per gal.; further goods exempt from retail sales tax; taxes suspended under agreement with Dominion

Alta.—gasoline tax increased from 7¢ to 9¢ per gal.; taxes suspended under new agreement with Dominion; Social Services Tax Act repealed from Jan. 1, 1947; Mineral Taxation Act, 1947, passed

B.C.—new agreement with Dominion: 5% corp. income tax passed as in P.E.I., N.S., N.B., Man., Sask., Alta.; taxation of Crown-granted forest lands revised; Report of the Commissioner on Provincial-Municipal Relations in British Columbia

1948 *Dom.*—Revised Income Tax Act passed, to come into effect Jan. 1, 1949; prepared and canned foods exempt from sales tax; retail sales tax removed from cutlery and alarm clocks, and amusement, cabaret, and bets taxes repealed; succession duty exemption increased from $5,000 to $50,000 and 50% limit on charitable gifts removed; 3% excise on imports from general tariff countries removed and tariff amended to implement undertaking under General Agreement; balance of additional and increased taxes of November, 1947, removed by order in council, July 1, 1948; non-bedded industrial minerals allowed 33⅓% depletion by regulation

P.E.I.—land tax (Land Assessment Act), poll tax, and horse tax repealed (Road Act)

N.S.—rates under Domestic, Dominion and Foreign Corp's. Act revised

N.B.—City of Fredericton Assessment Act implemented many of recommendations of Commission on Taxation

Que.—personal income tax suspended for 1948; Quebec City amusement tax broadened

Ont.—20% amusement tax enacted (Hospital Tax Act); premiums tax on fire and life co's. revised from 1¾% and 1⅔% (plus 25% surtax) to 2% without surtax; minor amendments in natural gas tax; Provincial-Municipal Conference at Toronto

Man.—tax on income from mining operations imposed under Mining Royalty and Tax Act; amusement tax increased from 10% to 25%; Winnipeg Brief on Provincial-Municipal Relations submitted to provincial government

Sask.—Mineral Taxation Act, 1948, passed

Alta.—amusement tax increased; Report of Royal Commission on Taxation (Judge Commission)

B.C.—3% retail sales tax introduced under Social Security and Municipal Aid Tax Act; coal and coke tax repealed; Mining Tax Act passed to impose 4% tax on mining income; Pari-mutuel Betting Tax Act passed imposing 12% tax; Amusement Tax Act revised and increased from 5% to 25%; 1948 consolidation of Taxation Act shows taxes of 1% on improved land, of 3% on wild land, of 7% on class A and 2% on class B coal land, 1½% on timber land, ½% on farm land; poll tax $5 where a municipality does not impose; Vancouver and New Westminster first B.C. municipalities to have business taxes; basis rental value, rate in Vancouver 9% and in New Westminster 11%

1949 *Dom.*—major post-war tax remissions in March budget; personal income tax exemptions increased to $1,000 and $2,000 and rates reduced; corporation income tax changed from 30% to 10% on first $10,000 and 33% on excess; 10% credit against personal income tax for dividends, carry-over of losses extended to 5 years forward and 1 year back; "recapture" system for depreciation comes into effect; excise taxes repealed on transportation tickets, berths and parlour car seats, soft drinks, candy, chewing gum, busses, telegrams, long distance tolls, and reduced on fountain pens and pencils, jewellery, lighters, luggage, matches, tires and tubes, toilet articles; in October, tax on light wines reduced and fuel oil exempt from sales tax

Nfld.—entered confederation on April 2; tariff repealed and under subsequent tax agreement with Dominion personal and corporation income taxes and death duties also repealed from April 1, 1949; Social Security Assessment Act, 1949, passed to levy 3% retail sales tax; Local Government Act passed

P.E.I.—no tax changes

N.S.—maximum for municipal poll taxes increased; Report on Reorganization of Provincial-Municipal Relations in Nova Scotia

N.B.—Saint John business tax assessments increased

Que.—personal income tax suspended for 1949; Montreal Catholic School Commission authorized to impose 1% retail sales tax for 3 years, bringing total rate in Montreal to 5% (2% prov., 2% mun., 1% school)

Ont.—succession duty exemption for class 1 beneficiaries increased from $25,000 to $50,000; personal income tax suspended for 1949, minor amendments to allocation formulae under Corporation Tax Act, and other minor changes

Man.—municipal commissioner's levy reduced following assumption by province of 12½% of cost of old age pensions formerly charged to municipalities; rates of amusement tax reduced

Sask.—no tax changes

Alta—wild lands tax repealed from Jan. 1, 1949; new Mines and Minerals Act passed

B.C.—wild land under 640 acres exempt from forest protection tax

1950 *Dom.*—privilege of paying 15% tax on undistributed surplus granted private companies and major revision made in income tax provisions relating to capitalization of income; other changes affected profit-sharing plans, prospectors, charitable organizations, etc.; ice cream exempt from sales tax and toilet soap from 5% excise tax. Fall session: corporation rates increased to 15% and 38%, liquor tax increased $1 per gal., malt tax increased to 21¢ per lb.; 10% excise taxes increased to 15% and new tax of 30% on candy, chewing gum, and soft drinks

Nfld.—5% corporation income tax (effective 1949) and tax on fire insurance premiums enacted; retail sales tax proclaimed Nov. 15.

P.E.I.—no tax changes
N.S.—no tax changes
N.B.—4% retail sales tax introduced under the Social Services and Education Tax Act
Que.—personal income tax suspended for 1950; fall session: gasoline tax increased from 11¢ to 13¢ per gal.; Quebec City Catholic School Commission given right to levy 1% sales tax
Ont.—personal income tax of 5% of Dominion tax and act authorizing collection agreement with Dominion passed but not proclaimed; minor amendments to corporation and mining tax acts; 9% tax on income from logging operations introduced; amusement tax reduced from 20% to 15% on theatres and similar amusements and tickets under 15¢ exempt; pari-mutuel bets tax increased from 10% to 12½%; provincial statutes revised and consolidated; Report of Royal Commission on Education; Report of Toronto Civic Advisory Council
Man.—no tax changes
Sask.—2% retail sales tax replaced by 3% tax under Education and Hospitalization Tax Act; Report of Committee on Provincial-Municipal Relations
Alta.—no tax changes
B.C.—amusement tax reduced from 25% to 17½%; important amendments to Hospital Insurance Act; provincial poll tax repealed effective Jan. 1, 1951; *Attorney-General for British Columbia* v. *Esquimalt and Nanaimo Railway Co.*, [1950] A.C. 87

1951 *Dom.*—April budget: sales tax increased from 8% to 10%; surtax of 20% levied on corporate and personal income tax rates; tax on cigarettes increased, new 15% taxes on electrical appliances and most excise taxes raised from 10% rate to 25% rate; system of deferred depreciation instituted. Fall session: under Old Age Security Act 2% of sales tax set aside for old age pensions and new taxes of 2 per cent on personal and corporate income introduced; Supplementary Income Tax Convention with U.S. ratified in Nov., 1951, effective from Jan. 1, 1951
Nfld.—minor provincial changes; tax provisions of Local Government Act amended; St. John's adopted rental value business tax in place of stock tax
P.E.I.—provincial statutes revised and consolidated for first time; no important tax changes
N.S.—gasoline tax increased from 13¢ to 15¢ per gal.; taxes on amusements, pari-mutuel bets, and long distance telephone calls also increased
N.B.—Report of Royal Commission on Rates and Taxes
Que.—succession duty exemption for preferred beneficiaries increased; several new municipalities introduce retail sales tax; business tax rate increased from 10% to 11% in Montreal and from 15% to 20% in Quebec City
Ont.—amusement tax reduced from 15% to 12½%; pari-mutuel bets tax revised
Man.—no tax changes
Sask.—no tax changes
Alta.—gasoline tax increased from 9¢ to 10¢ per gal.; auto licences reduced; increased grants to municipalities
B.C.—rates under hospital insurance raised; changes in taxation of privately owned forest lands; Vancouver business tax rate reduced from 9% to 6% and New Westminster rate reduced from 11% to 9%

1952 *Dom.*—old age security taxes of 2% on sales, 2% on corporate income, and 2% on personal income levied from July 1; 20% defence surtax on personal income replaced from July 1 by new rate schedule; corporate tax rates increased to 20% on first $10,000 and 50% on excess (concurrent with repeal of 5% uniform corporate tax in agreeing provinces); 5% tax credit offered for profits tax in non-agreeing province; 15% excise taxes on refrigerators, stoves, and washing machines repealed and most other excises reduced from 25% to 15%; tax on cigarettes reduced by 3¢ per package of 20; soft drinks tax reduced from 30% to 15%; validation fee on exported liquors repealed; Tax Rental Agreement Act 1952 enacted and new agreements entered into for five years 1952 to 1956 inclusive with all provinces but Quebec

Nfld.–5% profits tax repealed; foods made taxable under sales tax; tax agreement signed Sept. 22; first Assessment Act passed; taxes under Local Government Act revised; Revised Statutes of Newfoundland 1952

P.E.I.–5% profits tax repealed; first revised statutes issued; tax agreement signed July 31

N.S.–5% profits tax repealed; tax of 6¢ per ton on gypsum introduced where over 20,000 tons per annum mined; tax agreement signed Nov. 24

N.B.–5% profits tax repealed; Report of Royal Commission on Rates and Taxes Act issued; tax agreement signed Aug. 13; city service tax replaced poll tax in Saint John

Que.–no provincial tax changes

Ont.–At first session corporation profits tax revised to adopt depreciation on federal basis and provincial tax credits revised; pari-mutuel bets tax slightly reduced; province to pay property tax on its businesses; August: Government announces intention to enter into tax agreement with Dominion; at second session legislation for tax agreements passed; agreement signed Oct. 29, suspending corporation profits tax from Jan. 1, 1952

Man.–5% profits tax repealed; tax agreement signed Aug. 29; minor amendments to municipal, gasoline tax, mining royalty, amusement tax, and other legislation

Sask.–5% profits tax repealed; tax agreement signed Sept. 29; public revenue tax repealed effective Jan. 1, 1953

Alta.–5% profits tax repealed; tax agreement signed Sept. 22; minor revision in other taxing statutes

B.C.–5% profits tax repealed; tax agreement signed July 10

1953 *Dom.*–personal income tax rates reduced to 1949 level from July 1; dividend credit increased from 10% to 20%; ineligible amount of medical expenses reduced from 4% to 3% of income; corporation profits tax reduced to 18% on $20,000 and 47% on excess; provincial profits tax credit increased from 5% to 7%; excise duty on cigarettes reduced from $6 per 1,000 to $4 per 1,000; stamp taxes, security transfer tax, and sales tax on books, newsprint, and minor other items repealed; radio licence repealed and revenue from 15% excise on radios, TV sets, etc., earmarked for C.B.C.; many revisions made in Income Tax Act; income tax and succession duty conventions with France became effective

Nfld.–entertainment tax of 5¢ per ticket introduced for cancer control; minor revisions in Local Government and St. John's Municipal Acts

P.E.I.–no provincial tax changes; business tax introduced in Charlottetown

N.S.–tax of 33⅓% on profits from gypsum mining substituted for levy of 6¢ per ton enacted in 1952

N.B.–childrens' clothing and footwear exempted from sales tax; 10% cigarette tax converted to 4¢ per package and cigar tax revised; wild lands tax raised from 2¢ to 3¢ per acre and forest fire tax from 1¢ to 2¢ per acre

Que.—minor succession duty amendments

Ont.—succession duty on estates just over $50,000 alleviated for preferred beneficiaries; graduated pari-mutuel bets tax replaced by flat 8% rate; one-mill mortgage tax repealed; minor retroactive amendments to repealed corporation profits tax; Metropolitan Toronto Act, 1953 passed; acreage rates under Land Tax Act and Mining Tax Act increased

Man.—amusement tax reduced from 25% to 17½%; Report of the Provincial-Municipal Committee issued

Sask.—gasoline tax increased from 10¢ to 11¢ per gallon; hospital insurance rates increased effective Jan. 1, 1954; sales tax exemptions extended to include certain physical aids, natural gas, and domestic fuel oil

Alta.—provincial licence on mobile construction and other equipment introduced in lieu of municipal taxes; City Act amended to allow assessment of improvements at 60% of value

B.C.—auto licences reduced by 10% at spring session; at fall session new logging tax of 10% and tax of 1% on timberland held under lease introduced; mining tax raised from 4% to 10%; sales tax exemption on meals raised form 50¢ to $1.00; special 10% sales tax levied on liquor and other purchases in cocktail bars; social security and municipal aid tax renamed social services tax; provincial crown corporation for toll roads established; Assessment Equalization Act required equalized assessment and inclusion of industrial and commercial machinery and fixtures in assessment for educational tax levy; municipal business licences increased

1954 *Dom.*—15% excise tax repealed for furs, electrical appliances, firearms and ammunition, golf clubs and balls, fishing rods and reels, camera lenses, films and plates, projectors, luggage and vending machines; 15% excise tax reduced to 10% for cosmetics, motorcycles, lighters, coin operated amusement devices, smokers' accessories, automatic pens and pencils, matches, tires and tubes, clocks, watches, jewellery, etc., soft drinks, and candy and chewing gum; sales tax repealed on certain equipment purchased by municipalities, drain tiles, hearing aids, and other minor items; excise duty of 21¢ per lb. on malt replaced by duty of 38¢ per gal.; amendments under income tax included increase in pension deductions from $900 to $1,500, withdrawal of regulation 1100(4); revision of arm's length definition; income tax treaty signed with Eire

Nfld.—gasoline tax increased from 14¢ to 15¢ per gal.; amusement tax (cancer tax) broadened in scope

P.E.I.—no changes

N.S.—no changes

N.B.—sales tax reduced from 4% to 3% and gasoline tax increased from 13¢ to 15¢ per gal.

Que.—personal income tax enacted for 1954, 1955, and 1956 at approximately 15% of federal rates.

Ont.—pari-mutuel bets tax reduced from 8% to 7%

Man.—new petroleum royalties introduced

Alta.—no changes

B.C.—sales tax increased from 3% to 5% to finance hospital care and previous specific charges for this purpose repealed; 10% cocktail lounge tax repealed; amusement tax reduced from 17½% to 15%; children's shoes and clothing exempted from sales tax; vehicle licence fee for motor vehicles on first registration reduced from $10 to $1

Appendix B—Budget Speeches*

Dec.	7, 1867	Hon. John Rose
April	28, 1868	Hon. John Rose
May	7, 1869	Hon. John Rose
May	7, 1870	Sir Francis Hincks
March	10, 1871	Sir Francis Hincks
April	30, 1872	Sir Francis Hincks
April	1, 1873	Hon. S. L. Tilley
April	14, 1874	Hon. R. J. Cartwright
Feb.	16, 1875	Hon. R. J. Cartwright
Feb.	25, 1876	Hon. R. J. Cartwright
Feb.	20, 1877	Hon. R. J. Cartwright
Feb.	22, 1878	Hon. R. J. Cartwright
March	14, 1879	Hon. S. L. Tilley
March	9, 1880	Hon. S. L. Tilley
Feb.	18, 1881	Sir Leonard Tilley
Feb.	24, 1882	Sir Leonard Tilley
March	30, 1883	Sir Leonard Tilley
Feb.	29, 1884	Sir Leonard Tilley
March	3, 1885	Sir Leonard Tilley
March	30, 1886	Sir Leonard Tilley
May	12, 1887	Sir Charles Tupper
April	27, 1888	Sir Charles Tupper
March	5, 1889	Hon. George Foster
March	27, 1890	Hon. George Foster
June	23, 1891	Hon. George Foster
March	22, 1892	Hon. George Foster
Feb.	14, 1893	Hon. George Foster
March	27, 1894	Hon. George Foster
May	3, 1895	Hon. George Foster
Jan.	31, 1896	Hon. George Foster
April	22, 1897	Hon. William S. Fielding
April	5, 1898	Hon. William S. Fielding
May	2, 1899	Hon. William S. Fielding
March	23, 1900	Hon. William S. Fielding
March	14, 1901	Hon. William S. Fielding
March	17, 1902	Hon. William S. Fielding
April	16, 1903	Hon. William S. Fielding
June	7, 1904	Hon. William S. Fielding
July	6, 1905	Hon. William S. Fielding
May	22, 1906	Hon. William S. Fielding

*In *House of Commons Debates*, Ottawa, Queen's Printer.

Nov.	29, 1906	Hon. William S. Fielding
March	17, 1908	Hon. William S. Fielding
April	20, 1909	Hon. William S. Fielding
Dec.	14, 1909	Hon. William S. Fielding
April	4, 1911	Hon. William S. Fielding
March	13, 1912	Hon. William S. Fielding
May	12, 1913	Hon. W. T. White
April	6, 1914	Hon. W. T. White
Aug.	20, 1914	Hon. W. T. White
Feb.	11, 1915	Hon. W. T. White
Feb.	15, 1916	Hon. W. T. White
April	24, 1917	Hon. W. T. White
April	30, 1918	Hon. A. K. MacLean
June	5, 1919	Sir Thomas White
May	18, 1920	Sir Henry L. Drayton
May	9, 1921	Sir Henry L. Drayton
June	12, 1922	Hon. William S. Fielding
May	11, 1923	Hon. William S. Fielding
April	10, 1924	Hon. James A. Robb
March	24, 1925	Hon. James A. Robb
April	5, 1926	Hon. James A. Robb
Feb.	17, 1927	Hon. James A. Robb
Feb.	16, 1928	Hon. James A. Robb
March	1, 1929	Hon. James A. Robb
May	1, 1930	Hon. Chas. A. Dunning
June	1, 1931	Rt. Hon. R. B. Bennett
April	6, 1932	Hon. Edgar N. Rhodes
March	21, 1933	Hon. Edgar N. Rhodes
April	18, 1934	Hon. Edgar N. Rhodes
March	22, 1935	Hon. Edgar N. Rhodes
May	1, 1936	Hon. Chas. A. Dunning
Feb.	25, 1937	Hon. Chas. A. Dunning
June	16, 1938	Hon. Chas. A. Dunning
April	25, 1939	Hon. Chas. A. Dunning
Sept.	12, 1939	Hon. J. L. Ilsley
June	24, 1940	Hon. J. L. Ralston
April	29, 1941	Hon. J. L. Ilsley
June	23, 1942	Hon. J. L. Ilsley
March	2, 1943	Hon. J. L. Ilsley
June	26, 1944	Hon. J. L. Ilsley
Oct.	12, 1945	Hon. J. L. Ilsley
June	27, 1946	Hon. J. L. Ilsley
April	29, 1947	Hon. D. C. Abbott
May	18, 1948	Hon. D. C. Abbott
March	22, 1949	Hon. D. C. Abbott
Oct.	20, 1949	Hon. D. C. Abbott
March	28, 1950	Hon. D. C. Abbott
Sept.	7, 1950	Hon. D. C. Abbott
April	10, 1951	Hon. D. C. Abbott
April	8, 1952	Hon. D. C. Abbott
Feb.	19, 1953	Hon. D. C. Abbott
April	6, 1954	Hon. D. C. Abbott

Appendix C—Tables

TABLE 1

TOTAL REVENUE[a]—ALL GOVERNMENTS FOR SELECTED FISCAL YEARS ENDED NEAREST DECEMBER 31, 1866 TO 1954 (millions of dollars)

Year	Dominion	Provincial	Municipal	Total
1866[b]	[c]	14	6[d]	20
1874	22	3	8[d]	33
1896	30	6	[e]	[e]
1904	57	13	37[d]	107
1913	135	32	110	277
1921	333	77	230	640
1926	360	120	271	751
1930	314	158	317	789
1933	278	133	294	705
1937	461	221	304	986
1939	480	236	317	1,033
1941	1,389	302	331	2,022
1943	2,522	251	341	3,114
1945	2,694	317	356[f]	3,367
1947	2,663	534	413[f]	3,610
1948	2,575	636	463[f]	3,674
1949	2,411	731	512[f]	3,654
1950	2,906	827	560[f]	4,293
1951[g]	3,780[h]	945	650[f]	5,375
1952[g]	4,370[h]	907	739	6,016
1953[i]	4,450[h]	981	800	6,231
1954[i]	4,500[h]	959	843	6,302

[a]Exclusive of intergovernmental transfers.
[b]Province of Canada, Nova Scotia, and New Brunswick.
[c]Not applicable.
[d]An estimate.
[e]Not available.
[f]Includes an estimate for Quebec.
[g]Approximate.
[h]Includes old age security Taxes.
[i]Estimates.

SOURCES: *Canada Year Book 1954; Canada 1954; Comparative Statistics of Public Finance*, 1933, 1937, 1939, 1941, 1943; Royal Commission on Dominion-Provincial Relations, *Report*, Books I and III; *Submission to the Royal Commission on Dominion-Provincial Relations* by the Citizens Research Institute of Canada (1866 to 1950).

TABLE 2

TAX REVENUE—ALL GOVERNMENTS FOR SELECTED FISCAL YEARS ENDED NEAREST DECEMBER 31, 1866 TO 1954
(millions of dollars)

Year	Metropolitan[a]	Other urban municipalities[a]	Rural municipalities[a]	Total municipalities[a]	Provinces[b]	Federal
1866	[c]	[c]	[c]	4.8[d,e]	11.6[e]	[f]
1867	[c]	[c]	[c]	[c]	[c]	11.7
1874	[c]	[c]	[c]	6.5[d]	[g]	20.7
1896	[c]	[c]	[c]	[c]	.9	28.6
1904	[c]	[c]	[c]	30.5[d]	3.2	54.0
1913	32.5	39.8	24.5	96.8	9.3	127.5
1921	72.2	78.5	57.0	207.7	35.3	319.9
1926	87.2	89.4	63.7	240.3	53.9	347.0
1930	114.3	100.9	67.5	282.7	75.2	296.8
1933	109.7	96.4	46.3	252.4	74.7	272.2
1937	116.7	100.5	47.4	264.6	130.2	449.1
1938	118.3	100.5	50.4	269.2	133.0	436.3
1939	116.0	102.3	55.1	273.4	140.1	468.2
1940	119.0	104.3	55.4	278.7	174.4	778.2
1941	121.9	106.8	56.7	285.4	179.3	1,360.9
1942	117.8	107.7	58.9	284.4	105.6	2,066.7
1943	115.3	108.7	67.7	291.8	109.7	2,436.8
1944	115.8	107.9	76.7	300.4	112.5	2,154.6
1945	116.7	109.3	72.9	298.9	130.3	2,202.4
1946	124.7	116.5	78.0	319.2	160.3	2,427.7
1947	136.5	126.5	86.2	349.2	276.4	2,452.1
1948	148.3	143.5	99.1	390.9	347.7	2,436.1
1949	162.1	161.0	109.3	432.4	416.2	2,323.1
1950	183.2	182.9	117.5	483.6	476.3	2,785.3
1951	211.6	214.4	132.9	559.0	562.1	3,657.8[j]
1952	237.3	247.9	151.8	637.0	468.5	3,997.6[j]
1953	255.8[h]	270.9[h]	161.5[h]	688.2[h]	499.2[i]	4,003.6[j]
1954	271.5[h]	287.1[h]	170.6[h]	729.2[h]	531.2[h]	4,074.0[j h]

[a]For 1945 to 1950, includes a partial estimate for Quebec.
[b]Does not include revenue from public domain, liquor control, and motor vehicle licences.
[c]Not available.
[d]An estimate.
[e]Province of Canada, Nova Scotia, and New Brunswick.
[f]Not applicable.
[g]Less than $50,000.
[h]Estimates.
[i]Approximate.
[j]Excludes old age security taxes.

SOURCES: *Bank of Canada Statistical Summary; Public Accounts of Canada; Submission to the Royal Commission on Dominion-Provincial Relations* by the Citizens Research Institute of Canada, Charts B, D, and E; Royal Commission on Dominion-Provincial Relations, *Report*, Books I and III.

TABLE 3

TAXATION AND THE GROSS NATIONAL PRODUCT
1926–1953

Year	Gross national product at market prices[a]	Personal direct taxes	Indirect taxes	Corporation taxes	Total[b]	% of G.N.P.
	($ mm)	($ mm)	($ mm)	($ mm)	($ mm)	
1926	5,296	53	614	34	701	13.2
1927	5,650	59	637	38	734	13.0
1928	6,110	59	684	45	788	12.9
1929	6,171	68	686	48	802	13.0
1930	5,553	71	600	40	711	12.8
1931	4,578	63	575	33	671	14.7
1932	3,776	64	546	32	642	17.0
1933	3,560	69	545	37	651	18.3
1934	4,042	64	585	52	701	17.3
1935	4,368	80	608	65	753	17.2
1936	4,715	95	674	83	852	18.1
1937	5,365	112	714	101	927	17.3
1938	5,295	115	700	94	909	17.2
1939	5,690	112	716	115	943	16.6
1940	6,925	139	883	327	1,349	19.5
1941	8,591	296	1,128	510	1,934	22.5
1942	10,632	495	1,178	629	2,302	21.7
1943	11,394	698	1,328	640	2,666	23.4
1944	12,221	838	1,378	598	2,814	23.0
1945	12,112	809	1,265	599	2,673	22.1
1946	12,262	796	1,505	654	2,955	24.1
1947	13,948	791	1,784	701	3,276	23.5
1948	15,688	822	1,847	685	3,354	21.4
1949	16,539	789	1,907	731	3,427	20.7
1950	18,266	740	2,081	981	3,802	20.8
1951	21,602	1,030	2,606	1,429	5,065	23.4
1952	23,284	1,323	2,843	1,333	5,499	23.6
1953	24,459	1,432	3,017	1,174	5,623	23.0

[a]For comparability, subsidies have been added to the total since indirect taxes are shown in the gross without deducting subsidies.

[b]Excluding withholding taxes.

SOURCES: *National Accounts, Income and Expenditure, 1926–1950, 1950–1953,* D.B.S. (dollar figures only).

TABLE 4

Taxation and the National Income 1926–1953

Year	Net national income	Total taxes[a]	% of N.N.I.	Net national income	Personal and indirect taxes	% of N.N.I.
	($ mm)	($ mm)		($ mm)	($ mm)	
1926	4,185	701	16.8	4,185	667	15.9
1927	4,417	734	16.6	4,417	696	15.8
1928	4,823	788	16.3	4,823	743	15.4
1929	4,789	802	16.7	4,789	754	15.7
1930	4,283	711	16.6	4,283	671	15.7
1931	3,333	671	20.1	3,333	638	19.1
1932	2,630	642	24.4	2,630	610	23.2
1933	2,452	651	26.5	2,452	614	25.0
1934	2,897	701	24.2	2,897	649	22.4
1935	3,188	753	23.6	3,188	688	21.6
1936	3,487	852	24.4	3,487	769	22.1
1937	4,062	927	22.8	4,062	826	20.3
1938	4,018	909	22.6	4,018	815	20.3
1939	4,373	943	21.6	4,373	828	18.9
1940	5,263	1,349	25.6	5,263	1,022	19.4
1941	6,563	1,934	29.5	6,563	1,424	21.7
1942	8,337	2,302	27.6	8,337	1,673	20.1
1943	9,043	2,666	29.5	9,043	2,026	22.4
1944	9,826	2,814	28.6	9,826	2,216	22.6
1945	9,840	2,673	27.2	9,840	2,074	21.1
1946	9,821	2,955	30.1	9,821	2,301	23.4
1947	10,985	3,276	29.8	10,985	2,575	23.4
1948	12,560	3,354	26.7	12,560	2,669	21.3
1949	13,194	3,427	26.0	13,194	2,696	20.4
1950	14,550	3,802	26.1	14,550	2,821	19.4
1951	17,138	5,065	29.6	17,138	3,636	21.2
1952	18,221	5,499	30.2	18,221	4,166	22.9
1953	19,043	5,623	29.5	19,043	4,449	23.4

[a]Excluding withholding taxes.

Sources: *National Accounts, Income and Expenditure, 1926–1950, 1950–1953,* D.B.S. (dollar figures only).

TABLE 5

TAXATION AND PERSONAL INCOME
1926–1953

Year	Personal income	Personal direct taxes	% of personal income	Personal direct taxes and indirect taxes	% of personal income
	($ mm)	($ mm)		($ mm)	
1926	4,092	53	1.3	667	16.3
1927	4,305	59	1.4	696	16.2
1928	4,618	59	1.3	743	16.1
1929	4,657	68	1.5	754	16.2
1930	4,363	71	1.6	671	15.4
1931	3,692	63	1.7	638	17.3
1932	3,065	64	2.1	610	19.9
1933	2,843	69	2.4	614	21.6
1934	3,153	64	2.0	649	20.6
1935	3,373	80	2.4	688	20.4
1936	3,577	95	2.7	769	21.5
1937	4,042	112	2.8	826	20.4
1938	4,090	115	2.8	815	19.9
1939	4,320	112	2.6	828	19.2
1940	4,947	139	2.8	1,022	20.7
1941	5,896	296	5.0	1,424	24.2
1942	7,475	495	6.6	1,673	22.4
1943	8,176	698	8.5	2,026	24.8
1944	9,002	838	9.3	2,216	24.6
1945	9,239	809	8.8	2,074	22.4
1946	9,761	796	8.2	2,301	23.6
1947	10,390	791	7.6	2,575	24.8
1948	11,943	822	6.9	2,669	22.3
1949	12,757	789	6.2	2,696	21.1
1950	13,414	740	5.5	2,821	21.0
1951	15,693	1,030	6.6	3,636	23.2
1952	17,132	1,323	7.7	4,166	24.3
1953	18,096	1,432	7.9	4 449	24.6

SOURCES: *National Accounts, Income and Expenditure, 1926–1950, 1950–1953,* D.B.S. (dollar figures only).

TABL

DOMINION GOVERNMENT—
(mil

Fiscal years	Tax revenue									
	Customs duties	Excise duties	Net sales tax[a]	Miscellaneous indirect taxes	Total indirect taxes	Income tax				E p t
						Individuals	Corporations	Non-Resident	Total	
1868	8.6	3.0	—	0.1	11.7	—	—	—	—	
1869	8.3	2.7	—	0.1	11.1	—	—	—	—	
1870	9.4	3.6	—	0.1	13.1	—	—	—	—	
1871	11.8	4.3	—	0.2	16.3	—	—	—	—	
1872	12.8	4.7	—	0.2	17.7	—	—	—	—	
1873	12.9	4.5	—	0.2	17.6	—	—	—	—	
1874	14.3	5.6	—	0.2	20.1	—	—	—	—	
1875	15.4	5.1	—	0.2	20.7	—	—	—	—	
1876	12.8	5.6	—	0.2	18.6	—	—	—	—	
1877	12.6	4.9	—	0.2	17.7	—	—	—	—	
1878	12.8	4.8	—	0.2	17.8	—	—	—	—	
1879	12.9	5.4	—	0.2	18.5	—	—	—	—	
1880	14.1	4.2	—	0.2	18.5	—	—	—	—	
1881	18.4	5.3	—	0.2	23.9	—	—	—	—	
1882	21.6	5.9	—	0.1	27.6	—	—	—	—	
1883	23.0	6.3	—	—	29.3	—	—	—	—	
1884	20.0	5.5	—	—	25.5	—	—	—	—	
1885	18.9	6.5	—	—	25.4	—	—	—	—	
1886	19.4	5.8	—	—	25.2	—	—	—	—	
1887	22.4	6.3	—	—	28.7	—	—	—	—	
1888	22.1	6.1	—	—	28.2	—	—	—	—	
1889	23.7	6.9	—	—	30.6	—	—	—	—	
1890	23.9	7.6	—	—	31.5	—	—	—	—	
1891	23.3	6.9	—	—	30.2	—	—	—	—	
1892	20.4	7.9	—	—	28.3	—	—	—	—	
1893	20.9	8.4	—	—	29.3	—	—	—	—	
1894	19.1	8.4	—	—	27.5	—	—	—	—	
1895	17.6	7.8	—	—	25.4	—	—	—	—	
1896	19.8	7.9	—	—	27.7	—	—	—	—	
1897	19.4	9.2	—	—	28.6	—	—	—	—	
1898	21.6	7.9	—	—	29.5	—	—	—	—	
1899	25.2	9.6	—	—	34.8	—	—	—	—	
1900	28.2	9.9	—	—	38.1	—	—	—	—	
1901	28.3	10.3	—	—	38.6	—	—	—	—	
1902	31.9	11.2	—	—	43.1	—	—	—	—	
1903	36.7	12.0	—	—	48.7	—	—	—	—	
1904	40.5	12.9	—	—	53.4	—	—	—	—	
1905	41.4	12.6	—	—	54.0	—	—	—	—	
1906	46.1	14.0	—	—	60.1	—	—	—	—	
1907[d]	39.7	11.8	—	—	51.5	—	—	—	—	
1908	57.2	15.8	—	—	73.0	—	—	—	—	
1909	47.1	14.9	—	—	62.0	—	—	—	—	
1910	59.8	15.2	—	—	75.0	—	—	—	—	
1911	71.8	16.9	—	—	88.7	—	—	—	—	
1912	85.0	19.3	—	—	104.3	—	—	—	—	
1913	111.8	21.4	—	—	133.2	—	—	—	—	
1914	104.7	21.4	—	—	126.1	—	—	—	—	

[a]Gross less refunds of sales and other excise taxes for 1952 and preceding years, gross less refunds of sales ta 1953 and 1954 (see footnote *k*).

[b]Business profits tax (1917 to 1930).

ENUES, 1868 TO 1954
ollars)

			Non-tax revenues						
ession ities	Total direct taxes	Total tax revenue	Post office	Miscellaneous[c]	Total	Total ordinary revenue	Special receipts and other credits	Grand total revenue	Fiscal years
—	—	11.7	0.5	1.5	2.0	13.7	—	13.7	1868
—	—	11.1	0.5	2.8	3.3	14.4	—	14.4	1869
—	—	13.1	0.6	1.8	2.4	15.5	—	15.5	1870
—	—	16.3	0.6	2.4	3.0	19.3	0.1	19.4	1871
—	—	17.7	0.7	2.3	3.0	20.7	—	20.7	1872
—	—	17.6	0.8	2.4	3.2	20.8	0.2	21.0	1873
—	—	20.1	1.1	3.0	4.1	24.2	0.3	24.5	1874
—	—	20.7	1.2	2.7	3.9	24.6	—	24.6	1875
—	—	18.6	1.1	2.9	4.0	22.6	—	22.6	1876
—	—	17.7	1.1	3.2	4.3	22.0	0.9	22.9	1877
—	—	17.8	1.2	3.4	4.6	22.4	—	22.4	1878
—	—	18.5	1.2	2.8	4.0	22.5	4.5	27.0	1879
—	—	18.5	1.3	3.5	4.8	23.3	0.1	23.4	1880
—	—	23.9	1.4	4.3	5.7	29.6	—	29.6	1881
—	—	27.6	1.6	4.2	5.8	33.4	1.8	35.2	1882
—	—	29.3	1.8	4.7	6.5	35.8	1.0	36.8	1883
—	—	25.5	1.7	4.7	6.4	31.9	.9	32.8	1884
—	—	25.4	1.8	5.6	7.4	32.8	0.6	33.4	1885
—	—	25.2	1.9	6.1	8.0	33.2	0.3	33.5	1886
—	—	28.7	2.0	5.1	7.1	35.8	—	35.8	1887
—	—	28.2	2.4	5.3	7.7	35.9	—	35.9	1888
—	—	30.6	2.2	6.0	8.2	38.8	—	38.8	1889
—	—	31.5	2.4	6.0	8.4	39.9	—	39.9	1890
—	—	30.2	2.5	5.9	8.4	38.6	—	38.6	1891
—	—	28.3	2.7	5.9	8.6	36.9	—	36.9	1892
—	—	29.3	2.8	6.1	8.9	38.2	—	38.2	1893
—	—	27.5	2.8	6.1	8.9	36.4	—	36.4	1894
—	—	25.4	2.8	5.8	8.6	34.0	—	34.0	1895
—	—	27.7	3.0	5.9	8.9	36.6	—	36.6	1896
—	—	28.6	3.2	6.0	9.2	37.8	—	37.8	1897
—	—	29.5	3.5	7.6	11.1	40.6	—	40.6	1898
—	—	34.8	3.2	8.7	11.9	46.7	—	46.7	1899
—	—	38.1	3.2	9.7	12.9	51.0	—	51.0	1900
—	—	38.6	3.4	10.5	13.9	52.5	—	52.5	1901
—	—	43.1	3.9	11.1	15.0	58.1	—	58.1	1902
—	—	48.7	4.4	12.9	17.3	66.0	3.3	69.3	1903
—	—	53.4	4.7	12.6	17.3	70.7	—	70.7	1904
—	—	54.0	5.1	12.1	17.2	71.2	—	71.2	1905
—	—	60.1	5.9	14.1	20.0	80.1	—	80.1	1906
—	—	51.5	5.1	11.4	16.5	68.0	—	68.0	1907[d]
—	—	73.0	7.1	16.0	23.1	96.1	—	96.1	1908
—	—	62.0	7.4	15.7	23.1	85.1	0.4	85.5	1909
—	—	75.0	8.0	18.5	26.5	101.5	0.1	101.6	1910
—	—	88.7	9.1	20.0	29.1	117.8	0.1	117.9	1911
—	—	104.3	10.5	21.3	31.8	136.1	—	136.1	1912
—	—	133.2	12.1	23.4	35.5	168.7	—	168.7	1913
—	—	126.1	13.0	24.1	37.1	163.2	—	163.2	1914

ludes Chinese revenue and export tax on gold.
ıe months ended March 31; fiscal period changed from July 1–June 30 to April 1–March 31.

TABLE

Fiscal years	Tax revenue									
	Customs duties	Excise duties	Net sales tax[a]	Miscellaneous indirect taxes	Total indirect taxes	Income tax: Individuals	Income tax: Corporations	Income tax: Non-Resident	Income tax: Total	Ex pr ta
1915	75.9	21.5	—	.1	97.5	—	—	—	—	-
1916	98.6	22.4	—	3.7	124.7	—	—	—	—	-
1917	134.0	24.4	—	3.9	162.3	—	—	—	—	1
1918	144.2	27.2	—	4.0	175.4	—	—	—	—	2
1919	147.2	30.3	—	13.9	191.4	7.9	1.4	—	9.3	3
1920	168.8	42.7	—	17.7	229.2	13.2	7.1	—	20.3	4
1921	163.3	37.1	37.6	43.6	281.6	32.5	13.9	—	46.4	4
1922	105.7	36.8	61.3	14.6	218.4	39.8	38.9	—	78.7	2
1923	118.1	35.8	89.8	19.0	262.7	31.7	28.0	—	59.7	1
1924	121.5	38.2	98.0	25.0	282.7	25.7	28.5	—	54.2	
1925	108.1	38.6	63.2	25.1	235.0	25.1	31.1	—	56.2	
1926	127.4	42.9	72.9	27.9	271.1	23.9	31.7	—	55.6	
1927	142.0	48.5	81.2	27.2	298.9	18.1	29.3	—	47.4	
1928	157.0	57.4	70.6	22.6	307.6	23.2	33.3	—	56.5	
1929	187.2	63.7	62.6	22.9	336.4	24.8	34.6	—	59.4	
1930	179.4	65.0	44.1	21.2	309.7	27.2	41.8	—	69.0	
1931	131.2	57.7	20.1	16.7	225.7	26.7	44.4	—	71.1	-
1932	104.1	48.7	41.7	19.6	214.1	24.8	36.5	—	61.3	-
1933	70.1	37.8	56.8	27.7	192.4	26.0	36.1	—	62.1	-
1934	66.3	35.5	61.4	47.6	210.8	29.2	27.4	4.8	61.4	-
1935	76.6	43.2	72.4	45.9	238.1	25.2	35.8	5.8	66.8	-
1936	74.0	44.4	77.6	38.9	234.9	33.0	42.5	7.2	82.7	-
1937	83.8	46.0	112.8	42.0	284.6	35.5	58.0	8.9	102.4	-
1938	93.5	52.0	138.1	45.2	328.8	40.4	69.8	10.1	120.3	-
1939	78.8	51.3	122.1	42.1	294.3	46.9	85.2	9.9	142.0	-
1940	104.3	61.0	137.4	31.1	333.8	45.4	77.9	11.1	134.4	-
1941	130.8	88.6	179.7	107.0	506.1	103.5	131.6	13.0	248.1	2
1942	142.4	110.1	236.2	219.8	708.5	296.1	185.8	28.3	510.2	13
1943	119.0	138.7	232.9	268.1	758.7	484.1[e]	348.0	28.1	860.2	43
1944	167.9	142.1	304.9	341.4	956.3	698.4[e]	311.4	27.0	1,036.8	42
1945	115.1	151.9	209.4	341.9	818.3	672.8[e]	276.4	28.6	977.8	34
1946	128.9	186.7	212.2	293.7	821.5	686.6[e]	217.8	28.3	932.7	42
1947	237.4	196.0	298.2	290.5	1,022.1	670.5[e]	238.8	30.1	939.4	44
1948	293.0	196.8	372.3	272.3	1,134.4	659.8	364.2	35.9	1,059.9	22
1949	223.0	204.7	377.3	262.8	1,067.8	762.6	492.0	43.4	1,298.0	4
1950	225.9	220.6	403.4	172.4	1,022.3	622.0	603.2	47.5	1,272.7	-
1951	295.7	241.0	460.1	231.7	1,228.5	652.3	799.2	61.6	1,513.1	1
1952	346.4	217.9	573.5[h]	318.0	1,455.8	975.7[i]	1,130.7[j]	55.0	2,161.4	
1953	389.4	241.4	566.2[h]	288.7[k]	1,485.7	1,180.0[i]	1,240.1[j]	53.7	2,473.8	
1954	407.3	226.7	587.3[h]	310.5[k]	1,531.8	1,187.7[i]	1,191.2[j]	53.8	2,432.6	

[e]Excludes reserve for refundable tax as follows: 1943—$50 mm; 1944—$115 mm; 1945—$95 mm; 1946—$5 and 1947—$24 mm.

[f]Excludes reserve for refundable tax as follows: 1943—$20 mm; 1944—$40 mm; 1945—$124.5 mm; 1946—$67.5 and 1947—$6.2 mm.

[g]Includes excess reserve for refundable tax as follows: 1951—$25 mm; and 1952—$7.4 mm.

ontinued

uccession duties	Total direct taxes	Total tax revenue	Non-tax revenues: Post office	Non-tax revenues: Miscellaneous[c]	Non-tax revenues: Total	Total ordinary revenue	Special receipts and other credits	Grand total revenue	Fiscal years
—	—	97.5	13.1	22.5	35.6	133.1	—	133.1	1915
—	—	124.7	18.9	28.5	47.4	172.1	—	172.1	1916
—	12.5	174.8	20.9	37.0	57.9	232.7	—	232.7	1917
—	21.3	196.7	21.3	42.8	64.1	260.8	—	260.8	1918
—	42.3	233.7	21.6	57.6	79.2	312.9	—	312.9	1919
—	64.4	293.6	24.5	31.6	56.1	349.7	—	349.7	1920
—	87.2	368.8	26.7	38.9	65.6	434.4	2.5	436.9	1921
—	101.5	319.9	26.4	35.6	62.0	381.9	13.1	395.0	1922
—	72.7	335.4	29.0	30.2	59.2	394.6	15.0	409.6	1923
—	59.0	341.7	28.9	26.2	55.1	396.8	11.0	407.8	1924
—	58.9	293.9	28.8	24.1	52.9	346.8	5.7	352.5	1925
—	56.8	327.9	30.3	22.6	52.9	380.8	2.5	383.3	1926
—	48.1	347.0	29.1	22.6	51.7	398.7	2.4	401.1	1927
—	57.5	365.1	31.6	26.0	57.6	422.7	8.1	430.8	1928
—	59.9	396.3	30.6	28.6	59.2	455.5	6.2	461.7	1929
—	69.2	378.9	33.3	29.2	62.5	441.4	11.6	453.0	1930
—	71.1	296.8	30.2	22.6	52.8	349.6	8.1	357.7	1931
—	61.3	275.4	32.2	19.2	51.4	326.8	7.7	334.5	1932
—	62.1	254.5	30.9	21.2	52.1	306.6	5.1	311.7	1933
—	61.4	272.2	30.9	21.0	51.9	324.1	0.6	324.7	1934
—	66.8	304.9	31.3	22.3	53.6	358.5	3.5	362.0	1935
—	82.7	317.6	32.5	22.1	54.6	372.2	.4	372.6	1936
—	102.4	387.0	34.3	23.7	58.0	445.0	9.1	454.1	1937
—	120.3	449.1	35.5	25.7	61.2	510.3	6.4	516.7	1938
—	142.0	436.3	35.3	26.4	61.7	498.0	4.2	502.2	1939
—	134.4	468.2	36.7	36.7	73.4	541.6	20.5	562.1	1940
—	272.1	778.2	40.4	41.2	81.6	859.8	12.4	872.2	1941
7.0	652.4	1,360.9	46.0	56.9	102.9	1,463.8	24.7	1,488.5	1942
13.2	1,308.0	2,066.7	48.9	67.2	116.1	2,182.8	66.7	2,249.5	1943
15.0	1,480.5	2,436.8	61.1	72.2	133.3	2,570.1	194.9	2,765.0	1944
17.2	1,336.3	2,154.6	66.1	79.4	145.5	2,300.1	387.2	2,687.3	1945
21.5	1,380.9	2,202.4	68.6	92.2	160.8	2,363.2	650.0	3,013.2	1946
23.6	1,405.5	2,427.6	73.0	87.9	160.9	2,588.5	419.4	3,007.9	1947
30.8	1,317.7	2,452.1	77.8	99.9	177.7	2,629.8	241.9	2,871.7	1948
25.5	1,368.3	2,436.1	80.6	132.4	213.0	2,649.1	122.3	2,771.4	1949
29.9	1,300.8	2,323.1	84.5	121.1	205.6	2,528.7	51.4	2,580.1	1950
33.6	1,556.9	2,785.4	90.4	142.9	233.3	3,018.7	93.8[g]	3,112.5	1951
38.2	2,202.0	3,657.8	104.6	177.3	281.9	3,939.7	41.2[g]	3,980.9	1952
38.1	2,511.9	3,997.6	111.9	168.2	280.1	4,277.7	83.1	4,360.8	1953
39.1	2,471.7	4,003.6	111.0	207.2	318.2	4,321.8	74.5	4,396.3	1954

[h]Excludes old age security sales tax as follows: 1952—$24.3 mm; 1953—$141.6 mm; and 1954—$146.8 mm.
[i]Excludes old age security individual income tax as follows: 1952—$ .1 mm; 1953—$45.2 mm; and 1954—$90.7 mm.
[j]Excludes old age security corporation income tax as follows: 1952—$2 mm; 1953—$36.8 mm; and 1954—$55.6 mm.
[k]Other excise tax refunds deducted as follows: 1953—$2.9 mm; and 1954—$1.6 mm (see footnote *a*).
SOURCE: *Public Accounts of Canada.*

TABL

DOMINION GOVERNMENT—MAIN SOURCE
(thous

Fiscal years	Sugar and molasses	Spirits and wines	Tea	Cottons	Woollens	Fancy goods	Silks, satins, and velvets	Misc. iron & steel[b]	Fruits and vegetables	Grain and products	Tobacco products	Coal	Oils	F
1868	1,439	1,290	943	1,097	1,167	144	163	344	85	98	159	—	—	
1869	1,502	946	916	1,107	1,009	161	159	320	89	2	116	—	—	
1870	1,870	1,080	1,141	1,101	1,045	217	192	355	83	4	113	—	—	
1871	1,946	1,233	1,158	1,362	1,457	289	306	467	134	62	138	—	—	
1872	1,937	1,548	948	1,527	1,760	427	390	576	142	5	274	—	—	
1873	2,371	1,546	26	1,511	1,679	491	340	696	169	1	269	—	—	
1874	2,541	1,883	110	1,708	1,693	508	336	883	149	1	258	—	—	
1875	2,451	1,595	380	1,717	2,373	580	391	920	219	—	189	—	—	
1876	2,504	1,868	526	1,253	1,607	413	234	635	166	1	227	—	24	
1877	2,473	1,337	535	1,296	1,561	311	197	577	201	1	138	—	191	
1878	2,830	1,212	611	1,243	1,494	293	247	577	190	1	188	—	142	
1879	2,759	1,368	744	1,194	1,297	250	323	915	180	45	242	109	161	
1880	2,146	1,107	641	1,725	1,639	128	638	1,368	214	213	130	506	188	
1881	2,629	1,428	882	2,272	2,346	161	883	1,717	302	257	161	641	212	
1882	2,515	1,644	404	2,477	2,738	429	978	2,594	348	262	234	705	369	
1883	2,727	1,888	63	2,292	2,690	471	861	2,984	520	217	237	931	428	
1884	2,805	1,706	28	1,663	2,174	367	653	2,167	470	292	234	1,114	398	
1885	2,693	1,688	33	1,499	2,313	341	680	1,606	368	260	247	1,072	440	
1886	2,437	1,961	35	1,408	2,499	332	702	1,721	384	220	319	1,072	476	
1887	3,301	1,660	9	1,389	3,177	609	860	2,168	502	233	306	1,179	520	
1888	3,602	1,938	11	1,192	2,802	535	828	2,632	491	259	234	758	548	
1889	3,869	2,128	7	1,198	2,964	560	888	2,950	467	320	283	773	535	
1890	3,064	2,308	12	1,137	3,158	550	850	2,916	514	425	296	870	584	
1891	3,275	2,159	16	1,135	2,963	459	798	2,721	532	326	327	985	633	
1892	190	2,173	8	1,114	3,096	493	734	2,792	580	191	272	999	656	
1893	148	2,337	9	1,296	3,309	520	827	2,878	514	207	292	992	681	
1894	151	2,396	18	1,142	2,877	498	743	2,463	637	211	288	844	686	
1895	302	2,100	6	1,201	2,528	445	676	1,964	561	212	263	878	590	
1896	1,205	2,185	4	1,322	2,759	439	774	2,170	593	309	267	934	620	
1897	1,798	2,406	4	1,167	2,264	449	607	2,070	506	183	301	937	615	
1898	1,386	2,484	6	1,340	2,438	540	773	2,852	627	93	481	898	569	
1899	1,992	2,896	14	1,570	2,699	535	1,091	3,496	668	142	368	1,154	597	
1900	2,382	3,250	4	1,665	2,746	579	1,164	4,420	756	147	486	1,309	639	
1901	2,541	3,582	2	1,624	2,556	584	1,100	4,020	741	156	494	1,370	718	
1902	2,828	3,667	4	1,787	2,815	673	1,237	4,773	752	190	532	1,653	849	
1903	2,714	4,137	6	1,935	3,460	829	1,078	6,208	1,014	219	583	1,914	1,078	
1904	2,246	4,759	5	2,031	3,954	1,007	1,073	7,025	1,012	207	655	2,207	1,268	
1905	1,893	5,656	2	2,017	4,447	1,018	1,174	6,678	1,186	269	682	2,276	529	
1906	1,803	3,882	2	1,690	3,987	854	919	5,288	938	165	568	1,785	425	
1907[d]	1,759	4,071	3	2,213	4,380	877	957	7,829	978	164	733	2,093	437	
1908	2,725	5,583	2	3,767	6,112	1,055	1,399	10,932	1,253	245	908	3,599	542	
1909	2,921	5,398	4	2,715	4,635	896	1,248	7,262	1,302	272	791	3,148	587	
1910	3,083	5,774	7	4,197	6,443	1,077	1,544	10,918	1,540	273	829	3,210	685	
1911	3,371	6,737	4	4,712	6,739	1,140	1,533	16,470	1,704	272	1,026	3,561	813	
1912	3,560	7,907	4	5,155	6,829	1,217	1,671	21,007	2,292	234	1,272	4,908	890	
1913	4,182	9,270	4	6,617	8,591	1,408	2,115	29,642	2,717	482	1,551	5,055	1,057	
1914	3,715	9,681	6	6,312	7,934	1,362	2,197	21,413	2,641	349	1,532	6,145	998	
1915	5,423	8,545	10	4,798	5,578	878	1,812	11,583	2,408	668	1,009	3,943	708	
Total	116,004	149,397	10,317	98,890	151,781	28,399	41,343	230,962	34,839	9,365	21,502	66,527	23,086	2

[a]The fact that no revenue is shown does not necessarily indicate that there was no tariff; only that the item wa
a principal source of revenue in the year indicated.

[b]Principal item "Other Hardware" in earliest years.

TOMS REVENUE, 1868 TO 1915[a]
ollars)

d - s	Leather	Glass	Drugs	Carriages of all kinds	Electric motors	Metals	Meats	Books	Rubber and mftrs.	Brass and mftrs.	Export duty on logs	Total of previous columns	Total customs revenue[c]	Fiscal years
	—	—	—	—	—	—	—	—	—	—	18	6,947	8,819	1868
	—	—	—	—	—	—	—	—	—	—	14	6,341	8,299	1869
	—	—	—	—	—	—	—	—	—	—	38	7,239	9,463	1870
	—	—	—	—	—	—	—	—	—	—	36	8,588	11,844	1871
	—	—	—	—	—	—	—	—	—	—	25	9,559	13,046	1872
	—	—	—	—	—	—	—	—	—	—	20	9,119	13,018	1873
	—	—	—	—	—	—	—	—	—	—	15	10,085	14,422	1874
	—	—	—	—	—	—	—	—	—	—	7	10,822	15,361	1875
	64	158	—	—	—	—	—	—	—	—	5	9,778	12,833	1876
	69	137	—	—	—	—	—	—	—	—	4	9,129	12,548	1877
8	203	157	—	—	—	—	—	—	—	—	4	9,640	12,796	1878
0	220	125	—	—	—	—	—	—	—	—	4	10,170	12,940	1879
8	271	152	—	—	—	—	—	—	—	—	9	11,405	14,139	1880
7	332	204	—	—	—	—	—	—	—	—	8	14,898	18,501	1881
2	430	301	142	—	—	—	—	—	—	—	9	17,237	21,709	1882
0	453	331	178	—	—	—	—	—	—	—	10	18,134	23,172	1883
6	314	283	258	—	—	—	—	—	—	—	9	15,482	20,165	1884
8	329	291	263	—	—	—	—	—	—	—	12	14,621	19,134	1885
3	284	326	271	—	—	—	—	—	—	—	21	15,025	19,448	1886
4	359	362	330	—	—	—	—	—	—	—	31	17,623	22,470	1887
9	324	353	368	—	—	—	—	—	—	—	22	17,711	22,210	1888
5	338	352	358	—	—	—	—	—	—	—	42	18,792	23,785	1889
6	245	336	384	—	—	—	—	—	—	—	94	18,538	24,015	1890
6	202	317	408	—	—	—	—	—	—	—	65	18,037	23,481	1891
6	231	326	440	—	—	—	—	—	—	—	—	15,023	20,551	1892
9	259	325	435	—	—	—	—	—	—	—	—	15,730	21,162	1893
9	201	327	323	—	—	—	—	—	—	—	—	14,394	19,380	1894
5	241	301	260	—	—	—	—	—	—	—	—	13,036	17,887	1895
9	252	283	310	—	—	—	—	—	—	—	—	14,867	20,219	1896
1	269	293	316	—	—	—	—	—	—	—	—	14,623	19,892	1897
7	318	248	350	—	—	—	—	—	—	—	—	15,869	22,158	1898
6	325	323	394	406	—	—	—	—	—	—	—	19,149	25,734	1899
9	359	398	384	421	202	202	359	—	—	—	—	22,474	28,889	1900
6	340	380	421	332	217	204	389	—	—	—	—	22,455	29,107	1901
3	362	459	416	426	316	235	375	—	—	—	—	25,111	32,426	1902
8	377	489	432	355	390	288	276	—	—	—	—	28,636	37,110	1903
3	447	472	464	429	576	336	310	—	—	—	—	31,611	40,954	1904
0	530	449	461	368	693	348	288	—	—	—	—	32,182	42,024	1905
9	406	376	361	352	664	287	369	—	—	—	—	26,025	46,671	1906
2	554	462	449	317	632	387	395	—	—	—	—	30,745	40,290	1907[d]
8	797	691	630	513	792	599	492	675	—	—	—	44,902	58,331	1908
2	672	527	562	400	528	515	466	581	—	—	—	36,796	48,060	1909
6	873	659	639	483	885	709	470	669	399	—	—	47,115	61,024	1910
3	1,117	752	706	719	1,267	929	491	724	608	—	—	57,552	73,313	1911
8	1,392	883	794	1,268	1,470	1,226	798	854	763	513	—	69,520	87,576	1912
7	2,048	1,154	965	3,048	2,212	1,591	1,041	1,047	1,348	726	—	91,420	115,064	1913
9	1,886	1,104	967	6,256	2,198	1,453	1,081	1,106	1,291	652	—	85,570	107,181	1914
3	1,553	735	926	2,761	1,479	957	579	880	927	475	—	60,972	79,205	1915
0	20,246	16,601	15,365	18,854	14,521	10,266	8,179	6,536	5,336	2,366	522	1,140,697	1,491,825	

efore deducting refunds, drawbacks, etc.

ine months ended March 31.

JRCE: *Dominion of Canada Sessional Papers*, "Annual Report on Trade and Navigation" to 1908; "Customs" after.

TABLE 8

DOMINION GOVERNMENT—REVENUE FROM EXCISE DUTIES, 1868 TO 1954
(thousands of dollars)

Fiscal years	Spirits		Malt	Beer	Malt syrup	Validation fee	Cigars	Cigarettes	Tobacco	Canadian raw leaf tobacco	Petroleum inspection fees	Gross total[b]	Net total[c]
	Matured	Un-matured[a]											
1868	2,488	—	226	118	—	—	26	—	495	—	11	3,207	3,003
1869	2,391	—	287	21	—	—	23	—	554	—	163	2,968	2,710
1870	2,208	—	348	17	—	—	29	—	924	—	557	4,361	3,620
1871	2,664	—	295	9	—	—	38	—	998	—	247	4,301	4,296
1872	2,884	—	319	26	—	—	57	—	1,195	—	234	4,763	4,736
1873	2,825	—	358	27	—	—	57	—	957	—	238	4,484	4,461
1874	3,503	—	355	26	—	—	77	—	1,324	—	274	5,616	5,595
1875	2,977	—	351	30	—	—	125	—	1,310	—	269	5,090	5,070
1876	3,100	—	328	14	—	—	134	—	1,641	—	286	5,575	5,563
1877	2,651	—	389	7	—	—	127	—	1,503	—	235	4,951	4,942
1878	2,709	—	539	7	—	—	145	—	1,437	—	6	4,875	4,859
1879	3,297	—	463	8	—	—	158	—	1,427	—	8	5,412	5,391
1880	2,293	—	298	6	—	—	164	—	1,479	—	16	4,277	4,232
1881	3,226	—	317	6	—	—	210	—	1,568	—	19	5,389	5,343
1882	3,555	—	388	6	—	—	294	—	1,610	—	24	5,895	5,885
1883	3,903	—	405	6	—	—	351	—	1,535	—	25	6,306	6,260
1884	3,610	—	413	7	—	—	258	—	1,178	—	27	5,500	5,459
1885	4,281	—	477	7	—	—	318	—	1,271	—	28	6,486	6,449
1886	3,214	—	383	6	—	—	560	—	1,630	—	29	5,889	5,853
1887	3,737	—	433	7	—	—	524	—	1,668	—	32	6,360	6,308
1888	3,099	—	493	7	—	—	554	—	1,740	—	37	6,106	6,071
1889	3,874	—	518	13	—	—	563	—	1,841	—	36	6,910	6,887
1890	4,620	—	556	14	—	—	603	44	1,852	—	40	7,659	7,618
1891	3,547	—	591	10	—	—	614	55	1,872	—	40	7,052	6,915

[a]Included in "Matured" until 1923.

[b]Includes methylated spirits, acetic acid, vinegar, and other minor sources not itemized. Gross deposited to the credit of the Receiver General. In earlier years detailed analysis tabulated on an accrual basis, and, therefore, details may exceed total.

[c]The difference between net and gross represents refunds and drawbacks.

SOURCES: *Public Accounts of Canada; Annual Reports*, Dept. of National Revenue; and *Canada Year Books*.

TABLE 8—*Continued*

Fiscal years	Spirits: Matured	Spirits: Un-matured[a]	Malt	Beer	Malt syrup	Validation fee	Cigars	Cigarettes	Tobacco	Canadian raw leaf tobacco	Petroleum inspection fees	Gross total[b]	Net total[c]
1892	3,877	—	936	7	—	—	634	63	2,359	—	44	7,992	7,945
1893	4,142	—	1008	7	—	—	692	64	2,382	—	46	8,444	8,367
1894	4,134	—	957	6	—	—	700	83	2,366	—	41	8,465	8,381
1895	3,902	—	766	7	—	—	647	100	2,270	—	41	7,901	7,806
1896	4,011	—	782	7	—	—	661	121	2,231	—	40	8,018	7,926
1897	4,772	—	1,033	7	—	—	690	156	2,401	—	42	9,265	9,170
1898	3,594	—	590	7	—	—	689	240	2,654	—	45	7,976	7,872
1899	4,610	—	849	7	—	—	781	303	3,017	—	46	9,760	9,641
1900	4,821	—	911	7	—	—	826	347	2,935	—	6	9,994	9,868
1901	5,181	—	977	7	—	—	837	363	2,975	—	—	10,499	10,318
1902	5,621	—	1,078	7	—	—	897	400	3,164	—	—	11,347	11,197
1903	6,163	—	1,021	9	—	—	998	531	3,374	—	—	12,260	12,014
1904	6,672	—	1,138	9	—	—	1,071	629	3,499	—	—	13,191	12,959
1905	5,951	—	1,141	9	—	—	1,014	746	3,666	—	—	12,785	12,586
1906	6,796	—	1,292	10	—	—	1,147	805	4,037	—	—	14,263	14,010
1907[d]	5,808	—	1,043	7	—	—	913	793	3,272	—	—	11,971	11,805
1908	7,538	—	1,485	11	—	—	1,184	1,153	4,504	—	—	16,058	15,782
1909	6,951	—	1,396	18	—	—	626	893	5,071	—	—	15,133	14,938
1910	7,170	—	1,434	27	—	—	433	1,092	4,976	—	—	15,351	15,253
1911	7,913	—	1,529	53	—	—	470	1,416	5,368	—	—	17,004	16,870
1912	8,668	—	1,717	87	—	—	518	1,889	6,242	—	—	19,399	19,262
1913	9,474	—	1,865	149	—	—	602	2,358	6,834	—	—	21,604	21,447
1914	9,038	—	2,012	161	—	—	589	2,809	6,680	—	—	21,605	21,452
1915	8,706	—	2,616	143	—	—	626	3,005	6,348	—	—	21,738	21,497
1916	8,701	—	2,689	98	—	—	635	3,253	6,969	—	—	22,652	22,428
1917	9,881	—	2,368	109	—	—	730	3,929	7,268	—	—	24,699	24,412
1918	11,487	—	1,791	80	—	—	776	5,003	7,614	—	—	27,404	27,168
1919	6,964	—	1,478	19	—	—	1,262	8,852	11,396	—	—	30,486	30,342
1920	8,950	—	2,102	77	—	—	1,629	14,657	14,798	—	—	42,959	42,698
1921	5,757	—	2,468	84	—	—	1,244	14,651	12,481	—	—	37,390	37,118
1922	6,224	—	2,629	58	—	—	1,094	14,711	12,165	—	—	36,906	36,755

[d]Nine months ended March 31.

TABLE 8—*Continued*

Fiscal years	Spirits		Malt	Beer	Malt syrup	Validation fee	Cigars	Cigarettes	Tobacco	Canadian raw leaf tobacco	Petroleum inspection fees	Gross total[b]	Net total[c]
	Matured	Un-matured[a]											
1923	6,588	1,395	2,548	60	—	—	617	14,079	10,934	—	—	36,265	35,762
1924	8,095	1,272	3,278	85	—	—	597	14,767	10,469	—	—	38,606	38,182
1925	8,225	1,165	3,539	106	—	—	516	15,198	10,221	—	—	39,015	38,603
1926	9,783	1,145	3,839	108	—	—	533	17,308	10,608	—	—	43,369	42,924
1927	12,632	1,267	3,810	218	—	—	532	20,011	10,625	—	—	49,139	48,513
1928	17,104	1,157	4,275	234	—	—	545	23,570	11,140	—	—	58,062	57401
1929	18,173	1,165	4,755	347	—	—	573	27,651	11,652	—	—	64,360	63,685
1930	17,354	1,173	4,494	342	—	—	590	30,224	11,446	—	—	65,672	65,036
1931	10,694	1,121	4,139	384	—	—	534	30,499	11,200	—	—	58,615	57,747
1932	7,101	1,053	3,633	386	—	—	457	26,416	10,231	—	—	49,322	48,655
1933	5,722	881	2,876	303	—	—	368	19,998	9,333	—	—	39,526	37,834
1934	5,546	843	2,774	235	—	323	348	17,371	8,486	—	—	35,981	35,494
1935	6,459	947	6,263	1,144	169	444	376	19,837	8,066	—	—	43,750	43,190
1936	6,003	950	7,692	409	164	600	374	21,323	7,356	—	—	44,910	44,410
1937	7,299	725	8,050	390	160	1,056	372	23,346	4,989	—	—	46,427	45,957
1938	8,625	734	8,853	363	132	919	409	27,397	5,931	—	—	52,502	52,037
1939	8,846	749	8,177	255	113	391	384	27,654	5,187	—	—	51,789	51,319
1940	8,057	1,029	11,402	281	123	374	424	33,655	6,478	—	—	61,859	61,032
1941	15,133	1,108	16,802	324	109	665	523	45,149	9,570	175	—	89,602	88,608
1942	19,211	1,391	25,241	414	103	417	597	54,246	9,861	346	—	111,866	110,091
1943	28,750	1,726	33,952	580	73	513	614	65,269	9,918	570	—	142,004	138,721
1944	27,676	2,131	35,080	372	222	441	590	68,467	10,255	594	—	145,865	142,124
1945	26,834	2,197	35,121	7,103	244	634	603	72,083	9,962	494	—	155,312	151,922
1946	39,198	2,828	41,382	6,646	177	1,043	633	87,069	10,090	437	—	189,541	186,726
1947	42,181	2,880	49,209	2,511	92	948	295	90,128	10,345	394	—	199,023	196,044
1948	36,880	2,511	53,625	3,820	68	771	215	91,585	9,980	336	—	199,829	196,794
1949	38,598	2,037	55,853	3,740	52	825	208	95,407	10,303	324	—	207,385	204,652
1950	44,455	2,092	56,018	3,678	—	791	203	105,280	10,225	274	—	223,055	220,565
1951	57,757	2,369	65,409	2,746	—	1,108	204	103,650	10,375	257	—	243,914	241,046
1952	39,985	2,082	73,748	3,812	—	1,224	163	89,506	10,822	220	—	221,598	217,940
1953	39,105	1,954	80,584	5,294	—	747	213	104,749	11,703	249	—	244,636	241,360
1954	47,539	1,965	78,733	4,800	—	—	246	86,722	9,768	234	—	230,044	226,732

TABLE 9

DOMINION GOVERNMENT—REVENUES FROM MISCELLANEOUS TAXES, 1915 TO 1954
(thousands of dollars)

Fiscal years	Bank note circulation	Trusts & loan co's.	Insurance co's.	Electricity export	Fur export (N.W.T.)	Placer gold export[a] (Yukon)	Chinese immigration[b]
1915	—	—	—	—	—	116	294
1916	1,300	324	459	—	—	111	−32
1917	1,114	202	420	—	—	99	87
1918	1,116	269	497	—	—	82	209
1919	1,100	323	546	—	—	49	2,027
1920	1,170	274	639	—	—	41	132
1921	1,258	294	808	—	—	31	240
1922	1,294	284	750	—	—	31	395
1923	1,244	312	852	—	—	26	201
1924	1,237	309	858	—	—	28	326
1925	1,218	315	868	—	—	16	305
1926	1,177	327	950	288	—	22	21
1927	1,175	335	948	357	—	12	13
1928	1,225	345	999	374	—	14	14
1929	1,242	8	895	351	—	16	18
1930	1,408	—	74	318	—	17	14
1931	1,429	—	74	395	89[c]	16	22
1932	1,390	—	12	183	125	20	10
1933	1,328	—	826	88	113	19	9
1934	1,336	—	742	244	78	18	6
1935	1,368	—	750	266	148	18	6
1936	1,281	—	761	306	104	17	6
1937	1,210	—	774	390	70	23	7
1938	1,107	—	867	431	57	22	2
1939	1,014	—	891	450	98	34	2
1940	949	—	926	444	96	41	2
1941	898	—	971	560	76	37	2
1942	786	—	1,148	598	104	33	1
1943	665	—	10,893	621	102	40[d]	—
1944	458	—	6,481	641	111	20[d]	—
1945	350	—	7,182	639	63	11[d]	—
1946	270	—	7,951	695	57	15[d]	—
1947	221	—	8,797	599	91	21[d]	—
1948	188	—	3,004	471	141	22[d]	—
1949	166	—	3,339	436	96	29[d]	—
1950	121	—	3,789	432	94	39[d]	—
1951	—	—	4,228	609	102	44[d]	—
1952	—	—	4,752	743	100	36[d]	—
1953	—	—	12,361	673	6	37[d]	—
1954	—	—	13,756	684	2	31[d]	—

[a]First imposed in 1906.
[b]First imposed in 1885.
[c]First imposed in 1930.
[d]Royalty on placer gold.

SOURCE: *Public Accounts of Canada.*

TABLE

DOMINION GOVERNMENT—REVENUE FR
(thousa

Fiscal years	Do								
	Sales tax	Automobiles	Tires and tubes	Gasoline	Radios and musical instruments	Electric and Gas appliances	Trans-missions[a] (cables, telephones)	Trans-portation (tickets, berths, etc.)	Stam (inc. emboss cheque
1915	—	—	—	—	—	—	—	98[b]	—
1916	—	—	—	—	—	—	—	793	75
1917	—	—	—	—	—	—	—	1,166	90
1918	—	—	—	—	—	—	—	1,205	1,03
1919	—	3,797	—	—	446	—	—	1,487	1,15
1920	—	6,584	—	—	1,036	—	—	2,203	1,60
1921	27,910	6,492	—	—	768	15	—	2,633	7,02
1922	44,820	60	—	—	13	—	—	2,534	2,98
1923	62,686	1,363	—	—	—	—	—	2,234	5,53
1924	71,835	2,689	—	—	—	—	—	2,400	8,77
1925	51,253	2,411	—	—	—	—	—	2,421	9,32
1926	57,254	3,475	—	—	—	—	—	2,404	9,77
1927	63,940	2,209	—	—	—	—	—	2,453	9,32
1928	55,379	838	—	—	—	—	343	2,192	4,73
1929	49,152	1,026	—	—	—	—	392	2,256	4,07
1930	34,936	742	—	—	—	—	125	525	5,74
1931	16,587	398	—	—	—	—	—	—	3,79
1932	34,558	333	—	—	—	—	—	—	3,04
1933	49,276	220	—	—	—	—	702	330	3,39
1934	54,244	153	703	—	—	—	961	414	4,64
1935	64,012	262	980	—	—	—	1,078	385	4,63
1936	70,260	271	991	—	—	—	1,037	424	4,63
1937	99,421	418	899	—	—	—	1,149	434	5,7
1938	121,349	545	714	—	—	—	1,282	445	5,0
1939	107,928	460	711	—	—	—	1,215	425	4,7
1940	119,392	506	809	—	—	—	1,297	360	4,6
1941	156,749	8,212	2,075	—	1,243	1,549	1,410	438	4,5
1942	214,948	13,046	3,000	23,803	2,338	8,080	2,145	5,986	4,8
1943	224,289	1,182	1,742	24,336	1,151	4,995	3,457	12,626	12,5
1944	302,755	155	5,766	24,760	408	2,860	4,587	17,792	12,9
1945	372,428	171	6,123	29,524	975	3,604	5,087	19,119	12,9
1946	296,611	589	5,707	29,482	597	1,207	5,835	21,058	14,8
1947	278,824	7,895	4,253	35,014	2,202	7	6,491	21,440	16,2
1948	323,670	21,555	4,648	2,193	4,886	2,164	7,114	20,417	15,8
1949	342,075	28,337	4,640	—	3,499	3,620	7,868	21,166	14,0
1950	363,309	28,974	4,015	—	3,065	—	1,890	2,077	9,3
1951	406,351	51,173	8,619	—	5,372	1,607	—	—	10,9
1952	521,173	77,435	11,677	—	7,912	12,154	—	—	11,3
1953	611,362	68,180	10,631	—	10,086	4,742	—	—	10,5
1954	633,817	82,136	10,363	—	15,875	3,702	—	—	—

[a]Included with "Transportation" until 1928.
[b]Includes stamps.

cise Taxes, 1915 to 1954
dollars)

atches	Lighters	Playing cards	Jewellery, Watches, ornaments, etc.	Fountain pens and pencils	Amusements	Pari-mutuel bets	Cameras and films	Candy and chewing gum	Soft drinks[b]	Fiscal years
—	—	—	—	—	—	—	—	—	—	1915
—	—	—	—	—	—	—	—	—	—	1916
—	—	—	—	—	—	—	—	—	—	1917
—	—	—	—	—	—	—	—	—	—	1918
,535	—	126	415	—	—	—	160	—	—	1919
,781	—	182	751	—	—	—	241	—	—	1920
,789	—	250	1,044	—	—	—	67	1,320	—	1921
,694	—	231	108	—	—	—	—	351	—	1922
,677	—	207	—	—	—	—	—	442	372	1923
,602	—	177	—	—	—	—	—	177	162	1924
,404	—	203	—	—	—	—	—	—	39	1925
,192	—	278	—	—	—	—	—	—	38	1926
,875	—	286	—	—	—	—	—	—	28	1927
,148	—	225	—	—	—	—	—	—	—	1928
,502	—	269	—	—	—	—	—	—	—	1929
,795	—	291	—	—	—	—	—	—	—	1930
,838	—	290	—	—	—	—	—	—	—	1931
,949	—	277	—	—	—	—	—	—	—	1932
,600	—	206	—	—	—	—	—	—	—	1933
,672	—	240	—	—	—	—	—	—	—	1934
,457	—	244	—	—	—	—	—	—	—	1935
,567	19	278	—	—	—	—	—	—	—	1936
,496	26	223	—	—	—	—	—	—	—	1937
,610	24	233	—	—	—	—	—	—	—	1938
,728	22	230	—	—	—	—	—	—	—	1939
,033	27	250	—	—	—	—	—	—	54	1940
,940	88	250	—	—	—	—	111	—	307	1941
,555	154	372	—	—	7,710	1,082	142	—	6,539	1942
,662	163	564	—	505	10,778	1,287	323	8,184	14,316	1943
,768	63	627	3,707	837	12,019	1,683	342	12,602	19,299	1944
,969	124	641	5,306	993	12,284	1,904	453	12,860	19,693	1945
,292	285	729	6,847	1,193	13,387	2,188	236	11,417	16,939	1946
,616	319	691	8,117	1,672	14,552	2,510	358	12,793	18,925	1947
,498	350	512	8,343	1,001	15,369	2,518	563	17,139	24,103	1948
,994	404	614	8,648	1,298	2,482	105	829	19,544	28,017	1949
757	269	648	3,554	496	—	—	538	1,030	1,627	1950
755	242	834	4,959	542	—	—	692	9,914	7,338	1951
,387	320	665	7,326	697	—	—	1,164	10,846	19,537	1952
,071	236	724	5,960	587	—	—	930	11,216	12,557	1953
,019	218	710	7,256	574	—	—	1,104	11,813	11,798	1954

Includes carbonic acid gas.

TAI

Fiscal years	Domestic								
	Wines	Beer, ale, and porter	Furs	Luggage, trunks, etc.	Toilet articles	Toilet soaps	Sugars	Pipes, etc.	Ciga
1915	—	—	—	—	—	—	—	—	—
1916	—	—	—	—	—	—	—	—	—
1917	—	—	—	—	—	—	—	—	—
1918	—	—	—	—	—	—	—	—	—
1919	—	—	—	—	—	—	—	—	—
1920	—	—	—	—	—	—	—	—	—
1921	73	4,943	—	—	—	—	—	—	—
1922	123	1,247	—	—	—	—	—	—	—
1923	159	2,612	—	—	—	—	—	—	2
1924	152	4,235	—	—	—	—	—	—	3
1925	67	4,669	—	—	—	—	—	—	3
1926	95	5,467	—	—	—	—	—	—	3
1927	118	5,199	—	—	—	—	—	—	3
1928	171	6,321	—	—	—	—	—	—	3
1929	212	7,953	—	—	—	—	—	—	3
1930	299	7,475	—	—	—	—	—	—	3
1931	262	6,541	—	—	—	—	—	—	2
1932	258	6,298	—	—	—	—	—	—	2
1933	195	4,973	—	—	—	—	—	—	1
1934	214	4,928	—	—	698	164	14,123	—	1
1935	248	1,838	—	—	861	191	10,679	—	1
1936	203	—	—	—	891	187	10,038	—	1
1937	207	—	—	—	909	203	10,306	—	1
1938	240	—	—	—	942	215	10,549	—	1
1939	230	—	—	—	965	222	10,761	—	1
1940	420	—	—	—	1,034	238	11,891	—	1
1941	658	—	—	—	1,184	260	11,547	—	2
1942	1,445	—	—	—	3,140	315	21,402	—	3
1943	2,007	—	3,130	2,129	4,096	388	14,572	96	4
1944	1,710	—	4,146	4,051	4,946	349	12,769	251	1,4
1945	1,772	—	4,903	3,763	5,830	359	11,557	279	1,5
1946	2,066	—	4,509	4,281	6,428	392	9,672	550	1,5
1947	2,394	—	2,733	4,966	6,689	418	10,878	644	2,5
1948	2,342	—	2,860	4,348	6,269	545	10,101	390	2,6
1949	2,060	—	3,570	5,135	6,823	760	—	442	2,6
1950	2,126	—	2,774	2,036	3,602	645	—	248	2,7
1951	2,225	—	4,165	2,204	4,386	67	—	323	2,7
1952	2,167	—	4,222	3,231	8,234	—	—	560	2,5
1953	2,216	—	5,213	2,931	6,962	—	—	340	1,9
1954	2,231	—	3,366	2,655	6,769	—	—	250	2,0

[d]Includes some miscellaneous articles not itemized.
[e]No separate record of revenue; included in "Stamps."

Continued

rettes	Tobacco	Cigarette papers & tubes	Importations: Sales tax	Excise taxes	Special excise tax	War exchange tax	Gross total[d]	Net total	Fiscal years
—	—	—	—	—	—	—	98	98	1915
—	—	—	—	—	—	—	1,548	1,537	1916
—	—	—	—	—	—	—	2,065	2,060	1917
—	—	—	—	—	—	—	2,239	2,227	1918
—	—	—	—	—	—	—	11,938	11,889	1919
—	—	—	—	—	—	—	15,726	15,588	1920
—	—	—	10,218	9,840	—	—	79,318	78,803	1921
—	—	—	16,699	1,212	—	—	73,903	73,656	1922
—	—	—	28,577	768	—	—	107,990	106,483	1923
—	—	—	29,155	837	—	—	123,669	120,676	1924
—	—	—	15,454	724	—	—	89,331	85,811	1925
—	—	—	16,771	1,123	—	—	99,228	98,097	1926
—	—	—	18,366	1,577	—	—	106,723	105,613	1927
—	—	—	16,721	2,060	—	—	91,662	90,223	1928
—	—	—	14,495	2,130	—	—	84,014	83,007	1929
—	—	—	9,922	1,749	—	—	64,154	63,409	1930
—	—	—	4,197	887	—	—	35,372	34,735	1931
—	—	—	7,835	254	4,982	—	60,264	59,606	1932
—	—	—	8,702	35	13,378	—	83,355	82,192	1933
—	—	[e]	8,980	1,435	14,535	—	108,408	106,576	1934
—	—	[e]	10,432	1,510	15,007	—	114,076	112,192	1935
—	—	[e]	10,918	1,561	12,939	—	116,472	112,733	1936
—	—	[e]	16,718	1,890	15,415	—	155,780	152,473	1937
—	—	146	20,514	1,842	18,621	—	184,627	180,819	1938
—	—	242	17,999	1,760	15,591	—	165,498	161,711	1939
—	—	536	21,729	2,193	1,979	—	169,703	166,028	1940
—	—	1,313	27,787	4,014	1,008	61,932	289,002	284,167	1941
—	—	3,690	31,605	3,109	861	100,874	463,795	453,425	1942
996	4,860	3,531	26,189	3,408	480	94,554	506,261	488,712	1943
875	10,324	1,963	36,500	5,819	508	118,913	672,961	638,619	1944
918	10,817	4,901	31,680	4,187	545	98,164	737,784	543,065	1945
107	10,454	4,284	29,642	4,260	787	41,198	610,915	496,910	1946
908	11,708	6,509	49,249	10,463	1,185	338	608,869	579,024	1947
778	10,073	6,125	59,342	12,062	2,113	—	651,442	640,758	1948
296	11,552	6,706	48,099	6,681	279	—	649,009	636,138	1949
638	11,207	6,887	51,913	8,404	—	—	583,242	571,457	1950
979	11,512	7,370	64,276	17,825	—	—	697,275	686,768	1951
047	23,209	382	90,318	24,547	—	—	923,949[f]	910,226[f]	1952
844	25,838	—	114,036	21,310	—	—	1,003,948[f]	983,448[f]	1953
525	23,328	—	121,420	25,119	—	—	1,052,899[f]	1,030,189[f]	1954

ludes old age security sales tax as follows: 1952—$24,298,000; 1953—$141,558,000; and 1954—$146,883,000.
RCES: *Annual Reports*, Dept. of National Revenue; *Public Accounts of Canada; Canada Year Book.*

TABLE

DOMINION GOVERNMENT—REVENUE F
(thousa

Fiscal years	Individual income tax: General	Individual income tax: National defence tax	Individual income tax: Total	Individual income tax: Refundable tax reserve	Individual income tax: Net total	Corporation income tax	Withholding tax: Dividends and interest	Withholding tax: Rents and royalties	(t
1917	—	—	—	—	—	—	—	—	·
1918	—	—	—	—	—	—	—	—	·
1919	7,973	—	7,973	—	7,973	1,377	—	—	·
1920	13,195	—	13,195	—	13,195	7,069	—	—	·
1921	32,533	—	32,533	—	32,533	13,849	—	—	·
1922	39,820	—	39,820	—	39,820	38,864	—	—	·
1923	31,689	—	31,689	—	31,689	28,023	—	—	·
1924	25,657	—	25,657	—	25,657	28,547	—	—	·
1925	25,157	—	25,157	—	25,157	31,091	—	—	·
1926	23,849	—	23,849	—	23,849	31,723	—	—	·
1927	18,043	—	18,043	—	18,043	29,343	—	—	·
1928	23,223	—	23,223	—	23,223	33,348	—	—	·
1929	24,793	—	24,793	—	24,793	34,629	—	—	·
1930	27,238	—	27,238	—	27,238	41,783	—	—	·
1931	26,624	—	26,624	—	26,624	44,424	—	—	·
1932	24,773	—	24,773	—	24,773	36,481	—	—	·
1933	25,960	—	25,960	—	25,960	36,107	—	—	·
1934	29,184	—	29,184	—	29,184	27,386	4,829	—	·
1935	25,201	—	25,201	—	25,201	35,790	5,817	—	·
1936	32,789	—	32,789	—	32,789	42,519	7,208	—	
1937	35,358	—	35,358	—	35,358	58,013	8,910	—	
1938	40,071	—	40,071	—	40,071	69,769	10,152	—	
1939	46,591	—	46,591	—	46,591	85,186	9,903	—	
1940	45,009	—	45,009	—	45,009	77,920	11,122	—	
1941	75,636	27,672	103,308	—	103,308	131,566	12,282	760	
1942	189,237	106,637	295,874	—	295,874	185,836	26,642	1,627	
1943	453,717	80,198	533,915	50,000	483,915	347,970	26,711	1,370	
1944	809,183	388	809,571	115,000	694,571	311,379	25,671	1,272	1,
1945	763,896	—	763,896	95,000	668,896	276,404	27,053	1,546	
1946	689,507	—	689,507	5,000	684,507	217,834	26,823	1,486	
1947	691,989	—	691,989	24,000	667,989	196,819	28,428	1,708	1,
1948	656,873	—	656,873	—	656,873	351,535	33,929	1,960	2,
1949	760,152	—	760,152	—	760,152	488,550	40,965	2,480	1,
1950	619,263	—	619,263	—	619,263	602,073	47,475[d]	[e]	2,
1951	648,663	—	648,663	—	648,663	711,577	61,610[d]	[e]	3,
1952	975,676[h]	—	975,676[h]	—	975,676[h]	1,116,067[h]	55,017[d]	[e]	
1953	1,180,026[h]	—	1,180,026[h]	—	1,180,026[h]	1,229,706[h]	53,674[d]	[e]	
1954	1,187,656[h]	—	1,187,656[h]	—	1,187,656[h]	1,182,416[h]	53,761[d]	[e]	

[a]In Table 6 included under "Individuals."

[b]Under Part XVIII of Income War Tax Act and Part IA of Income Tax Act. In Table 6 included unde "Corporations."

[c]Amounts for 1917–32 are collections (including arrears) under business profits tax, repealed from December 31, 1920.

[d]Includes "Rents and royalties."

irect Taxes, 1917 to 1954
dollars)

1942 …ferred tax[a]	Tax on undistributed income[b]	Excess profits tax: Corporations	Individuals	Total	Refundable tax reserve	Net total[c]	Succession duties	Grand total	Fiscal years
—	—	—	—	12,507	—	12,507	—	12,507	1917
—	—	—	—	21,271	—	21,271	—	21,271	1918
—	—	—	—	32,970	—	32,970	—	42,320	1919
—	—	—	—	44,145	—	44,145	—	64,409	1920
—	—	—	—	40,841	—	40,841	—	87,223	1921
—	—	—	—	22,816	—	22,816	—	101,500	1922
—	—	—	—	13,031	—	13,031	—	72,743	1923
—	—	—	—	4,753	—	4,753	—	58,957	1924
—	—	—	—	2,704	—	2,704	—	58,952	1925
—	—	—	—	1,173	—	1,173	—	56,745	1926
—	—	—	—	710	—	710	—	48,096	1927
—	—	—	—	956	—	956	—	57,527	1928
—	—	—	—	455	—	455	—	59,877	1929
—	—	—	—	173	—	173	—	69,194	1930
—	—	—	—	34	—	34	—	71,082	1931
—	—	—	—	3	—	3	—	61,257	1932
—	—	—	—	—	—	—	—	62,067	1933
—	—	—	—	—	—	—	—	61,399	1934
—	—	—	—	—	—	—	—	66,808	1935
—	—	—	—	—	—	—	—	82,710	1936
—	—	—	—	—	—	—	—	102,365	1937
—	—	—	—	—	—	—	—	120,366	1938
—	—	—	—	—	—	—	—	142,026	1939
—	—	—	—	—	—	—	—	134,449	1940
—	—	23,847	148	23,995	—	23,995	—	272,138	1941
—	—	131,685	3,483	135,168	—	135,168	6,957	652,368	1942
—	—	443,201	11,380	454,581	20,000	434,581	13,273	1,308,043	1943
,318	—	447,300	21,418	468,718	40,000	428,718	15,020	1,480,495	1944
,326	—	441,618	24,187	465,805	124,500	341,305	17,251	1,336,314	1945
,309	—	465,558	28,638	494,196	67,500	426,696	21,448	1,380,873	1946
,002	41,973	421,045	27,652	448,697	6,200	442,497	23,576	1,405,531	1947
686	12,596	213,886	13,144	227,030	—	227,030	30,828	1,317,706	1948
779	3,440	38,737	6,055	44,792	—	44,792	25,550	1,368,341	1949
629	1,120	[f]	[f]	−1.788[g]	—	−1,788[g]	29 920	1 300,782	1950
548	87 620	[f]	[f]	10,141	—	10,141	33,599	1,556,876	1951
[i]	14,613	[f]	[f]	2,365	—	2,365	38,208	2,201,946[h]	1952
[i]	10,383	—	—	—	—	—	38,071	2,511,861[h]	1953
[i]	8,771	—	—	—	—	—	39,138	2,471,741[h]	1954

[e]Included in "Dividends and interest."
[f]Not available.
[g]Refunds exceeded payments.
[h]Excludes old age security tax.
[i]Included in "General."
SOURCES: *Taxation Statistics*, Dept. of National Revenue.

TABLE 12

PRINCE EDWARD ISLAND—PRINCIPAL REVENUES, 1901 TO 1954 FOR FISCAL YEARS ENDED WITHIN CALENDAR YEARS (thousands of dollars)

Fiscal years	Succession duties	Corporation taxes	Income tax[a][b]	Motor vehicles		Sales and amusement		Property, etc.			Liquor	
				Gasoline tax	Motor vehicle licences[c]	Amusement tax	Public health tax—tobacco	Land tax	Road taxes[d]	Personal property tax[b]	Public health tax—liquor	Liquor Control Board (licences, profits, etc.)[e]
1901	1	9	5	—	—	—	—	31	12	—	—	—
1902	4	13	7	—	—	—	—	35	15	—	—	—
1903	3	13	7	—	—	—	—	32	14	—	—	—
1904	4	13	6	—	—	—	—	28	12	—	—	—
1905	7	12	6	—	—	—	—	32	13	—	—	—
1906[f]	7	9	2	—	—	—	—	6	1	—	—	—
1907	5	16	6	—	—	—	—	32	13	—	—	—
1908	7	17	9	—	—	—	—	28	11	—	—	—
1909	4	17	9	—	—	—	—	35	15	—	—	—
1910	5	15	11	—	—	—	—	36	12	—	—	—
1911	3	16	8	—	—	—	—	41	17	—	—	—
1912[g]	2	23	25	—	—	—	—	73	15	—	—	—
1913	6	17	9	—	—	—	—	32	—	—	—	—
1914	8	17	10	—	1	—	—	45	—	—	—	—
1915	6	18	9	—	—	—	—	37	—	—	—	—
1916	10	17	13	—	1	—	—	52	—	—	—	—
1917	4	16	11	—	5	—	—	55	—	—	—	—
1918	4	22	12	—	14	—	—	54	—	—	—	—
1919	4	22	—	—	16	—	—	58	—	—	—	15
1920	8	35	80	—	31	5	—	106	30	12	—	52

[a]Does not include collections by federal government of 5 per cent provincial corporations income tax levied from 1947 to 1951.
[b]Does not include arrears in early years.
[c]Includes fees levied for Unsatisfied Judgment Fund.
[d]Includes horse, dog, and poll taxes.
[e]Includes net profits of the wholesale vendor and contributions from Prohibition Commission. Includes fines and penalties.
[f]Nine months ended September 30.
[g]Fifteen months ended December 31.

TABLE 12—Continued

Fiscal years	Succession duties	Corporation taxes	Income tax[a,b]	Motor vehicles: Gasoline tax	Motor vehicles: Motor vehicle licences[c]	Sales and amusement: Amusement tax	Sales and amusement: Public health tax—tobacco	Property, etc.: Land tax	Property, etc.: Road taxes[d]	Property, etc.: Personal property tax[b]	Liquor: Public health tax—liquor	Liquor: Liquor Control Board (licences, profits, etc.)[e]
1921	11	53	50	—	38	5	—	102	37	13	—	50
1922	21	40	34	—	47	6	—	101	33	22	—	28
1923	9	30	30	—	53	4	—	96	16	19	—	14
1924	6	33	36	14	55	5	—	101	—	17	—	44
1925	15	34	35	19	62	5	—	107	1	17	—	45
1926	19	116	33	28	72	5	—	102	1	21	—	57
1927	9	78	25	36	82	5	—	80	1	17	—	15
1928	17	81	32	63	99	7	—	90	30	18	—	—
1929	29	84	28	108	115	6	—	93	35	20	—	22
1930	26	85	27	124	146	8	—	83	31	18	—	23
1931	12	102	28	109	136	8	—	61	31	12	—	42
1932	35	117	23	131	122	7	—	59	52	13	—	32
1933	31	125	27	164	95	5	—	69	49	17	—	30
1934	50	133	35	175	101	6	—	69	46	19	—	30
1935	20	147	24	180	103	5	—	68	43	14	—	30
1936	43	161	35	201	112	12	—	98	50	21	—	55
1937	45	164	34	270	145	11	—	105	50	17	—	40
1938	68	166	51	286	155	11	—	89	42	14	—	64
1939	75	172	57	316	159	10	—	87	39	10	—	102
1940	44	172	86	301	159	10	—	85	35	3	—	68
1941	43	120	85	285	155	19	—	85	34	5	28	87
1942	57	—	11	233	142	26	38	128	28	—	52	130
1944[h]	46	—	24	279	154	40	56	114	31	—	73	205
1945	82	—	9	291	169	32	56	93	29	—	65	182
1946	109	—	4	365	177	49	69	91	29	—	108	356
1947	93	—	3	466	208	52	84	86	32	—	171	580
1948	63	—	1	698	230	55	89	82	31	—	168	539
1949	21	—	5	783	264	105	111	37	—	—	175	566
1950	6	—	6	856	292	99	125	21	—	—	195	692
1951	3	—	13	960	367	111	128	1	—	—	209	762
1952	12	—	20	1,002	409	118	129	—	—	—	235	800
1953	1	—	27	1,161	452	124	157	—	—	—	274	946
1954	—	—	30	1,202	474	133	148	—	—	—	270	913

[h]Fifteen months ended March 31

TABLE 13

NOVA SCOTIA—PRINCIPAL REVENUES, 1901 TO 1953 FOR FISCAL YEARS ENDED WITHIN CALENDAR YEARS
(thousands of dollars)

Fiscal years	Succession duties	Corporation taxes[a]	Motor vehicles		Amusement taxes	Property		Mineral royalties and rentals	Liquor Control Board (licences, profits, etc.)[c]
			Gasoline tax	Motor vehicle licences[b]		Provincial land tax	Highway tax		
1901	46	—	—	—	—	—	—	437[d]	—
1902	55	—	—	—	—	—	—	487[d]	—
1903	35	—	—	—	—	—	—	619[d]	—
1904	41	—	—	—	—	—	—	585[d]	—
1905	50	—	—	—	—	—	—	614[d]	—
1906	63	—	—	—	—	—	—	613	—
1907	65	—	—	—	—	—	—	602	—
1908	79	—	—	—	—	—	—	661	—
1909	71	—	—	—	—	—	—	605	—
1910	54	—	—	—	—	—	—	596	—
1911	42	—	—	—	—	—	—	633	—
1912	78	—	—	7	—	—	—	774	—
1913	53	43	—	11	—	—	—	839	—
1914	53	60	—	12	—	—	—	748	—
1915	107	66	—	26	—	—	—	716	—
1916	161	68	—	42	—	—	—	805	—
1917	131	93	—	35	20	—	—	724	—
1918	117	117	—	92	89	30	—	641	—
1919	181	276	—	148	131	32	416	607	—
1920	196	314	—	256	161	33	316	656	—
1921	159	541	—	372	157	32	440	606	75

[a]Includes long distance telephone tax and corporations income tax, but excludes collections by federal government of 5 percent corporations income tax levied from 1947 to 1951.
[b]Includes fees levied for Unsatisfied Judgment Fund.
[c]Includes net profits of Department of Vendors. Excludes revenue expended for enforcement.
[d]Includes licences, fees, and other miscellaneous revenue.

SOURCES: *Public Accounts of the Province of Nova Scotia;* and *The Control and Sale of Alcoholic Beverages in Canada, 1951*, D.B.S.

TABLE 13—*Continued*

Fiscal years	Succession duties	Corporation taxes[a]	Motor vehicles		Amusement taxes	Property		Mineral royalties and rentals	Liquor Control Board (licences, profits, etc.)[c]
			Gasoline tax	Motor vehicle licences[b]		Provincial land tax	Highway tax		
1922	121	559	—	418	123	65	490	530	280
1923	223	549	—	480	123	66	509	712	507
1924	136	695	—	535	116	83	462	728	367
1925	258	593	—	576	112	85	300	348	52
1926	537	731	158	601	115	121	479	682	122
1927	188	731	243	677	111	97	469	780	167
1928	222	692	476	755	122	88	467	711	244
1929	290	745	680	766	134	87	463	755	222
1930	312	772	811	996	163	90	464	661	307
1931	256	787	870	1,134	158	90	466	570	753
1932	515	830	926	1,281	134	86	469	448	525
1933	263	802	948	1,028	112	85	429	401	311
1934	298	963	1,161	1,028	129	88	437	615	394
1935[e]	463	1,115	1,794	1,286	180	104	516	722	697
1936	567	987	1,736	1,239	147	89	438	670	996
1937	606	1,015	2,006	1,392	148	82	444	723	1,314
1938	746	1,108	2,424	1,422	151	79	431	700	1,366
1939	557	1,169	2,608	1,486	153	83	452	728	1,718
1940	550	1,364	2,875	1,615	207	82	395	839	2,284
1941	410	1,543	3,031	1,755	245	82	417	795	3,358
1942	688	222	2,423	1,686	283	80	390	783	4,885
1943	662	55	2,163	1,680	346	82	487	681	5,613
1944	511	36	2,242	1,715	354	73	430	629	6,738
1945	879	40	2,642	1,833	385	75	511	576	7,429
1946	661	46	3,498	2,119	390	72	448	582	9,021
1947	513	47	5,179	2,485	377	78	445	446	8,246
1948	208	50	5,869	2,733	363	79	342	727	8,154
1949	73	54	6,246	2,943	435	76	251	750	8,154
1951[f]	26	82	8,419	4,135	669	101	272	932	10,030
1952	25	113	7,852	3,479	613	73	245	638	8,279
1953	12	171	8,820	3,676	699	73	245	786	9,256

[e]Fourteen months ended November 30.
[f]Sixteen months ended March 31.

TABLE 14

NEW BRUNSWICK—PRINCIPAL REVENUES,[a] 1901 TO 1953 FOR FISCAL YEARS ENDED WITHIN CALENDAR YEARS (thousands of dollars)

Fiscal years	Succession duties	Corporations		Motor vehicles		Sales, amusements, etc.		Property		Natural resources			Liquor Control Board (licences, profits, etc.)[d]
		Corporation taxes	Corporation profits tax[b]	Gasoline tax	Motor vehicle licences[c]	Amusement tax	Tobacco tax	Municipal road tax	Wild lands tax	Forest fire tax	Stumpage	Mining royalties	
1901	12	25	—	—	—	—	—	—	—	—	101	—	—
1902	17	26	—	—	—	—	—	—	—	—	108	—	—
1903	23	29	—	—	—	—	—	—	—	—	123	—	—
1904	25	30	—	—	—	—	—	—	—	—	176	—	—
1905	42	32	—	—	—	—	—	—	—	—	134	—	—
1906	12	37	—	—	—	—	—	—	—	—	171	—	—
1907	15	31	—	—	—	—	—	—	—	—	180	—	—
1908	32	34	—	—	—	—	—	—	—	—	134	—	—
1909	12	34	—	—	—	—	—	—	—	—	247	3	—
1910	33	37	—	—	—	—	—	—	—	—	330	5	—
1911	6	48	—	—	4	—	—	—	—	—	368	7	—
1912	45	47	—	—	8	—	—	—	—	—	340	5	—
1913	98	50	—	—	11	—	—	—	—	—	306	14	—
1914	20	51	—	—	15	—	—	—	—	—	386	13	—
1915	155	53	—	—	23	—	—	—	—	—	423	15	—
1916	78	109	—	—	38	—	—	—	—	—	354	18	—
1917	30	121	—	—	62	—	—	—	—	—	352	21	—
1918	95	131	—	—	90	17	—	21	102	31	476	42	—
1919	75	135	—	—	116	64	—	75	54	33	576	30	—
1920	90	222	—	—	197	72	—	93	56	32	1,293	28	—
1921	151	255	—	—	274	68	—	84	57	31	1,005	30	47
1922	262	249	—	—	301	54	—	81	56	32	380	43	305

[a]Receipts prior to 1918. Excludes social service and education tax revenue of: 1950, $2,293,000; 1951, $2,819,000; 1952, $7,207,000; and 1953, $7,742,000.
[b]Does not include collections by federal government of 5 per cent corporation income tax levied from 1947 to 1951.
[c]Includes revenue of Motor Carrier Board and Unsatisfied Judgment Fund.
[d]Includes revenue from Board of Liquor Commissioners. Excludes fines and confiscations.

SOURCES: *Public Accounts of the Province of New Brunswick;* and *The Control and Sale of Alcoholic Beverages in Canada, 1951*, D.B.S.

TABLE 14—*Continued*

Fiscal years	Succession duties	Corporations		Motor vehicles		Sales, amusements, etc.		Property		Natural resources			Liquor Control Board (licences, profits, etc.)[d]
		Corporation taxes	Corporation profits tax[b]	Gasoline tax	Motor vehicle licences[c]	Amusement tax	Tobacco tax	Municipal road tax	Wild lands tax	Forest fire tax	Stumpage	Mining royalties	
1923	134	248	—	—	374	60	—	72	56	31	740	49	415
1924	164	245	—	—	451	55	—	85	56	33	1,043	35	490
1925	299	244	—	—	501	58	—	76	57	32	888	33	329
1926	595	590	—	144	556	55	—	85	56	37	667	31	294
1927	461	393	—	230	615	62	—	74	56	33	790	33	317
1928	414	401	—	274	747	63	—	73	56	34	849	28	1,043
1929	320	416	—	538	781	69	—	82	57	34	814	26	1,522
1930	199	437	—	650	873	93	—	62	57	34	677	25	1,544
1931	294	443	—	690	866	80	—	75	58	33	279	23	1,220
1932	192	548	—	793	837	66	—	62	56	33	297	23	862
1933	259	517	—	802	759	59	—	41	57	33	126	32	545
1934	150	495	—	880	764	68	—	43	59	33	472	35	558
1935	415	495	—	1,017	839	75	—	44	58	33	445	35	601
1936	619	516	—	1,167	890	82	—	36	59	33	379	37	783
1937	398	522	—	1,468	1,063	89	—	55	58	33	768	40	1,105
1938	319	812	57	1,836	1,140	96	—	52	58	31	672	29	1,154
1939	177	828	41	1,914	1,156	87	—	49	59	34	452	45	1,276
1940	526	882	157	2,113	1,405	96	—	56	58	33	835	65	1,656
1941	383	899	248	2,026	1,499	109	260	50	59	33	926	56	2,220
1942	222	—	—	1,683	1,365	135	300	46	59	33	1,005	48	2,951
1943	600	—	—	1,555	1,270	167	393	65	60	33	1,028	45	3,055
1944	365	—	—	1,760	1,391	172	500	63	62	33	1,052	39	3,497
1945	677	—	—	2,086	1,403	189	581	—	62	33	1,069	40	4,247
1946	1,072	—	—	2,752	1,626	215	708	—	62	34	1,198	39	6,891
1947	432	—	—	4,196	2,021	229	728	—	61	34	1,655	35	6,880
1948	53	—	—	5,189	2,323	263	825	—	65	34	1,822	54	6,606
1949	46	—	—	5,536	2,424	280	856	—	60	34	1,753	53	6,484
1950	5	—	—	5,814	2,608	288	844	—	62	34	1,426	62	5,472
1951[e]	1	—	—	2,126	84	116	317	—	2	—	320	28	2,476
1952	1	—	—	6.323	2,847	326	872	—	62	69	2,602	98	5,409
1953	1	—	—	6,830	3,018	396	941	—	63	69	2,671	108	6,401

[e]Five months ended March 31.

TABLE

QUEBEC—PRINCIPAL REVENUE
FOR FISCAL YEARS ENDI
(thousan

Fiscal years	Succession duties	Corporations		Personal income tax	Motor vehicles		Sales, amu		
		Corporation taxes (capital, etc.)	Corporation profits tax		Gasoline tax	Motor vehicle licences[a]	Retail sales tax	Tobacco tax	Hospit tax (meals)
1901	164	214	—	—	—	—	—	—	—
1902	223	232	—	—	—	—	—	—	—
1903	154	226	—	—	—	—	—	—	—
1904	450	261	—	—	—	—	—	—	—
1905	183	304	—	—	—	—	—	—	—
1906	421	315	—	—	—	2	—	—	—
1907	568	464	—	—	—	3	—	—	—
1908	621	566	—	—	—	5	—	—	—
1909	634	653	—	—	—	9	—	—	—
1910	838	688	—	—	—	11	—	—	—
1911	1,072	712	—	—	—	27	—	—	—
1912	1,227	777	—	—	—	49	—	—	—
1913	1,064	941	—	—	—	71	—	—	—
1914	1,604	925	—	—	—	123	—	—	—
1915	1,661	983	—	—	—	180	—	—	—
1916	1,376	1,035	—	—	—	241	—	—	—
1917	1,741	1,102	—	—	—	489	—	—	—
1918	4,737	1,289	—	—	—	650	—	—	—
1919	1,459	1,530	—	—	—	880	—	—	—
1920	1,787	1,582	—	—	—	1,134	—	—	—
1921	2,100	1,641	—	—	—	1,387	—	—	—
1922	3,005	2,010	—	—	—	1,983	—	—	—
1923	2,620	2,213	—	—	—	2,145	—	—	—
1924	2,978	2,323	—	—	66	2,092	—	—	—
1925	2,423	2,461	—	—	653	2,492	—	—	—
1926	2,257	2,455	—	—	1,012	2,740	—	—	—
1927	3,654	2,524	—	—	1,290	3,299	—	—	—
1928	3,741	3,113	—	—	1,680	3,891	—	—	—
1929	4,184	3,066	—	—	3,250	4,742	—	—	—
1930	5,268	3,444	—	—	3,972	5,316	—	—	—
1931	6,675	3,425	—	—	4,405	5,410	—	—	—
1932	3,799	3,481	7	—	5,107	5,275	—	—	—
1933	3,070	3,287	674	—	4,920	5,027	—	—	545
1934	2,698	3,081	886	—	4,822	5,205	—	—	460
1935	3,402	3,038	1,025	—	5,115	5,503	—	—	462
1936	4,698	4,073	2,109	—	5,791	5,920	—	—	473
1937	7,637	5,148	2,189	—	6,565	6,484	—	—	518
1938	11,838	4,940	3,490	—	7,347	7,184	—	—	611
1939	12,277	9,733	2,430	—	7,883	6,878	—	—	719
1940	12,404	3,601	2,992	—	10,784	7,152	—	—	812
1941[f]	5,015	5,654	4,883	2,411	9,220	2,376	6,458	1,548	858
1942	12,076	7,202	8,983	1,897	12,142	7,300	12,000	3,023	1,176
1943	6,796	156	417	299	10,279	6,803	12,957	3,599	1,331
1944	6,505	41	69	269	9,965	7,122	13,292	4,030	1,697

[a]Does not include revenue of Transportation Board.
[b]Details of earlier years not available.
SOURCES: *Public Accounts, Province of Quebec;* and *The Control and Sale of Alcoholic Beverages in Canada, 1951*, D.B

1901 TO 1954
WITHIN CALENDAR YEARS
of dollars)

ments, etc.			Natural resources					Liquor		Fiscal years
Amusements tax[b]	Races tax[bc]	Stock transfers tax	Mining royalties	Mining profits tax	Development licences	Stumpage, ground rents, and timber bonuses[d]	Water power and storage rentals	Unemployment tax	Liquor Control Board (licences, profits, etc.)[e]	
—	—	—	—	—	—	1,234	—	—	—	1901
—	—	—	—	—	—	1,055	—	—	—	1902
—	—	—	—	—	—	1,242	—	—	—	1903
—	—	—	—	—	—	1,167	—	—	—	1904
—	—	—	—	—	—	1,380	—	—	—	1905
—	—	33	—	—	—	1,266	—	—	—	1906
—	—	39	—	—	—	1,018	—	—	—	1907
—	—	28	—	—	—	978	—	—	—	1908
—	—	60	—	—	—	906	—	—	—	1909
—	—	77	—	—	—	1,034	—	—	—	1910
—	—	66	—	—	—	1,127	—	—	—	1911
—	—	69	—	—	—	1,533	—	—	—	1912
—	—	71	—	—	—	1,510	—	—	—	1913
—	—	54	—	—	—	1,589	—	—	—	1914
—	—	20	—	—	—	1,737	—	—	—	1915
—	—	75	—	—	—	1,684	—	—	—	1916
—	—	77	—	—	—	1,568	—	—	—	1917
—	—	27	102	—	—	1,414	—	—	—	1918
—	—	61	257	—	—	2,024	—	—	—	1919
—	—	133	366	—	—	2,604	—	—	—	1920
—	—	99	689	—	—	3,035	47	—	—	1921
—	—	88	251	—	—	3,692	46	—	4,036	1022
—	—	109	146	—	—	3,148	183	—	4,565	1923
—	—	104	167	—	—	3,778	156	—	5,754	1924
—	—	130	154	—	112	4,320	181	—	5,462	1925
—	—	181	—	92	130	5,219	276	—	5,796	1926
—	—	287	—	117	189	5,757	345	—	6,778	1927
—	—	554	—	186	248	5,612	374	—	7,610	1928
—	—	980	—	321	243	5,179	495	—	9,688	1929
—	—	793	—	501	168	4,360	438	—	10,081	1930
—	—	398	—	386	163	3,812	443	—	8,262	1931
—	—	278	—	170	92	2,939	342	96	6,056	1932
723	146	421	—	219	106	1,757	386	322	5,445	1933
816	111	662	—	306	158	1,327	521	316	3,940	1934
781	81	393	—	371	170	2,429	626	354	5,209	1935
696	18	524	—	619	183	3,496	672	527	4,868	1936
984	43	917	—	1,010	297	3,317	663	646	5,487	1937
933	60	477	—	1,042	298	4,287	682	757	6,222	1938
914	63	482	—	1,208	231	6,605	762	749	6,471	1939
975	66	365	—	1,339	142	2,753	865	619	7,572	1940
738	40	173	—	216	86	4,789	727	541	7,271[g]	1941[f]
1,011	47	217	—	1,489	112	6,168	1,163	829	9,474	1942
1,186	50	213	—	1,860	105	6,255	1,282	1,024	12,333	1943
1,363	68	282	—	1,855	138	4,940	1,349	1,060	14,035	1944

[c]Includes licences.
[d]"Woods and forests" prior to 1931.
[e]Excludes fines and revenue expended for enforcement.

TABL

Fiscal years	Succession duties	Corporations		Personal income tax	Motor vehicles		Sales, amu		
		Corporation taxes (capital, etc.)	Corporation profits tax		Gasoline tax	Motor vehicle licences[a]	Retail sales tax	Tobacco tax	Hospita tax (meals)
1945	5,382	32	67	92	11,023	7,846	12,961	4,441	1,485
1946	6,299	71	8	52	12,949	8,174	15,235	4,986	1,676
1947	11,353	64	3	58	16,469	9,551	19,608	5,494	2,040
1948	9,085	6,237[h]	24,759	23	25,569	11,491	24,334	6,465	2,554
1949	11,834	9,548[h]	35,000	23	29,591	13,279	27,196	7,958	2,941
1950	13,325	10,211[h]	34,705	16	30,908	14,736	29,677	8,598	3,211
1951	13,007	11,676[h]	42,769[k]	21	37,180	16,542	32,810	9,031	3,233
1952	12,429	12,312[h]	55,834[k]	3	47,647	18,688	35,906	8,828	4,049
1953	12,833	12,748[h]	51,117[k]	—	50,532	20,402	38,783	10,313	4,166
1954	10,913	15,196[h]	48,879[k]	10	56,612	22,555	41,711	12,734	4,467

[f]Nine months ended March 31. [g]Eleven months ended March 31.

[h]Excludes revenue collected under Progress of Education Act on capital of refining and telephone compani 1948—$391,000; 1949—$490,000; 1950—$646,000; 1951—$738,000; 1952—$861,000; 1953—$1,020,000; and 1954 $1,105,000.

[i]Excludes revenue representing additional charges on forestry industries under Progress of Education Act: 1947 $113,000; 1948—$773,000; 1949—$806,000; 1950—$672,000; 1951—$475,000; 1952—$760,000; 1953—$856,000; a 1954—$625,000.

TABLE

ONTARIO—PRINCIPAL REVENUE FOR FISCAL YEARS END (thousan

Fiscal years	Succession duties	Corporations								Person incom tax
		Railways	Insurance companies	Banks	Other	Paid up capital	Place of business	Net revenue	Total	
1901	336	33	94	44	67	—	—	—	238	—
1902	236	34	102	45	65	—	—	—	246	—
1903	387	35	109	49	61	—	—	—	254	—
1904	459	188	116	53	64	—	—	—	421	—
1905	684	192	132	57	65	—	—	—	446	—
1906	1,016	376	138	61	69	—	—	—	644	—
1907	834	391	145	70	66	—	—	—	672	—
1908	1,155	401	153	69	72	—	—	—	695	—
1909[e]	682	417	158	70	74	—	—	—	719	—
1910	758	431	167	74	80	—	—	—	752	—
1911	1,051	453	183	74	115	—	—	—	825	—
1912	874	449	190	77	126	—	—	—	842	—
1913	1,146	463	211	76	128	—	—	—	878	—
1914	1,288	641	235	195	248	—	—	—	1,319	—

[a]Excludes: luxury tax—1925, $371,000; 1926, $347,000; 1927, $282,000; 1928, $308,000 and 1929, $46,000; v tax—1932, $65,000; 1933, $151,000; 1934, $132,000; 1935, $63,000; 1936, $119,000; and 1937, $25,000; logging ta 1951, $1,289,000; 1952, $923,000; 1953, $827,000; and 1954, $824,000.

[b]Includes fees levied for Unsatisfied Judgment Fund.

·*Continued*

s, etc.			Natural resources					Liquor		Fiscal years
ıse- ıts ι[b]	Races tax[bc]	Stock transfers tax	Mining royalties	Mining profits tax	Develop- ment licences	Stumpage, ground rents, and timber bonuses[d]	Water power and storage rentals	Unemploy- ment tax	Liquor Control Board (licences, profits, etc.)[e]	
29	178	346	—	1,685	255	6,205	1,458	1,213	17,121	1945
94	199	611	—	1,331	516	7,913	843	1,277	23,096	1946
35	243	783	—	897	649	13,208[i]	1,490[j]	1,501	29,715	1947
98	267	591	—	1,007	528	9,648[i]	1,727[j]	1,376	28,073	1948
60	344	509	—	1,376	429	12,157[i]	1,880[j]	1,296	27,458	1949
67	390	601	—	2,264	397	6,880[i]	1,737[j]	1,282	27,668	1950
63	420	1,150	—	2,370	444	10,739[i]	2,287[j]	1,399	30,508	1951
52	366	1,059	—	4,010	545	15,355[i]	2,512[j]	1,380	29,776	1952
85	719	913	—	5,018	557	12,234[i]	2,645[j]	1,491	32,858	1953
48	1,463	846	—	4,478	561	11,096[i]	3,312[j]	1,524	33,094	1954

xcludes additional charges on generation of electricity under Progress of Education Act: 1947—$1,566,000; —$1,842,000; 1949—$1,582,000; 1950—$1,675,000; 1951—$1,826,000; 1952—$2,111,000; 1953—$2,362,000; and —$2,497,000.

xcludes provincial share of income tax on power utilities collected by federal government: 1951—$1,247,000; —$559,000; 1953—$910,000; and 1954—$2,120,000.

ɩ TO 1954
HIN CALENDAR YEARS
ollars)

:otor vehicles		Amusements, etc.			Property		Natural resources		Liquor Control Board (licences, profits, etc.)[d]	Fiscal years
oline ax	Motor vehicle licences and fees[b]	Amuse- ment tax	Stock transfer tax	Race track meetings[c]	Provincial land tax	Land transfer tax	Mining profits tax	Timber dues and bonuses		
—	—	—	—	—	—	—	—	1,480	—	1901
—	—	—	—	—	—	—	—	1,331	—	1902
—	—	—	—	—	—	—	—	2,307	—	1903
—	1	—	—	—	—	—	—	2,584	—	1904
—	3	—	—	—	—	—	—	2,001	—	1905
—	6	—	—	—	—	—	—	1,831	—	1906
—	8	—	—	—	—	—	27	1,151	—	1907
—	10	—	—	—	—	—	101	1,719	—	1908
—	12	—	—	—	—	—	29	815	—	1909[e]
—	24	—	—	—	—	—	109	1,727	—	1910
—	51	—	14	16	—	—	176	1,600	—	1911
—	73	—	39	17	—	—	156	1,881	—	1912
—	106	—	42	17	—	—	174	1,869	—	1913
—	149	—	25	42	—	—	73	1,567	—	1914

ncludes race track meeting licences prior to 1922.

ncludes profits of Ontario Government Dispensaries and Liquor Authority transfer fees after deductions for reserves.

'en months ended October 31.

TAB

Fiscal years	Succession duties	Corporations								Pers inco ta
		Railways	Insurance companies	Banks	Other	Paid up capital	Place of business	Net revenue	Total	
1915	1,721	716	555	199	295	—	—	—	1,765	—
1916	2,452	731	418	199	310	—	—	—	1,658	—
1917	3,228	689	444	196	303	—	—	—	1,632	—
1918	3,158	764	502	195	294	—	—	—	1,755	—
1919	3,527	639	563	187	285	—	—	—	1,674	—
1920	4,014	869	554	415	293	—	—	—	2,131	—
1921	4,822	643	673	583	305	—	—	—	2,204	—
1922	6,523	944	723	542	300	—	—	—	2,509	—
1923	3,858	360	758	567	340	—	—	—	2,025	—
1924	4,175	1,086	813	524	305	—	—	—	2,728	—
1925	5,787	721	859	525	316	—	—	—	2,421	—
1926	8,762	742	905	531	324	—	—	—	2,502	—
1927	9,469	685	986	515	444	—	—	—	2,630	—
1928	4,667	685	1,069	534	458	—	—	—	2,746	—
1929	6,610	691	1,171	539	468	—	—	—	2,869	—
1930	11,229	689	1,272	595	514	—	—	—	3,070	—
1931	9,505	735	1,328	608	509	1,490	—	—	4,670	—
1932	6,137	735	1,986	731	678	1,403	555	801	6,889	—
1933	8,081	729	1,859	720	584	1,418	486	614	6,410	—
1934	6,515	719	1,777	682	553	1,238	484	698	6,151	—
1935[f]	3,469	—	—	—	22	115	—	—	137	—
1936	11,985	718	1,804	682	596	1,614	539	1,179	7,132	—
1937	15,991	711	1,824	728	657	2,121	601	2,415	9,057	4,9
1938	20,214	706	1,880	647	618	1,983	681	1,996	8,511	6,0
1939	15,315	699	1,961	1,182	597	2,063	717	2,286	9,505	6,8
1940	11,500	886	2,034	1,028	683	1,758	713	3,398	10,500	6,5
1941	11,172	875	2,547	860	367	1,328	716	15,267	21,960	6,9
1942	11,676	—	—	—	—	—	—	17,025	22,247[i]	4,6
1943	11,636	—	—	—	—	—	—	—	– 481[g]	6
1944	13,321	—	—	—	—	—	—	—	96[i]	4
1945	12,783	—	—	—	—	—	—	—	361[i]	2
1946	12,525	—	—	—	—	—	—	—	650[i]	2
1947	15,227	—	—	—	—	—	—	—	534[i]	1
1948	17,944	966	4,381	911	25	1,291	445	36,645	44,664	
1949	15,995	973	4,950	925	44	1,983	822	51,215	60,912	
1950	14,978	1,016	5,106	934	29	2,109	877	54,295	64,366	
1951	17,828	977	5,605	955	42	2,134	885	65,863	76,461	
1952	21,652	922	6,622	964	86	2,696	1,001	82,031	94,322	
1953	19,821	—	—	—	—	—	—	—	—	
1954	20,164	—	—	—	—	—	—	—	—	

[f]Five months ended March 31.
[g]Refunds exceeded collections.
[h]Estimated.

16—*Continued*

Motor vehicles		Amusements, etc.			Property		Natural resources			
Gasoline tax	Motor vehicle licences and fees[b]	Amusement tax	Stock transfer tax	Race track meetings[c]	Provincial land tax	Land transfer tax	Mining profits tax	Timber dues and bonuses	Liquor Control Board (licences, profits, etc.)[d]	Fiscal years
—	335	—	24	42	—	—	140	1,436	—	1915
—	640	244	37	136	—	—	141	1,242	—	1916
—	931	588	39	101	—	—	1,504	1,473	—	1917
—	1,214	532	18	—	—	—	864	1,474	—	1918
—	1,580	850	34	—	—	—	553	1,536	376	1919
—	1,991	1,374	46	770	—	—	713	2,315	820	1920
—	2,945	1,458	50	770	—	163	184	3,477	702	1921
—	3,477	1,362	77	2,982	—	521	161	3,762	769[e]	1922
—	4,293	1,269	76	2,493	—	475	253	2,083	988	1923
—	4,780	1,477	63	2,643	—	496	192	3,627	877	1924
1,974	5,594	1,459	86	2,702	—	452	287	4,235	847	1925
3,376	6,371	1,523	135	2,198	1	458	411	3,715	758	1926
4,033	5,917	1,568	223	2,152	76	515	341	3,646	3,318	1927
4,607	6,387	1,187	339	1,862	158	539	356	3,649	8,710	1928
8,498	7,753	1,316	620	1,880	128	634	397	3,855	10,651	1929
10,757	5,449	1,290	267	1,667	140	439	503	2,227	10,279	1930
10,951	5,521	1,096	147	1,318	132	430	480	2,649	9,351	1931
12,341	7,306	1,017	149	1,029	120	254	515	1,760	7,279	1932
12,629	7,352	827	504	813	119	202	680	961	5,906	1933
12,961	7,982	745	705	565	131	169	1,074	1,111	6,379	1934
4,790	7,127	302	242	—	107	74	—	359	2,957	1935[f]
15,022	9,064	2,179	757	653	132	187	1,401	2,071	8,242	1936
15,762	10,824	1,919	1,421	670	179	232	1,564	2,181	9,631	1937
17,644	8,681	228	868	045	235	228	1,801	2,929	10,645	1938
18,504	7,833	—	683	662	129	225	2,728	3,351	10,318	1939
25,105	8,614	—	457	612	134	225	1,907	2,300	11,276	1940
26,608	9,233	—	279	611	170	238	2,003	3,405	12,560	1941
27,641	10,063	—	241	649	147	319	2,391	3,695	15,377	1942
20,996	7,234	—	244	805	146	373	2,263	4,449[h]	18,890	1943
19,168	9,320	—	420	1,010	159	428	1,851	4,074[h]	21,344	1944
18,913	9,399	—	680	2,235	175	630	1,420	3,606	19,612	1945
24,167	9,724	—	1,336	2,558	209	788	1,821	4,948	31,501	1946
31,260	13,174	—	1,153	3,001	204	1,084	900	6,175	36,405	1947
47,420	14,533	—	792	2,833	185	1,060	2,267	6,246	38,976	1948
52,567	15,404	6,118	874	3,325	218	1,201	2,681	6,899	40,358	1949
58,228	17,860	8,038	938	3,670	242	1,361	2,721	6,147	41,391	1950
65,040	20,817	6,290	1,645	4,149	323	1,702	3,825	5,269	43,075	1951
71,382	21,691	6,329	1,797	4,014	368	1,836	5,223	8,325	43,485	1952
77,648	26,002	6,667	1,846	3,640	393	2,049	4,377	13,718	45,691	1953
86,239	27,551	6,747	1,788	3,968	563	2,487	3,925	10,255	47,000[h]	1954

[i]Details not available.

SOURCES: *Public Accounts of the Province of Ontario; The Control and Sale of Alcoholic Beverages in Canada, 1951,* D.B.S.; and *Annual Reports,* Liquor Control Board.

TABLE

Manitoba—Principal Revenu
for Fiscal Years Eni
(thousai

Fiscal years	Succession duties	Corporations		Individuals		Motor vehicles	
		Corporation taxes	Corporation profits tax[a]	Income tax	Wage tax	Gasoline tax	Moto vehicl licence
1901	3	64	—	—	—	—	—
1902	7	64	—	—	—	—	—
1903	5	108	—	—	—	—	—
1904	13	112	—	—	—	—	—
1905	12	123	—	—	—	—	—
1906	71	159	—	—	—	—	—
1907	13	182	—	—	—	—	—
1908	43	190	—	—	—	—	2
1909	52	223	—	—	—	—	3
1910	73	228	—	—	—	—	9
1911[e]	166	238	—	—	—	—	14
1912	344	262	—	—	—	—	20
1913	268	349	—	—	—	—	35
1914	283	362	—	—	—	—	40
1915	412	415	—	—	—	—	83
1916	296	417	—	—	—	—	111
1917	306	520	—	—	—	—	178
1918	198	540	—	—	—	—	236
1919	193	651	—	—	—	—	379
1920	478	714	—	—	—	—	400
1921	299	1,111	—	—	—	—	539
1922[g]	169	613	—	—	—	—	455
1923	291	793	—	—	—	56	681
1924	456	757	—	498	—	126	784
1925[h]	592	489	—	335	—	102	418
1926	422	1,053	—	549	—	432	668
1927	757	1,049	—	478	—	446	739
1928	607	952	—	461	—	562	864
1929	733	973	—	491	—	658	962
1930	1,034	1,014	—	623	—	811	1,099
1931	452	1,058	125	872	—	1,177	1,104
1932	347	1,124	252	841	—	1,228	995
1933	267	1,457	236	1,145	—	1,483	915
1934	423	1,310	292	982	1,509	1,610	901
1935	340	1,262	235	881	1,675	1,835	1,113
1936	375	1,334	371	815	1,756	1,855	913
1937	464	1,234	593	912	1,825	2,015	1,135
1938	404	1,247	607	964	1,825	2,316	1,330
1939	605	1,287	831	853	1,066	2,537	1,265
1940	875	1,280	1,026	1,051	1,014	2,789	1,468
1941	603	1,315	1,513	1,020	1,188	2,678	1,575
1942	737	3	375	319	364	2,776	1,726
1943	543	2	164	140	199	2,034	1,473
1944	344	—	94	131	48	2,040	1,668

[a]Does not include collection by federal government of the 5 per cent corporation income tax lev from 1947 to 1951.

[b]Includes revenue of Municipal and Public Utility Board and fees levied for Unsatisfied Judgm Fund.

[c]Levied by Municipal Commission.

1 TO 1954
THIN CALENDAR YEARS
dollars)

use- ent x	Property		Natural resources		Liquor Control Board (licences, profits, etc.)[d]	Other		Fiscal years
	Supplementary revenue tax	Unoccupied land tax[c]	Forests	Mines		Public Welfare Act levy[c]	Old age pensions levy[c]	
—	—	—	—	—	—	—	—	1901
—	—	—	—	—	—	—	—	1902
—	—	—	—	—	—	—	—	1903
—	—	—	—	—	—	—	—	1904
—	—	—	—	—	—	—	—	1905
—	—	—	—	—	—	—	—	1906
—	—	—	—	—	—	—	—	1907
—	—	—	—	—	—	—	—	1908
—	—	—	—	—	—	—	—	1909
—	—	—	—	—	—	—	—	1910
—	—	—	—	—	—	—	—	1911[e]
—	—	—	—	—	—	—	—	1912
—	—	—	—	—	—	—	—	1913
—	—	—	—	—	—	—	—	1914
11[f]	—	—	—	—	—	—	—	1915
12[f]	—	—	—	—	—	—	—	1916
30[f]	—	—	—	—	—	24	—	1917
135	625	138	—	—	—	48	—	1918
284	1,039	85	—	—	—	96	—	1919
359	1,330	115	—	—	—	193	—	1920
339	1,514	283	—	—	—	225	—	1921
199	1,150	200	—	—	95	150	—	1922[g]
272	1,417	299	—	—	151	226	—	1923
283	1,391	38	—	—	1,346	220	—	1924
194	895	30	—	—	982	151	—	1925[h]
356	1,326	40	—	—	1,315	230	—	1926
459	1,160	24	—	—	1,367	230	—	1927
379	624	21	—	—	1,345	245	—	1928
414	291	16	—	—	1,993	281	315	1929
433	425	14	—	—	2,045	384	616	1930
352	—	7	90	38	1,867	325	345	1931
254	—	—	105	36	1,490	—	263	1932
182	—	—	125	37	1,094	—	308	1933
156	—	—	143	52	992	—	395	1934
123	—	1	190	83	1,086	—	380	1935
161	14	—	195	54	1,293	20	274	1936
159	—	1	232	75	1,512	—	344	1937
175	—	—	261	55	1,753	—	378	1938
173	—	—	206	40	1,742	—	384	1939
198	—	—	231	33	1,781	—	392	1940
155	—	—	304	28	2,056	—	406	1941
156	—	—	293	26	2,740	—	441	1942
186	—	—	309	41	3,739	—	443	1943
246	—	—	346	50	3,831	—	476	1944

Includes profits of liquor vendor. Excludes fines and penalties and revenue allocated to enforcement enditure.

Eleven months ended November 30.

Tax imposed under The Theatre and Automatic Vending Machines Tax Act.

Nine months ended August 31.

TABLE

Fiscal years	Succession duties	Corporations		Individuals		Motor vehicles	
		Corporation taxes	Corporation profits tax[a]	Income tax	Wage tax	Gasoline tax	Motor vehicle licences[b]
1945	667	—	79	126	—	2,040	1,614
1946	767	—	69	43	—	2,681	1,788
1947[i]	809	—	34	32	—	3,036	1,658
1948	403	—	—	45	—	4,567	2,237
1949	92	—	—	30	—	4,890	2,467
1950	32	—	—	39	—	5,466	2,861
1951	28	—	—	23	—	5,901	3,286
1952	15	—	—	16	—	6,678	4,028
1953	8	—	—	4	—	7,423	4,065
1954	5	—	—	—	—	8,145	5,117

[h]Eight months ended April 30.
[i]Eleven months ended March 31.

TABLE 1

SASKATCHEWAN—PRINCIPAL REVE
FOR FISCAL YEARS ENDE
(thousand

Fiscal years	Succession duties	Corporations		Income tax[b]	Motor vehicles		Sales and bets	
		Corporation taxes	Railway tax		Gasoline tax	Motor vehicle licences	Pari-mutuel bets tax	Education and hospitalization taxes (retail sales)
1907[f]	2	—	—	—	—	—	—	—
1908	4	28	—	—	—	1	—	—
1909	3	35	—	—	—	—	—	—
1910	28	40	145[g]	—	—	1	—	—
1911	40	51	64	—	—	5	—	—
1912	34	63	64	—	—	13	—	—
1913	46	92	69	—	—	35	—	—
1914[h]	74	187	71	—	—	49	—	—
1915	64	204	143	—	—	66	—	—
1916	44	167	87	—	—	111	—	—
1917	70	189	115	—	—	252	—	—
1918	116	210	109	—	—	625	—	—
1919	145	195	131	—	—	744	—	—
1920	271	422	156	—	—	693	—	—
1921	324	417	107	—	—	946	—	—
1922	309	464	139	—	—	701	—	—
1923	276	507	271	—	—	1,003	—	—
1924	484	465	200	—	—	1,342	—	—

[a]Excludes hospitalization premiums of: 1948, $3,641,000; 1949, $3,617,000; 1950, $5,535,000 1951, $5,708,000; 1952, $5,810,000; 1953, $5,860,000; and 1954, $5,885,000.

[b]Consists of corporation and individual income taxes. Does not include collections by federal govern ment of the 5 per cent corporation income tax levied from 1947 to 1951.

[c]Does not include land titles assurance fees.

7—*Continued*

muse-ment tax	Property		Natural resources		Liquor Control Board (licences, profits, etc.)[d]	Other		Fiscal years
	Supplementary revenue tax	Unoccupied land tax[c]	Forests	Mines		Public Welfare Act levy[c]	Old age pensions levy[c]	
275	—	—	451	56	4,379	—	496	1945
507	—	—	375	68	6,101	—	515	1946
589	—	—	391	89	6,527	—	499	1947[i]
635	—	—	587	126	6,989	—	650	1948
900	—	—	567	599	7,291	—	788	1949
980	—	—	519	408	7,651	—	36	1950
979	—	—	669	669	7,958	—	—	1951
1,116	—	—	1,014	609	8,096	—	—	1952
1,215	—	—	1,038	554	8,481	—	—	1953
1,248	—	—	983	449	8,622	—	—	1954

SOURCES: *Public Accounts of the Province of Manitoba;* and *The Control and Sale of Alcoholic Beverages* *Canada, 1951*, D.B.S.

ES,[a] 1907 TO 1954
ITHIN CALENDAR YEARS
f dollars)

Property				Natural resources		Liquor Control Board (licences, profits, etc.)[e]	Fiscal years
Public revenue tax	Supplementary revenue tax	Wild lands tax	Land titles Act fees[c]	Forests	Mines[d]		
—	—	—	46	—	—	—	1907[f]
—	85	—	144	—	—	—	1908
—	254	—	191	—	—	—	1909
—	340	—	201	—	—	—	1910
—	321	—	268	—	—	—	1911
—	336	—	352	—	—	—	1912
—	385	—	452	—	—	—	1913
—	572	—	745	—	—	—	1914[h]
—	418	—	491	—	—	—	1915
—	564	—	337	—	—	200	1916
—	564	—	415	—	—	415	1917
929	607	—	466	—	—	656	1918
1,521	510	575	522	—	—	—	1919
1,729	495	1,033	620	—	—	—	1920
1,776	493	751	697	—	—	—	1921
1,819	596	680	602	—	—	—	1922
2,101	68	728	573	—	—	—	1923
2,242	47	710	548	—	—	—	1924

[d]Includes coal and mineral taxes.

[e]Includes revenue from Saskatchewan Liquor Store System. Excludes fines and revenue allocated o enforcement expenditures.

[f]Fourteen months ended February 28.

[g]Three years' revenue. [h]Fourteen months ended April 30.

Fiscal years	Succession duties	Corporations: Corporation taxes	Corporations: Railway tax	Income tax	Motor vehicles: Gasoline tax	Motor vehicles: Motor vehicle licences	Sales and bets: Pari-mutuel bets tax	Sales and bets: Education hospitalizat taxes (retail sal
1925	283	515	207	—	—	1,297	—	—
1926	333	488	349	—	—	1,718	—	—
1927	290	516	349	—	—	1,510	—	—
1928	363	508	349	—	—	2,266	—	—
1929	405	566	484	—	1,300	2,434	—	—
1930	463	582	404	—	982	2,018	—	—
1931	318	583	404	—	1,919	1,887	—	—
1932	199	521	190	—	1,211	1,067	—	—
1933	177	752	618	404	1,395	1,629	—	—
1934	149	705	404	372	1,421	1,572	—	—
1935	223	588	—	297	1,499	1,384	—	—
1936	324	615	808	425	1,749	1,542	13	—
1937	311	571	404	551	2,098	1,895	14	—
1938	241	519	404	634	1,995	1,581	14	1,292
1939	376	494	404	660	1,876	1,691	16	2,342
1940	352	735	404	728	3,000	2,142	19	2,716
1941	262	498	404	1,176	3,293	1,982	21	3,184
1942	330	222	—	1,306	3,758	2,721	19	3,806
1943	393	2	—	93	2,902	1,467	19	3,748
1944	454	—	—	62	3,272	2,785	22	4,228
1945	463	—	—	4	3,385	2,369	30	4,895
1946	618	—	—	16	4,390	1,917	35	5,592
1947[i]	641	—	—	8	4,724	1,638	42	5,433
1948	475	—	—	1	6,399	3,084	39	6,190
1949	101	1	—	44	6,642	3,343	40	6,820
1950	23	—	—	—	7,881	3,521	44	7,597
1951	127	—	—	—	8,331	3,802	42	11,185
1952	30	—	—	—	9,388	4,599	51	12,932
1953	13	—	—	—	11,759	4,761	56	15,629
1954	23	—	—	—	14,088	5,394	58	17,941

[i]Eleven months ended March 31.
[j]Includes transfer of Public Revenue Tax Reserve moneys held in suspense.

–*Continued*

Property				Natural resources			
ublic revenue tax	Supplementary revenue tax	Wild lands tax	Land titles Act fees[c]	Forests	Mines[d]	Liquor Control Board (licences, profits, etc.)[e]	Fiscal years
359	34	708	493	—	—	—	1925
449	20	604	501	—	—	1,930	1926
394	20	492	523	—	—	2,130	1927
971	21	389	536	—	—	2,458	1928
787	25	309	543	—	—	3,097	1929
727	10	232	479	—	—	2,406	1930
254	2	174	396	131	27	1,537	1931
021	1	133	278	169	56	873	1932
390	1	112	189	126	40	866	1933
484	—	50	163	109	49	920	1934
562	—	43	153	154	51	1,029	1935
666	—	27	190	218	74	1,280	1936
728	1	12	202	225	64	1,453	1937
959	—	6	150	286	88	1,247	1938
355	—	4	137	241	44	1,291	1939
155	—	5	165	312	47	1,706	1940
609	—	4	182	410	74	1,941	1941
787	—	5	203	551	88	2,407	1942
052	—	5	229	667	190	3,031	1943
215	—	8	356	692	224	3,661	1944
091	—	10	524	724	209	4,163	1945
158	—	14	489	583	889	6,605	1946
975	—	15	411	511	1,138	8,105	1947[i]
086[j]	—	6	390	634	1,428	7,920	1948
177[j]	—	2	398	675	1,514	8,546	1949
866[j]	—	3	582	588	1,771	8,891	1950
966[j]	—	—	569	629	1,859	8,720	1951
060[j]	—	3	658	742	2,880	9,596	1952
173[j]	—	1	640	621	4,059	10,993	1953
290	—	—	647	615	6,802	11,332	1954

OURCES: *Public Accounts of the Province of Saskatchewan;* and *The Control and Sale of Alcoholic rages in Canada, 1951,* D.B.S.

TABLE

ALBERTA—PRINCIPAL REV
FOR FISCAL YEARS END
(thousan

Fiscal years	Succession duties	Corporation taxes[a]	Income tax[b]	Motor vehicles: Gasoline taxes[c]	Motor vehicles: Motor vehicle licences[d]	Motor vehicles: Mileage tax (public service vehicles)	Sales, amusements, etc.: Amusements tax	Sales, amusements, etc.: Pari-mutuel bets	Sales, amusements, etc.: Sales tax	Sales, amusements, etc.: Unearn increme tax
1906	1	—	—	—	1	—	—	—	—	—
1907	—	152	—	—	2	—	—	—	—	—
1908	2	119	—	—	1	—	—	—	—	—
1909	10	109	—	—	5	—	—	—	—	—
1910	5	17	—	—	1	—	—	—	—	—
1911	31	134	—	—	4	—	—	—	—	—
1912	54	158	—	—	31	—	—	—	—	—
1913	67	171	—	—	46	—	—	—	—	5
1914	72	205	—	—	60	—	—	—	—	36
1915	110	208	—	—	106	—	—	—	—	—
1916	152	292	—	—	130	—	39	—	—	—
1917	147	320	—	—	270	—	77	—	—	—
1918	205	362	—	—	535	—	90	—	—	—
1919	174	379	—	—	611	—	144	—	—	—
1920	273	419	—	—	682	—	170	—	—	—
1921	177	452	—	—	719	—	181	—	—	—
1922	128	651	—	185	716	—	184	—	—	73
1923	164	725	—	241	743	—	204	—	—	54
1924	190	771	—	294	848	—	193	—	—	55
1925	460	690	—	311	954	—	193	—	—	68
1926	254	845	—	424	1,153	—	201	—	—	76
1928[h]	587	843	—	803	2,104	—	254	105	—	120
1929	383	821	—	1,307	2,125	—	246	101	—	138
1930	897	946	—	1,793	2,023	—	257	90	—	133
1931	553	977	—	1,932	1,694	—	163	78	—	62
1932	258	982	—	1,501	1,474	—	109	66	—	20
1933	471	1,174	650	1,517	1,553	—	118	41	—	16
1934	257	1,009	615	1,724	1,668	—	116	33	—	10
1935	293	998	470	1,945	1,618	—	121	28	—	16
1936	271	1,042	683	2,221	1,425	—	132	26	—	16
1937	343	1,074	1,065	2,455	1,112	—	137	21	947	16
1938	1,326	1,430	1,190	2,610	1,908	37	141	23	601	15
1939	372	1,566	1,467	2,953	2,186	46	158	27	68	24
1940	375	1,557	1,795	3,097	2,424	54	176	28	1	25
1941	415	1,515	2,205	3,222	2,574	53	180	28	—	28
1942	673	1,408	2,241	4,212	2,813	56	196	23	—	40
1943	459	6	426	3,525	2,851	59	236	18	—	41
1944	686	2	318	3,646	3,013	45	297	20	—	70
1945	903	1	240	3,808	3,072	48	311	57	—	159
1946	1,130	1	20	4,463	3,192	73	327	78	—	210
1947	855	2	29	5,404	3,550	140	339	96	—	356

[a]Includes railway taxes.

[b]Consists of individual and corporation income taxes. Does not include collections by federal government of 5 cent corporation income tax levied from 1947 to 1951.

[c]Includes fuel oil tax.

ES, 1906 TO 1954
ITHIN CALENDAR YEARS
f dollars)

Property						Natural resources						
Social service tax	Education tax[e]	Wild lands tax	Power lines tax	Pipe lines tax	Land Titles Act[f]	Timber areas tax	Mineral tax	Coal mine owner's tax	Fees, rents & royalties from minerals & petroleum	Timber fees, dues, & rentals	Liquor Control Board (licences, profits, etc.)[g]	Fiscal years
—	—	—	—	—	—	—	—	—	—	—	—	1906
—	—	—	—	—	132	—	—	—	—	—	—	1907
—	90	—	—	—	131	—	—	—	—	—	—	1908
—	91	—	—	—	135	—	—	—	—	—	—	1909
—	47	—	—	—	60	—	—	—	—	—	—	1910
—	—	—	—	—	239	—	—	—	—	—	—	1911
—	255	—	—	—	413	—	—	—	—	—	—	1912
—	81	—	—	—	471	—	—	—	—	—	—	1913
—	107	—	—	—	349	—	—	—	—	—	—	1914
—	130	157	—	—	261	18	—	—	—	—	—	1915
—	154	236	—	—	242	7	—	—	—	—	—	1916
—	134	599	—	—	284	12	—	7	—	—	—	1917
613	158	350	—	—	371	14	—	131	—	—	—	1918
782	113	734	—	—	492	9	—	208	—	—	292	1919
1,469	161	827	—	—	503	5	—	281	—	—	500	1920
1,102	127	652	—	—	439	4	—	276	—	—	250	1921
1,164	204	397	—	—	341	9	—	283	—	—	900	1922
1,561	241	547	—	—	310	7	—	247	—	—	1,033	1923
1,522	232	470	—	—	287	11	—	194	—	—	1,222	1924
1,489	199	509	—	—	278	21	—	250	—	—	1,672	1925
1,277	166	370	—	—	295	26	—	274	—	—	1,935	1926
1,184	169	357	—	—	395	6	—	42	—	—	2,785	1928[h]
1,166	150	295	—	—	373	11	—	3	—	—	2,856	1929
1,019	130	236	—	—	333	6	—	1	—	—	2,598	1930
828	103	156	—	—	291	5	—	—	371	122	1,888	1931
791	72	116	19	—	214	5	—	—	441	180	1,423	1932
797	63	106	59	—	167	2	—	—	388	127	1,412	1933
786	65	87	30	9	139	6	—	—	477	157	1,269	1934
915	69	45	30	30	138	14	—	—	473	227	1,538	1935
860	67	57	29	19	150	9	—	—	540	304	1,855	1936
1,150	58	14	31	20	142	9	—	—	751	331	2,391	1937
1,158	49	10	60	41	142	—	—	—	819	360	2,594	1938
1,394	45	24	32	46	158	—	48	—	1,033	298	2,740	1939
1,248	39	27	56	53	157	—	48	—	1,050	360	2,937	1940
1,169	30	22	43	56	161	—	48	—	945	612	3,207	1941
1,266	30	23	46	64	184	—	75	—	1,073	732	3,898	1942
1,314	38	27	—	1	194	2	94	—	1,216	777	5,050	1943
1,464	37	25	—	—	272	—	102	—	1,112	843	5,356	1944
1,206	14	18	—	—	371	—	93	—	1,663	844	6,026	1945
1,155	42	30	—	—	394	—	160	—	1,360	1,003	8,249	1946
1,083	28	26	—	—	437	—	357	—	1,236	1,260	9,705	1947

[d]Does not include fees collected for Unsatisfied Judgment Fund.
[e]In early years represents transfers from education tax trust accounts.
[f]General fees.
[g]Includes amounts transferred from Alberta Government Liquor Business. Excludes fines and confiscations.

TAB

Fiscal years	Succession duties	Corporation taxes[a]	Income tax[b]	Motor vehicles			Sales, amusements, etc.			
				Gasoline taxes[c]	Motor vehicle licences[d]	Mileage tax (public service vehicles)	Amuse-ments tax	Pari-mutuel bets	Sales tax	Unearn increme tax
1948	652	—	3	7,658	4,121	125	373	93	—	356
1949	149	—	14	8,578	4,776	134	441	113	—	427
1950	98	—	7	10,365	5,597	146	645	129	—	757
1951	101	—	6	11,609	6,384	159	695	140	—	737
1952	26	—	10	12,766	6,473	154	801	156	—	978
1953	37	—	—	15,379	7,502	162	938	297	—	1,025
1954	17	—	—	17,315	8,507	149	1,057	341	—	1,034

[h]Fifteen months ended March 31.

[i]Excludes revenue from auction of oil leases: 1949, $8,721,000; 1950, $23,181,000; 1951, $28,008,000; 1952, $12,518,000; 1953, $19,659,000; and 1954, $49,590,000.

—*Continued*

ial ice x		Property				Natural resources					Liquor Control Board (licences, profits, etc.)[g]	Fiscal years
	Educa-tion tax[e]	Wild lands tax	Power lines tax	Pipe lines tax	Land titles Act[f]	Timber areas tax	Mineral tax	Coal mine owner's tax	Fees, rents & royalties from minerals & petroleum	Timber fees, dues, & rentals		
14	27	20	—	—	450	—	474	—	1,891	1,539	9,971	1948
1	22	12	—	—	445	—	566	—	4,602[i]	1,640	11,199	1949
–	26	5	—	—	533	—	751	—	8,981[i]	1,557	11,979	1950
–	21	—	—	2	561	—	834	—	14,664[i]	2,030	12,194	1951
–	20	—	—	—	558	—	770	—	24,868[i]	2,227	13,086	1952
–	12	—	—	—	621	—	886	—	31,115[i]	2,993	14,960	1953
–	27	—	—	—	644	—	1,002	—	40,556[i]	2,747	15,436	1954

OURCES: *Public Accounts of the Province of Alberta;* and *The Control and Sale of Alcoholic Beverages in Canada, 1951,* .S.

TABLE 2

BRITISH COLUMBIA—PRINCIPA
FOR FISCAL YEARS ENDI
(thousand

Fiscal years	Successions		Income tax[b]	Individuals		Motor vehicles		Sales, amusements, etc.			
	Succession duties	Probate fees		Poll tax	Chinese revenue	Gasoline tax	Motor vehicle licences[c]	Amusements tax	Fuel oil tax	Race-tracks tax	Social security and municip aid tax
1871	—	—	—	—	—	—	—	—	—	—	—
1872	—	—	—	—	—	—	—	—	—	—	—
1873	—	—	—	—	—	—	—	—	—	—	—
1874	—	—	—	—	—	—	—	—	—	—	—
1875	—	—	—	—	—	—	—	—	—	—	—
1876	—	—	—	—	—	—	—	—	—	—	—
1877	—	—	1	—	—	—	—	—	—	—	—
1878	—	—	1	—	—	—	—	—	—	—	—
1879[f]	—	—	1	—	—	—	—	—	—	—	—
1880	—	—	1	—	—	—	—	—	—	—	—
1881	—	—	1	—	—	—	—	—	—	—	—
1882	—	—	1	29	—	—	—	—	—	—	—
1883	—	—	1	48	—	—	—	—	—	—	—
1884	—	—	1	49	—	—	—	—	—	—	—
1885	—	—	1	64	2	—	—	—	—	—	—
1886	—	—	1	66	—	—	—	—	—	—	—
1887	—	2	2	63	3	—	—	—	—	—	—
1888	—	3	3	53	1	—	—	—	—	—	—
1889	—	1	3	54	4	—	—	—	—	—	—
1890	—	3	5	55	10	—	—	—	—	—	—
1891	—	8	6	74	13	—	—	—	—	—	—
1892	—	3	7	43	26	—	—	—	—	—	—
1893	—	6	8	40	41	—	—	—	—	—	—
1894	—	5	6	45	27	—	—	—	—	—	—
1895	1	7	6	52	25	—	—	—	—	—	—
1896	8	5	6	59	17	—	—	—	—	—	—
1897	2	3	8	65	21	—	—	—	—	—	—
1898	3	6	9	85	30	—	—	—	—	—	—
1899	2	4	10	104	26	—	—	—	—	—	—
1900	19	12	18	96	53	—	—	—	—	—	—
1901	21	5	28	101	47	—	—	—	—	—	—
1902	64	7	47	138	41	—	—	—	—	—	—
1903	12	9	29	143	86	—	—	—	—	—	—
1904	30	12	72	149	258	—	—	—	—	—	—
1905	31	11	72	158	225	—	—	—	—	—	—
1906	30	6	84	180	—	—	—	—	—	—	—
1907	50	13	114	194	19	—	—	—	—	—	—
1908	35	8	153	208	345	—	—	—	—	—	—
1909[g]	78	15	16	154	305	—	—	—	—	—	—
1910	108	19	191	261	356	—	—	—	—	—	—
1911	200	37	193	313	1,066	—	—	—	—	—	—
1912	152	30	241	381	1,433	—	—	—	—	—	—

[a]Excludes hospitalization premiums of: 1949, \$6,092,000; 1950, \$10,660,000; 1951, \$11,439,000; 1952, \$15,303,00 1953, \$14,882,000; and 1954, \$14,149,000.

[b]Includes individual and corporation income taxes and other corporation taxes, but does not include collectio by federal government of 5 per cent corporation income tax levied from 1947 to 1951.

[c]Includes receipts *re* Public Utilities Act and Motor Carrier Act.

EVENUES,[a] 1871 TO 1954
ITHIN CALENDAR YEARS
dollars)

Property			Natural resources					
Land tax	Wild lands tax[d]	Personal property tax	Royalties, rentals, etc. (mainly timber)	Sales of land and timber	Coal and coke tax	Mineral output tax	Liquor Control Board (licences, profits, etc.)[e]	Fiscal years
—	—	—	11	11	—	—	—	1871
—	—	—	14	6	—	—	—	1872
—	1	—	12	12	—	—	—	1873
—	3	—	14	25	—	—	—	1874
—	1	—	12	21	—	—	—	1875
9	2	8	13	18	—	—	—	1876
25	8	13	12	23	—	—	—	1877
26	10	12	13	41	—	—	—	1878
11	7	11	4	26	—	—	—	1879[f]
11	5	11	10	22	—	—	—	1880
13	6	14	11	17	—	—	—	1881
12	6	13	9	24	—	—	—	1882
12	5	14	7	26	—	—	—	1883
15	5	15	13	92	—	—	—	1884
18	8	17	11	175	—	—	—	1885
22	8	17	16	78	—	—	—	1886
40	9	22	23	89	—	—	—	1887
47	14	35	32	81	—	—	—	1888
75	16	40	39	143	—	—	—	1889
77	21	45	40	245	—	—	—	1890
98	26	55	64	244	—	—	—	1891
97	53	69	68	214	—	—	—	1892
81	38	85	56	180	—	—	—	1893
67	36	85	75	34	—	—	—	1894
78	35	94	115	26	—	—	—	1895
93	36	84	143	64	—	—	—	1896
106	42	108	261	86	—	30	—	1897
109	62	112	274	104	—	36	—	1898
120	47	115	286	74	—	34	—	1899
118	49	73	365	53	6	32	—	1900
122	48	92	305	43	85	95	—	1901
130	51	90	348	86	86	84	—	1902
205	71	94	518	65	76	78	—	1903
287	112	175	570	118	96	66	—	1904
286	102	193	751	142	95	114	—	1905
302	101	135	846	189	108	162	—	1906
264	118	129	1,559	663	107	152	—	1907
269	194	135	2,579	548	126	113	—	1908
49	37	23	2,120	529	143	82	—	1909[g]
336	251	162	2,609	2,618	223	103	—	1910
352	316	179	2,919	2,431	248	91	—	1911
298	428	257	2,874	1,805	195	101	—	1912

[d]Includes coal and timber land taxes.

[e]Includes profits on liquor sold under Prohibition Act. Excludes fines and penalties, confiscations and revenue xpended for enforcement.

[f]Six months ended June 30.

[g]Nine months ended March 31.

Fiscal years	Successions		Income tax[b]	Individuals		Motor vehicles		Sales, amusements, etc.			
	Succession duties	Probate fees		Poll tax	Chinese revenue	Gasoline tax	Motor vehicle licences[c]	Amuse-ments tax	Fuel oil tax	Race-tracks tax	Soc secu an muni aid
1913	194	44	280	361	1,724	—	—	—	—	—	—
1914	249	45	348	4	1,279	—	99	—	—	—	—
1915	162	40	429	—	252	—	110	—	—	—	—
1916	140	65	329	—	—	—	95	—	—	—	—
1917	278	73	297	—	—	—	134	—	—	—	—
1918	241	49	671	330	—	—	193	124	—	—	—
1919	272	48	1,507	283	—	—	246	221	—	—	—
1920	374	77	2,013	256	—	—	354	320	—	—	—
1921	342	65	2,006	263	—	—	582	347	—	—	—
1922	564	70	2,911	168	—	—	803	318	—	—	—
1923	683	58	2,527	152	—	—	975	290	—	193	—
1924	773	82	2,762	166	—	51	1,048	274	28	227	—
1925	709	55	3,476	172	—	477	1,126	235	130	313	—
1926	565	122	3,450	123	—	579	1,371	245	81	170	—
1927	702	65	3,559	128	—	680	1,614	259	2	181	—
1928	758	105	4,723	132	—	784	1,772	197	—	210	—
1929	736	97	4,399[h]	119	—	905	2,007	209	—	220	—
1930	837	169	5,457[h]	147	—	1,086	2,239	221	—	217	—
1931	559	140	5,291[h]	118	—	1,753	2,189	206	—	180	—
1932	411	90	5,524[h]	83	—	1,749	1,985	172	—	169	—
1933	536	129	5,510	35	—	2,042	1,888	170	26	183	—
1934	383	95	4,655	16	—	2,055	1,943	161	543	123	—
1935	979	101	5,139[h]	16	—	2,264	2,093	176	458	128	—
1936	1,067	138	5,987[h]	13	—	2,530	2,294	195	484	135	—
1937	825	147	6,777[h]	66	—	2,720	2,627	209	483	146	—
1938	1,261	163	7,343[h]	63	—	3,163	2,871	220	508	169	—
1939	704	100	10,003	58	—	3,284	2,851	216	423	172	—
1940	1,162	228	8,124	54	—	3,455	3,257	222	461	162	—
1941	889	125	10,535	53	—	3,760	3,485	237	513	169	—
1942	761	128	705	40	—	4,006	3,471	247	558	150	—
1943	818	177	—	101	—	3,283	3,252	298	524	181	—
1944	1,450	171	—	93	—	3,139	3,295	359	508	383	—
1945	1,871	270	—	66	—	3,257	3,212	362	533	421	—
1946	1,723	275	—	54	—	4,331	3,486	400	593	468	—
1947	2,919	284	—	65	—	5,682	4,856	440	802	525	—
1948	1,049	200	—	75	—	9,296	5,945	478	971	607	—
1949	398	97	—	85	—	10,191	6,547	1,949	1,006	774	14,3
1950	161	96	—	88	—	11,222	7,464	2,366	1,009	800	24,6
1951	—	95	—	94	—	12,714	9,336	1,790	1,068	745	28,8
1952	—	116	—	83	—	13,839	9,702	1,999	1,243	807	31,4
1953	—	110	—	—	—	15,462	10,189	2,238	1,221	898	34,2
1954	—	127	—	—	—	16,988	10,377	2,378	1,375	959	35,4

[h]Includes personal property taxes.

[i]Does not include E. and N. Railway Belt land taxes: 1951, $345,000; 1952, $972,000; and 1953, $418,000; 1954, $863,000.

–*Continued*

	Property		Natural resources					
ınd ax	Wild lands tax[d]	Personal property tax	Royalties, rentals, etc. (mainly timber)	Sales of land and timber	Coal and coke tax	Mineral output tax	Liquor Control Board (licences, profits, etc.)[e]	Fiscal years
460	546	198	3,013	2,345	302	155	—	1913
501	659	212	2,950	1,173	193	154	—	1914
515	646	260	2,083	797	159	131	—	1915
493	534	279	1,834	192	173	163	—	1916
532	521	291	2,053	304	195	287	—	1917
014	691	521	2,117	529	192	294	17	1918
991	792	800	2,602	282	197	229	97	1919
149	1,132	954	2,457	530	195	158	653	1920
046	862	910	3,338	682	216	119	223	1921
995	693	626	2,803	778	221	100	2,367	1922
333	753	863	3,374	701	227	153	2,642	1923
296	745	899	3,263	740	179	189	3,207	1924
101	715	515	3,230	792	151	316	2,847	1925
755	808	593	3,302	842	198	474	3,493	1926
750	811	487	3,403	876	197	525	3,636	1927
469	767	55	3,408	871	211	391	3,940	1928
469	676	—	3,270	936	190	415	4,376	1929
479	633	—	3,233	995	172	498	4,837	1930
439	690	—	2,881	664	153	308	4,191	1931
431	544	—	2,428	576	139	78	3,422	1932
548	450	2	1,989	348	117	72	2,322	1933
392	439	2	2,017	337	102	155	2,314	1934
445	443	—	2,506	388	107	279	2,487	1935
435	420	—	3,008	433	93	403	3,062	1936
508	425	—	3,139	530	94	536	3,607	1937
559	419	—	3,244	703	101	809	4,095	1938
642	415	—	2,983	648	101	582	3,892	1939
661	452	—	3,121	805	155	716	4,457	1940
571	365	—	3,363	886	137	825	4,841	1941
862	351	—	3,713	1,093	144	806	5,928	1942
865	342	—	3,095	1,154	173	939	8,146	1943
933	337	—	3,050	1,430	163	714	6,946	1944
946	363	—	3,177	1,700	164	444	7,882	1945
947	388	—	3,303	2,053	127	562	11,194	1946
830	382	—	3,591	2,740	117	821	14,759	1947
072	394	—	4,426	3,942	110	1,215	16,608	1948
223	681	—	4,394	4,814	—	228	18,086	1949
697	662	—	4,155	5,545	—	1,914	17,931	1950
674[i]	662	—	4,369	7,307	—	1,273	18,789	1951
962[i]	710	—	4,843	11,155	—	1,372	19,875	1952
129[i]	821	—	6,162	15,895	—	2,126	20,764	1953
330[i]	130	—	6,544	15,390	—	1,562	21,260	1954

OURCE: *Public Accounts of the Province of British Columbia.*

TABLE 21

STATUTORY SUBSIDIES, GRANTS, AND CONDITIONAL SUBSIDIES PAYMENTS TO PROVINCES, 1868–1939
(millions of dollars)

Fiscal years[a]	Statutory subsidies	Special grants	Conditional subsidies				Total
			Old age & blind pensions	Relief	Other	Total	
1868–1912	203.5	—	—	—	—	—	203.5
1913	13.2	—	—	—	.5	.5	13.7
1914	11.3	—	—	—	.7	.7	12.0
1915	11.5	—	—	—	.8	.8	12.3
1916	11.5	—	—	—	.9	.9	12.4
1917	11.5	—	—	—	1.0	1.0	12.5
1918	11.4	—	—	—	1.1	1.1	12.5
1919	11.3	—	—	—	1.0	1.0	12.3
1920	11.5	—	—	—	1.7	1.7	13.2
1921	11.5	—	—	.3	2.6	2.9	14.4
1922	12.2	—	—	.5	5.6	6.1	18.3
1923	12.2	—	—	.9	8.1	9.0	21.2
1924	12.4	—	—	—	6.2	6.2	18.6
1925	12.3	—	—	—	4.1	4.1	16.4
1926	12.4	—	—	—	2.9	2.9	15.3
1927	12.5	—	—	.7	1.7	2.4	14.9
1928	12.5	1.6	.1	—	2.5	2.6	16.7
1929	12.6	1.6	.8	—	1.5	2.3	16.5
1930	12.5	1.6	1.5	—	.7	2.2	16.3
1931	17.4	1.6	5.6	3.2	.7	9.5	28.5
1932	13.7	1.6	10.0	33.5	.6	44.1	59.4
1933	13.7	1.6	11.5	33.8	.4	45.7	61.0
1934	13.7	1.6	12.3	28.0	.3	40.6	55.9
1935	13.8	1.6	14.9	43.4	.3	58.6	74.0
1936	13.8	4.0	16.8	40.7	.3	57.8	75.6
1937	13.7	3.2	21.1	51.5	.3	72.9	89.8
1938	13.7	8.1[b]	28.7	53.1	.7	82.5	104.3
1939	13.7	8.1[b]	29.0	33.8	1.0	63.8	85.6

[a]Ended March 31.
[b]Includes $600,000 awarded to Alberta in 1945.

TABLE 22

SUBSIDIES, GRANTS, TAX AGREEMENTS AND CONDITIONAL SUBSIDIES PAYMENTS TO THE PROVINCES FOR FISCAL YEARS ENDED MARCH 31, 1940 TO 1953
(millions of dollars)

Fiscal years	Statutory subsidies	Special grants	Wartime tax agreements	Gasoline revenue guarantee	1947 tax agreements[a]	5% provincial corporation income tax	Provincial share of utilities tax	Conditional subsidies: Old age and blind persons	Conditional subsidies: Relief	Conditional subsidies: Other	Conditional subsidies: Sub-total	Total pay-ment
1940	13.8	6.1[b]	—	—	—	—	—	30.0	29.3	1.2	60.5	80.4
1941	13.8	6.1[b]	—	—	—	—	—	30.0	16.6	2.9	49.5	69.4
1942	14.4	—	21.1	—	—	—	—	29.6	1.7	6.8	38.1	73.6
1943	14.5	—	85.9	8.3	—	—	—	30.0	.2	7.4	37.6	146.3
1944	14.4	—	83.7	11.8	—	—	—	33.4	.1	7.0	40.5	150.4
1945	14.4	—	83.0	10.4	—	—	—	41.0	—	4.6	45.6	153.4
1946	14.4	—	91.9	3.7	—	—	—	42.8	—	7.3	50.1	160.1
1947	14.4	—	88.4	—	6.0	—	—	45.4	—	15.3	60.7	169.5
1948	17.3	—	63.0	—	59.5	—	—	59.1	—	11.3	70.4	210.2
1949	17.1	—	—	—	84.4	—	—	66.8	5.0[c]	17.0	88.8	190.3
1950	19.2	6.5[d]	—	—	76.9	20.2	1.4	93.2	—	22.3	115.5	239.7
1951	18.7	6.5[d]	—	—	94.1	17.4	4.6	103.2	13.7[e]	32.2[f]	149.1	290.4
1952	20.1	6.5[d]	—	—	96.9	25.1	3.7	83.2	1.3[g]	45.1[f]	129.6	281.9
1953	20.1	5.6[d]	—	—	308.6[h]	[i]	4.4	22.1	.3[g]	49.8[f]	72.2	410.9

[a]After deducting offsets for collections under provincial corporation income taxes.
[b]Includes $600,000 awarded to Alberta in 1945.
[c]Fraser Valley flood relief (but does not include $4.5 million grant to Fraser Valley Dyking Board).
[d]Transitional grants to Newfoundland.
[e]Includes payments of $12.5 million to Manitoba *re* Red River flood and $1.2 million to Quebec *re* Rimouski and Cabano fires.
[f]Includes $7.2 million (1951), $12.8 million (1952) and $14 million (1953) *re* Trans-Canada Highway.
[g]Federal government's share of Rimouski and Cabano fires claims.
[h]Includes $284.8 million *re* 1952 Tax Agreements.
[i]The remaining liability of $91.8 million under this account was considered revenue of the federal government subsequent to agreements provided for by the Tax Rental Agreement Act, 1952.

SOURCE: *Public Accounts of Canada.*

TABLE

Assessed Valuations on which Taxes were Levied for Select

(thousa

Years	Halifax	Saint John	Montreal[b]	Quebec[b]	Toronto	Hamilt
1901	[d]	25,151	150,480	19,100	[d]	26,0
1902	[d]	[d]	154,594	20,211	[d]	26,7
1903	[d]	25,742	158,616	20,888	[d]	26,9
1904	[d]	25,654	163,269	21,677	[d]	27,0
1905	[d]	26,076	172,630	21,677	148,819	29,1
1906	[d]	26,542	200,965	23,771	167,862	32,3
1907	[d]	27,497	216,841	23,771	185,263	34,5
1908	[d]	28,689	234,823	27,110	206,385	37,1
1909	[d]	28,222	259,454	33,333	233,953	39,8
1910	[d]	28,952	319,342	38,424	270,086	42,1
1911	[d]	29,842	381,148	51,187	306,752	47,3
1912	[d]	30,625	500,217	55,268	343,740	53,1
1913	[d]	33,197	611,063	58,223	436,330	67,2
1914	[d]	35,312	623,200	63,899	513,381	75,5
1915	[d]	36,187	615,337	66,418	565,300	78,6
1916	[d]	37,639	611,294	66,288	585,936	79,9
1917	[d]	41,234	613,138	71,861	588,420	80,9
1918	[d]	43,916	623,821	72,955	602,939	83,2
1919	[d]	46,014	627,115	73,039	621,434	88,5
1920	[d]	50,709	663,532	78,193	641,454	95,6
1921	[d]	55,596	695,229	79,694	697,418	125,9
1922	[d]	54,079	709,324	88,576	776,135	136,0
1923	[d]	52,975	735,320	91,525	823,821	140,4
1924	[d]	53,360	766,699	95,916	849,121	145,6
1925	[d]	53,300	791,158	97,471	875,414	150,3
1926	[d]	51,476	814,228	99,593	886,840	151,6
1927	[d]	51,172	836,873	100,654	910,414	153,4
1928	54,248	51,004	868,542	107,536	923,972	153,6
1929	55,424	51,491	920,489	114,092	968,532	158,6
1930	56,771	52,980	962,732	117,490	1,013,409	165,4
1931	58,628	53,031	983,029	120,282	1,050,205	169,8
1932	59,943	50,220	983,145	120,475	1,063,798	171,7
1933	59,545	44,032	955,950	121,116	1,049,465	171,7
1934	58,949	41,040	948,895	119,490	1,027,224	169,1
1935	58,560	41,124	931,256	117,964	1,019,458	168,2
1936	58,264	46,348	920,006	118,234	978,170	163,6
1937	59,297	46,301	919,928	118,035	975,186	164,1
1938	59,567	46,792	921,700	117,769	972,383	164,8
1939	60,387	45,938	928,425	116,107	969,663	164,8
1940	61,307	46,531	928,797	116,621	963,231	165,2
1941	62,189	48,671	932,998	117,372	952,671	165,3
1942	63,941	37,144	912,924	120,221	954,928	167,8
1943	66,138	36,900	923,434	121,606	959,801	171,5
1944	66,649	41,792	931,638	122,635	951,763	175,8
1945	68,272	41,587	937,763	124,177	949,875	177,8
1946	68,811	44,088	944,647	127,881	954,585	182,2
1947	70,606	48,994	978,390	131,211	969,816	182,8
1948	72,672	53,105	1,081,766	136,148	987,840	190,3
1949	76,771	54,215	1,137,224	140,423	1,369,264	200,1
1950	80,601	53,968	1,193,741	145,716	1,378,698	212,3
1951	88,837	54,573	1,369,739	149,381	1,409,630	221,0
1952	93,979	56,662	1,459,077	181,321	1,445,148	347,1

[a]This historical table presents assessed valuations on which taxes were levied, and, as such, refl the statutory basis of assessments. This basis is not uniform from one municipality to another and varied through time. For example, real property, personal property, business, income, and househ have all been subject to assessments and taxes by one municipality (Saint John), but not all in year; whereas another municipality (Victoria) has only partially assessed real property, and noth more. In one municipality (Vancouver) partial assessment of improvements has varied chronologic from 50 per cent to 25 per cent, to nil, to 25 per cent and to 50 per cent. Businesses have in so municipalities been assessed at rates from 10 per cent to 150 per cent of property value, varying w the type of business; and, in other municipalities, business assessments are based on rental val Another complication is that the rates of tax imposed on property may vary for specific purp

UNICIPALITIES FOR FISCAL YEARS ENDED NEAREST DECEMBER 31, 1901 TO 1952[a]
dollars)

innipeg	Regina	Edmonton[c]	Calgary	Vancouver[c]	Victoria	Year
6,406	952	1,396	2,258	16,513	14,090	1901
8,616	[d]	1,724	2,339	16,954	14,113	1902
6,273	986	3,208	3,263	18,391	14,185	1903
8,215	1,873	3,960	4,099	19,565	14,279	1904
2,728	3,117	6,621	5,433	22,641	14,380	1905
0,512	5,890	17,047	7,782	28,624	14,631	1906
6,787	10,605	21,986	12,892	42,442	17,832	1907
6,101	11,427	22,535	17,942	46,673	20,013	1908
1,091	11,715	25,585	19,825	54,383	23,145	1909
0,970	13,753	30,105	30,796	76,882	32,090	1910
6,715	26,987	46,495	52,747	98,720	46,516	1911
8,980	55,027	123,475	111,599	138,558	71,671	1912
5,302	69,513	188,539	133,024	144,975	89,130	1913
7,365	70,889	191,284	134,886	150,466	89,152	1914
4,166	59,185	171,362	113,808	145,199	80,751	1915
3,710	51,240	132,475	84,161	139,463	62,642	1916
8,676	43,582	100,917	80,045	140,000	53,695	1917
7,676	42,705	92,405	78,051	151,839	45,967	1918
1,655	41,487	79,665	79,804	168,645	45,972	1919
3,449	43,221	79,192	76,086	170,738	46,108	1920
5,866	43,922	80,214	75,002	171,802	45,231	1921
7,945	43,927	62,929	69,657	172,085	47,862	1922
9,062	43,415	61,935	62,926	166,793	43,854	1923
5,345	41,503	61,065	61,867	166,904	43,725	1924
1,815	40,272	59,829	60,351	169,169	42,604	1925
9,989	39,535	58,827	59,035	170,321	39,306	1926
7,495	40,644	59,784	57,576	177,619	39,457	1927
6,036	41,351	60,340	59,372	180,173	39,125	1928
1,011	44,285	63,177	64,191	247,484	39,344	1929
5,528	47,428	65,687	68,592	258,036	39,976	1930
6,104	47,468	66,496	70,607	269,752	40,670	1931
6,725	46,465	66,099	70,824	272,514	43,903	1932
5,499	45,744	65,757	66,266	269,058	42,600	1933
2,581	45,510	56,476	64,716	254,971	39,893	1934
9,745	42,555	54,614	64,167	246,328	38,522	1935
7,327	42,146	54,063	61,236	224,856	37,532	1936
2,933	42,241	53,948	60,304	261,967	36,064	1937
7,931	41,252	53,407	59,116	214,081	35,786	1938
9,034	40,975	53,767	59,046	209,854	35,023	1939
8,800	40,681	54,783	58,958	208,064	35,255	1940
9,617	40,789	56,228	59,125	207,629	35,051	1941
1,404	40,877	57,665	60,119	209,944	36,118	1942
3,180	40,607	59,051	61,074	211,338	35,834	1943
4,909	40,383	69,925	61,841	211,910	36,172	1944
8,608	40,597	73,594	63,841	216,436	36,790	1945
4,484	41,357	77,248	66,370	226,337	37,620	1946
5,133	42,112	83,377	69,628	237,692	39,110	1947
5,319	43,148	90,835	74,160	257,350	40,314	1948
6,894	44,707	100,368	80,194	272,118	42,822	1949
2,862	45,960	120,413	86,616	289,014	45,702	1950
3,117	51,682	134,417	95,386	300,020	47,927	1951
2,633	53,206	179,267	117,435	324,030	51,034	1952

parate schools, etc.). Properties exempt from taxation vary considerably between municipalities. me of the variations in assessments also reflect annexations of territory and reassessments, the most table recent occurrence being the reassessment of Toronto for 1949. Although in principle the assess- nt figures represent assessed valuations on which taxes were levied for general purposes, it has been cessary in some cases to use total assessment figures in order to obtain reasonable comparability rough time.

[b]Assessed valuations of immovables.

[c]Does not include business tax assessments.

[d]Figures not available.

SOURCES: D.B.S.; municipal officials.

TABLE 24

TAXES LEVIED (INCLUDING LOCAL IMPROVEMENTS) FOR SELECTED MUNICI
(thousands

Years	Halifax	Saint John	Montreal[a]	Quebec[a]	Toronto	Hamilton
1901	[d]	413	1,846	505	[d]	517[c]
1902	[d]	416	1,894	512	[d]	530[c]
1903	[d]	444	1,943	528	[d]	534[c]
1904	[d]	478	2,128	515	[d]	547[c]
1905	[d]	498	2,251	577	[d]	574[c]
1906	[d]	547	2,692	618	[d]	614[c]
1907	[d]	576	2,892	625	[d]	661[c]
1908	[d]	579	3,111	659	[d]	710[c]
1909	[d]	604	3,576	679	[d]	820[c]
1910	[d]	632	4,291	720	[d]	953[c]
1911	[d]	638	5,225	803	6,426	975[c]
1912	[d]	661	6,831	845	7,380	1,171
1913	602	695	8,309	929	9,618	1,491
1914	668	728	8,439	985	11,178	1,674
1915	696	750	8,349	1,113	14,540	1,948
1916	738	835	8,537	1,257	14,990	2,002
1917	856	1,109	9,257	1,368	16,932	2,107
1918	944	1,042	13,550	1,588	20,135	2,570
1919	1,235	1,296	14,107	1,628	19,331	2,938
1920	1,484	1,613	15,421	2,007	21,219	3,509
1921	1,970	1,657	16,618	2,035	24,969	4,420
1922	1,875	1,722	16,646	2,347	26,029	5,037
1923	1,972	1,709	17,868	2,488	26,443	4,851
1924	1,788	1,738	18,581	2,665	26,692	5,081
1925	1,809	1,756	18,945	2,746	27,286	5,383
1926	1,841	1,833	19,478	2,914	27,162	5,575
1927	1,881	1,744	20,026	2,997	29,449	5,595
1928	1,926	1,619	21,762	3,239	30,045	5,668
1929	1,918	1,610	22,740	3,448	31,363	5,851
1930	1,964	1,633	24,752	3,824	33,535	6,082
1931	2,023	1,822	24,405	3,927	36,653	6,495
1932	2,038	1,854	24,825	4,078	37,352	6,884
1933	2,025	1,720	24,789	4,100	36,335	6,889
1934	2,040	1,809	25,040	4,058	34,857	6,682
1935	2,085	1,860	25,719	4,163	35,517	7,086
1936	2,057	1,867	25,479	4,172	34,619	7,021
1937	2,146	2,083	24,695	4,319	35,213	6,795
1938	2,210	2,045	24,666	4,205	35,267	6,569
1939	2,246	1,993	24,667	4,249	33,843	6,406
1940	2,293	2,018	27,135	4,177	33,619	6,705
1941	2,326	2,095	27,123	4,276	32,375	6,318
1942	2,417	2,235	26,565	4,324	30,497	6,142
1943	2,557	2,168	26,918	4,338	29,549	6,463
1944	2,769	2,357	27,074	4,239	30,586	6,392
1945	2,820	2,494	27,212	4,338	28,812	5,952
1946	3,011	2,543	27,389	4,397	31,394	6,423
1947	3,648	2,608	29,229	4,497	35,678	7,206
1948	3,681	2,870	32,222	4,935	36,625	8,720
1949	3,957	3,152	33,987	4,927	41,478	9,270
1950	4,148	3,321	35,954	5,086	45,142	10,401
1951	5,095	3,373	43,495	5,204	54,566	13,007
1952	6,262	3,720	46,535	6,564	59,281	16,352

[a]Real property taxes.
[b]Includes levy for Greater Winnipeg Water District for 1918 and subsequent years.
[c]Excludes business taxes.

ʟLITIES FOR FISCAL YEARS ENDED NEAREST DECEMBER 31, 1901 TO 1952
dollars)

'innipeg[b]	Regina	Edmonton	Calgary[c]	Vancouver[c]	Victoria	Year
823	[d]	33	[d]	330	282[e]	1901
876	[d]	37	[d]	339	339[e]	1902
1,035	26	55	[d]	367	340[e]	1903
1,087	42	76	[d]	391	343[e]	1904
1,585	62	116	[d]	475	345[e]	1905
1,909	81	193	[d]	670	351[e]	1906
2,329	163	328	[d]	985	428[e]	1907
2,401	187	375	[d]	1,089	500[e]	1908
2,533	189	482	[d]	1,258	612[e]	1909
2,709	253	563	[d]	1,773	842[e]	1910
3,428	440	687	[d]	2,304	983	1911
3,809	778	1,530	[d]	3,183	1,418	1912
4,861	982	3,471	[d]	3,403	1,677	1913
5,815	1,046	3,769	3,265	4,182	1,886	1914
5,857	1,563	3,358	2,740	4,234	1,556	1915
6,087	1,338	3,284	1,024	4,049	1,295	1916
5,953	1,215	3,189	2,726	4,348	1,260	1917
7,165	1,454	3,655	3,045	4,660	1,247	1918
7,534	1.646	3,702	3,455	4,911	1,337	1919
7,637	1,749	4,541	4,024	5,814	1,302	1920
9,758	2,064	4,103	4,168	5,846	1,415	1921
0,071	1,994	3,366	3,762	5,833	1,639	1922
9,794	1,833	3,293	3,622	5,640	1,848	1923
9,416	1,732	3,292	3,380	5,553	1,829	1924
9,298	1,778	3,644	3,200	5,581	1,780	1925
9,191	1,883	3,474	3,134	5,649	1,639	1926
9,586	1,856	3,607	3,387	5,907	1,606	1927
9,856	1,913	3,682	3,357	6,565	1,711	1928
0,489	2,043	3,865	3,544	10,899	1,718	1929
0,771	2,160	4,075	3,842	11,956	1,726	1930
0,958	2,567	4,285	4,035	12,674	1,816	1931
0,912	2,458	4,424	4,337	12,799	1,935	1932
0,071	2,448	4,136	3,837	12,635	1,858	1933
9,858	2,401	4,410	3,725	12,005	1,747	1934
9,468	2,418	3,743	3,603	11,064	1,690	1935
9,235	2,351	3,757	3,736	10,131	1,800	1936
8,971	2,355	3,694	3,424	10,436	1,680	1937
8,900	2,289	3,668	3,204	11,011	1,614	1938
8,415	2,269	3,595	3,049	10,945	1,547	1939
8,350	2,242	3,606	2,922	10,783	1,521	1940
8,303	2,225	3,676	2,848	10,816	1,443	1941
8,346	2,193	3,747	2,862	11,314	1,449	1942
8,378	2,146	3,695	2,823	11,385	1,438	1943
8,420	2,127	4,222	2,868	11,467	1,451	1944
8,510	2,115	4,401	2,983	11,691	1,658	1945
9,435	2,158	4,705	3,344	12,601	1,694	1946
0,041	2,297	4,980	3,829	13,496	1,895	1947
1,622	2,613	5,444	4,356	14,549	1,952	1948
3,507	2,835	6,028	5,145	15,361	2,407	1949
4,458	2,907	7,388	5,374	15,805	2,515	1950
5,893	3,316	9,253	6,211	17,313	2,772	1951
7,125	3,528	11,574	7,600	20,270	2,920	1952

[d]Not available.

[e]Estimated.

SOURCES: D.B.S.; municipal officials.

TABLE 25

UNITED CANADA—AVERAGE *Ad Valorem* TARIFF RATES—1850 TO 1867
(total duty collected expressed as per cent of total imports)

Fiscal years[a]	Total imports	Total duties	Average rate of duty
	($ 000)	($ 000)	%
1850	16,982	2,463	14.5
1851	21,435	2,950	13.8
1852	20,286	2,957	14.6
1853	31,981	4,115	12.9
1854	40,529	4,899	12.1
1855	36,086	3,526	9.8
1856	43,584	4,509	10.3
1857	39,431	3,925	10.0
1858	29,079	3,381	11.6
1859	33,555	4,438	13.2
1860	34,448	4,758	13.8
1861	43,055	4,768	11.1
1862	48,601	4,653	9.6
1863	45,964	5,169	9.6
1864	23,882	3,068	12.8
1865	44,620	5,663	12.7
1866	53,802	7,331	13.6
1867	59,049	7,002	11.9

[a]To 1863 ending Dec. 31; thereafter ending June 30.
SOURCE: Annual Report of the Trade of Canada, D.B.S. (1925), pp. 42, 44.

TABLE 26

DOMINION GOVERNMENT—AVERAGE *Ad Valorem* TARIFF RATES AND RELATED DATA, 1868 TO 1953

Years[b]	Rate on dutiable imports[a]			Rate on total imports[a]			Origin of imports		Duty collected per capita
	Total %	U.K.[c] %	U.S. %	Total %	U.K.[c] %	U.S. %	From U.K. %	From U.S. %	$
1868	20.2	—	—	13.1	—	—	56.1	33.8	2.61
1869	20.2	16.9	20.1	13.1	13.5	7.3	56.2	32.0	2.43
1870	20.9	16.8	19.5	14.1	13.4	7.8	56.1	32.4	2.73
1871	19.6	16.4	16.3	14.0	13.5	8.4	57.6	32.3	3.36
1872	19.1	16.4	18.0	12.4	12.7	7.1	59.7	32.1	3.61
1873	18.3	15.6	17.7	10.4	10.9	6.5	54.6	36.3	3.54
1874	18.9	16.5	17.4	11.7	12.8	7.1	49.9	42.0	3.77
1875	19.6	18.1	17.3	13.1	14.8	7.9	51.1	41.7	3.95
1876	21.3	18.8	19.2	13.9	15.0	9.3	43.8	47.7	3.72
1877	20.6	19.4	18.7	13.3	16.2	7.9	41.8	52.5	3.13
1878	21.4	20.1	20.4	14.2	17.3	9.4	41.2	53.1	3.14
1879	23.3	20.5	23.2	16.4	18.0	13.1	39.3	53.6	3.12
1880	26.1	24.0	23.1	20.2	20.0	16.0	48.3	40.3	3.35
1881	25.8	24.5	22.0	20.4	20.5	15.5	47.4	40.6	4.26
1882	25.3	24.1	21.5	19.5	19.9	15.0	45.3	42.3	4.95

[a]Duties collected expressed as per cent of imports; excludes war tax collections from 1915 to 1923.
[b]Years ended June 30 to 1906; nine months ended March 31, 1907, and thereafter 12 months ended March 31 to 1938; thereafter calendar year.

TABLE 26—*Continued*

Years[b]	Rate on dutiable imports[a]			Rate on total imports[a]			Origin of imports		Duty collected per capita
	Total %	U.K.[c] %	U.S. %	Total %	U.K.[c] %	U.S. %	From U.K. %	From U.S. %	$
1883	25.3	24.3	21.1	19.0	19.2	14.8	42.4	45.3	5.23
1884	25.2	24.4	20.7	19.0	19.1	14.9	39.6	47.0	4.49
1885	26.1	24.8	21.2	19.2	19.0	14.5	40.1	45.7	4.21
1886	27.5	25.7	22.8	20.2	20.0	15.8	40.7	44.6	4.23
1887	28.7	26.1	23.8	21.3	20.8	16.2	42.6	42.6	4.84
1888	31.8	29.1	26.2	22.0	22.9	15.3	38.9	46.1	4.73
1889	31.9	29.3	25.4	21.8	22.4	14.7	38.7	45.9	5.01
1890	31.0	28.8	26.6	21.4	22.1	15.8	38.8	46.0	4.99
1891	31.4	29.0	26.0	21.0	21.7	14.9	37.7	46.7	4.83
1892	29.7	29.4	26.5	17.8	22.1	15.1	35.7	44.9	4.20
1893	30.3	29.8	26.7	18.4	22.3	14.6	36.9	45.4	4.29
1894	30.9	30.0	27.0	17.8	22.3	13.7	34.0	46.5	3.89
1895	30.5	30.1	26.7	17.8	22.6	13.7	30.9	49.8	3.55
1896	30.0	30.2	26.7	19.2	22.4	14.5	31.2	50.8	3.98
1897	30.0	30.7	26.7	18.7	21.1	14.3	27.6	53.5	3.87
1898	29.7	29.5	26.1	17.5	20.8	13.3	25.4	59.2	4.26
1899	28.8	26.6	26.3	17.2	19.8	13.2	24.7	59.2	4.89
1900	27.7	25.6	25.0	16.7	18.2	13.2	25.7	59.2	5.43
1901	27.5	24.7	24.8	16.4	18.3	12.4	24.1	60.3	5.39
1902	27.3	24.0	25.2	16.5	17.2	13.2	25.0	58.4	5.86
1903	27.1	23.3	24.9	16.5	16.7	13.3	26.2	57.3	6.54
1904	27.5	24.1	25.2	16.8	17.6	13.6	25.3	58.7	7.03
1905	27.8	24.8	26.1	16.7	18.5	13.5	24.0	60.6	7.01
1906	27.0	24.6	24.8	16.4	18.7	13.1	24.4	59.6	7.56
1907	26.5	24.3	24.2	16.1	18.4	12.8	25.8	59.5	6.39
1908	26.7	24.2	24.6	16.5	18.3	13.2	26.8	58.2	8.99
1909	27.5	25.8	24.9	16.7	19.0	13.2	24.5	59.0	7.18
1910	26.8	25.1	24.8	16.5	18.9	13.5	25.8	58.9	8.82
1911	25.9	24.6	24.7	16.2	18.9	13.7	24.3	60.8	10.17
1912	26.1	25.0	25.0	16.8	19.1	14.8	22.4	63.4	11.89
1913	26.1	25.1	24.9	17.1	19.6	15.8	20.7	65.0	15.29
1914	26.1	25.2	24.8	17.3	19.5	15.6	21.4	64.0	13.93
1915	27.4	27.1	25.1	16.8	20.5	14.2	19.8	65.2	9.74
1916	27.2	28.4	25.0	15.5	19.1	13.5	15.2	73.0	9.79
1917	23.8	24.9	22.7	13.0	17.6	11.4	12.7	78.6	13.42
1918	21.5	24.3	20.5	12.1	17.3	11.1	8.4	82.3	14.00
1919	21.5	22.3	20.9	12.3	15.3	11.6	8.0	81.6	13.37
1920	22.5	22.1	22.5	14.7	16.2	14.0	11.9	75.3	18.09
1921	20.6	20.9	20.3	14.1	16.6	12.9	17.3	69.0	19.89
1922	24.5	24.8	23.0	16.2	20.1	13.9	15.7	69.0	13.64
1923	24.9	24.5	22.5	16.7	20.1	13.8	17.6	67.4	14.85
1924	22.9	22.3	22.3	15.1	18.3	13.2	17.2	67.3	14.78
1925	23.3	22.1	23.1	15.1	18.2	13.0	19.0	64.0	12.94
1926	24.7	21.6	23.9	15.5	18.4	13.3	17.6	65.6	15.23
1927	24.1	23.9	23.1	15.4	19.7	13.2	15.9	66.6	16.50
1928	24.2	25.6	23.3	15.5	20.6	13.5	16.7	64.9	17.48
1929	24.4	25.9	23.4	15.8	20.6	14.1	15.3	68.6	19.99
1930	24.3	25.5	23.3	15.9	20.0	14.4	15.2	67.9	19.50

[c]Due to the fact that the tariff on spirits replaces the internal excises normally payable and because of the large importations of spirits from the United Kingdom the rate shown is considerably higher than would be the case if the tariff on spirits were similar in effect to an ordinary tariff duty.

SOURCE: *Annual Report of the Trade of Canada*, D.B.S.

TABLE 26—*Continued*

Years[b]	Rate on dutiable imports[a]			Rate on total imports[a]			Origin of imports		Duty collected per capita
	Total %	U.K.[c] %	U.S. %	Total %	U.K.[c] %	U.S. %	From U.K. %	From U.S. %	$
1931	26.0	26.9	24.8	16.4	19.5	15.2	16.5	64.5	14.38
1932	29.3	29.2	27.4	19.7	21.9	17.9	18.4	60.8	10.85
1933	30.1	25.8	28.1	19.0	16.6	17.4	21.3	57.2	7.23
1934	29.2	26.2	28.6	16.9	14.2	16.8	24.2	54.9	6.76
1935	28.1	26.2	27.4	16.2	13.8	16.3	21.4	58.1	7.74
1936	26.7	26.7	26.3	14.7	12.7	15.6	20.9	56.8	7.60
1937	24.9	25.8	23.8	13.7	12.0	14.3	19.3	58.6	8.30
1938	23.9	23.8	22.9	13.0	11.0	13.6	18.1	61.0	9.31
1939	24.2	27.0	21.3	13.8	12.4	13.0	15.2	66.2	9.17
1940	23.9	24.8	20.3	12.9	8.4	12.4	14.9	68.8	12.23
1941	21.9	23.4	18.8	11.1	4.7	11.6	15.2	69.3	13.92
1942	21.5	24.2	19.0	9.4	5.8	9.2	9.8	79.3	13.22
1943	20.7	18.7	18.9	10.0	5.2	10.0	7.8	82.1	14.71
1944	20.1	16.3	18.7	10.1	6.1	10.2	6.3	82.3	14.89
1945	21.1	17.6	19.3	10.6	4.7	11.1	8.9	75.8	13.94
1946	21.2	17.5	19.4	11.9	4.5	12.7	10.5	72.9	18.64
1947	20.8	15.9	19.5	12.7	6.4	13.1	7.4	76.7	25.95
1948	17.6	17.1	15.7	9.2	7.7	9.1	11.4	68.5	18.94
1949	17.4	16.2	16.0	9.1	6.9	9.0	11.1	70.7	18.67
1950	17.1	16.6	16.3	8.7	6.2	9.0	12.7	67.1	20.17
1951	17.3	15.8	16.5	9.2	6.5	9.5	10.3	68.9	26.84
1952	18.2	16.5	16.8	9.8	7.2	9.6	8.9	73.9	27.29
1953	18.6	16.1	17.4	10.2	6.9	10.3	10.3	73.5	30.35

TABLE 27

DOMINION GOVERNMENT—LEVIES ON LIQUOR, BEER, AND CIGARETTES

LIQUOR

Excise duties levied on spirits[a]	
1846[b] per imperial proof gallon	2*d.*
1859[b] per wine gallon, proof	$ .06
1862[b] " " " "	.09
1864[b] " " " "	.30
1867 " " " "	.60
1868 " " " "	.63
1874 " " " "	.75
1875 per imperial proof gallon	.90
1879 " " " "	1.00
1885 " " " "	1.30
1891 " " " "	1.50
1895 " " " "	1.70
1897 " " " "	1.90

[a]The tax shown is the basic levy on spirits; other rates apply for spirits used in certain bonded manufactories such as drugs and perfumes, when used in the treatment of wines, etc.

[b]Rates in effect in United Canada.

[c]An excise tax on $2.00 per proof gallon in addition to the excise duty was imposed under the Special War Revenue Act on July 1, 1920. It was repealed as of May 10, 1921.

NOTE: Spirits are also subject to the 10 per cent sales tax on the manufacturer's price including the excise duties.

TABLE 27—*Continued*

LIQUOR

1914	"	"	"	"	2.40
1920[c]	"	"	"	"	4.40
1921	"	"	"	"	9.00
1932	"	"	"	"	7.00
1935	"	"	"	"	4.00
1939	"	"	"	"	7.00
1942	"	"	"	"	9.00
1943	"	"	"	"	11.00
1950	"	"	"	"	12.00

Excise duties levied on Canadian brandy

1936	per	imperial	proof	gallon	$ 3.00
1939	"	"	"	"	6.00
1942	"	"	"	"	7.00
1943	"	"	"	"	9.00
1950	"	"	"	"	10.00

BEER

Excise duties on malt used in beer[a]

1867	malt	per	lb		$ .01
1877	"	"	"		.02
1879	"	"	"		.01
1891	"	"	"		.02
1894	"	"	"		.01½
1914	"	"	"		.03
1930	malt	screened	per	lb	.03
1934	"	"	"	"	.06
1939	"	"	"	"	.10
1941	"	"	"	"	.12
1942	"	"	"	"	.16
1950	"	"	"	"	.21
1954	"	"	"	"	[b]

Excise duties on beer when brewed in whole or in part from substances other than malt

1867	per	wine	gallon	$ .03½
1877	per	imperial	gallon	.08
1883	"	"	"	.04
1891	"	"	"	.10
1914	"	"	"	.15
1934	"	"	"	.22
1939	"	"	"	.30
1941	"	"	"	.35
1942	"	"	"	.45
1952	"	"	"	.42
1954	"	"	"	.38

[a]As most beer brewed in Canada is brewed from malt this is the principal tax on beer.

[b]Repealed in 1954 and replaced by a gallonage levy at the rate of 38 cents per imperial gallon of beer.

NOTE: Beer is also subject to the 10 per cent sales tax on the manufacturer's price including the excise duties.

TABLE 27—*Continued*

CIGARETTES

Pre-1888 excise duties on tobacco generally, including cigarettes[a]

1867	manufactured from foreign leaf per lb	$ .10
1870	" " " " " "	.15
1874	" " " " " "	.20
1880	" " " " " "	.20
	" " Cdn " " "	.14
1882	" " foreign " " "	.20
	" " Cnd " " "	.08
1883	" " foreign " " "	.12
	" " Cnd " " "	.02
1885	" " foreign " " "	.20
	" " Cnd " " "	.05

Specific cigarettes duties since 1888 (since 1888 special rates have been provided for cigarettes; standard weight, i.e., not more than 3 lbs per 1,000 cigarettes)

1888	per thousand	$ .60
1889	" "	1.50
1897	" " from domestic leaf	1.50
	" " " foreign "	3.00
1908	" "	2.40
1914	" "	3.00
1918	" "	6.00
1922	" "	7.50
1923	" "	6.00
1932	" "	4.00
1939	" "	5.00
1940	" " (weighing not more than 2½ lbs per 1,000)	6.00
1953	" " (weighing not more than 2½ lbs per 1,000)	4.00

Combined rates since 1942; in 1942 a further tax was levied under the Special War Revenue Act (now Excise Tax Act)

1942	$6.00 per 1,000 + $2.00 per 1,000	$ 8.00
1943	6.00 " " + 4.00 " "	10.00
1951	6.00 " " + 5.50 " "	11.50
1952	6.00 " " + 4.00 " "	10.00
1953	4.00 " " + 4.00 " "	8.00

[a]These taxes would not amount to more than $.25 per 1,000 in 1867, and $.50 per 1,000 in 1885, for cigarettes of standard weight, i.e., weighing not more than 2½ lbs per 1,000.

NOTE: Other forms of manufactured and raw leaf tobacco are subject to excise duties and excise taxes. Tobacco and cigarettes are also subject to the 10 per cent sales tax on the manufacturer's price including the excise duties.

TABLE 28

DOMINION GOVERNMENT—CHANGES IN RATES OF EXCISE DUTIES, 1939 TO 1954

Date of change	Spirits[a]								Validation fee[d]
	General	Can. brandy	Spirits for use in manufactures						
			Medicines	Perfumes	Vinegar	Chemical compositions[b]	Domestic wines	Imported spirits[c]	
	$	$	$	$	¢	¢	$	¢	¢
Pre-war	4.00	3.00	1.50	1.50	60	15	nil	30	20
Sept., 1939	7.00	6.00	—	—	—	—	—	—	—
June, 1940	—	—	—	—	—	—	—	—	—
April, 1941	—	—	—	—	—	—	—	—	—
June, 1942	9.00	7.00	—	—	—	—	—	—	—
March, 1943	11.00	9.00	—	—	—	—	11.00	—	—
Oct., 1944	—	—	—	—	—	—	1.50	—	—
June, 1946	—	—	—	—	—	—	—	—	—
May, 1948	—	—	—	—	repealed	—	—	—	—
Sept., 1950	12.00	10.00	—	—	—	—	—	—	—
April, 1952	—	—	—	repealed	—	—	repealed	—	—
Nov., 1952	—	—	—	—	—	—	—	—	repealed
Feb., 1953	—	—	—	—	—	—	—	—	—
April, 1954	—	—	—	—	—	—	—	—	—
Rates after April, 1954, budget	12.00	10.00	1.50	nil	nil	15	nil	30	nil

[a]All spirit rates given are per proof gallon.
[b]As prescribed by order in council.
[c]An additional rate on imported spirits taken into bonded manufacture.
[d]On each proof gallon of spirits exported from Canada.

TABLE 28—*Continued*

Date of change	Malt[e]	Malt syrup[e]		Beer[f]		Tobacco		Cigarettes[g]		Cigars[g]
		Domestic	Imported	Domestic	Imported	Manufactured[e] (ex. cigars & cigarettes)	Raw leaf[e]	Standard weight[h]	Over standard[i]	
	¢	¢	¢	¢	¢	¢	¢	$	$	$
Pre-war	6	10	16	22	7	20	nil	4.00	11.00	3.00
Sept., 1939	10	15	21	30	—	25	—	5.00	—	—
June, 1940	—	—	25	—	—	35	10	6.00	—	—
April, 1941	12	18	30	35	12	—	—	—	—	—
June, 1942	16	24	40	45	to customs tariff	—	20	—	—	—
March, 1943	—	—	—	—	—	—	—	—	—	—
June, 1946	—	—	—	—	—	—	—	—	—	1.00
May, 1948	—	repealed Oct., 1948	repealed Oct., 1948	—	—	—	—	—	—	—
Sept., 1950	21	—	—	—	—	—	—	—	—	—
April, 1952	—	—	—	42	—	—	—	—	—	—
Nov., 1952	—	—	—	—	—	—	—	—	—	—
Feb., 1953	—	—	—	—	—	—	—	4.00	5.00	—
April, 1954	repealed[j]	—	—	38	—	—	—	—	—	—
Rates after April, 1954, budget	—	nil	nil	38	nil	35	20	4.00	5.00	1.00

[e]Per pound.
[g]Per one thousand.
[i]Over 3 lbs. per 1,000 to June, 1940; over 2¾ lbs. per 1,000 after that date.
[j]Replaced by a gallonage levy of 38 cents per gallon on all beer.
[f]Per gallon on beer brewed from substances other than malt or malt syrup.
[h]Not more than 3 lbs. per 1,000 to June, 1940; not over 2¾ lbs. per 1,000 after that date.

NOTES: 1. See also Table 29 for excise tax rates on these products.
2. The excise duty does not apply to spirits used in any article subject to a special excise tax (e.g. cosmetics).

TABLE 29

DOMINION GOVERNMENT—CHANGES IN RATES OF EXCISE TAXES, 1939 TO 1954

Date of change	Amusements	Automobiles	Bank note circulation	Bets on horse races	Carbonated beverages	Cabarets	Cameras	Candy	Carbonic acid gas	Chewing gum
	%	%	%	%	%	%	%	%	c. per lb.	%
Pre-war	—	Up to $650 — no tax Excess - - 5 Maximum tax - $250 Buses taxed as autos	¼ of 1	—	—	—	—	—	—	—
Sept., 1939	—	—	—	—	—	—	—	—	2	—
June, 1940	—	Up to $700 - - 10 Next $200 - - 20 Next $300 - - 40 Excess over $1,200 - 80 Buses - - 5	—	—	—	—	10	—	5	—
Dec., 1940	—	Up to $900 - - 20 Next $300 - - 40 Excess over $1,200 - 80 Buses - - 5	—	—	—	—	25	—	—	—
Apr., 1941	20	Up to $900 - - 25 Next $300 - - 40 Excess over $1,200 - 80 Buses - - 5	—	5	25	—	—	—	25	—
June, 1942	—	—	—	—	25, and 1c per bottle	20	—	30	50	30
Mar., 1943	—	—	—	—	—	25	—	—	—	—
June, 1944	—	—	—	—	—	—	—	—	—	—
May, 1945	—	10 Buses 5	—	—	—	—	10	—	—	—
Oct., 1945	—	—	—	—	—	—	—	—	—	—
June, 1946	—	—	—	—	—	—	—	—	—	—
Nov., 1947	—	Up to $1,200 - - 25 Next $800 - - 50 Excess over $2,000 - 75 Buses - - 5	—	—	—	—	25	—	—	—

TABLE 29—*Continued*

Date of change	Amusements	Automobiles	Bank note circulation	Bets on horse races	Carbonated beverages	Cabarets	Cameras	Candy	Carbonic acid gas	Chewing gum
May, 1948	Repealed	—	—	Repealed	—	Repealed	—	—	—	—
July, 1948	—	10	—	—	—	—	10	—	—	—
		Buses 5								
Mar., 1949	—	Buses—repealed	—	—	Repealed	—	—	Repealed	Repealed	Repealed
Mar., 1950	—	—	Repealed	—	—	—	—	—	—	—
Sept., 1950	—	15	—	—	30	—	15	30	50	30
Apr., 1951	—	25	—	—	—	—	25	15	—	15
Apr., 1952	—	15	—	—	15	—	15	—	25	—
Feb., 1953	—	—	—	—	—	—	—	—	—	—
Apr., 1954	—	—	—	—	10	—	Repealed	10	15	10
Rate after Apr., 1954	Nil	15 Buses—nil	Nil	Nil	10	Nil	Nil	10	15	10

Date of change	Cigarettes[a]	Cigarette papers[b]	Cigarette tubes[b]	Cigars[c]	Communications: Long distance calls[d]	Communications: Cables	Communications: Telephone extensions[e]	Electric and gas fixtures[f]	Electric and gas appliances	Electrical appliances[h]
	c	c	c		%	c	c	%	%	%
Pre-war	—	2	2	50c if value under $40 to $16 if value over $200	6	5	—	—	—	—
Sept., 1939	—	—	—	—	—	—	—	—	—	—
June, 1940	—	5	5	$1 if value under $40 to $32 if value over $200	—	—	—	—	—	—
Dec., 1940	—	—	—	—	—	—	—	25	25	25

TABLE 29—*Continued*

Date of change	Cigarettes[a]	Cigarette papers[b]	Cigarette tubes[b]	Cigars[c]	Communications			Electric and gas fixtures[f]	Electric and gas appliances[g]	Electrical appliances[h]
					Long distance calls[d]	Cables	Telephone extensions[e]			
	c	c	c		%	c	c	%	%	%
Apr., 1941	—	—	10	—	10	—	—	—	—	—
June, 1942	1	6	12	$1.25 if value under $40 to $40 if value over $200	15	7	25 per month	—	—	—
Mar., 1943	2	8	14	$6.25 if value under $40 to $55 if value over $200	—	—	—	—	—	—
June, 1944	—	—	—	$3.25 if value under $25	—	—	—	—	—	—
May, 1945	—	—	—	—	—	—	—	Repealed	Repealed	Repealed
Oct., 1945	—	—	—	—	—	—	—	—	—	—
June, 1946	—	—	—	25%	—	—	—	—	—	—
Nov., 1947	—	—	—	—	—	—	—	—	25 on refrigerators	25
May, 1948	—	—	—	—	—	—	—	—	—	—
July, 1948	—	—	—	—	—	—	—	—	Repealed	Repealed
Mar., 1949	—	—	—	—	Repealed	Repealed	Repealed	—	—	—
Mar., 1950	—	—	—	—	—	—	—	—	—	—
Sept., 1950	—	—	—	—	—	—	—	—	—	15
Apr., 1951	2¾	Repealed	Repealed	—	—	—	—	—	15 on stoves, refrigerators, washing machines	25
Apr., 1952	2	—	—	15%	—	—	—	—	Repealed	15
Feb., 1953	—	—	—	—	—	—	—	—	—	—
Apr., 1954	—	—	—	—	—	—	—	—	—	Repealed
Rate after Apr., 1954	2	Nil	Nil	15%	Nil	Nil	Nil	Nil	Nil	Nil

[a]Per 5 cigarettes

[b]Per 100.

[c]Per 1,000, graduated by value per 1,000.

[d]Calls under 15c exempt; flat charges on calls from pay phones.

[e]Domestic telephone extensions only.

[f]Fixtures, shades, globes, and reflectors.

[g]Electric and gas stoves, ranges, heaters, refrigerators, etc., for household use.

[h]A wide range of smaller electric appliances.

TABLE 29—*Continued*

Date of change	Firearms[i]	Fishing rods and reels	Fountain pens and pencils	Furs	Gasoline	Golf clubs and balls	Jewellery, watches, etc.[j]	Lighters
	%	%	%	%	c. per Gal.	%	%	%
Pre-war	—	—	—	—	—	—	—	20
Sept., 1939	—	—	—	—	—	—	—	—
June, 1940	—	—	—	12	—	—	—	—
Dec., 1940	—	—	—	—	—	—	—	—
Apr., 1941	—	—	—	—	3	—	—	25
June, 1942	—	—	35	25	—	—	25	—
Mar., 1943	—	—	—	—	—	—	—	—
June, 1944	—	—	—	—	—	—	—	—
May, 1945	—	—	—	—	—	—	—	—
Oct., 1945	—	—	—	10	—	—	—	—
June, 1946	—	—	—	—	—	—	—	—
Apr., 1947	—	—	—	—	Repealed	—	—	—
Nov., 1947	25	—	—	—	—	—	—	—
May, 1948	—	—	—	—	—	—	—	—
July, 1948	Repealed	—	—	—	—	—	—	—
Mar., 1949	—	—	10	—	—	—	10	10
Mar., 1950	—	—	—	—	—	—	—	—
Sept., 1950	15	15	15	15	—	15	—	15
Apr., 1951	25	25	25	25	—	25	25	25
Apr., 1952	15	15	15	15	—	15	15	15
Feb., 1953	—	—	—	—	—	—	—	—
Apr., 1954	Repealed	Repealed	10	Repealed	—	Repealed	10	10
Rate after Apr., 1954	Nil	Nil	10	Nil	Nil	Nil	10	10

[i]Includes ammunition after Sept., 1950.

[j]Retail tax until March, 1949, when converted to a manufacturers' tax.

TABLE 29—*Continued*

Date of change	Luggage[k]	Matches	Motorcycles	Ornaments, silverware, etc.[m]	Outboard motors	Photographic materials[n]	Playing cards
	%	c. per 100	%	%	%	%	c. per pack
Pre-war	—	$\frac{3}{4}$	—	—	—	—	10
Sept., 1939	—	—	—	—	—	—	—
June, 1940	—	1	—	—	—	—	—
Dec., 1940	—	—	—	—	—	—	—
April, 1941	—	—	—	—	—	—	15
June, 1942	35	—	—	25	—	25	20
March, 1943	—	—	—	—	—	—	—
June, 1944	—	—	—	—	—	—	—
May, 1945	—	—	—	—	—	10	—
Oct., 1945	—	—	—	—	—	—	—
June, 1946	—	—	—	—	—	—	—
April, 1947	—	—	—	—	—	—	—
Nov., 1947	—	—	25	—	25	25	—
May, 1948	—	—	—	—	—	—	—
July, 1948	—	—	Repealed	—	Repealed	10	—
March, 1949	10	10%[l]	—	10	—	—	—
March, 1950	—	—	—	—	—	—	—
Sept., 1950	15	15	15	15	—	15	—
April, 1951	25	25	25	25	—	25	—
April, 1952	15	15	15	15	—	15	—
Feb., 1953	—	—	—	—	—	—	—
April, 1954	Repealed	10	10	10	—	Repealed	—
Rate after Apr., 1954	Nil	10	10	10	Nil	Nil	20

[k]Includes trunks, suit-cases, bags, wallets, cases, etc.

[l]Converted to ***ad valorem*** tax in March, 1949.

[m]Retail tax until March, 1949, when converted to a manufacturers' tax; applies to ornamental articles of precious metals, ivory, amber, shell, china, pottery etc. Plated knives, forks and spoons, and articles for preparing and serving food are exempt.

[n]Includes films, plates, and projectors; industrial and professional use exempt.

TABLE 29—*Continued*

Date of change	Premium income (insurance companies)					Radios & phonographs[o]	Slot machines	Smokers' accessories[p]	Special import tax[q]
	Life	Fire & casualty	Mutual & Lloyds	Exchanges & premium deposits	British & foreign				
	%	%	%	%	%	%	%	%	%
Pre-war	—	1	—	2	10	—	—	—	3
Sept., 1939	—	—	—	—	—	—	—	—	—
June, 1940	—	—	—	—	—	10	—	—	—
Dec., 1940	—	—	—	—	—	25	25	—	—
April, 1941	—	—	—	—	—	—	—	—	—
June, 1942	2	2	3	4	10	—	—	35	—
March, 1943	—	—	—	—	—	—	—	—	—
June, 1944	—	—	—	—	—	—	—	—	—
May, 1945	—	—	—	—	—	10	—	—	—
Oct., 1945	—	—	—	—	—	—	—	—	—
June, 1946	—	—	—	3	—	—	—	—	—
April, 1947	—	—	—	—	—	—	—	—	—
Nov., 1947	—	—	—	—	—	25	—	—	—
May, 1948	—	—	—	—	—	—	—	—	Repealed
July, 1948	—	—	—	—	—	10	—	—	—
March, 1949	—	—	—	—	—	—	10	10	—
March, 1950	—	—	—	—	—	—	—	—	—
Sept., 1950	—	—	—	—	—	15	15	15	—
April, 1951	—	—	—	—	—	25	25	25	—
April, 1952	—	—	—	—	—	15	15	15	—
Feb., 1953	—	—	—	—	—	—	—	—	—
April, 1954	—	—	—	—	—	—	10[r]	10	—
Rate after Apr., 1954	2	2	3	3	10	15	10	10	Nil

[o]Includes radios, television sets, phonographs, and replacement tubes.
[p]Includes ash trays, pipes, holders, rolling devices, etc.
[q]Applied only to imports from general tariff countries.
[r]The tax that formerly applied to coin operated vending machines was repealed. Now applies only to amusement devices.

TABLE 29—*Continued*

Date of change	Stamps: Cheques	Stamps: Security transfers	Stamps: Postal notes	Stamps: Letters[a]	Sugar: General[t]	Sugar: Syrups	Sugar: Glucose	Tires	Tubes	Tobacco: Manu-factured	Tobacco: Raw leaf	Toilet soap	Toilet articles
	c		c	c	c per lb.	c per lb.	c per lb.	c per lb.	c per lb.	c per lb.	c per lb.	%	%
Pre-war	3 to $100 6 over $100	Bonds: 3c per $100; Stocks: vary with value.	1c to $1.00 3c over $1.00	1	1	1	½	2	3	—	—	5	10
Sept., 1939	—	—	—	—	—	—	—	—	—	—	—	—	—
June, 1940	—	—	—	—	—	—	—	5	5	—	—	—	—
Dec., 1940	—	—	—	—	—	—	—	—	—	—	—	—	—
April, 1941	—	—	—	—	2	2	1	—	—	—	—	—	25
June, 1942	—	—	—	—	1½	—	—	—	—	16	—	—	—
Mar., 1943	—	—	—	2	1 (Sept.)	—	—	—	—	32	8	—	—
June, 1944	—	—	—	—	—	—	—	—	—	—	—	—	—
May, 1945	—	—	—	—	—	—	—	—	—	—	—	—	—
Oct., 1945	—	—	—	—	—	—	—	—	—	—	—	—	—
June, 1946	—	—	—	—	—	—	—	—	—	—	—	—	—
April, 1947	—	—	—	—	—	1	—	—	—	—	—	—	—
Nov., 1947	—	—	—	—	Repealed	Repealed	Repealed	—	—	—	—	—	—
May, 1948	—	—	—	—	—	—	—	—	—	—	—	—	—
July, 1948	—	—	—	—	—	—	—	—	—	—	—	—	—
Mar., 1949	—	—	—	—	—	—	—	10%[u]	10%[u]	—	—	—	10
Mar., 1950	—	—	—	—	—	—	—	—	—	—	—	Repealed	—
Sept., 1950	—	—	—	—	—	—	—	15%	15%	—	—	—	15
April, 1951	—	—	—	—	—	—	—	25%	25%	80	20	—	25
June, 1951	—	—	Repealed	Repealed	—	—	—	—	—	—	—	—	—
April, 1952	—	—	—	—	—	—	—	15%	15%	—	8	—	15
Feb., 1953	Repealed	Repealed	—	—	—	—	—	—	—	—	—	—	—
April, 1954	—	—	—	—	—	—	—	10%	10%	—	—	—	10
Rate after Apr., 1954	Nil	Nil	Nil	Nil	Nil	Nil	Nil	10%	10%	80	8	Nil	10

[a]Applicable in addition to ordinary postage; in 1951 the tax was embodied in the postage charge.
[t]Includes refined sugar, raw sugar, invert sugar, and syrup enumerated in tariff items 134, 135, 135A, and 135B.
[u]Converted to *ad valorem* tax in March, 1949.

TABLE 29—*Continued*

Date of change	Transportation			War exchange tax[a]	Wines		
					Non-sparkling		Sparkling
	Tickets	Berths	Chairs		More than 7% of absolute alcohol but not more than 40% of proof spirits	Not more than 7% of absolute alcohol	
	%	%	c.	%	c. per gal.	c. per gal.	$ per gal.
Pre-war	—	10	10	—	7½	7½	.75
Sept., 1939	—	—	—	—	15	15	1.50
June, 1940	—	—	—	10	—	—	—
Dec., 1940	—	—	—	—	—	—	—
April, 1941	10	—	—	—	40	40	2.00
June, 1942	15	15	15	—	50	50	2.50
March, 1943	—	—	—	—	—	—	—
June, 1944	—	—	—	—	—	—	—
May, 1945	—	—	—	—	—	—	—
Oct., 1945	—	—	—	Repealed	—	—	
June, 1946	—	—	—	—	—	—	—
April, 1947	—	—	—	—	—	—	—
Nov., 1947	—	—	—	—	—	—	—
May, 1948	—	—	—	—	—	—	—
July, 1948	—	—	—	—	—	—	—
March, 1949	Repealed	Repealed	Repealed	—	—	—	—
Oct., 1949	—	—	—	—	—	25	—
March, 1950	—	—	—	—	—	—	—
Sept., 1950	—	—	—	—	—	—	—
April, 1951	—	—	—	—	—	—	—
April, 1952	—	—	—	—	—	—	—
Feb., 1953	—	—	—	—	—	—	—
April, 1954	—	—	—	—	—	—	—
Rate after Apr., 1954	Nil	Nil	Nil	Nil	50	25	2.50

[a]Applied to goods imported into Canada except under British Preferential Tariff or under trade agreements with British countries.

TABLE 30

DOMINION GOVERNMENT—RATES OF SALES TAX SINCE INCEPTION

Period covered	Nature of sales
May 19 to June 16, 1920	1 per cent on sales by manufacturers, on sales by wholesalers, and on imports
June 17, 1920, to May 9, 1921	Tax payable by purchaser to manufacturer or wholesaler: Domestic sales: 1 per cent on sales by manufacturers to wholesalers, and on sales by wholesalers 2 per cent on sales by manufacturers to retailers or consumers Imports: 1 per cent on imports by manufacturers and wholesalers 2 per cent on imports by retailers or consumers
May 10, 1921, to May 23, 1922	Domestic sales: 1½ per cent on sales by manufacturers to wholesalers and on sales by wholesalers 3 per cent on sales by manufacturers to retailers and consumers Imports: 2½ per cent on imports by manufacturers and by wholesalers 4 per cent on imports by retailers and consumers Lumber: 2 per cent on domestic sales and 3 per cent on importations
May 24, 1922, to Dec. 31, 1923	Domestic sales: 2¼ per cent on sales by manufacturers to wholesalers and on sales by wholesalers 4½ per cent on sales by manufacturers to retailers and consumers Imports: 3¾ per cent on importations by manufacturers and by wholesalers 6 per cent on importations by retailers and consumers Lumber: 3 per cent on domestic sales and 4½ per cent on importations
Jan. 1 to Apr. 10, 1924	6 per cent on sales by manufacturers or producers and 6 per cent on importations 3 per cent on a restricted list, both on domestic sales and on importations
Apr. 11, 1924, to Feb. 17, 1927	5 per cent on sales by manufacturers and on importations 2½ per cent on a restricted list of commodities, both on domestic sales and on importations
Feb. 18, 1927, to Feb. 16, 1928	4 per cent on sales by manufacturers and on importations 2 per cent on a restricted list, both on domestic sales and on importations

TABLE 30—*Continued*

Period covered	Nature of sales
Feb. 17, 1928, to Mar. 1, 1929	3 per cent on sales by manufacturers and on importations 1½ per cent on a restricted list, both on domestic sales and on importations
Mar. 2, 1929, to May 1, 1930	2 per cent on sales by manufacturers and on importations 1 per cent on a restricted list, both on domestic sales and on importations
May 2, 1930, to June 1, 1931	1 per cent on sales by manufacturers and on importations ½ of 1 per cent on a restricted list, both on domestic sales and on importations
June 2, 1931, to Apr. 6, 1932	4 per cent on sales by manufacturers and on importations ½ of 4 per cent on a restricted list, both on domestic sales and on importations
Apr. 7, 1932, to May 2, 1936	6 per cent on sales by manufacturers and on importations ½ of 6 per cent on a restricted list, both on domestic sales and on importations
May 3, 1936, to Apr. 10, 1951	8 per cent on sales by manufacturers and on importations ½ of 8 per cent on a restricted list, both on domestic sales and on importations
Apr. 11, 1951, to Dec. 31, 1951	10 per cent on sales by manufacturers and on importations ½ of 10 per cent on a restricted list, both on domestic sales and on importations
Since Jan. 1, 1952	General rate reduced to 8 per cent, and 2 per cent rate levied as an old age security tax, earmarked for Old Age Security Fund

TABLE 31

DOMINION GOVERNMENT—SUMMARY OF CHANGES IN SALES TAX,[a] 1939 TO 1954

Immediate pre-war rate	8%
Sept., 1939	Canned fish, salted or smoked meats, and electricity and gas used in dwellings, were made taxable
April, 1941	Building materials and lumber were made taxable
June, 1944	Baling twine and small grain loaders added to exempt list
May, 1945	Building materials added to exempt list
Oct., 1945	Apparatus used directly in process of manufacture or production of goods added to exempt list
Nov., 1947	Electricity and gas used in domestic dwellings added to exempt list
May, 1948	Substantially all food items not previously exempt were added to exempt list; also hay presses, internal combustion engines for farm implements, crushed stone and gravel, wheel chairs, and articles for exhibition in museums and schools

[a]A percentage tax levied upon the sales price at manufacturers' level, or upon the duty paid value when goods are imported. A wide range of articles listed in Schedule III of the Excise Tax Act are exempt.

TABLE 31—*Continued*

March, 1949	Diesel powered self-propelled trucks for off-highway use exclusively at mines or quarries, lactose, and malt syrup except for beverage purposes, were added to exempt list
Oct., 1949	All fuel oils (except those used in internal combustion engines) added to exempt list
March, 1950	Ice cream exempt from sales tax
April, 1951	Rate increased to 10%
Jan., 1952	General rate reduced to 8%, but old age security tax of 2% imposed, effective Jan. 1; combined rate was 10%
April, 1952	Miscellaneous items such as preserved fruits, steel pens for farm animals, etc., added to exempt list
Feb., 1953	Books, materials used in making newspapers and foodstuffs, and certain consumable materials added to exempt list
April, 1954	Oil and gas burners and stokers for furnace for heating of buildings, coal crushers and stokers for use in manufacture and production of goods, road making and cleaning and fire fighting equipment purchased by municipality if price in excess of $1,000, wall panels, drain tiles, sheet music, and hearing aids added to exempt list
Present tax	10%; exemptions include substantially all foodstuffs, a large group of products of farm, forest, mines, and fisheries, most building materials, religious and educational material, machinery and equipment used in production, and electricity and gas used in domestic dwellings (for complete list see Schedule III of Excise Tax Act)

TABLE 32

DOMINION GOVERNMENT—SUMMARY OF CHANGES IN RETAIL PURCHASE TAX,[a] 1939 TO 1954

Immediate pre-war rate	No tax
June, 1942	25%
Oct., 1945	Goods valued under $100 included in baggage of residents returning from abroad to be exempt
May, 1948	Plated knives, forks, and spoons, watches designed for use of the blind, and alarm clocks sold at not more than $10 each, to be exempt
March, 1949	Repealed; replaced by a 10% *ad valorem* tax at the manufacturers' level on the same items
Present tax	No retail tax; 15% *ad valorem* tax on jewellery and related articles including: clocks and watches (except railway men's watches, those designed for the use of the blind, and alarm clocks selling for less than $10); articles of ivory, jet, amber, etc.; goldsmiths' and silversmiths' products and pewter ware (except plated knives, forks, and spoons); precious or semi-precious stones for personal use or adornment; glassware and articles of china, marble, pottery, etc. (except articles for use in preparation or serving of food or drink and use in manufacture of electric lamps); tax does not apply where sale price by manufacturer or duty paid value does not exceed a minimum value.

[a]A percentage tax levied upon the "tax paid value" when goods are imported, or upon the retail sale price when sold by retailer to consumer; levied upon a wide range of articles including clocks, watches, jewellery, plated ware; articles of ivory, amber, shell, etc.; articles of china or other pottery ware except articles used in the preparation or serving of food or drink.

TABLE 33

DOMINION GOVERNMENT—PERSONAL INCOME TAX EXEMPTIONS AND DEDUCTIONS, 1917 TO 1954[a]

Tax year	Single status	Married status	Dependent children of the taxpayer	Other dependents	Charitable donations	Medical expenses	Aged taxpayers
1917	$1,500 (for normal tax only)	$3,000 (for normal tax only)	Nil	Nil	Amounts paid to patriotic funds	Nil	Nil
1918–9	$1,000 (for normal tax only)	$2,000 (for normal tax only)	$200 for children under 18 yrs. (for normal tax only)	"	"	"	"
1920–1	"	"	"	"	Nil	"	"
1922	"	"	$300 for children under 18 yrs. (for normal tax only)	"	"	"	"
1923–4	"	"	$500 for children under 18 yrs. (for normal tax only)	"	"	"	"
1925	$1,500	$3,000	$500 for children under 18 yrs.	"	"	"	"
1926–8	"	"	$500 for children under 21 yrs.	"	"	"	"
1929–30	"	"	"	$500	Up to 10% of income	"	"
1931	$1,200	$2,400	"	"	"	"	"
1932–8	$1,000	$2,000	$400 for children under 21 yrs.	$400	"	"	"
1939	"	"	"	"	Up to 50% of income	"	"
1940	$750	$1,500	"	"	"	"	"
1941	"	"	"	"	Up to 10% of income	"	"
1942–3	$660	$1,200	A tax credit for children under 18 yrs. or under 21 attending school For normal tax—$28 For graduated tax—$80	For normal tax—$28 For graduated tax—$80	"	In excess of 5% of income; maximum amounts, $400, $600, and $400	Taxpayers over 65 yrs. with incomes less than $5,000 did not pay refundable portion
1944	"	"	"	"	"	In excess of 4% of income; maximum amounts, $600, $900, and $600	"
1945–6	"	"	"	"	"	"	Nil

TABLE 33—*Continued*

Tax year	Single status	Married status	Dependent children of the taxpayer	Other dependents	Charitable donations	Medical expenses	Aged taxpayers
1947	$750	$1,500	$100 for children eligible for family allowance payments; $300 for those not eligible	$100 for other dependents eligible for family allowance payments; $300 for those not eligible	Up to 10% of income	In excess of 4% of income; maximum amounts, $600, $900, and $600	Nil
1948	"	"	"	"	"	"	For taxpayers over 65 yrs. an extra deduction of $500
1949–51	$1,000	$2,000	$150 for children eligible for family allowance payments; $400 for those not eligible	$150 for other dependents eligible for family allowance payments; $400 for those not eligible	"	In excess of 4% of income; maximum amounts—$750, $1,000, and $1,000	"
1952	"	"	"	"	"	In excess of 4% of income; maximum amounts—$1,500, $2,000 and $2,000	"
1953–4	"	"	"	"	"	In excess of 3% of income; maximum amounts,$1,500, $2,000, and $2,000	"

[a] *Re* national defence tax. A national defence tax was introduced in 1940 applicable to one-half the income for that year. For 1940 the starting points for this tax were $600 for single status and $1,200 for married status. The tax was not to reduce income below these amounts. A tax credit of $4 was allowed for dependent children under 21 yrs. and for other dependents. For 1941 the starting points were $660 and $1,200 and the tax credit was $14. In 1942 the national defence tax was replaced by the normal tax.

TABLE 34: DOMINION GOVERNMENT—PERSONAL INCOME TAX PAYABLE 1917 TO 1954; SINGLE PERSON WITHOUT DEPENDENTS[a]

Tax year	Incomes $700	$1,000	$1,500	$2,000	$2,500	$3,000	$5,000	$10,000	$15,000	$20,000	$30,000	$50,000	$100,000	$200,000
1917	—	—	—	20	40	60	140	420	870	1,320	2,520	5,320	14,820	43,820
1918	—	—	10	30	50	70	150	452	968	1,463	2,783	5,863	17,688	51,842
1919-24	—	—	20	40	60	80	160	662	1,334	2,132	4,127	9,692	32,792	97,892
1925	—	—	—	10	20	30	90	415	990	1,815	3,930	8,770	24,370	65,015
1926	—	—	—	9	18	27	81	374	891	1,634	3,537	7,893	21,933	58,514
1927-30	—	—	—	8	16	24	72	332	792	1,452	3,144	7,016	19,496	52,012
1931	—	—	6	16	26	36	102	464	1,084	1,966	4,196	9,290	25,702	68,401
1932-3	—	—	15	30	50	70	180	662	1,397	2,394	4,841	10,364	27,846	72,660
1934-8	—	—	15	30	50	70	180	662	1,428	2,583	5,450	12,023	32,918	86,657
1939	—	—	18	36	60	84	216	794	1,714	3,100	6,539	14,427	39,501	103,988
1940[b]	7	25	78	135	203	280	690	2,288	4,328	6,503	11,138	21,493	51,198	118,653
1941[b]	25	73	188	300	425	563	1,233	3,400	5,978	8,705	14,483	27,393	62,348	139,795
1942[cd]	10	46	124	220	313	412	864	2,156	3,790	5,515	9,198	17,452	40,169	89,152
	10	40	60	80	100	120	200	400	400	400	400	400	400	400
1943[d]	13	92	247	441	626	824	1,728	4,312	7,579	11,029	18,396	34,903	80,337	178,304
	13	80	120	160	200	240	400	800	800	800	800	800	800	800
1944[d]	13	92	247	441	626	824	1,728	4,312	7,579	11,029	18,396	34,903	80,337	178,304
	7	40	60	80	100	120	200	400	400	400	400	400	400	400
1945	13	88	237	423	601	791	1,659	4,140	7,276	10,588	17,660	33,507	77,124	171,172
1946	11	77	208	370	526	693	1,452	3,622	6,366	9,264	15,453	29,319	67,483	149,775
1947	—	42	150	266	386	506	1,020	2,645	4,745	7,208	12,564	24,773	59,323	138,248
1948	—	29	120	220	320	420	835	2,253	4,153	6,515	11,728	23,456	56,631	133,056
1949-50	—	—	75	150	235	320	700	1,960	3,760	5,960	10,660	21,814	53,714	126,414
1951	—	—	83	165	259	352	770	2,156	4,136	6,566	11,726	23,995	59,085	139,055
1952[e]	—	—	88	175	274	372	820	2,301	4,406	6,951	12,371	25,195	61,960	145,880
	—	—	5	10	15	20	30	30	30	30	30	30	30	30
1953[e]	—	—	80	160	250	340	750	2,105	4,030	6,355	11,305	23,084	56,859	133,909
	—	—	10	20	30	40	60	60	60	60	60	60	60	60
1954[e]	—	—	75	150	235	320	700	1,960	3,760	5,960	10,660	21,814	53,714	126,414
	—	—	10	20	30	40	60	60	60	60	60	60	60	60

[a]Investment income: From 1934 to 1940 inclusive there was a special tax on investment income under which all earned income in excess of $14,000 was treated as investment income. In calculating the above taxes for these years it has been assumed that all income under $14,000 was earned income. In calculating the above taxes for the years following 1940 it has been assumed that all incomes up to $30,000 were entirely earned incomes and that incomes of more than $30,000 included earned income of that amount and additional investment income to make up the total.

Dividend tax credit: In calculating these taxes no account has been taken of the deduction from tax allowed in respect of dividends received from a taxable Canadian corporation by individuals resident in Canada. The deduction allowed was 10 per cent for the years 1949 to 1952 inclusive and 20 per cent for 1953–4.

[b]Including national defence tax.

[c]The taxes shown for 1942 reflect the transition to the pay-as-you-go plan. As part of this process taxpayers were relieved of one-half the 1942 tax on earned income and on investment income up to $3,000. One-half the uncancelled tax on investment income in excess of $3,000 could be deferred.

[d]First row indicates fixed tax; second row, refundable tax. In calculating the refundable taxes for 1942, 1943, and 1944 the full amount of the liability has been

TABLE 35

Dominion Government—Personal Income Tax Payable 1917 to 1954
Married Person without Dependents[a]

Tax year	Incomes $1,500	$2,000	$2,500	$3,000	$5,000	$10,000	$15,000	$20,000	$30,000	$50,000	$100,000	$200,000
1917	—	—	—	—	80	360	810	1,260	2,460	5,260	14,760	43,760
1918	—	—	10	20	100	399	913	1,408	2,728	5,808	17,633	51,785
1919–24	—	—	20	40	120	620	1,292	2,090	4,085	9,650	32,750	97,850
1925	—	—	—	—	40	290	790	1,540	3,600	8,380	23,830	64,370
1926	—	—	—	—	36	261	711	1,386	3,240	7,542	21,447	57,933
1927–30	—	—	—	—	32	232	632	1,232	2,880	6,704	19,064	51,496
1931	—	—	2	12	58	355	911	1,730	3,919	8,963	25,248	67,859
1932–3	—	—	15	30	120	546	1,229	2,174	4,589	10,070	27,447	72,188
1934–8	—	—	15	30	120	546	1,260	2,363	5,198	11,729	32,519	86,184
1939	—	—	18	36	144	655	1,512	2,835	6,237	14,074	39,022	103,421
1940	15	55	100	165	505	1,970	3,960	6,110	10,680	20,890	50,300	117,210
1941	53	145	238	355	925	2,930	5,400	8,030	13,635	26,215	60,375	136,270
1942	{54	115	200	292	689	1,881	3,465	5,140	8,723	16,777	38,994	86,977
	{54	100	125	150	250	500	500	500	500	500	500	500
1943	{100	231	401	584	1,378	3,762	6,929	10,279	17,446	33,553	77,987	173,954
	{100	200	250	300	500	1,000	1,000	1,000	1,000	1,000	1,000	1,000
1944	{100	231	401	584	1,378	3,762	6,929	10,279	17,446	33,553	77,987	173,954
	{50	100	125	150	250	500	500	500	500	500	500	500
1945	96	222	385	561	1,323	3,612	6,652	9,868	16,748	32,211	74,868	166,996
1946	84	194	337	491	1,158	3,160	5,820	8,634	14,655	28,185	65,509	146,121
1947	—	94	206	326	821	2,356	4,401	6,814	12,151	24,342	58,817	137,667
1948	—	70	170	270	670	1,990	3,840	6,140	11,315	23,043	56,143	132,493
1949–50	—	—	75	150	510	1,660	3,360	5,510	10,160	21,264	53,064	125,714
1951	—	—	83	165	561	1,826	3,696	6,061	11,176	23,390	58,370	138,285
1952	{—	—	88	175	596	1,946	3,941	6,431	11,796	24,565	61,220	145,060
	{—	—	5	10	30	30	30	30	30	30	30	30
1953	{—	—	80	160	545	1,780	3,605	5,880	10,780	22,509	56,184	133,159
	{—	—	10	20	60	60	60	60	60	60	60	60
1954	{—	—	75	150	510	1,660	3,360	5,510	10,160	21,264	53,064	125,714
	{—	—	10	20	60	60	60	60	60	60	60	60

[a]The notes on Table 34 are also applicable to this table.

TABLE 36

DOMINION GOVERNMENT—SUMMARY OF SOME IMPORTANT CHANGES IN PERSONAL INCOME TAX, 1939 TO 1954[a]

Year	Changes
1939	Prior to 1939 rates ranged from 3% to 66%; a special graduated tax was also imposed on earned income over $14,000 and on investment income
1940	Rates increased to range from 6% to 78%
	National Defence tax imposed on total income if in excess of $600 and $1,200 at rates ranging from 2% to 3%; this tax was withheld at the source and applied to ½ of 1940 income
1941	Rates increased to range from 15% to 85%
	Rates of N.D. tax were increased beginning July 1, 1941, to 5% and 7%
	The special graduated tax on investment income and earned income was replaced by an additional tax of 4% on investment income in excess of $1,500; earned income no longer subject to special tax
1942	The N.D. tax was changed to a normal tax of 7, 8, or 9%; the rates of graduated tax were increased to range from 30% to 85%
	A part of the combined total tax was regarded as compulsory savings to be refunded after the war; this part was paid only to the extent that taxpayer could not offset it with other specified types of saving
	A deduction for medical expenses was instituted in 1942
	Beginning Sept. 1, 1942, withholding at the source, previously applied only to N.D. tax, was extended to collect approximately 90% of the total tax
1943	Only minor adjustments were made in rates but tax was placed on pay-as-you-earn basis; as part of this process one-half of tax liability for 1942 was cancelled, compulsory savings continued in effect
1944	No further collection of compulsory savings after June 30, 1944, and liability for savings part of 1944 tax was reduced by half
	Deduction allowed for medical expenses was increased
1945–6	Rates and exemptions unchanged but tax was reduced by 16% commencing Oct. 1, 1945 (this meant a 4% reduction for 1945 and 16% for 1946)
	Family allowance payments were begun July 1, 1945, and provision made for recovery of a portion of these payments through tax (recovery was 100% over $3,000 of income in 1945 and 100% over $3,200 in 1946)
1947–8	Budget of 1946 announced lower rates and increased exemptions which became effective Jan. 1, 1947
	The family allowance recovery provision was cancelled with introduction of new lower exemption for children eligible for family allowances
	Exemption for 4% tax on investment income was increased from $1,500 to $1,800 from Jan. 1, 1947
	Budget of 1947 announced new and lower rates ranging from 10% to 80% effective July 1, 1947; tax liability for 1947 was determined by average of rates effective Jan. 1, 1947, and rates effective July 1, 1947
	Tax liability for 1948 is based on rates effective from July 1, 1947
1949	New and lower rates ranging from 15% to 80% effective from Jan. 1, 1949
	Exemption for 4% tax on investment income increased to greater of $2,400 or personal exemptions
	Taxpayer allowed a credit against his tax equal to 10% of dividends received from taxable Canadian corporations
1950–1	No significant changes in 1950
	Budget of 1951 announced a defence surtax equal to 10% of income tax for 1951 and 20% of income tax for subsequent taxation years

[a] *Provincial income taxes:* Previous to 1941 all provinces except New Brunswick (where there were municipal taxes) and Nova Scotia levied a tax upon individual incomes at various rates. Under the Wartime Tax Agreements the provinces withdrew these taxes. The seven provinces which entered into Tax Agreements with the Dominion in 1947 and the nine provinces in 1952 agreed not to levy a tax on incomes. Quebec, which has not entered into such an agreement, reimposed its taxes on individual incomes in 1954.

TABLE 36—*Continued*

1952	Most of the weight of the 20% defence surtax was incorporated into a new rate schedule ranging from 17% to 86% effective July 1, 1952
	An old age security tax of 1% of taxable income up to a maximum of $30 was levied
1953	Budget of 1953 announced lower rates ranging from 15% to 80% effective July 1, 1953
	For 1953 the old age security tax was 2% of taxable income up to a maximum of $60
	The credit allowed a taxpayer against his tax for dividends received from taxable Canadian corporations was increased to 20%
1954	No significant changes in 1954

TABLE 37

DOMINION GOVERNMENT—COLLECTIONS UNDER PERSONAL INCOME TAX[a] BY FISCAL AND TAXATION YEARS
(thousands of dollars)

Collections during each fiscal year[b]		Collections in respect of each taxation year[c]	
1918–19	7,973	1917	11,646
1919–20	13,195	1918	18,451
1920–21	32,533	1919	33,279
1921–22	39,821	1920	39,214
1922–23	31,689	1921	29,435
1923–24	25,657	1922	24,657
1924–25	25,157	1923	25,133
1925–26	23,849	1924	24,531
1926–27	18,043	1925	19,417
1927–28	23,223	1926	21,475
1928–29	24,793	1927	22,318
1929–30	27,238	1928	26,060
1930–31	26,624	1929	26,977
1931–32	24,773	1930	26,748
1932–33	25,959	1931	26,831
1933–34	29,184	1932	28,590
1934–35	25,201	1933	26,168
1935–36	32,789	1934	34,135
1936–37	35,358	1935	35,102
1937–38	40,071	1936	39,654
1938–39	46,591	1937	45,731
1939–40	45,009	1938	42,359
1940–41	103,308	1939	54,781
1941–42	295,874	1940	152,246

[a]Includes national defence tax, but excludes deferred tax and gift tax except where otherwise specified.

[b]Prior to 1942 the bulk of tax from individuals was collected in April, May, and June of the fiscal year commencing April 1 on the income of the previous taxation year. (For example, the income tax paid in the fiscal year 1928–9 was largely upon income of 1927.) With the introduction of the pay-as-you-earn system in 1942 a substantial portion of the tax began to be collected in the year to which it applied. Collections in any fiscal year include arrears of taxes that were levied in previous years and also prepayment of taxes not due till a later year. These payments for other years formed an increasing proportion of the total following 1938–9.

[c]This column shows the total amount of tax paid upon the income of each particular taxation year irrespective of when collected. The taxation year, in the case of individuals, is almost always the calendar year.

TABLE 37—*Continued*

Collections during each fiscal year[b]		Collections in respect of each taxation year[c]	
1942–43	533,915[d]	1941	329,334
1943–44	809,571[d]	1942	391,194[d]
1944–45	763,896[d]	1943	825,782[d]
1945–46	689,507[d]	1944	809,113[d]
1946–47	691,989[d]	1945	710,478
1947–48	656,873	1946	742,755
1948–49	760,152	1947	622,327[e]
1949–50	619,263	1948	647,712[e]
1950–51	648,663	1949	500,989[e]
1951–52	975,776[f]	1950	574,936[e]
1952–53	1,225,276[f]	1951	812,067[e]
1953–54	1,278,356[f]	1952	1,071,783[e,g]

[d]Includes refundable tax.

[e]Tax declared compiled from a 10 per cent sample of T1 returns on a declared, prior to assessment, basis.

[f]Includes old age security tax, gift tax, and deferred tax.

[g]Includes old age security tax.

SOURCE: *Taxation Statistics*, 1949 to 1954, Taxation Division, Dept. of National Revenue.

TABLE 38

DOMINION GOVERNMENT—NUMBER OF TAXPAYERS, INCOME ASSESSED AND TAX COLLECTIONS UNDER PERSONAL INCOME TAX FOR FISCAL YEARS ENDED MARCH 31, 1919 TO 1943

Fiscal year[a]	Number of taxpayers	Income assessed[b]	Tax collections
		($ 000)	($ 000)
1918–19	[c]	[c]	7,973
1919–20	[c]	[c]	13,195
1920–21	190,561	[c]	32,533
1921–22	290,584	1,058,578	39,821
1922–23	281,182	823,101	31,689
1923–24	239,036	802,617	25,657
1924–25	225,514	701,893	25,157
1925–26	209,539	697,017	23,849
1926–27[d]	116,029	465,690	18,043
1927–28	122,026	604,736	23,223
1928–29	129,663	668,688	24,793
1929–30	142,154	781,174	27,238
1930–31	143,601	815,715	26,624
1931–32	133,621	660,107	24,773

[a]Prior to 1941 tax statistics were compiled for each fiscal year ending March 31 based upon the returns assessed in the fiscal year. These returns were almost entirely those covering the previous taxation year. As a result the income assessed shown in this table for a particular fiscal year relates to the previous taxation year. (For example, the assessed income shown for 1928–9 relates to the 1927 taxation year.)

As the number of taxpayers increased after 1939 due to lower exemptions and an increase in the number gainfully employed it became impossible to assess all returns in a twelve-month period and as a result the income assessed in the fiscal years after 1940–41 does not coincide with the amount of income which actually was taxed in the corresponding taxation years as indicated above.

[b]Gross income less allowable deductions but before statutory exemptions.

[c]Not available.

[d]For 1925 taxation year the exemption limit was raised from $2,000 to $3,000 for married, and from $1,000 to $1,500 for single persons.

TABLE 38—*Continued*

Fiscal year[a]	Number of taxpayers	Income assessed[b]	Tax collections
1932–33[e]	166,972	685,544	25,959
1933–34[e]	203,957	617,717	29,184
1934–35	184,195	655,381	25,201
1935–36	199,102	714,334	32,983
1936–37	217,049	728,044	35,442
1937–38	237,064	712,183	40,445
1938–39	264,804	729,640	46,937
1939–40	293,097	1,000,290	50,554[f]
1940–41	300,384	990,250	51,545[f]
1941–42[e,g]	95,249	370,885	25,445[f]
1941–42[e,h]	291,931	580,704	30,120[f]
1941–42[e,i]	545	1,368	190[f]
1942–43[j]	316,468	788,769	67,959[f]
1942–43[i]	325,126	636,813	47,935[f]
1942–43[k]	532	1,144	194[f]

[e]For 1931 taxation year the exemption limit was lowered from $3,000 to $2,400 for married, and from $1,500 to $1,200 for single persons; for 1932 taxation year it was again lowered to $2,000 for married and $1,000 for single persons; and for 1940 taxation year to $1,500 for married, and to $750 for single persons.

[f]Tax assessed. [g]Taxation year 1939 or earlier. [h]Taxation year 1940.

[i]Taxation year 1941. [j]Taxation year 1940 or earlier. [k]Taxation year 1942.

SOURCES: *Canada Year Books; Dominion Income Tax Statistics, 1943*, D.B.S.; *Dominion Income Tax, Excess Profits Tax and Succession Duty Statistics, 1944*, Taxation Division, Dept. of National Revenue.

TABLE 39

DOMINION GOVERNMENT—NUMBER OF TAXPAYERS, INCOME AND TOTAL TAX UNDER PERSONAL INCOME TAX FOR TAXATION YEARS 1941 TO 1952[a]

Taxation year[b]	Number of taxpayers	Income	Total tax[c]
		($ 000)	($ 000)
1941	871,484	1,980,160	222,929
1942	1,781,244	3,523,223	335,691
1943	2,163,354	4,298,824	801,320
1944	2,254,319	4,591,041	781,133
1945	2,254,246	4,548,174	662,111[d]
1946	2,353,122	4,810,396	647,711[d]
1947	2,366,456	5,580,958	622,327
1948	2,689,930	6,760,770	647,712
1949	2,231,970	6,431,266	500,989
1950	2,374,240	7,032,803	574,936
1951	2,777,950	8,747,550	812,067
1952	3,125,100	10,274,033	1,071,783[e]

[a]These statistics depend upon the number and size of incomes which are in excess of personal exemptions. They will therefore vary from year to year as a result of changes in the number gainfully employed, changes in the general level of incomes, and changes in the exemption levels.

[b]Prior to 1946 the statistics were taken almost entirely from the returns after assessments. For 1946 and subsequent years they have been compiled from a 10% sample of T1 returns on a declared, prior to assessment, basis.

[c]Tax assessed before 1946 and tax declared for 1946 and subsequent years.

[d]Including family allowance recoveries.

[e]Includes old age security tax.

SOURCES: *Taxation Statistics*, 1946 to 1954. Taxation Division, Dept. of National Revenue.

TABLE 4

DOMINION GOVERNMENT—DISTRIBUTION OF PERSONA

Fiscal year[b]	Total number of taxpayers	Under $2,000	$2,000–3,000	$3,000–4,000	$4,000–5,000	$5,000–6,000	$6,000–7,000	$7,000 8,000
1928–29	129,663	36,857	22,374	19,408	15,049	9,529	6,833	3,950
1929–30	142,154	38,709	20,090	24,429	17,468	10,980	7,349	4,620
1930–31	143,601	38,788	20,885	22,869	17,909	11,348	7,483	4,814
1931–32	133,621	37,002	19,595	21,160	16,555	10,410	6,839	4,573
1932–33	166,972	63,276	29,156	27,546	15,760	8,951	5,556	3,481
1933–34	203,957	93,316	46,207	27,778	13,312	6,670	4,082	2,770
1934–35	184,195	85,385	41,918	24,127	11,672	6,238	3,729	2,464
1935–36	199,102	89,724	46,198	26,804	12,766	6,759	4,267	2,816
1936–37	217,049	98,423	50,618	28,690	13,852	7,448	4,480	2,993
1937–38	237,064	106,764	56,026	30,973	14,727	8,016	5,148	3,344
1938–39	264,804	119,346	63,572	34,392	15,902	8,627	5,563	3,674
1939–40	293,097	124,132	68,420	39,700	19,409	11,563	7,243	4,924
1940–41	300,384	127,954	72,502	43,021	19,581	10,346	6,524	4,435
1941–42	387,725	229,789	83,592	32,542	14,403	8,390	4,988	3,219
1942–43	642,126	400,319	143,282	47,628	19,259	9,691	5,688	3,788
Taxation year[c]								
1941	871,484	534,337	198,252	65,421	26,626	13,849	8,382	5,586
1942	1,781,244	1,227,857	379,101	87,556	31,944	16,279	9,708	6,646
1943	2,163,354	1,434,243	513,875	114,707	39,229	18,955	10,919	7,363
1944	2,254,319	1,440,202	572,848	129,719	44,635	21,141	12,104	8,127
1945	2,254,246	1,487,984	529,202	122,821	44,448	22,207	12,630	8,427
1946	2,353,122	1,566,650	535,730	124,280	46,040	24,330	14,490	9,970
1947	2,366,456	1,238,560	773,780	186,400	63,400	30,200	18,480	12,360
1948	2,689,930	1,196,270	1,001,260	280,670	85,310	38,380	22,420	14,970
1949	2,231,970	745,520	848,960	368,090	117,040	49,110	26,870	17,420
1950	2,374,240	747,060	889,900	434,200	134,380	54,940	30,500	18,190
1951	2,777,950	732,910	961,620	643,650	211,750	84,620	41,320	23,520
1952	3,125,100	736,680	986,520	808,750	303,210	113,790	54,790	29,610

[a]The total number of taxpayers in a year depends upon the number of individuals receiving incomes above th exemption levels. The number varies as a result of changes in the number gainfully employed, changes in the level incomes, and changes in exemption levels. In the lower income classifications the changes in the number of taxpaye are largely a result of changes in exemptions, however all those who receive incomes above $4,000 or $5,000 are likely continue to be taxpayers regardless of the changes in exemption levels and the number of taxpayers in these classi cations should coincide with the number of individuals receiving these incomes.

[b]Prior to 1941 tax statistics were compiled for each fiscal year based upon the returns asesssed in that fiscal yea These returns were almost entirely those covering the previous taxation year. As a result the distribution of taxpaye shown in the above table for any fiscal year relates to the previous taxation year. (For example the distribution show for the fiscal year 1928–9 relates to the taxation year 1927.)

,000– ,000	$ 9,000– 10,000	$10,000– 15,000	$15,000– 20,000	$20,000– 25,000	$25,000– 30,000	$30,000– 50,000	Over $50,000	Fiscal year[b]
2,785	2,185	5,520	2,197	1,027	579	847	523	1928–29
3,313	2,607	6,575	2,540	1,181	674	1,016	603	1929–30
3,449	2,609	6,825	2,878	1,314	784	1,045	601	1930–31
3,238	2,462	5,901	2,405	1,123	646	1,098	614	1931–32
2,580	1,962	4,577	1,653	872	483	729	390	1932–33
1,937	1,445	3,284	1,254	665	349	581	307	1933–34
1,777	1,229	2,815	1,198	558	329	497	259	1934–35
1,898	1,422	3,303	1,290	654	345	552	304	1935–36
2,078	1,533	3,520	1,431	724	380	579	300	1936–37
2,290	1,691	4,121	1,613	763	452	754	382	1937–38
2,612	1,986	4,687	1,775	816	469	926	457	1938–39
3,355	2,534	6,409	2,408	1,084	582	851	483	1939–40
2,830	2,235	5,737	2,268	977	601	900	473	1940–41
2,318	1,574	3,768	1,391	679	317	474	281	1941–42
2,537	1,896	4,378	1,599	714	388	590	369	1952–53
								Taxation year[c]
3,693	2,815	6,897	2,417	1,170	652	881	506	1941
4,402	3,399	8,023	2,774	1,303	1,694		558	1942
4,933	3,784	8,797	2,912	1,333	1,762		542	1943
5,479	3,962	9,456	3,015	1,351	1,764		516	1944
5,734	4,244	9,821	3,055	1,433	1,744		496	1945
5,960	5,210	11,970	4,040	1,970	1,942		540	1946
8,750	6,400	16,240	5,800	2,527	2,772		787	1947
10,350	7,470	18,330	6,680	2,750	3,790		1,050	1948
11,640	8,530	21,770	7,810	3,880	4,240		1,090	1949
12,720	9,070	23,390	9,410	4,090	5,050		1,340	1950
16,350	11,080	28,280	10,070	4,520	6,690		1,570	1951
18,500	13,610	33,740	11,940	5,460	6,660		1,840	1952

As the number of taxpayers increased after 1939 due to lower exemptions and an increase in the number gainfully nployed, it became impossible to assess all returns in a twelve-month period and as a result the number of taxpayers ıown above for the fiscal years 1940–1 and 1941–2 do not coincide with the actual number of taxpayers in the taxation ars 1939 and 1940. Beginning in 1941 the statistics show the actual number of taxpayers in the taxation year.

[c]Prior to 1946 the statistics were taken almost entirely from returns after assessment, for 1946 to 1951 they were ımpiled from a 10% sample of T1 returns on a declared, prior to assessment, basis.

Sources: *Incomes Assessed for Income War Tax in Canada*, 1933 to 1940, Dept. of Trade and Commerce, D.B.S.; *ominion Income Tax Statistics*, 1942 and 1943, Dept. of Trade and Commerce, D.B.S.; *Dominion Income Tax, Excess rofits Tax and Succession Duty Statistics 1944*, Taxation Division, Dept. of National Revenue; *Taxation Statistics*, 46 to 1953, Taxation Division, Dept. of National Revenue.

TABLE 41

DOMINION GOVERNMENT—RATES OF CORPORATION INCOME TAX 1917 TO 1954
(including minimum excess profits tax (E.P.T.) and
old age security tax (O.A.S.T.))

Year[a]	Rate of corporation income tax[b]	Minimum E.P.T. and O.A.S.T.	Combined rate
	%	%	%
1917	4	—	4
1918	6	—	6
1919–24	10 up to $5,000[c]	—	10[c]
	10.5 over $5,000[c]	—	10.5[c]
1925	9	—	9
1926	8.1	—	8.1
1927–9	8	—	8
1930	10	—	10
1931	11 up to $5,000[c]	—	11[c]
	11.55 over $5,000[c]	—	11.55[c]
1932–3	12.5[d]	—	12.5[d]
1934	13.5[d]	—	13.5[d]
1935–9	15[e]	—	15[e]
1940	18[e]	12[f]	30[e]
1941	18[e]	22[f]	40[e]
1942–5	18[e]	12[f]	40[e]
		10[f]	
1946	18[e]	22[f]	40[e]
1947–8	30[e]	—	30[e]
1949 to Aug. 31, 1950	10 on first $10,000[e]	—	10[e]
	33 on excess over $10,000[e]	—	33[e]
Sept. 1 to Dec. 31, 1950	15 on first $10,000[e]	—	15[e]
	38 on excess over $10,000[e]	—	38[e]
1951	15 on first $10,000[g]	—	15
	45.6 on excess over $10,000	—	45.6
1952	20 on first $10,000	2[h]	22
	50 on excess over $10,000	2[h]	52
1953–4	18 on first $20,000	2[h]	20
	47 on excess over $20,000	2[h]	49

[a]Taxation years from 1917 to 1939 inclusive and calendar years thereafter. Since January 1, 1940 the portions of the taxation year falling on one or the other side of a tax change are taxed accordingly.

[b]An exemption of $3,000 was given in 1917 and 1918 and $2,000 from 1919 to 1931. There has been no exemption for corporations since the latter year.

[c]When the income exceeded $5,000 the tax was subject to a 5 per cent surtax.

[d]An additional 1 per cent was charged on consolidated returns for 1932 and 1933 and an additional 1½ per cent was charged for 1934.

[e]An additional 2 per cent was charged on consolidated returns.

[f]Minimum rates of excess profits tax payable by all corporations.

[g]The right to file consolidated returns was repealed for 1952 and subsequent taxation years.

[h]Old age security tax payable by all corporations.

TABLE 42

DOMINION GOVERNMENT—SUMMARY OF BUSINESS PROFITS WAR TAX, TAXATION YEARS 1915 TO 1920[a]

1915	1916	1917	1918	1919	1920
Incorporated businesses 25% on profits in excess of 7% of capital employed		*Incorporated businesses* 25% on profits in excess of 7% but not exceeding 15% of capital employed			*All businesses except small businesses* where profits do not exceed 10% of capital employed—no tax
Non-incorporated businesses 25% on profits in excess of 10% of capital employed	Same as 1915	50% on profits in excess of 15% but not exceeding 20% of capital employed	Same as 1917 with following addition:	Same as 1918	20% on profits in excess of 10% but not exceeding 15% of capital employed
		75% on profits in excess of 20% of capital employed	*Small businesses* (where capital is not less than $25,000 and under $50,000)		30% on profits in excess of 15% but not exceeding 20% of capital employed
		Non-incorporated businesses 25% on profits in excess of 10% but not exceeding 15% of capital employed	25% on profits in excess of 10% of capital employed		50% on profits in excess of 20% but not exceeding 30% of capital employed
		50% on profits in excess of 15% but not exceeding 20% of capital employed			60% on profits in excess of 30% of capital employed
		75% on profits in excess of 20% of capital employed			*Small businesses* (where capital is not less than $25,000 and under $50,000)
					20% on profits in excess of 10% of capital employed

[a]Tax base: The tax applied to all businesses incorporated and otherwise. It was levied on net profits in excess of a certain percentage of the capital employed. Such allowances as the Minister thought reasonable were permitted for depreciation in the case of all business and for depletion in the case of mines.

Definition of capital employed: For incorporated businesses it was the amount paid up on its capital stock plus any reserve or accumulated profits. For non-incorporated businesses it was the fair value of all assets used in connection with such businesses plus accumulated profits used in the business less any borrowed money used in the business.

Businesses exempt: Businesses, other than those employed in manufacturing munitions or war supplied, were not liable for tax unless their capital exceeded a certain amount. Up until 1918, this limit was $50,000, but in 1918 it was reduced to $25,000. Businesses more than 20% engaged in manufacturing munitions or war supplies were taxable regardless of amount of capital employed. Life insurance businesses and farmers were exempt from the tax and also businesses 90% or more owned by a province or municipality.

Duration of act: The tax was first applied to profits earned in accounting periods ending after December 31, 1914. It was originally provided that the tax would not continue in force after December 31, 1917, but subsequent amendments extended its life. It finally ceased to be in force at December 31, 1920.

TABLE 43

DOMINION GOVERNMENT—EXCESS PROFITS TAX ON CORPORATIONS, 1940 TO 1947[a]

1940	1941	1942	1943	1944	1945	1946	1947
12% of total profits or 75% of excess profits whichever is greater	22% of total profits or 75% of excess profits whichever is greater	(*a*) First six months—same as 1941 (*b*) Second six months—12% of total profits plus the greater of 10% of total profits or 100% of excess profits In the case of those taxable at the 100% rate on excess profits a portion equal to 20% of all profits in excess of 116 2/3% of standard profits is refundable after the war, effective from July 1, 1942	12% of total profits plus the greater of 10% of total profits or 100% of excess profits A portion equal to 20% of all profits in excess of 116 2/3% of standard profits is refundable	Same rates as 1943	Same rates as 1943	(*a*) Corporations not filing consolidated returns—22% of total profits plus 20% of that portion of profit in excess of 116.666% of standard profits (*b*) Corporations filing consolidated returns—22% of total profits plus 20% of that portion of profit in excess of 117.241% of standard profits No refundable portion after Dec. 31, 1945	(*a*) Corporations not filing consolidated returns—15% of that portion of profit in excess of 116.666% of standard profits (*b*) Corporations filing consolidated returns—15% of that portion of profits in excess of 117.241% of standard profits No refundable portion Repealed effective Dec. 31, 1947

[a]The excess profits tax was introduced in the budget of Sept. 12, 1939, to apply on profits of 1940. No tax was collected under the original Act and a new Act was passed in 1940 to apply to profits of 1940 and subsequent years. This Act applied to all forms of business enterprise whether conducted within a corporate partnership or sole proprietorship structure.

Excess profits are defined in the Act as profits in excess of "Standard Profits." Standard Profits are defined as the average yearly profits earned in the four year period from 1936 to 1939 inclusive. But if the profits in one of those years fall below 50% of the average in the three remaining years, then the average of the three best years may be used. Businesses which were depressed during the standard period might apply to the Board of Referees for the award of a Standard Profit based on some yardstick other than the actual profits of the business during the years 1936 to 1939. In the case of new businesses, those which commenced business between Dec. 31, 1937, and Jan. 1, 1939, could apply to the Board for the award of a Standard Profit and those commencing after Jan. 1, 1939, were automatically referred to the Board.

From Jan. 1, 1940, to Dec. 31, 1945, a minimum Standard Profit of $5,000 was established for all businesses. As of Jan. 1, 1946, the minimum was increased by a provision that all Standard Profits below $25,000 could be augmented by half the difference between the existing Standard Profit and $25,000. This raised the minimum Standard Profit to $15,000.

The excess profits tax was not restricted to the taxing of purely "excess profits" as defined above but also imposed for several years a tax on total profits, as indicated in the table above.

The tax on partnerships or sole proprietorships was repealed as of Jan. 1, 1947, and the tax on corporations was repealed as of Jan. 1, 1948.

TABLE 44

DOMINION GOVERNMENT—EXCESS PROFITS TAX ON PARTNERSHIPS AND INDIVIDUALS, 1940 TO 1946[a]

1940	1941	1942	1943	1944	1945	1946
12% of total profits or 75% of excess profits whichever is greater	15% of total profits or 75% of excess profits whichever is greater	(a) First six months—same as 1941 (b) Second six months—15% of total profits or 100% of excess profits whichever is greater	15% of total profits or 100% of excess profits whichever is greater	Same as 1943	Same as 1943	60% on that portion of the profits in excess of 117.647% of the standard profits
		In the case of those taxable at the 100% rate on excess profits a portion equal to 20% of all profits in excess of 117.64% of standard profits is refundable after the war effective from July 1, 1942	A portion equal to 20% of all profits in excess of 117.64% of standard profits in refundable			No refundable portion after Dec. 31, 1945

[a]Partnerships or sole proprietorships earning less than $5,000 per year before deduction for proprietors' salaries were not subject to excess profits tax. In computing taxable income a maximum allowance of $5,000 for each working proprietor was allowed.

No excess profits tax has been levied on profits of partners or individuals in business earned since Dec. 31, 1946. (See also footnote to Table 43.)

TABLE 45

DOMINION GOVERNMENT—COLLECTIONS UNDER CORPORATION INCOME TAX BY FISCAL AND TAXATION YEARS
(thousands of dollars)

Collections during each fiscal year[a]		Collections in respect of each taxation year[b]	
1918–19	1,377	1917	4,638
1919–20	7,068	1918	7,958
1920–21	13,849	1919	20,336
1921–22	38,864	1920	35,731
1922–23	28,022	1921	26,622
1923–24	28,547	1922	26,862
1924–25	31,091	1923	30,625
1925–26	31,722	1924	31,631
1926–27	29,343	1925	28,973
1927–28	33,348	1926	31,195
1928–29	34,629	1927	33,923
1929–30	41,783	1928	41,658
1930–31	44,424	1929	44,846
1931–32	36,482	1930	37,295
1932–33	36,107	1931	31,105
1933–34	27,386	1932	26,499
1934–35	35,790	1933	29,222
1935–36	42,519	1934	44,525
1936–37	58,013	1935	53,276
1937–38	69,769	1936	67,149
1938–39	85,186	1937	88,920
1939–40	77,920	1938	74,077
1940–41	131,566	1939	90,498
1941–42	185,836	1940	151,395
1942–43	347,970	1941[c]	224,471
1943–44	311,379	1942[c]	270,205
1944–45	276,404	1943[c]	278,508
1945–46	217,834	1944[c]	231,004
1946–47	196,819	1945[c]	191,072
1947–48	351,535	1946[c]	207,126
1948–49	488,550	1947	485,458[d]
1949–50	602,073	1948	568,259[d]
1950–51	711,577	1949	571,972[d]
1951–52	1,116,067[e]	1950	759,664[d]
1952–53	1,229,706[e]	1951	1,164,100[d]
1953–54	1,182,415[e]	1952	1,193,730[d,e]

[a]Collections during each fiscal year prior to 1940–1 relate almost entirely to the previous taxation year. For example, the information shown for 1928–9 relates to the 1927 taxation year. Includes excess profits tax not identified as such at time of collection.

[b]This column shows the total amount of tax paid upon the income of each taxation year irrespective of when collected. Includes excess profits tax not identified as such at time of collection.

[c]Refunds arising out of renegotiation of war contracts applicable to the years 1941 to 1944 have been deducted from the 1945 and 1946 figures. The true 1945 and 1946 figures are therefore higher and the 1941 to 1944 lower than shown.

[d]Tax declared compiled on a declared, prior to assessment basis.

[e]Excludes old age security tax.

[f]Not available.

SOURCE: *Taxation Statistics*, 1949 to 1953, Taxation Division, Dept. of National Revenue.

TABLE 46

DOMINION GOVERNMENT—NUMBER OF TAXPAYING CORPORATIONS, INCOME ASSESSED, AND TAX COLLECTIONS: FISCAL YEARS ENDED MARCH 31, 1919-43

Fiscal year[a]	Taxpaying corporations	Income assessed	Tax collections
		($ 000)	($ 000)
1918–19	1,560	[b]	1,377
1919–20	2,245	[b]	7,068
1920–21	3,696	[b]	13,849
1921–22	8,286	403,952	38,864
1922–23	6,010	269,307	28,022
1923–24	5,569	305,410	28,547
1924–25	6,236	297,267	31,091
1925–26	5,738	306,094	31,722
1926–27	5,777	278,495	29,343
1927–28	6,121	435,497	33,348
1928–29	7,438	526,715	34,629
1929–30	7,957	544,019	41,783
1930–31	7,603	555,764	44,424
1931–32	6,010	332,499	36,482
1932–33	6,483	258,548	36,107
1933–34	8,913	211,614	27,386
1934–35	10,458	273,174	35,790
1935–36	10,970	359,109	42,519
1936–37	12,146	352,846	58,013
1937–38	13,949	353,851	69,769
1938–39	13,809	397,572	85,186
1939–40	17,618	545,832	78,203[c]
1940–41[d]	15,884	537,331	75,400[c]
1941–42[d]	9,178	361,568	54,049[c]
1942–43[d]	9,956	443,019	70,999[c]

[a]The statistics shown are based upon the returns actually assessed in each fiscal year. Until after 1939–40 these returns were almost entirely applicable to the previous taxation year. (For example, the information shown for 1928–9 relates to the 1927 taxation year.)

[b]Not available. [c]Tax assessed.

[d]The information shown for these years does not give a correct picture of the corresponding taxation years due to greater volume of assessments following 1939. SOURCES: *Canada Year Books; Dominion Income Tax Statistics, 1943*, D.B.S.; *Dominion Income Tax, Excess Profits Tax and Succession Duty Statistics, 1944*, Taxation Division, Dept. of National Revenue.

TABLE 47

DOMINION GOVERNMENT—NUMBER OF COMPANIES, CURRENT YEAR PROFITS DECLARED, AND INCOME TAX DECLARED, TAXATION YEARS 1944 TO 1952

Taxation year	Taxable companies reporting a profit	Profits declared[a]	Tax declared
		($ 000)	($ 000)
1944	20,023	1,194,113	213,097
1945	21,331	1,198,791	212,504
1946	23,563	1,392,956	245,246
1947	27,272	1,776,554	485,458
1948	27,997	1,945,957	568,259
1949	28,570	1,864,582	571,972
1950	31,239	2,359,065	759,664
1951	33,720	2,795,350	1,164,100
1952	35,228	2,653,934	1,193,730[b]

[a]Before deducting prior years' losses. [b]Excludes old age security taxes.

SOURCE: *Taxation Statistics, 1954*, Taxation Division, Dept. of National Revenue.

TABLE 48

Dominion Government—Succession Duties
Aggregate Value of Resident Dutiable Estates Assessed by Size of Estate for Fiscal Periods Ended March 31, 1945 to 1951
(thousands of dollars)

Size of estate	June 14, 1941 to March 31, 1945	1945–6	1946–7	1947–8	1948–9[c]	1949–50	1950–1
$ 5,000–$ 6,000	—	5,334	6,482	6,065	1,836		
6,000– 7,000	—	5,501	7,084	6,596	2,093		
7,000– 8,000	—	5,068	6,703	6,492	1,942		
8,000– 9,000	—	5,466	6,835	6,645	2,272		
9,000– 10,000	83,740[a]	5,320	6,465	6,336	2,038	9,584	2,936
10,000– 15,000	—	21,945	28,732	27,831	8,363		
15,000– 25,000	158,801[b]	36,473	43,680	44,811	15,375		
25,000– 35,000	65,147	27,341	31,174	36,674	13,990		
35,000– 50,000	62,497	29,594	33,053	35,645	15,033		
50,000– 75,000	61,884	28,839	32,757	38,183	37,178	42,268	43,944
75,000– 100,000	36,148	19,853	21,857	21,073	25,357	30,055	30,906
100,000– 125,000	27,800	13,752	16,361	13,615	15,984	21,394	23,836
125,000– 150,000	17,768	10,124	9,275	12,008	11,662	15,746	15,548
150,000– 200,000	28,583	15,041	13,881	16,633	15,875	21,382	24,427
200,000– 300,000	30,573	18,761	23,187	23,654	26,484	30,038	32,546
300,000– 400,000	17,866	11,225	15,731	9,573	12,529	19,024	16,614
400,000– 500,000	13,693	12,201	12,724	9,216	10,401	12,915	12,889
500,000– 750,000	10,829	10,858	14,552	15,443	17,095	17,679	22,923
750,000– 1,000,000	19,674	6,100	9,299	13,280	7,181	8,334	9,700
Over $1,000,000	50,005	15,376	34,979	25,826	46,997	71,662	61,318
Total	684,908	304,172	374,811	375,599	289,685	300,081	297,587

[a]$5,000–$10,000.
[b]$10,000–$25,000.
[c]General exemption increased from $5,000 to $50,000.
Source: *Taxation Statistics*, Dept. of National Revenue.

TABLE 49

DOMINION GOVERNMENT—SUCCESSION DUTIES—NUMBER OF RESIDENT DUTIABLE ESTATES ASSESSED BY SIZE OF ESTATE FOR FISCAL YEARS ENDED MARCH 31, 1946 TO 1951

Size of estate	1945–6	1946–7	1947–8	1948–9[a]	1949–50	1950–1
$ 5,000–$ 6,000	973	1,181	1,101	337		
6,000– 7,000	852	1,071	1,017	324		
7,000– 8,000	677	900	863	262		
8,000– 9,000	646	810	777	269		
9,000– 10,000	561	682	661	216	538	181
10,000– 15,000	1,791	2,334	2,256	685		
15,000– 25,000	1,854	2,216	2,272	781		
25,000– 35,000	933	1,049	1,243	475		
35,000– 50,000	715	795	864	361		
50,000– 75,000	476	545	635	611	692	722
75,000– 100,000	230	245	245	295	350	359
100,000– 125,000	124	147	122	143	191	213
125,000– 150,000	72	68	87	86	115	113
150,000– 200,000	87	81	98	91	125	141
200,000– 300,000	77	96	95	109	124	135
300,000– 400,000	33	45	27	38	55	49
400,000– 500,000	27	28	21	23	29	28
500,000– 750,000	18	26	25	28	29	37
750,000– 1,000,000	7	11	16	8	10	11
Over $1,000,000	9	21	17	17	23	25
Total (residents in Canada)	10,162	12,351	12,442	5,159	2,281	2,014

[a]General exemption increased from $5,000 to $50,000.

SOURCE: *Taxation Statistics*, Dept. of National Revenue.

TABLE 50

PROVINCIAL GOVERNMENTS—YEAR IN WHICH MAJOR TAXES WERE FIRST INTRODUCED

Province	Succession duties[a]	Corporation taxes[b]	Corporation income taxes[b]	Personal income taxes[b]	Amusement taxes	Gasoline taxes	Sales taxes
P.E.I.	1894	1894	1920	1894	1920	1924	—
N.S.	1892	1912	1939	—	1917	1925	—
N.B.	1892	1892	1938	—	1918	1926	1950
Que.	1892	1882	1932	1939	1917	1924	1940
Ont.	1892	1899	1932	1936	1916	1925	—
Man.	1893	1900	1931	1923	1918	1923	—
Sask.	1903[c]	1907	1931	1932	—	1928	1937
Alta.	1903[c]	1907	1932	1932	1916	1922	1936[d]
B.C.	1894	1901	1901	1876	1917	1923	1948

[a]Repealed in all cases except Ontario and Quebec since 1947 under Tax Rental Agreements.

[b]Repealed in all provinces from 1941 to 1946 inclusive under Wartime Tax Agreements and since 1947 in all provinces which signed Tax Rental Agreements (excludes Ontario and Quebec under 1947 Agreement and Quebec under 1952 Agreement), except 5% profits tax imposed by agreeing provinces under the 1947 Tax Agreement. Quebec reimposed a tax on personal income in 1954.

[c]Under Northwest Territories Ordinance.

[d]Repealed in following year.

TABLE 51

PROVINCIAL GOVERNMENTS—RATES OF PRINCIPAL

			P.E.I.	N.S.	N.B.
SPECIFIC COMPANIES					
Life Insurance Companies					
On premium income	1929	%	1	2	1½
	1935	%	1	2½	1½
	1940	%	2	2½	2½
Banks					
(1) On volume of business[a]	1929	%	1/8	—	1/30
(loans, deposits, etc.)	1935	%	1/10	1/20	1/15
	1940	%	1/9	1/20	1/10
(2) On paid-up capital	1929	%	—	1/10	—
	1935	%	—	1/10	—
	1940	%	—	1/10	—
(3) On branches	1929	$	—	1,500–4,000[b]	—
Main (other)	1935	$	—	2,500–7,500[b]	—
	1940	$	—	2,500–7,500[b]	5,500 (550)[c]
Railways					
On miles of track	1929	$	agreed	20–50	50–100
(or percentage on assessed	1935	$	amounts	20–50	50–10
value of track)	1940	$	"	10–50	50–100
GENERAL					
Places of Business					
per place	1929	$	—	—	—
	1935	$	—	15–100[d]	—
	1940	$	3% on sales[d]	1/10% on sales[d]	—
Paid up on authorized capital	1929	%	—	1/10	$100-$400[e]
	1935	%	$200-$1500 on domiciled companies	1/8	$100–$400[e]
	1940	%	$50–$1,500 on domiciled companies	1/10	.1375%

[a]Tax based on monthly average of loans and deposits in Prince Edward Island and additional tax levied on volume of business in Nova Scotia.

[b]"Other" branches at a variety of rates.

CORPORATION TAXES, 1929, 1935 AND 1940

Que.	Ont.	Man.	Sask.	Alta.	B.C.
1¾	1½	2	1 -2	2	2
1¾	1¾	3	1½-3	2.2	2¼
2	2.19	3	1½-3	3	2¾
—	—	—	—	—	—
—	—	—	—	—	—
—	—	—	—	—	—
1/10	1/5	—	—	—	—
(1/10 plus) (45% surtax)	1/5	—	—	—	—
1/5	1/4	—	—	1/10 & 50% surtax	—
—	3,000 (200)	2,400 (1-300)	1200(50-300)	1,200 (200)	3,000 (500)
45% surtax	3,000 (200)	3-5,000 (4-750)	1500-3,000 (2-400)	2-4,000 (2-500)	4-10,000 (500)
3,000 (200)	3,750 (250)	as above ÷ 40%	1,500-3,000 (2-400)	3-6,000 (3-750)	4-10,000 (500)
40-60	85 max.	agreed	agreed	1%	2%
40-60	85 max.	amounts	amounts	1.1%	2%
40-60	50-75	"	"	1½%	2%
7.50-30	—	—	—	—	—
7.50-30	50	—	—	—	—
20-50	50	—	15-60[d]	—	—
1/10	—	—		40c per $1,000	—
1/10	1/10	—	$10 to $500	40c per $1,000	—
1/10	1/20	—	$10 to $500	50c per $1,000	—

[c]in lieu of volume of business tax where capital over $500,000.
[d]Chain stores only.
[e]Extra provincial companies only.

TABLE 52

PROVINCIAL REVENUE FROM CORPORATIONS BY INDIVIDUAL SOURCES FOR FISCAL YEARS ENDED NEAREST DECEMBER 31, 1913, 1929, 1935, 1940.

(thousands of dollars)

		General								Express			
		Profits	Capital[a]	Insurance[b]	Railways	Banks	Telephone	Gas and electric	Trust and loan	and telegraph	Tramways	Other	Total[c]
P.E.I.	1913	—	—	7	—	5	—	—	1	1	—	—	17
	1929	d	—	21	40	15	3	1	1	1	—	—	84[e]
	1935	d	58	22	40	16	2	3	3	1	f	1	147[e]
	1940	d	59	27	40	23	3	4	5	1	f	11[g]	172[e]
N.S.	1913	—	—	20	—	11	2	2	4	4	—	—	43
	1929	—	195	187	113	71	75	53	14	28	9	—	745
	1935[h]	—	228	278	132	142	118	113	40	43	7	14[g]	1,115
	1940	i	429	250	114	138	123	179	43	31	8	42[g]	1,364
N.B.	1913	—	—	25	—	15	3	—	2	2	2	—	50
	1929	—	34[j]	122	177	32	39	—	3	7	1	—	416
	1935	—	42[j]	172	182	55	36	—	3	5	1	—	495
	1940	157	196	217	170	102	75	91	6	22	1	2	1,039
Que.	1913	—	504	221	70	95	7	f	10	7	11	4	925
	1929	—	1,939	1,028	151	201	63	f	27	8	15	13	3,444
	1935	2,109	2,563	990	89	288	81	f	29	6	17	11	6,182
	1940[k]	8,461	2,247	1,533	118	450	134	1,831	117	31	289	385	15,596
Ont.	1913	—	—	211	463	76	14	14	36	47	14	2	875
	1929	—	—	1,171	691	539	99	131	134	83	6	15	2,869
	1935	1,179	2,153	1,804	718	682	189	200	164	32	f	10	7,132
	1940	15,267	2,044	2,547	875	860	317	f	f	39	f	11	21,960
Man.	1913	—	—	48	205	31	—	2	26	6	3	28	349
	1929	—	—	422	462	53	—	2	44	7	9	16	1,014
	1935	371	—	453	705	127	—	3	23	5	8	10	1,705
	1940	1,513	—	468	631	166	—	2	25	5	4	14	2,828
Sask.	1913[h]	—	—	65	71	47	—	—	31	28	—	16	258
	1929	—	79	393	404	55	f	f	33	11	f	10	986
	1935	169	85	355	404	102	f	f	27	11	f	35	1,188
	1940	700	70	282	404	79	f	f	33	14	f	34	1,603
Alta.	1913	—	—	43	74	23	—	2	11	3	—	15	171
	1929	—	137	361	239	64	—	25	17	12	—	89	946
	1935	305	150	275	342	79	—	16	21	12	—	146	1,346
	1940	1,187	183	307	482	303	—	47	32	12	—	149	2,702
B.C.	1913	138	—	23	145	37	4	25[l]	15	1	m	—	388
	1929	2,795	—	420	700	115	51	192[l]	37	14	m	—	4,324
	1935	2,190	—	474	713	140	135	578[l]	30	13	m	—	4,273
	1940	5,350	—	529	696	135	165	971[l]	40	14	m	158	8,058

[a]Includes place of business taxes.
[b]Includes taxes on accident and guarantee, and fire insurance companies.
[c]Does not necessarily add owing to rounding of figures.
[d]Details not available.
[e]Excludes general profits tax.
[g]Includes taxes on chain stores.
[h]Fourteen months.
[i]Not separable from other taxes.
[j]Extra-provincial companies.
[k]Twelve months ended June 30, 1941.
[l]Includes tramways.

TABLE 53

PROVINCIAL GOVERNMENTS—REGISTRATIONS OF MOTOR VEHICLES

Year	Passenger cars	Commercial vehicles	Motor cycles	Total[a]
1905	553	—	—	565
1910	5,890	—	55	9,158
1915	60,688	533	5,412	95,284
1920	251,945	22,310	8,195	408,790
1925	641,186	74,938	7,924	724,048
1930	1,055,514	167,548	9,427	1,232,489
1935	989,744	175,888	10,484	1,176,116
1936	1,041,529	187,770	10,825	1,240,124
1937	1,103,012	205,588	11,102	1,319,702
1938	1,159,604	223,176	12,073	1,394,853
1939	1,190,021	236,902	12,322	1,439,245
1940	1,234,637	252,813	13,379	1,500,829
1941	1,279,536	278,771	14,477	1,572,784
1942	1,216,950	291,385	15,818	1,524,153
1943	1,193,847	301,602	16,396	1,511,845
1944	1,177,558	309,964	15,045	1,502,567
1945	1,160,058	322,829	14,194	1,497,081
1946	1,234,006	371,294	17,163	1,622,463
1947	1,370,173	439,657	26,129	1,835,959
1948	1,496,784	504,220	33,939	2,034,943
1949	1,672,352	578,282	39,994	2,290,628
1950	1,907,169	649,672	43,670	2,600,511
1951	2,097,594	731,637	43,189	2,872,420
1952	2,296,435	817,304	42,085	3,155,824
1953	2,513,754	876,741	40,177	3,430,672

[a]Some of the provinces reported totals only prior to 1923.

SOURCE: *The Motor Vehicle*, D.B.S.

TABLE 54

PROVINCIAL GOVERNMENTS—EFFECTIVE DATE OF CHANGES IN GASOLINE TAX RATES

	Effective date	Rate per gallon
Newfoundland	Mar. 28, 1949	14c
	June 22, 1954	15
Prince Edward Island	May 1, 1924	2
	Mar. 31, 1926	3
	May 1, 1928	5
	May 2, 1932	6
	Apr. 15, 1933	8
	Apr. 23, 1937	10
	Apr. 1, 1947	13
Nova Scotia	Jan. 15, 1926	3
	Mar. 7, 1928	5
	Apr. 1, 1932	6
	May 1, 1934	8
	Mar. 15, 1938	10
	Apr. 1, 1947	13
	June 18, 1951	15

TABLE 54—*Continued*

	Effective date	Rate per gallon
New Brunswick	Apr. 30, 1926	3
	Jan. 1, 1929	5
	Apr. 1, 1932	7
	Apr. 1, 1934	8
	Mar. 20, 1938	10
	Apr. 1, 1947	13
	Apr. 1, 1954	15
Quebec	Apr. 1, 1924	2
	Apr. 1, 1925	3
	Apr. 1, 1928	5
	Dec. 17, 1931	6
	Apr. 18, 1939	8
	Apr. 1, 1947	11
	Nov. 8, 1950	13
Ontario	May 11, 1925	3
	Mar. 28, 1929	5
	Mar. 25, 1932	6
	Apr. 1, 1939	8
	Apr. 1, 1947	11
Manitoba	Apr. 27, 1923	1
	Mar. 5, 1925	3
	Apr. 14, 1930	5
	May 7, 1932	7
	Apr. 1, 1947	9
Saskatchewan	May 1, 1928	3
	Apr. 1, 1930	5
	May 1, 1932	6
	Apr. 1, 1935	7
	May 1, 1945	8
	Apr. 1, 1947	10
	Apr. 1, 1953	11
Alberta	Apr. 30, 1922	2
	July 1, 1927	3
	June 1, 1929	5
	Apr. 1, 1933	6
	Apr. 1, 1935	7
	Apr. 1, 1947	9
	Apr. 1, 1951	10
British Columbia	Dec. 21, 1923	3
	Mar. 25, 1930	5
	Apr. 13, 1932	7
	Apr. 1, 1947	10

SOURCE: *The Motor Vehicle*, D.B.S.

TABLE 55

PROVINCIAL GOVERNMENTS—GASOLINE TAX RATES IN EFFECT IN EACH PROVINCE AS AT DECEMBER 31, 1922 TO 1954
(cents per imperial gallon)

	Nfld.	P.E.I.	N.S.	N.B.	Que.	Ont.	Man.	Sask.	Alta.	B.C.
1922	—	—	—	—	—	—	—	—	2	—
1923	—	—	—	—	—	—	1	—	2	3
1924	—	2	—	—	2	—	1	—	2	3
1925	—	2	—	—	3	3	3	—	2	3
1926	—	3	3	3	3	3	3	—	2	3
1927	—	3	3	3	3	3	3	—	3	3
1928	—	5	5	3	5	3	3	3	3	3
1929	—	5	5	5	5	5	3	3	5	3
1930	—	5	5	5	5	5	5	5	5	5
1931	—	5[a]	5	5	6	5	5	5	5	5
1932	—	6	6	7	6	6	7	6	5	7
1933	—	8	6	7	6	6	7	6	6	7
1934	—	8	8	8	6	6	7	6	6	7
1935	—	8	8	8	6	6	7	7	7	7
1936	—	8	8	8	6	6	7	7	7	7
1937	—	10	8	8	6	6	7	7	7	7
1938	—	10	10	10	6	6	7	7	7	7
1939	—	10	10	10	8	8	7	7	7	7
1940	—	10	10	10	8	8	7	7	7	7
1941	—	10	10	10	8	8	7	7	7	7
1942	—	10	10	10	8	8	7	7	7	7
1943	—	10	10	10	8	8	7	7	7	7
1944	—	10	10	10	8	8	7	7	7	7
1945	—	10	10	10	8	8	7	8	7	7
1946	—	10	10	10	8	8	7	8	7	7
1947	—	13	13	13	11	11	9	10	9	10
1948	—	13	13	13	11	11	9	10	9	10
1949	14	13	13	13	11	11	9	10	9	10
1950	14	13	13	13	13	11	9	10	9	10
1951	14	13	15	13	13	11	9	10	10	10
1952	14	13	15	13	13	11	9	10	10	10
1953	14	13	15	13	13	11	9	11	10	10
1954	15	13	15	15	13	11	9	11	10	10

[a] 6c for months of June, July, and August.

TABLE 56

SALES OF GASOLINE IN CANADA
(millions of gallons)

Year	Total sales (gross)	Taxable sales (net)
1930	582	461
1931	557	463
1932	501	439
1933	485	422
1934	535	477
1935	574	500
1936	624	533
1937	718	603
1938	763	632
1939	808	663
1940	883	703
1941	980	747
1942	898	612
1943	904	530
1944	970	575
1945	916	663
1946	1,213	935
1947	1,372	1,033
1948	1,518	1,133
1949	1,684	1,253[a]
1950	1,843	1,390[a]
1951	2,050[b]	1,529[a]
1952	2,344[a]	1,718[a]
1953	2,549[a]	1,903[a]

[a]Includes Newfoundland.

[b]Includes Newfoundland for last four months of 1951.

SOURCES: *The Highway and The Motor Vehicle in Canada; The Motor Vehicle in Canada; The Motor Vehicle.*

TABLE 57

CORPORATION INCOME BY PROVINCE OF ORIGIN UNDER 5 PER CENT UNIFORM TAX, TAXATION YEARS 1947 TO 1951
(million of dollars)

Province	1947	1948	1949	1950	1951
Newfoundland	—	—	—	21.2	25.0
Prince Edward Island	3.8	3.8	4.1	5.9	3.9
Nova Scotia	38.6	47.3	42.9	49.7	56.5
New Brunswick	35.6	39.3	31.1	38.8	50.2
Manitoba	79.3	84.4	78.0	98.0	103.3
Saskatchewan	54.5	53.4	52.1	62.2	66.3
Alberta	71.0	87.8	93.4	117.5	128.8
British Columbia	226.3	248.8	189.8	284.4	303.0
Total, 8 provinces[a]	509.1	564.8	491.3	677.8	737.0
Total[b]	1,765.4	1,931.9	1,847.9	2,334.2	2,756.9

[a]Does not necessarily add due to rounding of figures.

[b]Net taxable income of taxable corporations. Includes corporation income with origin in Ontario, Quebec, Yukon and Northwest Territories, and foreign jurisdictions.

SOURCE: *Taxation Statistics*, 1954, pp. 73, 126.

Bibliography

GENERAL SOURCES

A Government of Canada

House of Commons Debates, 1870 to date. Ottawa, Queen's Printer. (A newspaper clipping record of debates from 1846 to 1869 is available in the Library of Parliament, Ottawa.)

Budget Speeches of the Ministers of Finance. Ottawa, Queen's Printer. (These speeches comprise an invaluable record of Canadian tariff, taxation, and fiscal policies and were a basic source in the writing of the sections of this book dealing with national developments. They will not be referred to again in the bibliography. The reader may consult the footnotes and the complete list of budget speeches in Appendix B.)

Public Accounts of Canada. Ottawa, Queen's Printer.

Statutes of Canada. Ottawa, Queen's Printer.

Miscellaneous Statistics of Canada, 1863–1873. Quebec and Ottawa, Hunter, Rose & Co. (An annual volume compiled in the Audit Office, Department of the Ministry of Finance, includes municipal as well as provincial financial and commercial statistics.)

Yearbook and Almanac of Canada, 1867–1870. Ed. by ARTHUR HARVEY, Finance Department. Ottawa and Montreal.

Canada: Statistical Abstract and Record, 1885–1904. Ottawa, Department of Agriculture.

Canada Yearbook, 1905 to date. Ottawa, Queen's Printer.

Dominion Bureau of Statistics. *Financial Statistics of Provincial Governments in Canada,* 1916 to date, Ottawa. (Annual.)

—— *Municipal Statistics,* 1931–8. Ottawa. (Annual, superseded by *Financial Statistics of Municipal Governments in Canada,* 1944 to date.)

For statement on existing financial statistics of municipalities see Appendix A of Dominion Bureau of Statistics, Finance Statistics Branch, *Memorandum on the Co-ordination and Publication of Municipal Statistics in Canada.* Ottawa, 1937.

B. Provincial Governments

See budget speeches of the Provincial Treasurers or Ministers of Finance, the Statutes of the various provinces, and the provincial *Gazettes.* All are publications of the provincial Queen's Printers.

C. Non-Official Publications

Canada and Its Provinces. ADAM SHORTT and A. G. DOUGHTY, general editors. Toronto, Publishers' Association of Canada, 1913–17. 23 vols.

Canadian Annual Review, 1901–1937/8. Founded by CASTELL HOPKINS. Toronto, Canadian Annual Review, Ltd.

Canadian Banker. Journal of the Canadian Bankers' Association, vol. I, Sept., 1893 to date. (Prior to July, 1936, published under title, *Journal of the Canadian Bankers' Association.*)

Canadian Bar Review, vol. I, Jan., 1923 to date. Ottawa, Canadian Bar Association.

Canadian Chartered Accountant, vol. I, 1911 to date. Toronto, Dominion Association of Chartered Accountants.

Canadian Journal of Economics and Political Science, vol. I, Feb., 1935 to date. Journal of the Canadian Political Science Association. Toronto, Univ. of Toronto Press. (Supersedes *Contributions to Canadian Economics* and *Papers and Proceedings of the Canadian Political Science Association.* Each issue up to Nov., 1952, contains classified list of writings in Canadian economics entitled "A Bibliography of Current Publications on Canadian Economics.")

Canadian Political Science Association. *Papers and Proceedings of the Annual Meetings,* vol. I, 1913, vols. II–VI, 1930–4.

Citizens Research Institute of Canada. *Proceedings of the Annual Convention of the Canadian Tax Conference,* 1st–9th, 1923–31. Toronto.

——— *Yearbook and Annual Report,* 1919 to date. Toronto.

Contributions to Canadian Economics. University of Toronto Studies, History and Economics. Vols. I–VII, 1928–34. Toronto, Univ. of Toronto Press. (Includes bibliography of Canadian economics and list of theses.)

For additional currently published "General Sources" see bibliography in the author's *Taxation in Canada.* Toronto, Univ. of Toronto Press. 1954.

Chapters 1–3

BACKGROUND OF UNION, 1867

Government Documents

Canada, Province of. *Parliamentary Debates on the Subject of the Confederation of the British North American Provinces.* 3rd session, 8th Provincial Parliament of Canada. Quebec, Hunter & Rose, Parliamentary Printer, 1865.

Canada, Audit office. *Miscellaneous Statistics of Canada for the Year 1867.* Part 1. *Municipal Returns, Ontario.* Part 2. *Municipal Returns, Quebec, and Partial Returns from New Brunswick.* Ottawa, Hunter Rose, 1868.

Canada. *Correspondence and Negotiations Connected with the Affairs of Nova Scotia.* Laid before Parliament by command of His Excellency the Governor General. Ottawa, Hunter, Rose, 1869.

Canada, Royal Commission on Dominion-Provincial Relations. *Report* (Rowell-Sirois). Ottawa, King's Printer, 1940. (Book I, *Canada: 1867–1939.*)

Durham, J. G. L., 1st Earl of. *Lord Durham's Report on the Affairs of British North America.* Ed. with an introduction by Sir C. P. Lucas. Oxford, Clarendon press, 1912.

Books and Pamphlets

Adarkar, B. P. *The Principles and Problems of Federal Finance.* London, King, 1933.

Boos, A. W. *The Financial Arrangements between the Provinces and the Dominion.* McGill Univ. Economic Studies, no. 12. Toronto, Macmillan, 1930.

Bourinot, J. G. *Local Government in Canada: An Historical Study.* Baltimore, Johns Hopkins Press, 1887. (Also in *Transactions of the Royal Society of Canada,* vol. IV, sec. 2, 1886, pp. 43–76.)

Brittain, H. L. *Local Government in Canada.* Toronto, Ryerson Press, 1951. (Chap. 1.)

BROWNSTEIN, CHARLES. *Taxation of Income in Canada.* M.A. thesis, McGill Univ., 1925.

CAHALL, R. D. *The Sovereign Council of New France.* Studies in History, Economics and Public Law, ed. by Faculty of Political Science, Columbia Univ., vol. LXV, no. 1. New York, Columbia Univ., 1915.

CLARK, R. M. *Some Aspects of the Development of Personal Income Tax in the Provinces and Municipalities of Canada up to 1930.* Vol. I. Ph.D. thesis, Harvard Univ., 1946. 2 vols.

CREIGHTON, D. G. *British North America at Confederation.* Appendix 2, *Report,* Royal Commission on Dominion-Provincial Relations. Ottawa, 1939.

DAWSON, R. M. *The Government of Canada.* 2nd ed. Toronto, Univ. of Toronto Press, 1954. (Chaps. 1, 2, and 3.)

DICEY, A. V. *Introduction to the Study of the Law of the Constitution.* 9th ed. London, Macmillan, 1939.

EGGLESTON, WILFRID. *The Road to Nationhood: A Chronicle of Dominion-Provincial Relations.* Toronto, Oxford Univ. Press, 1946.

ELLS, MARGARET. "A Study of Early Provincial Taxation: Being a Tabular Statement of Fiscal Legislation in Nova Scotia between 1751 and 1815, with an Introduction and an Appendix." In *Bulletin of the Public Archives of Nova Scotia,* vol. I, no. 2, Halifax, 1937.

GALT, A. T. *Speech on the Proposed Union of the British North American Provinces.* Delivered at Sherbrooke, Que., Nov. 23, 1864. Reprinted from Montreal *Gazette,* Montreal, Que., 1864.

HARVEY, D. C. "The Maritime Provinces and Confederation." In *Report of the Annual Meeting of the Canadian Historical Association,* 1927, pp. 39–45.

HEMMEON, J. C. "Trade and Tariffs in the British North American Provinces before Confederation." In *Papers and Proceedings of the Sixth Annual Meeting of the Canadian Political Science Association* 6: 51–9 (1934).

HOWE, J. E. "Quit Rents in New Brunswick." In *Report of the Annual Meeting of the Canadian Historical Association,* 1928, pp. 55–61.

INNIS, H. A., and A. R. M. LOWER, eds. *Selected Documents in Canadian Economic History, 1783–1885.* Toronto, Univ. of Toronto Press, 1933. (Esp. pp. 78, 111, 224, 318–67, 381, 638–42.)

KARVE, D. G. *Federation: A Study of Comparative Politics.* London, Oxford Univ. Press, 1932.

KENNEDY, W. P. M. *The Constitution of Canada, 1534–1938: An Introduction to Its Development, Law and Custom.* 2nd ed. London, Oxford Univ. Press, 1938.

KENNEDY, W. P. M., ed. *Documents of the Canadian Constitution, 1795–1915.* Toronto, Oxford Univ. Press, 1918.

KEIRSTEAD, W. C. "The Basis of the Federal Subsidies." In *Papers and Proceedings of the Sixth Annual Meeting of the Canadian Political Science Association* 6: 134–61 (1934).

LOWER, A. R. M. *Colony to Nation.* Toronto, Longmans, Green, 1946.

MCDIARMID, O. J. *Commercial Policy in the Canadian Economy.* Cambridge, Mass., Harvard Univ. Press, 1946.

MACKINTOSH, W. A. *The Economic Background of Dominion-Provincial Relations.* Appendix 3, *Report,* Royal Commission on Dominion-Provincial Relations. Ottawa, 1939.

MACLEAN, S. J. *Tariff History of Canada.* Univ. of Toronto Studies in Political Science, no. 4. Toronto, Warwick and Rutter, 1895.

MANNING, H. E. *Assessment and Rating: Municipal Taxation in Canada.* 3rd ed. Toronto, Cartwright, 1951.

MASTERS, D. C. *The Reciprocity Treaty of 1854.* London, New York, Longmans, Green, 1937.

MAXWELL, J. A. *Federal Subsidies to the Provincial Governments in Canada.* Cambridge, Mass., Harvard Univ. Press, 1937. (Chap. 1.)

——— *The Fiscal Impact of Federalism in the United States.* Cambridge, Mass., Harvard Univ. Press, 1946. (See Prologue and chap. 2.)

MILL, J. S. *Considerations on Representative Government.* London, Routledge, 1905.

POPE, JOSEPH. *Confederation Documents: A Series of Hitherto Unpublished Documents Bearing on the British North America Act.* Toronto, Carswell, 1895.

PORRITT, EDWARD. *Sixty Years of Protection in Canada, 1846–1907.* London, Macmillan, 1908.

SAUNDERS, S. A. *The Economic History of the Maritime Provinces: A Study Prepared for the Royal Commission on Dominion-Provincial Relations.* Ottawa, 1939.

SAWER, G., ed. *Federalism: An Australian Jubilee Study.* Melbourne, F. W. Cheshire Pty. Ltd., 1952.

SHIPPEE, L. B. *Canadian–American Relations, 1849–1874.* New Haven, Yale Univ. Press, 1939.

SHIRRAS, G. F. *Federal Finance in Peace and War, with Special Reference to the United States of America and the British Commonwealth.* London, Macmillan, 1944.

SHORTT, ADAM. "Municipal History, 1791–1867" (Ontario). In *Canada and Its Provinces* 18: 405–52 (1914).

SKELTON, O. D. *The Life and Times of Sir Alexander Tilloch Galt.* Toronto, Oxford Univ. Press, 1920.

TROTTER, R. G. *Canadian Federation: Its Origin and Achievement.* Toronto, Dent, 1924.

VINEBERG, SOLOMON. *Provincial and Local Taxation in Canada.* Studies in History, Economics and Public Law, ed. by Faculty of Political Science, Columbia Univ., vol. LII, no. 1. New York, Columbia Univ., 1912.

WHEARE, K. A. *Federal Government.* 3rd ed. London, Oxford Univ. Press, 1953.

WHITELAW, M. W. *The Maritimes and Canada before Confederation.* Toronto, Oxford Univ. Press, 1934.

WICKETT, S. M., ed. *Municipal Government in Canada.* Univ. of Toronto Studies, History and Economics, vol. II. Published by the Librarian of the Univ. of Toronto, 1907. (See esp. "Municipal Government in Ontario," an historical sketch, by ADAM SHORTT, pp. 61–87; "Municipal Institutions in the Province of Quebec," by R. S. WEIR, pp. 165–92.)

Periodical Articles

HALL, G. E. "Municipal Government's 100th anniversary." *Municipal World* 59: 369–74 (Dec., 1949).

HARVEY, D. C. "Confederation in Prince Edward Island." *Canadian Historical Review* 14: 143–60 (June, 1933).

JONES, R. S. "The Canadian Agricultural Tariff of 1843." *Canadian Journal of Economics and Political Science* 7: 528–37 (Nov., 1941).

MARTIN, CHESTER. "British Policy in Canadian Confederation." *Canadian Historical Review* 13: 3–19 (March, 1932).

——— "The United States and Canadian Nationality." *Canadian Historical Review* 18: 1–11 (March, 1937).

MORSE, CHARLES. "Municipal Institutions in England and Canada." *Canada Law Journal* 41: 505–21 (June 15, 1905).

——— "Robert Baldwin and the Municipal Act, 1869." *Municipal World* 59: 150–1 (May, 1949).

"Nationhood and the Constitution." *Canadian Bar Review* 29 (Dec., 1951).

TROTTER, R. G. "Some American Influences upon the Canadian Federation Movement." *Canadian Historical Review* 5: 213–27 (Sept., 1924).

WEAVER, S. R. "Taxation in New France: A Study in Pioneer Economics." *Journal of Political Economy* 22: 736–55 (Oct., 1914).

WILSON, C. E. "New Brunswick's Entrance into Confederation." *Canadian Historical Review* 9: 4–24 (March, 1928).

CHAPTER 4

FRUSTRATION LEADS TO A NATIONAL POLICY

Government Documents

Canada, Parliament, House of Commons, Select Committee on the Causes of the Present Depression of the Manufacturing, Mining, Commercial, Shipping, Lumber and Fishing Interests. Report [and minutes of evidence]. *Journals of the House of Commons*, 1876, vol. IV, Appendix no. 3. Ottawa. Printed by MacLean, Roger.

Canada, Royal Commission on Dominion-Provincial Relations. *Report.* Ottawa, King's Printer, 1940. (Book I, *Canada: 1867–1939.*)

Books and Periodical Articles

ANNETT, D. R. *British Preference in Canadian Commercial Policy.* Toronto, Ryerson, 1948.

COLQUHOUN, A. H. U. "Reciprocity Negotiations with the United States in 1869." *Canadian Historical Review* 8: 233–42 (Sept. 1927).

Encyclopedia of Canada. W. S. WALLACE, ed. Toronto, University Association of Canada. (See "Tarriffs," vol. VI, pp. 102–8.)

HINCKS, Sir FRANCIS. "Relations of Canada with the United States." *North American Review* 130: 338–55 (1880).

INNIS, H. A., and A. R. M. LOWER, eds. *Selected Documents in Canadian Economic History, 1783–1885.* Toronto, Univ. of Toronto Press, 1933. (See esp. pp. 809–22.)

MCDIARMID, O. J. *Commercial Policy in the Canadian Economy.* Cambridge, Mass., Harvard Univ. Press, 1946.

McGill Univ. 1925 Graduating Class in Commerce. *Reciprocal and Preferential Tariffs*, by Misses GLASSCO, PATTON, MITCHELL [and others]. McGill Univ. Economic Studies, no. 4, National Problems of Canada. Toronto, Macmillan [1925].

MACKINTOSH, W. A. *The Economic Background of Dominion-Provincial Relations.* Appendix 3, *Report*, Royal Commission on Dominion-Provincial Relations. Ottawa, 1939.

MACLEAN, S. J. *Tariff History of Canada.* Toronto Univ. Studies in Political Science, no. 4. Toronto, Warwick and Rutter, 1895.

PORRITT, EDWARD. *Sixty Years of Protection in Canada, 1846–1907.* London, Macmillan, 1908.

SKELTON, O. D. "General Economic History" (1867–1896). In *Canada and Its Provinces* 9: 95–191 (1913).

——— *Life and Letters of Sir Wilfrid Laurier.* Toronto, Oxford Univ. Press, 1921.

TANSILL, C. C. *The Canadian Reciprocity Treaty of 1854.* Johns Hopkins Univ. Studies in Historical and Political Science, ser. 11, no. 2. Baltimore, Johns Hopkins Press, 1922.

——— *Canadian–American Relations, 1875–1911.* New Haven, Yale Univ. Press, 1943.

Taylor, K. W. "Statistics of Foreign Trade." In vol. II of *Statistical Contributions to Canadian economic history*, Toronto, Macmillan, 1931. (Analyses total exports by commodity groups, 1869–75.)

Chapter 5

PORTENTS OF THINGS TO COME

Government Documents

New Brunswick, Commission upon Civic and Municipal Taxation. Report. *Journal of the House of Assembly*, 1894, Supplementary Appendix, pp. 58–62. Fredericton, Queen's Printer, 1894.

Ontario, Legislative Assembly, Select Committee on Exemptions from Taxation. Report. *Journal of the Legislative Assembly*, Appendix no. 4, 1878. Toronto, Queen's Printer, 1878.

Ontario, Select Committee on Taxation and Exemptions. Report. *Journal of the Legislative Assembly*, Appendix no. 3, 1879. Toronto, Queen's Printer, 1879.

Ontario, Commission on Municipal Institutions. *First Report*. Sessional Paper no. 42, 1888. Toronto, Queen's Printer, 1888.

——— *Second Report*. Sessional Paper no. 13, 1889. Toronto, Queen's Printer, 1889.

Ontario, Commission on Municipal Taxation. *Report*. Sessional Paper no. 73, 1893. Toronto, Queen's Printer, 1893.

Books and Periodical Articles

Biggar, C. R. W. *Growth of Municipal Institutions in Ontario*. Appendix to report of Ontario Bureau of Industries for 1896.

Clark, R. M. *Some Aspects of the Development of the Personal Income Tax in the Provinces and Municipalities of Canada up to 1930*. Ph.D. thesis, Harvard Univ., 1946. 2 vols.

MacKay, K. W. "Municipal History, 1867–1913" (Ontario). In *Canada and Its Provinces* 18: 455–510 (1914).

Mavor, James. "Finance and Taxation" (Ontario). In *Canada and Its Provinces* 17: 243–73 (1914).

——— "The Taxation of Corporations in Ontario." *Journal of the Canadian Bankers' Association* 7: 333–50 (July, 1900).

Raney, E. F. *Municipal Taxation in Canada: A Reconstruction*. Ph.D. thesis, Univ. of Toronto, 1912.

Vineberg, Solomon. *Provincial and Local Taxation in Canada*. Studies in History, Economics and Public Law, ed. by Faculty of Political Science, Columbia Univ., vol. LII, no. 1. New York, Columbia Univ., 1912.

Wickett, S. M. *Municipal Government in Canada*. Univ. of Toronto Studies, History and Economics, vol. II. Published by the Librarian of the Univ. of Toronto, 1907. (Esp. "The Municipal History of Manitoba," by A. C. Ewart, pp. 133–48; "Municipal Organization in Ontario," by K. W. MacKay, pp. 91–119; "Local Government in the Maritime Provinces," by W. C. Murray, pp. 221–67; "Municipal Government in the Northwest Territories," by M. S. Wickett, pp. 151–63.)

Chapter 6

NATIONAL POLICY IN TRANSITION

To avoid repetition, material dealing with commercial policy and the tariff which are listed for chapter 4, and which cover this period also, are not repeated here.

Government Documents

Canada. *Tariff Relations between the United States and the Dominion of Canada: Correspondence and Statements, 1911.* Ottawa, Govt. Printing Bureau, 1911.

Canada. *Correspondence between British Ambassador at Washington and the Government of Canada in Connection with Negotiations for a Reciprocity Treaty between Canada and United States.* Sessional Paper no. 82a, 1912. Ottawa, King's Printer, 1912.

Canada, Royal Commission on Dominion-Provincial Relations. *Report.* Ottawa, King's Printer, 1940. (Book I, *Canada: 1867–1939.*)

U.S. Tariff Commission. *Reciprocity with Canada: A Study of the Arrangement of 1911.* U.S. Govt. Printing Office, 1920.

Books

ANNIS, C. A. *A Study of Canadian Tariffs and Trade Agreements.* Ph.D. thesis, Cornell Univ., 1936.

BATES, STEWART. *Financial History of Canadian Governments.* A Study Prepared for the Royal Commission on Dominion-Provincial Relations. Ottawa, 1939.

ELLIS, L. E. *Reciprocity, 1911: A Study in Canadian–American Relations.* New Haven, Yale Univ. Press, 1939.

HARPELL, J. J. *Canadian National Economy: The Cause of High Prices and Their Effect upon the Country.* Toronto, Macmillan, 1911.

MACKINTOSH, W. A. *The Economic Background of Dominion-Provincial Relations.* Appendix 3, *Report,* Royal Commission on Dominion-Provincial Relations. Ottawa, King's Printer, 1939.

PORRITT, EDWARD. *Sixty Years of Protection in Canada, 1846–1912.* 2nd ed. rev. by ANNIE G. PORRITT. Winnipeg, Grain Growers' Guide, 1913.

SHORTT, ADAM. *Imperial Preferential Trade from a Canadian Point of View.* Toronto, Morang, 1904.

SKELTON, O. D. *Federal Finance.* Bulletin of the Departments of History and Political and Economic Science in Queen's Univ., no. 16, July, 1915. Kingston, Jackson Press, 1915.

——— "General Economic History, 1867–1912." In *Canada and Its Provinces* 9: 95–274 (1914), pp. 191–274.

Periodical Articles

LEWIS, JOHN. "The British Preference." *Annals of the American Academy of Political Science* 107: 198–203 (May, 1923).

MACE, B. M. "Imperial Preference in the British Empire." *Annals of the American Academy of Political Science* 168: 226–32 (July, 1933).

OSBORNE, J. B. "Commercial Relations of the United States with Canada." *Annals of the American Academy of Political and Social Science* 32: 330–42 (Sept., 1908).

SHORTT, ADAM. "Origin and Results of Canada's Preferential Tariff." *Annals of the American Academy of Political and Social Science* 112: 221–31 (March, 1924).

SIFTON, CLIFFORD. "Reciprocity." *Annals of the American Academy of Political and Social Science* 45: 20–8 (Jan., 1913).

SWARTZ, W. G. "The Proposed Canadian–American Reciprocity Agreement of 1911." *Journal of Economic and Business History* 3: 118–47 (Nov., 1930).

CHAPTER 7

EXPANSION BRINGS FIRST MAJOR TAXES

Government Documents

Canada, Royal Commission on Dominion-Provincial Relations. *Report.* Ottawa, King's Printer, 1940. (Book I, *Canada: 1867–1939.*)

Dominion-Provincial Conference on Reconstruction, 1945. *Corporation Taxes. Succession Duties.* [Ottawa, 1945.] (Reference books.)

British Columbia

Commission on Assessment Act. *Report.* Sessional Paper F27, 1905. Victoria, King's Printer, 1905.

Royal Commission on Taxation. *Synopsis of Report and Full Report.* Sessional Papers, 1912. Victoria, King's Printer, 1912.

Manitoba

Assessment and Taxation Commission. *Report* (E. M. WOOD, Chairman). Winnipeg, King's Printer, 1919. (Appendices include "Taxation in British Columbia," "Taxation in Alberta," "Taxation in Saskatchewan": Studies of provincial and municipal tax systems by Professor A. B. CLARK.)

Ontario

Royal Commission on Railway Taxation. *Report.* Sessional Paper no. 54, 1905. Toronto, King's Printer, 1905.

Books

BAYLY, R. A. *Succession Duty in Canada.* Toronto, Carswell, 1902.

BLUMENSTEIN, J. H. *The Taxation of Corporations in Canada.* McGill Univ. Economic Studies, no. 3, National Problems of Canada. Toronto, Macmillan, n.d.

BRADSHAW, T. "Taxation of Life Insurance Companies in Canada." In *Addresses and Proceedings of the Second International Conference of the International Tax Association,* 1908, pp. 343–61. (Formerly and subsequently the National Tax Association.)

CHAMBERS, E. T. D. "Provincial Taxation and Finance" (Quebec). In *Canada and Its Provinces* 15: 239–50 (1914).

CLARK, A. B. "Finance and Taxation" (Prairie Provinces). In *Canada and Its Provinces* 20: 351–62 (1914).

GOSNELL, R. E. "Public Administration" (British Columbia). In *Canada and Its Provinces* 22: 349–84 (1914).

MCKILLIGAN, J. B. "Taxation in British Columbia." In *Proceedings of the Second International Conference of the International Tax Association,* 1908, pp. 303–28.

MAVOR, JAMES. "Finance and Taxation" (Ontario). In *Canada and Its Provinces* 17: 243–73 (1914).

MORSE, CHARLES. "Provincial and Local Government: Nova Scotia, New Brunswick, Prince Edward Island." In *Canada and Its Provinces* 14: 435–508 (1913).

SELIGMAN, E. R. A. *Essays in Taxation.* 10th ed. New York, Macmillan, 1925. (See chap. 6, "The Taxation of Corporations.")

SKELTON, O. D. "The Taxation of Mineral Resources in Canada." In *Addresses and Proceedings of the Second International Conference of the International Tax Association,* 1908, pp. 385–94.

VINEBERG, SOLOMON. *Provincial and Local Taxation in Canada.* Studies in History, Economics and Public Law, ed. by Faculty of Political Science, Columbia Univ., vol. LII, no. 1. New York, Columbia Univ. Press, 1912.

Periodical Articles

COTTON, C. M. "Is the Tax on Stock Transfers in the Province of Quebec Constitutional." *Journal of the Canadian Bankers' Association* 13: 331–41 (July, 1906).

ECKARDT, H. M. P. "How Excessive Taxation of Banks Increase Discount Rates and Banking Charges." *Journal of the Canadian Bankers' Association* 20: 54–62 (Oct., 1912).

——— "Provincial Taxation of Banks." *Ibid.* 24: 337–9 (July, 1917).

HENRY, W. A. "Double Payment of Succession Duties." *Journal of the Canadian Bankers' Association* 24: 337–9 (July, 1917).

——— "Succession Duty and the Bank Act." *Ibid.* 26: 374–9 (July, 1919).

HOLT, C. M. "The Quebec Succession Duties Act." *Journal of the Canadian Bankers' Association* 10: 37–40 (July, 1903).

MAVOR, JAMES. "The Taxation of Corporations in Ontario." *Journal of the Canadian Bankers' Association* 7: 333–50 (July, 1900).

WYNNE, W. H. "The Taxation of Corporations in Canada." *Bulletin of the National Tax Association* 27: 66–79 (Dec., 1941); 98–111 (Jan., 1942).

CHAPTER 8

THE SINGLE TAX EXPERIMENT

Government Documents

Manitoba

Assessment and Taxation Commission. *Report* (E. M. WOOD, Chairman). Winnipeg, King's Printer, 1919. (Appendices include "Taxation in British Columbia," "Taxation in Alberta," "Taxation in Saskatchewan": studies of provincial and municipal tax systems by Professor A. B. CLARK.)

Winnipeg. *Report to the Mayor and Council of the City of Winnipeg* (Commissioners, F. H. PHIPPEN and A. L. JOHNSON). Feb. 1, 1909.

Winnipeg. *Report to the Mayor and Council of the City of Winnipeg* (Commissioners, F. H. PHIPPEN, A. L. JOHNSON, W. J. CHRISTIE). March 26, 1909.

Winnipeg, Board of Valuation and Revision and Systems of Assessment and Taxation. *Report.* Winnipeg, Telegram Job Printer, 1917.

New Brunswick

Saint John. *Report of the Assessment Law Commissioners.* 1906.

Civic Assessment Commission. *Report* (J. ROY CAMPBELL, Chairman). 1916.

Ontario

Assessment Commission. *Interim (or First Report) and Record of Proceedings of the Commission on Municipal Assessment and Taxation.* Sessional Paper no. 44, 1901. Toronto, King's Printer, 1901.

——— *Report.* Sessional Paper no. 48, 1902. Toronto, King's Printer, 1902.

Legislative Assembly, Select Committee on Municipal Taxation. Report. *Journals of the Legislative Assembly,* vol. XXXVII, 1903, pp. 258–9. Toronto, King's Printer, 1903.

——— Report. *Journal of the Legislative Assembly,* vol. XXXVIII, 1904, pp. 137–9. Toronto, King's Printer, 1904.

Saskatchewan

Municipal Commission. *Report of the Municipal Commission, August 30, 1907.* Sessional Paper no. 2, Session 1908. Regina, King's Printer, 1907.

Books

CLARK, A. B. "Municipal Institutions" (Prairie Provinces). In *Canada and Its Provinces* 20: 395–413 (1914).

FORMON, J. C. "Business Assessment as a Substitute for Personal Property Tax." In *Proceedings of the Second International Conference of the International Tax Association*, 1908, pp. 273–83.

GOSNELL, R. E. "Public Administration" (British Columbia). In *Canada and Its Provinces* 22: 349–84 (1914).

GEORGE, HENRY. *Progress and Poverty: An Enquiry into the Cause of Industrial Depressions, and of Increase of Want with Increase of Wealth: The Remedy.* 4th ed. New York, H. George Co. [1889].

HAIG, R. M. *The Exemption of Improvements from Taxation in Canada and the United States.* A Report Prepared for the Taxation Committee, New York City. New York, Brown Printing and Binding, 1915.

HUNT, T. A. "Taxation Systems of Northwest Canada." In *Proceedings of the Second International Conference of the International Tax Association*, 1908, pp. 285–98.

HURST, GEORGE. "Municipal Income Tax." In *Proceedings of the Eighth Annual Canada Tax Conference*, Citizens Research Institute of Canada, Toronto, 1930, pp. 85–91.

MCGILLIGAN, J. B. "Taxation in British Columbia." In *Proceedings of the Second International Conference of the International Tax Association*, 1908, pp. 303–28.

POST, L. F. *The Taxation of Land Values: An Explanation with Illustrative Charts, Notes and Answers to Typical Questions, of the Land-Labor-and-Fiscal Reform. Advocated by Henry George.* Chicago, The Public, 1912.

RANEY, E. F. *Municipal Taxation in Canada: A Reconstruction.* Ph.D. thesis, Univ. of Toronto, 1912.

SELIGMAN, E. R. A. *Essays in Taxation.* 10th ed. New York, Macmillan, 1925. (See chap. 2, "The General Property Tax," and chap. 3, "The Single Tax.")

Single Tax Association of Canada. *Brief* [presented to the] *Royal Commission of Dominion-Provincial Relations.* Toronto, 1938.

STALKER, ARCHIBALD. *Taxation of Land Values in Western Canada.* McGill Univ., pub. ser. 6, History and Economics, no. 4. Montreal, 1914.

VINEBERG, SOLOMON. *Provincial and Local Taxation in Canada.* Studies in History, Economics and Public Law, ed. by Faculty of Political Science, Columbia Univ., vol. LII, no. 1. New York, Columbia Univ. Press, 1912.

WICKETT, S. M. ed. *Municipal Government in Canada.* Univ. of Toronto Studies, History and Economics, vol. II. Published by the Librarian of the Univ. of Toronto, 1907.

Periodical Articles

DAVENPORT, H. J. "Theoretical Issues in the Single Tax." *American Economic Review* 7: 1–30 (March, 1917).

PATTERSON, H. S. "Single Tax in Alberta." *Dalhousie Review* 6: 362–6 (Oct., 1926).

CHAPTERS 9–10

TRADITIONAL PHILOSOPHY OF WAR FINANCE; PAYING THE COST

Government Documents

Canada, Dept. of Public Information. *Canada's Part in the Great War.* Ottawa, 1919.

Canada, Royal Commission on Dominion-Provincial Relations. *Report*. Ottawa, King's Printer, 1940. (Book I, *Canada: 1867–1936.*)

Books and Pamphlets

BROWN, F. W., J. D. GILSON, and A. F. W. PLUMPTRE. *War Finance in Canada*. Contemporary Affairs, no. 3. Toronto, Ryerson, 1940.

BROWNSTEIN, CHARLES. *Taxation of Income in Canada*. M.A. thesis, McGill Univ., 1925.

CURTIS, C. A. "The Canadian Banks and War Finance." In *Contributions to Canadian Economics* 3:7–40 (1931), Univ. of Toronto Studies, History and Economics, Univ. of Toronto Press, 1931.

HIGGINS, B. H. *Canada's Financial System in War*. Occasional Paper 19. New York, National Bureau of Economic Research, 1944.

PRENTICE, J. S. *Canadian Federal Finance*. Bulletin of the Departments of History and Political and Economic Science in Queen's Univ., no. 55, March, 1928. Kingston, Jackson Press, 1928.

SKELTON, O. D. *Federal Finance*. Bulletin of the Departments of History and Political and Economic Science in Queen's Univ., no. 16, July, 1915. Kingston, Jackson Press, 1915.

——— *Canadian Federal Finance*, II. Bulletin of the Departments of History and Political and Economic Science, Queen's Univ., no. 29, Oct., 1918. Kingston, Jackson Press, 1918.

WHITE, Sir THOMAS. *The Story of Canada's War Finance*. Montreal [Canadian Bank of Commerce], 1921.

Periodical Articles

CRAMMOND, EDGAR. "The Real Cost of the War." *Journal of the Canadian Bankers' Association* 28: 80–99 (Oct., 1920).

DEUTSCH, J. J. "War Finance and the Canadian Economy, 1914–20." *Canadian Journal of Economics and Political Science* 6: 525–42 (Nov., 1940).

HURD, W. B. "The Trend of Federal Taxation and Expenditures." *Journal of the Canadian Bankers' Association* 36: 19–28 (Oct., 1928).

MACKINTOSH, W. A. "Economics, Prices, and the War." *Queen's Quarterly* (April, May, June, 1919).

SKELTON, O. D. "Canadian War Finance." *American Economic Review* 7: 816–31 (Dec., 1917).

WHITE, Sir THOMAS. "Federal Financial Administration and the Banks." *Journal of the Canadian Bankers' Association* 29: 350–62 (April, 1922).

CHAPTERS 11–12

WAR ALSO BRINGS NEW PROVINCIAL TAXES; RUDE AWAKENING FOR THE CITIES

NOTE: The references for these chapters have been combined, since so many of them deal with provincial and municipal taxation simultaneously.

Government Documents

Canada, Dominion Bureau of Statistics, Finance Statistics Branch. *Municipal Tax Levies and Receipts by Provinces: Historical Analysis, 1913–1938*. Ottawa. (Special report.)

British Columbia

Board of Taxation. [First and second] *Reports with a Report on Taxation in the Province of British Columbia by R. M. Haig*. Sessional Papers, 1919. Victoria, King's Printer, 1919.

BRITTAIN, H. C. *The Taxation System of Vancouver*. Report to the Mayor and City Council of Vancouver, December, 1920.

Manitoba

Assessment and Taxation Commission. *Report* (E. M. WOOD, Chairman). Winnipeg, King's Printer, 1919. (Appendices include "Taxation in British Columbia," "Taxation in Alberta," "Taxation in Saskatchewan": studies of provincial and municipal tax systems by Professor A. B. CLARK.)

BRITTAIN, H. L. *The Present System of Taxation in Force within the City of Winnipeg, with Special Reference to the Incidence and Equitable Distribution of the Tax Burden*. Report Prepared for the Mayor and City Council, Winnipeg, Canada. Toronto, Citizens Research Institute of Canada, 1923.

Winnipeg, Board of Valuation and Revision on Systems of Assessment and Taxation. *Report*. Winnipeg, Telegram Job Printers, 1917.

Saskatchewan

Commission of Inquiry Respecting the Public Revenue Tax. *Synopsis of report*. Sessional Paper 19, 1921–2, vol. II. Regina, King's Printer, 1922.

HAIG, R. M. *Taxation in the Urban Municipalities of Saskatchewan*. A Report to the Government of the Province of Saskatchewan. Sessional Paper no. 10, Session 1918-19. Regina, King's Printer, 1917.

YORATH, C. J. *Special Report upon Taxation and Assessment*. Report to the Mayor and Aldermen of Saskatoon. Published by the City of Saskatoon, 1917.

Books

Canadian Annual Review, founded by J. CASTELL HOPKINS. Toronto, Canadian Annual Review. (The sparsity of other material on the period makes this yearbook an invaluable source of information on financial and legislative developments in Canada. In particular see reviews of provincial affairs in the volumes 1913 to 1919.)

CLARK, A. B. "Recent Tax Developments in Western Canada." In *Proceedings of the 13th Annual Conference of the National Tax Association*, 1921, pp. 48–69.

CLARK, R. M. *Some Aspects of the Development of the Personal Income Tax in the Provinces and Municipalities of Canada up to 1930*. Ph.D. thesis, Harvard Univ., 1946.

HAIG, R. M. "The Single Tax Limited in Wartime." In *Proceedings of the 11th Annual Conference of the National Tax Association*, 1917, pp. 375–81.

HURST, GEORGE. "Municipal Income Tax." In *Proceedings of the Eighth Annual Convention of the Canada Tax Conference*, Citizens Research Institute of Canada, Toronto, 1930, pp. 85–91.

MUTCH, D. A. *Brief on Taxation of the Metal and Asbestos Mining Industries, Province of Quebec, 1916–1941*. Prepared for the Western Quebec Mining Association and the Quebec Asbestos Producers' Association. Quebec, July 1, 1943.

——— *Brief on Taxation on the Ontario Metal Mining Industry, 1907–1941*. Prepared for the Ontario Mining Association, by DOUGLAS A. MUTCH, in Collaboration with BALMER NULLY. Toronto, March 1, 1943.

SCHEFTEL, YELTA. *The Taxation of Land Value: A Study of Certain Discriminatory Taxes on Land*. Hart, Schaffner and Marx Prize Essays, 22. Boston, Houghton-Mifflin, 1916.

Periodical Articles

APPLETON, JOHN. "Broadening the Basis of Municipal Taxation." *Journal of the Canadian Bankers' Association* 25: 284–8 (July, 1918).

BECKETT, S. E. "Taxation in British Columbia." *Journal of Political Economy* 32: 416–40 (Aug., 1924).

BELL, F. H. "Municipal Taxation in Nova Scotia." *Dalhousie Review* 1: 264–80 (Oct., 1921).

BRITTAIN, H. L. "Municipal Taxation in Canada." *Annals of the American Academy of Political and Social Science* 107: 221–6 (May, 1923).

ECKARDT, H. M. P. "Provincial Taxation of Banks." *Journal of the Canadian Bankers' Association* 21: 208–18 (July, 1914).

KEIRSTEAD, W. C. "Provincial Taxation of Companies in Canadian Provinces." *Journal of Political Economy* 31: 65–89 (Feb., 1923).

——— "Rural Taxation in the Province of New Brunswick." *Ibid.* 34: 669–90 (Dec., 1926).

NEWCOMER, MABEL, and R. G. HITCHISON. "Taxation of Land Values in Canada." *Journal of Political Economy* 40: 366–78 (June, 1932).

CHAPTERS 13–14

THE DOMINION ADOPTS THE SALES TAX; MAJOR CHANGES ALSO IN DIRECT TAXES

Government Documents

Canada, Royal Commission on Dominion-Provincial Relations. *Report*. Ottawa, King's Printer, 1940. (Book I, *Canada: 1867–1936*, chap. 5.)

Canada, Royal Commission on the Taxation of Annuities and Family Corporations. *Report*. Ottawa, King's Printer, 1945.

Books

BLUMENSTEIN, J. H. *The Taxation of Corporations in Canada*. McGill Univ. Economic Studies, no. 3, National Problems of Canada. Toronto, Macmillan, 1930.

BUEHLER, A. D. *General Sales Taxation: Its History and Development*. New York, Business Bourse, 1932.

Citizens Research Institute of Canada. *Proceedings of the Annual Convention of the Canadian Tax Conferences*, 1st–9th, 1923–31. Toronto. (See chapter footnotes for special references.)

DUE, J. F. *The General Manufacturers Sales Tax in Canada*. Canadian Tax Papers, no. 3. Toronto, Canadian Tax Foundation, 1951.

GORDON, T. M. *The Canadian Sales Tax*. McGill Univ. Economic Studies, no. 11, National Problems of Canada. M.A. thesis. Toronto, Macmillan, 1930.

KEMP, H. R. "Dominion Taxation." In *Proceedings of the First Annual Convention of the Canadian Tax Conference*, Citizens Research Institute of Canada, Toronto, 1923, pp. 9–15.

MCDIARMID, O. J. *Commercial Policy in the Canadian Economy*. Cambridge, Mass., Harvard Univ. Press, 1946.

MACKINTOSH, W. A. *The Economic Background of Dominion-Provincial Relations*. Appendix 3, *Report*, Royal Commission on Dominion-Provincial Relations. Ottawa, 1939.

PERRY, J. H. *Taxation in Canada*. 2nd ed. Toronto, Univ. of Toronto Press, 1954.

PLAXTON, C. P., and F. P. VARCOE. *A Treatise on the Dominion Income Tax Law*. Toronto, Carswell, 1921.

Periodical Articles

BATES, E. S. "Tariff Protection on Textiles." *Canadian Textile Journal* pp. 13–15 (July 29, 1932).

HODGINS, J. E. "The Canadian Sales Tax" (history and development). *Bulletin for International Fiscal Documentation* 4:5–12 (1950).
HURD, W. B. "The Trend of Federal Taxation and Expenditures." *Journal of the Canadian Bankers' Association* 36: 19–28 (Oct., 1928).
KEMP, H. R. "Dominion and Provincial Taxation in Canada." *Annals of the Academy of Political and Social Science* 107: 216–20 (May, 1923).
"The Sales Tax." *Canadian Forum* 3 (July, 1923).
WYNNE, W. H. "The Canadian Federal Sales Tax." *Canadian Chartered Accountant* 38: 176–93 (March, 1941). (Also in *Bulletin of the National Tax Association*, Oct., 1940.)

CHAPTER 15

GASOLINE AND LIQUOR PROVIDE NEW REVENUE

Government Documents

Canada, Dominion Bureau of Statistics. *The Control and Sale of Liquor in Canada,* 1930 to date. Ottawa. (Annual. See also *Canada Yearbook,* 1934–5, and later issues.)
——— *Financial Statistics of Provincial Governments in Canada,* 1921 to date. Ottawa. (Annual.)
——— *The Motor Vehicle in Canada,* 1921 to date. Ottawa. (Annual.) (See report of 1931 for summary history of gasoline taxation in the provinces and subsequent reports for provincial tax rates and revenues.)

Alberta

Advisory Committee on Taxation. *Report on Taxation* (H. M. TORY, Chairman). Edmonton, King's Printer, 1928.
Taxation Inquiry Board on Provincial and Municipal Taxation. *Report* (J. F. PERCIVAL, Chairman). Edmonton, King's Printer, 1935.

Books and Periodical Articles

BARBOUR, H. D. "Death Taxes in Western Canada." *Canadian Bar Review* 9: 641–9 (Nov., 1931); 10: 18–30 (Jan., 1932).
BATES, STEWART. *Financial History of Canadian Governments.* Study Prepared for the Royal Commission on Dominion-Provincial Relations. Ottawa, 1939.
BECKETT, S. E. "Taxation in British Columbia." *Journal of Political Economy* 32: 416–40 (Aug., 1924).
Citizens Research Institute of Canada. *Proceedings of the Annual Convention of the Canadian Tax Conference,* 1st-9th, 1923–31. Toronto. (See chapter footnotes for special references.)
JACOBY, NEAL, and J. E. ROBBINS. *The Problem of Securing Additional Sources of Revenue for Provincial Purposes.* Essays on Canadian Economic Problems, vol. III. Competition, 1929–30. Montreal, Royal Bank of Canada.

CHAPTER 16

SUB-DIVISIONS UNLIMITED BRING PROSPERITY AND PROBLEMS

Government Documents

Alberta, Advisory Committee on Taxation. *Report on Taxation* (H. M. TORY, Chairman). Edmonton, King's Printer, 1928.
British Columbia, Royal Commission on Municipal Taxation. *Report* (A. M. HARPER, Chairman). Victoria, Govt. Print. Bureau, 1934. (Mimeo.)
New Brunswick, Royal Commission to Inquire into the Taxation by Cities, Towns

and Municipalities of Non-Residents. Report. *Journal of the House of Assembly*, 1928. Fredericton, King's Printer, 1928.

Saskatchewan, Commission of Inquiry into Provincial and Municipal Taxation. *Report* (N. H. JACOBY, Chairman). Regina, King's Printer, 1936.

Books

Citizens Research Institute of Canada. *Proceedings of the Annual Convention of the Canadian Tax Conference*, 1st-9th, 1923–31. Toronto. (See chapter footnotes for special references.)

MACKINTOSH, W. A. *Economic Problems of the Prairie Provinces.* Toronto, Macmillan, 1935.

MANNING, H. E. *Assessment and Rating, Being the Law of Municipal Taxation in Canada.* 1st ed. Toronto, Canada Law Book Co., 1928. 3rd ed. Toronto, Cartwright, 1951.

Periodical Articles

APPLETON, JOHN. "After War Financial Problems of Western Municipalities." *Journal of the Canadian Bankers' Association* 27: 162–7 (Jan., 1920).

BELL, F. H. "Municipal Taxation in Nova Scotia." *Dalhousie Review* 1: 264–80 (Oct., 1921).

BRADSHAW, THOMAS. "Municipal Finance." *Municipal Review of Canada* 29: 12–15 (Dec., 1933); 30: 24–6 (Jan., 1934).

BRITTAIN, H. L. "Municipal Taxation in Canada." *Annals of the American Academy of Political and Social Science* 107: 221–6 (May, 1923). (See also reports prepared by this author for the mayors and city councils of Winnipeg and Vancouver respectively, listed for chapter 12.)

KEIRSTEAD, W. C. "Rural Taxation in the Province of New Brunswick." *Journal of Political Economy* 34: 669–90 (Dec., 1926).

NEWCOMER, MABEL, and R. G. HUTCHISON. "Taxation of Land Values in Canada." *Journal of Political Economy* 40: 366–78 (June, 1932).

CHAPTERS 17–18

INCOME TAXES FOR ALL; ALL OTHER TAXES EXPLOITED

Government Documents

Dominion

Bank of Canada. *Reports on the Financial Position of the Provinces of Manitoba, Saskatchewan, and Alberta.* Ottawa, 1937.

Dept. of Agriculture. *Taxation in Rural Ontario*, by H. C. HUDSON. Pub. 489, Technical Bulletin 4. Ottawa, King's Printer, 1936.

Dept. of Trade and Commerce. *Empire Tariff Preferences in Canada*, by WILLIAM GILCHRIST. Ottawa, 1930.

Dominion Bureau of Statistics. *Dominion Income Tax Statistics, Fiscal Year 1939–1940.* Ottawa, 1942. (Figures on the basis of tax collected rather than tax assessed as in previous issues.)

——— *Incomes Assessed for Income War Tax in Canada, 1935, and Income War Tax Collected Thereon, Classified by Provinces, by Size of Incomes and by Occupations.* Ottawa, 1936.

——— *Incomes Assessed for Income War Tax in Canada, 1939, and Income War Tax Collected Thereon, Classified by Provinces, by Size of Income and by Occupations.* Ottawa, 1940.

——— *The Public Debt of Canada, Dominion and Provincial Governments, 1937, and Municipalities, 1936.* Ottawa, 1938. (Appendix: "The Tax Systems of Canada: Dominion, Provincial, and Municipal Governments.")

——— *The Tax Systems of Canada, Dominion, Provincial and Municipal Governments.* Ottawa, 1940.

Imperial Economic Conference, 1932. *Report of the Conference* [with supplementary volume including the texts of the trade agreements concluded during the conference]. Ottawa, King's Printer, 1933. (For material relating to this conference, see bibliography in *Contributions to Canadian Economics* 6: 121–5 (1933)).

National Employment Commission. *Interim Report.* Ottawa, King's Printer, 1937. *Final Report.* Ottawa, King's Printer, 1938.

Royal Commission on Dominion-Provincial Relations. *Report.* Ottawa, King's Printer, 1940. (*Book I, Canada, 1867–1939.* For valuable material on the economic and financial history of the provinces and municipalities during this period the reader is referred to the submissions of the respective provincial and municipal governments and of various organizations to this Commission. See partial list of submissions on pp. 733–4.)

Provinces

Budget speeches of the Provincial Treasurers or Ministers of Finance published in pamphlet form by the provincial King's Printers are available for these years for the original nine provinces of Confederation excepting Nova Scotia and Prince Edward Island.

Alberta, Taxation Inquiry Board on Provincial and Municipal Taxation. *Report* (J. F. PERCIVAL, Chairman). Edmonton, King's Printer, 1935.

British Columbia, Committee to Investigate the Finances of British Columbia. *Report.* Victoria, King's Printer, 1932.

British Columbia, Royal Commission on Municipal Taxation. *Report* (A. M. HARPER, Chairman). Victoria, Govt. Print. Bureau, 1934. (Mimeo. Extracts from this report dealing with school finance are printed as appendix in *School Finance in British Columbia,* by H. B. KING.)

KING, H. B. *School Finance in British Columbia,* by H. B. KING, Technical Adviser to the Commission on School Finance. Victoria, King's Printer, 1935.

Manitoba. *Manitoba's Case: A Submission Presented to the Royal Commission on Dominion-Provincial Relations.* Winnipeg, King's Printer, 1938. (Part VI, *The Financial Problems of Municipalities and School Districts.*)

Manitoba, Economic Survey Board. *Agricultural Income and Rural Municipal Government in Manitoba,* by H. C. GRANT, C. B. DAVIDSON, and J. E. CHERNICK. [Winnipeg] 1939.

Manitoba, Royal Commission on the Municipal Finances and Administration of the City of Winnipeg, 1939. *Report* (H. C. GOLDENBERG, Chairman). Winnipeg, King's Printer, 1939.

Saskatchewan, Commission of Inquiry into Provincial and Municipal Taxation. *Report* (N. H. JACOBY, Chairman). Regina, King's Printer, 1936.

U.S. Library of Congress, Legislative Reference Service. *Income Tax in Canada and Other Dominion and Provincial Taxes.* Prepared for the Joint Committee on Internal Revenue Taxation, by ANDRE BERNARD. U.S. Govt. Print. Off., 1934.

Winnipeg, Commission on Assessment, Taxation, etc. *Report* (T. BRADSHAW, Commissioner). 1934.

Books and Pamphlets

ANNETT, D. R. *British Preference in Canadian Commercial Policy.* Toronto, Ryerson, 1948.

BATES, STEWART. *Financial History of Canadian Governments.* A Study Prepared for the Royal Commission on Dominion-Provincial Relations. Ottawa, 1939.

BRADSHAW, THOMAS. *A Discussion of Municipal Finance and Administration.* Dalhousie Univ. Bulletin on Public Affairs, 3. Halifax, Imperial Pub. Co., 1937.

Dominion Association of Chartered Accountants. *Provincial Taxation Respecting Corporations and Individuals.* 1936.

ELLIOTT, COURTLAND, and J. A. WALKER. *Report to Alberta Bondholders Committee: A Survey of the Fiscal Problems of the Province of Alberta in Relation to the Economic and Social Conditions Facing Them.* Edmonton, July 17, 1936. (Especially chaps. 5 and 7.)

GOLDENBERG, H. C. *Comparative Statement of the Financial Situation in Canadian Municipalities.* Dominion Conference of Mayors, March, 1936.

——— *Municipal Finance in Canada.* A Study Prepared for the Royal Commission on Dominion-Provincial Relations. Ottawa, 1939.

——— *Statistical Report on Taxable Valuation and Exemptions in Canadian Municipalities.* Montreal, Canadian Federation of Mayors and Municipalities, 1937.

JONES, J. M. *Tariff Retaliation, Repercussions of the Hawley-Smoot Bill.* Philadelphia, Univ. of Pennsylvania Press, 1934. (Chap. 6, "Canada Retaliates in Kind," pp. 176–210.)

LABRIE, F. E. "Recent Developments and Trends in Alberta Taxation." A Thesis submitted in partial fulfilment of the requirement for the Degree of Master of Laws, Univ. of Toronto, School of Law, Nov., 1944.

LOUGHEED, W. F. and W. C. MACKENZIE. *Provincial Finance in Nova Scotia: An Introduction.* Dalhousie Univ. Bulletin on Public Affairs, 10. Toronto, Nelson, 1940.

MCCORMICK, R. N., comp. and ed. *Sales Tax—Canada: The Special War Revenue Act, as Amended with Regulations Issued by the Department of National Revenue and with Rulings and Regulations re Sales Tax and Other Excise Taxes.* Toronto, Canadian Manufacturers' Assn., 1937.

MCDIARMID, O. J. *Commercial Policy in the Canadian Economy.* Cambridge, Mass., Harvard Univ. Press, 1946.

MACKINTOSH, W. A. "Canadian Tariff Policy." In *Canadian Papers, 1933, Prepared for the Fifth Biennial Conference of Institute of Pacific Relations,* pp. 1–18.

——— *Economic Problems of the Prairie Provinces.* Toronto, Macmillan, 1935. (Chaps. 7–11.)

MACGREGOR, D. C. "Outline of the Position of Public Finance." In *The Canadian Economy and Its Problems,* Canadian Institute of International Affairs, Toronto, 1934.

MANNING, H. E. *Local Taxation and Municipal Finance.* Dalhousie Univ. Bulletin on Public Affairs, 7. Halifax, Imp. Pub. Co., 1937.

PARKINSON, J. F. *Memorandum on the Basis of Canadian Commercial Policy, 1926–38.* Paris, International Institute of Intellectual Co-operation, Twelfth Session, International Studies Conference, 1939.

Tax Research Foundation. *Tax Systems of the World.* Chicago, Commerce Clearing House. 5th ed. 1934. 6th ed. 1935. 7th ed. 1938. (Canadian sections.)

TAYLOR, K. W. "The Results of the Imperial Economic Conference in Relation to the Trade of the Countries, Which are Members of the Institute of Pacific Relations." In *Canadian Papers, 1933, Prepared for the Fifth Biennial Conference of Institute of Pacific Relations.*

——— "The Commercial Policy of Canada." In H. R. KEMP, ed., *Canadian Marketing Problems,* Toronto, Univ. of Toronto Press, 1939, pp. 1–12.

Periodical Articles

ASHLEY, C. A. "Budgets: An Examination and a Suggestion." *Journal of the Canadian Bankers' Association* 39: 367–9 (April, 1932).

BLADEN, V. W. "Tariff Policy and Employment in Depression." *Canadian Journal of Economics and Political Science* 6: 72–8 (Feb., 1940).

BRADSHAW, THOMAS. "Municipal Finance." *Municipal Review of Canada* 29: 12–15 (Dec., 1933); 30: 24–6 (Jan., 1934).

——— "Municipal Debt." *Maclean's* (June 1, 1935).

HANSON, E. J. "Public Finance in Alberta since 1935." *Canadian Journal of Economics and Political Science* 18: 322–35 (Aug., 1952).

KEIRSTEAD, W. C. "Taxation for School Purposes." *Canadian Chartered Accountant* (Feb., 1937).

LABRIE, F. E. "Farm Taxation: Alberta's Trial & Error." *Canadian Tax Journal* 2: 119–22 (March-April, 1954).

MCDIARMID, O. J. "Canadian Tariff Policy." *Annals of the American Academy of Political and Social Science* 253: 150–7 (Sept., 1947).

MACGREGOR, D. C. "The Problem of Public Debt in Canada." *Canadian Journal of Economics and Political Science* 2: 167–94 (May, 1936).

MACDONNELL, J. M. "After the Ottawa Conference." *Foreign-Affairs* 11: 331–46 (Jan., 1933).

"Ottawa supplement." *Economist,* Oct. 22, 1932. (Details of Ottawa and pre-Ottawa concessions, Dominion tariffs, general comparisons and reflections.)

SHAUGHNESSY, E. C. "A Provincial Sales Tax." *Canadian Chartered Accountant* 33: 179–91 (Sept., 1938).

SKELTON, O. D. "Is our Economic System Bankrupt?" In *Papers and Proceedings of the Third Annual Meeting of the Canadian Political Science Association* 3: 67–87 (1931).

WAINES, W. J. "Federal Public Finance: Canada." *Canadian Journal of Economics and Political Science* 3: 181–96 (May, 1937).

——— "Problem of Public Finance in the Prairie Provinces." *Ibid.* 3: 355–69 (Aug., 1937).

CHAPTERS 19–20

TIME FOR RE-EXAMINATION; THE ROWELL-SIROIS REPORT

NOTE: Documentary material on the background for the Rowell-Sirois report is plentifully distributed in official and other publications of the thirties. This material is not listed again here. The reader is referred especially to the lists for chapters 17–18 and 34–36 and to the footnotes of the present chapters.

It has been considered worth while to list all the published documents of the Royal Commission on Dominion-Provincial Relations and submissions containing material relevant to the subject of taxation and fiscal relations.

Government Documents

Dominion-Provincial and Interprovincial Conferences from 1887 to 1926. Ottawa, Reprinted by the King's Printer, 1951.

Dominion-Provincial Conference, 1927. *Precis of Discussions, Dominion-Provincial Conference, November 3 to 10, 1927.* Ottawa, King's Printer, 1928.

Dominion-Provincial Conference, 1935. *Record of Proceedings, Ottawa, December 9–13, 1935.* Ottawa, King's Printer, 1936.

Royal Commission on Dominion-Provincial Relations. *Report of Proceedings, Nov. 1937–Dec. 1938.* (Mimeographed transcription.) Royal Commission on Dominion-Provincial Relations. *Report.* Book 1. *Canada, 1867–1939.* Book 2. *Recommendations.* Book 3. *Documentation.* Ottawa, King's Printer, 1940.

Appendices

1. *Comparative Statistics of Public Finance 1913, 1921, 1925 to 1939* (For Dominion with C.N.R. and provinces combined, and separately in sub-appendices A-H, J-K).
2. *British North America at Confederation,* by D. G. CREIGHTON.
3. *The Economic Background of Dominion-Provincial Relations,* by W. A. MACKINTOSH.
4. *National Income,* by D. C. MACGREGOR, J. B. RUTHERFORD, G. E. BRITNELL, and J. J. DEUTSCH.
5. *Labour Legislation and Social Services in the Province of Quebec,* by ESDRAS MINVILLE.
6. *Public Assistance and Social Insurance,* by A. E. GRAUER.
7. *Difficulties of Divided Jurisdiction,* by J. A. CORRY.
8. *Legislative Expedients and Devices Adopted by the Dominion and the Provinces,* by L. M. GOUIN and BROOKE CLAXTON.

Mimeographed Studies

Dominion Monetary Policy, by F. A. KNOX.
Dominion-Provincial Subsidies and Grants, by W. EGGLESTON and C. T. KRAFT.
Economic History of the Prairie Provinces, by S. A. SAUNDERS.
Financial History of Canadian Governments, by STEWART BATES.
The Growth of Government Activities since Confederation, by J. A. CORRY.
Housing, by A. E. GRAUER.
Labour Legislation, by A. E. GRAUER.
Municipal Finance in Canada, by H. C. GOLDENBERG.
Prairie Population Possibilities, by W. J. WAINES.
Public Health, by A. E. GRAUER.

Indexes

Royal Commission on Dominion-Provincial Relations. *Digests of Briefs and Evidence.* N.p., n.d. (Mimeo.)

British Columbia. *The Governments of Canada before the Rowell-Commission, 1937–1938: Index of Policies, Claims, Submissions, etc., Stated by Dominion and Provincial Governments (Exclusive of Alberta).* Victoria, King's Printer, 1938.

Provincial Submissions

Alberta. *The Case for Alberta.* Edmonton, King's Printer, 1938. (Not a direct representation to the Royal Commission but addressed to the Sovereign people of Canada and their government.)

British Columbia. *British Columbia in the Canadian Federation.* Victoria, King's Printer, 1938.

Manitoba. *Manitoba's Case: A Submission Presented to the Royal Commission on Dominion-Provincial Relations.* Winnipeg, King's Printer, 1938.

New Brunswick. *Submission by the Province of New Brunswick to the Royal Commission on Dominion-Provincial Relations.* Fredericton, King's Printer, 1938.

Nova Scotia. *Submission of the Government of the Province of Nova Scotia to the Royal Commission on Dominion-Provincial Relations.* Halifax, King's Printer, 1938.

Ontario. *Statement by the Government of Ontario to the Royal Commission on Dominion-Provincial Relations.* Toronto, King's Printer, 1938.

Prince Edward Island. *The Case of Prince Edward Island: A Submission Presented to the Royal Commission on Dominion-Provincial Relations.* Charlottetown, King's Printer, 1937.

Saskatchewan. *A Submission by the Government of Saskatchewan to the Royal Commission on Dominion-Provincial Relations.* Regina, King's Printer, 1937.

Of the briefs of the national organizations the reader is referred especially to the following as containing useful information relating to various aspects of Canadian taxation: Canadian Life Insurance Officers association, Chartered Banks of Canada, Citizens Research Institute of Canada, Dominion Mortgage and Investments Association, National Construction Council of Canada, Single Tax Association of Canada.

For a complete list of submissions to the Royal Commission including those of the various municipal governments, boards of trade, regional and municipal organizations, see the *Report,* Book 3, "Exhibits and Hearings," pp. 209–14.

Books and Periodical Articles

Brady, A. "Report of the Royal Commission on Dominion-Provincial Relations." *Canadian Historical Review* 21: 245-53 (Sept., 1940).

Brossard, R. and H. F. Angus. "The Working of Confederation." *Canadian Journal of Economics and Political Science* 3: 335–53 (Aug., 1937).

Carrothers, W. A. "Problems of the Canadian Federation." *Canadian Journal of Economics and Political Science* 1: 26–40 (Feb., 1935).

Citizens Research Institute of Canada. *Special Study of Taxation and Public Expenditure in Canada: Report to Donors* [to fund for Special Study on Taxation and Governmental Expenditure]. Toronto, 1937.

Corry, J. A. "The Federal Dilemma." *Canadian Journal of Economics and Political Science* 7: 215–28 (May, 1941).

Eggleston, Wilfrid. *The Road to Nationhood: A Chronicle of Dominion-Provincial Relations.* Toronto, Oxford Univ. Press, 1946.

Kemp, H. R. "Is a Revision of Taxation Powers Necessary?" In *Papers and Proceedings of the Annual Meeting of the Canadian Political Science Association* 3: 185–201 (1931).

Innis, H. A. "The Rowell-Sirois Report." *Canadian Journal of Economics and Political Science* 6: 562–71 (Nov., 1940).

Keirstead, B. S. "The Sirois Report: An Evaluation." *Public Affairs* 4: 1–7 (Aug., 1940).

Maxwell, J. A. "Provincial Conferences and Better Terms." In *Papers and Proceedings of the Sixth Annual Meeting of the Canadian Political Science Association* 6: 162–74 (1934).

"The Rowell-Sirois Report": A Canadian Reaffirmation of the Democratic Faith in Social Progress." *International Labour Review* 42: 347–76 (Dec., 1940).

Rogers, N. McLeod. "A Crisis of Federal Finance." *Canadian Forum* (Nov., 1934).

——— "One Path of Reform." *Canadian Forum* (Dec., 1934).

Saunders, S. A. and Eleanor Bach. *The Rowell-Sirois Commission.* Toronto, Ryerson, 1945.

Waines, W. J. "Federal Public Finance: Canada." *Canadian Journal of Economics and Political Science* 3: 181–96 (May, 1937).

Chapter 21

REVISED PHILOSOPHY OF WAR FINANCE

Government Documents

Canada at War. Recapitulation issue, no. 45, 1945. Ottawa, Wartime Information Board, 1945.

Dominion Bureau of Statistics. *Canada Year Book,* 1940–5. Ottawa, King's Printer, 1940–5. (See special articles in each edition on Canada and the war.)

Royal Commission on Prices. *Report.* Ottawa, King's Printer, 1949. (see vol. II, chap. 6.)

Wartime Prices and Trade Board. *Reports,* no. 1–5, Sept. 3, 1939/March 31, 1943–Jan./Dec. 31, 1946. Ottawa, King's Printer, 1943–7.

Books and Pamphlets

Blough, Roy. "The Individual Income Tax as a Method of Inflation Control." In *Curbing Inflation through Taxation.* New York, Tax Institute, 1944, pp. 112–25.

Brown, F. H., J. D. Gilson, and A. F. W. Plumptre. *War Finance in Canada.* Contemporary Affairs, no. 3. Toronto, Ryerson, 1940.

Buck, A. E. *Financing Canadian Government.* Chicago, Public Administration Service, 1949.

Citizens Research Institute of Canada. *Government Control and Finance in War.* Toronto, 1939.

Dawson, R. M. *Canada in World Affairs: Two Years of War, 1939–1941.* Toronto, Oxford Univ. Press, 1943.

Eaton, A. K. "Canadian Experience in Curbing Inflation through Fiscal Devices." In *Curbing Inflation through Taxation,* New York, Tax Institute, 1944, pp. 188–200.

Gibson, J. D. "Financing the War." In *Canadian War Economics.* J. F. Parkinson, ed., Toronto, Univ. of Toronto Press, 1941, pp. 33–46.

Herbert, C. H. *Why War Savings?* Contemporary Affairs, no. 7. Toronto, Ryerson, 1940.

Higgins, B. H. *Canada's Financial System in War.* Occasional Paper 19. New York, National Bureau of Economic Research, 1944.

Keynes, J. M. *How to Pay for the War.* London, Macmillan, 1940.

Lingard, C. C. and R. G. Trotter. *Canada in World Affairs, September 1941 to May, 1944.* Toronto, Oxford Univ. Press, 1950.

Plumptre, A. F. W. *Canadian War Finance: A Study of Wartime Economic, Financial and Price Policies and Developments in Canada, September 1939 to December, 1940.* Washington, D.C., Office of Price Administration and Civilian Supply, 1941.

——— *Mobilizing Canada's Resources for War.* Toronto, Macmillan, 1941.

Rasminsky, Louis. "Foreign Exchange Control in Canada: Purposes and Methods." In *Canadian War Economics,* J. F. Parkinson, ed., Toronto, Univ. of Toronto Press, 1941, pp. 89–127.

Shirras, G. F. *Federal Finance in Peace and War, with Special Reference to the United States of America and the British Commonwealth.* London, Macmillan, 1944.

Taylor, K. W. "The Wartime Control of Prices." In *Canadian War Economics,* J. F. Parkinson, ed., Toronto, Univ. of Toronto Press, 1941, pp. 47–71.

Wilson, K. R. *Price Control in Canada.* Booklet no. 1. Ottawa, King's Printer, 1941.

Periodical Articles

DOUGLAS, MONTEATH. "Limitations of the Financial Factor in a War Economy." *Canadian Journal of Economics and Political Science* 8: 351–63 (Aug., 1942).

JACK, L. B. "How Canada Finances the War." *Public Affairs* 3: 173–7 (June, 1940).

MACAULAY, J. A. "Destructive or Constructive Taxation." *Canadian Bar Review* 23: 424–34 (May, 1945).

MCIVOR, R. C. "Canadian Wartime Fiscal Policy, 1939–45." *Canadian Journal of Economics and Political Science* 14: 62–93 (Feb., 1948).

PARKINSON, J. F. "Some Problems of War Finance in Canada." *Canadian Journal of Economics and Political Science* 6: 403–23 (Aug., 1940).

PLUMPTRE, A. F. W. "An Approach to War Finance." *Canadian Journal of Economics and Political Science* 7: 1–12 (Feb., 1941).

SELIGMAN, H. L. "Patterns of Wartime Borrowing in the United States, the United Kingdom and Canada." *Federal Reserve Bulletin* 30: 1056–68 (Nov., 1944).

STEWART, S. I. "Statutes, Orders, and Official Statements Relating to Canadian War-time Economic Controls." *Canadian Journal of Economics and Political Science* 13: 99–114 (Feb., 1947).

TAYLOR, K. W. "Canadian Wartime Price Controls, 1941–46." *Canadian Journal of Economics and Political Science* 13: 81–98 (Feb., 1947).

CHAPTER 22

EXCESS PROFITS TAX: A CASE STUDY

Government Documents

Canada, Dept. of Reconstruction and Supply. *Encouragement to Industrial Expansion in Canada: Operation of Special Depreciation Provisions, November 10, 1944–March 31, 1949*. Ottawa, King's Printer, 1948.

Canada, Senate, Special Committee on the Income War Tax Act and the Excess Profits Tax Act, 1940. *Proceedings*. Session 1945. Ottawa, King's Printer, 1945.

——— *Proceedings*. Session 1946. Ottawa, King's Printer, 1946.

Books

CURRAN, K. J. *Excess Profits Taxation*. Washington, D.C., American Council on Public Affairs, 1943.

Dominion of Canada Income War Tax Act [including Excess Profits Tax Act, etc.]. Montreal, Toronto, CCH Canadian, 1940–6. (Rev. annually.)

"Excess Profits Taxation." In *Law and Contemporary Problems*, vol. X, no. 1, Durham, N.C., School of Law, Duke Univ., 1943.

FREARS, R. I. *Frears' annotated Income War Tax Act and Excess Profits Tax Act, 1947*. Toronto, Canadian Law List Pub. Co., 1947.

GILLAM, M. H. *The Incidence of Excess Profits Taxation*. Studies in History, Economics and Public Law, no. 514. New York, Columbia Univ. Press, 1945.

GILMOUR, A. W. *Income Tax Handbook*. Toronto, Dominion Association of Chartered Accountants, 1945. New ed. 1947.

GOPAL, M. H. *The Theory of Excess Profits Taxation*. Mysore, Bureau of Economic Research, Vanivilas Mohalla, 1947. (Bibliography, pp. 374–82.)

HICKS, J. R., U. K. HICKS and L. ROSTAS. *The Taxation of War Wealth*. 2nd ed. Oxford, Clarendon Press, 1942.

MCBAIN, A. G. *Concise Excess Profits Tax and National Defence Contribution* (inclusive of the E.P.T. and N.D.C. provisions of the Finance Act, 1944). 2nd ed. London, Sweet and Maxwell, 1944.

RUDICK, H. J. "The Controversy over E.P.T." In *Report of Proceedings of the Fourth Annual Tax Conference of the Canadian Tax Foundation*, 1950, pp. 39–46.

STIKEMAN, H. H., ed. and comp. *Income Tax and Excess Profits Tax, Canada, Consolidated Acts, 1944–45*. Annotated. Toronto, Richard de Boo, 1944.

Periodical Articles

BLOUGH, ROY. "Measurement Problems of the Excess Profits Tax." *National Tax Journal* 1: 353–65 (Dec., 1948).

BOULDING, K. E. "The Incidence of a Profits Tax." *American Economic Review* 34: 567–72 (Sept., 1944).

See *Canadian Chartered Accountant* and *Canadian Bar Review* for the period of operation of the Excess Profits Tax Act for editorial comment, amendments to the legislation, orders in council, and departmental regulations.

CARTER, K. Le M. "Taxation of Corporate Income by the Dominion Government." *Canadian Chartered Accountant* 42: 354–60 (May, 1943).

COLLINS, F. T. "Excess Profits Taxation." *Canadian Bar Review* 20: 584-604 (Aug.-Sept., 1942).

ELLIOTT, COURTLAND. "The Canadian Excess Profits Tax: The Administration of the Tax and the Board of Referees." *Public Affairs* 6: 20–2 (autumn, 1942).

"Excess Profits Tax on New Gold Mines." *Canadian Chartered Accountant* 44: 102–3 (Feb., 1944).

GILMOUR, A. W. "The Excess Profits Tax Act." *Canadian Chartered Accountant* 47: 141–60 (Sept., 1945).

HARRISON, W. H. "The Work of the Board of Referees under the Excess Profits Tax Act, 1940." *Canadian Bar Review* 20: 242–52 (March, 1942).

HOPPER, J. R. "Corporation Income and Excess Profits Tax." *Canadian Chartered Accountant* 17: 5–13 (July, 1945).

LEACH, C. W. "Excess Profits Taxation in Canada: A Business Man's View." *Canadian Journal of Economics and Political Science* 7: 363–70 (Aug., 1941).

LEETHAM, E. C. "The Preparation and Presentation of a Brief before the Board of Referees." *Canadian Chartered Accountant* 44: 73–91 (Feb., 1944); 142–53 (March, 1944).

MORGAN, LUCY. "The Canadian Excess Profits Tax: The Effect of the Tax on 80 Canadian Corporations." *Public Affairs* 6: 16–20 (autumn, 1942).

RATCHFORD, B. U. "The Federal Excess Profits Tax: Part one; Development and Present Status. Part two: Some Economic and Political Aspects." *Southern Economic Journal* 12: 1–16 (July, 1945); 97–114 (Oct., 1945).

SWIFT, C. E. "Points for Consideration in the Preparation of Standard Profits Claims." *Canadian Chartered Accountant* 45: 20–5 (July, 1944).

TOLMIE, J. R. "Excess Profits Taxation: The Canadian Act and Its Administration." *Canadian Journal of Economics and Political Science* 7: 350–63 (Aug., 1941). (Also in *Canadian Chartered Accountant*, Dec., 1941.)

WATTS, H. B. "Circumstances under which a Taxpayer is Eligible to File a Standard Profits Claim." *Canadian Chartered Accountant* 45: 16–20 (July, 1944).

CHAPTER 23

PERSONAL INCOME AND OTHER TAXES

Government Documents

Canada, Dept. of National Revenue, Income Tax Division. *Your 1942 Income Tax . . . a Simplified Explanation of the 1942 Income Tax for the Individual Taxpayer with a View to Answering Questions Most Frequently Asked*. N.d.

—— *National Defence Tax*. Ottawa, King's Printer, 1940.

Canada, Dept. of National Revenue, Succession Duty Division. *Dominion Succession Duty Act.* Explanatory brochure. Rev. Aug., 1942. Ottawa, King's Printer, 1942. Rev. ed. Ottawa, King's Printer, 1947.

Canada, Dept. of National Revenue, Taxation Division. *Taxation Statistics.* Ottawa, King's Printer, 1946. (Annual.)

Canada, Dominion Bureau of Statistics. *Dominion Income Tax Statistics Fiscal Year, 1939–40.* Ottawa, 1942.

——— *Dominion Income Tax Statistics, Fiscal Year 1940–1941.* Ottawa, 1943.

——— *Dominion Income Tax, Excess Profits Tax and Succession Duty Statistics.* Ottawa, 1944.

U.S. Treasury Dept., Division of Tax Research. *Comparisons of Taxes in the United States, United Kingdom and Canada.* Washington, D.C., 1943.

——— *Excise Taxes:* United States, Canada and United Kingdom. Washington, D.C., 1944.

Books and Periodical Articles

For text of Income War Tax Act as amended, with annotations, see FREARS, GILMOUR, and STIKEMAN, in list for chapter 22.

BAKER, C. E. "Income Tax Family Allowances." *Canadian Chartered Accountant* 45: 346–50 (Dec., 1944).

ELLIOTT, C. F. "The Dominion Succession Duty Act: A Reply." *Canadian Bar Review* 20: 141–5 (Feb., 1942).

GORDON, W. L. "Post-War Taxation." *Canadian Chartered Accountant* 45: 329–40 (Dec., 1944).

HERINGTON, H. P. "Comments on Corporation Income Tax." *Canadian Chartered Accountant* 45: 278–82 (Nov., 1944).

HOOD, WM. C. "Structural Changes in the Dominion Personal Income Tax, 1932–49." *Canadian Journal of Economics and Political Science* 15: 220–7 (May, 1949).

LADNER, L. J. "Post War Tax Impact." *Canadian Bar Review* 22: 652–69 (Oct., 1944).

MCTAGUE, C. P. "The War Contracts Depreciation Board." *Canadian Bar Review* 20: 575–83 (Aug.–Sept., 1942).

MIGNAULT, P. B. "The Dominion Succession Duty Act: Its Effect on the Succession Law of Quebec." *Canadian Bar Review* 19: 719–32 (Dec., 1941).

MUSGRAVE, R. A. "The Wartime Tax Effort in the United States, the United Kingdom and Canada." In *Proceedings of the 36th Annual Conference of the National Tax Association, 1943,* pp. 300–22.

PATTERSON, C. A. "Application of the Income War Tax Act to Corporations." *Canadian Chartered Accountant* 45: 270–8 (Nov., 1944).

ROBERTS, R. A. "Application of the Income War Tax Act to Individuals." *Canadian Chartered Accountant* 45: 282–90 (Nov., 1944).

STIKEMAN, H. H. "Canadian Experience in Financing the War." *In Proceedings of the 36th Annual Conference of the National Tax Association,* 1943, pp. 345–60.

"Taxation Statistics in Canada." *Canadian Chartered Accountant* 47: 66–88 (Aug., 1945).

CHAPTER 24

NEW PHILOSOPHY FOR PEACETIME

Government Documents

Canada, Dept. of Reconstruction. *Employment and Income, with Special Reference to the Initial Period of Reconstruction.* Presented to Parliament by the Minister of Reconstruction, April, 1945. Ottawa, King's Printer, 1945.

Canada, Dept. of Reconstruction and Supply. *Encouragement to Industrial Expansion in Canada: Operation of Special Depreciation Provisions, November 10, 1944–March 31, 1949*. Ottawa, King's Printer, 1948.

Dominion-Provincial Conference (1945). *Dominion and Provincial Submissions and Plenary Conference Discussions*. Ottawa, King's Printer, 1946.

——— *Proposals of the Government of Canada, August, 1945*. Ottawa, 1945.

Royal Commission on Prices. *Report*. Ottawa, King's Printer, 1949. (Vol. II.)

Books

ABBOTT, D. C. "Federal Budget Policy." In *Report of the 1948 Tax Conference, Canadian Tax Foundation*, pp. 73–7.

BLOUGH, ROY. "The Individual Income Tax as a Method of Inflation Control." In *Curbing Inflation through Taxation*. New York, Tax Institute, 1944. pp. 112–25.

Committee for Economic Development. *Jobs and Markets: How to Prevent Inflation and Depression in the Transition*. New York, McGraw-Hill, 1946.

HANSEN, A. H. Fiscal Policy and Business Cycles. New York, Norton, 1941.

HIGGINS, BENJAMIN. *Public Investment and Full Employment*. Studies and Reports, New Series, no. 3. Montreal, International Labour Office, 1946.

McLEOD, A. N. *Maintaining Employment and Incomes in Canada*. Unpublished Ph.D. Thesis. Cambridge, Mass., 1949.

PERRY, J. H. "Plans for Post-War Dominion Taxation in Canada." In *Proceedings of the 37th Annual Conference of the National Tax Association*, 1944, pp. 213–20.

Periodical Articles

CLARK, W. C. "Canada's Post-War Finance." *Canadian Tax Journal* 1: 6–12, 100–11 (Jan.-Feb., 1953). (Paper prepared for the annual meeting of the American Economic Association, Chicago, Dec., 1952.)

GLASSCO, J. G. "Trends in Post-War Tax Policy." *Canadian Chartered Accountant* 51: 256–66 (Nov., 1947).

GORDON, W. L. "Post-War Taxation." *Canadian Chartered Accountant* 45: 329–40 (Dec., 1944).

HIGGINS, BENJAMIN. "Postwar Tax Policy." *Canadian Journal of Economics and Political Science* 9: 532–56 (Nov., 1943).

LERNER, A. P. "Functional Finance and the Federal Debt." *Social Research* 10: 38–51 (Feb., 1943).

LINDAHL, ERIC. *Studies in the Theory of Money and Capital*. London, Allen and Unwin, 1939. (See Appendix, "The Problem of Balancing the Budget," pp. 351–84.)

MOSAK, J. L. "National Budget and National Policy." *American Economic Review* 36: 20–43 (March, 1946). See also rejoinder by A. G. HART and final reply by MOSAK, pp. 632–41 (Sept., 1946).

CHAPTERS 25–26

PERSONAL INCOME TAX REFORM; CORPORATE INCOME TAX REFORM

Government Documents

Canada, House of Commons, Standing Committee on Banking and Commerce. *Minutes of Proceedings and Evidence* [Consideration of Bill no. 338; An Act Respecting Income Taxes]. Session 1947–8. Ottawa, King's Printer, 1948. (Pp. 547–728.)

Canada, Senate, Special Committee on the Income War Tax Act and Excess Profits Tax Act, 1940. *Proceedings*. Session 1945. Ottawa, King's Printer, 1945.

——— *Proceedings.* Session 1946. Ottawa, King's Printer, 1946.

Royal Commission on Co-operatives. *Report* (E. M. W. McDougall, Chairman). Ottawa, King's Printer, 1945.

Royal Commission on the Taxation of Annuities and Family Corporations. *Report* (W. C. Ives, Chairman). Ottawa, King's Printer, 1945.

Books and Pamphlets

Canadian Tax Foundation. *Corporation Profits and Dividends under the Income Tax Act. 1: Double Taxation. 2: Undistributed Profits. 3: Private Companies.* Memorandum of Draft Proposals Prepared for the Third Tax Conference, December 5–6, 1949. Toronto, 1949.

——— *Corporation Profits and Dividends under the Income Tax Act.* Draft Report of the Third Tax Conference Held on December 5 and 6, 1949. [Toronto.]

——— *The Income Tax Act, Part 1A and Sections 73, 73A and 27, Respecting Private Companies and Controlled Operations.* Memorandum of Recommendations Submitted to the Minister of Finance and the Minister of National Revenue, February 12, 1951. Toronto, 1951.

——— *The Income Tax Bill, a Review and Analysis.* Toronto [n.d.]. (Reprinted in *Canadian Chartered Accountant,* Dec. 1947.)

Canadian Tax Foundation, Conference on the Income Tax Bill, Ottawa, December 8th and 9th, 1947. *Report of Proceedings.* Toronto, 1948.

Canadian Tax Foundation, Tax Conference, 2nd, 1948; 4th–6th, 1950–2. *Reports of Proceedings.* Toronto. (Contain papers and panel discussions on various aspects of personal and corporation income tax.)

Courtice, A. R. "Succession Duties." In *Report of 1948 Tax Conference of the Canadian Tax Foundation,* pp. 61–72.

Norman, H. G. "Income Receipts vs. Capital Gains under the Canadian Income Tax Act." In *Report of Proceedings of the Fifth Tax Conference of the Canadian Tax Foundation, 1951,* pp. 73–80.

Perry, J. H. "Development of the Corporation Income Tax." In *Report of Proceedings of the Fourth Tax Conference of the Canadian Tax Foundation, 1950,* pp. 16–30.

Phillips, Lazarus. "Capital Gains under the Canadian Income Tax Act." *Report of Proceedings of the Fifth Tax Conference of the Canadian Tax Foundation, 1951,* pp. 81–95.

Stikeman, H. H. "Computation of Taxable Income under the Income Tax Act." In *Report of 1948 Tax Conference of the Canadian Tax Foundation,* pp. 47–60.

Willis, John. *The Mitigation of the Tax Penalty on Fluctuating or Irregular Incomes.* Canadian Tax Papers, no. 2. Toronto, Canadian Tax Foundation, 1951.

Periodical Articles

Abbott, D. C. "Drafting the New Income Tax Act." *Canadian Chartered Accountant* 52: 191–200 (April, 1948).

"Constitution of the Income Tax Appeal Board." *Canadian Chartered Accountant Tax Review* [1949] 1–4 (Jan.).

Dominion Association of Chartered Accountants. "Briefs Submitted to Ives Commission." *Canadian Chartered Accountant* 46: 189–95 (April, 1945).

——— "Recommendations on Bill 454, Submitted to the Minister of Finance, March 25, 1948." *Canadian Chartered Accountant* 52: 265–312 (May, 1948).

Douglas, Monteath. "Double Taxation of Corporate Earnings." *Canadian Tax Foundation Bulletin to Members,* July, 1950, pp. 8–13.

——— "Income Tax Revision." *Canadian Bar Review* 26: 1212–27 (Oct., 1948).

GLASSCO, J. G. "The Proposed Income Tax Act." *Canadian Chartered Accountant* 52:133–42 (March, 1948).
——— "The Treatment of Depreciation under the Income Tax Bill." *Ibid.* 51: 324–35 (Dec., 1947).
GORDON, M. L. "The Taxation of Farmers." *Canadian Chartered Accountant Tax Review* [1950] 15–21 (Feb.).
IRWIN, F. R. "Some Recent Developments in Canadian Taxation: The Fifteen Percent Tax on Undistributed Income of Companies." *National Tax Journal* 4: 289–98 (Dec., 1951).
INNES, J. S. "Tax on Undistributed Income of Closely-Held Companies: Mechanics and Operation." *Canadian Chartered Accountant Tax Review* [1950] 136–9 (Sept.).
KEEPING, G. C. "Tax on Undistributed Income of Closely-Held Companies: Advantages and Disadvantages." *Canadian Chartered Accountant Tax Review* [1950] 133–6 (Sept.).
LADNER, L. J. "Post-War Tax Impact." *Canadian Bar Review* 22: 652–69 (Oct., 1944).
PETRIE, J. R. "Some Aspects of Recent Corporation Income Tax Legislation in Canada." *Canadian Tax Foundation Bulletin to Members*, Nov., 1950. pp. 1–8. Reprinted from *Tax Policy*, vol. 17 (Oct., 1950).
STIKEMAN, H. H. "The Income Tax Appeal Board and Its Place in the Profession of Accountancy." *Canadian Chartered Accountant* 50: 246–57 (May, 1947).
WILSON, J. R. "Report of the Royal Commission on the Taxation of Annuities and Family Corporations, 1945." *Canadian Journal of Economics and Political Science* 12: 87–92 (Feb., 1946).

CHAPTER 27

COMMODITY TAXES AND TARIFFS

Government Documents

Canada

Dept. of External Affairs. *Additional Protocols Concerning the General Agreement on Tariffs and Trade of October 30, 1947, Signed at Geneva, September 14, 1948.* Treaty Series, 1948, no. 30. Ottawa, King's Printer, 1949.
——— *Final Act of the Second Session of the Preparatory Committee of the United Nations Conference on Trade and Employment Held at Geneva from April 10 to October 30, 1947, and Related Documents.* Treaty Series, 1947, no. 27. Ottawa, King's Printer, 1947. (Schedule V to the General Agreement on Tariffs and Trade negotiated at the second session of the Preparatory Committee of the United Nations Conference on Trade and Employment, held at Geneva from April 10 to October 30, 1947, published as Treaty Series, 1947, no. 27A.)
——— *General Agreement on Tariffs and Trade of October 30, 1947, as Amended by Protocols Signed at Havana, March 24,1948, and at Geneva, September 14, 1948, and Related Documents.* Treaty Series, 1948, no. 31. Ottawa, King's Printer, 1949.
——— *General Agreement on Tariffs and Trade: Schedule V to Annex A to the Torquay Protocol, Negotiated at Torquay from September 28, 1950 to April 21, 1951.* Treaty Series, 1951, no. 6. Ottawa, King's Printer, 1951.
Dept. of External Affairs, Information Division. *Annecy Tariff Negotiations.* Press release no. 70, Oct. 9, 1949. Ottawa, 1949.
Dept. of Finance. [Speech by Mr. D. C. Abbott, Minister of Finance, broadcast over C.B.O., November 17, 1947, announcing the Government's emergency

programme to correct Canada's foreign exchange position.] Ottawa, 1947. (See also speech in House of Commons, December 16, 1947, on Emergency Exchange Conservation Act. *House of Commons Debates*, 1948, vol. I, p. 323.)

House of Commons, Standing Committee on Banking and Commerce. *Minutes of Proceedings and Evidence* [General Agreement on Tariffs and Trade]. Session 1947–8. Ottawa, King's Printer, 1948. (Pp. 1–465.)

Senate, Standing Committee on Canadian Trade Relations. *Proceedings* . . . [on General Agreement on Tariffs and Trade]. Session 1947–8. Ottawa, King's Printer, 1947–8.

United States

Dept. of State. *Proposals for Expansion of World Trade and Employment*. Publication 2411, Commercial Policy Series 79. U.S. Govt. Print. Off., 1945. (Also published in Canada, Dept. of External Affairs, Conference Series, 1945, no. 3.)

---- *Suggested Charter for an International Trade Organization of the United Nations*. Publication 2598, Commercial Policy Series 93. U.S. Govt. Print. Off., 1946.

Tariff Commission. [Report on] *Operation of the Trade Agreements Program*. No. 1–4, June, 1934/April, 1948–July, 1950/June, 1951. U.S. Govt. Print. Off., 1949–52.

International

Contracting Parties to the General Agreement on Tariffs and Trade. *Basic Instruments and Selected Documents*. Vol. I. *Text of the Agreement and Other Instruments and Procedures*. Vol. II. *Decisions, Declarations, Resolutions, Rulings and Reports*. Geneva, 1952.

---- *General Agreement on Tariffs and Trade: Consolidated Schedules of Tariff Concessions*. Geneva, 1952. 5 vols.

---- *General Agreement on Tariffs and Trade: The Torquay Protocol to the General Agreement on Tariffs and Trade and the Torquay Schedules of Tariff Concessions*. Geneva, 1951.

Interim Commission for the International Trade Organization. *The Attack on Trade Barriers: A Progress Report on the Operations of the General Agreement on Tariffs and Trade from January 1948 to August 1949*. Geneva, published by the Commission at the request of the Contracting Parties to the General Agreement on Tariffs and Trade [1949].

---- *Liberating World Trade: Second Report on the Operation of the General Agreement on Tariffs and Trade, June 1950*. Geneva, published by the Commission at the request of the Contracting Parties to the General Agreement on Tariffs and Trade, 1950.

---- *Gatt in Action: Third Report on the Operation of the General Agreement on Tariffs and Trade, January 1952*. Geneva, published by the Commission at the request of the Contracting Parties to the General Agreement on Tariffs and Trade, 1952.

United Nations Conference on Trade and Employment, Havana, Cuba, November 21, 1947 to March 24, 1948. *Final Act and Related Documents*. Havana, 1948. (Also published as Canada, Dept. of External Affairs, Treaty Series, 1948, no. 32; Great Britain, Parliament, House of Commons, Papers by Command, Cmd. 7375.)

Books

Canadian Sales and Excise Tax Guide. June, 1950. Toronto, Montreal, C.C.H. Canadian, 1950.

Canadian Sales and Tax Guide: 1950 Special Session Amendments, Supplement to Canadian Sales and Excise Tax Guide. September, 1950. Toronto, Montreal, C.C.H. Canadian, 1950.

DIEBOLD, WILLIAM. *The End of the I.T.O.* Essays in International Finance, no. 16. Princeton, N.J., International Finance Section, Dept. of Economics and Social Institutions, Princeton Univ., 1952.

DUE, J. F. *The General Manufacturers Sales Tax in Canada.* Canadian Tax Papers, no. 3. Toronto, Canadian Tax Foundation, 1951.

——— "The Manufacturer's Sales Tax." *Tax Bulletin* 2: 311–17 (Nov.-Dec., 1952). (Paper given at the conference of the National Tax Association, Toronto, Sept. 1952.)

——— "Manufacturers General Sales Tax." *Report of Proceedings of the Fifth Annual Tax Conference of the Canadian Tax Foundation, 1951,* pp. 55–66.

"The General Sales Tax." Round table. *Report of Proceedings of the Sixth Annual Tax Conference of the Canadian Tax Foundation, 1952,* pp. 41–6.

LETICHE, J. M. *Reciprocal Trade Agreements in the World Economy.* New York, King's Crown Press, 1948.

MCCORMICK, R. N., comp. and ed. *Sales Tax—Canada: The Excise Act as Amended, with Regulations Issued by the Department of National Revenue and with Rulings and Regulations re Sales Tax and Other Excise Taxes.* Canadian Manufacturers' Association, 1950.

"Manufacturers Sales Tax" [articles and comment by J. F. DUE, F. LORENZEN, G. MOLLER, W. GOODMAN]. *Tax Bulletin* 2: 1–32 (Jan.-Feb., 1952).

WILCOX, CLAIR. *A Charter for World Trade.* New York, Macmillan, 1949.

CHAPTER 28

TAXES FOR SECURITY—NATIONAL AND SOCIAL

Government Documents

Canada. *Bill 13, An Act to Provide for Old Age Security, as Passed by the House of Commons Nov. 8, 1951.* Ottawa, King's Printer.

Canada. Old Age Security Act, 1951 (2nd Sess.), c. 18. *R.S.C.* 1952, c. 200. Ottawa, Queen's Printer, 1952.

Canada, Dept. of National Health and Welfare. *Annual Report of Expenditures and Administration in Connection with the Old Age Security Act, for Fiscal Year Ended Mar. 31, 1953.* Ottawa, Queen's Printer, 1953.

——— *Report on the Administration of Old Age Assistance in Canada.* Ottawa, Queen's Printer. Yearly.

——— *Report on the Administration of Old Age Pensions and Pensions for Blind Persons in Canada.* Ottawa, Queen's Printer. (Annual.)

Canada, Dept. of Trade and Commerce. *Deferred Capital Cost Allowances—Explanatory Memorandum, with Order in Council P.C. 1778, dated Apr. 10, 1951.* Ottawa, Queen's Printer, 1951.

——— Deferred Capital Cost Allowances, Explanatory Memorandum no. 2, Dec. 3, 1951, with Order in Council P.C. 6384 dated Nov. 27, 1951. Published in the *Canada Gazette,* Part II, Nov. 27, 1951.

Canada, House of Commons, Special Committee on Defence Expenditure. *Minutes of Proceedings and Evidence.* Nos. 1–17. Ottawa, Queen's Printer, 1952.

Canada, Joint Committee of the Senate and the House of Commons on Old Age Security. *Minutes of Proceedings and Evidence.* Nos. 1–31. Ottawa, King's Printer, 1950.

——— *Report, June 28, 1950.* Ottawa, King's Printer, 1950.

"Prime Minister's Statement on Old Age Security." *Labour Gazette,* July, 1951.

Canada, Minister of Defence. *Canada's Defence Programme.* Ottawa, King's (Queen's) Printer. (Annual.)

Canada, Senate. *Proceedings of the Standing Committee on Finance on the Estimates for Fiscal Year Ending Mar. 31, 1952.* Nos. 1–12. Ottawa, King's Printer, 1951.

HOWE, C. D. Statement by Minister of Trade and Commerce re Amendments to Deferred Capital Cost Allowance Regulations in House of Commons, June 28, 1951. Order in Council P.C. 3237, printed in the *Canada Gazette*, Part II, June 30, 1951.

——— Statement on an Amendment to the Deferred Capital Cost Allowance Provisions Made in House of Commons, Nov. 27, 1951, with copy of Order in Council P.C. 6384.

Books and Periodical Articles

ABBOTT, DOUGLAS. *The Economic and Financial Demands of Defence.* Address by Minister of Finance to Couchiching Conference, Aug. 12, 1952.

——— *Savings and Inflation: The Problem and Its Setting.* Address by Minister of Finance to Conference on Savings, Inflation and Economic Progress, Univ. of Minnesota, Minneapolis, May 15, 1952.

ARMOUR, STUART. "Who Wants Controls and Why?" *Public Affairs* 13:1–9 (summer, 1951).

ARMSTRONG, P. C. "The Inflationary Prospect." *Public Affairs* 14: 41–6 (winter, 1952).

BRYCE, R. B. "Financial Administration and the Defence Programme." *Report of Proceedings of the Fifth Annual Tax Conference of the Canadian Tax Foundation, 1951*, pp. 5–18.

"The Canadian Budget." *Tax Bulletin* Budget Supplement 1: 37–43 (March-April, 1951).

"Canada: Economic Survey." First Canadian supplement to *The Statist*, May 31, 1952.

Canadian Depreciation Guide. 4th ed., rev. to Jan. 15, 1953. Toronto, CCH Canadian, 1953.

CLARK, W. C. "Canada's Post-War Finance." *Canadian Tax Journal* 1: 6–12 (Jan.-Feb., 1953).

COLDWELL, M. J. "The Case for Price Controls." *Public Affairs* 14: 18–20 (winter, 1952).

COYNE, J. E. *Monetary Developments in 1951.* Address by Deputy Governor of Bank of Canada at meeting of Young Men's Canadian Club, Toronto, Jan. 14, 1952.

"The Critical Question of Old Age Pensions." *Tax Bulletin* 1: 15–16 (Jan.-Feb., 1951).

"Deferred Capital Cost Regulations." *Tax Bulletin* 1: 105–8 (July-Aug., 1951).

Deferred Depreciation Allowances. Toronto, Toronto Type Foundry Company Limited, 1951.

DIRECTOR, AARON. "Defense without Inflation." *Public Affairs* 14: 1–10 (winter, 1952).

DOUGLAS, MONTEATH. *Financing Old Age Pensions: A Personal View.* Toronto, Canadian Tax Foundation, 1951.

——— "Welfare and Redistribution." *Canadian Journal of Economics and Political Science* 19: 316–25 (Aug., 1953).

DOUGLAS, MONTEATH, and J. R. PETRIE. *Taxation for Defence: A Policy Statement.* Toronto, Canadian Tax Foundation, Nov. 22, 1950. (Also printed in *Report of Proceedings of the Fourth Annual Tax Conference, 1950*, along with discussion, pp. 47–70.)

DUE, JOHN F. "The Sales Tax as an Anti-inflationary Measure." *Public Finance* 6: 385–94.

EASTMAN, H. C. "Recent Canadian Economic Policy: Some Alternatives." *Canadian Journal of Economics and Political Science* 18: 135–45 (May, 1952).

"The Economics of Defence from a Tax Viewpoint." *Tax Bulletin* 1: 3–14 (Jan.-Feb., 1951).

EATON, A. K. "Taxing Income in Canada." In *Proceedings of the Annual Conference of the National Tax Association,* 1952, pp. 21–31.

The Federal Tax Programme: Review and Prospect. Toronto, Canadian Tax Foundation, Memo. to Sixth Annual Tax Conference, Nov., 1952.

$40-per-Month-at-70 Universal Pension and Company Pension Plans. A panel discussion sponsored by Employee Relations Section of the Montreal Board of Trade, Jan. 24, 1952.

FIRESTONE, O. J. *Canada's Industrial Development: Role of Government.* Remarks to Toronto Junior Board of Trade, March 31, 1953.

FOSTER, HELEN G. "Living Standards Going up . . . because Productivity is Rising." *Canadian Business* 25: 46 (Sept., 1952).

GARDNER, K. A. "Finance and the Canadian Economy." *Industrial Canada* 54: 252–4 (July, 1953).

JAMES, F. CYRIL. "The Inflation Menace." *Canadian Banker* 59: 56–65 (winter, 1952).

KNOX, FRANK. "Can Canada Avoid Direct Controls?" *Banker* 97: 236–9 (Oct., 1951).

MCDOUGALL, JOHN L. "Taxes to Fight Inflation." *Canadian Business* 24: 22 (Feb., 1951).

MACGREGOR, D. C. "The Old Age Pension Legislation." In *Report of Proceedings of the Fifth Tax Conference of the Canadian Tax Foundation, 1951,* pp. 19–42.

——— *The Proposed Old Age Pension.* Canadian Tax Papers, no. 4. Toronto, Canadian Tax Foundation, Oct. 25, 1951.

MCGURRAN, H. D. "Deferred Depreciation." *National Tax Journal* 4: 299–303 (Dec., 1951).

MCIVOR, R. CRAIG. "Monetary and Fiscal Policy." *Canadian Tax Journal* 1: 15–25 (March-April, 1953).

MCIVOR, R. CRAIG, and JOHN H. PANABAKER. "Canadian Post-War Monetary Policy, 1946–52." *Canadian Journal of Economics and Political Science* 20: 207–26 (May, 1954).

MACKINTOSH, W. A. "Government Economic Policy: Scope and Principles." *Canadian Journal of Economics and Political Science* 16: 314–26 (Aug., 1950).

MOORE, A. MILTON. "Fiscal Policy for 1952." *Tax Bulletin* 2: 45–56 (March-April, 1952).

——— "Taxation as an Instrument of Economic Policy." *Canadian Chartered Accountant Tax Review* 1953: 169–75 (Dec.).

Pension Conference. Sponsored by Employee Relations Section of the Montreal Board of Trade, May 18, 1950.

PERRY, J. H. "Depreciation Allowances under the Canadian Income Tax." *Canadian Chartered Accountant* 64: 119–32 (Feb., 1954).

——— "Major Features of the Canadian Tax Structure." In *Proceedings of the Annual Conference of the National Tax Association,* 1952, pp. 8–20.

——— "Taxes in Canada." In *Canada: Nation on the March,* Toronto, Clarke, Irwin and Co. Ltd., pp. 37–41.

——— "Surveys of Canada's National Finances." *Canadian Business* 27:30–4 (Oct., 1954).

PETRIE, J. R. "How are we to Pay for Old Age Pensions?" *Tax Bulletin* 1: 119–23 (Sept.-Oct., 1951).

——— "Inflation and the Budget." *Canadian Business* 24: 48.

PETRIE, J. R., and MONTEATH, DOUGLAS. *Inflation and Price Control.* Toronto, Canadian Tax Foundation, 1951.

"The Poll of Canadian Executive Opinion on the Direction of Prices and Effects of Government's No Control Policy." Conducted by Division of Research, University of Western Ontario, London, Jan. 26, 1952.

"Postwar Financial Developments, Government of Canada." In Citizens' Research Institute, *Effective Government*, June 26, 1952.

RUDICK, HARRY J. "The Controversy over E.P.T." In *Report of Proceedings of the Fourth Tax Conference, 1950, of the Canadian Tax Foundation, 1950*, pp. 39–46.

"The Sales Tax Issue." *Tax Bulletin* 1: 19–23 (March-April, 1951).

SHARP, M. W. *Deferred Capital Cost Allowance.* Statement to Montreal Board of Trade, Apr. 17, 1951, by Associate Deputy Minister of Trade and Commerce.

——— "Deferred Depreciation." *Tax Bulletin* 2: 73–87 (March-April, 1952).

——— "Deferred Depreciation: A Canadian Anti-inflationary Measure." *Journal of Finance* 7: 331–46 (May, 1952).

——— "Deferred Depreciation: A Further Assessment." *Canadian Tax Journal* 1: 277–86 (May-June, 1953).

TAYLOR, K. W. "The Canadian Approach to the Control of Inflation." *Journal of Farm Economics* 33: 667–75 (Nov., 1951).

——— "Canadian Fiscal Policies in the War and Postwar Years." In *Proceedings of the Annual Conference of the National Tax Association*, 1952, pp. 235–43.

——— "Fiscal and Monetary Trends." *Industrial Canada* 54: 239–41.

TAYLOR, K. W., and J. A. CORRY. *Canada, the North Atlantic Community, and N.A.T.O.* Toronto, Univ. of Toronto Press, 1952.

WALLACE, ELISABETH. "Old Age Security in Canada: Changing Attitudes." *Canadian Journal of Economics and Political Science* 18: 125–34 (May, 1952).

WISMER, LESLIE E. "Control of Inflation is First Priority in Defence Preparedness." *Trades and Labor Congress Journal* 30: 32–7 (July, 1951).

CHAPTERS 29–30

LATENT PROBLEMS BECOME PRESSING; TAX AND OTHER CHANGES IN SUMMARY

Government Documents

Canada, Dept. of Trade and Commerce. *Private and Public Investment in Canada, 1926–1951.* Ottawa, 1951.

Canada, Dominion Bureau of Statistics. *The Motor Vehicle.* Ottawa. (Annual. Contains tabular presentation of gasoline tax rates and revenue by provinces.)

Alberta

Royal Commission on Taxation. *Report* (J. W. JUDGE, Commissioner). Sessional Paper no. 71, 1948. Edmonton, King's Printer, 1948.

British Columbia

Commission of Enquiry into Educational Finance. *Report* (M. A. CAMERON, Commissioner). Victoria, King's Printer, 1945.

Royal Commission on the Forest Resources of British Columbia. *Report* (G. McG. SLOAN, Commissioner). Victoria, King's Printer, 1945.

Royal Commission on Provincial-Municipal Relations. *Report* (H. C. GOLDENBERG, Commissioner). Victoria, King's Printer, 1947.

Manitoba

Manitoba, Provincial-Municipal Committee, *Report*. Winnipeg, 1953.

Winnipeg. *Brief on Provincial-Municipal Relations Submitted to the Government of the Province of Manitoba* [by] H. CARL GOLDENBERG, Special Counsel for the City of Winnipeg. May 15, 1948.

Saskatchewan

Committee on Provincial-Municipal Relations. *Report* (G. E. BRITNELL, F. C. CRONKITE, LOUIS JACOBS). Regina, King's Printer, 1951.

Dept. of Municipal Affairs. *The Municipal System of Saskatchewan*, by G. F. DAWSON. Rev. ed. Regina, 1952.

New Brunswick

Committee on Reconstruction. *Report* (N. A. M. MACKENZIE, Chairman). Fredericton, 1944.

Royal Commission [on the] Rates and Taxes Act. *Report* (R. J. LOVE, Chairman). Fredericton, 1951.

Fredericton, Commission to Investigate Taxation in the City of Fredericton. *Report* (J. R. PETRIE, Chairman). 1947.

Newfoundland

Dept. of Supply, Local Government Division. *Report*. St. John's. (Annual. Report for the year ending March 31, 1949, reviews the growth of local government in Newfoundland to that date.)

GOLDENBERG, H. CARL. *Report on Municipal Administration and Services in the Greater Corner Brook area of Newfoundland* [to the Town Council of Corner Brook West, Town Council of Corner Brook East, Town Council of Curling, and Bowaters Newfoundland Pulp and Paper Mills, Ltd. for the Townsite of Corner Brook]. Montreal, 1950.

Nova Scotia

Municipal Bureau. *The Reorganization of Provincial-Municipal Relations in Nova Scotia.* A Report Prepared for the Government of Nova Scotia by the Nova Scotia Municipal Bureau, D. C. ROWAT, Director of Research. Halifax, Dalhousie Univ., Institute of Public Affairs, 1949. (Contains a supplement on municipal organization and finance in the provinces of British Columbia, Alberta, Saskatchewan, Manitoba, Ontario, Quebec, and New Brunswick, pp. 166–215.)

Royal Commission on Provincial Development and Rehabilitation. *Report* (R. McG. DAWSON, Commissioner). Halifax, King's Printer, 1944.

Ontario

Royal Commission on Education in Ontario. *Report* (J. A. HOPE, Chairman). Toronto, King's Printer, 1950.

Royal Commission on Forestry. *Report* (HOWARD KENNEDY, Commissioner). Toronto, King's Printer, 1947.

Royal Ontario Mining Commission. *Report* (N. C. URQUHART, Chairman). Toronto, King's Printer, 1944.

Toronto, Civic Advisory Council. *Municipal Finance: A Report Prepared by the Civic Advisory Council of Toronto* (W. F. LOUGHEED, Chairman). Univ. of Toronto Press, 1950.

Toronto, Civic Advisory Committee, Committee on Metropolitan Problems. *First Report*. Toronto, 1949–50.

Prince Edward Island

LATTIMER, J. E. *Prince Edward Island Tax Survey Report.* [Pub. by Dept. of Reconstruction, Prince Edward Island, 1945.]

Books

Association of Ontario Mayors and Reeves. *Submission to the Provincial-Municipal Committee for the Adjustment of the Municipal Position and Tax Structure.* Jan. 18, 1952. Toronto, 1952.

BESLEY, LOWELL. *Taxation of Crown-Granted Timberlands in British Columbia.* Forestry Bulletin no. 1. Vancouver, Faculty of Forestry, Univ. of British Columbia, 1951.

BRACEWELL, B. C. "Plans for the Municipal Government of Metropolitan Areas—Annexation and other Alternatives." In *Proceedings of the Fifth Annual Conference of the Institute of Public Administration,* 1953, pp. 323–8.

BRITNELL, G. F. "Municipal Government Re-visited—Reports on Accomplishments and Results since the Recent Provincial-Municipal Reports in British Columbia, Alberta, Saskatchewan and Nova Scotia." In *Proceedings of the Fourth Annual Conference of the Institute of Public Administration,* 1952, pp. 231–8.

BRITTAIN, H. L. *Local Government in Canada.* Toronto, Ryerson, 1951.

Citizens Research Institute of Canada. *Submission to the Committee on Provincial-Municipal Relations of the Province of Ontario,* by the Citizens Research Institute of Canada, Supported by the Bureau of Municipal Research, Toronto. Toronto, 1952.

CLARK, R. M. *A Brief on the Proposed Business Tax By-law for Vancouver.* Vancouver, 1948.

——— *The Municipal Business Tax in Canada.* Canadian Tax Papers, no. 5. Toronto, Canadian Tax Foundation, 1952.

"More Aid from Senior Governments Would Reduce Need for Business Tax." *Civic Administration* (May, 1952).

CORBETT, D. C. *Urban Growth and Municipal Finance: An Analysis and Study Prepared for the Canadian Federation of Mayors and Municipalities.* Montreal, 1952.

CRAWFORD, K. GRANT. *Canadian Municipal Government.* Toronto, Univ. of Toronto Press, 1954.

——— "The Municipal Fiscal Problem—The Distribution of Functions and Revenue Sources between the Provinces and Municipalities." In *Proceedings of the Third Annual Conference of the Institute of Public Administration,* 1951, pp. 227–49.

DETWILLER, L. F. "Provincial Sales Tax." In *Proceedings of the First Annual Conference of the Institute of Public Administration,* 1949, pp. 60–81.

DUE, J. F. *Provincial Retail Sales Taxes in Canada.* Canadian Tax Papers, no. 1. Toronto, Canadian Tax Foundation, 1951.

GATHERCOLE, G. E. "Plans for the Municipal Government of Metropolitan Areas—Annexation and Other Alternatives." In *Proceedings of the Fifth Annual Conference of the Institute of Public Administration,* 1953, pp. 305–20.

GIMAIEL, PHILIPPE. "Evolution in Administration of Gasoline Tax." In *Proceedings of the Second Annual Conference of the Institute of Public Administration of Canada,* 1950, pp. 79–92.

GOLDENBERG, CARL. "Municipal Government Re-visited—Reports on Accomplishments and Results since the Recent Provincial-Municipal Reports in British Columbia, Alberta, Saskatchewan and Nova Scotia." In *Proceedings of the Fourth Annual Conference of the Institute of Public Administration,* 1952, pp. 211–18.

GREY, R. "Conditional Grants-in-Aid." In *Proceedings of the Fifth Annual Conference of the Institute of Public Administration,* 1953, pp. 353–8.

HARRIES, HU, and associates. *Some Aspects of Municipal Finance in the City of Edmonton.* A Study Prepared for the Edmonton Chamber of Commerce, Special Committee on Municipal Finance. Nov. 15, 1951.

HOBBS, W. E. *Report of Enquiry into Municipal and School District Finances in British Columbia, November 1951 to January 1952.* Made at the Request of the Union of British Columbia Municipalities [n.d.].

JUDGE, J. W. "Municipal Government Re-visited—Reports on Accomplishments and Results since the Recent Provincial-Municipal Reports in British Columbia, Alberta, Saskatchewan and Nova Scotia." In *Proceedings of the Fourth Annual Conference of the Institute of Public Administration,* 1952, pp. 221–8.

MACGREGOR, D. C. "Review of Provincial Fields of Taxation." In *Proceedings of the Fourth Annual Conference of the Institute of Public Administration,* 1952, pp. 359–69.

MANNING, H. E. *Assessment and Rating, Being the Law of Municipal Taxation in Canada.* 3rd ed. Toronto, Cartwright, 1951.

Ontario Tax Acts Consolidated. 1st ed. Toronto, Montreal, CCH Canadian, 1947. (2nd ed. 1949. Includes provincial and municipal tax legislation.)

PERRY, J. H. *Taxation in Canada.* 2nd ed. Toronto. Univ. of Toronto Press, 1954.

POWELL, C. W. "Problems Arising from lack of Organized Municipalities in Newfoundland." In *Proceedings of the First Annual Conference of the Institute of Public Administration,* 1949, pp. 168–82.

Quebec Tax Acts Consolidated. 1st ed. Toronto, Montreal, CCH Canadian, 1947. (2nd ed. 1949. Includes provincial and municipal tax legislation.)

ROWAT, D. C. "Municipal Government Re-visited—Reports on Accomplishments and Results since the Recent Provincial-Municipal Reports in British Columbia, Alberta, Saskatchewan and Nova Scotia." In *Proceedings of the Fourth Annual Conference of the Institute of Public Administration,* 1952, pp. 241–9.

STANTON, R. H. "Sales Taxation in the Provincial and Municipal Fields." In *Proceedings of the Third Annual Conference of the Institute of Public Administration of Canada,* 1951, pp. 471–91.

WAINES, W. J. "The Impact of the National Defense Programme on Provincial and Municipal Finance." In *Proceedings of the Third Annual Conference of the Institute of Public Administration,* 1951, pp. 217–24.

Periodical Articles

BRACEWELL, B. C. "Financial Policies in Intergovernmental Relations." *Municipal Finance* 27: 8–15 (Aug., 1954).

BRISEBOIS, EPHRIEM. "The Montreal Metropolitan Commission." *Municipal Finance* 24: 119–23 (Feb., 1952).

CLARK, R. M. "The Municipal Business Tax in Canada." *Canadian Journal of Economics and Political Science* 14: 491–501 (Nov., 1948).

CRAWFORD, K. G. "Some Aspects of Provincial-Municipal Relations." *Canadian Journal of Economics and Political Science* 16: 394–407 (Aug., 1950).

——— "What Hope is there for a Solution to Problems of Provincial-Municipal Relations." *Civic Administration* 6: 87–94 (Oct., 1954).

CURTIS, C. A. "Municipal Finance and Provincial-Federal Relations." *Canadian Journal of Economics and Political Science* 17: 297–306 (Aug., 1951).

HOBBS, W. E. "A New Deal for Municipal Taxation." *Civic Administration* 2: 67–9 (Sept., 1950).

LASCELLES, G. A. "Urban and Fringe Area Financial and Operating Problems in Large Municipalities." *Municipal Finance* 27: 21–6 (Aug., 1954).

MAXWELL, J. A. "Reports on Local Government." *Canadian Journal of Economics and Political Science* 17: 377–82 (Aug., 1951). (Review article on four of the reports on municipal government and finance listed above, i.e. JUDGE, ROWAT, LOUGHEED, LOVE.)

OUTRAM, E. A. "Municipal Grants: Comments on a Current Issue of Local Finance." *Canadian Tax Journal* 2: 158–60 (May-June, 1954).

STEWART, Andrew, and E. J. HANSON. "Some Aspects of Rural Municipal Finance in Canada." *Canadian Journal of Economics and Political Science* 14: 481–90 (Nov., 1948).

"Submissions on Behalf of the Municipalities of Ontario to the Government of Ontario." *Municipal World* 58: 341–4 (Nov., 1948).

CHAPTERS 31–33

SUBSIDIES AND FISCAL ARRANGEMENTS

Government Documents

Dominion-Provincial Conferences

Dominion-Provincial and Interprovincial Conferences from 1887 to 1926. Ottawa, Reprinted by King's Printer, 1951. (Reprint from document with title *Minutes of the Proceedings in Conference of the Representatives of the Provinces in the Years 1887, 1902, 1906, 1910, 1913, 1918, 1920,* n.p., 1926.)

Dominion-Provincial Conferences, November 3–10, 1927; December 9–13, 1935; January 14–15, 1941. Ottawa, Reprinted by King's Printer, 1951. (Originally published separately by King's Printer, Ottawa.)

Dominion-Provincial Conference, 1945. *Dominion and Provincial Submissions and Plenary Conference Discussions.* Ottawa, King's Printer, 1946.

——— *Dominion Subsidies to Provinces Including Other Transfers.* Ottawa, 1945. (Reference book.)

——— *Proposals of the Government of Canada, August, 1945.* Ottawa, 1945.

——— *Correspondence since the Budget of 1946 on Matters of Substance Regarding Tax Agreements with the Provinces.* Ottawa, King's Printer, 1947.

Conference of Federal and Provincial Governments, 1950. *Proceedings, Ottawa, December 4–7, 1950.* Ottawa, King's Printer, 1951.

Canada

Royal Commission on Industrial Training and Technical Education. *Report.* (J. W. ROBERTSON, Chairman). Ottawa, C. H. Parmelee, 1913.

Royal Commission on Maritime Claims. *Report* (A. R. DUNCAN, Chairman). Ottawa, King's Printer, 1927.

Royal Commission on Reconveyance of Land to British Columbia. *Report* (W. M. MARTIN, Chairman). Ottawa, King's Printer, 1928.

Royal Commission on the Transfer of the Natural Resources to Manitoba. *Report* (W. F. A. TURGEON, Chairman). Ottawa, King's Printer, 1929.

Royal Commission on the Natural Resources of Alberta. *Report* (A. K. DYSART, Chairman). Ottawa, King's Printer, 1935.

Royal Commission on the Natural Resources of Saskatchewan. *Report* (A. K. DYSART, Chairman). Ottawa, King's Printer, 1935.

Brief of the Dominion of Canada [submitted to the Commission on Financial Arrangement between the Dominion and the Maritime Provinces]. Ottawa, King's Printer, 1935. (Appendices: 1, Exhibits; 2, Maps; 3, Memoranda.)

Royal Commission on Financial Arrangements between the Dominion and the Maritime provinces. *Report* (THOMAS WHITE, Chairman). Ottawa, King's Printer, 1935.

Dept. of Finance. *Federal Subsidies and Grants to Provinces of Canada; Summary of Legislation; Payments Made from Confederation to the Close of the Fiscal Year 1936–37.* 1937. (Processed.)

Bank of Canada. *Reports on the Financial Position of the provinces of Manitoba, Saskatchewan and Alberta.* Ottawa, 1937.

Royal Commission on Dominion-Provincial Relations. *Report* (Rowell-Sirois). Ottawa, King's Printer, 1940. (Book I, *Canada: 1867–1939;* Book II, *Recommendations.* For list of provincial submissions to the Royal Commission see chapters 19–20.)

Dept. of Finance. [Statement of Mr. D. C. Abbott, Minister of Finance, in the House of Commons, July 9, 1947, on tax agreements] *Debates of the House of Commons, 1947.* Ottawa, King's Printer. (Vol. VI, pp. 5305–19.)

——— *Federal-Provincial Fiscal Relations.* Address by Mr. D. C. Abbott to Canadian Club of Montreal, Nov. 2, 1953.

Joint Committee of the Senate and House of Commons on Old Age Security, April and May, 1950. Minutes of Proceedings and Evidence. Ottawa, 1950.

Dept. of Finance. *Tax Rental Agreement between the Government of Canada and the Government of the Province of Alberta, dated Sept. 22, 1952.* Ottawa, Queen's Printer, 1953.

Same for British Columbia, July 10, 1952; Manitoba, Aug. 29, 1952; New Brunswick, Aug. 13, 1952; Newfoundland, Sept. 22, 1952; Nova Scotia, Nov. 24, 1952; Ontario, Oct. 29, 1952; Prince Edward Island, July 31, 1952; Saskatchewan, Sept. 29, 1952.

Dept. of National Health and Welfare. *Five Year Report, National Health Programme.* Ottawa, 1954.

British Columbia

The Case of British Columbia for Better Terms. Victoria, King's Printer, 1905.

Federal-Provincial Co-operation in Economic Development. Brief submitted to Government of Canada by Government of British Columbia, December 14, 1953. Victoria, mimeo.

New Brunswick

The Case of New Brunswick for an Increase in the Federal Subsidy. [N.d.] (Prepared subsequent to publication of report of Royal Commission on Maritime Claims, 1927.)

Nova Scotia

A Submission on Dominion-Provincial Relations and the Fiscal Disabilities of Nova Scotia within Canadian Confederation. (N.d.) (Presented by Norman McL. Rogers to the Royal Commission of Economic Enquiry, 1924, on behalf of the Nova Scotia Government.)

A Submission of Its Claims with Respect to Maritime Disabilities within Confederation as Presented to the Royal Commission [on Maritime Claims]. Halifax, 1926.

Books and Pamphlets

Binns, K. J. *Federal Financial Relations in Canada and Australia.* Report Prepared for the Government of Tasmania. Hobart, Tasmania, Govt. Printer, 1948.

Boos, A. W. *The Financial Arrangements between the Provinces and the Dominion.* McGill Univ. Economic Studies, no. 12. Toronto, Macmillan, 1930.

Buck, A. E. *Financing Canadian Government.* Chicago, Public Administration Service, 1949.

Canadian Federation of Mayors and Municipalities. *Municipal and Intergovernmental Finance, 1930–1951*. Montreal, 1953.

COHEN, MAXWELL. *The Dominion-Provincial Conference: Some Basic Issues*. Toronto, Ryerson, 1945.

EGGLESTON, WILFRID. *The Road to Nationhood: A Chronicle of Dominion-Provincial Relations*. Toronto, Oxford Univ. Press, 1946.

EGGLESTON, WILFRID, and C. T. KRAFT. *Dominion-Provincial Subsidies and Grants*. A Study Prepared for the Royal Commission on Dominion-Provincial Relations. Ottawa, 1939.

FOWLER, R. M. "Intergovernmental Fiscal Relations in Canada." In *Proceedings of the 33rd Annual Conference of the National Tax Association*, 1940, pp. 207–13.

GARSON, S. S. "Effects of the War upon Canadian Provincial Fiscal Systems." In *Proceedings of the Thirty-fourth Annual Conference of the National Tax Association*, 1941, pp. 57–64.

GETTYS, C. L. *The Administration of Canadian Conditional Grants: A Study in Dominion-Provincial Relationships*. Chicago, Public Administration Service, 1938.

KEIRSTEAD, W. G. "The Basis of the Federal Subsidies." *Papers and Proceedings of the Sixth Annual Meeting of the Canadian Political Science Association* 6: 134–61 (1934).

LAMONTAGNE, MAURICE. *Le Fédéralisme canadien: evolution et problèmes*. Quebec, Laval Univ., 1954.

MARTIN, C. B. *The Natural Resources Question: The Historical Basis of Provincial Claims*. Winnipeg, King's Printer, 1920.

MAXWELL, J. A. *Federal Subsidies to Provincial Governments in Canada*. Cambridge, Harvard Univ. Press, 1937.

——— "Provincial Conferences and Better Terms." In *Papers and Proceedings of the Sixth Annual Meeting of the Canadian Political Science Association* 6: 162–74 (1934).

MOORE, A. M., and PERRY, J. H. *Financing Canadian Federation*. Canadian Tax Papers, no. 6. Toronto, Canadian Tax Foundation, March, 1953.

PERRY, J. H. "Intergovernmental Fiscal Arrangements in Canada." In *Proceedings of the Fifth Annual Conference of the Institute of Public Administration*, 1953, pp. 53–70.

"Recent Development in Tax Coordination in Canada." In *Proceedings of the 34th Annual Conference of the National Tax Association*, 1941, pp. 673–7.

——— *Recent Developments in Dominion-Provincial Relations in Canada*. (Occasional Paper, no. 5. New York, National Bureau of Economic Research, 1948.

Tax Institute. *Federal-State-Local Tax Correlation*. A Symposium. Princeton, 1954.

Periodical Articles

ANGUS, H. F. "An Echo of the Past: The Rowell-Sirois Commission." *Canadian Tax Journal* 1: 439–49 (Sept.-Oct., 1953).

BIRCH, A. H. "Federalism and Finance." *Manchester School of Economics and Social Science* 17: 163–85 (May, 1949).

CRONKITE, F. C. "Federal Aid for Roads: A Proposal for Federal Grants." *Canadian Tax Journal* 2: 106–10 (March-April, 1954).

EGGLESTON, WILFRID. "Recent Trends in Federal-Provincial Relations." *Canadian Banker* 59: 66–78 (winter, 1952).

GATHERCOLE, GEORGE. "Co-ordination of Tax Systems in Canada and the United States: A Provincial Viewpoint." *Tax Bulletin* 2: 334–43 (Nov.–Dec., 1952).

GREY, R. "Federal Aid–A Critique." *Canadian Tax Journal* 2: 111–15 (March-April, 1954).

GROVES, H. M. "New Sources of Light on Inter-governmental Fiscal Relations." *National Tax Journal* 5: 234–8 (Sept., 1952). (Contrasts achievements of Scandinavian countries with those in Switzerland, Germany, Great Britain, and Canada.)

MACGREGOR, D. C. "Federal-Provincial Financial Relations in Canada." *Economic Journal* 46: 171–8 (March, 1936).

——— "The Provincial Incidence of the Canadian Tariff." *Canadian Journal of Economics and Political Science* 1: 384–95 (Aug., 1935).

MACKINTOSH, W. A. "Federal Finance." *Canadian Tax Journal* 1: 335–40.

MCQUEEN, R. "The Economic Aspects of Federalism." *Canadian Journal of Economics and Political Science* 1: 348–67 (Aug., 1935).

MAXWELL, J. A. "The Adjustment of Federal-Provincial Financial Relations." *Canadian Journal of Economics and Political Science* 2: 374–89 (Aug., 1936).

MOORE, A. M. "The Tremblay Commission: A Review of the Submissions." *Canadian Tax Journal* 2: 142–9 (May-June, 1954). "Further Submissions." 2: 311-14 (Sept.-Oct., 1954).

——— "What Alternative to the Tax Rental Agreements?" *Canadian Tax Journal* 2: 281–9 (Sept.-Oct., 1954).

PERRY, J. H. "The New Tax Agreements" [editorial notes]. *Tax Bulletin* 2: 143–4 (July-Aug., 1952).

——— "Fiscal Relations in the Canadian Federation." *Bulletin for International Fiscal Documentation* 7: 65–87 (1953).

——— "Federal Tax Credit: Conflict with Quebec Corporation Profits Tax." *Canadian Tax Journal* 2: 6–11 (Jan.-Feb., 1954).

ROWAT, D. C. "Federal Aid–A Commentary." *Canadian Tax Journal* 2: 115–18 (March-April, 1954).

——— "Recent Developments in Canadian Federalism." *Canadian Journal of Economics and Political Science* 18: 1–16 (Feb., 1952).

SHINK, G. H. "Co-ordination of Tax Systems in Canada and the United States: The Viewpoint of Quebec." *Tax Bulletin* 2: 344–52 (Nov.-Dec., 1952).

SMITH, E. H. "Co-ordination of Tax Systems: The Federal Viewpoint." *Tax Bulletin* 2: 326–33 (Nov.-Dec., 1952).

Index